# Slavery, Freedom, and Abolition in Latin America and the Atlantic World

CHRISTOPHER SCHMIDT-NOWARA

University of New Mexico Press ✢ Albuquerque

© 2011 by the University of New Mexico Press
All rights reserved. Published 2011
Printed in the United States of America
16  15  14  13  12  11      1  2  3  4  5  6

LIBRARY OF CONGRESS CATALOGING-IN-PUBLICATION DATA

Schmidt-Nowara, Christopher, 1966–
Slavery, freedom, and abolition in Latin America and the Atlantic world /
Christopher Schmidt-Nowara.
p. cm. — (Diálogos)
Includes bibliographical references and index.
ISBN 978-0-8263-3904-1 (paper : alk. paper) —
ISBN 978-0-8263-3905-8 (electronic)
1. Slavery—Latin America—History. 2. Slaves—Emancipation—Latin
America—History. 3. Antislavery movements—Latin America—History.
4. Latin America—History. 5. Latin America—Biography. I. Title.
HT1052.5.S36 2011
306.3'62098—dc22

2011006201


Text is composed in Janson Text LT Std 10/13.5
Display type is Bernhard Modern Std

Slavery, Freedom, and Abolition
in Latin America and the Atlantic World

❧

SERIES ADVISORY EDITOR:
Lyman L. Johnson,
University of North Carolina at Charlotte

*To my students*

# Contents

# Illustrations, Maps, and Tables

## Illustrations

## Maps

## Tables

# Acknowledgments

More than ten years of teaching Latin American, Caribbean, and Atlantic history at Fordham University and as a visitor at other universities gave me the opportunity to explore and discuss this topic, so I dedicate this work to the many students, especially at Fordham, who impressed me with their hunger for knowledge. They always wanted to know more, so I tried my best to learn more.

Working with the University of New Mexico Press has also been a boon. Thanks to David Holtby, who first urged me to write this book over an excellent lunch at Richard's Mexican Restaurant in Albuquerque, and to Clark Whitehorn and Lyman Johnson for their support and ready feedback.

An early conversation with Rebecca Scott in Ann Arbor convinced me to get to work on this book; my thanks to her for the encouragement. Lyman Johnson read more than one draft of the manuscript and provided most helpful comments throughout. Robin Blackburn, Rafael de Bivar Marquese, Erik Seeman, and Dale Tomich also read versions of the manuscript, and I greatly valued their criticisms and enthusiasm.

Thanks to Tim Cannon, John McNeill, Cassie Spieler, and Ben Spieler for their help with several of the book's maps.

At Fordham, collaborating with my colleagues Arnaldo Cruz-Malavé, Héctor Lindo-Fuentes, Viviane Mahieux, Beth Penry, Clara Rodríguez, and Irma Watkins-Owens led to numerous lively discussions and presentations over the past ten years.

Visiting at other universities, especially in Latin America, provided new perspectives along the way. At the Universidad de Puerto Rico, Río Piedras, thanks to Astrid Cubano-Iguina, a source of inspiration since my grad school days, for the invitation to teach a class in 2003 and to many others for their hospitality and engaging conversations: María del Carmen Baerga, Jorge Duany, Humberto García Muñíz, Jorge Giovanetti, Juan Giusti, María Dolores de Luque, Fernando Picó, Mayra Rosario, César Solá-García, and Lanny Thompson. Rafael de Bivar Marquese's invitation in 2007 to teach at the Universidade de São Paulo was pivotal: many thanks to him and to Márcia Berbel for eye-opening conversations and for the introduction to a remarkable historiography. Thanks also to Valdei Lopes de Araujo and Andréa Lisley Gonçalves at the Universidade Federal de Ouro Preto for inviting to me to give talks to their seminar on cultural and intellectual history. Every historian of Latin American slavery should spend time in Minas Gerais. At the University of Arizona, Karen Anderson, Bill Beezley, Kevin Gosner, and Scott Whiteford made it possible for me to teach a very lively seminar on Afro-Latin America at the Center for Latin American Studies. Jeremy Adelman generously arranged for me to be a visiting fellow in the Princeton History Department in 2007–2008. I benefited not only from being a hundred yards away from Firestone Library but also from conversations with Jeremy, Arcadio Díaz Quiñones, and Stanley Stein, with whom I talked at length and with much pleasure about research and the history of our field. Longtime friends and colleagues in Madrid and Barcelona helped and inspired in innumerable ways: Jim Amelang, Josep Maria Delgado, Josep Maria Fradera, Albert Garcia Balañá, Luis Miguel García Mora, Stephen Jacobson, Consuelo Naranjo Orovio, José Antonio Piqueras, and Martín Rodrigo y Alharilla.

Support for research trips and time to write came from several sources. My thanks to Fordham's Office of Research, Dean of Faculty, and Graduate School of Arts & Sciences; the Program for Cultural Cooperation between Spain and the United States; and Spain's Ministry of Science and Innovation (grant number HAR2009–07103).

My friends and family have shown interest and support for this undertaking all along. My most heartfelt thanks go to my parents, sister, and brother, and to Miranda Spieler for unwavering generosity and help. Thanks finally to Mickey and Sammy, great New Yorkers.

—Fort Greene, Brooklyn, Summer 2010

# Introduction

❧

✦ In the early 1880s, the members of the Spanish Abolitionist Society wrote with outrage about the continued use of the stock (*el cepo*) and shackles (*el grillete*) as punishment for slaves in Cuba. At the time, Cuba, along with Puerto Rico, was Spain's last colony in the Americas. It was also the biggest slave society in almost four centuries of Spanish colonial history. Slavery was not abolished there until 1886. Only Brazil maintained slavery longer, finally abolishing the institution two years later in 1888.

Cuban slave owners clung to enslaved labor for as long as possible, especially in the rich western and central sugar regions of the island. The Spanish government abolished the slave trade to Cuba in 1867. It also passed gradual emancipation laws in 1870 and 1880. While the government and its allies sought to portray these measures as humane and enlightened, critics argued that they did not go far enough, pointing to the violence and lawlessness that thrived on the Cuban plantations in the form of unchecked corporal punishment. For even the most minor offenses, slave owners were able to put slaves in the stock. The suffering was horrific: "Any person can imagine what the headstock is like. A refinement of the old and barbarous

FIGURE 1. El cepo de cabeza.

torture of burying someone up to the head. The mosquitoes, flies, and insects of all kinds, whose number is infinite in the Antilles, fatten themselves upon the head and face of the poor slave, who cannot use his hands to defend himself."[1] The use of shackles was equally cruel: "Naturally, this punishment produces many illnesses. The black field hands suffer from sunstrokes or fevers, hernias and kidney ailments. The first of these results from the harshness of the work, which takes place under the open sky in an extreme climate with a sun that burns like no other."[2]

The authors of the pamphlet noted that in metropolitan Spain, shackles were still employed as punishment but only for the gravest forms of treason or acts of violence. In Cuba, slave owners resorted to the stock and shackles for the most trivial offenses, real or perceived. The law denied the rights of slaves by allowing owners to terrorize them into hard work and obedience: "They do not punish *crimes*. Reader take note. What they punish is the resistance of the black stolen from Africa or from his family. Coerced, wronged, reviled, pressed into laboring gratis for the benefit of a master who forces him to work without the least consideration of his interests."[3]

FIGURE 2. El grillete. Spanish abolitionists included these images in a pamphlet in order to depict and denounce punishments still practiced on Cuban plantations in the 1880s, during the final days of slavery on the island. Slave owners fought to the last to retain control over enslaved labor. Slaves and their allies faced bitter resistance throughout Latin America during the various stages of abolition. Sociedad Abolicionista Española, *El cepo y el grillete* (Madrid: Sociedad Abolicionista Española, [188?]).

The abolitionists' indignation derived from a series of contrasts that highlighted not only the cruelty of slavery but also its archaism. From the perspective of the lawyers, engineers, journalists, and politicians who composed the Abolitionist Society, most American and Western European nations of the era sought to govern themselves according to the rule of law, constitutional regimes, and market economies based on contract and the freedom of labor. Slavery was the historical residue of absolutist regimes in which power was arbitrary and capricious and unfree labor and monopolies dominated the economies. In this view of progress, slavery must give way to the imperatives of individual liberty.

However, the resurgence and persistence of slavery in nineteenth-century Cuba, far from being the inverse of economic and civil progress, were products of revolutionary changes that had reshaped Latin America and the Atlantic world beginning in the previous century. Hostility to the African slave trade and New World slavery began to flourish in different corners of the Atlantic world in the mid-eighteenth century. This hostility coalesced into major challenges to both institutions. Slaves in the French colony of Saint-Domingue (Haiti) threw off their bondage between 1791 and 1804 in the greatest slave rebellion the Americas would ever see. Opposition to the slave trade spread through the British Isles in the same era, leading the parliament of the most energetic slave-trading nation to abolish the traffic to its colonies in 1806. In Spanish America, the wars of independence of the 1810s and the 1820s gravely weakened slavery. The newly independent nations passed emancipation laws, usually of a gradual nature, and banned the slave trade altogether.

Yet merchants, planters, and government officials in some regions of the Atlantic world were fully capable of weathering and even exploiting these changes. In the United States, southern slave owners amassed considerable political clout and fended off serious challenges to their power until the Civil War. In Latin America, Cuba and Brazil saw a spectacular resurgence of the slave trade and the opening of new territories to slave-worked agriculture on an unprecedented scale. The decline of competitors such as Saint-Domingue and Jamaica on the world market presented Antillean and Brazilian planters with new opportunities, which they eagerly seized.

A look at the slave population of Latin America is revealing. In 1800 there were 718,000 slaves in Brazil, 212,000 in Cuba, and 112,000 in Venezuela, the three largest slave populations in the Iberian empires. Venezuela soon experienced a violent and tortuous war for independence against Spain. One outcome of the war was the suppression of the slave trade and the passing of a gradual emancipation law in 1821. The number of slaves declined until final abolition in 1854. Brazil also gained its independence from Portugal in this period but through a largely negotiated process that involved little social or military upheaval. The slave trade and slavery continued to thrive. By 1822, the year of independence, the slave population had grown to more than 1.1 million and would increase until slave trade abolition in 1850. Cuba remained loyal to the Spanish metropolis during the era of revolution, partly because of the growth of the slave trade and plantation slavery. By 1842 the slave population had expanded to more than 320,000. After 1800, the transatlantic slave trade brought more than 700,000 captives to Cuba and more than 2 million to Brazil.[4]

These data illustrate that even as political and economic liberalism took hold in much of Latin America and the imperial centers, broad commitment to the legitimacy of the enslavement of Africans and their descendants persisted almost until the end of the nineteenth century.

Why these deeply entrenched ideas and institutions were so resilient and how they were ultimately overcome are the questions that this book will explore.

This work is organized as a narrative of slavery's uneven rise and fall in Latin America and those parts of the Atlantic world to which the region was inextricably connected. The story begins in the eastern Atlantic in the fifteenth century and extends to Cuba and Brazil at the end of the nineteenth. Since much ground will be covered, it might be useful for the reader to keep several organizing ideas in mind:

- The rise of African slavery in Latin America was related to the conquest, subordination, and, in some cases, the decimation of the indigenous population.
- Slavery existed in relation to a broad pattern of unfree and free labor in the Americas, Africa, and the imperial centers.
- In the Americas, Brazil, as a Portuguese colony and then as an independent state, was the most constant and most massive importer of enslaved Africans over the centuries. According to estimates from *Voyages: The Trans-Atlantic Slave Trade Database* (www.slavevoyages. org), Brazil received close to 5 million of the 10.7 million captives disembarked in the Americas (between the early sixteenth and mid-nineteenth centuries). As a destination for the transatlantic slave trade, Spanish America—with almost 1.3 million captives prior to slave trade suppression to Cuba in 1867—trailed far behind Brazil and the British and French colonies of Jamaica and Saint-Domingue. This situation changed significantly in the late eighteenth century when Cuba emerged as the biggest plantation society in Spanish American history, fully rivaling its Caribbean neighbors.
- Plantation labor was the most powerful motor of the transatlantic traffic. At the same time, enslaved men and women worked throughout the economies of Brazil and Spanish America.
- Enslaved Africans and their descendants in the Americas frequently sought to recreate their religions and forms of social organization in the New World. Paradoxically, the centrality and pervasiveness of the Catholic Church in the Iberian empires often facilitated this process.
- Flight (maroonage) and other forms of resistance by enslaved people, coupled with legally and religiously sanctioned pathways to

emancipation, created large free populations in Brazil and Spanish America even as slavery and the slave trade flourished.

- Latin American societies were simultaneously inclusive and hierarchical. Because of the Iberian monarchies and the Church, all members of society, as long as they were nominally Christian, had some place within the larger social and cultural order. At the same time, inequality of status and privilege was the norm. Discrimination based on lineage, color, and gender was widely accepted and legally enforced. Nonetheless, social hierarchies were not static; indeed, frequent assertions of status and privilege indicated their permeability.

- International and anticolonial warfare in the eighteenth and nineteenth centuries had the most decisive impact on slavery's survival in most of Latin America. War was the most common spur to abolition, in part because it presented slaves and free people of color with opportunities to demand the end of slavery and to claim inclusion as free and equal citizens in the emerging Latin American nations.

The reader should also keep in mind the necessary Atlantic dimension of this study of slavery, freedom, and abolition in Latin America. The Atlantic world was a space that brought into contact and conflict the peoples, polities, and economies of Africa, Europe, and the Americas. The Iberian explorers and conquerors of the late Middle Ages were the pioneers of this world; the commercial networks, trading forts, and settlements they established in the eastern Atlantic islands and along the west coast of Africa in the fourteenth and fifteenth centuries were the jumping-off point to the Americas, unbeknownst to them before 1492. Over the course of the sixteenth century they incorporated parts of the Americas into this world through conquest and settlement. Iberian priests, administrators, soldiers, and merchants flowed to the New World, as did African servants and slaves. Old World diseases decimated the indigenous peoples, while the flora and fauna imported by the conquerors, such as the horse and sugar cane, took root. In the reverse direction, American

MAP 1. Volume and direction of the transatlantic slave trade. David Eltis and David Richardson, *Atlas of the Transatlantic Slave Trade* (New Haven, CT: Yale University Press, 2010). Courtesy of Yale University Press.

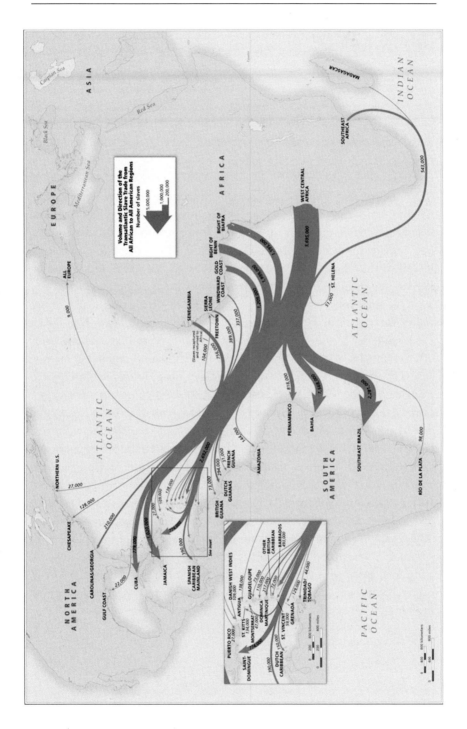

silver and agricultural products like tobacco and the potato would transform European and African tastes and economies. Exchange among the
American colonies was also important. The licit and illicit movement of
goods, people, and ideas across the Americas was a fundamental aspect of
the Atlantic empires, despite the efforts of regimes to control the flows to
and from their colonial territories. All of the colonial empires participated
in the transatlantic slave trade, a far from unified system. Different colonial
powers competed for control, though the Portuguese (and the Brazilians)
and later the British were the most important carriers of African captives
to the Americas.[5] The Portuguese and Brazilians would cement a south
Atlantic slave trade in the seventeenth century that conjoined Brazil and
Angola until the middle of the nineteenth century. The Caribbean, the
other major terminus of the trade, was part of a north Atlantic system
linked to the Gold Coast and the Bights of Biafra and Benin, in which
Britain was the major, though far from the only, slaving power.

One final coordinate will help the reader to situate this history: if we
follow the circuit of some of these goods and voyagers, we will find that
the boundaries of the Atlantic world were not hard and fast. The streams
of Peruvian and Mexican silver did not halt in Spain but made their way
across the world to China, brought there by European merchants eager to
trade with the world's largest economy. Mexican silver reached China not
only via Europe but also through the galleon trade that linked Acapulco
and Manila across the Pacific Ocean. The circuits of enslaved and unfree
labor also stretched beyond the confines of the Atlantic. Portuguese slavers trafficked in captives from the east coast of Africa, while Spaniards
sent captives from the Philippines to Mexico. Later in the nineteenth century, as the slave trade from Africa waned, indentured workers from China
and India arrived in the Caribbean and Latin America in huge numbers.
These examples show us that while the coming together (or collision) of
Africa, Europe, and the Americas created a dynamic economic, cultural,
and social space with African enslavement and the transatlantic traffic in
captives at its heart, the Atlantic complex was also part of an emerging and
evolving global system.

## CHAPTER ONE

# Slavery and Iberian Colonization

❧

[T]o me it seems harsh to make slaves of those whom God and nature made free.

— Miguel de Cervantes, *Don Quixote*, 170

## The Iberian Empires and the Atlantic World

✝ AT THE END OF HIS FIRST VOYAGE, THE GENOESE MARINER Christopher Columbus sent a letter to Spain in which he reported on the lands that he called the Indies and the great wealth that would flow from them to his Spanish patrons, the Catholic Kings Ferdinand and Isabella: "their Highnesses can see that I will give them as much gold as they require, if they will render me some very slight assistance." He also promised spices, cotton, mastic, rhubarb, cinnamon, and "countless other things in addition." The natives of these lands, whom he called Indians, would be cooperative because they were gentle and generous. They seemed eager to convert to Christianity, in his view. He also thought they would make

MAP 2. Eastern Atlantic around the time of Columbus. Courtesy of Ben Spieler.

good servants for European overlords, as he promised to bring Ferdinand and Isabella "as many slaves" as they required.[1]

Columbus's automatic appeal to slavery was rooted in medieval European conceptions of the globe and the different peoples that inhabited

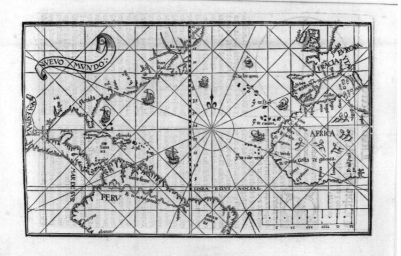

FIGURE 3. Spanish nautical chart from the mid-sixteenth century. This map shows the developing contours of the Iberian Atlantic world several decades after Columbus's first voyage, divided by the boundary agreed upon in the Treaty of Tordesillas (1494). Note the importance of the eastern Atlantic islands in the transatlantic voyages. Pedro de Medina, *Arte de navegar* (Valladolid, 1545). Courtesy of the John Carter Brown Library at Brown University.

it. Because of climate and innate capacities, some peoples were born to be free, others to be enslaved. His reaction also arose from his familiarity with the complex of exploration, trade, colonization, and slavery that the Portuguese and Spanish were constructing in the eastern Atlantic at the same time that he traveled to the ocean's distant western shores. The beginnings of African slavery in Latin America are to be found in these Portuguese and Spanish sallies into the Atlantic Ocean and in the widely, though not universally, held conviction that some peoples were natural slaves.

In the Middle Ages, the Iberian Peninsula was a patchwork of kingdoms, some Christian, others Muslim. By the fifteenth century, Christian kingdoms held the upper hand. These included Portugal, Aragon, Navarre, and the largest of all, Castile. Castile became even more preeminent in the later part of the century when the crowns of Aragon and Castile were united in the persons of the Catholic Kings Ferdinand and Isabella. The last Muslim stronghold was Granada in the southeast of the peninsula.

The Portuguese and Spanish kingdoms were imbued with the crusading spirit against Islam. They aspired not only to drive Islamic princes from the peninsula but also to take the battle to North Africa, the Holy Lands, and beyond. In the early fifteenth century, the Portuguese landed in Morocco and conquered the city of Ceuta. From there they hoped to undercut Muslim strength by taking over trade routes of gold and slaves. Later in the century, they hoped to do the same by finding a path to India and China and controlling the rich trade in spices and other luxury goods. The spirit of religious warfare was thus intertwined with the spirit of commerce.

These ambitions drove the Iberians into the Atlantic world and down the coast of Africa. Initially, gold was the major harvest of Portuguese exploration. By exploring southward and finally rounding Cape Bojador in 1434, they hoped to trade directly at the source. To that end, they established trading outposts such as Arguin and El Mina in the mid- to late fifteenth century.

Traffic in slaves was also at the heart of Portuguese endeavors. Slavery was a well-rooted institution in the African societies with which they traded. As the historian John Thornton has observed of West and Central Africa in this period: "the necessary legal institutions and material resources were available to support a large slave market, one that anyone could participate in, including Europeans and other foreigners. Those who held slaves and did not intend to use them immediately could also sell them, and indeed, this is why the number of African merchants who dealt in slaves was large."[2] Slavery was an important form of property, and the capture of slaves was one of the goals of the frequent wars among polities in West and Central Africa. Slavery was not as universally associated with debasement, as it would be in the European colonial empires. Slaves worked in a wide variety of tasks, from agricultural and skilled labor to positions of military and political leadership. There was also a greater emphasis on assimilation into the social group of the slave owner.

Moreover, long before the arrival of the Portuguese, other slave trades out of sub-Saharan Africa flourished. One crossed the Sahara into the Mediterranean world. Another linked East Africa to the Indian Ocean. Historians have traced both routes back to the seventh century. The Atlantic system would favor men over women as slaves by two to one. The Sahara and Indian Ocean traffics were exactly the reverse, women captives outnumbering men. Many of these slaves found homes in their new societies through marriage and other forms of kinship and service. Manumission—formal release of the enslaved person from her or his servitude—was frequent. While the Saharan and Indian Ocean routes were older than the Atlantic, the latter would surpass the others in the number of captives transported during its relatively short but intense life span. Pier Larson estimates that between 650 and 1900, the Saharan trade took 7,450,000 slaves, the Indian Ocean trade, 4,200,000. The Atlantic system, by his statistics, took 11,313,000 African slaves between 1400 and 1900, the overwhelming majority of them in the eighteenth and nineteenth centuries.[3]

The Portuguese were therefore European pioneers in the African slave trade but a relatively minor force within the larger African slave market in the fifteenth and sixteenth centuries. Portuguese explorers usually set up trading forts on islands off the coast of Africa such as São Tomé because they were generally unable to impose their will on African polities. Exchange with local merchants and officials was, for the most part, the mechanism of the Atlantic slave traffic, not direct conquest and slaving (with the important exception of Angola at the end of the sixteenth century, discussed in chapter 2). As Herbert Klein observes: "European buyers were totally dependent on African sellers for the delivery of slaves."[4]

Slaves purchased by the Portuguese were destined for work and service in various locales controlled by Iberian powers. The Portuguese cities Lisbon and Evora had an ample African and African-descended population at the end of the fifteenth century. The same was true of Seville, the jumping-off point for Spanish voyages to the Americas in the sixteenth century. Slaves also labored on sugar plantations on the Atlantic islands controlled by the Portuguese and Spanish—Madeira, São Tomé, and the Canary Islands—harbingers of the plantation complex that would arise in the Americas over time.

Sugar plantations worked by unfree labor had a long history in the Iberian world, beginning in the Mediterranean. Italian and Iberian merchants established plantations in Cyprus, Sicily, and the southern part of the Iberian Peninsula. They found a ready market for their goods throughout Western Europe. They recruited workers from numerous sources: Muslim captives from the Crusades, Slavs from the Black Sea area, and increasingly, Africans from beyond the Sahara. This latter source of bonded labor became preeminent in the fifteenth century as the Portuguese built their commercial networks in Africa and founded productive plantations in

Madeira and São Tomé. In contrast to the medieval Mediterranean world, the early modern Atlantic world would increasingly associate enslavement with Africa and blackness, though this process developed over time.[5]

Thus, by the late fifteenth century, the precedents for African slavery in the Americas were taking shape in the Iberian world. The Portuguese had established a slave trade in the eastern Atlantic, sugar plantations were exporting their product to European markets, and African slaves were prominent in various Iberian settings, from the plantation to the city. Moreover, both Portugal and Castile possessed Roman, Visigothic, and medieval law codes that would shape slavery's development in the Americas. Slavery never faded as an institution in this corner of the defunct Roman Empire, so the laws that pertained to it continued to function and to find expression in legal codes. Among the important features of Roman law that survived in late medieval Iberia was the *peculium*, the slave's personal wealth, which could be used to purchase freedom from the master, even though it was already technically the property of the master. The scale of slave societies in Latin America far surpassed that of their Iberian predecessors, but laws inherited from the Roman Empire would play an important role in the New World, often leading to unintended consequences.[6]

It was from this commercial, colonial, and legal world that Christopher Columbus set sail in 1492 as an agent of the Spanish monarchy. His ambitions paralleled those of the Portuguese. He too sought to establish an oceanic path to India and China. He was also familiar with the budding sugar complex of the Atlantic islands. During a decade's residence in Portugal, he traveled to the slaving fort of El Mina and established ties to Portuguese enterprises in Madeira (merchants from his hometown, Genoa, were instrumental in providing the capital and carrying networks that supported the production and trade of sugar).[7] He also hoped that his discoveries would strike a blow against Islam. Indeed, one of his stated goals was to amass a fortune that would fund a new crusade to the Holy Lands. Unlike the Portuguese, he believed that he could reach the Indies by a westward *and* southerly route. This latter trajectory has recently received new attention. At the fore of Columbus's endeavor was the goal of trade with India and China, far richer economies than Europe's in this era. Always present in the background, however, was a plan of conquest and colonization. Columbus and other medieval geographers believed that an archipelago of islands extended from the Indian subcontinent far to the south and east, into the equatorial regions that they called the Torrid

Zone. The conviction that Columbus shared was that precious metals and gems came exclusively from torrid climes and that the people who dwelled there were naturally weak and inferior, suitable as servants of the European powers.[8]

This latter strategy, associated with the Torrid Zone, was what quickly won out. Columbus did not arrive in Asia, but his projection of an Indian archipelago led him to call the islands of the Caribbean the Indies and their inhabitants Indians. He established settlements on the island of Hispaniola and explored the Caribbean and the coasts of Central America and South America. Spaniards desiring wealth soon followed. By the early sixteenth century, there were settlements throughout the Caribbean and the Central American isthmus.

Though Columbus and his royal patrons were in search of trade with the rich Asian economies, they were also interested in gold, which Columbus found in small amounts in the Caribbean rivers on his first voyage. The Taíno Indians of the Greater Antilles, where the Spaniards concentrated their first settlements, lived in large villages and subsisted on agriculture, fishing, and hunting. They possessed a small number of locally mined gold ornaments that whetted the appetites of Columbus and his fellows. However, it was immediately evident that they could not offer to the Spaniards the luxury goods that they anticipated finding in places like China, Japan, and India. Wealth was to be gotten by other means. The conquerors turned to mining, cattle ranching, and farming to exploit the potential of the new colonies. The question of labor quickly leapt to the fore. Indeed, Columbus noted to himself in the logbook of his first voyage that the peoples he encountered in 1492 "should be good servants." The vision of a tropical overseas empire based on domination of the indigenous population had immediately sprung to mind.[9]

The Spanish immigrants to the Caribbean who followed Columbus on subsequent voyages were adventurers in search of riches, not hard labor. The peninsula would never provide a steady stream of pliant work-ers to the New World. Settlers thus preyed upon the indigenous popula-tion. The Spaniards extracted native labor through an institution known as *encomienda*. This royal grant gave the Spanish holder, the *encomendero*, the right to receive tribute and labor from Indian villages. In exchange, the encomendero was to offer Christian tutelage to the Indians to facilitate the process of conversion. The conquerors imposed the system of encomienda with great brutality, terrorizing local chiefdoms through extreme acts of violence. The governor of Hispaniola, Nicolás de Ovando, who arrived in 1502, sought to settle the unrest on the island by carrying out massacres of Indian notables and warriors. In the chiefdom of Higüey, the Spaniards knifed to death hundreds of Indian men, whose bodies were then openly displayed. In the chiefdom of Xaraguá, Ovando lured dozens of notables into a meeting and then burned them to death in a locked building.

The Spanish settlers in Hispaniola, Puerto Rico, and Cuba supplemented encomienda with Indian slavery. They opened trade with other islands, such as the Bahamas, which were completely depopulated by the slavers. They also used Spanish jurisprudence to justify enslaving Indians. The Spanish Crown permitted the enslavement of those Indians who were captured while resisting the authority of the monarchy. One version of this justification for Indian slavery was drafted in 1512 to limit the settlers' slaving. But it had the opposite effect. Spanish conquistadors would read to Indians a legal document called the *requerimiento*. The requerimiento spelled out a short history of Christianity and the Spanish monarchy. It invited the Indians to submit to the authority of the pope and the Spanish monarchs. Should they do so, they would be treated justly and their way of life respected. Should they resist, "we shall take you and your wives and your children, and shall make slaves of them, and as such sell and dispose of them as Their Highnesses may command; and we shall take away your goods, and shall do you all the mischief and damage that we can, as to vassals who do not obey, and refuse to receive their lord, and resist and contradict him; and we protest that the deaths and losses which shall accrue from this are your fault, and not that of Their Highnesses, or ours, nor of these cavaliers who come with us."[10]

Such legal mechanisms became valuable tools for securing domination of the Indian population. Spanish conquerors were known to read the requerimiento in Spanish or from a great distance so that it was incomprehensible or could not be heard; it thus provided a useful legal pretext for carrying war to newly encountered peoples and enslaving them. The conqueror and governor of Puerto Rico, Juan Ponce de León, used such measures to great effect. Faced with an uprising by the *cacique* (the Taíno name for their rulers) Agüeybana in 1511 and raids by Carib Indians from the Lesser Antilles, Ponce de León launched devastating reprisals. Finding themselves at war, he and his men were free to reduce captured Taínos to slavery and make them work in the island's mining centers. They also felt themselves entitled to carry out slaving expeditions against the Caribs from the Lesser Antilles. Alongside the Indians compelled to work through encomienda in Puerto Rico were Carib and Taíno slaves, distinguished by the *F* (for Ferdinand, king of Spain) branded upon their brows.[11]

The violent imposition of encomienda and slavery quickly engendered controversy within the expanding empire. Clerics such as Bartolomé de las Casas, himself an encomendero in Cuba for a short time, denounced the Spanish settlers for their abuse of the Indians and their utter indifference toward the work of evangelization. Las Casas argued that the conquerors were depopulating the colonies through their wanton violence and the harsh labor demands that they imposed on the Indians. Indeed, the conquerors went far beyond the limits of encomienda by trafficking in Indian slaves. Unless the monarchy acted to rein in the abuses, the Indians would be annihilated and their souls would be damned to hell, "having perished without ever learning the truths of the Christian religion and without the benefit of the Sacraments."[12]

The ecclesiastical attack on the violence of conquest and colonization was welcomed by the monarchy. The Spanish monarchs were concerned about establishing effective political control over the conquerors. They were loath to see an independent landed class that defied royal authority arise in the new colonies.

Moreover, the Catholic Kings Ferdinand and Isabella were engaged in a process of religious homogenization in their Iberian domains that would have important consequences for the colonies. Not only had they conquered the last Islamic kingdom of the peninsula, Granada, in 1492, but in the same year they also expelled all Jews who refused to convert to Christianity. Even earlier, in 1478, they had established an Inquisition under royal (as opposed to papal) authority to track down all Jewish converts to Christianity (*conversos*) suspected of practicing their old faith in private. When Columbus returned from the Caribbean in 1493, the rulers received a special charge from the pope to carry out the conversion of the peoples of the New World. The Spanish monarchs, in short, while always interested in wealth and political control, were also motivated by religious zeal. That encomienda interfered with conversion was therefore a most serious charge.

Royal and ecclesiastical efforts to curb encomienda and the power of the settlers were only sporadically effective for much of the sixteenth century. For example, in Peru, conquered under the leadership of the Pizarro brothers in the 1530s, the conquistadors revolted against royal authority in the 1540s when the Crown's representative sought to enact new legislation that would sharply curtail the spread and value of encomienda.

The clashes over the institution's legitimacy shaped not only relations between Spaniards and Indians in the New World but also the trajectory of the African slave trade to Spanish America. The attempts to limit encomienda and the settlers' control of the indigenous population reopened the question of labor. If the Crown and the Church successfully regulated the labor of Indians, then how would the owners of land, mines, and other enterprises find enough workers? The urgency of this question increased with the demise of the native population in the conquered lands. Highly vulnerable to the diseases introduced by the conquerors and dislocated by warfare and the imperatives of the colonial economy, the indigenous population declined precipitously and would not rebound until well into the seventeenth century in once densely populated regions like Mexico. In the Caribbean, the Taínos were virtually extinct by the middle of the sixteenth century. Many Spaniards suggested that the solution to these crises was to be found in the African slave trade forged by the Portuguese in the fifteenth century. Even Las Casas, the fierce defender of the Indians, briefly advocated enslaved Africans as a substitute labor force. The early slave trade to Spanish America thus opened out of the conflicts over Indian servitude and the destruction of the native population reaped by the conquerors as they built their new tropical empire.

## Why African Slavery?

African slaves and freedmen were already present in Spanish America when these controversies erupted in the early sixteenth century. Because the Portuguese had opened a slave trade from West Africa to the Iberian Peninsula and eastern Atlantic by the mid-fifteenth century, it is unsurprising that many of the Spanish conquistadors and settlers brought slaves and servants with them. One such example was a man named Juan Garrido, who was taken as a slave from West Africa to Lisbon sometime in the late fifteenth century. He ultimately gained his freedom there or in Seville. From the latter city he embarked for the Caribbean as the servant of the Spaniard Pedro Garrido. While in the Caribbean he participated in the wars of conquest in Puerto Rico and Cuba and later in the conquest of Mexico. For most of the rest of his life he took part in Spanish expeditions that explored the new colony before passing away in Mexico City some-time in the late 1540s.[13]

Juan Garrido's life in Africa, Europe, and the Americas tells us some-thing about slavery in the early phases of European colonization of the New World. Garrido was what the historian Ira Berlin has called an "Atlantic Creole," a man of African origin who adapted to the dominant European culture, taking a European name, speaking Spanish, practic-ing Christianity, and working in various capacities over his lifetime: as a soldier, doorman, town crier, and overseer of slave miners. Because he was familiar with Iberian ways from an early age, he was able to negoti-ate freedom and then make a living as a free man. Berlin argues that this pattern was common at the beginnings of colonization, before European settlers turned to more labor-intensive enterprises that demanded a more ruthlessly subordinated work force, particularly plantation agriculture.[14]

We can infer aspects of Garrido's life and career that were specific to the Iberian empires within the wider Atlantic context. For example, pro-cesses for gaining freedom were prescribed in Iberian law codes and prac-tice. In Spain and its American empire, slaves were permitted to purchase their freedom from their owners if they had gathered a peculium. Slaves might also be manumitted for various kinds of service, from military ser-vice to the king to personal service to a private slaveholder. Sometimes private acts of manumission required that the freed slave continue to per-form service for the former master. The law codes of Castile, regnant in Spanish America, also spelled out the necessity of slaves receiving the sacraments of the Church, including marriage. The role of the Catholic Church, in fact, was crucial in shaping slavery in the Iberian world. Not only were slaves to receive the sacraments, but they were also allowed to form their own confraternities—lay religious associations—which would play a significant role in shaping urban slavery and freedom.

African slavery was therefore a familiar alternative for royal officials and colonial settlers as they fought over the place of Indians in the empire. Why, however, did Spaniards believe that it was legitimate to enslave Africans but not Indians? Or for that matter, why did they not open a trade in unfree European workers?[15]

In Europe, such a population certainly did exist. Various groups were enslaved in the Iberian Peninsula during the era of overseas ex-pansion, and different kinds of coerced and unfree labor that greatly resembled enslavement also grew in this period.[16] Enslaved Muslim war captives were common in sixteenth- and seventeenth-century Spain as the Habsburg monarchs clashed with the Ottoman Empire for supremacy in the Mediterranean. *Moriscos* (Muslims converted to Christianity in Spain, whose number increased after the conquest of Granada) deemed renegades and traitors were also enslaved. Both groups were royal slaves, their fate ultimately controlled by the monarchy. Penal servitude was also widespread. Convicted criminals spared capital punishment were sentenced to long terms of hard labor, which frequently turned into de facto life sentences.

The Habsburg war machine generated the vast demand for coerced and enslaved workers. Slaves and convicts (*forzados*) supplied the brute labor for the war galleys active in the Mediterranean. Slaves and forzados rowed side by side in the huge crews (*chusmas*) of the galleys, the largest of which were manned by over three hundred oarsmen. Though forzados were supposed to serve sentences of no more than ten years, the demands of constant warfare encouraged the royal administration to keep men on for as long as they were useful through various administrative tricks. Slaves and convicts also manned the royal mercury mines at Almadén (supplier of the mercury used in silver refining in New Spain), the presidios that dotted the Spanish and North African coastlines, and when the use of galleys declined in the eighteenth century, the great arsenals of the Spanish navy.

Property in human beings defined the boundary between slavery and other types of forced labor. In actual treatment, they often came to resemble one another. Convicts who labored on the galleys were dispatched in chain gangs from prisons to port cities such as Cartagena on the Mediterranean coast. In Cervantes's novel, published in the early seventeenth century, Don Quixote and Sancho Panza witnessed this spectacle in their wanderings through La Mancha and pondered its essential similarity to slavery:

> Don Quixote looked up and saw coming toward him on the same road he was traveling approximately twelve men on foot, strung together by their necks, like beads on a great iron chain, and all of them wearing manacles. Accompanying them were two men on horseback and two on foot; the ones on horseback had flintlocks, and those on foot carried javelins and swords; as soon as Sancho Panza saw them, he said:

"This is a chain of galley slaves, people forced by the king to go to the galleys."

"What do you mean, forced?" asked Don Quixote. "Is it possible that the king forces anyone?"

"I'm not saying that," responded Sancho, "but these are people who, because of their crimes, have been condemned to serve the king in the galleys, by force."

"In short," replied Don Quixote, "for whatever reason, these people are being taken by force and not of their own free will."

"That's right," said Sancho.[17]

The demand for this kind of coerced labor within Spain itself perhaps curtailed the possibility of redirecting chain gangs to the New World in vast numbers.[18] In Portugal, the monarchy did force some groups, such as orphans and widows, to migrate to the overseas territories, especially in Asia.[19] But unlike the French and British colonizers, who in the seventeenth century would experiment with European indentured workers, those contractually bound to masters for a term of service, the Iberians never put in place a large-scale traffic of laborers from Europe to the Americas. The huge native populations of their New World territories, coupled with Iberian development of the African slave trade, made other forms of forced labor more immediately attractive to the Spanish and Portuguese conquerors.

As we have seen, exploitation of Native Americans quickly provoked controversy, especially in the Spanish Empire.[20] Regarding the natives of the New World, Spanish jurists insisted that the conquered peoples were the rightful possessors of the land and had their own legitimate lords before the arrival of the conquistadors. Conquest rightfully transferred sovereignty to the Spanish monarchy. It also made the peoples of the New World the subjects of the monarchs and therefore entitled to their protection. Moreover, because of the charge from the papacy to convert pagans to Christianity, the Spanish monarchy had a special obligation to oversee the just treatment and education of the conquered.

There were exceptions to this view. The conquistadors and their representatives to the Spanish court believed that the Spanish, as a conquering race, had demonstrated their superiority over the Indians, whom they must now rule as natural slaves. Conversion should be carried out not by education but through force. The monarchy was generally resistant to the claims of the conquistadors and settlers, whom it wished to keep in check.

However, there were certain exceptions to the ban on the enslavement of Indians, as we have seen. Rebels and war captives could be justifiably enslaved. More to the point, Indians were still subject to other kinds of labor coercion. Encomienda continued to spread with the Spanish conquistadors, while in rich mining centers like Peru the royal bureaucracy adapted preconquest labor systems to the mining industry. In Peru, the *mita* system forced all male Indians to spend a set period of time working in the mines of Potosí. The Crown's commitment to evangelization was thus tempered by the political realities of the colonies and by the promise of fabulous wealth in silver and gold (the Crown received one-fifth of all proceeds from mining).

Still, the situation of conquered Indians differed significantly from that of enslaved Africans. Fewer protections pertained to Africans in Spain or Spanish America. As one historian of Latin American slavery has observed, "no Las Casas ever came to the aid of the African." Because African slaves were imported into the peninsula or the colonies from territories beyond Spanish sovereignty, they were legally considered foreigners resident in Spanish domains. The same was true of their descendants.[21]

The Iberian slavers and slave owners also believed that there were religious sanctions for African slavery. One story that was extrapolated from the Old Testament concerned the curse placed upon Ham by his father, Noah. According to this story, Africans were descendants of Ham, cursed by his father for mocking his drunkenness and nakedness. Ham's children, beginning with his son Canaan, would thereafter form a race of slaves. In the late middle ages and early modern period, Christian and Jewish commentaries came to associate Ham's offspring with blackness, a corollary to the curse that gave the enslavement of Africans even more justification and apparent inevitability.

The Spanish Jesuit Alonso de Sandoval voiced these beliefs in his treatise on Africa, the slave traffic, and slavery. Sandoval was well situated to discuss such matters: based in the major Spanish American slaving port of the seventeenth century, Cartagena de Indias, he greeted the slave vessels and catechized those who survived the Middle Passage. Even this unusually compassionate figure subscribed to the explanations and justifications for slavery current in his time:

> One could infer, not without some basis, that the black skin of
> the Ethiopians not only comes from the curse Noah put on his

son Ham but also is an innate or intrinsic part of how God created them, so that in this extreme heat, the sons engendered
were left this color, as a sign that they descend from a man who
mocked his father, to punish his daring. Thus the Ethiopians
descend from Ham, the first servant and slave that there ever was
in the world, whose punishment darkened the skin of his sons and
descendants.[22]

While Iberian law codes and religion did protect the enslaved in certain ways, they still provided sanction for slavery. A sermon preached by the
Portuguese Jesuit Antonio Vieira in seventeenth-century Brazil shows how
broad and complex the commitment was to slavery in the Iberian world.
Preaching before a congregation of masters and slaves in the Brazilian city
of Bahia in 1633, Vieira asked the enslaved to accept their condition in spite
of the cruelty of their masters. He told them that their worldly enslavement was promise of their freedom before God in the next world. The
physical enslavement of the body was nothing compared to the spiritual
enslavement of the soul: "We have seen that just as human beings consist of
two parts or two halves—the body and the soul—just so slavery is divided
into two slaveries—one, the enslavement of the body in which bodies are
involuntarily captives and slaves of men; another, the slavery of the soul, in
which through one's own will souls are sold and become the captives and
slaves of the Devil."[23] Slaves therefore must not revolt against their worldly
condition; no matter how cruel the treatment of masters in this world,
enslavement and punishment were signs of liberation in the next: "when
you serve your masters you do not serve as one who serves men, but as one
who serves God. Thus you do not work as slaves but as free men, nor do you
obey as slaves but as sons. You do not work as slaves but as free men because
God will pay you for your work, and you do not obey as slaves but as sons
and daughters because God . . . will make you His heirs."[24]

Yet, while preaching resignation to the enslaved, Vieira heaped contempt and warnings upon the masters. They might seek comfort in their
present state: "'I,' each one of you is saying, 'I, thanks to God, am White
and not Black, free and not captive, master and not slave; in fact, I own
many of them.'" Vieira warned them, though, that their condition was
temporary. He asked them to consider the plight of the Jews in Egypt.
God was willing to allow their captivity and enslavement but liberated
them and punished Pharaoh and his people when the sufferings of the

enslaved became too great. Was not the same possible in Brazil? "What theology can there be that would justify the inhumanity and cruelty of the extreme punishments with which these slaves are mistreated? Mistreated indeed, but that is a very short word to cover the meaning that it conceals and hides. Tyrannized, we should say, or martyrized. For this is more like martyrdom than punishment for the miserable injured ones, squeezed, sealed with hot wax, slashed, ground up, and victims of even worse excesses about which I will be silent."[25]

Complacency in the face of such violence could only lead to violent redemption: "Oh, how I fear that the Ocean will be for you like the Red Sea, your houses like those of the Pharaoh, and all Brazil like Egypt! . . . If your hearts, like those of the Pharaoh, are hardened, that is tragic, because you will suffer the ultimate punishment. May God grant that I am wrong in this sad thought."[26]

Vieira justified slavery but in complicated and apparently contradictory terms. Enslavement of the body in this world promised the liberation of the soul in the next. Slaves must accept their fate here to reap the promise of salvation in the afterlife. The Jesuit likened the slaves to the Christian martyrs and to the "sons of Israel," the chosen people of the Old Testament. But acceptance of slavery in the here and now did not imply that the abuses of the masters had no consequences. While he preached passivity and martyrdom to the slaves, Vieira denounced their masters for their cruelty and violence. Should they continue to mistreat their slaves, Vieira warned that the fate of the Pharaoh awaited them. In other words, while slavery was part of the flawed human world, divine justice nonetheless limited its abuses.[27]

Commitment to enslaved African labor, justified by experience in the eastern Atlantic and by religious and legal sanctions, did not immediately translate into an unbridled slave trade, either to Brazil or to Spanish America. From its beginnings, the slave trade to Spanish America operated through highly regulated licenses awarded by the monarchy to Italian, Spanish, and Portuguese merchants. In the late sixteenth century, *asientos* (exclusive contracts) were granted to foreign slavers, initially Portuguese, later French and British. Spanish and Spanish American merchants became slave traders only much later, at the end of the eighteenth century. One reason for this reliance on foreign traders was that Spain had no trading forts or colonies on the west coast of Africa, as did the Portuguese and, later, other European nations. In the Treaty of

Algaçovas (1479), Castile ceded exploration and settlement of Africa to the Portuguese, a division reinforced after 1492 by subsequent treaties. Spain's historic distance from direct trade with Africa would shape slavery in its colonies over the centuries.

When the Crown did authorize the slave traffic to the American colonies in the early sixteenth century, it stipulated that slaves were to come only from the Iberian Peninsula so as to guarantee the introduction of Christians into the New World domains. This restriction came to an end in 1518 when the Emperor Charles V permitted the direct shipment of slaves from Africa to Spanish America, though still under licenses awarded by the Crown. São Tomé was the leading entrepôt in Africa in the early to mid-sixteenth century. From that base, the Portuguese entered into lucrative commercial relations with the mainland Kingdom of Kongo. Slaves were at the heart of this trade, many destined to work on São Tome's plantations but many others reexported to Europe and the Americas. Later in the sixteenth century São Tomé would be surpassed by Luanda as the major Portuguese slave port.[28]

The Caribbean colonies, where the controversy over encomienda had first erupted and where the destruction of the native population was most thorough, were early patrons of the slave trade. Planters in Cuba, Hispaniola, and Puerto Rico experimented with sugar plantations, consciously imitating the methods forged in the fifteenth century in the islands of the eastern Atlantic. They imported slaves from Africa and Iberia and brought in technology and skilled workers from the Atlantic islands, such as Madeira, where the plantation complex was in full swing. When the Spanish monarch Philip II took over the Portuguese throne in 1580, there was a spike in the slave traffic to Cuba, especially to the major port of Havana, as Portuguese traders gained exclusive privileges as the holders of the first asiento. These efforts, though, were sporadic. The costs of owning slaves could become prohibitive, while competition from other sugar producers, including from Spain itself, drove down profits. The first experiments in Caribbean sugar plantations were therefore limited. The real boom in Caribbean sugar production would take place in the insular possessions of rival empires in the seventeenth and eighteenth centuries (Barbados, Jamaica, Saint-Domingue).[29]

More than economic factors produced this hiatus. By the mid-sixteenth century the focus of Spanish rule in the New World had shifted from the Caribbean. Cortés's conquest of the Aztec Empire in the 1520s and the Pizarros' conquest of the Inca Empire in the 1530s brought to prominence the new Viceroyalties of New Spain (Mexico) and Peru. Rich in mineral wealth, densely populated, and possessed of sophisticated political and economic systems, the Aztec and Inca realms now attracted the bulk of Spanish immigration, investment, and royal and ecclesiastical personnel. They also absorbed most of the African slaves imported into Spanish America in the sixteenth and seventeenth centuries.

In Mexico and Peru, the conquistadors and encomenderos struggled against efforts by the Crown and Church to restrict the use of Indian labor. Encomienda and the system known as *repartimiento*, the forced distribution of indigenous workers, did compel Indian communities to supply labor to Spanish overlords and ventures. But the decline of the native population and the continual efforts to regulate Indian labor forced landowners and employers to turn to other sources. During the sugar harvest in Mexican regions such as Morelos, hacendados contracted with Indian notables to supply extra workers during peak times. There was also a precocious wage-labor system in mining sectors such as Potosí, high in the Andes in the Viceroyalty of Peru (later the Viceroyalty of La Plata, after administrative reshuffling in the eighteenth century), in which employers contracted with free workers—Indian, Spanish, and, increasingly, mixed-race—for wages.

African slaves were an important part of this patchwork of labor. By 1650 approximately 350,000 African captives had been transported to the colonies of Spanish America, principally Mexico and Peru.[30] The combination of the Spanish and Portuguese Crowns between 1580 and 1640 spurred the flow of captives to the Spanish Indies, as the premier slave-trading nation now enjoyed access to those colonies. Though often thought of as a substitute for the declining Indian population, slaves never came close to replacing the population lost in the catastrophe of conquest. They did, however, work throughout the economies of Mexico and Peru. Sugar haciendas in Veracruz and Morelos in Mexico relied upon a mix of workers—free Spaniards receiving wages, Indians recruited through a variety of means including encomienda, and African slaves. A study of the sugar haciendas of Hernán Cortés and his descendants shows that in the early seventeenth century, African slaves were most likely to work in the milling and purging section of the hacienda because the colonial regime forbade the use of Indian workers in those areas. Indians were field hands, while Spaniards filled most of the skilled

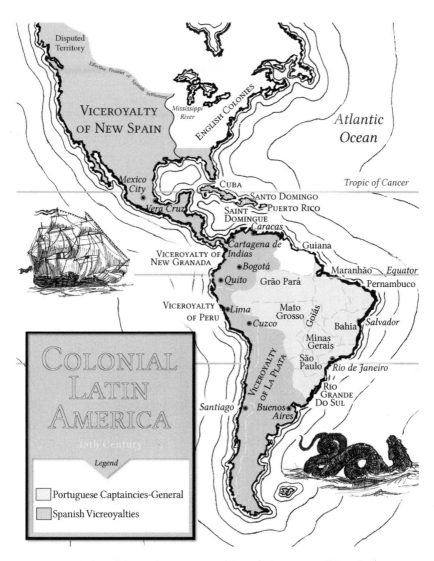

MAP 3. Colonial Spanish America and Brazil. Courtesy of Tim Cannon.

and administrative positions. Slaves were found far beyond the haciendas of Mexico. Many were concentrated in the viceregal capital, Mexico City, where they labored as skilled workers and domestic servants. The silver mines of Mexico also employed a significant number of slaves in the sixteenth and seventeenth centuries.[31]

Veracruz, on the Gulf of Mexico, was the viceroyalty's main slaving port. Peru did not possess an Atlantic port, so the traffic in captives followed a more roundabout path. The major port for Spanish South America was Cartagena de Indias in Nueva Granada (present-day Colombia). From there, merchants arranged a traffic that carried slaves from Cartagena through the isthmus at Panama and finally to Lima's port, Callao, which in turn served as the great entrepôt for the Viceroyalty of Peru and adjacent realms such as the Kingdom of Chile.

As in Mexico, slaves worked in a variety of capacities in Peru and other regions of Spanish South America. Peruvian agriculture relied heavily upon slave labor. Tasks ranged from work on small truck farms near Lima to large estates that specialized in cattle ranching and the production of export crops like sugar. The great bulk of slave workers were to be found in the environs of Lima, but slavery spread throughout the agricultural regions of the viceroyalty (Indian labor continued to predominate in the highlands). Frederick Bowser found that slavery made its way into practically every branch of Peru's coastal economy.[32] Slaves worked on ships, in mule trains, as household servants, and as skilled workers hired out by their owners in cities such as Lima. In the ports of Callao and Guayaquil, the majority of skilled black laborers were slaves. They were shipwrights, joiners, caulkers, and carpenters rented from owners. Slaves and later free people, especially women, were also instrumental as vendors in the urban centers. They brought produce to market in town, prepared food for sale, and sometimes became owners of taverns and stores. The one area of the viceregal economy where slave labor was minimal was in the rich mining sector. Though the Crown and its representatives voiced concern over the abuse of Indian labor through the mita system, they nonetheless bowed to the interests of mine owners who preferred to rely on the entrenched and reliable mita as opposed to slave labor, which was expensive and erratic in its supply. Thus, in what was Spain's richest colony in the sixteenth and seventeenth centuries, there developed an "African coast and Indian sierra."[33]

## Brazil

In the Portuguese Empire, slavery was associated with sugar and plantation labor from an early date. Madeira and São Tomé pioneered the African slave trade and the production of sugar for export to western European markets long before the rise of the Middle Passage to the Americas. It is curious to note, then, that even with these precedents, the slave trade and the sugar plantation were slow in coming to Brazil. But once they took hold, Brazil would far surpass, in volume and in duration, any other New World colony or independent nation in the import of African slaves.

Though the Portuguese were the first Europeans to institutionalize the slave trade to their colonial possessions, their primary concern as explorers, traders, and conquerors was with the route to the Indian Ocean, which they opened at the end of the fifteenth century when Vasco da Gama established a string of trading outposts along the east coast of Africa and South Asia. Following da Gama's route in 1500, Pedro Álvares Cabral unintentionally landed on the northeast tip of Brazil while seeking to traverse the Cape of Good Hope. The Portuguese quickly recognized this as territory hitherto unknown to the Europeans. They also claimed it as their own because it fell on the eastern side of the line drawn by the pope and the Iberian monarchs when they divided the world between themselves after Columbus's first voyage. Though according to the Treaty of Tordesillas (1494) the Spaniards were meant to explore westward and the Portuguese eastward, Brazil happened to fall to the latter's share.

With the eastern vocation by which they reaped great wealth from their Asian outposts, the Portuguese initially paid little attention to this new possession. The major lure was the extraction of brazilwood, source of a coveted red dye. The intentions of European rivals, especially the French, served as a goad for a more durable colonization. Through much of the sixteenth century, French merchants and privateers sought to establish trade connections on the Brazilian coast. At midcentury, French Protestants attempted to found a permanent colony at Guanabara Bay, present-day Rio de Janeiro. To head off "France antartique," the Portuguese Crown created incentives to attract colonizers. Huge land grants known as captaincies were doled out. The most successful in attracting European immigrants and establishing the economic foundations of a permanent colony were in the northeast: Pernambuco and Bahia.

Pernambuco and Bahia were major sugar producers and importers of African slaves, but planters established the sugar plantation before the African slave trade. To recruit labor, they preyed first upon the indigenous population of coastal Brazil. The peoples of the Brazilian littoral formed a broad linguistic and cultural group known as the Tupí, including the inhabitants of the northeast, the Tupinamba. They lived according to a subsistence economy. There were no great economies of scale or state structures like those the Spanish found and exploited in Mexico and Peru. Barter for brazilwood and food was the initial medium of Portuguese and Tupinamba relations. But once planters introduced sugarcane into the region, they sought to enslave the Tupinamba or coerce them through other means onto their plantations as workers.

The Portuguese Crown was less adamant than the Spanish about restricting the enslavement of the Indians. Though officially opposed, the Crown appeased settlers by permitting de facto enslavement through various legal fictions, such as the enslavement of captives in a "just war" or the rescue (*resgate*) of Indian captives from other tribes. The slave trade from Africa was still expensive and erratic in the mid-sixteenth century, so Brazilian Indians formed the core of the plantation labor force. These included the Tupinamba and eventually groups from interior regions, as the planters and their allies began to mount vigorous slaving expeditions.

The major opposition to the planters' predations came from the Jesuits, though as Stuart Schwartz has argued, the role of the Jesuits was perhaps more complementary than otherwise. Like the Dominicans in the early phase of Spanish colonization in the Caribbean, the Jesuits insisted that the purpose of colonization was the conversion of the Indians to Christianity. To that end they established *aldeias*, villages, in which they gathered the Tupinamba and carried out the work of conversion and education in European ways. (In the Spanish Empire the Jesuits founded similar communities, known as *reducciónes*.) Among the customs they hoped to instill was settled agricultural work. They sought to transform the Tupinamba into a settled peasantry that worked the land. The Jesuits, though they opposed the violence of the planters and the outright enslavement of the natives, were willing to let planters rent Indian workers from the aldeias to labor on the plantations. In other words, they too endeavored to transform the Tupinamba into a pliant and reliable workforce for the nascent export economy.[34]

Planters did ultimately turn aggressively to the African slave trade in the late sixteenth century. As in Spanish America, the arrival of the Europeans shattered native Brazilian society. Epidemics of Old World diseases like smallpox and measles decimated Indians, who had no resistance and were weakened by the disruptions of colonization. The Crown and the Church also began to throw up more concerted opposition to the enslavement of the native population, though planters and slavers continued to resist these prescriptions, especially the backwoodsmen of São Paulo in the Brazilian southeast, the so-called *bandeirantes*, who carried out epic slave raids in the interior well into the seventeenth century. These included the sacking of Spanish Jesuit reducciónes on the boundaries that separated Spanish and Portuguese America and the enslavement of thousands of Guaraní Indians settled there. Moreover, wherever the Portuguese expanded the frontier of settlement in the seventeenth century, such as the Amazon region, the colonists sated their hunger for labor by enslaving newly encountered tribes despite prescriptions to the contrary.[35]

But planters in more settled regions like Pernambuco and Bahia were certainly willing to employ enslaved African instead of Indian labor. The transition was uneven. Experience with the slave trade and slavery in Portugal and the Atlantic islands left settlers in Brazil well disposed toward African workers. Africans were experienced in the techniques of the sugar mill in places like Madeira and São Tomé. They also had their own traditions of manufacture and skilled labor that Europeans found useful. Even when Indians formed the vast bulk of the labor force on Brazilian plantations, the few African slaves filled the most skilled positions in the refining process. As planters accumulated capital and established viable commercial networks with European markets, they purchased more and more slaves from Africa. By the early seventeenth century, the African slave trade supplanted the internal Brazilian slave trade as the main conduit for unfree labor on the northeastern plantations and became the lifeblood for the first great sugar boom in the New World.[36]

The slave trade to Brazil was thereafter a constant until its suppression in 1850. Brazil alone imported close to half of all the Africans carried in the Middle Passage. Many were destined for labor on sugar plantations in the northeast. But over the centuries sugar would decline relative to other sources of tropical wealth. At the beginning of the eighteenth century, Minas Gerais emerged as a rival to Pernambuco and Bahia. The lure there was to be found in the region's mines, where tremendous fortunes were made from gold, diamonds, and a variety of other gems and minerals. When Brazil achieved its independence from Portugal in the nineteenth century, coffee in the southeastern Paraíba Valley soon supplanted sugar as the major agricultural export. In all of these cases, African and African-descended slaves formed the core of the labor force.

## The Middle Passage and Colonial Culture

By the late sixteenth century, most slaves imported into Latin America came directly from Africa. In the early days of colonization many slaves came from the Iberian Peninsula or other Iberian domains. They came in smaller numbers and were often integrated into the dominant culture. But as the demand for enslaved labor grew dramatically in Peru, Mexico, and Brazil, captives from Africa became the great majority. Political circumstances dovetailed with economic and social factors when the Spanish king took hold of the Portuguese throne in the late sixteenth century. The Portuguese kingdom continued to enjoy considerable autonomy from Philip of Spain's other domains. This arrangement was in keeping with the nature of the Iberian monarchies, which were a composite of diverse jurisdictions, privileges, and institutions. Nonetheless, the Portuguese-Spanish connection had an impact on the slave trade to the Americas. Portuguese slavers, with their long experience in Africa, came to dominate the traffic. And greater numbers of slaves began to arrive from the Portuguese outpost at Luanda, the terminus for extensive slave networks through Central Africa.

The passage from Africa to the Americas was long and uncertain.[37] It began with brutal travails in Africa itself. Slaves might spend between six months and a year in Africa from the time of their capture or purchase to embarkation to America. The networks from the coast reached deep into the hinterlands, especially around the great rivers of West and Central Africa such as the Senegal, Gambia, Niger, and Congo. A Portuguese physician, writing in the late eighteenth century, recounted the harsh welcome at Luanda after the long trek from the interior: "When they are first traded, they are made to bear the mark of the backlander who enslaved them, so that they can be recognized in case they run away. And when they reach a port . . . they are branded on the right breast with the coat of arms of the king and nation, of whom they have become vassals and under whom they will live subject to slavery. This mark is made with a hot silver instrument in the act of paying the king's duties, and this brand mark is called a *carimbo*."[38]

The wait on the coast might last as long as three months, as European slavers traversed the region looking for a full shipment of human cargo. Once loaded on the slave ships, captives were packed into tight decks layered in the ship's hold. The journey to Brazil from Central Africa could last a month, that from West Africa to the Caribbean, two months. The Portuguese physician described conditions of extreme physical hardship, as the crew strictly limited the space, movement, food, and water of the enslaved: "the slaves are afflicted with a very short ration of water, of poor quality and lukewarm because of the climate—hardly enough to water their mouths. The suffering that this causes is extraordinary, and their dryness and thirst cause epidemics, which, beginning with one person, soon spread to many others. Thus, after only a few days at sea, they start to throw the slaves into the ocean."[39]

Recent findings in the history of the slave trade show that the mortality rate on these voyages was high but not as high as once believed in spite of the treatment described above. Slavers had a strong interest in arriving in the Americas with as many survivors as possible. Over the long history of the trade mortality rates averaged between 10 and 20 percent. However, averages tell only a small part of the story. On some ships diseases could hit with devastating effect, taking the lives of slaves and crews alike. This randomness was one constant feature of the trade: "Very high mortality rates tend to be associated with unexpectedly long voyages, or to unusual outbreaks of disease, but, in general, it is the very broad range of outcomes rather than any bunching at specific mortality rates that has been the main characteristic of the transatlantic slave trade for most of its existence."[40] The main killers were malaria, yellow fever, and gastrointestinal diseases such as dysentery (the "bloody flux"). Scurvy and smallpox took the lives of many captives, though these declined by the eighteenth century. Some captives committed suicide; others banded together to stage revolts against the slavers, a perpetual feature of this violent traffic.

Historians have had a more difficult time reconstructing the health and mortality of African slaves once disembarked in the Americas. However, they have been able to document the hardships they encountered over time. Kenneth Kiple's studies of the diet of slaves in the Caribbean and its impact on their health are revealing. He found widespread malnutrition among slave populations that led to "night blindness," scurvy, anemia, suicidal depression, and calcium deficiencies, among other maladies. Malnutrition was especially devastating among slaves born in the Caribbean. It "tormented [them] twice, working much of its debilitating and often deadly effects through poor maternal nutrition before even touching the child via his own nutritional intake."[41] The result was infant and child mortality rates that took half of all those born in the Caribbean. Because of this

"slaughter," as Kiple calls it, slave populations in the Caribbean were maintained only through the trade, not natural increase, which tells us much
about the institution's cruelty.

The cultural impact on the enslaved of enslavement and transport
to the coast of Africa and thence to the Americas is a question that has
attracted widespread debate.[42] Those who survived the horror of the Middle Passage arrived in the Spanish and Portuguese colonies in a weakened physical condition. They were alien to the dominant culture, did not
speak the language of power, and usually practiced religions distinct from
Iberian Catholicism. From the vantage point of slave owners, the marginal
position of African slaves in the colonial world made them more vulnerable to control by the master class and the colonial state.

The anthropologists Sidney Mintz and Richard Price have argued that
African slaves and their descendants overcame the potentially dehumaniz-
ing experience of enslavement by responding tenaciously and creatively to
their circumstances in the New World. They defied the masters' and officials' desire to make them into their instruments. In doing so, they necessarily invented new forms of culture and community in the Americas. For
Mintz and Price, this process began during the Middle Passage. Peoples
of distinct linguistic and cultural groups were forced together in the slave
pens of entrepôts such as El Mina and Luanda. Those who survived transport through Africa and the Middle Passage forged new bonds among
themselves, thereby creating novel relations and identities. This process
continued in the Americas as the enslaved adapted to the different situations of colonial society. Language, religion, work, family, the law: all
were new. Survival required adaptation to these settings: "the people in
African-American societies, in which oppression was pervasive, quite literally built their life-ways to meet their daily needs."[43]

Other scholars, in contrast, have argued that enslaved Africans endured
by re-creating their Old World cultures in the hostile environment of the
New World. They have demonstrated that there were broad cultural and
linguistic groupings in West and Central Africa that crossed the myriad
regions and polities. Slaves were able to recognize their shared beliefs and
to compose forms of social organization and ritual life that approximated
more familiar settings. Such was especially true in those places where the
European overlords exercised less intimate control. These spaces might
include plantation belts like the Recôncavo of Bahia, where Africans outnumbered Europeans, or communities of runaway slaves beyond the reach

of the plantation and the colonial state. Thus, "Africa arrived in the various destinations of the colonial world in all of its social and cultural richness, informing the institutions that Africans created and providing them with a prism through which to interpret and understand their condition as slaves and as freed people."[44]

Rather than reenact this debate, I propose to explore aspects of the various positions. We can find rich examples that illustrate the thesis of cultural innovation and others that speak to the re-creation of Africa in America.

Nowhere are these processes more vividly illustrated than in the zestful religious life of the Iberian empires. Though the Iberian colonizers treated Africans distinctly from Indians, they at least paid lip service to converting the enslaved to Christianity. In Spanish South America, for example, the Jesuits greeted the arriving slave ships in Cartagena de Indias to begin the process of evangelization and conversion. Many Africans were Christians or had exposure to Christianity before arriving in the Americas, especially those from the Kingdom of Kongo, which was ruled by Christian princes.

In the cities of colonial Latin America, slaves and freed people often formed their own lay Catholic associations and participated in civic and ecclesiastical rituals. Salvador da Bahia in the Brazilian northeast was home to a rich associational life. Membership in lay brotherhoods devoted to particular saints was generalized and reproduced the divisions characteristic of urban slave society: Portuguese- and Brazilian-born whites had their own brotherhoods, as did mulattoes and blacks, the Brazilian- and the African-born, and the enslaved and the free. Among Africans, different ethnic groups such as Angolans, Jejes, and Nagôs joined separate brotherhoods. Within the African brotherhoods, members elected kings who re-created forms of authority and ideas of the mediation between heaven and earth, inscribing African practices and organization in colonial institutions. Though the brotherhoods thus helped to strengthen the hierarchies of colonial society, they also facilitated a shared civic life and provided a space in which Africans could approximate their cultures.[45]

That the dominant religion was more than a tool of social control is evident from the ways in which slaves made use of its rules to further their autonomy or to shield themselves from the abuse of their masters. The royal slaves of El Cobre in eastern Cuba relied on their link to the

shrine of the local patron saint, Our Lady of Charity, to defend their sense
of community and their autonomy from the rigors of the slave economy.
The royal slaves, as this phrase suggests, were the property of the Spanish
monarchy. They became royal slaves when the private operator of a local
copper mine that employed slave labor forfeited his control in the later
seventeenth century. Over the decades the slaves of El Cobre made constant reference to their special relation to the Spanish monarch and to the
local shrine to the Virgin. Through these appeals they convinced colonial
officials to keep their community intact. For instance, in their petitions
they frequently intimated that Our Lady of Charity would be angered if
her longtime caretakers were dispersed.[46]

In New Spain some slaves were able to force the Inquisition to intervene against abusive masters. The Spanish monarchy introduced the Inquisition into the Viceroyalties of New Spain and Peru to police the colonial
Christian population (in contrast, the Portuguese monarchy did not create a seat of the Holy Office in Brazil. Instead, Portuguese Inquisitors
carried out extended visits to the colony). Among the accused brought
before the Holy Office were slaves who had blasphemed while being physically punished by their masters. One such slave was Juan Bautista, who in
1598 declared "I renounce God!" after his master covered him with hot
pitch and forced a firebrand in his mouth. Blaspheming like Bautista's was
apparently a desperate choice made by the slaves because they hoped that
it would provoke the intervention of the Inquisition. In their testimony
they could then denounce their masters because the extreme violence of
their punishments had forced them to blaspheme and thus endanger their
salvation. In other words, though the slaves were guilty themselves, their
masters were guilty of a far worse crime in pushing their slaves to the
brink: "they used Christian religion as a 'language of contention'—that
is, as a 'common ground' shared with the Inquisitors upon which they
could establish their innocence and hold their masters—the true 'bad'
Christians and God's enemies—responsible for provoking their blasphe-
mies and putting at risk the salvation of their souls."[47]

Religion as a set of institutions was thus important in the making of
African-American cultures and the shaping of colonial slavery. As a set of
beliefs about life and the world, it was also essential. Comparable attitudes
toward the world of the living and the afterlife made possible the convergence of European and African religions in the Americas. Europeans and
Africans alike "conceived the cosmos as being divided into two separate

but intimately connected worlds: 'this world,' the material world that we all live in and that can be perceived by the five normal senses, and the 'other world,' normally imperceptible except to a few gifted individuals and inhabited by a variety of beings or entities." Both groups placed special emphasis on revelations and the interpretation of revelations as the foundation of religious belief and practice. Christian priests admitted that Africans received revelations, though they often condemned these as ploys of the devil. Africans, meanwhile, accepted the ancient revelations at the core of European Christianity when they dovetailed with their own.[48]

If we jump ahead slightly in time we find an especially fascinating and vibrant example of this convergence in the formation of Santería, the way of the saints. In the late eighteenth and early nineteenth centuries there was a huge surge in the number of Yorubas, a people from present-day Nigeria and Benin, transported to the Americas because of political and military upheaval in that area of Africa. Most of the enslaved Yoruba were destined for the great plantation societies of that era: Brazil and Cuba.

In Cuba the newly arrived Yoruba, called Lucumí in the colony, were organized in confraternities and *cabildos de nación*, mutual aid societies that grouped slaves according to their African ethnicities.[49] The cabildos helped Africans practice their Old World social and ritual ways, though under the gaze of the colonial Church. In the case of the Yorubas in Cuba, the Lucumí cabildos offered a space in which to honor the *orisha*. The orisha form "a pantheon of spiritual beings" who embody different aspects of *ashe*, "the blood of cosmic life" or "a divine current." For example, the orisha Ogun represents iron. He is patron to blacksmiths and also the embodiment of iron's value as a force of war and strength. His counterpart is Oshun, who represents water and rivers, bringer of life, coolness, and health.[50]

While the Yoruba of Cuba could continue to evoke the orisha, they did so under watchful Christian eyes and within a form of organization and ritual calendar intended to honor the Christian God and saints. Accordingly, homage to the orisha began to take place under cover of Christian holidays such as the Epiphany (Día de los Reyes) and saints such as Christopher and Barbara. Over time these practices led to a fusion of the orisha and the saints in Santería (see table 1). Rather than mere cover for Old World practices, worship of the saints complemented the worship of the orisha. Santo Niño de Atocha, for example, was not a mask for Eleggua but a distinct and related manifestation of his qualities.

TABLE 1. Orisha and saints

| Orisha | Saint | Principle |
|--------|-------|-----------|
| Agayu | Christopher | Fatherhood |
| Eleggua | Niño de Atocha, Anthony of Padua | Way-opener, messenger, trickster |
| Ogun | Peter, Santiago | Iron |
| Oshun | Caridad | Eros |
| Shango | Barbara | Force |

*Source:* Adapted from Joseph M. Murphy, *Santería: African Spirits in America* (Boston: Beacon, 1993), 42–43.

## Slavery, Freedom, and Lineage in Colonial Society

Religious associations permitted slaves to carve out some autonomy within colonial society. But some of the enslaved struggled for more than autonomy; they sought freedom. How could they attain it? From the beginnings of the slave trade to the Americas, slaves found legal and extralegal ways to freedom. Flight—maroonage—was common throughout colonial Latin America. Slaves could resort to flight as a short-term bargaining tactic with their masters. They could also seek to flee slave society altogether and establish free communities on the edges of empire, called *palenques* in Spanish America, *quilombos* and *mocambos* in Brazil.[51] Members of these communities sometimes found shelter among unvanquished Indian societies on the colonial frontier. Sometimes Indians and Africans on the run established them together.

Such was the case in the Bahoruco Mountains of Hispaniola, where a mixed group of Indians, Africans, and mestizos resisted Spanish military expeditions for years in the early sixteenth century, led by the heroic Taíno leader Enrique. As African slavery grew on the island, especially after the French took control of the western end at the close of the seventeenth century, more maroons established settlements in the mountains beyond the reach of the colonial governments. In his short history of the region that accompanied a map of a maroon settlement in the late eighteenth century, the Spanish official Antonio Ladrón de Guevara noted that the mountains are "high, rugged, and sprinkled with virgin woods that are impregnable." This setting constantly frustrated the European expeditions against the maroons despite "the most active and effective" preparations. While speaking dismissively of the settlement—the maroons lived in "hovels" (*malas chozas*)—he recognized the wisdom of its location, whose "proximity to the forests offered them shelter." Despite the best efforts of the French and Spanish to subdue the maroons of the region, the author lamented that they could not be "reduced to a Civil and Christian life."[52] So tenacious and persistent was maroon resistance to reenslavement that on the French side, officials reached a formal peace with the settlement of Le Maniel in 1785, the kind of compromise that runaways had forced the Spanish to make as far back as the time of Enrique's rebellion in the early sixteenth century.[53]

Events in the Bahoruco Mountains show that colonial officials and slave owners were adamant about capturing runaways and wiping out maroon settlements. They established local forces dedicated to tracking runaways and returning them to slavery. In some cases they organized military expeditions to lay siege to large communities, such as the famous quilombo Palmares in Pernambuco, which resisted concerted attacks against it for decades.

However, throughout the Spanish and Portuguese Empires, making peace with maroons was often a necessity. In the Kingdom of Quito in the later sixteenth century, local officials admitted their inability to suppress the maroons and their descendants in the remote coastal region of Esmeraldas.[54] The community's origins lay in a shipwreck in the mid-sixteenth century from which several slaves escaped and found a safe haven among local Indians. Over the decades, officials in Quito sent expeditions to break up the maroon settlement and enslave its mixed-race members. None met with success; Esmeraldas was isolated and practically inaccessible from the capital. When Spaniards did reach the coast, they found few traces of the people they pursued. Finally, the administration in Quito decided to make a pact with the people of Esmeraldas, recognizing their autonomy in exchange for their vow of loyalty to the Spanish monarchy. In New Spain in the eighteenth century, officials had to make a similar compromise with runaways whom they were unable to capture in the frontier between Veracruz and Oaxaca. Over the decades, the runaways had established free towns in the region, including Nuestra Señora de Guadalupe de los Morenos de Amapa. The parish priest of Amapa recounted that "the cimarrones [runaways] could not be subdued by force. On the contrary, armed sorties into the mountains in pursuit of the cimarrones only gave them more reason for revenge to the detriment of the sugar mills, travelers, and the inhabitants of the entire region."[55] In both Quito and New Spain, one of the conditions of recognition was that the former runaways would in turn become slave catchers themselves and return maroons to their masters, a tactic hammered out earlier by the Spaniards in the Caribbean. In 1533 the peace struck between the colonial power and the rebel community led by Enrique in Hispaniola required that he and his people capture runaway slaves and Indians.[56]

Requirements that maroon communities track and return other fugitives suggest that slavery and freedom coexisted in the Iberian empires in complicated ways. Maroonage did not necessarily represent a total rejection of slavery but an individual or group effort to obtain freedom on the margins of colonial society. Legal routes to freedom also indicate the limits and durability of Latin American slavery. The medieval legal culture that the Iberian conquerors implanted and adapted in the New World had important consequences for the development of African-American slavery. As Frederick Bowser argues for Spanish America, the *Siete Partidas*, the most important body of medieval Castilian jurisprudence, treated slavery at length and allowed for legal methods to gain freedom: "The *Partidas* viewed slavery as a necessary evil, as a transitory condition which did not alter or diminish the nature of the slave, while liberty was proclaimed as one of the greatest of human possessions. The compilation could therefore not fail to declare that freedom remained a legitimate goal for the slave, which intention society should facilitate by sanctioning means such as manumission by the master, liberation by a third person, and self-purchase with gift money."[57]

These legal routes to freedom were connected and demonstrate the importance of family and patronage networks. Masters might manumit slaves with whom they had forged a close connection, intimate or not, or their own children from informal relations with enslaved women. Self-purchase through the slave's peculium, or personal wealth, was possible in

FIGURE 4. Map of maroon community, island of Hispaniola, 1785. This map details the environs of the Bahoruco Mountains, refuge for runaway slaves from the Spanish colony of Santo Domingo and the French colony of Saint-Domingue, both on the island of Hispaniola. The left side of the image shows the maroon village of Le Maniel, the right side a bird's-eye view of the region, in the southwestern corner of Santo Domingo. The text in the center gives a brief history of the unsuccessful Spanish and French efforts to capture escaped slaves. Though the map describes conditions in 1785, this region long sheltered runaways from European colonization. Archivo General de Indias, Mapas y planos, Santo Domingo, 515.

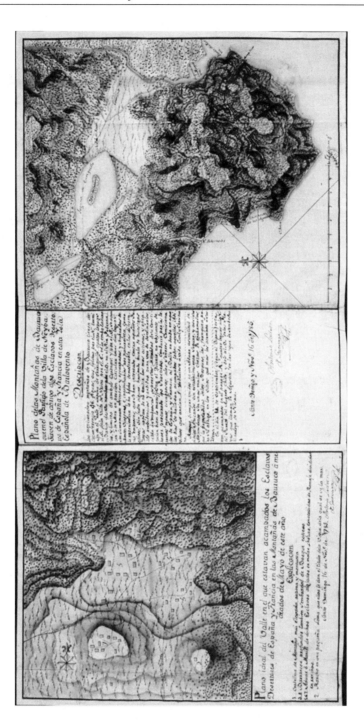

many colonial Latin American societies because slaves worked in multiple sectors of the economy, sometimes for wages. Slaves in urban settings were more likely to achieve freedom in this way than were slaves in the countryside, as they had greater access to money and to government officials. Bowser cites the example of Polonia Negra in seventeenth-century Lima, whose master required her labor only until midday after her free mulatto sons provided half of her purchase price. The rest of the working day was her own, which she used to gather savings to buy her way out of slavery. In Cuba self-purchase was formalized in an institution called *coartación* that functioned in more or less similar fashion. Cuban slaves had the right to register their price with a public official, thus becoming *coartados*, slaves en route to freedom. Even if sold to another master, they carried with them their status as coartados. Thus, a coartado who had paid half of his price owed his present and subsequent owners only half of his time.[58]

In colonial Brazil slaves enjoyed similar opportunities. They could come to an agreement with their owners to purchase their *carta de alforria*, a certificate of freedom. Colonial authorities were known to force masters to respect this process. Slaves working in the cities and in the mining regions of Brazil were more likely than those in the sugar regions of the northeast to obtain their freedom in this way. In Minas Gerais slave labor was less closely scrutinized and regulated than it was on the plantations of Pernambuco and Bahia. So-called *faisqueiros* worked under their own supervision, prospecting for gold. They would then return their bounty to their masters. Some faisqueiros received payment; others could gradually accumulate enough gold to purchase their freedom. Slaves working in the diamond mines of the region, despite close inspections during and after work, sometimes spirited away gems that would bring enough money to liberate them. In the cities of Brazil not only skilled labor and marketing led to freedom; religious brotherhoods would sometimes lend their members the sum needed to purchase the carta de alforria.[59]

Given slaves' determined efforts to purchase their freedom or that of family members, we cannot diminish the importance of escape from enslavement and the desire for freedom. Yet freedom from slavery in slave societies was a cramped and confined condition.[60] The Spanish and Portuguese colonial regimes sought to segregate freed people and to limit their access to large areas of the economy and society. Africans and African-descended people were banned from professions such as law and the priesthood. They were excluded from higher education. Laws prohibited them from carrying arms and subjected them to sumptuary restrictions. They paid special tribute because of their race. They were forbidden from living in Indian villages and intermarriage was proscribed.

In spite of these formal limits, free people carved out niches for themselves in colonial society. If whites "retained crushing pre-eminence in those fields which held genuine interest for them," such as the law, free people, along with slaves, came to dominate skilled labor positions in the cities.[61] They also might find mobility and prestige through military service. Arming slaves and free people of color in wartime had a long history in Latin America. In the mid-seventeenth century Portugal faced a major struggle with the Dutch for control of the rich sugar region of Pernambuco, which the Dutch West India Company captured and occupied in 1630 (more on this conflict in the next chapter). Among the leaders in the initial resistance to the Dutch invasion was the free black Henrique Dias, who controlled his own unit of black troops, the Terço da Gente Parda, also called the Henrique Dias Regiment.[62] In 1638 the Portuguese Crown rewarded Dias by making him a *fidalgo*, a minor aristocrat, and granting him a knighthood in one of Portugal's military orders. When a full-scale assault on the Dutch began in the 1640s, dubbed the War of Divine Liberty by one of its leaders, Dias and his troops played a prominent role. After the expulsion of the Dutch in 1654, the Crown again sought to reward Dias, this time with a title from the prestigious Order of Christ. Because of Dias's ancestry, however, it was decided that the honor would be bestowed upon the men who married his daughters in the future, rather than upon Dias himself. The rules for membership in the order dictated that no one with Jewish, Moorish, or Gentile (indigenous or African) ancestry would be admitted. Rather than forcing Dias to undergo proof of his ancestry, this leapfrogging passed it on to his future sons-in-law.

What do historians know of Henrique Dias before his ascent to military fame? In his 1656 petition to the Crown for rewards, he said that he was born in Pernambuco but says nothing of his parentage. Chroniclers of the era said that he was born enslaved in Brazil but was freed before he rose to prominence. It appears that many of those who served in his unit were slaves, usually of African birth. Contemporary documents refer to the "Angolas, Minas, and Ardras" who fought in the Portuguese units. These names refer grossly to the African trading forts or regions from which the slaves came to Brazil. They also provide some clues as to why the men of the Henrique Dias Regiment and other slave or freed soldiers were so effective; many likely had military experience in Africa before they were transported to the Americas.

After the defeat of the Dutch in 1654, Brazilian and Portuguese officials were undecided about the fate of the Henrique Dias Regiment. Some believed that it represented a threat to the stability of local slave society because it might encourage slaves to flee in search of freedom for service. Others expressed unease about arming former slaves at all. In contrast, some officials believed that maintaining the Henrique Dias Regiment was vital; it might play a role should war with the Dutch resume, or it might be invaluable in the battles against communities of runaway slaves (quilombos) in the Brazilian hinterlands. The Portuguese government opted to keep the regiment standing during Henrique Dias's lifetime and then decide upon its fate. In the event, the regiment survived its illustrious founder, seeing action in Angola and in battles against the greatest Brazilian quilombo, Palmares, which the Portuguese finally subdued in 1694, almost a full century after its establishment.

The career of Henrique Dias shows that soldiering offered a career in which free people and slaves could make themselves indispensable to the colonial regime and thereby reap rewards and freedoms otherwise forbidden to them. Dias achieved renown, while many of his troops were able to secure freedom for themselves. A military career was one avenue by which Africans and African-descended people could expand the boundaries of colonial society.

Nonetheless, we can also see the limits imposed by slavery and racial hierarchies in the colonial era. Dias's ancestry counted against him in official circles in spite of his many years of service. The foundation of the colonizers' segregationist and discriminatory laws and attitudes was the belief that Africans, Indians, and Europeans should live apart from one another and under separate jurisdictions. Different laws applied to different groups in colonial society. Indians were to live physically separated from Europeans and Africans. Penalties for infractions were harsh. In Peru, for instance, "a black man who sexually abused an Indian woman was to be castrated; other abuse would be punished with one hundred lashes."[63]

The preoccupations of Spanish and Portuguese imperial authorities with preventing the mixture of different groups arose in part from similar concerns with ethnic and religious boundaries in the Old World. The purpose of the Spanish Inquisition was to detect and punish Judaizers (Christian converts from Judaism suspected of practicing their old religion), a mission it would also carry out in the colonies.[64] Introduced at the late date of 1478 (papal Inquisitions took root in other parts of Europe centuries earlier), Spain's Holy Office reflected not only the wish of the Catholic Kings to impose orthodoxy on their subjects but also the obsession with lineage that was widespread throughout the Iberian Christian kingdoms. Even before the introduction of the Inquisition, corporate bodies in the Kingdom of Castile began to require that members and officeholders demonstrate their *limpieza de sangre* (purity of blood); that is to say, they had to document that they were free of Jewish ancestry. In crossing the Atlantic, this concern with purity and lineage shaped colonial mentalities. Particularly central to the sense of order and privilege was an emphasis on pure lineages free of African ancestry. This blatant discrimination against African-descended people would persist throughout the colonial era; it was one of the colonial legacies that independent Latin American nations promised to shed.

Despite the concern with blood purity and with dividing the colonial world into distinct groups, segregation proved difficult to enforce. The union of people across the formal boundaries of colonial society was pervasive. In Spanish America officials and local elites sought to keep pace by constructing categories that supposedly encapsulated the different degrees of mixture. In New Spain in the eighteenth century, this preoccupation with categorization and the prescription of putative traits manifested itself in the well-known *tablas de castas*, paintings that named and depicted the outcomes of different types of mixture. However, rather than representing the legitimacy of such categories, the castas paintings betrayed an obsession with neatly organizing an unruly, heterogeneous society that escaped official labels: "The elaborate efforts of these artists to depict in sets of exotic paintings family groups representing every conceivable blend of racial mixture and colour combination look like a doomed attempt to impose order on confusion."[65]

In the late eighteenth century the Bourbon monarchy sought to recognize and benefit from this confusion by allowing free people of color to purchase legal whiteness. Purchasing whiteness was expensive and within the reach of only the very few who had risen to positions of wealth and prominence. Nonetheless, the outcry from sectors of the colonial elite was virulent and forced the monarchy to abolish the process. If mixture was a reality beyond the control of the state, whiteness was still a marker of privilege and superiority that the dominant groups policed and protected.[66]

## Slavery in the Era of Iberian Colonization

When Don Quixote expressed his dismay at the sight of galley slaves in Spain and his belief in the essential freedom of all people, he summed up the views of many Iberian jurists and ecclesiastical officials. Slavery was an unnatural condition and laws and institutions should promote freedom. Iberian law codes that defined legal routes to freedom for the enslaved took root in the American colonies, allowing many slaves to escape from their condition or to liberate family members. The growth of free populations throughout colonial Latin America was ample proof that Don Quixote's revulsion toward enslavement found expression in many ways in the Iberian empires. Indeed, some historians have seen the large free population within colonial Latin American slave societies as evidence of a lenient form of bondage that favored liberation and assimilation.[67]

But this belief in humanity's innate freedom existed in metropolitan and colonial societies where different forms of enslavement and coercion were widespread. In Europe, convicts, orphans, so-called vagabonds, the mad, and other vulnerable groups were routinely swept up by royal officials and consigned to galley slavery, hard labor in presidios and arsenals, or confinement in correctional houses of various kinds. War captives from the clashes between Islamic and Christian Spain were legally enslaved, as were the Africans transported in significant numbers from West and Central Africa to the Iberian Peninsula and other Iberian domains in the eastern Atlantic.

Nowhere, however, was the commitment to slavery and other forms of coerced labor greater than in the American empires of Spain and Portugal. Though royal and church officials lamented and resisted the enslavement of Indians, they were often powerless to stop the colonists from opening outright slave trades within the Americas in places like the Brazilian backlands, the circum-Caribbean region, or the northern marches of New Spain. Legal mechanisms like the requerimiento in the Spanish Empire facilitated Indian slavery during the early decades of exploration and conquest. Even where widespread enslavement was successfully opposed, coercive systems such as the encomienda, mita, or Jesuit aldeias and reducciónes provided the colonists and the monarchy with the unfree labor force needed to work the lands and mines of the Americas.

As Indian labor declined in Brazil and Spanish America, the slave trade and African slavery increased significantly, though both would expand even more greatly once rival European powers—the Dutch, English, and French—staked their own claims in the Americas (the subject of the next chapter). Long familiar with the slave trade from the African coast and the sugar plantations of the Mediterranean and the eastern Atlantic, the Iberian conquerors were well poised to transplant these institutions in American soil. Religious and legal sanctions, such as the story of Ham and the corpus of medieval Iberian jurisprudence, leant legitimacy to enslavement, the traffic, and the condition of slavery in the colonies.

Masters and colonial officials did not have it all their own way in colonial Latin America. Outright defiance was common. There were rebellions throughout slave societies in Latin America. There was also widespread maroonage, which local officials and slave owners could control only unevenly despite their efforts to police runaways and crush palenques and quilombos such as Esmeraldas and those in the Bahoruco Mountains of Hispaniola.

Perhaps more significantly, the legal and religious culture of the Iberian empires, though supporting slavery, placed some checks on the power of slave owners and the state and permitted many slaves to win significant autonomy or freedom. Slaves could purchase their freedom or appeal to the Church for protection in some circumstances. Proof of the effectiveness of these avenues to freedom was the large free population of color throughout the Iberian empires, even in those zones such as the Brazilian northeast that were most plugged in to the Atlantic economy. Slavery was not reducible to the interests of the master class; similarly, freedom after slavery escaped the formal confines imposed by the colonial regimes. Free people worked to expand their sphere of activity in colonial society and frequently circumvented the segregationist ambitions of colonial governance.

Still, these challenges to the authority of masters and the colonial regime did not seriously weaken slavery as an institution in the Iberian empires. Commitment to African slavery and, in some quarters, to Indian slavery was hard and fast. Slaves worked throughout the colonial economies, from the great sugar mills in the environs of Salvador da Bahia in Brazil to the many trades of city life in places like Havana, Lima, and Mexico City. The slave trade continued to thrive, more so in Brazil than in Spanish America. While the power of the state and the slave owner was not absolute but negotiated and mediated, these regimes, as they implanted themselves in the Americas, proved able to accommodate manumission, self-purchase, rebellion, and flight.

# Estevanico and the Exploration of the Spanish Borderlands

❧

✢ IN HIS 1542 ACCOUNT OF HIS LONG YEARS OF WANDERING AND captivity in the mysterious land that the Spaniards called Florida, the would-be conquistador Álvar Núñez Cabeza de Vaca reported that an expedition undertaken in 1527 with hundreds of men was reduced to four survivors:

> It is appropriate that I mention those whom our Lord was served to allow to escape from these sufferings, and the places in these kingdoms from which they come. The first is Alonso del Castillo Maldonado, a native of Salamanca, son of Doctor Castillo and of Doña Aldonza Maldonado. The second is Andrés Dorantes, son of Pablo Dorantes, a native of Béjar and a resident of Gibraleón. The third is Álvar Núñez Cabeza de Vaca, son of Francisco de Vera and grandson of Pedro de Vera, the one who conquered [Gran] Canaria, and his mother was named Doña Teresa Cabeza de Vaca, a native of Jerez de la Frontera. The fourth is named Estevanico; he is an Arabic-speaking black man, a native of Azamor.[1]

The last of the four survivors listed by Cabeza de Vaca, Estevanico, was the slave of another survivor, Dorantes, one of the captains of the large and ill-fated expedition led by Panfilo de Narváez and licensed to explore and settle Florida, a vaguely understood place name encompassing for the Spaniards of the era those virtually unknown lands north of Cuba and Mexico, what the U.S. historian Herbert Bolton would one day dub the Spanish Borderlands.[2] Estevanico's presence on the expedition was not surprising. Like Juan Garrido, a servant and participant in the conquest of Mexico, Estevanico accompanied his Spanish master in the work of exploration, conquest, and settlement. Unlike Garrido, Estevanico did not achieve security or freedom in the New World.

The expedition landed on the west coast of present-day Florida. From the start things went badly, as harsh weather and violent encounters with indigenous groups disrupted Narváez's plans. Soon the leaders of the expedition had to admit that they had lost their bearings and were unsure how to make their way to Spanish settlements in Cuba or on the east coast of Mexico. As the expedition dwindled and dispersed under worsening conditions, Cabeza de Vaca, Estevanico, and several other Spaniards ended as castaways along the shores of Texas and northern Mexico. For years they lived as the slaves of Indians, surviving on the meager rations provided by the land and the sea. Over time they acquired reputations as healers. This reputation proved to be the key that unlocked them from captivity. They undertook an epic journey westward, hoping to reach the South Sea (the Pacific Ocean). During their years of wandering, their skills as healers eased their passage, until finally, in 1536, nine years after setting sail from Spain and almost eight years since they were marooned, the four survivors met with a group of Spaniards in the northern marches of Mexico, in a province called Nueva Galicia, not far from the Sea of Cortés (Gulf of California).

Their years of hardship did not quench their thirst for exploration and wealth. Cabeza de Vaca rushed back to Spain and soon undertook another expedition to the Americas, to the Río de la Plata at the other end of the Spanish Indies. Estevanico's career as an explorer was also far from finished. Spaniards pushing north from the Valley of Mexico heard rumors of fabulous cities of gold somewhere to the north, called Cíbola, perhaps close to the route that the Narváez survivors had traversed. Estevanico was pressed into service as an advance scout for an expedition headed by Francisco Vásquez de Coronado. He guided a Franciscan friar, Fray Marcos de Niza, and a large contingent of indigenous allies with the understanding that they would return and lead Coronado to Cíbola and its great wealth. In 1539 Estevanico and Fray Marcos reached the towns of the Zuni Indians on the western edge of present-day New Mexico. There Estevanico met his end under hazy circumstances. Fray Marcos beat a retreat to Mexico, where he reported that he and Estevanico had discovered the fabulously wealthy cities of Cíbola, a claim that Coronado, to his dismay, would soon disprove.

Over his lifetime, Estevanico journeyed from Morocco to New Mexico, literally from A to Z: Azemmour to Zuni. The forced travels of this remarkable man reveal key elements of slavery in the early phase of Iberian exploration and colonization. First, his origins in a Moroccan city within the Portuguese orbit show the close links between Iberian expansion in the eastern Atlantic and the subsequent transatlantic expeditions. Because the transatlantic slave trade to the Iberian domains in the New World developed slowly, a servant/soldier/explorer like Estevanico or Juan Garrido was perhaps a typical representative of slavery in sixteenth-century Spanish America: men of many talents and skills who were not reduced to the most brutal plantation conditions. Second, though from Morocco, Estevanico was a Christian. Many African slaves were Christians even before forced transportation to the Americas. Indeed, in the early sixteenth century, the Spanish monarchs ordered that all African slaves brought to the New World be *ladinos*, that is to say, African Christians assimilated to Spanish ways, as opposed to *bozales*, African captives who had not been converted or assimilated. The reason for this decision was the fear that non-Christians would corrupt the Indians during the conversion to Christianity. By the time Estevanico set sail with his master Dorantes in 1527, however, the Crown had reversed itself. Officials now believed that ladinos were too independent and unruly and that only bozales should be introduced into the new colonies because they would be easier to govern. Dorantes probably had to receive special permission to bring the Christian Estevanico with him on the expedition. Finally, though Cabeza de Vaca lists Estevanico along with himself and the other two survivors, he omits any reference to the slave's parentage. In contrast, he carefully lists his own illustrious lineage. This omission illustrates that while Estevanico and Cabeza de Vaca shared the same travails on the Narváez expedition—both were enslaved and suffered through years of hunger and depravation—the sense of difference and status remained strong. That emphasis on lineage, or the lack thereof, would play a powerful role in structuring colonial slave societies in Latin America as they matured.

## Additional Reading

Adorno, Rolena, and Patrick Charles Paultz. "Estevanico." In *Álvar Núñez Cabeza de Vaca: His Account, His Life, and the Expedition of Pánfilo de Narváez*, 2: 414–22. Lincoln: University of Nebraska Press, 1999.

Restall, Matthew. "Black Conquistadors: Armed Africans in Early Spanish America." *The Americas* 57 (2000): 171–205.

Rout, Leslie B. *The African Experience in Spanish America*. Princeton, NJ: Markus Wiener, 2003.

## CHAPTER TWO

# Bewtiful Empyre

## Challenges to Iberian Dominance
## and the Transformation of New World Slavery

∿

✦ IN THE 1770S, THE SCOTTISH SOLDIER JOHN GABRIEL STEDMAN served the Dutch colonial regime in a protracted war against runaway slaves in Surinam. The Dutch had settled in Surinam in the mid-seventeenth century, taking it from the British in exchange for the North American colony of New Amsterdam at the end of one of their several wars. Dutch settlers forged a plantation belt that produced sugar, cotton, and rice. The labor force was composed of enslaved Africans, brought in the trade that the Dutch had learned from the Portuguese. Surinam was an unruly colony. Its large, unsettled tracts, rivers, and ample forest provided protective shelter for slave runaways from the plantations.

This population was the target of Stedman's military excursions. His descriptions of service in Surinam are rife with scenes of tremendous brutality and sadism by planters. They also convey the danger in combating the resourceful maroon population in the colony's backlands. The fate of a small squad of European troops is indicative of the fierce resistance to recapture:

Mr. Lepper having been informed that between the rivers Pata-
maca and Upper Cormootibo a village of negroes had been discovered by the rangers some time before, he determined with his small
party, . . . to sally through the woods and attack them. But the rebels being apprized of his intentions by their spies, which they constantly employ, immediately marched out to receive him; in his way
they laid themselves in ambush, near the borders of a deep marsh,
through which the soldiers were to pass to the rebel settlement.
No sooner had the unfortunate men got into the swamp and up
to their armpits, then their black enemies rushed out from under
cover, and shot them dead at their leisure in the water. . . . Their
gallant commander, being imprudently distinguished by a gold-
laced hat, was shot though the head in the first onset.[1]

Maroons who fought hard against troops sent to capture or kill them
were not a new phenomenon in the Americas. Since the beginning of
Iberian colonization, runaway slaves from Hispaniola to Bahia had claimed
their freedom and autonomy by flight and armed resistance in remote
corners of the colonies. What was novel about the situation Stedman
described were the place and the people involved: Scottish soldiers serving
a Dutch colonial regime in the settlement of Surinam. European settlers
had incorporated more American spaces into the Atlantic system of slavery and slave trading; and the Spanish and Portuguese found themselves
on the defensive as rivals such as the Dutch staked their own claims to
overseas colonization and slaving.

After Columbus's first voyage the Spanish and Portuguese monarchies, with the mediation of the papacy, claimed to divide the world
between them. According to the Treaty of Tordesillas (1494), a line drawn
west of the Cape Verde Islands divided the world into respective areas of
Spanish and Portuguese dominance. To the west lay the lands that the
Spaniards were to explore and colonize, to the east were those that the
Portuguese were to control. Brazil, where Cabral landed in 1500 while
seeking to retrace da Gama's route to Asia, would fall to the Portuguese
share, unbeknownst to the Iberians at the time.

The European rivals of the Spanish and Portuguese never accepted the
authority of this division. Almost from the start, the Dutch, English, and
French sought to benefit from the Iberian empires. They resorted to various

strategies in varying combinations over time. These included privateering, territorial conquest, smuggling, and trade agreements that broke the commercial monopolies that were to govern the colonial economies of Spain and Portugal. Spanish silver fleets crossing the Atlantic were irresistible and enviable targets. Cargoes of Brazilian sugar also attracted pirates like flies.

The rivals to the Iberian empires coveted the wealth of the New World. They also feared the awesome military power of the Spanish monarchy and hoped to undermine it by striking a blow at its American fortunes. The Dutch were engaged in a decades-long struggle to free themselves from Spanish rule (1566–1648). England and France, meanwhile, vacillated between hot and cold wars with Spain as they vied for preeminence on the European continent and control of the seas. Religious war sharpened the conflict, as Protestant England and the Netherlands defied Spanish attempts to reassert Catholic orthodoxy upon Europe. Portugal found itself sucked into these great power conflicts not only because its American, African, and Asian possessions tempted foreign rivals but also because of its union with Spain (1580–1640), brought about by dynastic vicissitudes. Raids on the weaker Portuguese also distracted and weakened Spain. The low-level yet constant fighting in the Americas was thus connected to power politics and religious controversy within Europe.[2]

One of the English explorers of the late sixteenth and early seventeenth centuries, Sir Walter Ralegh, justified his excursions into lands claimed by Spain by arguing that the great wealth of the Spanish kings Charles V and Philip II directly threatened the security of England. The treasures of Peru that flowed back to Seville allowed the fearsome rival to field armies and navies and to buy friends and allies:

> But if we now consider of the actions both of *Charles* the fifte, who had the Maydenhead of *Peru*, & the aboundant treasures of *Atabalipa*, together with the affaires of the Spanish king now living [Philip II], what territories he hath purchased, what he hath added to the actes of his predecessors, how many kingdoms he hath indangered, how many armies, garrisons, and navies, he hath & doth maintaine, the greate losses which he hath repayred, as in [1588] above 100 sayle of greate shippes with their artillery, and that no yere is lesse unfortunate but that many vessels, treasures, and people are devoured, & and yet notwithstanding he beginneth againe like a storme to threaten shipwracke to us all, we shall

finde that these abilities rise not from the trades of sackes, and Civil Orenges, norfrom ought else that either Spaine, Portugal, or any of his other provinces produce: It is his Indian Golde that indaungereth and disturbeth all the nations of Europe, it purchaseth intelligence, creepeth into Councels, and setteth bound loyalty at libertie, in the greatest Monarchies of Europe. If the Spanish king can keepe us from forraine enterprizes, and from the impeachment of his trades, eyther by offer of invasion, or by beseiging us in Britayne, Ireland, or else where, he hath then brought the worke of our perill in greate forwardnes.[3]

Ralegh dedicated the last years of his life to finding the legendary kingdom of Eldorado (the Golden One) somewhere in the northern reaches of the South American continent, a "bewtiful empyre" thought to be endowed with fabulous riches like those secured by the Spaniards in Peru and Mexico. He hoped to gain personal wealth and to protect England against Spanish might and treachery. He imagined treasures filling his monarch's coffers (and his own, too); he also considered the possibility of an alliance with the Inca to overthrow their Spanish rulers, thus subverting the source of Spain's military strength in Europe.

Though Ralegh's dreams of Eldorado proved unfounded, his belief that he could undermine Spanish power by chipping away at Iberian exclusivism in the Americas ultimately bore fruit. As John Elliott has observed, "If Spain in the sixteenth century had furnished the model to be followed, . . . in the later seventeenth it was the model to be shunned. The encouragement of commerce, so neglected by the Spaniards, was coming to be seen as central to Britain's true interest. With the encouragement of commerce went a growing appreciation of the potential value to the mother country of its transatlantic colonies."[4] Britain defended itself against Catholic Spain and surpassed it in terms of wealth and military might. But the sources of power derived from its overseas empire came not from Eldorado or other cities of gold: they came from places named Barbados and Jamaica that produced not bullion but sugar. Instead of the silver mines of Potosí worked by coerced Indian laborers, Britain relied on the plantations of the West Indies manned by enslaved Africans transported to the Caribbean in steadily increasing numbers. Though Britain once sought to emulate Spain, in the end it developed a different model of New World colonialism and in the process transformed the nature and

MAP 4. Colonial Caribbean. Courtesy of Tim Cannon.

scale of slavery, a process to which the Dutch and the French also contributed mightily.

Efforts to establish colonies met with great difficulties, including hostility from the Iberians. A Spanish expeditionary force massacred a settlement of French Huguenots in Florida in the sixteenth century. In the same era, another Huguenot colony in Brazil's Guanabara Bay was dispersed by the constant pressure of the Portuguese and allied Indian groups. By the seventeenth century, however, the challengers to the Iberian mare clausum were beginning to carve out footholds for themselves, sometimes by claiming lands on the margins of the main Spanish settlements, such as Barbados in the eastern extreme of the Caribbean, other times by directly seizing Iberian colonial possessions, such as Jamaica, taken by the British in 1655, or Pernambuco in Brazil, occupied by the Dutch from 1630 to 1654.

The eastern Caribbean proved especially suitable for European aims.[5] French, Dutch, and British adventurers settled on islands such as Antigua, Martinique, and Guadeloupe. Early on, they sought to establish tobacco as a cash crop for export back to Europe. Privateering flourished from secure harbors. The islands also functioned as bases for large-scale smuggling operations that circumvented the restrictions of the Spanish imperial economy. Goods from Europe flowed from these entrepôts into the black market of the Spanish Indies. These European incursions into lands claimed by the Iberians transformed New World slavery, nowhere more so than in Brazil and the Caribbean, which over the history of the transatlantic slave trade would combine to import fully 80 percent of all the Africans brought forcibly to the Americas.

## From Servants to Slaves: Unfree Labor in the Non-Hispanic Caribbean

African slavery grew to new proportions in the Caribbean possessions of the northern European powers over time. Settlers initially made peace with the island Caribs of the Lesser Antilles, joined by their animosity toward the Spanish and a robust trade in tobacco and other goods. The growth of the European population soon ruptured this coexistence. The Caribs found their hunting, fishing, and agricultural grounds under threat. After many years of hard fighting, the British and the French confined the Caribs by midcentury to two island reservations: Dominica and St. Vincent.

Unlike the Spanish in Santo Domingo, Cuba, and Puerto Rico or the Portuguese in Brazil, the British and French settlers did not rely on the coercion of the Indian population in their Caribbean settlements for labor. Their first experiment was with indentured European servants, though like their Iberian predecessors, they would eventually turn to the African slave trade and expand this trade beyond existing levels.

The short-lived Puritan settlement on Providence Island, off the coast of present-day Nicaragua, essayed the different means of recruiting and controlling workers.[6] The Puritan backers of the venture hoped to found a settlement similar to the Puritan colony of Massachusetts in New England—that is to say, a community of the godly. The Providence Island Company also wished to strike a blow at Spanish supremacy by diverting some of the riches of the New World to England. The settlers of Providence Island were to cultivate tobacco. Privateering and trade with Moskito Indians on the Central American coast supplemented the colony's earnings.

With agriculture at the heart of the endeavor, labor was essential to its arrangements. Initially the wealthy Puritan investors hoped to supply the colonists with a steady stream of indentured British laborers. Indenture was entrenched in metropolitan society, where young men and women of modest means entered into yearly contracts with masters until they saved enough to establish themselves independently. Service in Providence Island required longer commitments but also held out the lure of greater benefits. Servants owed their masters three years of labor, at the end of which time the company would give them access to their own land and their own servants.

This tidy arrangement never developed as planned. Some masters were accused of abusing or illegally selling the contracts of their servants. The company had difficulties supplying former servants with the rewards promised them upon completion of their contracts. It also had trouble recruiting enough servants to satisfy the demands of the colonists and the need for laborers on public works projects.

With the flow of servants unpredictable and the costs of their service increasing, the colonists urged the company to turn to enslaved African labor. The settlers bought slaves from Dutch contraband traders and perhaps from Moskito Indians who had captured runaways on the isthmus. Despite hesitation on the part of the company directors, by the time the colony fell to Spain in 1641, Providence Island's slave population outnumbered the British population (381 slaves, 350 British, free and servant). The directors ultimately rationalized this development by acknowledging the advantages of "Negroes being procured at cheap rates, more easily kept, and perpetually servants." In other words, unlike indentured European workers, slaves would not become free in the short term. Nor did the company or local masters feel it incumbent upon them to treat the enslaved as well as they would fellow Britons.[7]

This process played out on a much larger scale on the island of Barbados, the first great Caribbean sugar producer. Settled by the British in 1627, Barbados exported various crops, especially tobacco, cotton, and indigo. Planters employed British servants on their farms. Beginning in the 1640s, the island experienced a sugar boom that would persist for several decades. While other export crops thrived and the number of indentured British servants rose, enslaved Africans started arriving in greater numbers. For the period between 1650 and 1657, historians have been able to estimate that there were 18.4 servants and 24 slaves per Barbadian estate that they surveyed. In the ensuing years, the balance tipped decisively toward slavery. In the period between 1658 and 1670 there were 3.1 servants per estate compared to 111.1 slaves.[8] Barbadian planters found that they could exercise greater control over enslaved workers. They could also import them in growing numbers as British and Dutch merchants and shippers invested in the African slave trade, successfully challenging Portugal's dominance of the traffic. Capital for investment in land and technology was also forthcoming from the metropolis, so that by the later seventeenth century large plantations that combined agriculture and refining were spreading across the island, worked by large captive labor forces.

Barbados represented a type of colonial exploitation quite different from that exercised by the Iberian powers. Barbados became an island of outsiders, both European and African. Though European planters and merchants held the upper hand, the population was increasingly African and African-descended. In contrast, the Spanish and Portuguese had latched onto large indigenous populations, usually with devastating consequences. The African slave trade existed in combination with the domination of indigenous workers, some enslaved as in Brazil, others subject to coercive regimes such as encomienda and the mita. Colonists also flowed to the New World possessions, so there were significant settler populations throughout the Iberian empires. Slaves were never in the majority, as they were in Barbados, Jamaica, or the French colony Saint-Domingue.

The absence of a crusading Catholic church dedicated to mass conversion in Barbados was another important distinction. While the British Empire did not lack publicists who fretted about its religious mission in the Americas or who played upon the rivalry with Catholic Spain and Portugal, the dynamic pluralism and conflict of metropolitan religious life impeded a coherent justification or ecclesiastical unity in the overseas empire. Barbados's sugar boom, for instance, took place in the 1640s during a civil war in England in which the number of Protestant religious sects multiplied, a situation far different from the Iberian kingdoms, which successfully preserved religious orthodoxy and unity. In the British Caribbean merchants and planters were the dominant figures, not friars and royal officials, as in the Iberian colonies.[9]

The weakness of an institutional church in the British possessions was parallel to the underdeveloped legal regime of the new colonies. Historians have carefully demonstrated that the Iberian colonizers implanted medieval law codes in their American territories. Together with the role of the Catholic Church in regulating almost all aspects of social life, the law in the Iberian empires provided slaves with important tools for achieving greater autonomy and freedom in many cases. Hence the large free black and mixed populations of colonial Brazil and Spanish America. In contrast, British colonists, who enjoyed a greater measure of local administrative control than did their Spanish and Portuguese counterparts, found a void in metropolitan law codes regarding slavery. They thus had a much freer hand in drafting local laws that enshrined their interests by seeking to cut down the avenues to legal freedom to as great a degree as possible. In Barbados and elsewhere in the British West Indies, slave owners' power felt few checks upon it.[10]

From Barbados, British power soon spread to Jamaica. The conquest of the island in 1655 had fateful consequences for the history of African slavery in the Americas as the colony became the destination for more than one million captives. The shifting scale of British involvement in the slave trade and plantation slavery is demonstrated by comparing the trade to Barbados and Jamaica. From the conquest and settlement of the islands until the suppression of the British slave trade in 1807, close to five hundred thousand slaves were disembarked in Barbados, over one million in Jamaica. Indeed, in the decades before slave trade abolition the traffic to Jamaica was attaining new heights; well more than three hundred thousand slaves reached the island between 1776 and 1800.[11]

The British thus forged a colonial society in Jamaica that was quite different from the Spanish one that preceded it. Like other Spanish Caribbean settlements, Jamaica had stagnated in the sixteenth century once the gold euphoria ended and the bulk of Spanish migration and investment shifted from the Caribbean to Mexico and Peru. The initial British inhabitants of the island after it was taken from Spain in 1655 were pirates and small planters, many of whom migrated from the much smaller

British settlements of the eastern Caribbean as sugar and slavery took over those islands. Richard Dunn tells us that until the end of the century the metropolis referred to the colony as "the Dunghill of the Universe" because of its boisterous and outlaw settler population.[12] By century's end, however, big planters were making more permanent arrangements. They chased out the pirates and took over many of the holdings of small farmers. They also turned almost exclusively to sugar, as had happened before in Barbados, building a colony that embodied "the sugar and slave system in its starkest and most exploitative form."[13] Contemporaries, such as the parliamentarian and political theorist Edmund Burke, shared this judgment: "The negroes in our colonies endure a slavery more complete, and attended with far worse circumstances, than what any people in their condition suffer in any other part of the world, or have suffered in any other period of time. Proofs of this are not wanting. The prodigious waste which we experience in this unhappy part of our species, is a full and melancholy evidence of this truth."[14]

There were, though, some limits on the planters' power. The main challenge came from one of the inheritances from the Spanish colony: the maroon communities.[15] Under Spanish rule, Jamaica was sparsely populated. Even slaves enjoyed a significant degree of autonomy, while runaways and manumitted slaves were able to establish themselves on abundant lands and ranges. When the British invaded in 1655, Spanish resisters allied with maroon communities in scattered palenques. It took the British several years to subdue the resistance and drive the last Spaniards from the island to Cuba. An important measure in securing the island was making peace with some of the maroon communities, including one led by Juan Lubolo, a "Spanish negro" who finally came over to the new rulers in 1660, his band of rebels converted into a "Black militia" that now hunted maroons, a role reversal not at all uncommon, as we have seen.[16]

As slavery grew on the island so did maroonage, facilitated by safe havens like the rugged and soaring Blue Mountains of eastern Jamaica or the crater-like Cockpit Country in the colony's central region. By the 1720s maroons numbered in the thousands. In response, the local government and the planter class organized a full-scale offensive in the 1730s. They successfully routed the maroons led by Nanny in the Blue Mountains but were unable to subdue those led by Cudjoe in the Cockpit Country. The British complained that "the service here is not like that in Flanders or any part of Europe. Here the greatest difficulty is not to beat, but to see the enemy."[17] Cudjoe's tenacity and elusiveness forced the British to strike a peace at decade's end. The settlement resembled those reached by Spanish authorities in other colonies. The government recognized the autonomy and freedom of the maroons and allotted them land for their own cultivation near the Cockpit Country. However, it also required them to participate in slave catching and to serve as an auxiliary military force. Once more in the New World, the freedom of some slaves rested on the continued enslavement of the majority.

A more serious threat to Jamaican slavery came several decades later, during Tacky's Revolt in 1760. Led by slaves, the rebels' goal was the overthrow of slavery and British rule. With military forces spread thin by the global conflict with France (the Seven Years' War, 1756–1763), local authorities were hard pressed to crush the uprising. Several decades later one Jamaican planter and historian looked back on Tacky's Revolt and compared it to events in his own day, namely the Haitian Revolution (1791–1804) that wiped out slavery and colonial rule in France's richest possession. The state of conflict and insecurity in the British West Indies led metropolitan observers like Edmund Burke to argue that if reforms were not made to lessen the cruelty of plantation slavery, then the enslaved would soon take matters into their own hands. Burke did not question slavery's legitimacy; rather, he expressed doubts about its viability should the present system continue: "I am far from contending in favor of an effeminate indulgence to these people. I know that they are stubborn and intractable for the most part, and that they must be ruled with the rod of iron. I would have them ruled, but not crushed with it. I would have a humanity exercised which is consistent with steadiness."[18]

Similar criticisms would arise in the French Empire in the eighteenth century. The origins of France's Caribbean colonies were similar to the British. Beginning in the eastern Caribbean, colonists established themselves in Martinique, Guadeloupe, and St. Christopher. They combined privateering and smuggling with the cultivation of tobacco and other goods, employing both slaves and indentured servants. But by midcentury sugar and slavery overtook the small planters, leading to an outflow of French settlers. In Martinique, for example, the French population numbered 12,000 in 1656. By 1671 it had dwindled to 3,083.[19]

Many of these emigrants, some of whom were former servants, moved to the western end of the Spanish colony of Santo Domingo, called Saint-Domingue by the French settlers and pirates whose numbers increased

over the second half of the seventeenth century. Spain had largely abandoned the western part of the island because the local administration
found it impossible to impede smuggling. In the absence of the Spanish,
the so-called Brothers of the Coast used Saint-Domingue as a site for privateering and for cultivating tobacco. The French monarchy kept on eye
on this fledgling settlement, dispatching a governor whose seat was the
small island of Tortuga from the 1640s onward.

In a 1697 treaty Spain ceded formal control to France. Soon after
the recognition of French sovereignty, sugar and slavery expanded, especially on the northern plain around the town of Le Cap. Between 1681
and 1713 the slave population increased by more than 1,000 percent and
came to outnumber the free population by almost five to one (24,156 slave,
5,648 free).[20] Meanwhile, the colony's southern peninsula thrived as an
entrepôt for smuggling by retaining close connections to other Caribbean
islands. It also developed a more robust and mixed settler population than
the north, where the sort of absenteeism characteristic of Jamaica and
Barbados was the norm.[21]

France was a Catholic monarchy like Spain and Portugal. The Iberians
strove to maintain Christian religious orthodoxy and conformity against
Judaism and Islam in the same era that they colonized the Americas, while
the French kings contended with strife between Christians during the
early colonization process. The sixteenth century was a time of fierce religious wars between Catholics and Protestants in France. The Edict of
Nantes of 1598 stabilized relations between the warring cults, but during
the long reign of Louis XIV (1643–1715) the Crown revoked the compromise that established peace between Catholicism and Protestantism.
Louis and his allies sought orthodoxy and homogeneity in the kingdom,
not unlike the Catholic Kings of Spain in the late fifteenth century. To
that end they drove most Protestants out of France and barred them from
the colonies.

These concerns with religious conformity shaped the Code Noir of
1685, drafted by the Crown in consultation with colonial interests as slavery grew in the French Caribbean. Striking to the modern reader is a provision in the first article of this new slave code banning Jews from residing
in France's overseas colonies. Subsequent articles banned Protestants and
spelled out the religious mission toward the enslaved. Article II instructed:
"All the slaves who will be in our Islands will be baptized and instructed
in the Catholic, Apostolic, and Roman religion. We charge the planters

who will buy newly arrived *negres* to inform the Governor and Intendant of the said islands within a week at the latest or face a discretionary fine, these [officials] will give the necessary orders to have them instructed and baptized within an appropriate time." Religion was also to govern work and the rhythms of economic life in the colonies. According to Article VI: "We charge all our subjects, whatever their status and condition, to observe Sundays and holidays that are kept by our subjects of the Catholic, Apostolic, and Roman religion. We forbid them to work or to make their slaves work on these days from the hour of midnight until the other midnight, either in agriculture, the manufacture of sugar or all other works, on pain of fine and discretionary punishment of the masters and confiscation of the sugar, and of the said slaves who will be caught by our officers in their work." The new code also spelled out the rights of manumitted slaves and gave masters broad prerogatives in freeing their slaves.[22]

The society that flourished in Saint-Domingue only slightly resembled the one prescribed in the Code Noir. While Spain introduced the Inquisition into its American colonies and the Portuguese Holy Office carried out lengthy visitations in Brazil, in the French Caribbean the ecclesiastical presence was comparatively small. The colony's origins in piracy, smuggling, and planting defined its trajectory. For example, despite Article I, Jewish merchants from Jamaica settled in the southern peninsula of Saint-Domingue in the early eighteenth century and carried out a healthy trade with other Caribbean colonies without interference from the Church or the Crown.[23]

The spirit of some of the code's provisions regarding manumission and the rights that accrued to the free did apparently take hold in the colony in the first half of the eighteenth century. A significant free population grew in the colony, especially in the south. French planters with mulatto offspring often recognized their paternity and freed their children at the baptismal font. Some of these free men were destined for intermediary positions within colonial society. For example, they staffed the rural gendarmerie charged with tracking down runaways. Some rose to more exalted positions, becoming planters and slaveholders. They studied in France and inherited substantial properties from their fathers.

However, by the second half of the eighteenth century the more numerous settlers from France and a stronger colonial administration became grudging about recognizing the legitimacy of mulattoes. New laws openly discriminated against free people of color. Professions such as law and medicine were to be racially exclusive, intermarriage was discouraged, and new sumptuary laws that prescribed how different groups in the colony were to dress were enforced. Moreover, colonial record-keepers now carefully scrutinized the ancestry and color of the free population. Where once ancestry had gone unnoted, it now received close measurement in parish and administrative records. In short, the administration sought to drive a wedge between the free white and free colored populations, systematically discriminating against the latter. The tensions caused by these measures would have a decisive impact on the colony's future at the end of the century.[24]

For the enslaved, the Code Noir was less pertinent. Though the code proposed to mitigate the brutality of slavery through religious sanctions and the lure of manumission, colonial planters built a plantation complex geared toward extracting labor from its workers no matter the human toll. Historians estimate that over the course of the eighteenth century Saint-Domingue imported close to one million slaves. In the single year of 1790, the traffic brought 44,472 captives to the French colony (in comparison to 14,640 to Jamaica) right on the eve of the great slave rebellion. The volume of the traffic was driven not only by the constant demand for labor but also by the use of those laborers. There was no natural increase among the colony's slave population. Laurent Dubois has summarized the planters' strategy: "They worked their slaves to death, and replaced them by purchasing new ones."[25]

Slaves acted in different ways when they tried to liberate themselves from such wanton brutality. With slavery came maroonage. The contiguity with the Spanish colony of Santo Domingo, along with the extent and ruggedness of the French territory, provided a particularly hospitable setting for maroon communities. The most stubborn of these communities was Le Maniel, in the southeast of the colony in the Bahoruco Mountains, home to rebels and runaways since the early sixteenth century (see figure 4). The French district of Cayes de Jacmel was one of the least populated in the colony. There were few roads and few settlers. Moreover, Spanish administrators encouraged the maroons by turning a blind eye to trade for food and weapons and by generally refusing permission for the French to pursue the inhabitants of Le Maniel across the border. The most famous of these colonial rebels was Makandal, a maroon who fled from enslavement on the northern plain of Saint-Domingue. In addition to securing his freedom and that of other maroons, Makandal struck against the dominant class through a network of slaves that allowed him to carry out a campaign of terror by poisoning planters, slaves suspected of treachery, and livestock. The French captured him and burned him alive in the plaza of Le Cap in 1758. However, many in the colony—both slave and free—believed that he lived on. The specter of Makandal and other slave rebels did not go unnoticed in the metropole. The violence of the Saint-Domingue plantation complex led enlightened critics of empire to foresee the emergence of a black Spartacus, an avenger of the New World, who would redeem his fellows. They demanded action to preclude his arrival.[26]

## Slavery and Freedom in the Spanish Caribbean

The sense of potential crisis that emerged in the writings of French and British critics was absent in the Hispanic world in the seventeenth and eighteenth centuries. Spanish colonies experienced neither the huge volume of the slave trade nor the centrality of the sugar plantation (until Cuba did so at the end of the eighteenth century). Moreover, there were broader avenues to freedom, creating an utterly distinct balance between enslavement and freedom.

Spain's support for maroons in neighboring colonies was not limited to the island of Hispaniola. Encouraging the flight of slaves from neighboring colonies was one of the countermeasures taken by Spain during the onslaught of European rivals. In Florida in the eighteenth century, the Crown freed all British slaves who fled from Georgia and the Carolinas, settling them in the town Santa Teresa de Gracia de Mose, where they helped defend St. Augustine and other Spanish towns from periodic British invasions. Puerto Rico was also a sanctuary for Caribbean runaways in the seventeenth and eighteenth centuries. When fugitive slaves began arriving from neighboring islands such as St. Thomas, St. Croix, or the Lesser Antilles, Spanish authorities devised a policy whereby they would be granted freedom once they were rebaptized and educated as Catholics. Ultimately, the number of fugitives was so significant that royal and ecclesiastical officials decided to create a new town, San Mateo de Cangrejos, just across the bridge from the capital, San Juan. By 1795 the settlement's population had grown to 1,290. It flourished as a supplier of food and other essentials to the nearby capital city.[27]

Puerto Rico and other border territories devised a sanctuary policy because of their proximity to foreign rivals. Perched on the eastern edge of

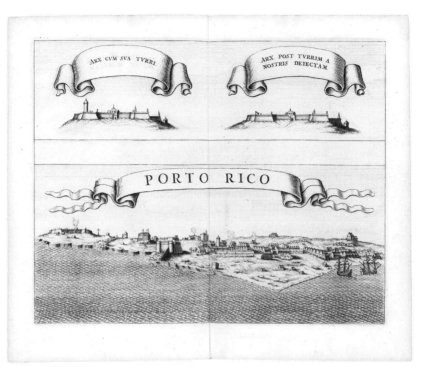

FIGURE 5. Dutch view of the fortifications at San Juan, Puerto Rico. The fortifications at Spanish Caribbean port cities such as San Juan, Havana, and Cartagena de Indias date from the early seventeenth century, when the Spanish Crown finally took steps to protect its settlements and shipping from smugglers, pirates, and imperial rivals. Inter-imperial conflict and smuggling had a decisive impact on the spatial coordinates and the scale of African slavery in the Americas. Shut out of the rich bullion centers in Peru, Mexico, and Brazil, English, Dutch, and French settlers eventually turned to export agriculture (primarily sugar) in Caribbean colonies. In the seventeenth and most of the eighteenth centuries it was the British and French who imported the vast majority of captive laborers. Puerto Rico and Cuba, however, eventually became major sugar producers as Spain sought to catch up with its economically more vigorous rivals. From the end of the eighteenth century to the final suppression of the trade in 1867, Cuba dominated the market for slaves in the Caribbean. Joannes de Laet, *Historie ofte Iaerlijck verhael van de verrichtinghen der Geoctroyeerde West-Indische Comapagnie* (Leiden, 1644). Courtesy of the John Carter Brown Library at Brown University.

the Caribbean, Puerto Rico brushed against the footholds secured by rival powers. It was also a target of their ambitions, which changed over time. Initially, the British and the Dutch made concerted efforts to wrest the island from Spanish control, though all were repulsed. Sir Francis Drake led a British expedition against the colony in 1595, as part of grand scheme to undermine Spanish might. His fleet was pummeled by shore batteries and fled without landing. A more substantial British force under the Earl of Cumberland landed in 1598 but failed to extend its control beyond the environs of San Juan and soon evacuated. In 1625 the Dutch landed but were unable to take the fortress at San Juan, from which the Spanish soon counterattacked and forced the Dutch back to sea.[28]

Thwarted militarily, European neighbors turned instead to smuggling and met with much greater success in Puerto Rico. Outside the capital of San Juan, the majority of the island's population lived within a self-sufficient economy. Plentiful land for settlement and squatting gave rise to a large peasantry that raised cattle and produced small surpluses of foodstuffs and other goods. The capital's control of the countryside was weak. Moreover, though a strategic hotspot, Puerto Rico lay outside the main commercial networks of the Spanish imperial system. Thus, the opportunities and incentives for smuggling were great. In exchange for Puerto Rican cattle, agricultural products, and the small amount of Mexican silver in circulation, smugglers from Curaçao, the French Antilles, and especially Jamaica, the center of British smuggling to Spanish America, brought slaves and finished products otherwise unavailable.[29]

Under these political and economic circumstances—irregular regional warfare, economic underdevelopment, weak metropolitan control—slaves found numerous opportunities to free themselves or to exert significant control over their lives in the Spanish Caribbean. Many of the royal slaves of El Cobre in eastern Cuba, for example, took advantage of laws, administrative and ecclesiastical institutions, and local customs and memories to carve out freedom and rights for themselves. María Elena Díaz recounts the history of the Cosme family to demonstrate these dynamics of slavery and freedom. In the late seventeenth century the slaves Manuel Cosme and Hilaria de Villavicencio wed and later purchased their freedom. They also purchased the freedom of some (but not all) of their children over time. They invested their wealth by purchasing slaves of their own. In the early eighteenth century the widowed Hilaria de Villavicencio owned two slaves. Over successive generations the Cosme family inherited and purchased slaves, always in small numbers. Not everyone in the clan was free; some remained royal slaves. However, even some of those who remained slaves themselves were slaveholders. Such was the case of Manuela Matamba, the daughter-in-law of Manuel Cosme and Hilaria de Villacencio and wife of Juan Luis Cosme, who had purchased his freedom in 1708, some twenty years after his parents. Later generations of the Cosmes continued this pattern of manumission and slave-holding. They also rose to positions of authority within El Cobre as civil and military officials.[30]

Louisiana, a colonial crossroads in the circum-Caribbean, illustrates that even when slavery expanded, Spanish laws and customs regarding the getting of freedom continued to operate. Spain took over governance of the Louisiana territories in a secret treaty with France in 1762. While France had sought to emulate the success of its Caribbean island colonies, it never established effective control over Louisiana outside of New Orleans. As a result, there was little investment and settlement beyond the environs of the city. When the Spaniards took over Louisiana under the governorship of Alejandro O'Reilly, a military man with ample experience in Europe and the Caribbean, they expanded their control in the hinterlands and set the stage for the growth of the slave trade as plantation agriculture blossomed. To establish an effective bulwark against British encroachment in the Gulf of Mexico, the Crown subsidized the new colony through a tobacco monopoly and other economic privileges. The result was a significant growth of tobacco and sugar production and the slave population. Historians of the colony have found that there was also a large growth in the rate of manumission and coartación, especially in the urban setting of New Orleans where slaves had greater access to wages and currency. The new laws also had an impact on the plantation zones. The historian Gwendolyn Midlo Hall recounts how officials and planters complained that the enslaved were all too aware of laws that endowed them with certain rights and were willing to trek to the capital city to claim them.[31]

Settlements like Cangrejos in Puerto Rico, El Cobre in Cuba, Mose in Florida, and New Orleans in Louisiana indicate that very different slave societies coexisted in the Caribbean in the seventeenth and eighteenth centuries. While there were spaces of freedom in the British and French colonies—Le Maniel in the Bahoruco Mountains and Cudjoe's maroon communities in Jamaica's Cockpit Country—slaves and maroons had created them only through irregular or open warfare, not by appeal to local laws, religion, or customs. The colonial regimes viewed places like

Le Maniel as threats and sought to destroy them and reduce the residents to slavery. In the Spanish Caribbean in this era, local economic and military conditions in combination with the laws and institutions of the Spanish colonial regime allowed many slaves to achieve freedom, marry and raise families, own property (including slaves), and occupy minor positions of authority, even in settlements experiencing rapid integration into the Atlantic slave trade, such as New Orleans and Louisiana.

## Brazil: Sugar, Gold, Diamonds, and Angola

As Spain saw its Caribbean domain infiltrated by foreign colonists and contraband, the Portuguese Empire suffered even more heavily at the hands of its European rivals, including Spain. The virtual collapse of the Portuguese monarchy and aristocracy precipitated major changes. In 1578 the Portuguese king Sebastian, along with thousands of his leading vassals, was killed on the battlefields of Morocco during a short-lived crusade. His death set off a succession crisis in Portugal. The eventual successor was Philip II of Spain, already the most powerful monarch in Europe. He and his heirs would rule until a national uprising in 1640 broke Portugal loose from Spain, with independence finally secured by a peace treaty between Lisbon and Madrid in 1668.

The incorporation of Portugal into the Spanish monarchy had complicated implications for its overseas empire. In the late sixteenth century the metropolis still considered the East Indies the heart of the imperial venture. However, the impact of warfare with Spain's enemies, especially the Dutch, and eventually with Spain itself, would shift Portugal's focus decisively toward Angola and Brazil. Brazilian slavery and the slave traffic from Angola would grow to unprecedented heights. Initially, Pernambucan and Bahian sugar were the motor of the slave trade. But at the end of the seventeenth century the discovery of fabulous gold, and later diamond, deposits in Minas Gerais would transform the space of Brazilian slavery.

Spain incorporated its neighboring Iberian kingdom by respecting existing laws, customs, and jurisdictions. This strategy of incorporation was characteristic of the Spanish monarchy, at least in its European possessions. Portuguese remained the language of government, Castilian laws were not applied in Portugal and its overseas possessions, and Portugal continued to control its own trade. Moreover, the Portuguese were now free to travel and conduct business with the other realms of the Spanish

monarchy. One consequence of this measure was that Portuguese conversos became prominent in Spanish and Spanish American cities as merchants and bankers, a source of friction with the Spanish Inquisition and
its American branches. Another outcome of union was the preeminence
of the Portuguese in supplying slaves to the Spanish Indies through the
concession of the monopoly contract known as the asiento. Incorporation
brought with it grave difficulties, too. The Portuguese increasingly felt
themselves subject to a Castilian viceroy and viceregal court out of touch
with their interests. The effective machinery of government was located
hundreds of miles away in Madrid.[32]

Perhaps more seriously, Portugal now found itself immersed in Spain's
struggle for European and overseas dominance. It did not fare well. In
the early seventeenth century the Dutch and the British preyed upon
Portugal's trading forts and outposts on the African coast and in the East
Indies. Both took over a large portion of the transatlantic slave trade while
also dispossessing Portugal of many of its Asian strongholds. Under these
circumstances it became urgent to strengthen Portugal's grip on Brazil
and on the African ports that provisioned it with enslaved workers. Spanish
views of the situation were different from those of the Portuguese. What
interested Spanish officials was the protection of Peru and other Spanish
American colonies from Dutch and British incursions. Brazil was a useful buffer. But for the Portuguese, the colony's sugar and slave complex
was becoming the colonial lifeblood. Yet here, too, the Dutch intervened,
briefly taking Bahia in 1624 and then occupying Pernambuco from 1630
to 1654. To this challenge, however, the Portuguese and the Brazilians
responded vigorously.

The Dutch entity that captured the Brazilian northeast was the West
India Company, a chartered company created to expand Dutch power and
wealth in the Atlantic world. In 1628 its naval forces captured a fabulously rich Spanish treasure fleet departing from the Caribbean. With
this fortune it was able to finance the campaign against Portuguese Brazil,
successfully establishing itself in 1630. Ensconced in Brazil, company officials quickly realized the need for slave labor. To that end, it attacked
Portuguese strongholds in Africa, taking the trading fort at El Mina and
a few years later Luanda in Angola.

The apotheosis of Dutch power in the Atlantic world was its undoing.
The historian Pieter Emmer has recently argued that the Brazilian adventure was expensive and unsustainable. Planters, many of them Portuguese,

in the Brazilian northeast purchased slaves from the company with credit rather than cash, which created large shortfalls. These debts were impossible to collect once the Portuguese, now free of Spanish dominance, rose against the Dutch in 1645. Thus, while the West India Company sank into debt and a costly war in Brazil, it lost valuable time, capital, and expertise to the British and French, who were establishing themselves in the Caribbean. Once expelled from Brazil in the 1650s, the Dutch had to content themselves with supplying slaves to the British and French (until they were cut out of the trade to those colonies a few years later) and smuggling slaves from Curaçao to Spanish colonies such as Venezuela. Its own plantation settlement at Surinam on the northeast shoulder of South America never rivaled its Caribbean neighbors.[33]

The Portuguese war against the Dutch led to important changes in colonial slavery and the relation between the colony and the metropole. Of greatest consequence was the consolidation of the axis joining Brazil and Angola. The Portuguese opened fronts against the Dutch in both places. Warfare in Angola soon spread and involved neighboring African kingdoms such as Kongo. Portuguese forces included not only local and metropolitan troops but also large contingents of Brazilians. The colony's connection to slaving ports was so crucial that officials and colonists helped raise levies to secure the Portuguese dominion in Angola and surrounding kingdoms. The Dutch withdrew from Brazil in 1654, but fighting in Central Africa continued for much of the second half of the seventeenth century. At stake for the Portuguese and the Brazilians was what kind of colonization they sought in Angola. Some royal officials advocated opening a corridor between the African coasts that would join the Portuguese settlements in Angola and Mozambique. Salvador de Sá, the most important military commander of the era, was a proponent. He believed that continuous Portuguese settlement would secure the trade with Asia, now more perilous in an age of imperial competition. Defenders of this policy foresaw an effective exploitation of Central Africa's natural resources and a diminution of the slave trade's importance.[34]

This vision of empire lost out to those who favored strengthening the slave trade and the Brazil-Angola connection. Slaving and Brazilian products, not African mines, were to provide the wealth of the empire. Officials who favored this policy were skeptical about the cost of territorial control in Africa and opted for the reinforcement of trade. Writing an opinion in the 1680s, a Portuguese official from the royal body the

Conselho Ultramarino observed, "In Angola the only conquest we need is that which secures commerce. . . . Experience shows that nothing is worse for business than battles."[35]

Over decades of hard warfare with the Dutch and the Kingdom of Kongo, Brazil and Angola emerged as the crucial components of the Portuguese Empire. While still under Portuguese sovereignty, Brazilians themselves became key players in restructuring and defending the imperial system. Colonists from Pernambuco, Bahia, and Rio de Janeiro saw the slave trade as the necessary foundation of the Brazilian economy. They sent troops to fight in Angola and carved out new markets for their goods there, such as sugar cane, brandy, and tobacco, which they used to purchase captives. They also aggressively lobbied in Lisbon for privileges that would protect the Angola-Brazil traffic. Basing themselves in Luanda and intermarrying with African notables, the Brazilians carried out massive slave raids in the interior of the colony, much like the São Paulo bandeirantes (slave-trading backwoodsmen) across the ocean in Brazil.[36]

Thus, by the second half of the seventeenth century Brazil was becoming a colonial society unique in the Iberian world. What was most distinctive was its direct, two-way traffic with Angola and, to a lesser extent, other African regions, such as the Gold Coast. Until the suppression of the slave trade in 1850, no site in the New World would import more slaves. Moreover, the movement of Brazilians *to* Africa was significant and lasted for the duration of the slave trade. Merchants, soldiers, and in some cases ex-slaves seeking to return home were among those who made the transatlantic journey in the reverse direction (more on this topic in chapter 4).

The affirmation of this link transformed Brazil. The slave population and the free population of color expanded. More territory came under cultivation, and more military pressure was brought to bear on recalcitrant quilombos like Palmares in Pernambuco. The sum of these changes had dangerous consequences for the indigenous Brazilians. As we have seen, at the dawn of Portuguese colonization in Brazil, settlers enslaved Indians at a ferocious rate, opening internal traffics from the interior to the coastal enclaves. However, once the Portuguese and the Brazilians staved off the Dutch and solidified their hold on Angola, colonists preferred to buy African slaves. Metropolitan and colonial merchants and officials alike came to envision a colony increasingly populated by European settlers and African slaves. There was little room for Indians in this vision. In response, the Crown and local settlers unleashed a war of extermination against Brazilian Indians that lasted until the early eighteenth century, so that they could open more lands to settlement and exploitation. The historian Luiz Felipe Alencastro has shown that Brazilian veterans of the wars in Angola were important in carrying war to the indigenous population and that they took part in the destruction of Palmares. He also recounts the colonial imagery that justified the new goals and tactics by describing a painting from the era. It depicts black and white corpses strewn on the ground, the bodies covered with gory bite marks. Departing from the scene are naked Indians, sated by their feast of human flesh. In Alencastro's reading, this anonymous painting from the late seventeenth century was the representation of a colonial society that joined white masters and black slaves against natives who, because of their cannibalism, "could be killed like wild beasts."[37]

One of the regions opened to settlement and slavery in this era was Minas Gerais, an inland captaincy in the Brazilian southeast. It was unusual among the major New World slave societies because, unlike older Brazilian centers like Bahia and Pernambuco or the British and French Caribbean sugar islands, this massive slave system was landlocked and had no direct access to the maritime roads of the Atlantic Ocean. The explorers of this region were bandeirantes from São Paulo. Though one of the oldest settlements in the colony, São Paulo was an inland city separated from the port at Santos by rugged terrain and from Rio de Janeiro by mountains. While Rio, Bahia, and Recife were firmly entrenched in the Atlantic system that joined the Brazilian coast to Africa, São Paulo oriented itself toward the vast interior. The Paulistas hunted and traded Indian slaves. In the second half of the seventeenth century they became Indian fighters, frontiersmen opening new territories under Portuguese control. On one of these long expeditions in the 1690s, Paulista bandeirantes struck gold.

Though news of the strike and this new source of wealth made its way slowly to Portuguese officials, the discovery set off a gold rush. The effects would be magnified when diamonds were discovered in another corner of the captaincy in the 1720s. Settlers flocked to Minas, and they brought with them enslaved workers. The wealth of the gold mines and the tremendous growth of the population spurred a huge influx of slaves into the region despite the Crown's efforts to regulate the trade. One reason for this policy was the fear that the rich sugar regions were losing slaves to Minas because of escalating demand and prices. Demand was so great that Brazilian slavers established new factories on Africa's Gold

Coast and purchased slaves from Dutch and British factors. Even Angola was not enough for the vast hunger of Mineiro slaveholders, so the Crown relented and the slave traffic to the mining regions developed without official impediments.[38]

Though the slave trade flowed powerfully into Minas Gerais, the mechanisms for attaining freedom in colonial Brazil continued to function. Indeed, historians have found that the particular conditions of work in the region allowed manumission and self-purchase to flourish, leading to the development of a vast free population. Slave workers in the diamond strikes labored under close scrutiny at the workplace. However, their condition differed from the enslaved workers on the plantations. On the plantations of the northeast, slaves often lived in common *senzalas* (barracks) and were sometimes locked in at night. Their labor was dedicated to the upkeep of the plantation and the harvesting of its crop. In the mining region, owners rented out their slaves to the mines. Enslaved workers collected wages, which were paid to their masters, but they were often able to accumulate their own savings. They might also live on their own rather than under the tight security of the senzala or the master's gaze. In the gold-mining regions enslaved workers had even greater autonomy in many cases. They ranged far and wide, searching for alluvial gold to meet a quota set by their masters. Whatever exceeded the quota was theirs to keep.[39]

A description from one of the diamond-mining sites captures both the duress of the labor and the opportunities for liberation. During a visit to the diamond center of Tejuco (now Diamantina), the French traveler August de Saint-Hilaire recorded the harsh work conditions: "Forced to stand constantly in water during the time when they are panning for diamonds and consuming foods of little nutritive value, their intestinal tract is weakened and they become morose and apathetic. Aside from this, they often run the risk of being crushed by rocks which, undermined from the mineral beds by digging, loosen themselves and fall. Their work is constant and agonizing. Ever under the watchful eye of the overseers, they cannot enjoy a moment of rest." Yet Saint-Hilaire noted that enslaved workers seemed to prefer mining because the chance of freedom was greater than in other kinds of work: "The money they acquire by stealing diamonds and the hope they nourish of acquiring their freedom if they find stones of great value are undoubtedly the main reasons for this preference." He also described the range of rewards bestowed upon those who found large diamonds, from goods of various kinds to freedom and wages.[40]

The autonomy of the enslaved created by the nature of the captaincy's economy pervaded religious and associational life. The great mineral wealth promised by the gold and diamond strikes motivated the Portuguese Crown to assert its control over Minas to a degree not found in the plantation zones. In the latter, the Portuguese Church played a significant role in shaping relations between settlers, Indians, slaves, and the Crown. The Jesuits, for example, not only pushed the frontier of settlement but also became large landholders and slaveholders. In Minas, by contrast, the Crown banned the entry of the regular orders. It also required the secular clergy to register with the civil authorities, who had the power to expel them.

The assertion of royal preeminence at the expense of the Church had the perhaps unintended effect of creating a robust lay religious culture. Lay brotherhoods spread through the new towns of Minas Gerais. In the administrative center, Vila Rica (now Ouro Preto), twenty-nine brotherhoods were founded in the eighteenth century, ten of these before 1720.[41] The members of some brotherhoods came from the various strata of colonial society: black, white, and mulatto, enslaved and free. But over time the brotherhoods tended to separate into distinctive groupings, as was the case in older colonial centers such as Bahia.[42]

One of the most active brotherhoods was the Brotherhood of Our Lady of the Rosary of the Blacks. The Rosary was a religious order with roots in medieval Portugal. Portuguese missionaries and officials helped spread it to Africa in the sixteenth and seventeenth centuries because they considered it an especially suitable mechanism for conversion. Brotherhoods were founded on São Tomé in 1526, in São Salvador in the Kingdom of Kongo in 1610, and in Luanda in 1690. Thus, some of the Africans who arrived in Brazil in the seventeenth and eighteenth centuries were Catholics and some were perhaps familiar with the Rosary. Moreover, in the Portuguese colonial imagination the link between Africans and the Rosary was a powerful one.[43]

Africans and African-descended people in Minas Gerais had their own motives for their devotion to the Rosary. The brotherhoods allowed their members autonomy and community and space for the enactment of ritual life: "Within the brotherhoods people organized their religious lives, engaged in charitable acts, participated in lavish public festivals, provided social services, and took care of the bodies and souls of their members after death."[44] The black brotherhoods of the Rosary, composed

FIGURE 6. View of Saint Iphigenia Church (on distant hilltop) from San Francisco Church, Ouro Preto, Brazil. Black lay brotherhoods participated actively in the communal and ritual life of Brazilian cities such as Ouro Preto, center of the great gold-mining regions in the eighteenth century. Note, however, the physical distance that separates the black church Saint Iphigenia from the centrally located San Francisco Church. Black churches were on cities' edges, simultaneously incorporated and on the margins. Photograph by the author.

of both enslaved and free members, first made their homes in the main churches of the urban centers, supporting chapels within the church. Over time, some were able to raise enough funds to build their own churches in sight of but also distant from the civil and ecclesiastical center of towns such as Mariana and Vila Rica (Ouro Preto). Thus developed one of the most singular and dynamic colonial slave societies in the Americas, a place of great wealth and suffering and of remarkable cultural adaptation and creativity.

## Slavery and Reform in the Spanish Empire

As rival European powers established colonies in the Americas, especially the Caribbean, the African slave trade grew; more and more enslaved workers labored in New World economies. But African slavery was differentiated across the American empires. In Brazil, the intimate connection to Angola reaffirmed the centrality of slaving to the colonial economy. Along with the Caribbean colonies of the British and French, Brazil would import the overwhelming majority of captives in the seventeenth and eighteenth centuries. Despite the high volume of the trade, slavery in Brazil differed significantly from slavery in the French and British Caribbean. The counterpart to the trade in Brazil was *alforria* and manumission. As the slave population grew, so too did the free population, unlike in the British and French Caribbean colonies such as Jamaica and Saint-Domingue, where the enslaved made up the vast majority of the colonial population. Spanish America diverged from the other colonial regimes because the slave trade, until the end of the eighteenth century, was always regulated and mediated through contracts with foreign providers. Though slavery was a major institution throughout Spanish America, the overall slave population was much smaller than in Brazil. In the Spanish Caribbean, colonies such as Cuba and Puerto Rico differed from their British and French neighbors because they were marginal to the slave trade and because, as in Brazil, laws and institutions in combination with local conditions provided the enslaved with mechanisms to achieve freedom. The free population (white and of color) always outnumbered the slave population in the Spanish Caribbean as well. Nonetheless, the persistence of imperial warfare continuously altered the nature of the slave trade and of slavery in the Iberian realms. Britain's gains in the global war that erupted in the mid-eighteenth century forced Spanish officials to consider a new kind of colonial economy with slavery at its center.

As Spain ceded ground to the British and French in the Caribbean in the seventeenth and eighteenth centuries, it found itself trapped between the ambitions of these rising powers in Europe itself. The efforts of Philip IV (1621–1665) and his minister the Count-Duke of Olivares to forge closer unity among the disparate parts of the Spanish monarchy in order to halt its decline ended in disaster. By 1640 Portugal and Catalonia were in open rebellion against Madrid, Portugal eventually gaining its independence under British protection. On the European continent, military setbacks finally forced Spain to cease its efforts to pacify the Dutch and to recognize independence. France emerged from this period of continental warfare and peninsular revolt as Europe's preeminent military power.[45]

Spain soon reached its imperial nadir with the death of Charles II in 1700. This Habsburg king died without an heir. Rivals from the Austrian Habsburgs and from the French ruling dynasty, the Bourbons, put forward their claims. Quickly, Spain found itself the theater of a proxy war between the French and the British. France sought to cement an alliance of the French and Spanish crowns by installing a Bourbon prince in Madrid. Britain and its European allies supported the Habsburg claim so as to limit France's power and access to Spanish American markets and products. After more than a decade of war, a compromise was reached. The Bourbons could claim the Spanish throne but with the condition that the Spanish and French crowns would never be united under the same monarch. Moreover, the British gained a most important economic concession: the coveted asiento, which permitted the British to expand their smuggling operations into the Spanish colonies under the cover of legality.

The new Bourbon dynasty confronted an American empire that was still rich in silver and other exports. But much of that wealth ended up in the hands of foreign merchants and rulers. Military and economic subordination to France and Britain forced the Spanish Crown to recognize the cracks in the imperial façade. How to reassert its control over the colonies was a problem that vexed the Bourbon kings throughout the eighteenth century.[46]

The Seven Years' War (1756–1763) forced the Bourbons into more aggressive reforms because it revealed just how vulnerable the Spanish colonies were to British military power. The war was a global struggle between Britain and France for overseas preeminence. By the end of the war, Britain had expelled France from Canada and crushed its rival's colonial ambitions in North America. It achieved a similar result in India as well, emerging as the dominant European power on the subcontinent. Spain figured in the war and peace only at the end of the conflict. In 1762 it entered the war as an ally of France. Britain struck back immediately, capturing two of the nodal points of the Spanish colonial system: Havana and Manila. In the subsequent peace, Spain regained those two ports. It also took control of Louisiana from France. However, the Spanish did make territorial concessions to Britain, including Florida, which placed the feared rival right in the Gulf of Mexico, close to Spain's Caribbean colonies and to its richest possession, the Viceroyalty of New Spain, the great producer of silver in this era.

The fall of Havana compelled the Bourbon king Charles III (1759–1788) and his advisers to undertake major military, fiscal, and economic reforms in the Americas, beginning with the Caribbean. Spain needed more troops on the ground in the colonies, more fortifications in key sites such as Havana, and more revenue with which to pay for these invigorated defenses. Here the question of the slave trade and slavery entered into the equation, leading the Spanish Crown ultimately to deregulate the slave traffic for the first time and to commit to the kind of plantation agriculture heretofore found primarily in Brazil and the French and British Caribbean.

The Caribbean was the testing ground. After the war, Bourbon officials made tours of the islands to report on local conditions and to suggest reforms. They were dismayed by the laxness of Spanish control over the colonies, the sparse population, and the weak economies, which were shot through with contraband. They reported back to Madrid that these were potentially rich territories gone to waste after centuries of metropolitan indifference. The reforms they advocated came in part from their observations of the much richer colonies that surrounded the Spanish Antilles, such as French Saint-Domingue and Danish St. Croix. If these islands could produce abundant exports, then Puerto Rico and the other Spanish possessions could emulate their success.

Field Marshall Alejandro O'Reilly was one of Madrid's agents who traveled to both Cuba and Puerto Rico to inspect their military preparedness. In his view, imperial defenses could be upgraded only when founded on economic revival, which meant sugar and slavery: "To encourage the rapid growth of the island of San Juan de Puerto Rico, I believe it is indispensable that men of wealth establish themselves here and set up sugar mills."[47] He pointed to the success of Danish St. Croix as an example of what could take place in Puerto Rico. France ceded the island to Denmark in 1734. The Danish crown established a chartered company to manage the new colony and granted it important privileges and incentives to attract investment. Among these was the free entry of slaves carried by ships of any nationality. Towns and plantations spread across the island, supported by an ample supply of servile labor.[48]

Several years after O'Reilly's tour Spanish observers were still suggesting a transition to a plantation economy. The friar Iñigo Abbad y Lasierra penned an extensive study of Puerto Rico's history and current conditions. Like O'Reilly, he was critical of the stasis into which the colony had fallen after the early decades of conquest and colonization. He repeatedly intimated that the colonists had returned to the primitive state in which the island had existed before the conquest. Though the Spaniards had destroyed the Indian population, they had in effect become Indians themselves: "The inhabitants of Puerto Rico have acquired from the ancient dwellers of this Island the indolence, frugalness, disinterest, hospitality, and other characteristics of the Indians. They have also conserved many of their habits and customs."[49] Like the Indians, the present-day colonists maintained a subsistence economy, thus depriving the Crown of trade, taxes, and revenues.

In an economy geared toward local needs, slavery was a minor institution. Abbad noted that manumission and self-purchase were widespread. Once slaves gained their freedom, they fled from the population centers and squatted on the abundant empty lands. The same was true of Spaniards who arrived in the colony. Rather than stimulate the export economy by farming or investing, they squatted, wandered from town to town, or turned to banditry and piracy. The richness of the island's produce supported a dispersed and vagabond population.[50] To make Puerto Rico a source of wealth for the Crown, Abbad insisted that the population should be settled in towns and put to work producing rich export crops like sugar. He looked to the British and French Caribbean colonies as sources of inspiration. Those governments encouraged the immigration of Europeans who would invest in land and in labor. They also facilitated the entry of slaves. As a consequence, colonies such as Martinique and Saint-Domingue housed large populations, thriving plantations, and lucrative trade: "In the convent of the Dominican friars in . . . Martinique I saw in 1774 1,500 slaves employed in two sugar mills. . . . If one looks at the island of Santo Domingo, one will find that Guarico [Saint-Domingue], which is occupied by the French, is full of perfectly cultivated plantations whose products are the object of a splendid commerce. The Spanish part of the island, despite being better and more extensive, is covered by forests and devoid of colonists." Should the Spanish Crown act like the French and the British, "Puerto Rico could easily and without expense receive the population and cultivation that it requires."[51]

Cuba, the largest and most populous of the Spanish Antilles, was the object of the most ambitious reforms. The island was the cornerstone of

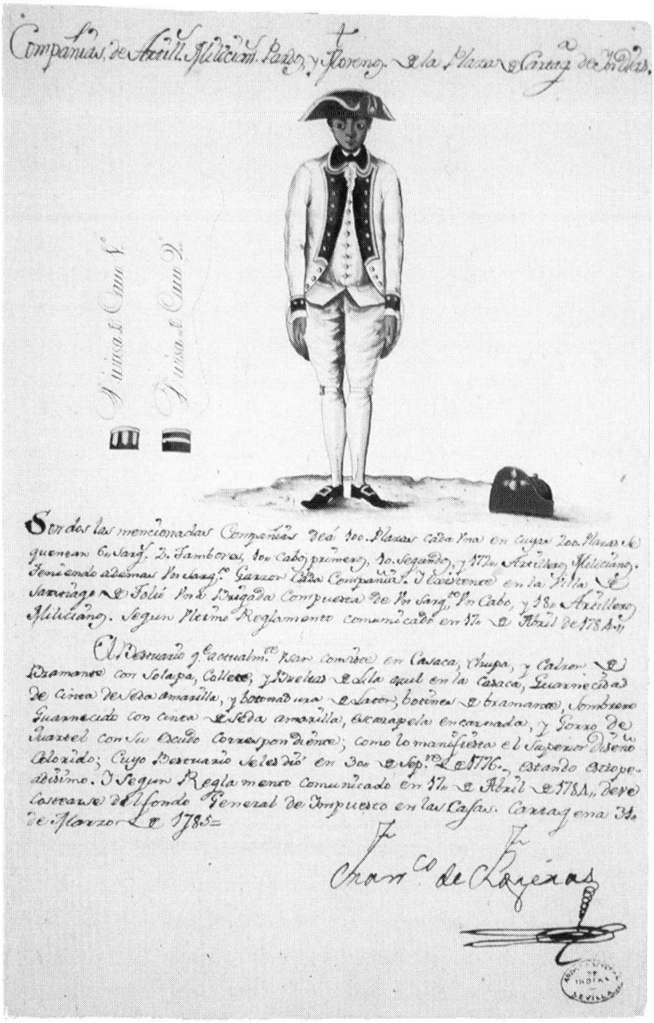

FIGURE 7. Militiaman, Cartagena de Indias, 1780s. In response to the setbacks of the Seven Years' War, the Spanish Crown expanded its colonial defenses, raising more troops directly in the colonies themselves. This image represents the pardo and moreno units of Cartagena de Indias. Military service by free blacks, and in some cases by slaves, dated from the era of the Spanish conquest of the Americas. Free black militias existed in the Caribbean, the front line of colonial warfare, from the sixteenth century. In the early nineteenth century, military service by the enslaved and free-colored population in much of Spanish South America was a crucial factor in the wars of independence. Archivo General de Indias, Mapas y Planos, Uniformes, 6.

Spain's imperial defenses, and Havana was a major port. Moreover, the local planters and merchants were eager to invest heavily in the slave trade and plantation production in Havana's environs. Bourbon officials cut an important deal with creole elites in Havana: in exchange for paying higher taxes, Cubans could trade with more Spanish ports and they could use their own ships for carrying. Moreover, Cubans would provide volunteer troops to the new, disciplined militias that would complement the veteran troops garrisoned on the island. Though this measure was expensive for local elites—they had to provide time and service to the militias and to pay for equipment—it also provided significant benefits, including prestige and the right to enjoy the *fuero militar*, a bundle of legal and fiscal privileges and exemptions. This military reform reached deeply into Cuban and later other Spanish American societies. Creole elites formed the officer corps of the disciplined militias. But free people of color also served in their own units, usually divided between *morenos* (blacks) and *pardos* (mulattoes).[52]

These were significant innovations that challenged vested interests in the Iberian Peninsula. Under the Habsburgs, all colonial trade had been routed through one port, initially Seville and later Cádiz. Bourbon officials were eager to weaken the power and privileges of the Cádiz merchants. They believed that deregulating trade would increase the monarchy's tax base and produce the revenues needed to bolster imperial defenses. In the deal worked out with Havana immediately after the Seven Years' War, Madrid opened trade far beyond Cádiz. Cuba could now trade directly with ports around the Spanish periphery: Alicante, Málaga, Cartagena, Barcelona, Santander, Gijón, La Coruña, and Seville. The tilt toward colonial interests was clear: "In the political chemistry that prevailed after the Seven Years' War, the concerns of Havana carried more weight than those of Cádiz."[53]

This pact between Madrid and Havana also gave Cubans leverage for negotiating the opening of the slave trade. Over the course of the eighteenth century merchants and planters had sought to expand plantation agriculture on the island. However, the limitations of the asiento hindered their efforts. The terms of the asiento capped the number of slaves to be legally introduced each year. It also fixed prices artificially high. Thus slave labor in Cuba was expensive and scarce. Madrid raised the number of slaves that could be introduced into the island. It also introduced a policy known as *comercio libre de negros* that permitted foreign merchants to enter Spanish American ports if they were also trafficking in slaves. But it was not until 1789 that Madrid, under intense lobbying from Havana in the person of the brilliant young planter and official Francisco Arango y Parreño, finally relented and lifted almost all restrictions on the slave trade between Africa and Cuba and between the island and neighboring colonies such as Jamaica. The stage was set for Cuba's takeoff. From the late eighteenth century until the trade's suppression in 1867 the island would import almost eight hundred thousand captives. Cuba would also remain firmly in the Spanish orbit even when most of Spanish America fought for independence in the 1810s and 1820s, in no small part because of slavery's centrality to the colonial economy (see chapter 4).[54]

The reforms in commercial policy and the slave trade produced mixed results as the Crown introduced them to other Caribbean islands and eventually to the empire at large. In the 1770s *comercio libre* (free trade) was opened to virtually all American ports. That is to say, Spanish American ports could now trade directly with Spanish ports other than Cádiz. They could also trade among themselves in limited fashion. The Crown also instituted the comercio libre de negros, though it did not meet with as much success as anticipated. Slavery was stagnating or on the decline in Mexico and Peru in the eighteenth century as the Indian population rebounded in both mining regions. In New Granada, there was little demand for slaves because the export economy faltered. Even in Venezuela, which saw tremendous growth over the eighteenth century due to the rising demand for its chief crop, cacao, the volume of the slave trade actually declined at the same time that it was booming in Cuba. Though the new viceregal capital at Buenos Aires experienced a surge in slave imports from Africa and from Brazil, they were on a scale far below Cuba's: approximately forty-five thousand between 1750 and 1810.[55]

## Slavery Questioned

The slave trade and plantation slavery were gaining traction, albeit unevenly, in Spanish America after the Seven Years' War. Yet as the Spanish Bourbons sought to copy the successes of the French and the British in the Caribbean, in those empires, as we have seen, the nature of colonial slavery was coming under closer and more critical scrutiny. Ironically, some critics suggested that it was they who should seek to learn from Spanish slave societies.

The most consequential questioning of the humanity and legitimacy of slavery came from within the British Empire.[56] When abolitionism took hold in Britain at the end of the eighteenth century, it would have a far-reaching impact not only within the British imperial orbit but also throughout the Atlantic world, not least in Brazil and Spanish America (to be discussed in detail in chapters 3 and 4). The sources of antislavery thought in the British Empire were diverse and scattered. They would come together to form serious challenges to slavery and the slave trade only in the aftermath of the American Revolution. Before then, the colossal struggles of the Seven Years' War had produced what one historian of the British Empire has called "antislavery with abolitionism."[57] With Britain poised to make serious territorial gains in Spanish America from new bases in North America and the Caribbean, and absent a serious French opponent in the Americas, British officials and reformers pondered how a new imperial system might benefit from a tempered form of slavery or even from colonies without slaves.

Desire for imperial expansion and consolidation shaped the first stirrings of antislavery imaginings. Maurice Morgann, an official connected through his patron to the Board of Trade, contemplated how Britain might best utilize its gains from the Seven Years' War. The taking of Florida and Caribbean settlements, in his view, placed Britain on the verge of even further expansion into Spanish America. He envisioned the new possessions as colonies in which free Africans would intermix with white colonists to produce a population well adapted to tropical climes and thus suited to serve as a vanguard in British operations against Spain throughout the Torrid Zone.[58]

Other writers and legislators put forward proposals intended to lessen the brutality of West Indian slavery and to set the stage for its (distant) suppression. In 1776 Granville Sharp called attention to the "Spanish Regulations," by which he meant coartación, as a measure that should be introduced into the British colonies.[59] Giving slaves the right to purchase their freedom would not only gradually undo slavery but also prepare the enslaved for the exercise of freedom by instilling in them the values of hard work and saving. But these habits and relations needed incentives to thrive, preoccupations that would remain constant in the British antislavery movement. Edmund Burke took note of Sharp's arguments in preparing his Negro Code of 1780, intended to check the wanton brutality of the West Indian planters and to stabilize colonies periodically shaken by uprisings such as Tacky's Revolt. Burke, like Sharp, also hoped to promote the formation of families among the enslaved population by making it more difficult for owners to separate legally recognized family members. The intent of these proposals was not the immediate suppression of slavery, far from it, but rather to make the institution more humane and more stable. The laws that endowed the enslaved with certain protections in the Spanish Empire appeared to offer a way forward.[60]

Contradictory currents were thus at work in the European Atlantic empires in the aftermath of the Seven Years' War. British and French critics questioned the institution of slavery with increasing skepticism as the slave trade to their Caribbean colonies peaked. In Brazil the centrality of the slave trade was reaffirmed as the Portuguese and the Brazilians defended Brazil and Angola against the ambitious attacks of European rivals. In Spanish America the setbacks suffered over the seventeenth and eighteenth centuries, dramatically signaled by the British capture of Havana in 1762, led the Bourbon rulers to foment the slave trade and plantation slavery for the first time as they braced themselves for a new round of warfare. When war among the great slave-holding empires did come, it would have an unforeseen consequence: the shattering of slavery's unquestioned legitimacy and apparent permanence.

# Jacqueline Lemelle and Chica da Silva

## Slavery, Freedom, and Family

❧

✦ IN THE SEVENTEENTH AND EIGHTEENTH CENTURIES AVENUES TO freedom remained open for some slaves even as the total enslaved population grew in plantation and mining regions in Spanish America and Brazil. Women were more likely to benefit from manumission than were men because of their ability to earn wages and because of their personal relations with free men. The change of colonial regime in Louisiana from French to Spanish changed the life of the enslaved woman Jacqueline Lemelle. She was sold to Santiago Lemelle in New Orleans in 1762, just as Spain was set to take control of the colony. Her master was a ship's captain and merchant, so Jacqueline likely managed his household while he was away and helped to market his goods in the city. When the Spanish governor Alejandro O'Reilly solidified Spanish rule at the end of the decade, he introduced Spain's Laws of the Indies, supplanting the French Code Noir. Spanish laws provided more protection and opportunities for the enslaved, including ownership of property, the ability to purchase their freedom, and more lenient manumission rules for slaveholders. Jacqueline Lemelle and her three daughters by Santiago Lemelle were beneficiaries of these changes. In the 1770s Santiago manumitted Jacqueline and their daughters and made them heirs to his estate. Jacqueline was also able to purchase the freedom of two other children, a son and a daughter, from whom she had been separated earlier.[1]

In Brazil in the eighteenth century, the captaincy of Minas Gerais underwent a terrific expansion of its slave population after the discovery of gold and diamonds. In the early formation of Mineiro society, some enslaved women found opportunities to free themselves and their children and to rise to positions of considerable wealth and influence. In Tejuco (now called Diamantina) the 1774 census reported that free or freed women headed almost half of the households; 86 percent of them were black. In contrast, of male householders, only 31.5 percent were black.[2]

Why were women more likely to become free and to become property owners than were men in Minas Gerais? Ties of affection, formal and informal, were important in shaping these dynamics: "Sex was a determining factor in access to manumission: the majority of freed women achieved manumission in adulthood, while the reverse is true of freed males, most of whom were sons born of mixed relationships who were given their liberty at baptism. The economic and social makeup of the region thus explains why wage-earning black women who could put together some savings, and slave women who lived as concubines to white men stood a better chance of being manumitted than other slaves."[3]

The life of Chica da Silva, a former slave who became a free woman of great wealth is illustrative. Unlike Jacqueline Lemelle in New Orleans, who married Santiago Lemelle, Chica da Silva never married her companion, the wealthy judge, João Fernandes de Oliveira, but had several children with him. This informal relationship, concubinage, was frequent in Minas because of colonial mentalities and rules that discouraged marriage between people of unequal status. Nonetheless, Chica saw her condition and that of her children improve dramatically over the years because of her link to Fernandes, despite prejudices against her origins. Fernandes freed his companion not at his death, as was common, but early in their relationship. As a free woman Chica could acquire her own, independent wealth and her children would be unequivocally free people. They would reinvent the family lineage, remaining silent about slavery and gradually working their way through education, wealth, and respectability into the dominant groups in the colony.

## Additional Reading

Lauderdale Graham, Sandra. *Caetana Says No: Women's Stories from a Brazilian Slave Society.* New York: Cambridge University Press, 2002.

Martínez-Alier, Verena. *Marriage, Class, and Colour in Nineteenth-Century Cuba.* 2nd ed. Ann Arbor: University of Michigan Press, 1989.

Socolow, Susan. *The Women of Colonial Latin America.* New York: Cambridge University Press, 2000.

Twinam, Ann. *Public Lives, Private Secrets: Gender, Honor, Sexuality, and Illegitimacy in Colonial Spanish America.* Stanford, CA: Stanford University Press, 1999.

## CHAPTER THREE

# An Era of Emancipation

## Slavery and Revolution in the Americas

∿

### A Letter from Cádiz

✦ AROUND NEW YEAR'S 1812, DOÑA JOSEFA GIRALT OF SAN JUAN, Puerto Rico, received a letter from her son don Ramón Power, Puerto Rico's representative to the Cortes of Cádiz in Spain.[1] The Cortes was a parliament convened in 1810 to resist the French occupation of the Iberian Peninsula and to draft a constitution that would govern the monarchy in the absence of the Spanish king Ferdinand VII, held captive by Napoleon Bonaparte since the French invasion in 1808. Though Ferdinand capitulated, most Spaniards and Spanish Americans did not. They professed their loyalty to the legitimate ruler and sought means to govern themselves during his captivity. The Cortes was the most sustained and controversial effort. Deputies from the colonies took part in the Cortes, including Power from Puerto Rico. As they debated the nature of the new constitution, completed in 1812, they touched on the most sensitive topics that bound Spain and the Americas together, including the slave trade to Spanish America and slavery itself. Spanish and American deputies raised the possibility of banning the trade in 1811; they also briefly discussed the gradual abolition of slavery altogether. While defenders of slavery quickly prevailed and halted any further action, the language of abolition and liberation swirled around Cádiz and soon made its way across the Atlantic to the colonies.

Power's letter to his mother was reputedly one of the bearers of this language. A government investigation of how slaves responded to news arriving from Cádiz reported that in his letter, the Puerto Rican deputy advised his mother: "if [the government in Cádiz] ordered that liberty be granted to the slaves, she should be the first to carry it out with hers." Apparently, doña Josefa was so moved that she "burst into tears . . . and tore up the letter," though whether out of joy, anger, fear, or some other emotion is unclear. Those who did receive the news with joy were her slaves Jacinto and Fermín, who, if they did not read the letter, told others that they had heard doña Josefa read it aloud. They took it to mean that they, and all of Puerto Rico's slaves, would be liberated. They quickly spread the news among enslaved friends in the neighborhood.[2]

Also in January 1812, sailors arriving in San Juan from Cádiz brought similar reports, which were warmly received by enslaved men and women in the city and, soon, in the surrounding countryside. When the brig *Cazador* anchored in San Juan, the ship's carpenter, Benito, possibly a *liberto* (freed slave) because he did not have a last name, began spreading the "false rumor" that the Cortes "had conceded liberty to the black slaves."[3] What worried Puerto Rico's governor was that Benito had set sail before he could be interrogated, and he was on his way to Havana, which had a much larger slave population.

In reporting back to the government at Cádiz, the island's Spanish governor, Salvador Meléndez, explained that such rumors of liberation spread rapidly in an environment already influenced by news of slavery's demise in other Caribbean colonies. The overthrow of slavery in the French colony of Saint-Domingue during the revolution there between 1791 and 1804 echoed in Puerto Rico, in part because some French slaveholders had fled to the Spanish colony with their slaves in tow. Moreover, Puerto Rico was getting news of unrest among Venezuela's enslaved and free-colored population.[4]

The claim that the Cortes of Cádiz had liberated Puerto Rico's slaves thus found fertile ground in 1812. According to Meléndez, enslaved men and women in the capital and the countryside, and in more distant towns such as Aguadilla on the west coast, were talking about their freedom and spreading the news. So, too, were free blacks, including Joaquín Morales, an officer in the moreno militia unit who urged slaves to claim their freedom. In the face of a potential uprising, Meléndez formed an emergency militia force of white troops in San Juan and arrested and interrogated anyone suspected of causing unrest. In the end, he detained twenty-six slaves and free blacks, though not all received punishment. The eleven whom he judged most culpable suffered thirty to fifty lashes.[5]

The events of 1812 in Puerto Rico show us that protest against slavery and claims of freedom spread throughout the Americas and Europe during the age of revolution. From the outbreak of the American Revolution through Spanish American independence in the 1820s, the language of liberty resonated in many New World slave societies, undermining the legitimacy of human bondage. This development was partly an expression of Enlightenment and religious ideologies that saw slavery as cruel, backward, and immoral. Perhaps more important, however, were the social and political transformations that took place in the midst of imperial and anti-colonial warfare. Enslaved men and women and free blacks took part in the battles between empires and for national liberation. Their broad participation shook the foundation of New World slavery to its core, enabling many slaves to claim freedom for themselves and for their families while also forcing military and political leaders to take the first halting steps toward complete abolition of both the slave traffic and slavery. Yet the consequences of warfare were far from linear. If we look again at Puerto Rico in 1812, we see that slaves and free people leapt at the chance to spread ideas of emancipation. At the same time, the Spanish colonial government responded rapidly and effectively to suppress these emancipatory urges: slavery would persist in the island for another six decades. The same was true elsewhere in Latin America. Even as independent Venezuela, Peru, Colombia, and other Spanish American nations passed abolition laws and banned the slave trade, Cuba and Brazil (and the United States) came to rely upon enslaved labor more than ever. Indeed, though abolition gained ground in the Atlantic world, so did slavery: more slaves labored on plantations in the nineteenth century than at any other time in the history of the Atlantic slave complex.

That slavery and emancipation simultaneously flourished in Latin America was not unprecedented. In 1800 the three largest Latin American slave societies, Brazil, Cuba, and Venezuela, all had large free black and mulatto populations even as slave imports remained steady or increased.

In none of them were slaves in the majority. The same would be true throughout the nineteenth century even in Cuba and Brazil, where the slave trade continued to boom until midcentury.

TABLE 2. Population in Brazil, Cuba, and Venezuela, 1800

|  | Brazil | Cuba | Venezuela |
| --- | --- | --- | --- |
| Slaves | 718,000 | 212,000 | 112,000 |
| Free blacks | 587,000 | 114,000 | 440,000 |
| Whites | 576,000 | 274,000 | 185,000 |
| Indians | 61,000 | n.a. | 161,000 |
| Total population | 1,942,000 | 600,000 | 898,000 |

*Source:* George Reid Andrews, *Afro-Latin America, 1800–2000* (New York: Oxford University Press, 2004), 41.

What these figures indicate, in part, is that since the sixteenth century individual slaves regularly had achieved emancipation, sometimes by their own efforts, sometimes by the actions of individual owners or the colonial state. But the freedom of some came in the context of the enslavement of many others and the continuation of the traffic in captives from Africa, which thrived for more than three centuries. This chapter asks: What conditions and transformations altered this balance between slavery and freedom in Latin America? When and why did the freedom of some ultimately come to seem incompatible with the enslavement of others? To answer these questions, it is necessary to look beyond the legal and religious institutions and customs that facilitated liberation over the centuries in Brazil and Spanish America. Direct attacks on the slave trade and on the political structures that protected slavery ultimately undermined this entrenched institution, giving the enslaved and their allies opportunities to claim freedom not only for themselves but for all people in Latin American societies.

## Slavery Affirmed, Slavery Destroyed: The American and Haitian Revolutions

To understand the forces that simultaneously weakened and strengthened slavery in Latin America, it is necessary to take a detour through the empires of Spain's rivals, Britain and France, as they regrouped in the aftermath of the Seven Years' War. Their clashes for supremacy in the Atlantic world would continue to have profound effects in the Iberian colonies.

Events on the ground in British and French America transformed slavery, though in a paradoxical, unpredictable fashion. The short-lived peace that followed the Seven Years' War left Britain in a commanding position, but the extent of its victories also turned out to have weakened British legitimacy in its North American colonies. While metropolitan officials pondered further expansion in the Western Hemisphere, colonists bitterly denounced the increased number of regular troops stationed in North America and the efforts of the government to impose new taxes to pay for those troops and the war. In the short period that witnessed British imperial ascendancy in the Americas—from the end of the Seven Years' War in 1763 until the outbreak of the American Revolution in 1775—settlers denounced the power of the Crown and the metropolitan parliament and demanded greater right of self-government and less meddling from Europe.

When settlers took up arms to overthrow British rule, they did so in the midst of colonies in which slavery figured quite diversely.[6] The Chesapeake and Carolina Lowcountry colonies were significant plantation societies. In mid-Atlantic cities such as Philadelphia and New York, slaves were a large part of the urban workforce. In the agrarian and urban north, however, slavery was a minor institution, though ports did a thriving business with the sugar islands in the British Caribbean. In the northern colonies, antislavery sentiment had been on the rise since midcentury, especially among the Quakers of Pennsylvania, who were in close touch with their British brethren. Many divested themselves of investments related to the slave trade and slavery, freed their own slaves, and in some cases freed those whom their families had sold long ago. Some northern colonies, including Pennsylvania, passed abolition laws during the revolution, and even before 1775 some had moved to limit or restrict the slave traffic.

Given this uneven terrain, the role of the enslaved and of free blacks varied during the American Revolution. In the first days of fighting, northern militias welcomed black volunteers, some of them formerly enslaved men freed by their owners so that they could serve. Black militia service had precedents. Benjamin Quarles shows that militias from colonies north and south had free black members in the 1750s and 1760s. But by 1776 local governments and the Continental Congress barred free blacks and slaves from the militias throughout the North American colonies.

Northern colonies such as Massachusetts were reversing their earlier policies. Southern colonies had refused to admit black troops from the first moment and would continue to refuse even when hard-pressed by metropolitan counterattacks.

British initiatives forced the rebellious Americans to reconsider their views. In November 1775 the British governor of Virginia, Lord Dunmore, issued a proclamation inviting slaves and servants to flee their masters and side with the British. In return, they would receive their freedom: "I do hereby further declare all indented servants, Negroes, or others, (appertaining to Rebels,) free, that are able and willing to bear arms, they joining His Majesty's Troops, as soon as may be, for the more speedily reducing the Colony to a proper sense of their duty, to His Majesty's crown and dignity."[7] Despite fierce resistance from Virginia colonists who introduced measures to control the enslaved population and harsh punishments for captured runaways, several hundred enslaved men reached the British lines and carried British arms in Dunmore's Ethiopian Regiment. Across the breast of their uniforms they bore the inscription "Liberty to Slaves."[8] Dunmore suffered defeat early on in Virginia, but British forces occupied much of South Carolina during the Revolution and there, too, they encouraged slaves to run away and serve in the British army.

The colonists soon went back on their efforts to eliminate free blacks and slaves from the militias, at least in the north. In 1778 Rhode Island raised a slave regiment, while local governments throughout New England disregarded color when recruiting troops. The southern colonies (with the exception of Maryland), in contrast, resisted arming their slaves even in the face of British assaults and requests from the Continental Congress and George Washington's staff. South Carolina's assembly rebuffed envoys from Washington, as did Georgia's, in spite of British successes and the need for more troops.

The British and the colonists were not the only forces to employ black troops during the American Revolution. So did Britain's European foes, France and Spain, both hungry for revenge and territory after the humiliation at midcentury. Supporting the North American rebellion offered them the opportunity. Among the troops that Spain dispatched from Cuba were moreno and pardo battalions that participated in the victories at Pensacola and Mobile. France sent hundreds of black and mulatto troops organized in the Chasseurs volontaires d'Amérique, units founded in Saint-Domingue during the Seven Years' War. They served in the failed siege of Savannah, Georgia, in 1779, after which they occupied the Caribbean island of Grenada, which the French had taken from Britain.[9]

In spite of the broad participation of slaves and free blacks (from several empires) in the war for independence, and in spite of the language of liberty that the new nation inscribed in its founding charters, after defeating Britain, the Americans consolidated a government with slave-holding at its economic and political core. The new regime fortified slavery because it relied heavily on the support of Southern planters. The holdouts against black military service in South Carolina and Georgia signified the dynamics of postindependence political and economic arrangements. After the British evacuated in 1783 (including thousands of black refugees, many of whom settled first in Nova Scotia, later in Sierra Leone), slaveholders in the Carolina Lowcountry and Georgia turned to the transatlantic traffic to restore and to augment their enslaved workforces. Such was their demand that they imported captives at an unprecedented rate. Moreover, with the opening of the cotton frontier in the Deep South in the early nineteenth century, the quest for enslaved workers took on new urgency. In a bitter historical irony, even as Britons were organizing to fight against slavery, their industrializing textile sector galvanized the market for slave-produced cotton. The United States agreed to abolish the transatlantic slave trade in 1808, but planters in the new cotton regions opened a vast internal traffic that brought captives from older plantation societies in the Chesapeake. Far from enjoying liberty, many slaves in the independent United States suffered new forms of subjugation as they were transported far from their communities to the expanding southeastern frontier.[10]

The American Revolution did unleash an antislavery movement—but in Britain, not in the newly independent republic. Britain's defeat in its North American colonies provided the impetus for more direct action against the slave traffic, which some Britons had sporadically criticized even before the American Revolution. Ever since the emergence of evangelical Christianity in the Anglo-American world in the mid-eighteenth century, religious activists denounced British colonial slavery. The Methodists and the Quakers were at the forefront of these expressions of outrage. Among the enslaved themselves there was a religious revival in the Caribbean and North American colonies, led by Baptists and other sects outside the Anglican Church. However, principled condemnations of the planters and the slavers did not threaten the institution.

The transition from criticism to direct action originated in the circle of Anglican reformers who gathered around the minister James Ramsay in the 1780s. Ramsay had spent more than a decade in Saint Kitts trying to minister to the enslaved population. Stout opposition from the planters eventually led to his expulsion from the island and his return to England. The timing was propitious. Many Britons were convinced that defeat at the hands of the American colonists was a sign of divine displeasure. Ramsay and his circle believed that the way to redeem Britain was to propagate the gospel throughout the empire, especially among the enslaved population of the Caribbean. One of Ramsay's admirers, the Anglican bishop Beilby Porteus, imagined slave societies harmonized and mellowed by the effective spread of Christianity: "a little society of truly Christian Negroes, impressed with a just cause, and living in the habitual practice, of the several duties they owe to God, to their masters, to their fellow labourers and to themselves; governed by fixed laws, and by the exactest discipline, yet tempered with gentleness and humanity."[11]

Though initially concerned with atonement after the debacle of the American Revolution, these religious reformers soon became active enemies of the slave trade and of Caribbean slavery. Ramsay's 1784 publication, *An Essay on the Treatment and Conversion of African Slaves in the British Sugar Colonies*, galvanized debate in Britain about slavery and the slave traffic. Like a latter-day Bartolomé de las Casas, Ramsay could speak from direct experience in the Caribbean about the sufferings of the enslaved and the cruelty and indifference of the master class. In the face of resistance from the West Indian lobby, Ramsay and his circle, which included highly placed officials and parliamentarians such as William Wilberforce, decided to press publicly for the abolition of the slave trade to the West Indies, seeking to awaken the British public to "that spirit of freedom, which runs throughout the Old and the New Testament."[12] Their goals were manifold. They wished to bring to an end the traffic, the brutality of which was brought to light by Thomas Clarkson's research in British slaving ports. They also hoped that with the traffic in captives suppressed, planters would have no choice but to treat their slaves more humanely, not least by allowing the spread and observation of the gospel. Ramsay argued that the consequence would be "the union of liberty and religion both slowly advancing together."[13]

Such objectives would be difficult to attain; the slave trade to the British West Indies, especially to Jamaica, was very much a going concern at the end of the eighteenth century. The number of captives disembarked in Jamaica and elsewhere was growing as the antislavery movement gained traction in the metropolis (see table 3). Though it has been argued that the profitability of the West Indian sugar and slave complex was on the decline, subsequent studies have shown that Britain was actually well poised to expand plantation production in Guiana and Trinidad. The New World plantation complex remained not only viable but, in the eyes of many, crucial to British economic well-being. Yet, from this small but influential circle of religious reformers, British antislavery efforts grew into a mass movement that became a major force in defining British politics and self-image for the next century.[14]

TABLE 3. Slaves disembarked in British Caribbean colonies, mid-eighteenth to early nineteenth centuries

|           | Trinidad and Tobago* | British Guiana | Barbados | Jamaica |
|-----------|---------------------|----------------|----------|---------|
| 1751–1775 | 1,925               | 0              | 106,898  | 232,235 |
| 1776–1800 | 18,732              | 30,647         | 28,307   | 301,769 |
| 1801–1825 | 20,128              | 41,725         | 6,813    | 68,901  |
| Totals    | 40,785              | 72,372         | 142,018  | 602,905 |

*The British took Trinidad from Spain in 1797.
Source: Estimates Database, 2009, *Voyages: The Trans-Atlantic Slave Trade Database*, http://www.slavevoyages.org, accessed January 7, 2011.

Among the most vocal advocates of suppressing the slave trade were Afro-Britons, who spoke and wrote about their direct experience with enslavement. Afro-Britons found themselves in a more favorable position in the later eighteenth century after the Somerset Case (1772), a legal decision concerning the fate of an enslaved man, James Somerset, whose master wanted to send him back to the West Indies. Though in strictest terms the decision forbade the master's specific action, many held it to mean that slavery was banned on British soil. As the poet William Cowper wrote in response: "Slaves cannot breathe in England; if their lungs / Receive our air, that moment they are free."[15] Critics of slavery and of the colonial planter class celebrated the Somerset decision as an affirmation of British liberty and a defense of the rule of law in the face of the lawlessness and private power of the slaveholder.

Afro-Britons assumed a more visible presence in British public life after 1772. Though their numbers were small, several became well-known poets and memoirists; others participated in public debates about the slave trade and its suppression. The most prominent black abolitionist at the end of the eighteenth century was Olaudah Equiano, also known as Gustavus Vassa.[16] Equiano published his autobiography, the *Interesting Narrative of the Life of Olaudah Equiano, or Gustavus Vassa, the African*, in 1789 and in several editions thereafter. A subscription supported publication of the work, and the list included eminent abolitionists and reform advocates of various stripes. Like his abolitionist friends and colleagues, such as Thomas Clarkson, Equiano took his *Narrative* and his argument for suppressing the slave traffic on the road. He spoke before large gatherings and offered his book for sale. Readers would find harrowing accounts of the cruel treatment meted out to the enslaved during the Middle Passage and by the master class of the Americas. For example, Equiano described a gruesome encounter on a Virginia plantation where he labored as a youth: "I was very much affrighted at some things I saw, and the more so as I had seen a black woman slave as I came through the house, who was cooking the dinner, and the poor creature was cruelly loaded with various kinds of iron machines; she had one particularly on her head, which locked her mouth so fast that she could scarcely speak; and could not eat nor drink. I was much astonished and shocked at this contrivance, which I afterwards learned was called the iron muzzle."[17]

But readers would also find inspiring tales of liberation, struggles to preserve his freedom against those who would reenslave him, religious conversion to Methodism, and economic rationales for suppressing the slave trade. As did leading abolitionists such as Granville Sharp, Equiano argued that trading with Africa in goods other than human beings would be a boon to the British and African economies alike:

> This I conceive to be a theory founded upon facts, and therefore an infallible one. If the blacks were permitted to remain in their own country, they would double themselves every fifteen years. In proportion to such increase will be the demand for manufactures. Cotton and indigo grow spontaneously in most parts of Africa; a consideration this of no small consequence to the manufacturing towns of Great Britain. It opens a most immense, glorious, and happy prospect—the clothing, &c. of a continent ten thousand

miles in circumference, and immensely rich in productions of every denomination in return for manufactures.[18]

Abolitionists like Sharp and Equiano were willing to back up these commercial arguments with money and work. Many invested in a company whose mission was to resettle freed slaves in Sierra Leone, where they would work as free people and demonstrate the lucrative trade to be forged between Britain and Africa. Among the settlers were the black veterans of the American Revolution who served in the British army in return for liberation.[19]

Combining religious fervor, economic liberalism, and mass political mobilization, British antislavery efforts drove Parliament to outlaw the slave traffic to the British colonies in 1807 and were a crucial factor in the suppression of slavery in the 1830s. Moreover, British initiatives against the slave trade became international in their scope. Beginning with the Congress of Vienna (1815), the British government sought to implement slave trade abolition throughout the Atlantic world by securing treaties to that effect with other governments. British warships patrolled off the coast of Africa, Cuba, and Brazil, while British-backed courts condemned captured slavers. In 1850 the navy took its most direct action by invading Brazilian ports and destroying slaving vessels. The traffic from Africa would persist until the Spanish government relented in 1867, but the rise of British antislavery groups nonetheless represented a significant blow that would finally bring three centuries of the transatlantic slave trade to an end.[20]

An even more definitive movement against slavery was taking place not in Europe but back in the Americas. In the same era in which Evangelicals and popular groups throughout the British Isles were demanding the end of the slave trade, and as planters in South Carolina and Georgia sought to rebuild their fortunes by avidly buying African captives, slaves in the French colony of Saint-Domingue were taking direct action to throw off their bonds. Like the British movement to suppress the slave traffic, the Haitian Revolution (1791–1804) had complicated effects. Revolutionaries destroyed slavery forever in the former French colony of Saint-Domingue (and eventually in the neighboring Spanish colony, Santo Domingo). The Haitian events became a symbol of liberation for enslaved and free people of color around the Caribbean, inspiring revolts in Venezuela and Cuba. At the same time, the destruction of slavery in the Caribbean's richest colony was a spur to slavery's growth in other corners of the Caribbean and Latin America, especially in Cuba and Brazil, where planters, merchants, and governments took advantage of new openings for their goods and new anxieties about the consequences of slave emancipation.[21]

The French colony of Saint-Domingue on the western end of the island of Hispaniola was a highly efficient, and deadly, producer of sugar, indigo, and coffee.[22] A small free population, divided between great planters and smaller property owners, shopkeepers, professionals, soldiers, and administrators ruled over a towering slave population, largely African-born. The free population included whites and people of color. Many of the latter were freed by European fathers and assumed leading positions in the colony through education and the inheritance of wealth, though they found their prerogatives increasingly curtailed in the second half of the century. Some were planters in their own right, though usually of coffee and indigo as opposed to sugar. Others filled positions in the colonial militia or the *maréchausée*, the gendarmerie dedicated to tracking down runaway slaves. Though discriminated against, they generally identified strongly with the dominant colonial culture.

When revolution broke out in France in 1789, Saint-Domingue's *gens de couleur* saw the new regime as a potential ally against the "aristocrats of the skin" who sought to disbar them from the full enjoyment of their liberty. They found advocates for equality in France. But to their dismay, since many owned slaves, they also confronted a small but influential abolitionist society, the Société des Amis des Noirs, founded in 1788 and dedicated to the gradual abolition of colonial slavery. By the later eighteenth century, more and more enlightened French had come to see New World slavery as a gross injustice. They also saw it as a powder keg ready to explode at any moment.

French abolitionists differed significantly from their British counterparts. Evangelical Christianity played no role in their criticisms of slavery; they were not moved by a desire to spread the gospel to the enslaved or by the wish to redeem their nation in the face of divine wrath. They believed instead in natural rights that were universally applicable to all peoples. Compared to the British, they were small in number, limited to enlightened intellectuals and officials who sought amelioration of the slave's condition and the extension of full rights of citizenship to free people of color. France never witnessed the kind of mass mobilization characteristic of British antislavery efforts, though the intersection of revolution and slave

FIGURE 8. Portrait of Vincent Ogé (d. 1791): "He loves liberty just as he knows
how to defend it." A wealthy free-colored merchant and landowner from Cap
Français, Saint-Domingue, Ogé was in Paris in 1789, where he gathered with
other prominent members of Saint-Domingue's free-colored population to lobby
for equal rights for all free people in the colony regardless of lineage. Their
demands met with staunch resistance from white settlers, rich and humble, even
though all agreed on the preservation of their property in slaves. John Garrigus
argues that Ogé's Parisian experience convinced him of the strong link between
militia service and active citizenship, a claim that would resonate among the free-
colored population of the colony. Among Ogé's co-conspirators after his return to
Saint-Domingue were many veterans of the Chasseurs volontaires who had served
during the American Revolution and were frustrated by the efforts to marginalize
their class in the colony and to exclude them from revolutionary citizenship after
1789. Archivo General de Indias, Mapas y Planos, Estampas, 30 (2).

rebellion in Saint-Domingue beginning in 1791 did place slavery's fate at the center of French colonial politics.[23]

Though the members of the Amis des Noirs were cautious about abolishing slavery, they were firm advocates of enfranchising the free black population of Saint-Domingue and other colonies and actively promoted this cause. But these proposed reforms ran into fierce opposition from white settlers and their allies in the revolutionary assembly. When it became clear that the whites of Saint-Domingue and their French allies would stall on extending citizenship, several free-colored leaders, such as Vincent Ogé, returned to the colony in 1790 and took up arms to force their claims. Though he gathered several hundred militia veterans about him, Ogé and his supporters dispersed after little more than a skirmish with troops from Cap Français. Ogé and others crossed the colonial border into Santo Domingo, but Spanish officials returned him to the French side, where he was broken on the wheel and beheaded in 1791.[24]

Later that year, a new rebellion led by free-colored veterans broke out near Port-au-Prince, this time with crucial support from a contingent of well-trained slave troops whom they called "the Swiss." After scoring victories over forces from Port-au-Prince, the gens de couleur reached an agreement with local officials to abolish color discrimination among the free population. Tellingly, the Swiss were excluded from this pact; their reward was deportation from the colony because slaveholders saw armed and trained slaves as a menace. When no neighboring colonies would accept the deportees, French officials imprisoned them offshore in hulks. Many were executed, others died of disease and starvation. Their fate spoke eloquently to the limits of revolutionary liberty.[25]

But openings for action against slavery were presenting themselves, as both the colony and metropolis were divided. While the dominant groups fought among themselves around Port-au-Prince in 1791, slaves in the northern part of the colony seized the opportunity to assert their own demands for freedom. Led by the slave and religious figure Boukman and inspired by African and European ideas of justice and freedom, a huge slave rebellion erupted in 1791 across the northern plain of the colony. The ideology of the French Revolution was important in shaping expectations and initiatives in revolutionary Saint-Domingue, but the African background was also crucial. The majority of slaves in the northern plain were from the Kingdom of Kongo, and through the early phases of their rebellion, several leaders steadfastly spoke the language of kingship to justify their actions and their political loyalties. After the burning of the city of Le Cap in 1793, the rebel leader Macaya rejected the overtures of the representatives of republican France, Léger Félicité Sonthonax and Étienne Polverel, in a royalist idiom: "I am the subject of three kings: of the King of Congo, master of all the blacks; of the King of France who represents my father; of the King of Spain who represents my mother. These three Kings are the descendants of those who, led by a star, came to adore God made Man."[26]

Macaya's expression of fealty to three kings demonstrated not only the import of Kongo political ideology but also the rivalry among European states in Saint-Domingue. France's rivals saw in the rebellions that shook Saint-Domingue a chance to advance their own cause, as both Britain and Spain aimed to incorporate the rich colony into their empires. Both sought allies, occupied territory, and supported proxy forces. The British tried to build their support on the great planters of the north and occupied territory there. Spain, from the adjoining colony of Santo Domingo, supported Toussaint Louverture, a well-educated former slave who, according to legend, was a reader of the Abbé Raynal, a philosophe who had augured the violent destruction of New World slavery by a black Spartacus. From obscure origins, Toussaint became one of the leading black generals in the early phase of the revolution. In 1794 he switched his allegiance from Spain to France when the revolutionary government in Paris endorsed the measure of its representative Sonthonax, who had declared slavery abolished the year before in an effort to rally the enslaved masses of Saint-Domingue to fight for France against the British and Spanish invaders, a tactic that reached fruition with Toussaint's conversion to the French side. The leverage against slavery provided by revolutionary and international war was more effective in the Saint-Domingue rebellion than in the American Revolution. In Spanish America a few years later, warfare also proved to be the most powerful solvent of slavery.

For the next several years, Toussaint was the ruler of the colony, which he successfully defended against foreign powers. He respected the abolition of slavery, but he also tried to restore plantation discipline and the export economy through various measures that would compel freedmen to continue laboring on the big estates. Despite Toussaint's loyalty and his efforts to keep the plantations working, France in 1802 sought to restore slavery in its colonies. The French successfully reenslaved freed people in their other Caribbean colonies (Guadeloupe, Martinique, French Guiana).

In Saint-Domingue they captured Toussaint and deported him to France, where he perished in the Fortress of Joux in the Jura Mountains in 1803. But resistance quickly stiffened. The black generals Henri Christophe and Jean-Jacques Dessalines defeated a large European expedition and proclaimed the independence of the new nation, Haiti, in 1804.[27]

When Haiti proclaimed its independence from France in 1804, slavery and the slave trade were facing major challenges to their survival in parts of the Atlantic world. Haitian independence, won largely by the formerly enslaved whose actions compelled the metropole to abolish slavery, definitively ended both slavery and the slave trade on the island of Hispaniola. A few years later, the British antislavery movement would score a major victory when Parliament voted to ban the slave traffic to the British colonies. The revolutionary era in British North America, France, and the French Caribbean brought about the destruction or weakening of slavery in major plantation societies (Saint-Domingue, Jamaica). At the same time, it ushered in the conditions for slavery's expansion into new territories. Slaveholders in the independent United States saw their hand strengthened by greater political control, consolidation of the southeastern frontier, and burgeoning demand on the world market for their slave-produced cotton.

The Iberian empires would experience similarly uneven developments soon after the American and Haitian revolutions. There, too, anticolonial movements spread and threw into doubt the future of bonded labor and the traffic in captives from Africa. In many regions of revolutionary Spanish America, the slave trade was suppressed and emancipation laws enacted. At the same time, planters in Cuba and Brazil, much like their U.S. counterparts, took advantage of new political and economic arrangements to open frontiers to slave-produced commodities on a vastly enlarged scale.

### Independence and Abolition in Spanish America

The French Revolution would exert important and unpredictable influence in New World slave societies well beyond the confines of the French colonial empire. France's military occupation of the Iberian Peninsula in 1808 threw the empires of Spain and Portugal into profound crisis.[28] The invasion had differing effects on slavery in the two empires. The Portuguese court embarked for Rio de Janeiro under British escort and remained there until 1822. With Rio as the new capital of the empire and the protection

FIGURE 9. Portrait from an apology for Ferdinand VII of Spain.
Ferdinand VII briefly succeeded his father, Charles IV, by means
of a palace coup in 1808. He then capitulated before Napoleon Bonaparte
at a meeting in Bayonne and relinquished his throne, which was taken
over by Napoleon's brother Joseph Bonaparte (Joseph I of Spain).
Ferdinand's abdication threw Spain and its overseas empire into political
crisis, from which came the revolutions that would undermine slavery
in much of Spanish America. This printed portrait of Ferdinand
was meant to circulate among his European and American domains
and explain that "the beloved King of Spain and the Emperor of
the Indies . . . like no other Sovereign . . . resolved to relinquish his
sovereignty, rather than see the blood of his Vassals spilled."
Archivo General de Indias, Mapas y Planos, Estampas, 141(1).

of Europe's dominant economic and naval power, Brazilian ports enjoyed greater freedom, urban and plantation slavery boomed, and political order reigned, at least in the short term (more on Brazil in chapter 4).

In contrast, a political vacuum opened in Spain and its overseas empire. The Spanish ruler Charles IV and his heir, Ferdinand, fell captive to Napoleon Bonaparte in 1808, and Bonaparte's legions commenced the occupation of Spain. However, all did not go as planned by the French. The country was submerged in a violent resistance to the occupying force between 1808 and 1814 as Spanish patriots gathered first in Seville and then in Cádiz to form a new government in the monarch's absence. The most lasting achievement of the Cádiz government was a constitution composed by peninsular and colonial framers in 1812. One of the major goals of the Constitution of Cádiz was to redefine the relationship between the peninsula and the overseas colonies, incorporating the latter into a constitutional regime that gave them broad political representation in a metropolitan assembly. But even as the framers at Cádiz sought to forge a new political order, events in the colonies were overtaking them. The overthrow of the Bourbon monarchy led to an acute crisis of legitimacy in the colonies, which the constitution failed to solve (indeed, as we will see, in some cases it exacerbated the crisis). Though Cádiz tried to assert its authority over all of the Spanish domains, Caracas, Buenos Aires, Cartagena, and other colonial centers formed juntas, or governing assemblies, that argued that in the absence of the monarch political power devolved to self-governing municipalities. As the opportunities for compromise between Cádiz and the American juntas receded, many Spanish American patriots saw this as the moment to fight for independence; in doing so, they set in motion a chain of events that would lead to the dismantling of Spanish dominion from the northern reaches of New Spain to the austral lands of South America. These far-reaching conflicts dramatically altered Spanish American slave regimes.

The Caracas junta's rupture from Spain showed that, as in other Atlantic revolutions, the fate of slavery would figure in the independence struggle in Spanish South America, though slavery was less central in these colonies than it was in Saint-Domingue, the Carolina Lowcountry, Brazil, or Cuba (see table 4).[29] Like other cities in Spain and Spanish America, Caracas, upon receiving news of the captivity of the Bourbon rulers, declared its opposition to the French and formed a local junta that would govern in the absence of the legitimate monarch. Within the governing coalition were strong advocates of independence—including Simón Bolívar, a wealthy planter from an old creole family—who ultimately prevailed upon their colleagues to declare Venezuela's independence in 1811. The Venezuelan constitution of that year spoke directly to the question of slavery and reflected the interests of the dominant economic and social groups. Among its provisions was a distinction between active and passive citizens. Only those possessing substantial property would enjoy the vote. The constitution also continued the segregation of African-descended people typical of Spanish rule by organizing its militia along color lines. The new regime declared the slave trade abolished—the hope of receiving recognition from Britain dictated the necessity of such a ban—but took no action against slavery itself. Thus, while enshrining liberty, the first champions of Venezuelan independence understood that only some would exercise it fully: those with property, often in slaves.[30]

TABLE 4. Slave population of Spanish South America on the eve of independence

| Colony | Slave population |
| --- | --- |
| Quito | 5,000 |
| Chile | 6,000 |
| Río de la Plata | 30,000 |
| Peru | 40,000 |
| New Granada | 78,000 |
| Venezuela | 87,800 |

*Source:* Peter Blanchard, *Under the Flags of Freedom: Slave Soldiers and the Wars of Independence in Spanish South America* (Pittsburgh, PA: University of Pittsburgh Press, 2008), 8.

But the best-laid plans of creole oligarchs could not necessarily survive the course of events. The independence wars threatened the interests of slaveholders throughout Spanish America because they gave enslaved people opportunities for liberation. The most important development was war itself. Spain struck back at colonial rebels after the restoration of the Bourbon monarch Ferdinand VII in 1814, waging a temporarily successful war of reconquest in Chile, Peru, Nueva Granada, and Venezuela under commanders such as General Pablo Morillo, a seasoned veteran of combat against the French in the Iberian Peninsula. As the wars quickened, so did the demand for troops on both sides. Here is where slaves and free blacks gained important leverage.

Royalist and patriotic forces alike mobilized slaves to fight on their sides during the long years of warfare on the South American continent. Royalists could draw on old precedents by promising freedom in exchange for a term of military service. Such a compromise had existed throughout the colonial period and recognized the basic legitimacy of slavery as an institution in Spanish America, while also honoring the mechanisms for acquiring freedom enshrined in Spanish law since the Middle Ages. Throughout the nineteenth century, from the wars in Venezuela to the final battles against Cuban patriots between 1868 and 1880 (more on this in chapter 4), Spain was able to attract military recruits from the slave population, trading freedom for service to the king and nation, as it had done throughout the old regime. Patriot armies often tried to strike a similar bargain. Many of their initial leaders were slave owners themselves, such as Bolívar in Venezuela, who gradually freed his more than one hundred slaves. But patriot armies found it harder to defend the persistence of slavery in the context of liberal and republican aspirations, the breakdown of traditional forms of order, and the spread of the language of liberation. As Bolívar conceded, "It seems to me madness that a revolution for freedom expects to maintain slavery."[31]

Soon after Spain was definitively expelled from South America in the 1820s, Bolívar looked back, with mixed feelings, on the wars and commented on how the need for manpower had dramatically shaken societies characterized by slave-holding and racial hierarchies:

> In the first years of Independence, we needed men who were above all brave, who could kill Spaniards and make themselves feared; blacks, *zambos*, *mulattos*, and whites, all were welcome as long as they fought bravely. No one could be rewarded with money, for there was none; the only way of maintaining ardour, rewarding exceptional actions and stimulating valour was by promotion, so that today men of every caste and colour are among the generals, leaders, and officers of our forces, though the majority of them have no other merit than brute strength. This was once useful to the Republic but now, in peacetime, is an obstacle to peace and tranquility. But it was a necessary evil.[32]

Bolívar's assessment of the transformative impact of war on the post-colonial social order had more than a twinge of pessimism about it. Now

free of Spanish rule, how would traditionally hierarchical societies organize themselves once those hierarchies were called into question? Yet
Bolívar's gloomy ruminations should not blind us to the vigor of the challenges to colonial slavery and racial prejudice enabled by the independence
movements. These challenges become more apparent when we contrast
them to Spain's efforts to maintain the old order in these years, as the metropolitan government consistently foundered on the questions of slavery
and political equality for the *castas*.

The Spanish Constitution of Cádiz, drafted in 1812, spoke eloquently
to the question of slavery in the colonies. Its answers reaffirmed the institution's centrality. Though some critics advocated abolishing the slave
trade in emulation of the British, Cuban planters prevailed upon the assembly to suppress any public utterances against the traffic or against slavery.
The recent deregulation of the traffic to Cuba had set the stage for a tremendous expansion of the sugar complex around Havana. In deference to
the Havana planter class's interests, the Cádiz constitution not only left
the traffic untouched but also formalized slavery and racial discrimination
in the colonies. This defense of hierarchy and property could be seen in
the prescriptions around citizenship. The Constitution of Cádiz barred
Africans and African-descended people from the active exercise of citizenship, which affected the proportional representation of the colonies in the
Cortes, diminishing their power in relation to the metropole. Lineage thus
became one of the qualifications for full political rights, a situation that
differed little from the discrimination that had prevailed against the castas
over the centuries. Moreover, though seeking to incorporate the colonies,
Spanish politicians nonetheless rigged the new regime so that metropolitan supremacy would remain intact.

This defense of aspects of the old order would necessarily marginalize large sectors of the colonial populace. Take, for example, the family of
Pedro de Ayarza, a well-to-do merchant from Portobello in Panama, just
a few years before the independence movements would erupt in Spanish
America. Ayarza was a pardo who had risen to wealth and local prominence
as a merchant and officer in the pardo militia. He was able to educate his
three sons in style. The eldest, José Ponciano, studied law in Bogotá, the
viceregal capital of Nueva Granada. However, when the young man was
on the verge of completing his studies, the university registrar refused
him his degree because he was a man of color and thus legally barred from
the university and the practice of law. In 1795 Ayarza sought to remedy the

situation by taking advantage of a new Bourbon policy that allowed people to purchase legal whiteness, a measure that was known as *gracias al sacar*, and the right to use the honorific title *don*. Ayarza hoped to acquire legal whiteness and the use of the honorific for himself and his three sons. The process was lengthy and expensive. Ayarza had to apply four times over the next several years, employing an agent in Madrid to pursue his case. In the end, the Council of the Indies granted these privileges only to the eldest son, José Ponciano. The decision "extinguished" his color, he could use the title *don*, and he could receive his diploma and exercise his profession. But the council repeatedly turned down the applications of his father and his two brothers, so that while José Ponciano became legally white, the other Ayarzas were pardos and remained subject to various kinds of legal discrimination.[33]

Such was the hierarchical and segregated colonial order that the Constitution of Cádiz would uphold. In contrast, Spanish officials in the colonies, who were desperate for manpower and local political support, realized how self-defeating the exclusionary policies were and recommended that the government take steps to reward and incorporate the castas. The captain general of Caracas, don José Ceballos, urged such measures in a report to the metropolitan government written in the midst of an effective Spanish counterattack against patriot forces in Venezuela and New Granada. Though General Pablo Morillo had temporarily gained the upper hand, Ceballos was dubious that the four thousand troops under his command could hold the colony for any length of time without widespread political support. Analyzing the local population and which sectors might be convinced to side with the monarchy, he concluded that since European and American Spaniards were a tiny minority, it made little practical sense to uphold their privileges. Instead, the crown should rebuilt its support among the castas by "extract[ing] them legally from their inferior class."[34] Ceballos wrote that one means of doing so would be to use existing legal mechanisms by which castas could be declared legally white and thus freed of the handicaps from which they suffered, which the Constitution of Cádiz and the restored monarchy had unwisely enforced.

Spanish intransigence on the question of slavery, the slave traffic, and lineage created new possibilities for the patriot movements. Though often led by traditional oligarchs like Bolívar, the independence movements required and attracted ever greater support from all sectors of society. Slaves were recruited as soldiers. Free blacks and mulattoes not only served in but also rose through the ranks of the insurgent armies. When Bolívar returned to Venezuela in 1816 after several years of exile in Jamaica and Haiti, he was greeted by men of color such as Manuel Piar, a general who organized and commanded effective fighting forces that served as the new foundations of the liberation movement.

Most of those who took part in the independence movements filled more humble but nonetheless crucial positions. Throughout the struggles in South America, enslaved men and women claimed their freedom because of their service or that of a family member to the *patria*. The historian Peter Blanchard has recovered many of these claims. In the 1820s, on the eve of independence, an official in the liberating armies in Peru recognized that favoring the freedom of soldiers' spouses was urgent: "I believe that this woman and other slave wives of the soldiers of this Army must be given preference in the lottery offered by the Government to benefit this unfortunate caste; for it is only fair that the first fruits of the endeavors of those who fought for freedom should be their families." This recommendation reflected the wisdom accumulated in the long years of conflict against Spain on the South American continent as slave soldiers and their families became active in the campaigns from the beginning. In 1813 the slave Francisco Estrada went before the court in Buenos Aires to demand freedom for serving the local forces in the invasion of the Banda Oriental (Uruguay). Estrada had taken his family with him, and after two years of hard service he requested that they all be liberated. The enslaved woman Juliana García made similar demands for herself and her children in Buenos Aires in 1818. She and her husband had fled captivity in Montevideo to join the Buenos Aires forces. They trekked throughout the continent, from Montevideo to the heights of Upper Peru (Bolivia), in support of the independence movement. Like other enslaved people, she claimed that the patria must reward such dedicated service with liberation.[35]

Thus, as the liberators fought back against Spain and gradually achieved independence between 1820 and 1824, they had to acknowledge that years of warfare and demands for liberation and equality from the slaves and free blacks serving in the military had weakened slavery and colonial-era racial hierarchies. Political leaders drafted constitutions that did away with the explicit discrimination and segregation that the Constitution of Cádiz defended. Color and lineage would no longer be criteria for active citizenship (though in some places, property would). The new regimes also suppressed the slave trade and passed emancipation laws. Even though these laws in the main Spanish American slave-holding countries—Argentina, Venezuela, Colombia, and Peru—were of a decidedly gradual nature and would not end slavery until midcentury (see table 5), they nonetheless differed significantly from the Spanish effort to preserve slavery and to foment the slave trade during the revolutionary crisis. When it came to deciding to abolish slavery in Spanish America, independence mattered.

Table 5. Dates of abolition of slavery in independent Spanish America

| | |
|---|---|
| Argentina | 1853 |
| Bolivia | 1851 |
| Central America | 1824 |
| Chile | 1823 |
| Colombia | 1852 |
| Ecuador | 1851 |
| Mexico* | 1829 |
| Paraguay† | 1869 |
| Peru | 1854 |
| Uruguay | 1842 |
| Venezuela | 1854 |

*With the exception of Texas, still part of Mexico but also caught up in the expansion of slavery in the southeastern United States.

†Forced by Brazil when its armies occupied Asunción during the Paraguayan War (1864–1870).

*Source:* George Reid Andrews, *Afro-Latin America, 1800–2000* (New York: Oxford University Press, 2004), 57.

External forces also explain why abolition laws took hold: the British government effectively enforced the suppression of the slave trade to the newly independent republics. In the 1820s Britain made slave trade abolition a condition of recognizing independence. One of the questions that its envoys had to put to new regimes was explicit: "Has it abjured and abolished the Slave Trade?"[36] Though the independent governments banned the trade, in some cases even before opening negotiations with Britain, there was pressure after independence to reopen it in some quarters. Peru opened a trade in slaves from Colombia in the 1840s. It also turned to the traffic in indentured Chinese workers, while slaveholders advocated the resumption of the African slave trade. Uruguay and Argentina circumvented agreements by allowing Portuguese and Brazilian slavers to outfit their ships and to fly their flags for illegal expeditions to Brazil. Britain would respond aggressively to these subterfuges by demanding new treaties (including with Spain and Portugal) that permitted the Royal Navy to seize and destroy ships found with slaving equipment.

British diplomacy and new laws and expectations combined to weaken slavery in the independent republics. Yet slaveholders did not give up without a fight. Chile, Mexico, and the Central American Federation abolished slavery soon after independence, but where slavery was more widespread in South America, efforts to impede final abolition were stubborn; there was in effect a backlash by slaveholders, who sought to reassert the primacy of property rights and, in some countries, to reopen the slave traffic or a close alternative, the trade in indentured Chinese workers.

Despite slaveholders' stubbornness, enslaved people in the newly independent South American republics took advantage of political and legal conditions to force slavery's decline and ultimate demise. Slaves continued to resort to flight, escaping from rural haciendas and seeking cover in urban centers such as Lima and Buenos Aires. Under the new regimes, they could appeal for liberation or transfer to another owner in cases of cruelty or violent treatment. They might win their freedom through lotteries established to liberate a certain number of slaves each year. In several Spanish American cities, emancipation funds managed by political parties and religious associations purchased the freedom of enslaved men, women, and children. In Guayaquil, Ecuador, the local government established a *junta de manumisión* that was to oversee the purchase of freedom by banking deposits from enslaved men and women and by collecting an inheritance tax dedicated to manumission, though the latter source of revenue was less reliable than the former. Indeed, slaves had shown their commitment to such an undertaking from the moment of independence. In 1822 a group of enslaved men petitioned the new government for the right to establish their own manumission fund, whereby each would contribute a portion of their wages to a common pool to be used to purchase the freedom of all. "Liberty for captives has always been a privileged concept," they wrote in their petition. "We hope it will be even more so under the just, humane and honorable government we now enjoy."[37]

Abolition became a political issue after independence. Liberal parties attacked slavery as a vestige of the colonial past that denied the liberty and equality promised by the new governments. They used abolitionism as a means to attract electoral support in regions with large free black populations, such as Cauca in southwestern Colombia, where one Liberal Party leader observed that "the slaves who lose their chains bring to society gratitude for the government that has lifted the yoke off them."[38] Such tactics reflected how the wars for independence had changed attitudes toward slavery in Spanish American societies. Colonial hierarchies and forms of domination were denuded of their veneer of inevitability. What took shape during the independence struggles in the new Spanish American nations were ideologies that formally declared the equality of all peoples regardless of lineage or status under the colonial regime. These were not slaveholding republics like the United States (or a slave-holding monarchy like Brazil) but republics committed, at least in their stated intentions, to fraternity and equality or, in the words of a recent study of early independent Colombia, to "racial harmony" after long centuries of discrimination. In such political and ideological circumstances, slaveholders could hold onto their property as best they could, but they could not convince the majority that slavery was a social good.[39]

In this regard, the Spanish American republics differed notably from their North American counterpart. One of the most acute and knowledgeable observers of the New World, the Prussian scientist and traveler Alexander von Humboldt, in 1826 noted the impact that the wars of independence across the Americas had had upon slavery. An advocate of gradual abolition, Humboldt wrote with dismay about the rapid spread of slavery through the southeastern section of the independent United States. In contrast, he praised the leaders of the newly independent Spanish American republics for showing foresight superior to their North American counterparts: "One cannot sufficiently praise the prudence of the legislation of the new republics of Spanish America. Since their origin, they have seriously occupied themselves with the total extinction of slavery. This vast part of the world has in this regard an immense advantage over the meridional part of the United States, where the whites during the war with England established liberty for their own benefit and where the slave population, which now numbers 1.6 million, is growing even faster than the white population."[40]

As Humboldt's observations show, the impact of revolution and independence on slavery was far from homogenous. By the early decades of the nineteenth century, the traffic in enslaved Africans had ceased to flow to such major plantation centers as Jamaica, Saint-Domingue, and the southern United States. The abolition of slavery was widespread, from the northern states of the independent United States to the independent regimes of Spanish America, though only in Saint-Domingue/Haiti did slavery come to a sudden and radical end. Abolition was seldom a decisive moment of truth but rather the culmination of many struggles, local and international, against the slave trade and slavery. Slavery lingered in much of Spanish America after independence, but the actions of enslaved people, abolitionists, and political parties in combination with the effective ban of the slave trade overcame the rearguard measures of slaveholders who were determined to defend their property.

The Spanish American republics were distinct from other revolutionary American societies in their espousal of racial harmony. The United States disenfranchised most blacks and made slavery even crueler by opening a new slave trade from the old plantation regions to the new cotton frontier. Haiti drove whites from its boundaries as former slaves and free people of color secured their independence from France. In both, independence accentuated racial antagonisms.[41] Spanish American republics did not instantly rid themselves of the colonial legacies of discrimination, but the long wars of independence gave rise to broadly supported efforts to overcome them. During those years the former Spanish colonies traveled a long way from the era of colonization, when even critics of slavery's brutality such as Alonso de Sandoval had justified the institution with the story of Noah's curse on Ham and other biblical sanctions. During the revolutionary era and after independence, in contrast, the language of liberty and equality took root among much of the population; slavery's defenders found themselves in the minority. However, the same could not be said for Latin America as a whole. Huge slave-worked plantations and a flourishing traffic in African captives were still to be found. Both emerged more vital than ever in the independent Brazilian monarchy and in Spain's last American colonies, Cuba and Puerto Rico.

# Simón Bolívar and the Problem of Equality

❦

✤ THE SPANISH AMERICAN WARS OF INDEPENDENCE UNDERMINED slavery in South America and led many free people of color to aspire to the dismantling of the colonial legal handicaps that enforced inequality. While revolutionary leaders were wary, they ultimately came to understand that such challenges to the colonial order would help them to overthrow Spanish rule. If Spain stood for slavery and legal discrimination, then the independent republics of South America would represent liberty and equality. But doubts persisted among the old colonial elite that now aspired to control free republics. Among the skeptics was the most prominent of the revolutionary leaders, the Venezuelan Simón Bolívar.

Bolívar was keenly attuned to how Spanish American societies had changed because he found himself involved in the clash between the desire for equality and mobility and the need for political and social order during the battles against Spain and then in the postindependence effort to create viable states. In 1816 Bolívar returned to the South American continent after several years of exile in the Caribbean, where he had become an abolitionist. While in Haiti, he promised his benefactor Alexandre Pétion that he would abolish slavery when he defeated Spain and achieved independence. His major ally upon his return to Venezuela was the mulatto general Manuel Piar, who had organized and trained effective forces in the eastern regions of Venezuela around the Orinoco River. Here Bolívar found the manpower and the regional base from which to begin the reconquest of his home and then to take war to the Spaniards in neighboring colonies. Despite their successes in the region, Bolívar and Piar soon found themselves at odds for control of the revolution. Bolívar took decisive action by having Piar arrested and executed for treason and insubordination. What he feared was that Piar would lead the free population of color against the white leadership, creating a *pardocracia* (rule by the pardos), inspired by the ruler of Haiti and Bolívar's erstwhile supporter, Pétion. Justifying the execution, Bolívar denounced Piar "for proclaiming the odious principles of race war."[1]

After independence, Bolívar again confronted what he considered an attempt to impose pardocracia, this time in Gran Colombia by the general José Padilla. Padilla had risen from humble origins in Caribbean Colombia and taken part in the epic struggles of the era, including naval service for Spain at Trafalgar in 1805 (where the British admiral Nelson destroyed the Spanish and French fleets). As Spanish authority began to break down, he chose to serve the cause of independence in Cartagena and Venezuela. He was in exile in Haiti with Bolívar and returned with him to Venezuela in 1816, proving himself in numerous actions against the Spaniards and loyalists, including the liberation of Cartagena in 1821. Yet Padilla soon ran afoul of white elites who distrusted him for his origins and his popularity among the pardos of Gran Colombia. Passed over for the high offices he considered his due, he several times issued manifestoes that denounced the machinations of white leaders. In 1824 he wrote to the people of Cartagena that: "this is not the first attempt by my enemies, the enemies of my class, to discredit me before the government, before my fellow citizens, before the entire world; one can see right away, I don't belong to the *old families*, nor do I draw my origin from . . . the ferocious Spaniards."[2] His vindication of his rights alarmed Bolívar, still fighting in Peru to drive the Spaniards from their last South American redoubt. To one of his allies, he wrote that Padilla and his admirers "want absolute equality, in the public and domestic areas alike; and next they will want pardocracia, which is their natural and unique propensity, in order to then exterminate the privileged class."[3] Though nothing came of the conflict in

1824, when Padilla plotted with other military leaders to take control of Cartagena, in 1828 Bolívar had him arrested and executed, while sending into exile his white coconspirator, Francisco de Paula Santander. Bolívar admitted in letters that his actions spoke of a double standard for whites and nonwhites: "what torments me even more is the just clamor with which those of the class of Piar and Padilla will complain."[4]

## Additional Reading

King, James F. "A Royalist View of the Colored Castes in the Venezuelan War of Independence." *Hispanic American Historical Review* 33 (November 1953): 526–37.

Lasso, Marixa. *Myths of Harmony: Race and Republicanism during the Age of Revolution, Colombia, 1795–1831.* Pittsburgh, PA: University of Pittsburgh Press, 2007.

Lombardi, John V. *The Decline and Abolition of Negro Slavery in Venezuela, 1820–1854.* Westport, CT: Greenwood, 1971.

Masur, Gerhard. *Simón Bolívar.* Rev. ed. Albuquerque: University of New Mexico Press, 1969.

Sanders, James E. *Contentious Republicans: Popular Politics, Race, and Class in Nineteenth-Century Colombia.* Durham, NC: Duke University Press, 2004.

## CHAPTER FOUR

# The Resurgence and Destruction of Slavery in Cuba, Puerto Rico, and Brazil

∿

When we reached the beach, and stood on the sand, oh! how I wished that the sand would open and swallow me up. My wretchedness I cannot describe. It was beyond description. The reader may imagine, but anything like an outline of my feelings would fall very short of the mark. . . . The next boat that was put to sea, I was placed in; but God saw fit to spare me, perhaps for some good purpose. I was then placed in that most horrible of all places,
THE SLAVE SHIP.[1]

✦ SOMETIME IN THE MID-1840S, THAT SLAVE SHIP TRANSPORTED Mahommah Gardo Baquaqua from the great slave port of Ouidah (in present day Benin) to Pernambuco in the Brazilian northeast, a route traversed by hundreds of thousands of captives over the centuries. In Pernambuco the local free population flocked to the newly arrived *tumbeiro:* "When a slaver comes in, the news spreads like wild-fire, and down come all those that are interested in the arrival of the vessel with its cargo of living merchandize." Baquaqua's master in Pernambuco was a baker who lived in the environs of Recife. He was one of five slaves owned by the family. His immediate task was helping with the construction of a new house, hard labor "such as none but slaves and horses are put to."[2]

Baquaqua was captured, enslaved, and then transported to Brazil in the 1840s. His fate illustrates how, even as abolitionists suppressed the slave traffic to some parts of the Americas and as revolutionary movements wrecked slavery in Haiti and much of Spanish America, slavery and the traffic became more entrenched in Latin America's largest slave-holding societies: Brazil and Cuba. Though all of the Spanish and Portuguese colonies relied upon slavery and the traffic, the major recipients of the transatlantic trade in the Iberian world were these two countries. Together they accounted for more than half of the 10.7 million captives disembarked on American shores via the Middle Passage from the sixteenth century to the nineteenth century, when the traffic was finally suppressed (in 1850 in Brazil, 1867 in Cuba). The nineteenth century remained an era of ferocious slaving, with Brazil receiving over 2 million captives, Cuba more than 700,000.[3]

The main impetus for the slave traffic from Ouidah and Angola to Brazil continued to be the plantation economy, particularly the coffee fazendas in the southeast (in the period 1826–1850 close to eight hundred thousand slaves were disembarked in the southeast). However, slave-holding was pervasive throughout Brazil's economy and society. That Baquaqua's Pernambucan master was an artisan of modest fortune hints at why the institution was so resilient in Brazil. Brazilians of limited means could hope to enhance their wealth by buying and selling slaves and exploiting their labor in a variety of ways. For example, the freed African Antonio José Dutra became a slaveholder because slaves were the form of property most within the reach of Brazil's middling groups, at least until the suppression of the slave traffic in 1850. Dutra went from enslavement to slave-holding, owning some thirteen slaves whom he employed in his barbershop and his musical band in Rio de Janeiro before his death in 1849.[4]

Yet other elements of Baquaqua's life story reveal that even as the slave traffic continued to flow between Africa and the Americas, commitment to abolition was rooted in many regions of the Atlantic world and influenced Brazil and Cuba. The Pernambucan baker sold Baquaqua to a Rio de Janeiro ship's captain. On a voyage to the United States in 1847, abolitionists in New York City encouraged Baquaqua and other

MAQUINAS DE MOLER.

FIGURE 10. Sugar mill, mid-nineteenth-century Cuba. The Cuban sugar
complex was more than a repetition of previous sugar booms in Jamaica
and Saint-Domingue because the productive capacity of Cuba's sugar
haciendas far surpassed that of its Caribbean predecessors. Planters
harnessed cutting-edge technology to slave labor. This image from the Flor
de Caña plantation depicts a steam-driven mill with horizontal rollers, both
significant improvements on earlier mills that had vertical rollers and were
driven by animals, wind, or water. Samuel Hazard, *Cuba with Pen and Pencil*
(London: Sampson Low, Marston, Low, and Searle, 1873), 366.

slaves aboard ship to flee from their enslavement. The great emporium
was once a center of slave-holding, but the state of New York had abolished slavery several decades earlier, as had many of the northern states.
Local judges ruled that Baquaqua was not legally entitled to flee from his
Brazilian master, but members of the Underground Railroad engineered
his escape from New York to Massachusetts and thence to Haiti. In Haiti
he joined American Free Baptists who were committed to spreading the
gospel and abolishing slavery, much like the British abolitionists of the
late eighteenth century. His involvement in those circles ultimately led

him to journey to evangelical and abolitionist strongholds around the Atlantic world, including the Canadian end of the Underground Railroad in Chatham, and finally to Liverpool, where he hoped to find support for a Christian mission to Africa.[5]

The conditions of the Atlantic economy encouraged the expansion of the slave trade, the introduction of new technologies on Latin American plantations, and the opening of vast hinterlands to plantation production, but the currents of abolition and emancipation touched even those places where slavery and the traffic in captives seemed most resilient. The specter of the Haitian Revolution haunted plantation belts and port cities, the Royal Navy and the British government heightened pressure on those governments that protected the slave trade, slaves such as Baquaqua fled their captivity or rebelled against it, and abolitionists like those in New York City who encouraged the Brazilian slave to jump ship agitated against slavery throughout Europe and the Americas. This simultaneous apotheosis and vulnerability of Latin American slavery is the defining feature of its last century of existence.

FIGURE 11. Sugar refining in Antigua, 1820s. William Clark, *Ten Views in the Island of Antigua* (London: T. Clay, 1823).

FIGURE 12. Sugar refining in Cuba, 1850s. These images give some sense of the new scale of sugar production in Cuba from the 1830s onward. Cuban and Spanish planters far outpaced their British and French competitors and predecessors by successfully industrializing the process and moving far beyond the more artisanal methods depicted in the view from Antigua. Justo G. Cantero and Eduardo Laplante, *Los ingenios. Colección de vistas de los principales ingenios de azúcar de la isla de Cuba* (Havana: Impreso en la litografia de Luis Marquier, 1857).

## The Space and Scale of Nineteenth-Century Slavery

Slavery was a protean institution in Latin America. Enslaved men and women worked on great sugar, tobacco, coffee, and cotton plantations. They also labored on small farms or their own plots of land. They occupied the urban trades and provisioned urban markets. Some owned slaves of their own. But in the nineteenth century, as global demand for sugar, coffee, and cotton boomed, planters and investors introduced steam-driven mills to extract and refine sugar, railways to carry their goods to port, and steamships to haul them across the Atlantic. Improved transportation and growing markets allowed planters to expand the frontiers of cultivation east and south from Havana into the center of the island of Cuba and west into the hinterlands of Rio de Janeiro and São Paulo.[6] The first Latin American railway, Cuba's fifty-one-kilometer-long Havana-Güines line,

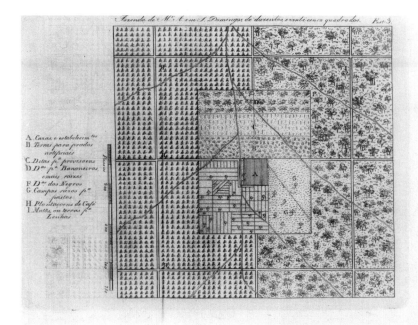

FIGURE 13. Plan of a coffee plantation, Saint-Domingue, 1799. José
Mariano da Conceiçao, *O fazendeiro do Brazil* (Lisbon, 1799). Courtesy
of the John Carter Brown Library at Brown University.

connected the sugar frontier to the Atlantic world. Opened in 1837, it was
the foundation for a railway network throughout the western and central
sugar regions that would carry sugar to the mills for grinding and the finished product to ports for export. Large estates could produce two or three
thousand tons of sugar annually in the mid-nineteenth century, compared
to three or four hundred a few decades earlier. In Brazil, coffee cultivation
was less reliant on technological innovation: land and labor remained the
main sources of investment. Nonetheless, railways introduced in the 1850s
and 1860s opened new southeastern territories to planting, expanding the
limits of the slave plantation and confirming planters in their resistance
to abolition.[7]

The greater size and capacity of the nineteenth-century plantation in
Cuba and Brazil had a harsh impact on the lives of the enslaved. Planters
bought more enslaved men and women, worked them harder, and policed

FIGURE 14. A senzala (slave dwelling), Fazenda Pau D'alho, São José do Barreiro, São Paulo, Brazil. In the nineteenth century coffee surpassed sugar as Brazil's major export crop and slaves flowed to the country's southeast, both from Africa and, after the suppression of the transatlantic trade at midcentury, from other regions. This plan showed Brazilian readers the layout of a Saint-Domingue coffee plantation. Coffee had been in rapid ascent as an export from the French colony in the later eighteenth century, before the Haitian Revolution. After the revolution, Brazilian planters moved to fill the gap in the world market, with slave labor forming the foundation for its new export boom. The slave barracks demonstrate the heightened vigilance and surveillance on the coffee fazendas. Photograph by Dale Tomich, used with his permission.

their movements more closely. The traffic in slaves from Africa grew until midcentury despite British pressure to end the slave trade. In the late 1850s and early 1860s Spanish and Cuban slavers used steamships to carry huge cargoes of captives, as many as fifteen hundred in one voyage.[8] When the transatlantic traffic entered into crisis, Cuban and Brazilian planters turned to other sources. In Cuba traffic in indentured Chinese workers from the 1840s to the 1870s brought more than one hundred thousand unfree laborers to the island; there was also a trade in defeated Maya rebels from Yucatán in the 1860s. Puerto Rico lagged far behind Cuba in the scale of its plantation complex. Nonetheless, when faced with the virtual end of the traffic in slaves to the island in the 1840s, planters relied on the colonial state to coerce nominally free peasants onto the large estates as laborers. In Brazil an internal slave traffic decisively shifted the enslaved population to the southeastern coffee regions. This process was already under way before slave-trade abolition in 1850, as the overwhelming number of slaves disembarked in Brazil in the first half of the nineteenth century landed in the southeast. Table 6 gives some indication of this shift from older slave-holding centers in the north (Bahia, Pernambuco) to the center and south (Rio de Janeiro, Minas Gerais, São Paulo).

Table 6. Slave population of Brazil, 1819 and 1872

|  | 1819 | 1872 |
|---|---|---|
| North | 606,251 | 508,846 |
| Center | 375,855 | 752,013 |
| South | 125,283 | 249,947 |
| Total | 1,107,389 | 1,510,806 |

*Source:* Laird Bergad, *The Comparative Histories of Slavery in Brazil, Cuba, and the United States* (Cambridge: Cambridge University Press, 2007), 120–21.

Abolitionists were dismayed at how slavery's growth in Cuba and Brazil eluded their intentions. In 1822 the British antislavery leader Thomas Clarkson published a short tract against the African slave trade that was quickly translated into Portuguese, Spanish, and French. The author sounded a bitter and desperate note at the resilience of the traffic in Africa and thence to the Americas: "The melancholy facts which we are going to announce, have generally a reference to the slave-trade, as formerly carried on by the English, yet they are applicable to the same trade as carried on by any nation whatever. . . . Human nature is alike in all the countries of the universe. The evils attendant upon it are not casual: they are inseparable from the very nature of the traffic. Consider, that it is the demand for any article which occasions it to be sold. In the present case, the article consists of *men, women, and children.*"[9]

The abolitionists had gained a tremendous victory when Parliament voted to abolish the traffic to the British colonies in 1807. Moreover, the government followed up on promises of more far-reaching action by negotiating with other states to bring the traffic to a close. Initially, it appeared that these measures were having some success. The United States banned the trade in 1808. During the negotiations at the Congress of Vienna at the end of the Napoleonic Wars in 1815, Britain brought other governments to the table, including those with the most vested interests in perpetuating the traffic: Spain and Portugal. But by the time Clarkson published his *Cries of Africa to the Inhabitants of Europe*, it was clear that those governments were actively circumventing the treaties signed with Britain. Indeed, the traffic to Cuba and Brazil would reach new heights in spite of formal commitments to restricting or abolishing it. As Clarkson regretfully observed, the market for enslaved people continued to flourish, propelled by the vast demand for tropical commodities like Cuban sugar and Brazilian coffee.

## Cuba: Capital of Spanish American Slavery

When the Spanish Crown deregulated the slave trade to Cuba at the end of the eighteenth century, it did so in fits and starts, effectively breaking with more than 250 years of policy. Unlike Portugal with its vast trading network and colonies on the African continent, Spain had no African presence aside from small footholds across the Straits of Gibraltar. The Crown had early on decided to farm out slave trading, first through a system of licenses granted to private individuals and then through the asientos sold, or conceded under duress, to foreign powers, most recently in the eighteenth century to the British. After the Seven Years' War, the Crown decided that it needed to develop the plantation economies of its Caribbean colonies to provide greater revenues that would pay for its ongoing clashes with Britain. To that end, it took gradual steps toward developing the slave traffic under its own control. Such measures included the acquisition from Portugal of the islands of Anabón and Fernando Po in the Gulf of Guinea. The hope was that the islands would serve as the kind of trading forts used by the Portuguese, British, French, and other powers to participate in the trade in captives on Africa's west coast. However, for a variety of reasons this sort of regulated trading system did not develop as planned. Instead, under intense lobbying from Havana, Spanish officials opened Cuba and other Caribbean colonies to a virtually free trade in slaves in 1789. Spanish and creole traders could traffic directly with the forts of rival powers in Africa or in neighboring Caribbean colonies such as Jamaica, while foreign slavers could carry slaves to Havana. Spain had resisted such a system for centuries, but under tremendous military pressure from Britain and lobbying from colonial planters, it finally committed to the wealth promised by plantation production in Cuba and the smaller Caribbean islands.

Havana planters led the charge in urging such reforms, and they were amply rewarded. Madrid implemented a wide array of policies that made planters more secure in their property rights and more attuned to the commercial possibilities of the Atlantic economy. From the end of the eighteenth century Spanish and creole traders begin to participate directly in the traffic, carrying human cargoes of vast numbers, such as the Spanish slave ship *Moctezuma*, which disembarked 820 slaves in the early nineteenth century.[10]

Opposition to the traffic, while overcome, was widespread, both in Cuba and in Spain. Events in the colony and the metropolis during the resistance to the French occupation of the Iberian Peninsula (1808–1814) give us some sense of the slave trade's opponents. In 1811 the Cortes of Cádiz, while drafting the new constitution, debated a ban on the slave trade to the Americas. One deputy, the Spaniard Agustín de Argüelles, who had spent time in England during the debates over slave trade abolition, sought to take the debate even further; he publicly addressed how slavery itself could be abolished. Havana's pro-slave-trade advocates overcame these first stirrings of Spanish antislavery sentiment in 1811; as we know, the Constitution of 1812 was eloquently mute on the question of slaving and slavery, but pleas for suppression of the traffic continued to circulate in the metropolis. Joseph Blanco White, one of the most astute and persistent critics of the Spanish colonial regime, published an anti-slave-trade tract from his London exile with assistance from the British Foreign Office. Blanco White was acquainted with the leading British abolitionist, William Wilberforce, having translated some of his writings into Spanish. He was also widely read on the topic. Central to his objections to the slave trade was the evidence presented by the explorer Mungo Park, who traveled extensively in West Africa and recounted the machinations of the internal and transoceanic traffics.[11] In his antislavery tract of 1814, Blanco White reserved especially harsh words for the Cuban planters who so vigorously defended the slave trade. He asked his Spanish readers to put themselves in the place of the Africans torn from their families and their homes. Having just freed themselves from the French occupation, they must identify with captives victimized by warfare:

Do not forget that you too have seen foreigners set foot in your homeland. Leave in peace that of others. Leave those unhappy Africans the scarce portion of goods that Heaven has bestowed on their land. Leave them in peace so that they can advance little by little along the road of civilization. You should not treat them worse than you would the beasts in the wilderness just because they are poor. They are poor and ignorant. But the same blood runs in their veins that runs in yours. The tears that their eyes shed are just like yours. Like you, they are parents, children, and siblings. Martyrs of Spanish patriotism! . . . From this day forward stop the *Spaniards* from going to the coast of Africa to surpass in cruelty and injustice those invaders that destroyed your soul. You, who know what it is to have them ripped from your homes by foreign soldiers, leave the father his children, the husband his wife.[12]

More direct attacks came from within Cuban slave society. In spite of the profound changes to the Spanish Antilles and the surrounding Caribbean islands, there was strong continuity in many of the legal and religious aspects of slavery in Cuba and Puerto Rico.[13] Throughout the nineteenth century, enslaved men and women purchased their freedom and demanded the right to change owners once they were coartados. They also continued to gather in religious and military associations with long histories in the Caribbean. Free men of color served in pardo and moreno militia units. Slaves gathered in the cabildos de nación, associations based on African ethnic affiliations. The laws, customs, and forms of sociability that had developed over the centuries clashed with the new rigors of the plantation and the deregulated slave trade.

The friction between two different types of slave society sparked into open rebellion in 1812 when Spanish authorities uncovered, and then suppressed with great violence, an island-wide conspiracy of slaves and free people of color intended to abolish slavery.[14] The leader of the aborted uprising was José Antonio Aponte, a free man of color who served in the colonial militia, like his father and grandfather before him, and who belonged to a cabildo. The sociability protected in the militias and cabildos allowed conspirators, free and enslaved, to gather and to plan and communicate with like-minded groups around the island. Though enslaved and free people lived under different circumstances and had different interests, both suffered increased discrimination and discipline during the plantation and

DULCE-SELLER.

FIGURE 15. Dulce seller, Havana, Cuba. Amid the plantation boom in nineteenth-century Cuba, older forms of enslavement and labor persisted. Not all slaveholders were sugar planters, and not all enslaved people worked cutting and grinding cane. Many slaveholders owned but a single slave, whose labor was their source of income. Enslaved women had for centuries provisioned the cities of colonial Latin America. Working in a cash economy, they might save enough money to begin the process of coartación. Their owners might also manumit them, a practice more common in the cities than in the country and more frequent among enslaved women than enslaved men. Samuel Hazard, *Cuba with Pen and Pencil* (London: Sampson Low, Marston, Low, and Searle, 1873), 167.

slave traffic boom. Moreover, their common monarchical political imaginations—references to the king of Spain and the king of Kongo were current in the conspiracy—allowed them to come together to fight against slavery. Surrounding Caribbean influences were also apparent. Aponte recruited supporters to his cause by showing them his *libro de pinturas*, a book of paintings of revolutionary and monarchical figures (which has never been recovered by historians but is known through the voluminous testimony of Aponte and others). Among the book's portraits were those of the great Haitian generals Toussaint Louverture, Henri Christophe, and Jean François. The last was well known in Cuba as Juan Francisco because he had allied with Spanish forces during the battles for control of Saint-Domingue. When Spain signed a peace treaty with France and evacuated its forces in 1795, Juan Francisco arrived in Cuba, where his brief presence clearly had a lasting effect. Thus, even where planters and slavers were most triumphant in the nineteenth century, they still contended with the diverse antislavery forces unleashed in the revolutionary era.

But the traffic's defenders were also highly motivated and actively depicted the trade to Cuba as a positive and necessary factor in the imperial economy as they combated opponents in Spain and in the colony. Even during the revolution in neighboring Saint-Domingue, Cuban planters such as Francisco Arango y Parreño insisted that such a rebellion could never take place in a Spanish colony "because the French looked at slaves as beasts, and the Spanish looked at them as men" protected by wise laws and customs.[15] Two decades later in 1811, in a petition that Arango y Parreño authored on behalf of the municipality of Havana intended to discourage government action against the slave trade, Cuba's planters drew attention to the "immense profit that all branches of our national industry have drawn from devoting the negroes to the service of all of our rural estates." They argued that "without negro slaves, there would not be colonies," an ominous warning to political and business leaders in the metropole.[16] In 1821 one of Cuba's representatives to the Spanish Cortes published a pamphlet to counter those critics of the traffic to Cuba. "I am not, let it be said, a defender of slavery," wrote the priest Juan Bernardo O'Gavan, "but of *work*, without which there is no production, population, energy, wealth, or power; nor is there any means by which to perfect the intelligence of men and to keep them from falling into barbarism, brutality, disorder, and misery."[17] In other words, not only was the traffic vital to the colony and to the metropole but it was also a means of civilizing barbarous Africans by carrying them to Cuba and forcing them to submit to the salutary labor of the plantation: "Black Africans are the most indolent and lazy of all known people. But they become open to work on the Antillean haciendas, and their creole children are truly robust. . . . In the name of a *well understood* humanity, and to improve the lot of these savages, wise legislators should not only compel them to work but also facilitate and protect their conveyance to the gentle climate of our Antilles."[18]

What Arango y Parreño and O'Gavan requested of Madrid, they received, at least in part. Spain offered protection for the slave trade, but in exchange, especially after Spanish American independence, it demanded greater political control and conformity. The slave traffic flowed unabated to Cuba even though Spain signed a treaty with Britain that would bring it to an end in 1820. It soon became clear to contemporaries that Madrid had no intention of enforcing the treaty, as the volume of the traffic actually increased through the 1830s. Puerto Rico, too, tapped into the traffic despite the treaty banning it. Though the traffic and the sugar plantations grew to a new scale in both islands, the slave regimes of the last Spanish colonies differed considerably. A glance at the populations of Cuba and Puerto Rico quickly shows that slavery took root much more deeply in the former (table 7).

Table 7. Population of Puerto Rico and Cuba, 1800

|  | Slave | Free-Colored | White | Total |
|---|---|---|---|---|
| Puerto Rico | 25,000 | 65,000 | 72,000 | 162,000 |
| Cuba | 212,000 | 114,000 | 274,000 | 600,000 |

*Source:* George Reid Andrews, *Afro-Latin America, 1800–2000* (New York: Oxford University Press, 2004), 41.

Cuba and Puerto Rico remained Spanish colonies for the rest of the nineteenth century, in no small part because of the slave trade and the great wealth that flowed from Antillean plantations. After the Spanish American revolutions, Spanish investors and merchants descended upon Cuba in particular, now the focus of Spain's much reduced American empire. To the displeasure of creole elites who wanted to direct the local economy, the Spanish immigrants, such as the Basque Julián Zulueta, came to dominate credit and slaving on the island. They also turned to planting

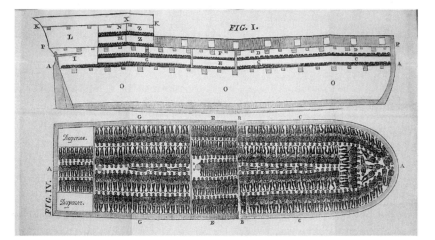

FIGURE 16. Diagram of the slave ship *Brookes*. Spanish critics of the slave
trade to Cuba sometimes borrowed from foreign antislavery advocates.
British abolitionists spread this image of the British slave ship *Brookes*
throughout the Atlantic world. The Barcelonan translator of the book in
which the image appeared wrote that news from Havana of the capture of
the slave ship *Relámpago*, carrying more than 150 captives, moved him to
publish in Spanish the British abolitionist's bitter denunciation of the slavers.
Outraged that the Spanish government refused to enforce the treaty signed
with Britain in 1817, he wrote that the traffic was "the most criminal act that
man can commit. All of us are horrified to have as a relative or as a friend
a man so depraved that he dedicates himself yet to this barbarous traffic."
Thomas Clarkson, *Grito de los africanos contra los europeos, sus opresores, o sea
rápida ojeada sobre el comercio homicida llamado Tráfico de Negros*, trans. Agustín
de Gimbernat (Barcelona, Spain: Imprenta de José Torner, 1825).

themselves, like their creole rivals opening haciendas of vast scale and
technological sophistication.[19] As planters and slavers constructed robust
plantation belts in the early decades of the nineteenth century, they kept
a wary eye on the changes that had taken place around them. The period
after Spanish American independence witnessed a hardening of Spanish
rule in the two islands, despite their loyalty. The demise of slavery elsewhere in the Caribbean benefited the Spanish colonies but it also threatened their stability, shaping official and elite attitudes and policies. Cuba
and Puerto Rico were surrounded by independent nations and colonies

that the Spanish government considered enemies and grave threats: Haiti, the British West Indies, and the United States.

The actions and intentions of independent Haiti always preoccupied Spanish officials. In the 1830s Spain finally made a lasting transition to constitutional government after the death of the hated monarch Ferdinand VII. In earlier constitutional eras, 1810–1814 and 1820–1823, Spain had extended new political rights to the colonies. This time, in contrast, Spanish politicians decided to rule the remaining colonies with an iron fist. They voted to expel from the new parliament the Cuban and Puerto Rican deputies until "special laws" applicable to the colonies could be drafted (more on this below). In the meantime, the Spanish captain general of the colony would assume almost unlimited authority. One of the rationales given for this drastic move was the possibility of a slave rebellion like the Haitian Revolution taking place in Cuba. Until well into the nineteenth century, Spanish officials in Havana and San Juan passed rumors back to Madrid about suspected invasions from Haiti. Related to the fear of Haiti was the specter of "Africanization" conjured by Spanish officials and by some Cuban critics of the slave trade. Haiti thus served not only as a symbol of emancipation for some Cubans but also as a pretext for fierce political repression.[20]

Events in the British Empire also echoed in the Spanish Antilles. The British government sought to terminate the slave trade to Cuba and Puerto Rico through bilateral treaties, naval patrols, and mixed courts in the Caribbean. Spanish governments signed treaties with Great Britain banning the trade in 1817, 1835, and 1845, though they consistently turned a blind eye toward the burgeoning contraband trade to both islands. British pressure could bring Madrid's officials to the bargaining table, but it could not convince them to act decisively to close the trade.[21] In spite of this complicity, officials and planters feared that the Spanish government would capitulate to British demands, not only banning the trade but also freeing the thousands of slaves illegally imported into the colonies. Such rumors raged in the metropolis and colonies in the early 1850s after the British took preemptive action, using its full naval might, to suppress the Brazilian trade.[22]

The abolition of slavery in the British West Indies between 1834 and 1838 was also cause for concern in Cuba and Puerto Rico. Planters and officials worried about abolitionist provocateurs infiltrating the colonies. For instance, in 1837 the Spanish consul in Kingston, Jamaica, reported to Madrid that antislavery activists "are trying to send some agents from their seat here to the province of Cuba (I fear that some might already be there) with the end of trying to induce the blacks to stage an uprising."[23] Ominous reports also arrived periodically from Spanish representatives in the United States about abolitionist and independence plots.

Finally, Spaniards and Antilleans felt the looming presence of the United States. Though the persistence of slavery in the United States provided ideological and political cover for Spain and its Caribbean colonies, the ambitions of southern slaveholders to annex Cuba as a slave state was yet another regional menace. In the 1840s and 1850s southern filibusters launched raids on Cuba and other Caribbean islands. In the 1850s rumors spread through Cuba and Puerto Rico that five thousand armed men were departing the United States for Santo Domingo. According to reports from San Juan and Havana, once they availed themselves of Santo Domingo and its secure deepwater harbor at Samaná Bay, they would easily take Cuba and Puerto Rico.

Threats to the colonial order came not only from neighbors but also from within the colonies. Apologists like Arango y Parreño and O'Gavan glossed over the nature of the emerging plantation complex by heralding the wisdom of Spanish laws and congratulating themselves for evangelizing and civilizing barbarous Africans. The reality was quite different. Cuban planters resisted the state's efforts to impose new slave codes meant to mitigate the violence of plantation slavery. They sought to reserve justice to themselves as they pressed their slaves into the brutal work conditions of the sugar mills. Like Saint-Domingue and Jamaica in the eighteenth century, Cuba became a slave society marked by great unrest and appalling violence. Homicides and suicides increased during the nineteenth century as some slaves took matters into their own hands, either by killing their tormentors or by seeking release from their suffering on the plantation. While some planters diagnosed suicide as a symptom of African barbarism, less disingenuous observers such as the count of Villanueva, a powerful planter and official, admitted that "their state of servitude should be considered as the main cause of their suicides."[24] More organized acts of defiance also took place. The Aponte rebellion of 1812 was but the tip of the iceberg. Smaller uprisings on plantations, often led by African-born slaves, became a feature of the colonial landscape. So did more widespread conspiracies like that of Aponte. In 1844 officials uncovered a plot, known later as the Conspiracy of La Escalera, among free blacks, slaves, and British abolitionists, the goal of which was to abolish slavery and create a free country under British protection. Spanish officials suppressed the conspiracy in spectacular and brutal fashion, traumatizing colonial society.[25]

The contentiousness of plantation society was not lost on Spanish governors. In this regional and internal context, the Spanish state opted to clamp down on its Caribbean colonies. Even as Spanish political leaders consolidated constitutional government in the metropole in the 1830s, they erected a regime based on extraordinary military rule in Cuba and Puerto Rico. After the independence of the great majority of the American colonies, Spanish leaders were in no mood to make political compromises with creoles in Cuba and Puerto Rico. Justifying their decision to deny the colonies elected representation and constitutional rights by reference to the threat of slave rebellion, invasion, and other forms of foreign subversion and internal rebellion, Spanish political leaders gradually formulated a colonial regime characterized by "centralization of [military] command, absence of political representation, and degradation of the institutions of the late imperial period."[26] Despotic rule nonetheless appeased some sectors of the colonial elite because of the economic trade-offs: with Spanish rule came the continuation of the slave trade in the face of British demands to end it.

## Brazil and the South Atlantic

Brazilian slave society differed from Antillean because the slave trade had been entrenched since the sixteenth century and because Brazil's planter class was the ruling class of an independent state. Brazilian independence was a far less conflictive process than the getting of independence in neighboring South American countries such as Venezuela, Argentina, and Peru. The arrival of the royal family in Rio de Janeiro in 1808, in flight from the invading armies of Napoleon and under British protection, signaled a major shift in Portuguese rule. Brazil was now the center of a global empire. Rio's new status as the home of the Court stimulated trade and the export of slave-produced goods. When a revolutionary government in Lisbon insisted that the monarchy return to Europe in 1821, the heir to the Braganza throne, Dom Pedro, made a pact with colonial elites and broke from Portugal in 1822 with minimal use of force.

The independent Brazilian monarchy consolidated economic and social trends at work in the later stages of Portuguese rule. An important consequence of the Court's arrival in 1808 was the conversion of Rio into a major center of urban slavery. In 1799 slaves made up slightly more than one third of the city's population: 14,986 out of a total population of 43,376. On the eve of independence in 1821 slaves were almost half of the much larger total population of Rio and its environs: 40,376 out of 86,323. Rio was also a very African city: in 1832, 73.3 percent of enslaved people were from Africa; in 1849, 66.4 percent.[27]

The traffic in slaves to other regions in Brazil increased during the last days of Portuguese rule and the early years of independence. In 1810 and 1815 Portugal signed treaties with its protector, Britain, placing limits on the traffic and calling for its eventual demise. In the short term, the Portuguese agreed to limit slaving to their possessions south of the equator, keeping alive the longtime connection between Brazil and Angola but shutting down operations from the Bight of Benin, the source of hundreds of thousands of enslaved Africans destined for Bahia in the northeast. After independence, the Brazilians not only kept alive the Angola connection but also rejuvenated the traffic from Ouidah on the Bight of Benin.

Bahian merchants had established their dominance in this African region since the early eighteenth century. In the nineteenth century the Bahian-born trader Francisco Félix de Souza, resident in Africa since 1804, reopened the traffic from Ouidah to his native region, which was undergoing a short-lived resurgence in sugar production. Moreover, he founded a new quarter in the city of Ouidah called Brazil, home to his extensive family and to other Brazilian-born merchants and ships' captains. Ouidah's Brazil neighborhood bordered on another district, Maro, home to dozens of Brazilian slaves forcibly returned to Africa after the suppression of a Muslim-led rebellion in Bahia in 1835. Other enslaved and freed Brazilians sojourned in Africa in this era. One such traveler was Rufino José Maria, a Mâle, the Brazilian term for Muslim Yorubas. Rufino most likely arrived in Brazil as a captive shortly after independence. By the 1830s he was a free man crisscrossing the Atlantic as a sailor and trader on slavers such as the *Paula* and the *São José* that regularly voyaged to Angola in search of human cargo. On one of Rufino's voyages, aboard the *Ermelinda*, the ship was detained by a British patrol and taken to Sierra Leone, where Rufino settled for several years before returning to Brazil.[28]

The careers of de Souza and Rufino indicate that Brazil's intimate connection to Africa was uninterrupted by independence. Even as a

FIGURE 17. Coffee vendors, Rio de Janeiro, nineteenth century.

colony, Brazil had carried on much of this traffic outside Portuguese control. What would change after independence was that the local planter class would assume greater political control over their own affairs. Moreover, the weight and direction of the slave traffic would shift from the northeastern sugar regions and the mines of Minas Gerais to the southeastern coffee plantations, as coffee supplanted sugar, gold, and diamonds as the most lucrative export. In 1820, on the eve of independence, 539,000 arrobas of coffee were exported through Rio de Janeiro; by 1859–1860, 10,606,394 arrobas passed through Rio to Atlantic markets (the Brazilian arroba equaled 31.7 pounds). The price fetched by coffee also increased significantly during that time.[29]

The great coffee barons of Rio de Janeiro, Minas Gerais, and São Paulo were the political stalwarts of the independent slave-holding state, though there were moments of conflict between planters and the monarchy. The most profound came in 1831 when the emperor Pedro I moved to enforce an earlier agreement with Britain that would squeeze the slave

FIGURE 18. Barbers, Rio de Janeiro, nineteenth century. After the
arrival of the Portuguese Court in 1808, Rio de Janeiro's population
surged. Slaves and freed people continued to fill many sectors of the
urban economy. Jean Baptiste Debret, *Voyage pittoresque et historique au
Brésil*, 3 vols. (Paris: Firmin Didot Frères, 1834–1839).

traffic, one of the pillars of the new regime carried over from the old.
Pedro I's acquiescence threw Brazil into a temporary crisis. When Pedro
abdicated his throne in favor of his young son and a regency government,
the Court loosened its control over the vast Brazilian periphery. What
ensued was a decade of turmoil that witnessed numerous revolts against
the central authority in Rio. Slave uprisings, especially the Muslim revolt
in Bahia in 1835, also challenged the dominant order. In response, a new
conservative party took shape in the southeastern coffee zones of Rio
de Janeiro and São Paulo, dedicated to restoring the monarchy's authority and defending the slave trade in the face of British pressure. By the
1840s the conservative political group called the *saquaremas* (named for
a town in the coffee regions of Rio de Janeiro province) forged a new

FIGURE 19. Senzalas (slave quarters), Fazenda São Luis, Vassouras, Brazil.

partnership with the young emperor Pedro II (r. 1831–1889) upon the pillars of centralized political authority and defense of the slave trade and of slavery.[30]

One pillar of the new order was shakier than the others: the slave trade. Though Pedro I had sought to assuage Britain, the Brazilian government that succeeded him allowed the traffic to flourish; between 1826 and 1850 the various plantation regions of Brazil combined to import more than one million slaves. Some diehard saquaremas went so far as to advocate openly cancelling the agreement with Britain. In the face of Brazilian defiance, hardened with the ascendancy of Pedro II and the conservatives, the Royal Navy decided to apply decisive force against slavers. In 1850 British warships entered Brazilian ports such as Santos and Cabo Frio, where they bombarded, captured, and burnt ships outfitted for slaving voyages. Brazilian shore batteries were impotent in the face of Britain's superior firepower. These actions provoked an immediate response from the Brazilian monarchy and Council of State. Weighing its options, the council decided that the lesser evil was to pass an effective law prohibiting the slave trade so as to preserve national sovereignty in the face of British aggression. Within a few days the Chamber of Deputies and then the Senate passed a new law with teeth in it for the suppression of the traffic.

FIGURE 20. Man working on drying terraces, Fazenda Cachoeira Grande, Vassouras, Brazil. The historian Stanley Stein took these photographs in the late 1940s in the heart of Brazil's coffee-growing country, the Paraíba Valley. The slave quarters and other buildings, including the planter's home, storehouses, and shelters for animals were built around a beaten earth square, the terreiro. After the slaves picked the coffee beans, they stored them in drying terraces in thin layers, which were turned over the course of the day. The Brazilian coffee fazendas relied on fairly simple techniques and tools. The major inputs were land and labor. The planters of Vassouras resisted abolition, clinging tenaciously to an aging labor force. They also worked the land to the point of exhaustion. By the later nineteenth century, the once-booming export economy of Vassouras was in crisis. Dynamism in the coffee sector was to be found in frontier territories in the Paraíba Valley, where planters opened new fazendas with fresh land and relied increasingly on free immigrant labor. Arquivo Edgard Leuenroth/Unicamp.

Brazil's transatlantic trade, the most potent current of enslaved Africans to the Americas, was finally running its course.[31]

The abolition of the slave trade transformed the dynamics of Brazilian slavery, but it did not strike a fatal blow against the great planters of the southeast. They were able to adapt, much like their North American counterparts, by opening an internal traffic that sent slaves from declining or stagnant regions such as the northeast to the expanding coffee zones in Rio de Janeiro and São Paulo. While they experimented with free labor and pondered the viability of mass immigration of Asian and European workers, the southeastern planters stubbornly clung to slaves as the core of their labor force until abolition.[32]

Middling property owners like Antonio José Dutra, the freed African-born slave who established himself in Rio as a barber, musician, and slaveholder, saw their interests and possibilities most damaged by the traffic's suppression. While the traffic from Africa remained open, slaves represented the most accessible form of property in the Brazilian economy: "Slavery was truly ubiquitous in Brazilian life in the early nineteenth century: slaves made up nearly half of Rio's population, and nearly all wealthholders participated in slaveholding." After abolition, the price of slaves in Brazil steadily increased, ultimately pushing middling owners like Dutra out of the market. Slave-holding thus became more concentrated within Brazilian society and more regionally concentrated in the southeastern coffee sector.[33]

## Slaves, Free People, and Constitutions

Dutra's world illustrates one of the key characteristics not only of Brazilian but also of Antillean slave society: the large free population. In Brazil, Cuba, and Puerto Rico, the enslaved might gain their freedom through self-purchase or manumission. This system had thrived for centuries. However, the equilibrium between slavery and freedom in Cuba and Puerto Rico differed from that in Brazil. In the latter, the free black population had grown in tandem with a large slave population, which was constantly replenished through the south Atlantic slave trade. In Cuba and Puerto Rico, in contrast, the large-scale slave trade was a relatively recent phenomenon. The trade and the rigors of the expanding sugar plantations clashed with the kind of slave societies that had grown in the islands since the sixteenth century. The tension between slavery and freedom was perhaps greater in the Spanish Antilles than it was in Brazil.[34]

Spain heightened this tension through the constitutional reforms it introduced beginning with the Constitution of Cádiz. Though the metropole governed Cuba and Puerto Rico through exceptional rule, it did so through the fiction of a temporary measure whose contradictions would be ironed out in the future. That is to say, Spain considered the islands to be provinces within the constitutional regime solidified in the 1830s and the residents of the islands to be Spaniards who would one day enjoy the same political and civil rights. However, this fiction of metropolitan and colonial unity carried within it important exclusions. First, the category of Spaniard applied only to those who were free. The hundreds of thousands of slaves in the Caribbean colonies were tacitly excluded from the political community. Second, even free people of color, though considered Spaniards, were barred from the exercise of political rights because of their African lineage. This act of exclusion also affected a large sector of the Antillean population. When the struggles over the legitimacy of Spanish rule and the dismantling of slavery converged later in the century, much of the Cuban and Puerto Rican populace found itself legally and politically marginalized within the Spanish colonial system. Independence would thus gain more adherents among those who found no recourse from Spain, a process parallel to that which unfolded during the breakdown of empire in Spanish America earlier in the century.[35]

We have seen that this exclusiveness unintentionally provided one of the levers of independence and liberation during the Spanish American revolutions. Though many patriot leaders were deeply wary of recruiting and freeing slaves, once they had decided to do so they found it impossible to proclaim national liberation without demanding the liberation of the enslaved as well. While Spain fought to maintain slavery and a racially exclusive political community, patriot forces, in response to the participation of slaves and free people of color in the wars, turned against slavery and embraced a broad view of citizenship. Over time, Spain found itself increasingly isolated and finally defeated, in no small part because of the loss of loyalty among slaves and free blacks in Spanish America. A similar dilemma would confront the Spanish colonizers when rebellion broke out in Cuba in 1868.

In contrast to Spanish intransigence, independent Brazil adopted a more flexible and open political community that incorporated free Brazilian-born (but not African-born) blacks as citizens. Those creoles liberated from slavery would thus find some inclusion within the fledgling state, though wealth and property remained qualifications for the full exercise of political rights.

During the revolutionary era, the Portuguese Court had avoided the fate of its Spanish counterpart by fleeing the Iberian Peninsula under British protection and reestablishing itself in Rio de Janeiro. With the imperial center now located in the Americas, the Portuguese were especially sensitive to events in the neighboring Spanish American colonies. They were also well aware of the constitutional debates taking place in Cádiz. Indeed, when the Lisbon Cortes met in 1821 and 1822 to remake the Portuguese domains as a constitutional monarchy, it borrowed heavily from Spain's 1812 constitution.[36] However, in this foundational moment the Portuguese and Brazilian divergence from Spanish attitudes toward the enslaved and free blacks was striking. Portuguese deputies proposed duplicating the measures from the Constitution of Cádiz that openly discriminated against large sectors of the colonial populace. They met with strong resistance from Brazilian deputies who insisted that banning the free Brazilian-born population from the exercise of political rights would lead to significant unrest in the colony. Ultimately the Portuguese deferred to the Brazilians. Soon thereafter Dom Pedro led the break from Portugal and oversaw the drafting of the Brazilian constitution. Once more defenders of enfranchisement carried the day.

Brazilian framers were not necessarily more egalitarian than their Spanish counterparts. They were responding to a distinct colonial reality and adapting it to the new regime. Colonial Brazil differed from colonial Spanish America in that it had a direct link to Africa, especially Angola, via the slave trade and other commercial networks over the centuries. The traffic to Brazil was thus more constant and more voluminous. Historians have argued that the counterpart to the constant traffic in slaves was a steady reliance on alforria, manumission or self-purchase, as a means of maintaining social equilibrium in the colony. Not only did Brazil have a huge enslaved population, but it also had a huge and growing free black and mulatto population. Such was the system that Brazilian political leaders sought to protect after independence: stalwart commitment to the slave trade and to slavery coupled with a modest policy of alforria and political and economic inclusion among the free population. Ironically, then, commitment to broader political rights in Brazil derived in part from a staunch pro-slavery and pro-traffic ideology.[37]

## Abolition

If slavery was so firmly entrenched in the economic, social, and political orders of these nineteenth-century Latin American slave societies, how did it finally come to an end? Unlike the United States, where civil war destroyed slavery suddenly, in Brazil and the Spanish Antilles abolition was a gradual, tortuous process. Multiple antislavery initiatives involving armed uprisings, legislation, and the actions of enslaved people and abolitionists chipped away at the rambling but sturdy edifice of slavery in Brazil and the Spanish Antilles. The governments and the big planters used delaying tactics as best they could so that enslaved labor would remain at the core of the plantation. But broad mobilization against slavery would ultimately force them to relent (see table 8).

TABLE 8. Benchmarks in the abolition process, Spanish colonies and Brazil

| | |
|---|---|
| **1868** | Uprising for independence takes root in Cuba's eastern provinces (i.e., outside the major plantation and population centers). The war would continue until 1878. Leaders of the rebellion abolish slavery in the regions they control. |
| **1870** | Moret Law passed in Spain. Gradual measure affecting Cuban and Puerto Rican slavery: frees those born to enslaved mothers but binds them to owners until adulthood. Frees those age sixty and over. |
| **1871** | Rio Branco Law passed in Brazil. Similar to the Moret Law. Frees those born to enslaved mothers, also binding them to owners. |
| **1873** | Spanish Cortes abolishes Puerto Rican slavery. Libertos (freed slaves) required to sign three-year contracts with former owners. |
| **1878** | The Pact of Zanjón brings to an end the war in Cuba. One of the measures emancipates those slaves who fought in the separatist insurgency. |
| **1880** | *Patronato* system promulgated by Spanish government. Cuban slaveholders, now called *patronos*, still entitled to labor of *patrocinados* (the enslaved). Sets 1888 as deadline for complete abolition. |
| **1885** | Saraiva-Cotegipe Law in Brazil liberates the elderly (sixty-five and over). |
| **1886** | Definitive abolition of Cuban slavery. |
| **1888** | Princess Isabel, regent of Brazil, signs the Golden Law, abolishing slavery. |

The decade of the 1860s was the turning point for Antillean slavery. The U.S. Civil War and slave emancipation, along with a renewed British initiative against the slave trade, forced the Spanish government to begin tinkering with the colonial regime. Most importantly, discussions of slavery's fate commenced. The Spanish Abolitionist Society, composed mostly of Puerto Rican and Spanish liberals and republicans, organized in Madrid. The government definitively banned the slave trade in 1867. It also convened a body of Spanish and Antillean experts to deliberate on the amelioration and gradual abolition of slavery. At the time, the slave populations of the two islands differed significantly: that of Cuba was over 370,000, that of Puerto Rico around 40,000.[38]

The most disruptive events occurred in 1868—the outbreak of revolution in Spain, Cuba, and Puerto Rico. Like the French invasion of Spain in 1808, the political tumult of 1868 initiated a period of unrest and uncertainty that tested the strong commitment to colonial slavery. The most central of these in shaping the fate of colonial slavery was the Cuban uprising in the island's eastern end. Slavery's fate came to the fore because of warfare, as in the Spanish American revolutions. Once again the Spanish government sought to protect the interests of slaveholders, even as it initiated abolition, while the independence movement soon turned against slavery, in no small part because of the support it received from the enslaved in the regions where it was active. Led by slaveholders on the margins of the colonial regime, the rebellion had the unintended effect of crippling slavery because slaves fled from their masters to the insurgency. The language of national liberation became entwined with the idea of liberation from slavery. Ultimately, the rebel leadership capitulated to facts on the ground and declared slavery abolished in its territories soon after the uprising.[39]

Developments in the colonies had an impact on metropolitan politics. Under a new constitutional monarchy (the Bourbon monarch Isabel II had fled into exile after the 1868 revolution) led by liberals and republicans after decades of conservative dominance, the Spanish government formulated a gradual emancipation law, the Moret Law of 1870, named for Segismundo Moret y Prendergast, the minister of overseas provinces. Moret sought to assuage the concerns of Antillean planters, the military, and metropolitan merchants and producers with vested interests in the colonial market. The law liberated all children born to enslaved women but tempered their freedom by binding them to their mother's owner until they reached adulthood. It also liberated the elderly (those sixty and over) and sought to curb excessive corporal punishment.[40]

Resistance and criticism were immediately forthcoming. Public demonstrations in Spanish cities denounced the government for catering to the interests of the Antillean planter class rather than to the enslaved workers of Cuba and Puerto Rico. A report from an antislavery demonstration in

Seville in 1873 showed the jubilation at these new challenges to the Cuban and Spanish defenders of slavery. Among those carrying banners bearing antislavery slogans was a black man who "was hailed by a black woman from a balcony. She asked for liberty for her race. The black man answered her, waving his banner. Energetic and frantic applause and cries of long live liberty for the slaves interrupted his sentences."[41]

The Spanish Abolitionist Society attacked the Moret Law as timid, unjust, and impolitic. The abolitionists argued that immediate abolition would undercut the Cuban uprising by winning the loyalty of the enslaved population. They also believed that immediate abolition was in the best interest of the Antillean and Spanish economies. Diehard economic liberals in the society held that once true market relations and individual liberty were introduced in the colonies, wealth would expand significantly. Citing the examples of emancipation in other New World settings, they argued, somewhat misleadingly, that only such radical action would avert a crisis in the Antillean economies. Puerto Rican abolitionists were instrumental in developing this argument in cooperation with doctrinaire liberals in Spain. With slavery declining on the island, many reformers, and some planters, believed that abolition with indemnification would benefit the plantation sector.

In contrast, Cuban slavery continued to thrive and planters there remained defiant. For Cuban planters, the Moret Law was a grave threat to their property and to the productivity of their plantations. Like planters in the Brazilian southeast, they clung to a core slave labor force until the final moment of abolition. Laird Bergad has shown that one effect of the Moret Law, which freed tens of thousands of slaves on both islands, was to concentrate enslaved workers in the most productive sugar-producing regions of Cuba. Astrid Cubano-Iguina has shown a similar dynamic at work in Puerto Rico, where planters were generally more amenable to some form of compensated abolition. The arch-conservative planter José Ramón Fernández opened perhaps the largest sugar plantation in the colony in the environs of Manatí in the 1850s. He fought bitterly against the abolitionists through the 1860s and 1870s while he continued to buy slaves to work on his Hacienda Esperanza.[42]

In Puerto Rico, such planter resistance was less successful. Indeed, slaves on the Hacienda Esperanza found allies among Puerto Rican abolitionists, who encouraged them to flee or helped them secure freedom through legal means.[43] Moreover, the Spanish Abolitionist Society and its political allies were more inclined to attack Puerto Rican slavery head on because the total slave population was so much smaller than Cuba's. In 1873 the Spanish Cortes passed an abolition law that freed the more than twenty thousand men and women who remained enslaved in Puerto Rico. However, conservative opponents did succeed in throwing up one more hurdle to freedom. The libertos (freed slaves) of Puerto Rico were legally required to work for their former masters for an additional three years.

In Cuba, the path to abolition was longer and more treacherous. When the Spanish general Arsenio Martínez Campos negotiated a peace agreement with the independence movement after ten years of warfare, the Pact of Zanjón, he recognized the emancipation of slaves who had joined the rebel ranks. But during the war the Spanish military had successfully controlled the western and central regions, home to the vast majority of the plantations and the enslaved men and women who toiled on them. In 1880 the metropolitan government passed a new law that abolished slavery in name but upheld it in practice. Beginning in that year, slaveholders were to be called *patronos* and their slaves *patrocinados*. Implied in this language was the idea of protection rather than domination. In reality, the new system, called the *patronato*, maintained prerogatives traditionally exercised by slaveholders, including the right to use corporal punishment and to sell their patrocinados (see figures 1 and 2). This measure was another concession to the big sugar planters who were determined to hold onto their enslaved workers.

Yet the new regime did include some significant innovations that proved to be "a set of weapons with which those patrocinados willing and able to press their claims could attack their masters."[44] Among these were a firm date for abolition in eight years, quotas that liberated a large percentage of patrocinados beginning in 1884, the right of patrocinados over eighteen to receive stipends for their labor, measures to ensure the integrity of families and proper supply of food and clothing, education and provision for freed children, and an enhanced process of self-purchase. The government also established greater oversight of its own rules, weakening the usual predominance of the slaveholder. Moreover, once the rebellion came to an end in 1878, abolitionist sentiment spread among sectors of colonial society that were eager to make the full transition to free labor and to help patrocinados take advantage of their new protections.

In this transformed legal and political setting, many patrocinados pushed hard to liberate themselves and their families. Of the 113,887 patrocinados, some 13,003 (11 percent) achieved freedom by indemnifying their patrono; 7,423 (7 percent) gained their liberation when oversight juntas ruled that their patronos were not living up to the measures prescribed by the patronato. In other words, enslaved people hastened their liberation by buying their way out of the patronato or by denouncing their patrono for violation of the 1880 law. This latter tactic was used by twenty-nine patrocinados who in 1881 denounced the plantation owner for failing to pay them their stipend. When he responded that he had given them credit at the plantation store, they answered that they paid for their own goods by bartering with the storekeeper. Ultimately the junta in Havana sided with the patrocinados and ordered them freed.[45] So effective were these initiatives that in 1886 the government abolished the patronato, two years before it was set to expire. Latin American slavery was now limited to one country: Brazil.

As in most Latin American countries, war disrupted the stability and legitimacy of slavery in Brazil. During the Paraguayan War that pitted Brazil, Uruguay, and Argentina against Paraguay between 1864 and 1870, several thousand slaves were freed for fighting for the Brazilian army when the government purchased them from their owners. There were also some runaways who found shelter in the army.[46] Nonetheless, politics, not warfare, were paramount in ending Brazilian slavery. Though the southeastern planters adapted successfully to the Atlantic trade's suppression, they faced a serious challenge from an unsuspected quarter: Pedro II, the emperor whose throne they had strengthened. In response to the war, emancipation in the United States, and the Spanish government's tentative first steps toward abolition, the emperor undertook a campaign within the corridors of power to begin an emancipation process in Brazil. Through parliamentary maneuvering, Dom Pedro succeeded in securing the Rio Branco Law of 1871, a free womb law that resembled in many ways the Moret Law of 1870, though it did not liberate the elderly as the Spanish law did.[47]

The resemblance was no coincidence. The Brazilian government closely followed the emancipation process in Cuba and Puerto Rico. Its representative in Madrid regularly dispatched copies of Spanish laws and debates as well as summaries of the latest news from the Antilles. These would come to include the Moret Law (which was also debated actively in learned and political circles in provincial capitals such as Pernambuco), the law abolishing slavery in Puerto Rico in 1873, and information about the traffic in indentured Chinese workers that flourished in Cuba from the 1840s to the 1870s.[48]

Once again, however, Brazilian planters effectively countered the measure despite being overridden by the emperor. The Rio Branco Law gave slaveholders the choice of reserving for themselves the labor of those children until they reached adulthood or turning them over to the imperial government when they reached the age of eight. The government would then assume responsibility for their education and compensate the owner. Historians have found that they overwhelmingly opted for the first choice. By 1884 the government reported that of the 363,307 children registered as free, only 113 were in the care of the state. Those born free by the letter of the law found themselves bound to slaveholders in practice.[49]

The futility of the Rio Branco Law and the 1885 Saraiva-Cotegipe Law that would free the elderly but strengthened certain slaveholder prerogatives ultimately provoked a widespread antislavery movement in Brazil, one instigated not by the monarchy but by frustrated enslaved people, politicians, professionals, and artisans in cities such as Rio de Janeiro, São Paulo, and Santos. Local governments in regions peripheral to the slave economy, such as Ceará, also took matters into their own hands when it became clear that conservative politicians in Rio and southeastern planters were more than able to thwart abolition. The diagnosis of the most prominent abolitionist, Joaquim Nabuco, son of an eminent politician from Pernambuco and himself a rising star in the capital, points to the sense of betrayal and distrust felt by many Brazilians after the obvious failures of the Rio Branco Law to make serious inroads against slavery:

> Since the law of September 28, 1871, was passed, the Brazilian government has been trying to make the world believe that slavery has ended in Brazil. Our propaganda has tried to spread to other countries the belief that the slaves were being freed in considerable numbers, and that the children of the slaves were being born *entirely* free. . . .
>
> The Brazilian people, however, understand the entire matter. They know that after the passage of the law of September 28 the life of the slaves did not change, except for those few who managed to redeem themselves by begging for their freedom.[50]

FIGURE 21. Sign from an immigrant hostel, São Paulo, Brazil. Although
Brazilian government and business leaders had sounded the idea of large-scale
immigration of free laborers since independence, only with the approaching
demise of slavery did serious efforts at recruitment, carried out by various
branches of government and by private organizations, get underway. Workers,
in turn, were less than eager to migrate to a society where slavery, and
therefore the legal possession and abuse of labor, was still in place. But as
slavery came to an end, the floodgates to São Paulo and other parts of Brazil
were opened. In total, from 1882 to 1934 more than 2.3 million immigrants
came to São Paulo, mostly from southern Europe but also from Asia. Cuba,
too, became a site of mass migration, largely from Spain. Between 1880 and
1930 approximately one million Spaniards immigrated to the island. There was
also significant intra-Caribbean immigration in the early twentieth century.
One goal among planters and other employers in encouraging immigration was
to flood the labor market to keep down wages. Photograph by the author.

Spurred by skepticism concerning the government's intentions, different groups and governments throughout the Brazilian Empire worked
against slavery. Many cities had private emancipation funds, such as the
Emancipadora of São Paulo, that purchased the freedom of slaves from
their owners. Also in São Paulo, Luiz Gama, a *rábula* (a type of attor-
ney) who was sold as a child into slavery by his own Portuguese father,

specialized in winning the freedom of people illegally enslaved according to the terms of the anti-slave-trade agreement with Britain. Before his death in 1882 he helped liberate more than five hundred enslaved people. By the 1880s these small-scale efforts to liberate some slaves were coalescing to undermine slavery as a whole. By that time, such an attack was necessarily aimed at the southeastern coffee plantations where the internal traffic had concentrated the vast majority of the empire's slaves.[51]

The planters were sensitive to their isolation and took some measures to counter it. They sought to increase their policing power by deputizing the military, but the army refused to cooperate. Even though they had aggressively traded with other Brazilian provinces since the ban on the transatlantic traffic in 1850, they sponsored legislation banning the internal trade so as to preserve significant slave populations, and thus slaveholding interests, in other provinces. Some also promoted immigration from Europe as a way of recruiting new workers once slavery came to an end, though it was only when slavery was finally abolished that European immigrants started arriving in significant numbers.[52]

These maneuvers failed to win allies or to impede the increasingly confrontational tactics of the abolitionists and slaves. Ceará and other peripheral provinces abolished slavery within their borders. Abolitionists in the core regions undertook more aggressive actions, especially those based in São Paulo and Santos. Leaders such as Antônio Bento organized raids on coffee plantations, the goal of which was to encourage mass flight by slaves. Slaves led by the abolitionists escaped on foot or by rail to the cities so that the quilombos of Santos and Rio de Janeiro swelled. The quilombo in the Rio neighborhood of Leblon became famous as a site of abolitionism. The main product of the local economy was the camellia, known as the *camélia da liberdade* (the camellia of liberty), a symbol and secret password for abolitionists in the southeast that joined opponents of slavery across the social spectrum, from the runaways of Leblon to Princess Isabel, daughter of the emperor, who was known to wear them at public events. Increasingly isolated and faced with unrelenting civil disobedience by abolitionists and the enslaved, the conservatives of São Paulo finally relented as Princess Isabel, regent of Brazil while her father, Dom Pedro, was absent from the country, signed the Golden Law of 1888 that brought Brazilian slavery to an end.[53]

In both Brazil and Cuba the abolition of slavery brought with it the subversion and overthrow of the regime created to defend slavery. In Cuba abolition would strengthen the independence movement. The ideal of an egalitarian nation forged in the struggles for independence and the abolition process remained potent. The convergence of anticolonial and anti-slavery mobilization undermined the regime constructed in the first half of the nineteenth century on the foundations of the slave trade, slavery, and political exclusion of various kinds. Just nine years after the abolition of slavery, a new and much larger war for Cuban independence broke out in 1895 with an explicitly egalitarian, anti-racist political ideology. As in Spanish South America in the 1810s and 1820s, the long legacy of slavery and formal discrimination came to be seen as incompatible with the promises of an independent nation.[54]

The actions of former slaves were essential in pushing Spanish rule in Cuba to the brink. In Brazil the actions of slaves and abolitionists in the 1880s precipitated a political crisis and abolition, but it was the planters who helped to bring down the imperial government a year later in 1889.[55] The Crown's efforts since the 1860s to abolish slavery created a rift with the southeastern planters who had formed the backbone of its legitimacy since independence. The decision to capitulate to the civil disobedience of the 1880s, abolishing slavery immediately and without indemnification, turned the planter class against the monarchy. When the military rose and declared a republic in 1889, the monarchy was isolated because, without slavery, it could no longer count on the powerful slave-holding allies who had defended it since independence. They watched passively and approvingly on the sideline as the Braganza dynasty came to an inglorious end.

The dynasty's passing was historically significant. Since the fifteenth century, African slavery had been entwined with Iberian expansion and colonization in the Atlantic world. That the offshoot of the Portuguese monarchy in Brazil capitulated underscored the close link between slavery and the old political and social order, as had the overthrow of the Spanish monarchy earlier in the century. Such connections were clear to contemporaries. In 1892, four hundred years after Columbus's first voyage to the Caribbean, when the admiral pondered enslavement as the core of new overseas settlements, the writer and political leader Juan Gualberto Gómez commented during the festivities marking the anniversary in Havana that: "One would imagine that we Cubans are all fraternally united in the effort to commemorate in the same manner and with equal passion the Fourth Centennial of the discovery of America; that we have suspended the political fights, put aside all opposing ideas and tendencies, and forgotten all that divides and separates us."[56] Such equanimity was impossible, he argued. The four hundredth anniversary of Columbus's voyage confronted Cubans with the divisive legacies of conquest and colonization: the subordination of the colony to Spain and the whole bundle of practices and institutions that perpetuated inequality based on wealth, color, and lineage. Like other Latin Americans, Gómez hoped that the end of slavery would lead to a new era of equality. While abolition was the crucial first step, it was also the beginning of the new struggle to bring all people into the full exercise of freedom as citizens in independent nations.

# Abolitionists of the Second Slavery

❧

✦ REBELLION AND REVOLUTION IN 1868 FORCED CUBANS AND SPAN-
iards to confront the question of abolition. In Spain, the most important
abolitionist of the era was Rafael María de Labra, a young lawyer from a
military and aristocratic background born to Spanish parents in Cuba. Labra
was an enthusiastic advocate of abolition from the founding of the Spanish
Abolitionist Society in Madrid in 1865, a date that coincided with the end of
the Civil War in the United States. Initially quite conservative, the Spanish
Abolitionist Society sought to guide the opinion of political leaders toward
a gradual and controlled emancipation process, beginning with the suppression of the slave trade in 1867. However, once the Cuban separatist rebellion
broke out in 1868 and showed staying power, Labra and other abolitionists
demanded more radical action. He believed that Spain had to learn from
the experience of the Spanish American revolutions earlier in the century.
The fatal mistake then was staunch defense of slavery, even as it was coming
apart in the colonies. If the metropole repeated that error in Cuba, Labra
feared that the slaves would embrace the cause of Cuban independence; if
Spain acted decisively to end slavery, then it might win their loyalty.

Religion, particularly evangelical Christianity, was fundamental to antislavery thought and action in Britain. Not so in Spain, where abolitionists were secular in outlook and often anticlerical. Spanish Protestants supported the antislavery cause, but they were few in number and had little influence. The Catholic Church was absent from Spanish antislavery efforts. Rather than evangelization among the enslaved, what motivated Spanish abolitionists was maintaining the bond between Spain and Cuba—not through force, as Spanish conservatives urged, but through political and economic liberalization, including the emancipation of the slaves.

Abolitionists also protested the violence of slavery, the lack of rights, and the breakup of families, forms of tyranny that they equated with their own political subjugation by conservatives in Spain. That so few Spanish abolitionists had been in the colonies perhaps made it easier for them to draw the parallel between their own plight and that of the enslaved; men of wealth, status, and significant political power identifying their situation with that of the most vulnerable members of colonial society seems far-fetched to say the least (for the large number of Puerto Rican members of the society, the situation differed). Yet as distant as their conditions were, making these connections did resonate in Spain during moments of political confrontation in the course of the abolition process in the 1870s and 1880s. For example, in 1872 in Barcelona, a city with a history of protest against Cuban slavery but also with powerful vested interests in the slave trade and the colonial economy, a speaker at a public meeting insisted on the identity of interests and values between the abolitionists and the slaves: "If there is an insurrection in Cuba, it is because there is slavery. The slave owners hide behind the farce of national integrity. . . . If they demand soldiers, it is to guard their slaves, not to save their country. Catalans, you are the most liberal people in Spain. You cannot permit a few scoundrels to get rich from the blood of the unhappy blacks, our brothers. Catalans, down with slavery! Long live reforms in the Antilles! . . . The enslaved man has the right to rebel against his master. Long live liberty!"[1] Labra made a similar appeal a year later, when he told his audience in Madrid that by combating slavery in Cuba "what we are committed to is the liberty of Spain."[2]

Some Brazilian abolitionists were like Labra in that they came from their country's social and political elite. The most well known was Joaquim Nabuco, the son of a leading imperial statesman who followed in the paternal footsteps by crafting a successful political and diplomatic career. The

Nabucos were from Pernambuco, an old sugar region where slavery was in decline in the later nineteenth century. Brazil's regional conflicts were important in shaping opposition to slavery, pitting declining or marginal slave societies against the robust plantation belts in the southeast where planters tenaciously resisted abolition.

But Brazilian antislavery efforts were much more closely connected to the everyday politics of slavery than was Spanish abolitionism. Such was particularly true in the 1880s, when more Brazilians rallied to the cause because it was clear that the southeastern planters and their political allies would subvert abolition laws like the Rio Branco Law of 1871. The far northern province of Ceará was one of the centers of more concerted action against the interests of slaveholders. Like other peripheral regions, Ceará had since the suppression of the transatlantic slave trade in 1850 sent many of its slaves to the coffee plantations of Rio de Janeiro and São Paulo. This internal trade became the target of radical abolitionists gathered in the Sociedade Cearense Libertadora, founded in December 1880 in the capital, Fortaleza. Among the most active members targeting the trade was Francisco José do Nascimento, a mulatto *jangadeiro* (fisherman who used the *jangada*, a raft), and the port pilot, nicknamed O Dragão do Mar (the Dragon of the Sea). He organized his fellow Fortaleza jangadeiros in a strike against the slave trade. When slavers from the south arrived in Fortaleza, Nascimento and his fellows refused to transport captives from the beach to the awaiting ships, giving rise to the rallying cry against the slave traders: "From the port of Ceará no more slaves will be embarked!"[3] Three years later, in 1884, Ceará abolished slavery altogether in its borders, a process that started on the most local level, as city blocks, neighborhoods, and municipalities declared slavery abolished until the provincial government responded. Not only local leaders like the Dragão do Mar but also abolitionists from other parts of the country were instrumental in orchestrating these diverse actions, especially the renowned journalist and orator José do Patrocínio, who spent several months in Ceará in 1883, finding more fertile ground there than in Rio or São Paulo, the political center of recalcitrant anti-abolitionism, though soon to be the site of dramatic and effective gestures against slavery.

## Additional Reading

Alonso, Angela. *Joaquim Nabuco*. São Paulo: Comphania das Letras, 2007.

Corwin, Arthur F. *Spain and the Abolition of Slavery in Cuba, 1817–1886*. Austin: University Texas Press, 1967.

Drescher, Seymour. *Abolition: A History of Slavery and Antislavery*. New York: Cambridge University Press, 2009.

Garcia Balañà, Albert. "Antislavery before Abolitionism: Networks and Motives in Early Liberal Barcelona, 1833–1844." In *Slavery, Antislavery, and Empire: Spain and Spanish America in Comparative Perspective*, ed. Josep M. Fradera and Christopher Schmidt-Nowara. Forthcoming.

Machado, Maria Helena. *O Plano e o pânico: Os movimentos sociais na década da abolição*. Rio de Janeiro: Editora UFRJ; São Paulo: EDUSP, 1994.

Nabuco, Joaquim. *Abolitionism: The Brazilian Antislavery Struggle*. Trans. and ed. Robert Edgar Conrad. Urbana: University of Illinois Press, 1977.

# Conclusion

## Legacies of Latin American Slavery

❧

✦ THE ABOLITION OF CUBAN AND BRAZILIAN SLAVERY IN 1886 AND 1888 closed a cycle that began more than four hundred years before in the eastern Atlantic domains of Spain and Portugal. Because slavery was so integral to Latin American societies for centuries, its abolition could not wipe the historical slate clean, though many hoped that it would. What were the legacies of slavery that lived on beyond the late nineteenth century?

The main employer of slave labor, the plantations, left parts of Latin America dependent on shifts in Atlantic and global markets because they were oriented toward the export of goods such as sugar, tobacco, and coffee. When demand for plantation goods slowed or collapsed, so did the local economy. Planters were interested in controlling and exploiting enslaved workers, not in providing for their well-being, their education, or their mobility. They also sought to wring as much wealth from their land as possible. Plantation societies were thus left vulnerable to foreign demand, and their people and environment were bent to the rigors of slavery: "paralleling the ruthless use of natural resources was an equally ruthless exploitation of man."[1]

But the cruel logic of the plantation and economic dependency do not tell the full story of slavery and its aftermath in Latin America. Planters could not always bend their workers to their will. The long history of rebellions, covert acts of resistance, flight, and maroon communities shows that slaves resisted their subordination stubbornly and frequently. Indeed, historians now find that the very landscape and quotidian culture of the plantation might contain the proof of slave resistance. On the nineteenth-century coffee plantations of Brazil's Paraíba Valley, planters laid out their trees in grids to maximize their ability to survey slave workers. They did so because slaves often fled into the surrounding forests, trying to escape from the plantation or to tend to hidden provision grounds stocked with stolen pigs, chickens, and crops. Such acts of defiance not only shaped the landscape but also found their way into the songs, called *jongos*, of the slaves on these plantations, some of which were recorded by Stanley Stein in the 1940s during his research among the ruins of Vassouras's once-thriving coffee economy: "jongos were songs of protest, subdued but enduring. Jongo form—that of the riddle—lent itself well in phrasing the slaves' reactions, for, as with all riddles, the purpose was to conceal meaning with words, expressions, or situations of more than one possible interpretation."[2]

Slaves not only chafed at the bonds of slavery but also made their way to freedom in significant numbers over the centuries. In the United States, when emancipation came during the Civil War, the vast majority of the country's black population was enslaved. Such was not the case in Latin American countries, even in Cuba and Brazil, the largest slave societies. There, the free black population usually outnumbered the enslaved population because laws and religious customs provided that a steady stream of enslaved men and women would achieve freedom even as slavery endured. Over the centuries, Africans and African-descended people such as the Rio de Janeiro barber Antonio José Dutra, the New Orleans slave woman Jacqueline Lemelle, or the Mineira Chica da Silva might become free through self-purchase or manumission. Jacqueline Lemelle and Chica da Silva gave birth to free children after their own liberation; they also purchased the freedom of their children who were still enslaved. What their lives and efforts show us is that even though slavery was entrenched in Latin America, and despite laws and norms that discriminated against free blacks, there was some mobility in the system, partly created by laws and religious expectations and greatly expanded by the actions of enslaved and freed people struggling to make a place for themselves and their descendants in free society. The argument here is not that Latin American slavery was gentle or that these societies were egalitarian. Rather, it is that freedom for some was integral to the slave systems of Latin America, by design and by historical development. Moreover, though brutally hierarchical, Latin American societies also had means to integrate different groups and to promote in limited fashion some mobility after slavery.

One area where the flexibility of Latin American slave societies was most apparent was, oddly enough, in religion. I say oddly because the most common image of Iberian religiosity is the intolerance of the Inquisition; just as Spain was embarking upon expansion in the New World, it was stamping out religious pluralism in the Old World. Yet the peoples of the New World, like many of those in the Old, proved resistant to the defenders of orthodoxy.[3] Catholic institutions like lay religious brotherhoods and beliefs like the cult of the saints unintentionally provided African slaves with means by which they could reproduce aspects of their social and religious worlds by giving them limited autonomous spaces of sociability and some form of inclusion within the ritual life of the colonies. Iberian Catholicism thus became a meeting ground of sorts for all sectors of colonial society; it was also a source of vibrant cultural creativity that lives on today in religions such as Santería, Candomblé, and Umbanda.

Finally, this capacity for negotiation and integration was crucial in shaping the simultaneous struggles against slavery and against colonialism in much of Latin America. Until recently, historians characterized Latin American independence as a superficial event that did little to change the fundamental structures of colonial society. However, studies of slavery and abolition have shown that independence brought with it significant transformations. Even in Brazil, the staunchest defender of slavery as a colony and as an independent monarchy, there were attempts to incorporate free, Brazilian-born blacks into the political system of the Brazilian Empire. In Spanish America, the challenge to colonial structures was more far-reaching. The fierce confrontation between Spain and its colonies in the 1810s and 1820s gave slaves leverage to demand freedom and free blacks the chance to dismantle the laws that discriminated against them. Later in the century, Cubans resisted efforts to impose Jim Crow–like restrictions on rights and citizenship during the U.S. occupation of the island (1898–1902) because the previous struggle against Spain, intersecting with the destruction of slavery on the island, had forged broad commitment to overcoming the racial divisions of colonialism.[4] Cuba's defiance of the United States shows that one of the legacies of Latin American slavery was the fight against it; the forms of social, political, and cultural solidarity created in that fight could at times countervail the stubborn colonial inheritance and the scientific racism and belief in white supremacy that would grip much of the western world in the modern age.

# Notes

## Introduction

1. Sociedad Abolicionista Española, *El cepo y el grillete (la esclavitud en Cuba)* (Madrid: Sociedad Abolicionista, 1882 [?]), 12–13. Unless otherwise noted, all translations are mine.

2. Sociedad Abolicionista, *El cepo y el grillete*, 19.

3. Sociedad Abolicionista, *El cepo y el grillete*, 21 (emphasis in the original).

4. George Reid Andrews, *Afro-Latin America, 1800–2000* (New York: Oxford University Press, 2004), 41; Leslie Bethell and José Murilo de Carvalho, "1822–1850," in *Brazil: Empire and Republic, 1822–1930*, ed. Leslie Bethell (Cambridge: Cambridge University Press, 1989), 45–46; Rebecca J. Scott, *Slave Emancipation in Cuba: The Transition to Free Labor, 1860–1899* (Princeton, NJ: Princeton University Press, 1985), 7. On the number of slaves who reached Latin American shores via the transatlantic traffic, see Estimates Database, 2009, *Voyages: The Trans-Atlantic Slave Trade Database*, http://www.slavevoyages. org, accessed June 21, 2010. Note that the database at slavevoyages.org is an ongoing research project, so the figures undergo refinement.

5. See the cogent summary in David Eltis, "Was the Abolition of the U.S. and British Slave Trade Significant in the Broader Atlantic Context?," *William and Mary Quarterly* 66 (October 2009): 715–36.

## Chapter One

1. Christopher Columbus, "Letter of Columbus to Various Persons Describing the Results of His First Voyage and Written on the Return Journey," in *The Four Voyages*, ed. and trans. J. M. Cohen (New York: Penguin, 1969), 122.

2. John Thornton, *Africa and Africans in the Making of the Atlantic World, 1400–1800*, 2nd ed. (Cambridge: Cambridge University Press, 1998), 108.

3. Pier Larson, "African Diasporas and the Atlantic," in *The Atlantic in Global History, 1500–2000*, ed. Jorge Cañizares-Esguerra and Erik R. Seeman (Upper Saddle River, NJ: Pearson Prentice Hall, 2007), 134. See also Paul Lovejoy, *Transformation in Slavery: A History of Slavery in Africa*, 2nd ed. (Cambridge: Cambridge University Press, 2000). Larson's estimates for the transatlantic slave trade are from an earlier iteration of the Trans-Atlantic Slave Trade Database. The most recent estimates are higher, at more than 12.5 million Africans embarked on slaving vessels. See Estimates Database, 2009, *Voyages: The Trans-Atlantic Slave Trade Database*, http://www.slavevoyages.org, accessed June 28, 2010.

4. Herbert S. Klein, *The Atlantic Slave Trade* (Cambridge: Cambridge University Press, 1999), 103. See also Thornton, *Africa and Africans*, chaps. 2–4.

5. A. C. de C. M. Saunders, *A Social History of Black Slaves and Freedmen in Portugal, 1441–1555* (Cambridge: Cambridge University Press, 1982); William D. Phillips Jr., *Slavery from Roman Times to the Early Transatlantic Trade* (Minneapolis: University of Minnesota Press, 1985); Philip D. Curtin, *The Rise and Fall of the Plantation Complex: Essays in Atlantic History*, 2nd ed. (Cambridge: Cambridge University Press, 1998), chaps. 1–3; and David Wheat, "Mediterranean Slavery, New World Transformations: Galley Slaves in the Spanish Caribbean, 1578–1635," *Slavery and Abolition* 31 (September 2010): 327–44.

6. Alan Watson, *Slave Law in the Americas* (Athens: University of Georgia Press, 1989).

7. On Columbus's early career in the Mediterranean and eastern Atlantic, see William D. Phillips Jr. and Carla Rahn Phillips, *The Worlds of Christopher Columbus* (Cambridge: Cambridge University Press, 1992), 37–111.

8. See the fascinating reappraisal in Nicolás Wey Gómez, *The Tropics of Empire: Why Columbus Sailed South to the Indies* (Cambridge, MA: MIT Press, 2008).

9. Christopher Columbus, "Digest of Columbus's Log-Book on His First Voyage Made by Bartolomé de las Casas," in *Four Voyages*, 56.

10. "The Requirement (1513)," in *Early Modern Spain: A Documentary History*, ed. Jon Cowans (Philadelphia, PA: University of Pennsylvania Press, 2003), 35–36.

11. Carl O. Sauer, *The Early Spanish Main* (Berkeley: University of California Press, 1966); Irving Rouse, *The Tainos: Rise and Decline of the People Who Greeted Columbus* (New Haven, CT: Yale University Press, 1992), 150–61; and Francisco Scarano, *Puerto Rico: Cinco siglos de historia* (San Juan, Puerto Rico: McGraw-Hill, 1993), chaps. 6–7.

12. Bartolomé de las Casas, *A Short Account of the Destruction of the Indies*, ed. and trans. Nigel Griffin (London: Penguin, 1992), 26.

13. Matthew Restall, "Black Conquistadors: Armed Africans in Early Spanish America," *The Americas* 57 (2000): 171.

14. Ira Berlin, *Generations of Captivity: A History of African-American Slaves* (Cambridge, MA: Harvard University Press, 2003), chap. 1.

15. This latter question is at the core of David Eltis's *The Rise of African Slavery in the Americas* (Cambridge: Cambridge University Press, 2000).

16. Ruth Pike, *Penal Servitude in Early Modern Spain* (Madison: University of Wisconsin Press, 1983).

17. Miguel de Cervantes, *Don Quixote*, trans. Edith Grossman (New York: Ecco, 2005), 163.

18. David Wheat has recently recounted the dispatch of Mediterranean galleys to the Caribbean colonies, powered by Muslim and morisco slaves. See Wheat, "Mediterranean Slavery."

19. Timothy Coates, *Convicts and Orphans: Forced and State-Sponsored Colonizers in the Portuguese Empire, 1550–1755* (Stanford, CA: Stanford University Press, 2001).

20. See Anthony Pagden, *The Fall of Natural Man: The American Indian and the Origins of Comparative Ethnology* (Cambridge: Cambridge University Press, 1982).

21. Frederick Bowser, *African Slavery in Colonial Peru, 1524–1650* (Stanford, CA: Stanford University Press, 1974), 26; and Tamar Herzog, *Defining Nations: Immigrants and Citizens in Early Modern Spain and Spanish America* (New Haven, CT: Yale University Press, 2003).

22. Alonso de Sandoval, *Treatise on Slavery: Selections from De instauranda Aethiopum salute*, ed. and trans. Nicole von Germeten (1627; Indianapolis: Hackett, 2008), 20. For more discussion, see Robin Blackburn, *The Making of New World Slavery: From the Baroque to the Modern, 1492–1800* (London: Verso, 1997), 64–76; and Jonathan Schorsch, *Jews and Blacks in the Early Modern World* (Cambridge: Cambridge University Press, 2004). See also Wey Gómez, *Tropics of Empire*, 229–91, on the parallel belief that the inhabitants of the Torrid Zone, where most of Africa lay, were natural servants of the Europeans who dwelled in the Temperate Zone.

23. "Two Slaveries—The Sermons of Padre Antônio Vieira, Salvador, Bahia (ca. 1633) and Sao Luís do Maranhao (1653)," in *Colonial Latin America: A Documentary History*, ed. Kenneth Mills, William Taylor, and Sandra Lauderdale Graham (Wilmington, DE: Scholarly Resources, 2002), 223. On Vieira's attitudes toward slavery, see Joan Meznar, "Our Lady of the Rosary, African Slaves, and the Struggle against Heretics in Brazil, 1550–1660," *Journal of Early Modern History* 9 (2005): 371–97.

24. "Two Slaveries," 225.

25. "Two Slaveries," 227–28.

26. "Two Slaveries," 228.

27. The Church did produce criticisms of the slave trade and of slavery that went beyond those of Vieira, though these never translated into a broadly based movement seeking their suppression. See Richard Gray, "The Papacy and the Atlantic Slave Trade: Lourenço da Silva, the Capuchins, and the Decisions of the Holy Office," *Past and Present*, no. 115 (1987): 52–68. Gray relates the story of the Afro-Brazilian Lourenço da Silva, who managed to present a petition to the papacy in the late seventeenth century to the effect that black Christians were being mistreated as slaves in both Africa and the New World and should therefore be released from their bondage. Papal authorities, after consulting with missionaries, concurred. However, they never acted forcefully against the Portuguese and Spanish monarchies. Thanks to Rebecca Scott for calling this article to my attention.

28. Klein, *African Slave Trade*, chaps. 3 and 4.

29. Curtin, *Rise and Fall of the Plantation Complex*, chaps. 4–6; Stuart B. Schwartz, ed., *Tropical Babylons: Sugar and the Making of the Atlantic World, 1450–1680* (Chapel Hill: University of North Carolina Press, 2004); and Alejandro de la Fuente with César García del Pino and Bernardo Iglesias Delgado, *Havana and the Atlantic in the Sixteenth Century* (Chapel Hill: University of North Carolina Press, 2008).

30. Estimates Database, 2009, *Voyages: The Trans-Atlantic Slave Trade Database*, http://www.slavevoyages.org, accessed June 6, 2010.

31. Ward Barrett, *The Sugar Haciendas of the Marqueses del Valle* (Minneapolis: University of Minnesota Press, 1970); Colin Palmer, *Slaves of the White God: Blacks in Mexico, 1570–1650* (Cambridge, MA: Harvard University Press, 1976); Patrick Carroll, *Blacks in Colonial Veracruz: Race, Ethnicity, and Regional Development* (Austin: University of Texas Press, 1991); R. Douglas Cope, *The Limits of Racial Domination: Plebian Society in Colonial Mexico City, 1660–1720* (Madison: University of Wisconsin Press, 1994); and Herman Bennett, *Africans in Colonial Mexico: Absolutism, Christianity, and Afro-Creole Consciousness, 1570–1640* (Bloomington: Indiana University Press, 2005).

32. Bowser, *African Slave in Colonial Peru*, chaps. 4–6.

33. Bowser, *African Slave in Colonial Peru*, 124.

34. Stuart Schwartz, *Sugar Plantations in the Formation of Brazilian Society: Bahia, 1550–1835* (Cambridge: Cambridge University Press, 1985), chaps. 1 and 2. Moreover, the Jesuits would eventually hold thousands of African slaves on their extensive Brazilian properties, which included sugar plantations. See Dauril Alden, *The Making of an Enterprise: The Society of Jesus in Portugal, Its Empire, and Beyond, 1540–1750* (Stanford, CA: Stanford University Press, 1996).

35. John Hemming, "Indians and the Frontier," in *Colonial Brazil*, ed. Leslie Bethell (Cambridge: Cambridge University Press, 1987), 145–89.

36. Schwartz, *Sugar Plantations*, chap. 3; and Schwartz, "A Commonwealth within Itself: The Early Brazilian Sugar Industry, 1550–1670," in *Tropical Babylons*, 158–200.

37. Thornton, *Africa and Africans*; Klein, *Atlantic Slave Trade*. On the reconstruction of the patterns of the slave trade, see the remarkable collaborative project *Voyages: The Trans-Atlantic Slave Trade Database* (http://www.slavevoyages.org). See also David Eltis and David Richardson, eds., *Extending the Frontiers: Essays on the New Transatlantic Slave Trade Database* (New Haven, CT: Yale University Press, 2008).

38. "A Portuguese Doctor Describes the Suffering of Black Slaves in Africa and on the Atlantic Voyage (1793)," in Robert E. Conrad, *Children of God's Fire: A Documentary History of Black Slavery in Brazil* (Princeton, NJ: Princeton University Press, 1983), 20–22.

39. "Portuguese Doctor," 22.

40. Klein, *Atlantic Slave Trade*, 136.

41. Kenneth Kiple, *The Caribbean Slave: A Biological History* (Cambridge: Cambridge University Press, 1984), 103.

42. For illuminating discussions of these debates, see Richard Price and Sally Price, *The Root of Roots; or, How Afro-American Anthropology Got Its Start* (Chicago: Prickly Paradigm Press, 2003); David Scott, *Conscripts of Modernity: The Tragedy of Colonial Enlightenment* (Durham, NC: Duke University Press, 2004); and Vincent Brown, "Social Death and Political Life in the Study of Slavery," *American Historical Review* 114 (December 2009): 1231–49. One of the most careful empirical studies testing these questions is Philip Morgan, *Slave Counterpoint: Black Culture in the Eighteenth-Century Chesapeake and Lowcountry* (Chapel Hill: University of North Carolina Press, 1998).

43. Sidney Mintz and Richard Price, *The Birth of African-American Culture: An Anthropological Perspective* (Boston: Beacon, 1992), 83. See also Paul Gilroy, *The Black Atlantic: Modernity and Double Consciousness* (Cambridge, MA: Harvard University Press, 1993).

44. James H. Sweet, *Recreating Africa: Culture, Kinship, and Religion in the African-Portuguese World, 1441–1770* (Chapel Hill: University of North Carolina Press, 2003), 2. See also Thornton, *Africa and Africans*; and Paul Lovejoy, "The African Diaspora: Revisionist Interpretations of Ethnicity, Culture, and Religion under Slavery," *Studies in the World History of Slavery, Abolition, and Emancipation* 2 (1997): 1–23.

45. See "Brotherhoods and Baroque Catholicism," in João José Reis, *Death Is a Festival: Funeral Rites and Rebellion in Nineteenth-Century Brazil*, trans. H. Sabrina Gledhill (Chapel Hill: University of North Carolina Press, 2003), 39–65; and Elizabeth W. Kiddy, "Who Is the King of Congo? A New Look at African and Afro-Brazilian Kings," in *Central Africans and Cultural Transformations in the American Diaspora*, ed. Linda M. Heywood (Cambridge: Cambridge University Press, 2002), 153–82.

46. María Elena Díaz, *The Virgin, the King, and the Royal Slaves of El Cobre: Negotiating Freedom in Colonial Cuba, 1670–1780* (Stanford, CA: Stanford University Press, 2000).

47. Javier Villa-Flores, "'To Lose One's Soul': Blasphemy and Slavery in New Spain, 1596–1669," *Hispanic American Historical Review* 82 (August 2002): 436, 467. Slaves might also make use of royal laws to provoke intervention against abusive masters. See Marcela Echeverri's study of infanticide in the Kingdom of Quito, "'Enraged to the limit of despair': Infanticide and Slave Judicial Strategies in Barbacoas, 1788–1798," *Slavery and Abolition* 30 (2009): 403–26.

48. Thornton, *Africa and Africans*, 235–71, quote on 236. Though European Christian priests sought to monopolize revelation and its interpretation, they always ran afoul of African Christianity, which accepted continuous revelation and its interpretation by non-priests. Moreover, in Europe itself, historians have shown that the laity insisted upon the importance of continuous revelation through apparitions and miracles. While the church hierarchy might seek to control the laity, it generally had to compromise in the face of ever-proliferating shrines and vows. See William Christian, *Local Religion in Sixteenth-Century Spain* (Princeton, NJ: Princeton University Press, 1981); and Allan Greer and Kenneth Mills, "A Catholic Atlantic," in Cañizares-Esguerra and Seeman, *Atlantic in Global History*, 3–19.

49. Philip A. Howard, *Changing History: Afro-Cuban Cabildos and Societies of Color in the Nineteenth Century* (Baton Rouge: Louisiana State University Press, 1998).

50. Joseph M. Murphy, *Santería: African Spirits in America* (Boston: Beacon, 1993), 7–20.

51. The best introduction to maroonage is Richard Price, ed., *Maroon Societies: Rebel Slave Communities in the Americas* (Baltimore, MD: Johns Hopkins University Press, 1996).

52. Archivo General de Indias, Mapas y planos, Santo Domingo, 515.

53. Carolyn E. Fick, *The Making of Haiti: The Saint-Domingue Revolution from Below* (Knoxville: University of Tennessee Press, 1990), 51–52. On Enrique and early sixteenth-century Española, see Ida Altman, "The Revolt of Enriquillo and the Historiography of Early Spanish America," *The Americas* 63 (2007), 587–614.

54. Esmeraldas has received extensive attention. See Thomas B. F. Cummins and William B. Taylor, "The Mulatto Gentlemen of Esmeraldas," in Mills, Taylor, and Graham, *Colonial Latin America*, 159–61; Kris Lane, *Quito 1599: City and Colony in Transition* (Albuquerque: University of New Mexico Press, 2002), chap. 1; and Charles Beatty Medina, "Caught between Rivals: The Spanish-African Maroon Competition for Captive Indian Labor in the Region of Esmeraldas during the Late Sixteenth and Early Seventeenth Centuries," *The Americas* 63 (2006): 113–36.

55. "The Foundation of Nuestra Señora de Guadalupe de los Morenos de Amapa, Mexico (1769)," in Mills, Taylor, and Graham, *Colonial Latin America*, 322.

56. Altman, "Revolt of Enriquillo," 602–8.

57. Frederick P. Bowser, "Colonial Spanish America," in *Neither Slave nor Free: The Freedman of African Descent in the Slave Societies of the New World*, ed. David W. Cohen and Jack P. Greene (Baltimore, MD: Johns Hopkins University Press, 1972), 21–22.

58. Bowser, "Colonial Spanish America," 26; Herbert S. Klein, *Slavery in the Americas: A Comparative Study of Virginia and Cuba* (Chicago: Quadrangle Books, 1971), 57–85; Lyman Johnson, "Manumission in Colonial Buenos Aires, 1776–1810," *Hispanic American Historical Review* 59 (1979): 258–79; and Alejandro de la Fuente, "Slavery and Claims-Making in Cuba: The Tannenbaum Debate Revisited," *Law and History Review* 22 (2004): 339–69.

59. A. J. R. Russell-Wood, "Colonial Brazil," in Cohen and Greene, *Neither Slave nor Free*, 84–133.

60. Russell-Wood, "Colonial Brazil"; Bowser, "Colonial Spanish America"; Magnus Mörner, *Race Mixture in the History of Latin America* (Boston: Little, Brown, 1967); and Cope, *Limits of Racial Domination*.

61. Bowser, "Colonial Spanish America," 47.

62. Francis Dutra, "A Hard-Fought Battle for Recognition: Manuel Gonçalves Doria, First Afro-Brazilian to Become a Knight of Santiago," *The Americas* 56 (July 1999): 91–113; Hendrik Kraay, "Arming Slaves in Brazil from the Seventeenth Century to the Nineteenth Century," in *Arming Slaves: From Classical Times to the Modern Age*, ed. Christopher Leslie Brown and Philip D. Morgan (New Haven, CT: Yale University Press, 2006), 146–79; and Hebe Mattos, "'Black Troops' and Hierarchies of Color in the Portuguese Atlantic World: The Case of Henrique Dias and His Black Regiment," *Luso-Brazilian Review* 45 (2008): 6–29.

63. Susan Migden Socolow, *The Women of Colonial Latin America* (Cambridge: Cambridge University Press, 2000), 39.

64. See Joseph Pérez, *The Spanish Inquisition: A History*, trans. Janet Lloyd (New Haven, CT: Yale University Press, 2005); and Richard Kagan and Abigail Dyer, eds., *Inquisitorial Inquiries: Brief Lives of Secret Jews and Other Heretics* (Baltimore, MD: Johns Hopkins University Press, 2004).

65. J. H. Elliott, *Empires of the Atlantic World: Britain and Spain in America, 1492–1830* (New Haven, CT: Yale University Press, 2006), 171. For an example of the castas paintings, see Ignacio Maria Barreda, *Casta Painting*, 1777, "Gallery: 1700s," in Dana Leibsohn and Barbara E. Mundy, *Vistas: Visual Culture in Spanish America, 1520–1820*, http://www.smith.edu/vistas, 2009.

66. Ann Twinam, "Pedro de Ayarza: The Purchase of Whiteness," in *The Human Tradition in Colonial Latin America*, ed. Kenneth J. Andrien (Wilmington, DE: SR Books, 2002), 194–210. See also Herzog, *Defining Nations*, 141–63.

67. The most influential expression of this perspective is Frank Tannenbaum, *Slave and Citizen, the Negro in the Americas* (New York: Vintage, 1946).

## Portrait One

1. Rolena Adorno and Patrick Charles Pautz, "The 1542 *Relación* (Account) of Álvar Núñez Cabeza de Vaca," in *Álvar Núñez Cabeza de Vaca: His Account, His Life, and the Expedition of Pánfilo de Narváez* (Lincoln: University of Nebraska Press, 1999), 1:277–79. Azemmour is a city on the northwest coast of Morocco. In the early sixteenth century, it paid tribute to the king of Portugal.

2. Herbert E. Bolton, *The Spanish Borderlands: A Chronicle of Old Florida and the Southwest* (1921; repr., Albuquerque: University of New Mexico Press, 1996).

## Chapter Two

1. John Gabriel Stedman, *Narrative of a Five Years' Expedition against the Revolted Negroes of Surinam in Guiana on the Wild Coast of South America from the Years 1772 to 1777* (Amherst: University of Massachusetts Press, 1972), 66.

2. J. H. Elliott, *Imperial Spain, 1469–1716* (London: Penguin, 1963); Geoffrey Parker, *The Dutch Revolt* (Ithaca, NY: Cornell University Press, 1977); and Jonathan I. Israel, "The Emerging Empire: The Continental Perspective, 1650–1713," in *Oxford History of the British Empire*, vol. 1, *The Origins of Empire: British Overseas Enterprise to the Close of the Seventeenth Century*, ed. Nicholas Canny (Oxford: Oxford University Press, 1998), 423–44.

3. Sir Walter Ralegh, *The Discoverie of the Large, Rich, and Bewtiful Empyre of Guiana*, with an introduction by Neil L. Whitehead (Manchester, UK: Manchester University Press, 1997), 127–28. Emphasis in the original.

4. Elliott, *Empires of the Atlantic World*, 220–21.

5. Philip P. Boucher, *Cannibal Encounters: Europeans and Island Caribs, 1492–1763* (Baltimore, MD: Johns Hopkins University Press, 1992).

6. Karen Ordahl Kupperman, *Providence Island, 1630–1641: The Other Puritan Colony* (New York: Cambridge University Press, 1993).

7. Kupperman, *Providence Island*, 172. See also Edmund Morgan, *American Slavery, American Freedom: The Ordeal of Colonial Virginia* (New York: Norton, 1975), for a close study of indentured servitude and slavery in British North America in the seventeenth century.

8. John J. McCusker and Russell R. Menard, "The Sugar Industry in the Seventeenth Century: A New Perspective on the Barbadian 'Sugar Revolution,'" *Tropical Babylons*, ed. Schwartz, 292–94.

9. See David Armitage, *The Ideological Origins of the British Empire* (Cambridge: Cambridge University Press, 2000). See also Elliott's comparison of Spanish and British colonization in *Empires of the Atlantic World*, chap. 5.

10. This dichotomy between British and Iberian legal and religious backgrounds finds its clearest formulation in Tannenbaum, *Slave and Citizen*. For more fine-grained studies of British slave societies, see Morgan, *American Slavery, American Freedom*; Morgan, *Slave Counterpoint*; and Richard S. Dunn, *Sugar and Slaves: The Rise of the Planter Class in the English West Indies, 1624–1713* (Chapel Hill: University of North Carolina Press, 2000).

11. Estimates Database, 2009, *Voyages: The Trans-Atlantic Slave Trade Database*, http://www.slavevoyages.org, accessed January 6, 2011.

12. Dunn, *Sugar and Slaves*, 149.

13. Dunn, *Sugar and Slaves*, 151. See also Trevor Burnard, *Mastery, Tyranny, and Desire: Thomas Thistlewood and His Slaves in the Anglo-Jamaican World* (Chapel Hill: University of North Carolina Press, 2004).

14. Edmund Burke, "An Account of the European Settlements in America" (1777), in *The Portable Edmund Burke*, ed. Isaac Kramnick (New York: Penguin, 1999), 233.

15. Michael Craton, *Testing the Chains: Resistance to Slavery in the British West Indies* (Ithaca, NY: Cornell University Press, 1982).

16. Maureen Warner Lewis, *Central Africa in the Caribbean: Transcending Time, Transforming Cultures* (Mona, Jamaica: University of West Indies Press, 2003), 69; Craton, *Testing the Chains*, 70–71.

17. British colonial governor Edward Trelawny quoted in Craton, *Testing the Chains*, 83.

18. Craton, *Testing the Chains*, 125. See also Burnard, *Mastery, Tyranny, and Desire*, 137–74; and Burke, "Account," 235.

19. John Garrigus, *Before Haiti: Race and Citizenship in French Saint-Domingue* (New York: Palgrave Macmillan, 2006), 25.

20. Garrigus, *Before Haiti*, 32.

21. See Garrigus, *Before Haiti*, 21–50.

22. The text of the Code Noir, translated by John Garrigus, is available from Dr. Sue Peabody, Department of History, Washington State University, Vancouver, "French Colonial Texts," http://directory.vancouver.wsu.edu/people/sue-peabody/french-colonial-texts.

23. On the tepid support for the missionary church in the French Caribbean, see Sue Peabody, "'A Dangerous Zeal': Catholic Missions to Slaves in the French Antilles, 1635–1800," *French Historical Studies* 25 (2002): 53–90.

24. See Garrigus, *Before Haiti*; and Laurent Dubois, *Avengers of the New World: The Story of the Haitian Revolution* (Cambridge, MA: Belknap Press, 2004), 60–90.

25. Dubois, *Avengers of the New World*, 40.

26. See the essays and excerpts in Price, *Maroon Societies*, 105–48; Garrigus, *Before Haiti*, 26–28; and Dubois, *Avengers of the New World*, 51–59.

27. Jane Landers, *Black Society in Spanish Florida* (Urbana: University of Illinois Press, 1999); and David Stark, "Rescued from Their Invisibility: The Afro-Puerto Ricans of Seventeenth- and Eighteenth-Century San Mateo de Cangrejos, Puerto Rico," *The Americas* (April 2007): 551 86.

28. Arturo Morales Carrión, *Puerto Rico and the Non-Hispanic Caribbean: A Study in the Decline of Spanish Exclusivism* (Río Piedras: University of Puerto Rico Press, 1952), 1–34.

29. Morales Carrión, *Puerto Rico and the Non-Hispanic Caribbean*, 35–45, 83–99; and Francisco Scarano, *Sugar and Slavery in Puerto Rico: The Plantation Economy of Ponce, 1800–1850* (Madison: University of Wisconsin Press, 1984), 3–34.

30. Díaz, *Virgin, King, and Royal Slaves of El Cobre*, 184–87.

31. See Gwendolyn Midlo Hall, *Africans in Colonial Louisiana: The Development of Afro-Creole Culture in the Eighteenth Century* (Baton Rouge: Louisiana State University Press, 1992), 275–315. Cf. Thomas N. Ingersoll, "Slave Codes and Judicial Practice in New Orleans, 1718–1807," *Law and History Review* 13 (Spring 1995): 23–62; and Ingersoll, *Mammon and Manon in Early New Orleans: The First Slave Society in the Deep South, 1718–1819* (Knoxville: University of Tennessee Press, 1999), 211–39. Ingersoll argues that there was no practical difference between the French and Spanish colonial regimes and laws regarding slavery and freedom, even though his own data demonstrate that the frequency of manumission and coartación rose significantly throughout the Spanish period. His skepticism seems to arise from concern that Frank Tannenbaum's rosy view of slavery and race relations in the Iberian empires would blind historians to the brutality of the slave regimes in Louisiana. However, acknowledging the impact of Spanish laws and customs does not necessarily bring with it all of Tannenbaum's baggage. For a recent discussion of the Tannenbaum thesis and its pitfalls, see the contributions by Alejandro de la Fuente, Christopher Schmidt-Nowara, and María Elena Díaz in the forum "What Can Frank Tannenbaum Still Teach Us about the Law of Slavery?" *Law and History Review* 22 (Summer 2004): 339–88.

32. Stuart B. Schwartz, "Luso-Spanish Relations in Hapsburg Brazil, 1580–1640," *The Americas* 25 (July 1968): 33–48; and J. H. Elliott, "The Spanish Monarchy and the Kingdom of Portugal, 1580–1640," in *Conquest and Coalescence: The Shaping of the State in Early Modern Europe*, ed. Mark Greengrass (London: Edward Arnold, 1991), 48–67.

33. Pieter C. Emmer, "The Dutch and the Slave Americas," in *Slavery in the Development of the Americas*, ed. David Eltis, Frank D. Lewis, and Kenneth L. Sokoloff (Cambridge: Cambridge University Press, 2004), 70–86; and Emmer, *The Dutch Slave Trade, 1500–1850*, trans. Chris Emery (New York: Berghan Books, 2006).

34. C. R. Boxer, *Salvador de Sá and the Struggle for Brazil and Angola* (London: Athlone Press, 1952); and Luiz Felipe de Alencastro, *O trato dos viventes: Formação do Brasil no Atlântico Sul* (São Paulo: Companhia Das Letras, 2000).

35. Alencastro, *O trato dos viventes*, 334.

36. Joseph C. Miller, "A Marginal Institution on the Margin of the Atlantic System: The Portuguese Southern Atlantic Slave Trade in the Eighteenth Century," in *Slavery and the Rise of the Atlantic System*, ed. Barbara L. Solow (Cambridge: Cambridge University Press, 1991), 120–50.

37. Alencastro, *O trato dos viventes*, 336–40. See also Rafael de Bivar Marquese, "A dinâmica da escravidão no Brasil: Resistência, tráfico negreiro e alforrias, séculos XVII a XIX," *Novos Estudos* 74 (March 2006): 107–23.

38. C. R. Boxer, *The Golden Age of Brazil: Growing Pains of a Colonial Society, 1695–1750* (1962; New York: St. Martin's, 1995), 1–60; Elizabeth W. Kiddy, *Blacks of the Rosary: Memory and History in Minas Gerais, Brazil* (University Park: Pennsylvania State University Press, 2005), 39–63.

39. Boxer, *Golden Age of Brazil*, 204–25; Kathleen J. Higgins, *"Licentious Liberty" in a Brazilian Gold-Mining Region: Slavery, Gender, and Social Control in Eighteenth-Century Sabará, Minas Gerais* (University Park: Pennsylvania State University Press, 1999); and Andrea Lisly Gonçalves, "Alforrias resultants a troca de cativos (Comarca de Ouro Preto, século XIX)," in *Termo da Mariana: História e documentação*, ed. Andrea Lisly Gonçalves and Ronaldo Polito de Oliveira (Mariana, Brazil: Imprensa Universitária da UFOP, 2004), 47–55. This last article documents that some slaves were able to acquire their freedom by providing their owners with another slave in their stead.

40. "Slave Workers at the Diamond Washings of Tejuco, Minas Gerais, in the Early Nineteenth Century," in Conrad, *Children of God's Fire*, 140–42. See also Boxer's description of labor conditions in diamond mining in *Golden Age of Brazil*, 216–18.

41. Kiddy, *Blacks of the Rosary*, 83.

42. Kiddy, *Blacks of the Rosary*, 81–84; and Reis, *Death Is a Festival*.

43. Kiddy, *Blacks of the Rosary*, 15–63; Joan Meznar, "Our Lady of the Rosary, African Slaves, and the Struggle against Heretics in Brazil, 1550–1660," *Journal of Early Modern History* 9 (2005): 371–97; and Thornton, *Africa and Africans*, 235–71.

44. Kiddy, *Blacks of the Rosary*, 37.

45. See Elliott, *Imperial Spain*; and Elliott, *Richelieu and Olivares* (Cambridge: Cambridge University Press, 1984).

46. On the change of dynasties and the halting reforms of the early Bourbon rulers, see Stanley J. Stein and Barbara H. Stein, *Silver, Trade, and War: Spain and America in the Making of Early Modern Europe* (Baltimore, MD: Johns Hopkins University Press, 2000).

47. "Memoria de D. Alexandro O'Reilly a S. M. sobre la Isla de Puerto Rico, en 1765," *Boletín Histórico de Puerto Rico* 8 (1921) (New York: Kraus Reprint, 1968), 114.

48. "Memoria de D. Alexandro O'Reilly," 112–14.

49. Fray Iñigo Abbad y Lasierra, *Historia geográfica, civil y natural de la Isla de San Juan de Puerto Rico* (Río Piedras, Puerto Rico: Editorial Universitaria, 1966), 185.

50. Abbad, *Historia geográfica*, 154–56.

51. Abbad, *Historia geográfica*, 157–58.

52. See the cogent summary of Cuban reforms in Allan J. Kuethe, "The Early Reforms of Charles III in the Viceroyalty of New Granada, 1759–1776," in *Reform and Insurrection in Bourbon New Granada and Peru*, ed. John R. Fisher, Allan J. Kuethe, and Anthony MacFarlane (Baton Rouge: Louisiana State University Press, 1990), 25–29. See also Kuethe's in-depth study *Cuba, 1753–1815: Crown, Military, and Society* (Knoxville: University of Tennessee Press, 1986); and Aline Helg, *Liberty and Equality in Caribbean Colombia, 1770–1835* (Chapel Hill: University of North Carolina Press, 2004).

53. Kuethe, "Early Reforms of Charles III," 27.

54. See the summary in Hubert H. S. Aimes, *A History of Slavery in Cuba, 1511–1868* (New York: G. P. Putnam's Sons, 1907), 20–53; and David R. Murray, *Odious Commerce: Britain, Spain and the Abolition of the Cuban Slave Trade* (Cambridge: Cambridge University Press, 1980), 1–21. For an important overview of Spanish policies regarding the slave trade, see Josep M. Delgado i Ribas, "De la marginalidad a la centralidad: La trata de esclavos en el sistema imperial español," in *Slavery, Antislavery, and Empire: Spain and Spanish America in Comparative Perspective*, ed. Josep M. Fradera, Stephen Jacobson, and Christopher Schmidt-Nowara (forthcoming). On Arango y Parreño and his vision of Cuban plantation society, see Manuel Moreno Fraginals, *The Sugarmill: The Socioeconomic Complex of Sugar in Cuba, 1760–1860*, trans. Cedric Belfrage (New York: Monthly Review Press, 1976); and Dale Tomich, "The Wealth of Empire: Francisco Arango y Parreño, Political Economy, and the Second Slavery in Cuba," in *Interpreting Spanish Colonialism: Empires, Nations, and Legends*, ed. Christopher Schmidt-Nowara and John Nieto-Phillips (Albuquerque: University of New Mexico Press, 2005), 55–85.

55. See Jacques A. Barbier, "Commercial Reform and *Comercio Neutral* in Cartagena de Indias, 1788–1808," in Fisher, Kuethe, and MacFarlane, *Reform and Insurrection*, 96–120; P. Michael McKinley, *Pre-Revolutionary Caracas: Politics, Economy, and Society, 1777–1811* (Cambridge: Cambridge University Press, 1985); and Johnson, "Manumission."

56. The origins and motivations of British antislavery efforts are matters of long-standing debate and controversy. A good introduction can be found in Thomas Bender, ed., *The Antislavery Debate: Capitalism and Abolitionism as a Problem in Historical Interpretation* (Berkeley: University of California Press, 1992).

57. Christopher Leslie Brown, *Moral Capital: Foundations of British Abolitionism* (Chapel Hill: University of North Carolina Press, 2006), 33–101. See also David Brion Davis, *The Problem of Slavery in the Age of Revolution, 1770–1823* (Ithaca, NY: Cornell University Press, 1975).

58. Christopher Leslie Brown, "Empire without Slaves: British Concepts of Emancipation in the Age of the American Revolution," *William and Mary Quarterly* 56 (April 1999): 280.

59. Sharp became involved in imperial matters through his defense of enslaved blacks in Britain. See Simon Schama, *Rough Crossings: Britain, the Slaves, and the American Revolution* (New York: Ecco, 2006), 21–57.

60. Brown, "Empire without Slaves," 286–91.

## Portrait Two

1. L. Virgina Gould, "Urban Slavery-Urban Freedom: The Manumission of Jacqueline Lemelle," in *More than Chattel: Black Women and Slavery in the Americas*, ed. David Barry Gaspar and Darlene Clark Hine (Bloomington: Indiana University Press, 1996), 298–314.

2. Júnia Ferreira Furtado, *Chica da Silva: A Brazilian Slave in the Eighteenth Century* (New York: Cambridge University Press, 2009), 131–32.

3. Furtado, *Chica da Silva*, 111.

## Chapter Three

1. My account of the events in Puerto Rico comes from the documents collected in "Intento de sublevación, 6 de mayo de 1812," in Centro de Investigaciónes Históricas, *El proceso abolicionista en Puerto Rico: Documentos para su estudio*, vol. 1, *La institución de la esclavitud y su crisis, 1823–1873* (San Juan: Instituto de Cultura Puertorriqueña, 1974), 115–32.

2. "Intento de sublevación," 125–26.

3. "Intento de sublevación," 126.

4. "Intento de sublevación," 117.

5. See Guillermo A. Baralt, *Esclavos rebeldes: Conspiraciónes y sublevaciónes de esclavos en Puerto Rico (1795–1873)*, 3rd ed. (Río Piedras, Puerto Rico: Ediciones Huracán, 1989), 27–28.

6. This discussion draws upon Benjamin Quarles, *The Negro in the American Revolution* (1961; Chapel Hill: University of North Carolina Press, 1996); Ira Berlin and Ronald Hoffman, eds., *Slavery and Freedom in the Age of the American Revolution* (Charlottesville: University Press of Virginia, 1983); and Davis, *Problem of Slavery*.

7. Quoted in Quarles, *Negro in the American Revolution*, 19.

8. Quarles, *Negro in the American Revolution*, 28.

9. See Allan J. Kuethe, *Cuba, 1753–1815: Crown, Military, and Society* (Knoxville: University of Tennessee Press, 1986), 78–112; Leví Marrero, *Cuba: Economía y sociedad*, vol. 13 (Madrid: Editorial Playor, 1986), 134–42; and Garrigus, *Before Haiti*, 205–10.

10. See the essays by Philip D. Morgan and Allan Kulikoff in Berlin and Hoffman, *Slavery and Freedom*.

11. Quoted in Brown, *Moral Capital*, 362.

12. James Ramsay, "Examination of The Rev. Mr. Harris's Scriptural Researches on the Licitness of the Slave Trade" (1788), in *The Slave Trade Debate: Contemporary Writings For and Against* (Oxford, UK: Bodleian Library, 2007), 249.

13. James Ramsay, "An Inquiry into the Effects of Putting a Stop to the African Slave Trade, and of Granting Liberty to the Slaves in the British Sugar Colonies," (1784), in *Slave Trade Debate*, 46.

14. Eric Williams, *Capitalism and Slavery* (Chapel Hill: University of North Carolina Press, 1944); Seymour Drescher, *Econocide: British Slavery in the Era of Abolition* (Pittsburgh, PA: University of Pittsburgh Press, 1977). See also the critique of Williams and Drescher in Dale Tomich, "Spaces of Slavery, Times of Freedom: Rethinking Caribbean History in World Perspective," *Comparative Studies of South Asia, Africa, and the Middle East* 17 (1997): 67–80.

15. Quoted in Adam Hochschild, *Bury the Chains: Prophets and Rebels in the Fight to Free an Empire's Slaves* (Boston: Houghton Mifflin, 2005), 50. See also Schama, *Rough Crossings*, 44–57.

16. Equiano identified himself in his work as "Olaudah Equiano, or Gustavus Vassa, the African." Until recently historians, including Vincent Carretta, accepted his claim of African birth, his recounting of his capture and enslavement in Africa, and his description of the Middle Passage. However, Carretta has raised questions about Equiano's origins because of documentary evidence he uncovered: baptismal and naval records that indicate South Carolina as Equiano's birthplace. See his book *Equiano, the African: Biography of a Self-Made Man* (Athens: University of Georgia Press, 2005). Carretta has debated this question with Paul Lovejoy. Lovejoy defends the accuracy of Equiano's claims by inferring his Igbo identity and worldview, while Carretta concludes that, short of new evidence, historians cannot decide if he was African- or American-born. See Paul Lovejoy, "Autobiography and Memory: Gustavus Vassa, alias Olaudah Equiano, the African," *Slavery and Abolition* 27 (December 2006): 317–47; Vincent Carretta, "Response to Paul Lovejoy's 'Autobiography and Memory: Gustavus Vassa, alias Olaudah Equiano, the African,'" *Slavery and Abolition* 28 (April 2007): 115–19; and Lovejoy, "Issues of Motivation—Vassa/Equiano and Carretta's Critique of the Evidence," *Slavery and Abolition* 28 (April 2007): 121–25. See also Hochschild, "Where Was Equiano Born?" in *Bury the Chains*, 369–72. The question, and relevance, of Equiano's origins is also taken up in James Sweet, "Olaudah Equiano,

Domingos Álvares, and the Methodological Challenges of Studying the African Diaspora," *American Historical Review* 114 (April 2009): 279–306.

17. Olaudah Equiano, "The Interesting Narrative of the Life of Olaudah Equiano, or Gustavus Vassa, the African. Written by Himself," (1789), in *The Interesting Narrative and Other Writings*, ed. and intro. Vincent Carretta (New York: Penguin, 1995), 62–63.

18. Equiano, "Interesting Narrative," 235.

19. On the travails of the Sierra Leone endeavor, see Schama, *Rough Crossings*.

20. On British mobilization and the politics and ideology of abolitionism, see Davis, *Problem of Slavery*; Seymour Drescher, *Capitalism and Antislavery: British Mobilization in Comparative Perspective* (New York: Oxford University Press, 1987); Drescher, *The Mighty Experiment: Free Labor versus Slavery in British Emancipation* (New York: Oxford University Press, 2002); and Howard Temperley, *British Antislavery, 1833–1870* (London: Longman, 1972). On British efforts against the major slavers in Portugal, Spain, Brazil, and Cuba, see Leslie Bethell, *The Abolition of the Brazilian Slave Trade: Britain, Brazil, and the Slave Trade Question, 1807–1869* (Cambridge: Cambridge University Press, 1970); Murray, *Odious Commerce*; and João Pedro Marques, *The Sounds of Silence: Nineteenth-Century Portugal and the Abolition of the Slave Trade*, trans. Richard Wall (New York: Berghan Books, 2006).

21. See David Patrick Geggus, ed., *The Impact of the Haitian Revolution in the Atlantic World* (Columbia: University of South Carolina Press, 2001); and Dale Tomich, *Through the Prism of Slavery: Labor, Capital, and World Economy* (Lanham, MD: Rowman and Littlefield, 2004).

22. This discussion of the Haitian Revolution relies on C. L. R. James, *The Black Jacobins: Toussaint L'Ouverture and the San Domingo Revolution*, 2nd ed. (New York: Vintage, 1963); Robin Blackburn, *The Overthrow of Colonial Slavery, 1776–1848* (London: Verso, 1988), 161–264; Fick, *Making of Haiti*; David Patrick Geggus, *Haitian Revolutionary Studies* (Bloomington: Indiana University Press, 2002); Dubois, *Avengers of the New World*; and Miranda Frances Spieler, "The Legal Structure of Colonial Rule during the French Revolution," *William and Mary Quarterly*, 3rd ser., 66 (April 2009): 365–408.

23. See Drescher's comparison of antislavery movements in *Capitalism and Antislavery*, 52–57.

24. John D. Garrigus, "Thy Coming Fame, Ogé! Is Sure: New Evidence on Ogé's 1790 Revolt and the Beginnings of the Haitian Revolution," in *Assumed Identities: The Meanings of Race in the Atlantic World*, ed. John D. Garrigus and Christopher Morris (College Station: Texas A&M University Press, 2010), 19–45; and Garrigus, *Before Haiti*, 195–263.

25. Geggus, "The 'Swiss' and the Problem of Slave/Free Colored Cooperation," in *Haitian Revolutionary Studies*, 99–118.

26. Quoted in John K. Thornton, "'I am the Subject of the King of Congo': African Political Ideology and the Haitian Revolution," *Journal of World History* 4 (Fall 1993): 181.

27. The new nation was initially divided. In the north, home to the great sugar estates, the rulers Dessalines and Christophe tried to maintain Toussaint's system on the plantations. In the south, the free-colored rulers Alexandre Pétion and Jean-Pierre Boyer divided lands among the free population, creating a large peasantry. During a period of political turmoil in the north, the southerners invaded and instituted a system similar to theirs while unifying the country. Under Boyer, Haiti also invaded Santo Domingo in 1822, suppressing slavery and again dividing lands, though this latter measure eventually provoked widespread resistance to Haitian rule, which brought about the end of the occupation in 1844. On the Spanish and French ends of the island during the revolution and after Haitian independence, see Wendell G. Schaeffer, "The Delayed Cession of Spanish Santo Domingo to France, 1795–1801," *Hispanic American Historical Review* 29 (February 1949): 46–68; and Frank Moya Pons, "The Land Question in Haiti and Santo Domingo: The Sociopolitical Context of the Transition from Slavery to Free Labor, 1801–1843," in *Between Slavery and Free Labor: The Spanish-Speaking Caribbean in the Nineteenth Century*, ed. Manuel Moreno Fraginals, Frank Moya Pons, and Stanley L. Engerman (Baltimore, MD: Johns Hopkins University Press, 1985), 181–214.

28. There is a huge literature on this topic. On the independence movements in Latin America, see John Lynch, *The Spanish American Revolutions, 1808–1826* (New York: Norton, 1973); and John Charles Chasteen, *Americanos: Latin America's Struggle for Independence* (New York: Oxford University Press, 2008). On resistance and collaboration in Spain and Portugal, see Charles Esdaile, *The Peninsular War: A New History* (New York: Palgrave Macmillan, 2003).

29. Important overviews of slavery and the Spanish American revolutions are Andrews, *Afro-Latin America*, chaps. 1–3; and Peter Blanchard, *Under the Flags of Freedom: Slave Soldiers and the Wars of Independence in Spanish South America* (Pittsburgh, PA: University of Pittsburgh Press, 2008).

30. John Lynch, *Simón Bolívar: A Life* (New Haven, CT: Yale University Press, 2006), 41–64.

31. Bolívar quoted in Peter Blanchard, "The Language of Liberation: Slave Voices in the Wars of Independence," *Hispanic American Historical Review* 82 (2002): 514.

32. Quoted in Lynch, *Simón Bolívar*, 108.

33. Twinam, "Pedro de Ayarza," 194–210. See also Jordana Dym, *From Sovereign Villages to National States: City, State, and Federation in Central America, 1759–1839* (Albuquerque: University of New Mexico Press, 2006), 91–92, 116–20; 135–38. Even in politically stable Central America, municipal governments that professed loyalty to Spain during the French occupation incorporated free people of color into local governance, showing the significant divergence between Spain and the American colonies.

34. James F. King, "A Royalist View of the Colored Castes in the Venezuelan War of Independence," *Hispanic American Historical Review* 33 (November 1953): 537.

35. See Blanchard, *Under the Flags of Freedom*, 1–2, 141, 151.

36. James Ferguson King, "The Latin-American Republics and the Suppression of the Slave Trade," *Hispanic American Historical Review* 24 (August 1944): 391.

37. Camilla Townsend, *Tales of Two Cities: Race and Economic Culture in Early Republican North and South America: Guayaquil, Ecuador, and Baltimore, Maryland* (Austin: University of Texas Press, 2000), 191; and Townsend, "In Search of Liberty: The Efforts of the Enslaved to Attain Abolition in Ecuador, 1822–1852," in *Beyond Slavery: The Multilayered Legacy of Africans in Latin America and the Caribbean*, ed. Darién Davis (Lanham, MD: Rowman and Littlefield, 2007), 38.

38. Manuel María Alaix quoted in James E. Sanders, *Contentious Republicans: Popular Politics, Race, and Class in Nineteenth-Century Colombia* (Durham, NC: Duke University Press, 2004), 76. Other studies of abolition in postindependence Spanish America include John V. Lombardi, *The Decline and Abolition of Negro Slavery in Venezuela, 1820–1854* (Westport, CT: Greenwood, 1971); George Reid Andrews, *The Afro-Argentines of Buenos Aires, 1800–1900* (Madison: University of Wisconsin Press, 1980); Peter Blanchard, *Slavery and Abolition in Early Republican Peru* (Wilmington, DE: Scholarly Resources, 1992); Carlos Aguirre, *Agentes de su propia libertad: Los esclavos de Lima y la desintegrción de la esclavitud, 1821–1854* (Lima: Pontífica Universidad Católica del Perú, 1993); Christine Hünefeldt, *Paying the Price of Freedom: Family and Labor among Lima's Slaves, 1800–1854* (Berkeley: University of California Press, 1994); Guillermo Feliú Cruz, *La abolición de la esclavitud en Chile*, 2nd ed. (Santiago de Chile: Editorial Universitaria, 1973); Jerry W. Cooney, "Abolition in the Republic of Paraguay: 1840–1870," *Jarbuch für Geschichte von Staat, Wirtschaft und Geselischaft Lateinamerikas* 11 (1974): 149–66; Alberto R. Crespo, *Esclavos negros en Bolivia* (La Paz: Academia Nacional de Ciencias, 1977); and Dennis N. Valdés, "The Decline of Slavery in Mexico," *The Americas* 44 (October 1987): 167–94. On Uruguay, Nelson Martínez Díaz, "La resistencia a la abolición en los países del Río de la Plata," in *Esclavitud y derechos humanos: La lucha por la libertad del negro en el siglo XIX*, ed. Francisco de Solano and Agustín Guimerá (Madrid: Consejo Superior de Investigaciónes Científicas, 1990), 625–34; and O. Nigel Bolland, "Colonialism and Slavery in Central America," *Slavery and Abolition* 15 (August 1994): 11–25. See also the references in note 37.

39. Marixa Lasso, *Myths of Harmony: Race and Republicanism during the Age of Revolution, Colombia, 1795–1831* (Pittsburgh, PA: University of Pittsburgh Press, 2007).

40. Alejandro von Humboldt, *Ensayo político sobre la isla de Cuba* (Madrid: Ediciones Doce Calles / Junta de Castilla y León, 1998), 305–6.

41. Lasso, *Myths of Harmony*, 156–58.

## Portrait Three

1. Quoted in Lynch, *Simón Bolívar*, 107.
2. Padilla quoted in Helg, *Liberty and Equality*, 195 (emphasis in original).
3. Bolívar quoted in Helg, *Liberty and Equality*, 196.
4. Bolívar quoted in Helg, *Liberty and Equality*, 209.

## Chapter Four

1. *The Biography of Mahommah Gardo Baquaqua: His Passage from Slavery to Freedom in Africa and America*, ed. Robin Law and Paul Lovejoy (1854; Princeton, NJ: Markus Wiener, 2007), 151–52. Baquaqua's is one of the very few slave narratives of Latin America, though it was written in North America with assistance. From Brazil there is the brief sketch by Luiz Gama in Roberto Schwarz, "Autobiografía de Luiz Gama," *Novos Estudos*, no. 25 (October 1989): 136–41, penned as a letter to a friend in 1880. Two others are from Cuba: Juan Francisco Manzano, *Autobiography of a Slave / Autobiografía de un esclavo*, trans. Evelyn Picon Garfield (Detroit, MI: Wayne State University Press, 1996) (originally published as an English translation in 1840; the original Spanish edition would not appear until the twentieth century); and Miguel Barnet, *Biography of a Runaway Slave*, trans. W. Nick Hill (Willimantic, CT: Curbstone Press, 1994), the story of Esteban Montejo as narrated by the Cuban anthropologist and novelist Miguel Barnet, who interviewed the ancient Montejo in the 1960s. For an incisive study of Afro-Latin American writing during the era of slavery and abolition, see William G. Acree Jr., "Jacinto Ventura de Molina: A Black *Letrado* in a White World of Letters, 1766–1841," *Latin American Research Review* 44, no. 2 (2009): 37–58. Scholars have sought out other genres of black writing and narrative during the era of Latin American slavery. See Kathryn Joy McKnight and Leo J. Garofalo, eds., *Afro-Latino Voices: Narratives from the Early Modern Ibero-Atlantic World, 1550–1812* (Indianapolis: Hackett, 2009).
2. *Biography of Baquaqua*, 158, 159.
3. Estimates Database, 2009, *Voyages: The Trans-Atlantic Slave Trade Database*, http://www.slavevoyages.org, accessed January 12, 2011.
4. Zephyr Frank, *Dutra's World: Wealth and Family in Nineteenth-Century Rio de Janeiro* (Albuquerque: University of New Mexico Press, 2004). See also B. J. Barickman, *A Bahian Counterpoint: Sugar, Tobacco, Cassava, and Slavery in the Recôncavo, 1780–1860* (Stanford, CA: Stanford University Press, 1998).
5. See Robin Law and Paul Lovejoy, "Introduction: The Interesting Narrative of Mahommah Gardo Baquaqua," in *Biography of Baquaqua*, 1–84.
6. Blackburn, *Overthrow of Colonial Slavery*; Berlin, *Generations of Captivity*; and Tomich, *Through the Prism of Slavery*.

7. For cogent summaries, see Dale Tomich, "The 'Second Slavery': Bonded Labor and the Transformation of the Nineteenth-Century World Economy" and "World Slavery and Caribbean Capitalism: The Cuban Sugar Industry, 1760–1868," in *Through the Prism of Slavery*, 56–71, 75–94; and Rafael de Bivar Marquese, *Feitores do corpo, missionários da mente: Senhores, letrados e o controle dos escravos nas Américas, 1660–1860* (São Paulo: Companhia das Letras, 2004). The cotton plantations of the Deep South in the United States were similarly characterized by their voracious need for enslaved labor and the new scale of cultivation and export. See Berlin, *Generations of Captivity*, 161–244; and Walter Johnson, *Soul by Soul: Life inside the Antebellum Slave Market* (Cambridge, MA: Harvard University Press, 1999).

8. Murray, *Odious Commerce*, 298.

9. Thomas Clarkson, *The Cries of Africa to the Inhabitants of Europe: or, A Survey of the Bloody Commerce Called the Slave-Trade* (London: Harvey and Darton, 1822), iv (emphasis in the original).

10. Josep M. Fradera, "La participació catalana en le tràfic d'esclaus (1789–1845)," *Recerques* no. 16 (1984): 124.

11. The Scotsman Mungo Park traveled in West Africa in the 1790s at the behest of Britain's African Association in search of the Niger River's source. His published account of his travels included vivid descriptions of slaving and warfare. Though Park himself was reserved on the question of slave-trade abolition, British abolitionists eagerly read and cited his work for its descriptions of the traffic in captives in Africa and the depredations of European and African slavers.

12. José María Blanco White, *Bosquejo del comercio de esclavos*, ed. and intro. Manuel Moreno Alonso (1814; Seville, Spain: Ediciones Alfar, 1999), 195–96 (emphasis in the original).

13. Cogently discussed in Alejandro de la Fuente, "Slaves and the Creation of Legal Rights in Cuba: *Coartación* and *Papel*," *Hispanic American Historical Review* 87 (November 2007): 659–92.

14. This discussion draws upon Matt Childs, *The 1812 Aponte Rebellion in Cuba and the Struggle against Atlantic Slavery* (Chapel Hill: University of North Carolina Press, 2006).

15. Francisco Arango y Parreño, *Representación hecha a S. M. con motivo de la sublevación de esclavos en los dominios franceses de la isla de Santo Domingo* (1791), quoted in Tomich, "Wealth of Empire," 74.

16. Francisco Arango y Parreño, *Representación de la ciudad de la Habana a las Cortes* (1811), quoted in Tomich, "Wealth of Empire," 73.

17. Juan Bernardo O'Gavan, *Observaciónes sobre la suerte de los negros del África, considerados en su propia patria, y trasplantados a las Antillas Españolas: Y reclamación contra el tratado celebrado on los ingleses el año 1817* (Madrid: Imprenta del Universal, 1821), 4 (emphasis in the original).

18. O'Gavan, *Observaciónes*, 7 (emphasis in the original).

19. Scarano, *Sugar and Slavery*; and Moreno Fraginals, *The Sugarmill*. On Spanish immigrants in the Cuban plantation complex, see Angel Bahamonde and José Cayuela, *Hacer las Américas: Las elites coloniales españolas en el siglo XIX* (Madrid: Alianza, 1992). On immigration to Puerto Rico, in addition to Scarano, see Astrid Cubano-Iguina, *El hilo en el laberinto: Claves de la lucha política en Puerto Rico (siglo XIX)* (Río Piedras, Puerto Rico: Ediciones Huracán, 1990).

20. Josep M. Fradera, *Gobernar colonias* (Barcelona, Spain: Ediciones Península, 1999); Christopher Schmidt-Nowara, *Empire and Antislavery: Spain, Cuba, and Puerto Rico, 1833–1874* (Pittsburgh, PA: University of Pittsburgh Press, 1999), 1–50; Sibylle Fischer, *Modernity Disavowed: Haiti and the Cultures of Slavery in the Age of Revolution* (Durham, NC: Duke University Press, 2004); and Ma. Dolores González-Ripoll et al., *El rumor de Haití en Cuba: Temor y rebeldía, 1789–1844* (Madrid: C.S.I.C., 2005).

21. Murray, *Odious Commerce*; Robert L. Paquette, *Sugar Is Made with Blood: The Conspiracy of La Escalera and the Conflict between Empires over Slavery in Cuba* (Middletown, CT: Wesleyan University Press, 1988); and Joseph Dorsey, *Slave Traffic in the Age of Abolition: Puerto Rico, West Africa, and the Non-Hispanic Caribbean, 1815–1859* (Gainesville: University Press of Florida, 2003).

22. In Spain in the 1850s, numerous translations of the U.S. antislavery novel *Uncle Tom's Cabin* were in circulation, as were adaptations for the stage. Their presence indicated considerable anxiety over British efforts to suppress the slave traffic to Cuba. See Lisa Surwillo, "Representing the Slave Trader: *Haley* and the Slave Ship; or, Spain's *Uncle Tom's Cabin*," *PMLA* 120 (2005): 768–82.

23. Consulado de S.M. Cátolica en Jamaica, Kingston, May 22, 1837, in Archivo Histórico Nacional (Madrid)/Estado, legajo 8036, expediente 1, number 23.

24. Count of Villanueva quoted in Manuel Barcia Paz, *Seeds of Insurrection: Domination and Resistance on Western Cuban Plantations, 1808–1848* (Baton Rouge: Louisiana State University Press, 2008), 81.

25. On La Escalera, see Paquette, *Sugar Is Made with Blood*, and Barcia Paz's typology of rebellions in nineteenth-century Cuba in *Seeds of Insurrection*, 25–48.

26. Josep Maria Fradera, *Colonias para después de un imperio* (Barcelona, Spain: Edicions Bellaterra, 2005), 326.

27. Mary C. Karasch, *Slave Life in Rio de Janeiro, 1808–1850* (Princeton, NJ: Princeton University Press, 1987), 62 (on total population), 11–28 (on African origins), 8 (on Africans as percentage of enslaved population).

28. On de Souza and Ouidah, see Robin Law, "The Evolution of the Brazilian Community in Ouidah," *Slavery and Abolition* 22 (April 2001): 3–21; and Alberto de Costa e Silva, *Francisco Félix de Souza, Mercador de Escravos* (Rio de Janeiro, Brazil: Editora Nova Frontera, 2004). On Rufino, see João José Reis, Flávio dos Santos Gomes, and Marcus J. M. de Carvalho, "África e Brasil entre margens: Aventuras e desaventuras do africano Rufino José Maria, c. 1822–1853," *Estudos Afro-Asiáticos* 26 (May–August 2004): 257–302.

29. Stanley J. Stein, *Vassouras, a Brazilian Coffee County, 1850–1900: The Roles of Planter and Slave in a Plantation Society* (1957; Princeton, NJ: Princeton University Press, 1985), 53. See also Laird Bergad, *The Comparative Histories of Slavery in Brazil, Cuba, and the United States* (Cambridge: Cambridge University Press, 2007), 157–64.

30. Ilmar Rolhoff de Mattos, *O tempo Saquarema* (São Paulo: Editora Hucitec, 1987); José Murilo de Carvalho, *Teatro de sombras: A política imperial* (São Paulo: Ediçoes Vértice, 1988); and João José Reis, *Slave Rebellion in Brazil: The Muslim Uprising of 1835 in Bahia*, trans. Arthur Brakel (Baltimore, MD: Johns Hopkins University Press, 1993).

31. Bethell, *Abolition of the Brazilian Slave Trade*. For a recent assessment of the factors leading to the trade's suppression, see Jaime Rodrigues, *O infame comércio: Propostas e experiências no final do tráfico de africanos para o Brasil, 1800–1850* (Campinas, Brazil: Editora da UNICAMP, 2000). See also the assessment of the political situation in Murilo de Carvalho, *Teatro de sombras*.

32. Stein, *Vassouras*; and Emília Viotti da Costa, *Da senzala à colônia*, 4th ed. (São Paulo: Editora UNESP, 1997).

33. Frank, *Dutra's World*, 41.

34. For an excellent evocation of these tensions, see Childs, *1812 Aponte Rebellion*.

35. Fradera, *Gobernar colonias*; Jaime Rodríguez O., *The Independence of Spanish America* (Cambridge: Cambridge University Press, 1998); Herzog, *Defining Nations*; and Christopher Schmidt-Nowara, *The Conquest of History: Spanish Colonialism and National Histories in the Nineteenth Century* (Pittsburgh, PA: University of Pittsburgh Press, 2006), 15–52.

36. The following discussion relies on Rafael de Bivar Marquese and Márcia Regina Berbel, "The Absence of Race: Slavery, Citizenship, and Pro-slavery Ideology in the Cortes of Lisbon and in the Rio de Janeiro Constituent Assembly (1821–1824)," *Social History* 32 (November 2007): 415–33; Márcia Berbel, Rafael Marquese, and Tâmis Parron, *Escravidão e política: Brasil e Cuba, 1790–1850* (São Paulo: Editora Hucitec, 2010), chap. 2; João Paulo G. Pimenta, *Brasil y las independencias de Hispanoamérica*, trans. Víctor y Pablo García Guerrero (Castellón de la Plana, Spain: Publicacions de la Universitat Jaume I, 2007); and Jeremy Adelman, *Sovereignty and Revolution in the Iberian Atlantic* (Princeton, NJ: Princeton University Press, 2006), chap. 6.

37. Marquese and Berbel, "Absence of Race." On manumission and its function, see also Stuart B. Schwartz, "Sugar Plantation and Slave Life," in *Slaves, Peasants, and Rebels: Reconsidering Brazilian Slavery* (Urbana: University of Illinois Press, 1992), 39–63; Marquese, "Dinâmica da escravidão no Brasil." On the limits of citizenship under the Brazilian monarchy, see Richard Graham, *Politics and Patronage in Nineteenth-Century Brazil* (Stanford, CA: Stanford University Press, 1990).

   Another question that warrants closer study is the role of colonial jurisprudence in shaping the nineteenth-century constitutional regimes.

Tamar Herzog shows that under the Spanish monarchy, Africans and African-descended people were legally classified as foreigners resident in Spanish domains, a measure that shaped metropolitan attitudes under constitutional rule. Were Portuguese and Brazilian attitudes different because of Portuguese rule in Angola and other parts of Africa? Did Africans and African-descended people within the Portuguese domains enjoy the same legal status as other groups? See Herzog, *Defining Nations*; and Herzog, "Communities Becoming a Nation: Spain and Spanish America in the Wake of Modernity (and Thereafter)," *Citizenship Studies* 11 (May 2007): 151–72.

38. Arthur F. Corwin, *Spain and the Abolition of Slavery in Cuba, 1817–1886* (Austin: University of Texas Press, 1967); and Schmidt-Nowara, *Empire and Antislavery*, 100–125.

39. Karen Robert, "Slavery and Freedom in the Ten Years' War, Cuba, 1868–1878," *Slavery and Abolition* 13 (December 1992): 181–200; and Ada Ferrer, *Insurgent Cuba: Race, Nation, and Revolution, 1868–1898* (Chapel Hill: University of North Carolina Press, 1999).

40. Scott, *Slave Emancipation in Cuba*, 63–83.

41. Schmidt-Nowara, *Empire and Antislavery*, 153.

42. Laird Bergad, *Cuban Rural Society in the Nineteenth Century: The Social and Economic History of Monoculture in Matanzas* (Princeton, NJ: Princeton University Press, 1990); and Astrid Cubano-Iguina, "Freedom in the Making: The Slaves of Hacienda La Esperanza, Manatí, Puerto Rico, on the Eve of Abolition, 1868–1876," *Social History* (forthcoming), cited by permission of the author.

43. Shown with exquisite detail in Cubano-Iguina, "Freedom in the Making."

44. Scott, *Slave Emancipation in Cuba*, 141.

45. See Scott, *Slave Emancipation in Cuba*, 148, 159–60.

46. See the summary of the debate over the impact of the Paraguayan War on Brazilian slavery in Kraay, "Arming Slaves in Brazil," 167–70. Kraay himself sees limited consequences beyond those slaves who actually became free through service.

47. Murilo de Carvalho, *Teatro de sombras*, 50–83. See also Roderick J. Barman, *Citizen Emperor: Pedro II and the Making of Brazil, 1825–1891* (Stanford, CA: Stanford University Press, 1999), 193–274; and Jeffrey Needell, *The Party of Order: The Conservatives, the State, and Slavery in the Brazilian Monarchy, 1831–1871* (Stanford, CA: Stanford University Press, 2006).

48. Celso Castilho, "Brisas atlánticas: La abolición gradual y la conexión brasileña-cubana," in *Haití: Revolución, independencia y emancipación*, ed. Rina Cáceres and Paul Lovejoy (San José, Costa Rica: Editorial UCR, 2008), 128–39. See also, for example, the report on the effects of the Moret Law in Cuba dated Madrid, September 25, 1875, Biblioteca Itamaraty, Madri, Oficios 1875–1880, 220/1/15.

49. Sidney Chalhoub, "The Politics of Silence: Race and Citizenship in Nineteenth-Century Brazil," *Slavery and Abolition* 27 (April 2006): 81. See also Stein, *Vassouras*; and Viotti da Costa, *Da senzala à colônia*, on coffee planters and abolition.

50. "'We Are Seeking Our Country's Highest Interests': An Abolitionist Analyzes Slavery and Calls for a Break with the Past (1883)," in Conrad, *Children of God's Fire*, 452. This passage is excerpted from Nabuco's book *O abolicionismo*, available in an English translation: *Abolitionism: The Brazilian Antislavery Struggle*, trans. and ed. Robert Edgar Conrad (Urbana: University of Illinois Press, 1977). For more on Nabuco, see Angela Alonso, "O abolicionista cosmopolita: Joaquim Nabuco e a rede abolicionista transnacional," *Novos Estudos* no. 88 (November 2010): 55–70.

51. See the memoirs of the abolitionist Antonio Manuel Bueno de Andrada, "A abolição em São Paulo. Depoimento de uma testemunha," *O Estado de São Paulo*, May 13, 1918. His mother directed the Emancipadora in cooperation with the Liberal Party. As a student in the Escola Polytechnica in Rio de Janeiro, he moved in abolitionist circles among students and faculty, including the director, Rio Branco, maestro of the 1871 law. For an overview of the many abolitionist initiatives, see Robert Edgar Conrad, *The Destruction of Brazilian Slavery, 1850–1888* (Berkeley: University of California Press, 1972). See also Seymour Drescher, "Brazilian Abolition in Comparative Perspective," *Hispanic American Historical Review* 68 (August 1988): 429–60. On emancipation funds, see Celso T. Castilho and Camilla Cowling, "Funding Freedom, Popularizing Politics: Abolitionism and Local Emancipation Funds in 1880s Brazil," *Luso-Brazilian Review* 47, no. 1 (2010): 89–120.

52. For a close study of race and labor after emancipation, see George Reid Andrews, *Blacks and Whites in São Paulo, Brazil, 1888–1988* (Madison: University of Wisconsin Press, 1991). For data on immigration to São Paulo, see Thomas H. Holloway, *Immigrants on the Land: Coffee and Society in São Paulo, 1886–1934* (Chapel Hill: University of North Carolina Press, 1980). On mass migration to Latin America in the late nineteenth and early twentieth centuries in broader perspective, see José Moya, "Modernization, Modernity, and the Trans/formation of the Atlantic World in the Nineteenth Century," in Cañizares-Esguerra and Seeman, *Atlantic in Global History*, 179–97. On Cuba, see Jordi Maluquer de Motes, *Nación e inmigración: los españoles en Cuba (ss. XIX y XX)* (Oviedo, Spain: Ediciones Jucar, 1992).

53. Conrad, *Destruction of Brazilian Slavery*, 239–77; Robert Brent Toplin, "Upheaval, Violence, and the Abolition of Slavery in Brazil: The Case of São Paulo," *Hispanic American Historical Review* 49 (November 1969): 639–55; Maria Helena Machado, *O plano e o pânico: Os movimientos sociais na década da abolição* (Rio de Janeiro, Brazil: Editora UFRJ; São Paulo: EDUSP, 1994), 143–73; and Eduardo Silva, "Black Abolitionist in the *Quilombo* of Leblon, Rio de Janeiro: Symbols, Organizers, and Revolutionaries," in Davis, *Beyond Slavery*, 109–22.

54. See Ferrer, *Insurgent Cuba;* and Rebecca J. Scott, *Degrees of Freedom: Louisiana and Cuba after Slavery* (Cambridge, MA: Harvard University Press, 2005).

55. Emília Viotti da Costa, "1870–1889," in Bethell, *Brazil,* 161–213.

56. Juan Gualberto Gómez, "Crónica política," *Revista Cubana* (Havana), October 31, 1892, quoted in Schmidt-Nowara, *Conquest of History,* 86.

## Portrait Four

1. Schmidt-Nowara, *Empire and Antislavery,* 151.

2. Schmidt-Nowara, *Empire and Antislavery,* 139.

3. Conrad, *Destruction of Brazilian Slavery,* 179. See also Edmar Morel, *Dragão do Mar: O jangadeiro de abolição* (Rio de Janeiro, Brazil: Edições do Povo, 1949); and Raimundo Girão, *A abolição no Ceará* (Fortaleza, Brazil: A. Batista Fontenele, 1956).

## Conclusion

1. Stein, *Vassouras,* 289.

2. Rafael de Bivar Marquese, "African Diaspora, Slavery, and the Paraiba Valley Coffee Plantation Landscape: Nineteenth-Century Brazil," *Review: A Journal of the Fernand Braudel Center* 31, no. 2 (2008): 195–216; Stein, *Vassouras,* 207. See also the recent study, including a CD, of the jongos Stein recorded: Silvia Hunold Lara and Gustavo Pacheco, eds., *Memória do jongo: As gravações históricas de Stanley J. Stein, Vassouras, 1949* (Rio de Janeiro, Brazil: Folha Seca; Campinas, Brazil: CECULT, 2007).

3. Christian, *Local Religion;* and Stuart Schwartz, *All Can Be Saved: Religious Tolerance and Salvation in the Iberian Atlantic World* (New Haven, CT: Yale University Press, 2008).

4. Andrews, *Afro-Latin America;* and Scott, *Degrees of Freedom.*

# Glossary

(sp) = Spanish
(port) = Portuguese

**aldeias** (port): Indian settlements under clerical control.

**asiento** (sp): Exclusive contract to provide slaves to the Spanish colonies, generally conceded to foreign traders.

**bandeirantes** (port): Backwoodsmen, usually associated with São Paulo and the slave trade in Brazilian Indians.

**bozal** (sp): Slave brought to the Americas from Africa, not acculturated.

**cabildo de nación** (sp): Associations of enslaved Africans in Cuba. Organized according to ethnic groupings (nations).

**carta de alforria** (port): Certificate of freedom.

**casta** (sp): Person of mixed parentage, often associated with African lineage.

**coartación** (sp): Self-purchase.

**confraternity**: Lay religious association.

**converso** (sp): Convert from Judaism to Christianity.

**encomienda** (sp): Grant by which the holder, the *encomendero*, received tribute and labor from the subject population.

**feitoria** (port): Factory, trading post.

**indenture**: A service contract by which a servant is bound to a master for a specific term. Hence, indentured servitude.

**junta** (sp): Governing assembly.

**ladino** (sp): Hispanized slave or free person.

**manumission**: Formal release of the enslaved person from her/his servitude. Sometimes an unconditional grant of freedom, sometimes freedom with strings attached, whereby the manumitted person would still owe some services to the former master.

**Mineiro** (port): Of Minas Gerais.

**mita** (sp): A system of forced labor that the Spanish conquerors adapted from the Inca Empire in the Andes.

**moreno** (sp): Black.

**morisco** (sp): Convert from Islam to Christianity.

**pardo** (sp and port): Mulatto, person of mixed African and European lineage.

**peculium**: Slave's personal wealth.

**repartimiento** (sp): Forced distribution of indigenous workers in the Spanish colonies.

**senzala** (port): Slave barracks.

**tumbeiro** (port): A slave ship, literally "floating tomb."

# Further Reading

The notes in this book give ample evidence of the richness of the field. In several, I indicate important debates, which will offer the interested reader additional food for thought. These include the debate over the origins of African-American cultures; the significance of religion and the law in shaping Latin American slavery and freedom; the social, economic, and ideological causes of abolitionism; and the birthplace of Olaudah Equiano and its meaning for reading slave narratives. For newcomers to the study of Latin American slavery, I will also indicate some fundamental works, though this list is far from exhaustive.

For more background on Latin American history there are several excellent surveys, including Mark A. Burkholder and Lyman L. Johnson, *Colonial Latin America*, 7th ed. (New York: Oxford University Press, 2010); James Lockhart and Stuart B. Schwartz, *Early Latin America: A History of Colonial Spanish America and Brazil* (New York: Cambridge University Press, 1983); and John Charles Chasteen, *Born in Blood and Fire: A Concise History of Latin America*, 2nd ed. (New York: W. W. Norton, 2006).

On the transatlantic slave trade, see Philip D. Curtin, *The Atlantic*

*Slave Trade: A Census* (Madison: University of Wisconsin Press, 1969); Sylvaine A. Diouf, ed., *Fighting the Slave Trade: West African Strategies* (Athens: Ohio University Press, 2003); David Eltis and David Richardson, eds., *Extending the Frontiers: Essays on the New Transatlantic Slave Trade Database* (New Haven, CT: Yale University Press, 2008); David Eltis and David Richardson, *Atlas of the Transatlantic Slave Trade*, 2nd ed. (New Haven, CT: Yale University Press, 2010); and Herbert S. Klein, *The Atlantic Slave Trade*, 2nd ed. (New York: Cambridge University Press, 2010). Specifically on the slave trade, slave markets, and Latin America, see Colin A. Palmer, *Human Cargoes: The British Slave Trade to Spanish America, 1700–1739* (Urbana: University of Illinois Press, 1981); Joseph Calder Miller, *Way of Death: Merchant Capitalism and the Angolan Slave Trade, 1730–1830* (Madison: University of Wisconsin Press, 1988); Laird W. Bergad, Fe Iglesias García, and María del Carmen Barcia, *The Cuban Slave Market, 1790–1880* (New York: Cambridge University Press, 1995); Luiz Felipe de Alencastro, *O trato dos viventes: Formação do Brasil no Atlântico sul, séculos XVI e XVII* (São Paulo: Comphania das Letras, 2000); and Linda A. Newson and Susie Michin, *From Capture to Sale: The Portuguese Slave Trade to Spanish South America in the Early Seventeenth Century* (Leiden: Brill, 2007).

The Latin American plantations were the main destination for enslaved workers, but the construction of the plantation belt was halting, as we learn in Stuart B. Schwartz, ed., *Tropical Babylons: Sugar and the Making of the Atlantic World, 1450–1680* (Chapel Hill: University of North Carolina Press, 2004). For studies of major sugar plantation societies, see Schwartz, *Sugar Plantations in the Making of Brazilian Society: Bahia, 1550–1835* (New York: Cambridge University Press, 1985); Franklin Knight, *Slave Society in Cuba during the Nineteenth Century* (Madison: University of Wisconsin Press, 1970); Peter L. Eisenberg, *The Sugar Industry in Pernambuco: Modernization without Change, 1840–1910* (Berkeley: University of California Press, 1974); Manuel Moreno Fraginals, *The Sugarmill*, trans. Cedric Belfrage (New York: Monthly Review Press, 1976); Moreno Fraginals, *El ingenio*, 3 vols. (Barcelona, Spain: Editorial Crítica, 2001); and Laird W. Bergad, *Cuban Rural Society in the Nineteenth Century: The Social and Economic History of Monoculture in Matanzas* (Princeton, NJ: Princeton University Press, 1990). On the Brazilian coffee plantations, see Stanley J. Stein, *Vassouras, a Brazilian Coffee County, 1850–1900: The Roles of Planter and Slave in a Plantation Society* (1957; Princeton, NJ: Princeton

University Press, 1985); and Emilia Viotti da Costa, *Da senzala à colônia*, 4th ed. (São Paulo: Editora UNESP, 1997). To understand the resurgence of Latin American plantation slavery in the nineteenth century, see Dale Tomich, *Through the Prism of Slavery: Labor, Capital, and World Economy* (Lanham, MD: Rowman and Littlefield, 2004); and Márcia Berbel, Rafael Marquese, and Tâmis Parron, *Escravidão e política: Brasil e Cuba, 1790–1850* (São Paulo: Editora Hucitec, 2010).

Slavery existed beyond the plantation in cities, mines, households, and small farms throughout Latin America. Among the many works that address these places, see Frederick P. Bowser, *The African Slave in Colonial Peru, 1524–1650* (Stanford, CA: Stanford University Press, 1974); Colin A. Palmer, *Slaves of the White God: Blacks in Mexico, 1570–1650* (Cambridge, MA: Harvard University Press, 1976); Mary C. Karasch, *Slave Life in Rio de Janeiro, 1808–1850* (Princeton, NJ: Princeton University Press, 1987); B. J. Barickman, *A Bahian Counterpoint: Sugar, Tobacco, Cassava, and Slavery in the Recôncavo, 1780–1860* (Stanford, CA: Stanford University Press, 1998); Kathleen J. Higgins, *"Licentious Liberty" in a Brazilian Gold-Mining Region: Slavery, Gender, and Social Control in Eighteenth-Century Sabará, Minas Gerais* (University Park: Pennsylvania State University Press, 1999); and Alejandro de la Fuente, César García del Pino, and Bernardo Iglesias Delgado, *Havana and the Atlantic in the Sixteenth Century* (Chapel Hill: University of North Carolina Press, 2008).

Efforts to gain freedom and to exercise it were constant and multifaceted in Latin American slave societies. Works that have explored these challenges include David W. Cohen and Jack P. Greene, eds., *Neither Slave nor Free: The Freedman of African Descent in the Slave Societies of the New World* (Baltimore, MD: Johns Hopkins University Press, 1972); João José Reis, *Slave Rebellion in Brazil: The Muslim Uprising of 1835 in Bahia*, trans. Arthur Brakel (Baltimore, MD: Johns Hopkins University Press, 1993); Jane Landers, *Black Society in Spanish Florida* (Urbana: University of Illinois Press, 1999); María Elena Díaz, *The Virgin, the King, and the Royal Slaves of El Cobre: Negotiating Freedom in Colonial Cuba, 1670–1780* (Stanford, CA: Stanford University Press, 2000); Ben Vinson III, *Bearing Arms for His Majesty: The Free-Colored Militia in Colonial Mexico* (Stanford, CA: Stanford University Press, 2001); Leslie B. Rout Jr., *The African Experience in Spanish America* (1976; Princeton, NJ: Markus Wiener, 2003); and Zephyr Frank, *Dutra's World: Wealth and Family in Nineteenth-Century Rio de Janeiro* (Albuquerque: University of New Mexico Press, 2004).

Changing racial identities and status in colonial societies, spurred in part by growing free populations, are discussed in the classic work by Magnus Mörner, *Race Mixture in the History of Latin America* (Boston: Little, Brown, 1967) and more recently in R. Douglas Cope, *The Limits of Racial Domination: Plebeian Society in Colonial Mexico City, 1660–1720* (Madison: University of Wisconsin Press, 1994); Ann Twinam, *Public Lives, Private Secrets: Gender, Honor, Sexuality, and Illegitimacy in Colonial Spanish America* (Stanford, CA: Stanford University Press, 1999); and Júnia Ferreira Furtado, *Chica da Silva: A Brazilian Slave of the Eighteenth Century* (New York: Cambridge University Press, 2009).

The age of revolution set the stage for attempts to destroy slavery altogether. Essential to understanding Latin America in the broader context of this period is Robin Blackburn, *The Overthrow of Colonial Slavery, 1776–1848* (London: Verso, 1988). For revolutionary Latin America, see George Reid Andrews, *Afro-Latin America, 1800–2000* (New York: Oxford University Press, 2004); and Peter Blanchard, *Under the Flags of Freedom: Slave Soldiers and the Wars of Independence in Spanish South America* (Pittsburgh, PA: University of Pittsburgh Press, 2008).

Planters held out against the revolutionary currents in the Spanish Caribbean and Brazil. On Puerto Rico, see Francisco Scarano, *Sugar and Slavery in Puerto Rico: The Plantation Economy of Ponce, 1800–1850* (Madison: University of Wisconsin Press, 1984); Christopher Schmidt-Nowara, *Empire and Antislavery: Spain, Cuba, and Puerto Rico, 1833–1874* (Pittsburgh, PA: University of Pittsburgh Press, 1999); and Luis Figueroa, *Sugar, Slavery, and Freedom in Nineteenth-Century Puerto Rico* (Chapel Hill: University of North Carolina Press, 2005). To understand the dismantling of slavery in the most recalcitrant slave societies, Brazil and Cuba, see Robert Brent Toplin, *The Abolition of Slavery in Brazil* (New York: Atheneum, 1971); Robert Edgar Conrad, *The Destruction of Brazilian Slavery, 1850–1888* (Berkeley: University of California Press, 1972); Rebecca J. Scott et al., *The Abolition of Slavery and the Aftermath of Emancipation in Brazil* (Durham, NC: Duke University Press, 1988); Maria Helena Machado, *O plano e o pânico: Os movimentos sociais na década da abolição* (Rio de Janeiro, Brazil: Editora UFRJ; São Paulo: EDUSP, 1994); Ada Ferrer, *Insurgent Cuba: Race, Nation, and Revolution, 1868–1898* (Chapel Hill: University of North Carolina Press, 1999); Rebecca J. Scott, *Slave Emancipation in Cuba: The Transition to Free Labor, 1860–1899* (Pittsburgh, PA: University of Pittsburgh Press, 2000); and Scott, *Degrees of Freedom: Louisiana and Cuba after Slavery* (Cambridge, MA: Harvard University Press, 2005).

# Index

Page numbers in italic text indicate illustrations, maps, or tables.

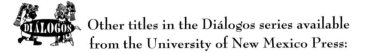 Other titles in the Diálogos series available
from the University of New Mexico Press:

# CAREERS WITHOUT BORDERS

*Careers without Borders* analyzes the challenges, debates and developments in global careers using a critical management perspective. Starting in the early nineties, the flow of information became more fluid, and, with this, managers and professionals started operating across borders, crossing different contexts in greater numbers than ever before.

In this edited collection, contributors from around the world examine how context, culture and social relations of power all impact on how professionals interact with new structural and ideological frameworks. Issues such as regulation and law, policies, history, identities and inequalities are explored. The book covers a wide range of countries, including USA, China, Brazil, and Hungary, offering strong theoretical analyses, as well as practical implications.

This book aims to help students and managers understand the career issues involved when they do business in other countries. It will appeal to students on human resource management or international business courses.

**Cristina Reis** is Associate Professor of Management and has been teaching in US and other European countries. Her research has been sponsored by the Portuguese Foundation for Science and Technology. She is also the recipient of an Academic Management Award and Emerald Award of Excellence.

**Yehuda Baruch** is a Professor of Management and Associate Dean for Research at Rouen Business School, France and Middlesex University, UK. His research interests and writing have been extensive and wide ranging, with particular focus on Careers and Global HRM, including over 100 refereed papers, including *JoM*, *HRM*, *OD*, *JVB*, *HuRel* and *OrgSt*, and over 30 books and book chapters. He is also former Editor of *Group & Organization Management* and *Career Development International*, and former Chair, Careers Division, Academy of Management.

# CAREERS WITHOUT BORDERS

## Critical Perspectives

*Cristina Reis and Yehuda Baruch*

NEW YORK AND LONDON

First published 2013
by Routledge
711 Third Avenue, New York, NY 10017

Simultaneously published in the UK
by Routledge
2 Park Square, Milton Park, Abingdon, Oxon OX14 4RN

*Routledge is an imprint of the Taylor & Francis Group, an informa business*

*Library of Congress Cataloging in Publication Data*
Careers without borders: critical perspectives/[edited by] Christina Reis &
    Yehuda Baruch.
    p. cm.
    Includes bibliographical references and index.
    1. International business enterprises—Employees. 2. Employment
    in foreign countries. 3. Career development. I. Reis, Christina.
    II. Baruch, Yehuda.
    HF5549.5.E45C337 2012
    331.702—dc23                                     2012014661

ISBN: 978–0–415–50116–3
ISBN: 978–0–415–50115–6
ISBN: 978–0–203–13326–2

Typeset in Bembo
by Florence Production Ltd, Stoodleigh, Devon


Printed and bound in the United States of America by Publishers Graphics,
LLC on sustainably sourced paper.

To all who supported me in a world where careers
are always in a constant transformation.
—Cristina Reis


To my students, on their way to boundaryless
global careers.
—Yehuda Baruch

# CONTENTS

# CONTRIBUTORS

## Chapter 1: Understanding Global Careers from a Critical Perspective

**Cristina Reis** is Associate Professor of Management and has been teaching in the US and Europe. Her research has been sponsored by the Portuguese Foundation for Science and Technology. She is also the recipient of an Academic Management Award and Emerald Award of Excellence.

**Yehuda Baruch** is a Professor of Management and Associate Dean for Research at Rouen Business School, France and Middlesex University, UK. His research interests and writing have been extensive and wide ranging, with particular focus on Careers and Global HRM, including over 100 refereed papers and over 30 books and book chapters. Former Editor of *Group & Organization Management* and former Chair of the Careers Division, Academy of Management.

## Chapter 2: The Situation of Global Careers in Canada

**Anthony R. Yue** is Assistant Professor in the Department of Communication Studies at Mount Saint Vincent University, Canada. His areas of research interest broadly concern how the individual navigates their organized world. He is also keenly interested in a variety of research methods and is a co-author of *Business Research Methods* (Oxford University Press, 2011).

**Scott MacMillan** is Assistant Professor in the Department of Business and Tourism at Mount Saint Vincent University, Canada. He conducts research on meaning in work, and his Ph.D. thesis was entitled 'Towards an existential approach to the meaning of work'.

### Chapter 3: Global Careers: Perspectives from the United Kingdom

**Tracy Scurry** is Lecturer in HRM at Newcastle University Business School, UK. Her main research interests are in the area of careers. She has recently completed a British Academy funded project exploring undergraduate future career expectations, career management, and notions of career success. Her current work focuses on identity narratives of global workers.

**John Blenkinsopp** is Reader in Management and Assistant Dean (Research) at Teesside University Business School, UK. His research focuses on how individuals make sense of, and cope with, their work and careers.

**Amanda Hay** is Senior Lecturer in HRM/OB at Nottingham Business School, UK. She has authored articles in journals such as *Career Development International* and *Management Learning*. She is a member of the international editorial board for *Management Learning*.

### Chapter 4: In and from the Heart of Europe: Global Careers and Austria

**Astrid Reichel** is Assistant Professor in the Interdisciplinary Group for Management and Organizational Behavior at WU Vienna, Austria. Previously, she held a teaching and research position at the University of Vienna, Austria. Her work on societal contingency of HRM and careers has appeared in a number of edited books and journals. She is a member of two international research networks (Cranet, 5C) focusing on country comparative research.

**Christiane Erten-Buch** is Managing Director of an Austrian SME in the field of heating and ventilation, and partner of AT Consult Austria. She has worked as Research Assistant and Assistant Professor at WU Vienna, Austria, as well as Consultant in the field of strategic process planning. Her research and teaching interest lies in cross-cultural management and training (with focus on Asian and Islamic countries), expatriation research and IHRM.

**Katharina Chudzikowski** is Assistant Professor for the Interdisciplinary Group for Management and Organizational Behavior at WU Vienna, Austria. Her work on careers in different settings, partly together with members of the Cross Cultural Collaboration on Contemporary Careers (5C), has appeared in numerous book chapters and journals. She served as guest editor for *Cross Cultural Management* and *An International Journal*, and is a member on the editorial board of the *European Journal of Cross-Cultural Competence and Management*.

**Wolfgang Mayrhofer** is Professor of Business Administration and has a chair for Management and Organizational Behavior at WU Vienna, Austria. Previously, he held teaching and research positions at a number of German universities. His research focuses on international comparative research in HRM, careers, and leadership.

## Chapter 5: The Embodiment of Unhealthy Global Careers Among Swedish Professionals

**Anna Essén** is a post-doctoral scholar employed at Stockholm University School of Business and Karolinska Institutet, Sweden. She is currently studying the emergence of quantitative measures in health care and how these articulation practices affect micro-level work orders and power relationships as well as macro-level structures such as legislation and national reimbursement systems. Anna has previously published papers on embodiment and habitual innovation in different empirical contexts, the multi-level dynamics of routines and the involvement of laggards in the design of new care services.

**Torkild Thanem** is Professor of Management and Organization Studies at Stockholm University School of Business, Sweden. His research focuses on the politics of embodiment and health and identity in organizational life. His recent publications include *The Monstrous Organization* (Edward Elgar, 2011).

**Sara Värlander** is Senior Lecturer at the Stockholm University School of Business, Sweden, and currently a visiting scholar at the Center for Work, Technology and Organization, Stanford University, USA. In her current research, using ethnography, Sara is studying global work and how culture is intertwined with the enactment of work practices, innovation, and spatial design in globally distributed teams. Previously, Sara has published papers on how organizational space affects flexibility and creativity, the emergent outcomes of the implementation of new technology in organizations, and the embodied and material dimensions of knowledge work.

## Chapter 6: Global Moves from and to Brazil

**Alan P. Marcus** is Assistant Professor in the Department of Geography and Environmental Planning, Towson University, USA. He is the author of several articles and book chapters on geography, race, immigration, and Brazil, and is the author of *Towards Rethinking Brazil* (Wiley & Sons, 2011).

## Chapter 7: Making Sense of Global Careerism in Argentina: The Structure, Culture and Context

**Hugo Gaggiotti** is Principal Lecturer of Organisation Studies at Bristol Business School, UK. He takes a constructionist perspective on organizing, most recently exploring the connections between nomadism and professional culture. He was Chair of the Standing Conference of Organisation Symbolism and is author of a number of books and papers, including 'The rhetoric of synergy in a global corporation: Visual and oral narratives of mimesis and similarity', in the *Journal of Organizational Change Management*, 25(2), 265–282 (2012).

## Chapter 8: The Global Careers of Australians and New Zealanders

**Kerr Inkson** recently retired following a 47-year career as an academic in management studies, mainly in New Zealand. He is the author or co-author of many papers and 16 books, including *The New Careers* (Sage, 1999), *Cultural Intelligence* (Berrett-Koehler, 2004) and *Understanding Careers* (Sage, 2007).

**Yvonne McNulty** is on the faculty at Shanghai University, PR China. She serves on the editorial board of *Journal of Global Mobility*, and is co-author (with Kerr Inkson) of the forthcoming book *Expatriate Return on Investment* (Business Expert Press, 2013).

**Kaye Thorn** is Senior Lecturer at Massey University's School of Management where she teaches a postgraduate paper in Career Management, while managing the internship program and postgraduate research. Her recent research has been exploring the motives behind the self-initiated expatriation of New Zealanders. She is also interested in self-initiated serial mobility (the highly mobile), patterns of mobility and the impact of mobility on careers.

## Chapter 9: Global Careers in Portugal

**Susana Costa e Silva** is Professor of International Marketing at the Catholic University of Portugal. She holds a Ph.D. in Marketing from University College Dublin, Ireland. She is author of several articles, book chapters and books on International Marketing and International Business. She has been teaching in Brazil and Guinea.

**Paulo Duarte** is Professor of Marketing at University of Beira Interior, Portugal. He has a Ph.D. in Management and has been doing research in satisfaction and consumer behavior. He is reviewer and member of the editorial board of several international journals and has published several articles on these topics.

**Sílvia Ferraz** is Trade Marketing Manager for Foreign Markets at Unicer. She researched on expatriates during her MSc in Marketing at the Catholic University of Portugal.

## Chapter 10: Global Careers: The Russian Experience

**Konstantin Korotov** is Associate Professor and Director of the Center for Leadership Development Research at the European School of Management and Technology in Berlin, Germany. His research interests involve leadership development, executive coaching, career development, and executive education.

**Sheila M. Puffer** is University Distinguished Professor and Cherry Family Senior Fellow of International Business at the D'Amore-McKim Business School, Northeastern University, Boston, USA. She has published widely on business and management in Russia, and has served as the editor of *The Academy of Management Executive*.

**Daniel J. McCarthy** is the McKim-D'Amore Distinguished Professor of Global Management and Innovation at the D'Amore-McKim Business School, Northeastern University, Boston, USA. His numerous publications include several co-authored books on Russian business and management, most recently, *Corporate Governance in Russia* (Edward Elgar, 2004). He also serves on the governing board of the Northeastern University Center for Entrepreneurship Education.

**Vlad Vaiman** is Professor of International Management and a Director of graduate programs at the School of Business of Reykjavik University, Iceland, and is a visiting professor at several top universities around the world. He is also a co-founder and the Editor-in-Chief of the *European Journal of International Management*.

### Chapter 11: Global Careers in Hungary

**Irén Gyökér** is Professor of Management and Human Resources Management at Budapest University of Technology and Economics, Hungary. She was the founder–director of the first MBA course in the country introducing modern business education. Evaluating intellectual capital and challenges in HRM is her main research area. She is the author of a number of books and articles in this field.

**Henrietta Finna** is Assistant Professor of Management and Human Resources Management at Budapest University of Technology and Economics, Hungary. Her research field includes HRM topics, such as alternative forms of employment. She has numerous publications in the field of HR practices mainly on the subject of Hungarian small and medium-sized enterprises.

### Chapter 12: Global Careers Within and Outside an Emerging Country: The Case of Turkey

**Burak Koyuncu** is Assistant Professor of Management at Rouen Business School, France. He received his Ph.D. from IE Business School, Spain. His research interests include executive careers, CEO succession, international careers, and corporate governance.

**Julia Richardson** is Associate Professor in the School of Human Resource Management at York University. She has a long-standing interest in global careers and specifically the impact of international mobility on work experiences and employment opportunities. Dr. Richardson has published widely in this field and has extensive personal experience having worked in Australasia, North America and Europe. She is currently Chair of the Careers Division of the Academy of Management.

### Chapter 13: Global Careers in China

**Victor P. Lau** is Assistant Professor at the Hang Seng Management College in Hong Kong. Before that, he was a faculty member at the Chinese University of

Hong Kong and the Hong Kong Polytechnic University, respectively. He received his Ph.D. from the Hong Kong Polytechnic University. His research interests include entrepreneurial behavior, career success, and business ethics. He has published in such journals as *Journal of International Business Studies*, *Journal of International Management*, and *Journal of Business Ethics*.

**Yu-Shan Hsu** is a doctoral candidate at the University of Wisconsin-Milwaukee, USA. Her research interests are international HRM and interpersonal and interdomain relationships. Her work has been published in journals such as *The International Journal of Human Resource Management* and *International Journal of Cross Cultural Management*.

**Margaret A. Shaffer** is the Richard C. Notebaert Distinguished Chair of International Business and Global Studies at the University of Wisconsin-Milwaukee, USA. She received her Ph.D. from the University of Texas at Arlington, USA. She is an active researcher in expatriation and cross-cultural organizational behavior and has published extensively in journals such as *Academy of Management Journal*, *Journal of Applied Psychology* and *Journal of International Business Studies*.

### Chapter 14: Global Careers from a Japanese Perspective

**Mami Taniguchi** is Professor of International Business at Waseda Business School and Graduate School of Commerce, Waseda University, Japan. She runs corporate executive education on global leadership and diversity management for Japanese multinational companies. Also, she plays an active role as a committee member on diversity and value creation at the Japan Ministry of Economy, Trade, and Industry.

**Chikae Naito** is a doctoral student at the School of Commerce, Waseda University, Japan. Her interests are in diversity management and career development.

### Chapter 15: Global Careers: An Indian Perspective

**Sushanta K. Mishra** is Assistant Professor in the Organizational Behavior and Human Resource Management Area at Indian Institute of Management Indore (IIM Indore), India. He is in the review panel of many journals and currently the editor of *Indore Management Journal*, a quarterly journal of IIM Indore.

**Pawan S. Budhwar** is Professor of International HRM and Associate Dean (Research) at Aston Business School, Birmingham, UK. He is also Director of the Aston India Foundation and President of the Indian Academy of Management. Pawan has published over 70 articles in a number of leading journals on International HRM/OB related topics with a specific focus on India. He has also written and co-edited books on HRM related topics such as Asia-Pacific, Middle East, Performance Management, India, developing countries, research methods,

and major works in international HRM. Pawan is also an advisor to the Common-wealth Commission, and a Fellow of the British Academy of Management and the Higher Education Academy.

### Chapter 16: Global Careers in the United States

**S. Gayle Baugh** is Associate Professor at the University of West Florida, USA. She has published in journals including *Journal of Vocational Behavior, Career Development International,* and *Journal of Business Ethics.* She is currently the Editor of *Group & Organization Management* as well as a member of the Board of Governors for the Academy of Management. She is a past Division Chair for the Gender and Diversity in Organizations Division of the Academy of Management and a Past President of the Southwest Academy of Management. Her research interests include mentoring, career theory, and leader–member exchange.

**Sherry E. Sullivan** is Associate Professor at Bowling Green State University, Ohio, USA, and has served as Chair and Historian for the Careers Division of the Academy of Management (AOM) as well as on the board for AOM's Gender and Diversity in Organizations Division. She is the co-editor of *Research in Careers,* Associate Editor of the *International Journal of Family Business* and an Associate Editor for *Group & Organization Management.* In 2002 was the recipient of the AOM's Gender and Diversity in Organizations Division's Janet Chusmir Life-time Achievement Award for Outstanding Service. She was named a Southern Management Association Fellow in 2006. She is the co-author of *The Opt-Out Revolt: Why People are Leaving Companies to Create Kaleidoscope Careers* (Davies-Black, 2006) and co-editor of *Winning Reviews* (Palgrave, 2006). She has over 60 journal articles, 10 book chapters, 40 proceedings and 80 presentations to her credit.

**Shawn M. Carraher** received his Ph.D. from the University of Oklahoma and was awarded the Oxford Journal Distinguished Research Professorship at Cambridge University in June 2011. He is the Hodson Endowed Chair in Entre-preneurship and Business at Indiana Wesleyan University. His recent work has been published in a number of journals including *Organizational Research Methods, Journal of Occupational & Organizational Psychology, Journal of International Business Studies, Academy of Entrepreneurship Journal,* and the *Journal of Applied Management & Entrepreneurship.* He is currently the editor of the *Journal of Management History, International Family Business Journal* and the *Academy of Health Care Management Journal* as well as serving on the editorial review boards for over 20 other journals. He has been named a Fellow of the Allied Academies in 2009 and 2010 and of the Academy of Global Business Advancement in 2010.

# 1

# UNDERSTANDING GLOBAL CAREERS FROM A CRITICAL PERSPECTIVE

*Cristina Reis, Foundation for Science and Technology, Portugal, and Yehuda Baruch, Rouen Business School, France, and Middlesex University, UK*

The ever-increasing globalization processes of business activities, fueled by economic, social, and technological factors that started in the twentieth century, have continued in the twenty-first century, with new trends. Moreover, additional intervening factors have influenced the extent and direction of global mobility. In this book, we go beyond description, to delve into critical thinking about the meaning of "being global."

The new trends and additional intervening factors have introduced changes into the nature of firm-led expatriation. There are more types of global mobility (Baruch, Dickmann, Altman, & Bournois, 2013), and these do not necessarily mean the same thing in different countries. Some countries tend to be a source of highly professional, skilled employees (e.g., Finland, for the telecom industry), whereas others are a source of manual labor (e.g., Romanians, for the construction industry).

Has there been a real change from what Hu (1992) pointed out as the fallacy of global firms' perceptions? In fact, firms can change their strategies and move to become more global (Bartlett & Ghoshal, 1989), but the majority cannot follow the ideal model of true transnationalism. Very few can operate under a truly global strategy, whereas others follow niche strategies to select and manage their expatriates (Baruch & Altman, 2002).

Due to the growing interest in global careers, there has been a surge in writing on various types and trends in global careers, including recent books that have focused on global careers. In particular, Dickmann and Baruch (2011) wrote a scholarly book about global careers with a clear focus on its conceptual contribution. They explored the wide range of global careers, mostly seen from a Western viewpoint, and compared individual and organizational perspectives, as well as overall cross-cultural points. They offered comprehensive coverage of

both theoretical and practical issues for firms and individuals dealing with expatriation (including before, during, and after expatriation). However, their book lacks a fully global view, and as such it cannot adequately reflect how global careers are perceived in different countries, or how the meaning of "being global" is considered by people from various cultures, as well as the various structural and contextual opportunities that exist for engaging in a global career.

Overall, people's careers are becoming increasingly global (Tams & Arthur, 2007). Both scholarly and practitioner literature provide ample evidence for the large and growing number of people opting for a career that transcends national borders. For example, Briscoe, Hall, and Mayrhofer (2012) offer an examination of 11 countries' cultural context characteristics that were relevant to career theory. However, this analysis was limited to discursive meanings of career success and transition at the national level (i.e. not global careers). Other career books have tended to be less global in their focus. For example, in Gunz and Peiperl's (2007) handbook, which develops a theory and consists of a number of chapters, only the chapter by Peiperl and Jonsen (2007) touches on the global perspective.

The aspirations of people leaving their countries are different, too, and these are subject to a range of factors. Individual motives can be analyzed using Baruch's (1995) push/pull model. Organizations operate under various constraints and they may ask or instruct their employees to move across borders. At the national level, cross-border moves can be easy for people and provide them with the ability to practice their professions (e.g., within the EU, or in US–Canada moves). Sometimes, they may only enable the movement of people, but not employment freedom, given the need to obtain a general work permit or a specific qualification to accredit professional qualifications. Moreover, some countries will prevent moves or will restrict people's ability to enter the country. As can be seen in the different chapters presented here, the stories of different global careers manifest different aspirations and different expectations. For example, in Portugal, it seems that there is a historical tendency for people to go abroad, either because of curiosity about distant places or necessity, due to economic depression, since there is huge division between the social classes. Similar reasons of curiosity and the desire to find one's place in the global rather than the local characterizes many people's reasons for mobility in the Netherlands. In Argentina, the focus is on the dominant discourse and the meanings of foreign global careers that take place in large corporations. In the UK, the value of international experiences is questioned in the context of a scientific career because work in the UK is regarded as being of a much higher quality than work abroad. In Austria, there seems to be a focus on individuals who work as foreigners, rather than on Austrians who go abroad, and very little is known about the subject. China presents contrasting stories of individuals from different backgrounds and situations, where some become superstars and others are marginalized in the making of global careers.

Although all of the countries represented in this book present *different global career situations* they all have many citizens engaged in different forms of global career—(see Baruch et al. (2013) for a framework and glossary of different types

and dimensions of global careers, mainly related to expatriation and repatriation career strategies, policies, and practices).

Careers have become unpredictable, and there are various ways of building a career. In the past, definitions of "career" have included a sequence of work–life experiences over the individual life cycle (e.g., Levinson, 1978; Arthur, Hall, & Lawrence, 1989), while recent descriptions of the global career propose that this occurs "when part of that sequence takes place in more than one country" (Dickmann & Baruch, 2011: 7). Since there is more to building a career than the application of mainstream skills and techniques, in this book we propose that how people live and interpret the situation of the global structures of their societies, cultural contexts, as well as contextual opportunities and barriers, all contribute to the making of a global career.

## Which People, which Organizations, which Societies?

At the individual level, when firms are selecting people for global assignments, they employ various criteria, of which the most important for US firms are performance, interest in international assignments, and functional expertise (Korbin, 1994). Different sets of personality traits are offered to help find who may be best suited to embark on a global assignment. Nonetheless, Baruch (2002) argued that there cannot be any clear criteria for success for a prospective global manager, apart from being open-minded culturally.

There are also demographic issues, such as gender, family status, and chronological and career age. In terms of gender, the role of women has changed a great deal since the early days of corporate expatriation (Adler, 1984). In this new era, women are chosen by organizations for expatriation (Altman & Shortland, 2008) and many opt for self-initiated expatriation (Tharenou, 2009). Under specific circumstances, women can manage self-initiated expatriation well, even to countries in which women have few legal rights (Bozionelos, 2009). Family support for corporate men managing their international assignments is typically different than that provided for women. Reis (2004) studied how *male expatriate managers* negotiated support from their wives in order to get ahead in expatriate assignments and their careers. Male managers still tend to have less conflict in family arrangements than women managers.

At the organizational level, different organizations may apply different strategies for the management of expatriation and repatriation practices (Baruch & Altman, 2002). What works for giant firms would not be applicable to small enterprises (Reis, 2010).

Within societies, national culture is another factor: What is acceptable in a high-power-distance culture will not work in a low-power-distance culture. Collectivist societies will have different motives for agreeing to organizational expatriation; individualistic societies will observe higher rates of self-initiated expatriation. Economic situation, as well, plays a role in generating the push-and-pull factors that influence immigration decisions.

The interpretation of the global situation structures of each society has had much to do with the diverse visible forms of historical development of those who have gone abroad and sometimes returned to the home country. Most of the chapters in this book focus on discourses of immigration development as they are connected with contemporary global careers in their countries. Cultural contexts help explain how individuals and institutions in a certain society are affected and forced to adjust, convening with these forces independently of their individual values and views. The role of culture interplays with the behaviors of people, which can vary greatly across social spaces.

There are several typologies and frameworks that use cultural communalities and distinctions, most notably Hofstede (1980), Schwartz (1999), and Ronen and Shenkar (1985). We have followed a model of clustering countries based on attitudinal dimensions, as presented by Ronen and Shenkar (1985). This model enables us to make a clear distinction between countries suggested by specific attitudes, which are analyzed in this book. We elected to use the attitudinal dimensions from Ronen and Shenkar (1985) rather than a different set of clusters that would depend upon the dimensions under investigation. Different sets of Hofstede's five dimensions, via factor analysis present the differences in the cultural dimensions of each country. For example, one dimension is "avoidance of uncertainty," which, according to Ronen and Shenkar (1985),

> measures the degree to which a society deals with the uncertainty and risk present in everyday life. People with high uncertainty avoidance tend to worry more about the future, have higher job stress, tolerate less change, and stay with one employer for a longer time.

This dimension has also been used to check whether people from certain countries are eager to become entrepreneurs (Reis, 2010). It is important to notice that the Hofstede's concept of culture is different from our definition. While Hofstede (2001) defines culture as the collective mental programming of the human mind that distinguishes one group of people from another, we focus on cultural contexts by examining the behavioral role of culture, which can vary enormously among social spaces.

Since our focus is on social spaces, societies or countries, Ronen and Shenkar's (1985) review of country membership clusters seems to be a more appropriate way of defining culture. They define cluster membership, as opposed to cultural dimensions of analysis, by assuming three dimensions: geography, language, and religion (see Table 1.1 for the countries in this book representing various cluster memberships). For example, cluster membership integrates colonization issues. Spain and Portugal colonized Latin America, and this suggests strong cultural ties. The same can be said for Great Britain and its former colonies. Although Ronen and Shenkar (1985) wrote about cluster memberships when communist economies still existed, and countries such as Japan, China, India, and Russia were

**TABLE 1.1**  The countries represented in the order of Ronen and Shenkar's (1985) framework

| Ronen and Shenkar (1985) cluster | Countries in this book representing this cluster |
| --- | --- |
| Anglo | UK; USA; Canada; Australia; New Zealand |
| Germanic | Austria |
| Nordic | Sweden |
| Latin Europe | Portugal |
| Latin America | Brazil; Argentina |
| Near East | Turkey |
| Far East | China; Japan; India |
| Arabic | United Arab Emirates |
| Eastern Europe (not represented at the time in Ronen and Shenkar (1985)) | Hungary; Russia |

difficult to include in scholarly studies due to the lack of researchers representing these countries, we believe that, in this book, we have brought the necessary knowledge to break through both Western and non-Western parts of the globe in the application of global career theory.

*The contextual opportunities and barriers* that emerge in the making of a global career have to do with external forces that are beyond cultural, historical, legal, or any other institutionalized forms. This focuses on how individuals interpret their way out of their contextual systems to engage in a global career, and how different contextual aspects influence the desire for, and perception of, a global career. We ask, for instance: What is a desirable target country? Some people are led by curiosity, others by the need for income. For others, the geo-climate is an important factor. At the same time, local customs and possible discrimination against foreigners might deter people from attempting to build a career in certain countries. Moreover, what is normal for EU citizens is an impossible dream for people in most developing countries. Indeed, how "global" is a move from France to Belgium, or from New Zealand to Australia, compared to a move from Cameroon to Belgium, or from China to Australia? Although global education helps to bridge such gaps, there are still legal constraints, even within the developed OECD countries.

Some people engage in a global career in response to organizational offers or demand (Baruch & Altman, 2002), whereas others choose it on their own initiative (Al Ariss, 2012; Altman & Baruch, 2012; Dickmann & Harris, 2005; Howe-Walsh & Schyns, 2010). The trend crosses traditional directions and sectors; it is no longer restricted to the diplomatic service or transportation and trade, nor to the production and services that are delivered from different corners of the world. It is subject to competitiveness, in terms of cost-effectiveness. However, different societies have a great deal of influence on the ideological meanings of what constitutes a talented person or who is useful (if we think of

now marginalized people) for the making of a global career, much in the same way product or service is accepted or not accepted as good and useful in a given country.

Our main intentions in this book were, first, to break new theoretical ground for the field of global careers within critical theory, and, second, to identify unexplored elements of global careers in a small collection of different countries.

Each chapter provides the contributors' perspectives on their countries' opportunities and barriers to engaging in global careers. We tried to maintain a certain coherence and fit across the chapters to facilitate comparison across the various countries.

The common thread woven throughout this book comprehends four main elements, which are divided into sections: the situation of global careers in each country; the relevance of contemporary career concepts; structural, cultural, and contextual difficulties and opportunities; and critical perspectives.

The section on the *situation of global careers* includes the exploration of data relevant to the specific country, including historical, legal, religious, and/or other important factors. Most chapters depict recent trends on employment and particularities of the wider labor market, focusing on issues specific to each country.

All chapters are followed by a section on the *relevance of contemporary career concepts*. The contributors offer a discussion on how global career theory could be applied to the situation in the countries discussed in their chapters. Many of the chapters utilize contemporary career concepts, such as boundaryless and protean careers (e.g., Sullivan & Baruch, 2009). Contributors present their own analyses of these career conceptual developments within local career systems, at the individual, organizational, and national levels. In this section, some chapters introduce the focus of their main discussions, which covers a wide range, including expatriation and repatriation, immigration and emigration, the brain drain at the labor-market and national level, and the impact of multinational or international organizations on the local career systems. It was clear in this section that each chapter provides a different perspective from the American model of global career. The latter is typically depicted by the expatriate being sent by a firm to perform certain roles in an overseas subsidiary (Black, Gregersen, & Mendenhall, 1992). This conceptual model is insufficient and it cannot represent the full range of contemporary global careers (Baruch et al., 2013). In particular, as we present in this book, going global may mean different things to different people in different corners of the globe.

The section on the *structural, cultural, and contextual difficulties or opportunities* is probably the most original, if not the most innovative, part of every chapter. We did not offer our contributors any particular definition of countries' structures, cultures, and contexts. Therefore, each contributor was free to interpret these terms in their own way. Nonetheless, all have included these concepts in their chapters, though these are not always clearly defined and they are often interrelated.

Most chapters include stories of how people managed a global career in their countries, although some contributors include individual career stories throughout the entire chapter. It is interesting to note that each chapter presents different interpretations of the ideological meaning of global careers. Some chapters present stories of traditional expatriation, repatriation through international organizations or multinationals, self-initiated assignments, or foreign assignments taken by those expatriated in the countries of each chapter. Other chapters focus on comparative narratives of illegal immigrants and global superstars. The stories in these chapters, which present how people have perceived and overcome difficulties, and have identified opportunities to develop a global career, are quite remarkable indeed.

Finally, all chapters present a section on critical perspectives just before the conclusion, which includes implications and recommendations for future research on global careers.

Unfortunately, the current body of literature in the field lacks the exploration of global careers from a critical perspective, which would address the various meanings that "being global" might have to different people in different societies. We introduce the concept of *global career from a critical perspective*, which opens up a different understanding of the contemporary discursive meaning of global careers (see Reis, 2012, for our understanding of material discursive practices in organizations).

This meaning draws on both global career theory and on critical theory to build an understanding of how dominant practices are shaping individuals' careers in their countries.

We asked the contributors of these chapters to use any critical theory in their analyses and, in particular, to write a section that combined career theory and critical theory, and the authors engaged with this reflection. Most of the authors provide critical reflections within their chapters and stories, though not all have necessarily used critical theory explicitly in their analyses. Particularly useful critical applications can be found in the chapters on Canada, Austria, the UK, Sweden, Brazil, and Argentina.

Our initial aim was to explore dominant global career practices by investigating the opportunities and difficulties in different countries, and to provide an analysis in the light of a framework that would combine global career theory and critical theory. Our critical perspective on global careers has commonalities with the established field of critical management studies regarding the use of critical theory. While critical management studies analysis tends to focus on labor process analysis (e.g., Braverman, 1974) and Foucault's work, we were open to any critical theory that provided a reflection on individual careers in various societies, with the aim of understanding the struggles, barriers, and opportunities. Critical management studies concentrate on processes of liberation within working-class struggles, while our critical perspective seeks processes of liberation for all individuals, of all classes. For example, in the chapter on China, where authors present stories both of the marginalized and of the privileged. In both stories,

there is a tentative liberation from the structures, culture, and contextual dynamics of their countries in their making of a type of living in the global world, perhaps a new way of making global careers.

We assume that most individuals see their individual career needs validated in their structures, cultures, and contexts. Eventually, they see the difficulties and opportunities as they engage in what is best for their lives. Those who aim or are forced to engage in a global career produce what they are best at. However, both the marginalized and the privileged individuals may not be pleased with their global careers. Even if those in privileged positions could provide some relief for those who are marginalized, they do not necessarily see different ways of organizing their careers and lives. As John Stuart Mill (1869) noted: Was there ever an oppression that did not seem natural and just to the oppressor? Therefore, the most privileged do not necessarily see their own global-career dynamics or the opportunities they had to become so privileged. In this sense, we aim to explore the dynamics of the global careers of both the marginalized, as they have seized opportunities in their societies, and of the most privileged.

Since critical theory is concerned with the critique of ideology in order to emancipate people from pervasive forms of domination that are not common sense, we proposed its application as a means to understand the contemporary transformations in global career theory. We do not seek to extol career techniques regarding how to succeed in a global world, but rather to understand the transformation of ideological meanings of global careers on different countries' structures, cultures, and contexts.

Critical theorists believe that people can be autonomous because they have the capacity to reflect on the reliance on various forms of subordination and inequality, which suggests various relations of social power. We present a critique of different forms of knowledge and its recognition in the present informal global economy. This recognition is not sufficient for change, but it does challenge established ideas and practices that preclude the development of unfair or non-diversified careers for future generations. Consequently, critical awareness of different global-career meanings and engagement in the ways of making a global career implies a discussion on the new forms of subordination and inequality—how we interconnect with each other and how we are collectively responsible for each other. A discussion on self-identities and insecurities may also be relevant (see the chapter from the UK, which highlights how migrants construct and negotiate their own identities and positions within the UK context).

Habermas (1974) suggests that, "The higher level of reflection coincides with a step forward in the progress toward autonomy of the individual, with the elimination of suffering and the furthering of concrete happiness" (254). Individual autonomy, in the Habermas (1974) sense, proposes a reflection on global careers that sees those who seek this as aiming for the elimination of suffering through the making of a global career, with ultimate integration into the global informal economy with a dignified status.

## Concluding Remarks

Endorsing the true meaning of academic freedom, we did not force our views on the contributors of the chapters of this book, and the views and research presented in this book are entirely their responsibility. The impetus for writing this book began with the first co-editor, following discussions with colleagues. This book includes several collaborations between junior and senior researchers, and there are also newcomers to the field of global careers and critical perspectives, including newcomers from other fields, such as geography or anthropology.

The primary audience for the book includes students, scholars, and practitioners in the fields of careers, international management, critical management studies, and media studies. They will hopefully be attracted to the book due to its emphasis on the possibility of blending theories from their fields with practice, as well as its collection of visible and esteemed authors. We anticipate that students and scholars will enjoy this innovative approach, while practitioners may appreciate the fresh ideas presented.

## The Structure and Content of the Book

We begin with chapters that use critical theory in their analyses.

The contributors from Canada use a critical sensemaking approach to analyze the situation of global careers in a young country intersected by colonialist immigration policies and influenced by the people, policies, and media of its close neighbor, the United States. Their contribution reflects on how power weighs down the sensemaking of a pluralistic global career which is simultaneously inhibited by a sense of identity based on multiculturalism.

The UK chapter focuses on the Bourdieusian concept of the institutionalized state of cultural capital. The contributors argue that certain groups are marginalized in the UK and within the existing careers literature. They focus in particular on low-skilled workers and irregular migrants, both of which are important groups to consider in the context of the UK. They suggest that, in spite of figures suggesting a healthy circulation of global talent to and from the UK, the reality is less optimistic and in fact shows evidence of the misuse of talent.

Similarly to the contributors from Austria, the contributors from the UK bring up issues of formal educational qualifications, which are not easily recognized because of national-based protectionism and lack of experience in local contexts. There is now a movement to avoid this trend at the academic level in the EU countries, which are trying to implement the Bologna agreement in three educational cycles: Bachelor, Master's and Ph.D.

Chapter 4, from Austria, uses a Bourdieusian perspective, and the contributors argue that global careers in the Austrian context are often characterized as constituting particular forms of working internationally when they have been explored in the literature, such as the Austrian citizens who work for international

organizations in Vienna. The authors find this lack of research disturbing and believe that it points to an ideological bias. The Austrian contributors are also concerned with the attitudes and political positions regarding migrants. National discussions seem to be based on migrants' movement across national borders, rather than hard, empirical data about their life and career goals. It is interesting to note that the contributors from Hungary, Austria's eastern neighbors, have similar concerns.

Contributors from Austria introduce the term "proximal flexpatriation" for those individuals who cross national borders for their daily work. This chapter examines the meaning of this proximal-flexpatriation movement for the local context, culture, and economic development.

The chapter from Sweden uses embodied theories in order to make sense of how individuals experience, act out, and deal with their global careers.

The contributors draw their arguments from the experiences of Swedish professionals. In other words, their focus on the "bodily and emotional strains and problems of global careers," caused by extensive traveling that is regarded as a normal part of the job, and the unhealthy side effects. They reflect on embodied experiences, which have been largely ignored, unacknowledged, and trivialized to understand global careers. The authors see the embodiment of global careers as a strategic issue in need of management, and they explore the powers and limitations of managerial responsibility in the non-invasive management of employee health and well-being.

The contributor of the chapter on Brazil uses theories from Castles and Miller (2003) to demonstrate the complexity and multi-layered nature of immigrant activities and behaviors, and immigrant labor market success. The author rejects neo-classical economic theories, since these do not explain the situation of global careers. The engagement in a global career is not a rational economic choice, to maximize benefits by migrating, nor is it a search for the best place to reside. The author claims that, in the case for Brazilian immigrants, there is a particular "culture of migration" that has been encouraged by the political and social elites in sending communities from Brazil. The author further explains how these elites benefit from promoting the "illusion" of immigration movements, since they are the owners of property and benefit directly from any increase in local real-estate values. Another important claim is the use of language and identity. While some contributors in this book see language as a barrier to managing a global career in local contexts (see e.g., the chapters from Japan, Turkey, and Hungary), this author sees language as an identity and an important decision-making factor in the management of a global career. For example, while immigrants from Spanish-speaking countries have their identities associated with ethnic issues, this is not the case for Brazilians, who are a Portuguese-speaking immigrant population. Mainly, those who return to their home country, Brazil, face socio-economic challenges based on social class, rather than facing ethnicity-related bias, as is the case for those from Spanish-speaking countries.

The chapter from Argentina follows the narrative approach that rejects the ideals of neoliberalism and other rationalizations based on the production of capitalist subjectivity. The author claims that local Argentineans who work for multinational companies as expatriates did not play a significant role in deciding their assignments and had no narrative on the issue. The meaning of global careers in Argentinean global corporations is constructed in such way that it is a prospective dimension for the future of a global career. It is also a dimension that creates a mythical place to emigrate, in order to start or continue a professional career or a new life. This explanation affects how expatriates live their global careers by denying important contextual aspects of Argentina. Adding to this point, the author's research does not differentiate between the meaning of being a local or a foreigner, since Argentineans who are placed in leading positions belong to the second or third generation of immigrants, and therefore they are all regarded either as foreigners or locals.

The next chapters are largely descriptive, because these authors used positivistic research methodologies that were mainly of a quantitative nature. The contributors from New Zealand and Australia, Russia, Hungary, Portugal, China, Turkey, Japan, and India did not follow critical theoretical approaches, but rather introduced the exploration of important critical issues.

The chapter from New Zealand and Australia focuses on the importance of geographical isolation and, in opposition to the claim made regarding Argentina, argues that global careers in New Zealand and Australia are self-directed. The authors see self-initiated expatriation as a growing research field, mainly related to the contextual issues of their countries. The focus on the trend of self-initiated assignments contradicts the focus on traditional corporate international careers, taking on controllable settings where global careers are promoted and expected. The editors of this book would like to add that there is research that illustrates that the engagement in a global career in a large multinational can be a process of self-discovery, in a similar way to that found in a self-initiated assignment, but within a corporation (see Reis 2004).

According to the authors of the chapter on Australia and New Zealand, there are more global careerists per head of population than any other developed country. Through a discussion in this chapter, the concept of "brain circulation" emerges to describe the phenomenon in which many Australians and New Zealanders return to the country where they were born. The authors discuss their concern that the voices of those who are in international labor markets or in foreign settings whose voices have not been heard. They claim that Australian and New Zealand global careers are based on westernized practices, and are often made possible by the efforts of those who may not think of themselves as pursuing careers and who are in positions to potentially become exploited. Moreover, the authors emphasize that the experiences of their countries' natives and their immigrants in pursuing global careers seem to have to do with their individual actions and the local government policies, as well as those of the other governments, wherever

they go, rather than to any practices of international corporations. However, it is still only a small fraction of the population who has access to the development of a global career. In Australia, those most disadvantaged in their access to making global careers seem to be the Aboriginal people. In New Zealand, the local Maori have been strongly protectionist about any westernizing practices and they have had to implement a governmental policy to restrict the number of white migrants allowed to arrive from countries such as South Africa, England, and the United States, as they brought with them critical attitudes towards the Maori.

Back to Europe, the chapter from Portugal focuses attention on the polarization of social classes in the making of global careers. There are those who leave the country for career development, and those who leave because of financial necessity. Brain drain is a serious problem in Portugal, where the most qualified face difficulties in securing a satisfactory position in their home country. The reasons for the brain-drain issue are somewhat similar to those presented in the chapter from Russia, where many family-owned companies still lack human resource management (HRM) practices. Mainly there is a lack of willingness to apply practices pertinent to organizational equality, such as performance appraisal systems, succession planning, and diversity policies. In public universities, it is still possible to find academic departments occupied by one family that has gained speedy doctorates to fulfill the EU requirements. The social power dominance of certain families and long-standing friendships in different public and private arenas prevails in Portugal.

In their examination of Portugal these authors' research focuses on classic expatriate assignment issues transferred to Portuguese companies, who have workers working abroad who are not necessarily highly qualified. These situations do not show the typical patterns of the corporate expatriate assignments. The authors' accounts of these workers assignments abroad show that these workers are mainly concerned with improving the social and financial status of their families in Portugal.

The chapters from Eastern Europe include Hungary and Russia.

The contributors of the Russian chapter describe two major challenges to the making of a global career in Russia. First, they point to the perceived lack of importance of HRM and the resulting low level of investment in human resources. Second, they note difficulties with the motivation and retention of a young, talented workforce. The authors claim that Russian employees and managers lack basic business knowledge and skills, mostly due to the lack of Western-style business education in the Soviet Union.

Among the many important issues presented by the contributors of the Russian chapter, we would like to mention a few here. In general terms, there are unfavorable conditions for developing and pursuing a global career within Russia. Partially for the same reasons for brain drain in Portugal, in Russia, many globally oriented careerists opt to go abroad for education and to initiate their global career. At times, they may return to Russia, but they repeatedly remain

abroad. Russian private companies are still owned and managed by their founders, who demand obedience and family/club membership. These conditions are simply unacceptable for many highly talented professionals, which causes them to leave.

Russia also has a youth-market-oriented business culture, and many Russian employees expect rapid promotions. This situation may parallel that discussed in the chapter on India, which will be described below.

The chapter from Hungary also presents the brain-drain issue, which includes both Hungarian professionals emigrating to the West and the re-entry of Hungarian citizens from neighboring Eastern European countries. The authors estimate that at least 30 percent of the young, highly qualified workers between 25 and 44 years of age do not return to work in Hungary. Other less qualified workers, or people in specific occupational groups (e.g., construction specialists or butchers), are also exposed to migration, but they tend to be under temporary-labor or short-term assignments. It is interesting to note that the authors transformed the concept of "brain circulation," first used by the contributors from Australia and New Zealand, to "migration circulation," since these workers commute between Hungary and their host countries.

Like the contributors from Austria, the authors from the neighboring country of Hungary also show concerns about immigrants' acceptance. The Hungarian authors present a discussion on "migration tolerance," with particular attention paid to Hungarian citizens who return to their home country from Eastern countries.

The contributors from the chapter on Turkey are less concerned with the brain-drain issue because the economy is growing and there is an expanding labor market. In the view of these authors, Turkey is a good place to track a global career. However, Turkey is one of the biggest exporters of students, mainly to the US; thus the brain-drain issue is nevertheless still present in Turkey.

Interestingly, these authors focus on women—women's career experiences, and potential career advancement—either as Turkish nationals or as expatriates. The authors suggest there is an optimistic environment for women's global careers in organizations with high ratios of women in senior level positions, but there is still a need for improvement in the political arena.

We view positions of power and influence as contextual. While Nordic countries may have a high ratio of women in the political arena, they lack similar high participation in senior level positions, for example, in certain influential multinational corporations (MNCs). Positions of power and influence in Turkey may be concentrated in the political arena and less in organizations, and consequently there are fewer women in politics.

We now depart to the Far East—Asia: China, Japan, and India—before presenting the situation of global careers in the US.

The contributors to Chapter 13, on China, see more foreign investment and more global assignments coming into China. However, the authors are concerned

with what they call a "glass ceiling for Chinese locals." While foreign expatriates take top management positions in their organizations, the local Chinese population has been neglected in general in their career development and in their well-being.

An important question that emerges in this chapter is how Chinese culture will mix with the expectations from organizations that would like to implement westernized career-management concepts with their Chinese employees.

Brain drain is also an issue in China, and the authors question the effectiveness of government policies to retain talented people. The extreme stories presented in this chapter—that of the NBA superstar Yao Ming and Foxconn's local workers—illustrate well the different consequences of global career building in these people's lives.

Remaining in Asia, we present the chapter from Japan. The authors argue that the globalization of Japanese companies and their employees is a recent phenomenon. The authors present the situation of foreign employees in Japan as one in which they face multiple barriers in socialization.

At the same time, Japanese employees feel underappreciated in terms of global careers and take a passive role, assuming there is slow change in their organizations. Remarkably, Japanese employees rely on their peers to get information about their careers and organizations.

The contributors from India focus on the virtual career experiences in the Indian offshore industry. They claim these experiences are relevant to a global career, although no physical borders are crossed. Like the contributors from the US, the contributors from India highlight the importance of technology, which is generally underrepresented in the global careers literature. However, we urge caution with such virtual definitions, since global careers have generally been represented in this book within material contextual issues that imply real consequences for people's careers and lives. In our view, the significance of virtual experiences in the making of global careers remains unclear.

There have been several labor-market transformations in India, mainly with the appearance of technology. In India, families used to exert a high level of control over their children's fate. With the emergence of technology, this sort of power has been dissipated, mainly because the previous generations have a limited understanding of the use of technology. There is a young, talented population in this industry with the expectation of quick promotion, similar to Russian youth. According to the authors, this situation has caused high job rotation in organizations in this industry. In a similar way, the contributors from Russia claim that their youngest population has high expectations of being promoted quickly. However, it is possible that in India, specifically in the growing offshore industry, job rotation is not regarded as lack of loyalty, and so this situation may be better tolerated in India than in Russia.

Finally, we return to the Anglo cluster, as proposed by Ronen and Shenkar (1985), with the contributors from the US, in Chapter 16. We did not include

this chapter in the beginning of this section alongside the other Anglo countries, because we first presented the chapters that applied critical theory.

The contributors from the US were surprised at the lack of historical data on the migration rates of U.S. citizens and were also concerned about the relative lack of empirical research on global careers in the US, since most research on global careers in the US focuses on organization-initiated expatriate assignments, with scholars studying self-initiated expatriate assignments only more recently. They offer a review on what US scholars need to devote more attention to regarding global careers, such as international virtual work teams, or collaboration with colleagues across national borders. Like the contributors from India, the authors emphasize virtual experiences in the making of a global career.

According to the authors, the experiences of marginalized groups in the US, such as undocumented immigrants, are not well reported. We are shocked by this finding, given the remarkable documentaries on these issues presented in the media. The reasons that the US literature on global careers might neglect these situations are something to explore. The authors of this chapter claim that in the US, being an illegal worker places individuals at the mercy of unscrupulous employers, mainly because of their illegal status.

We suggest there is also a "mercy tip culture" promoted among marginalized employees in the US, not necessarily just among undocumented employees, which is deeply settled in the imaginary ways of making quick and good money. For example, restaurant servers idealistically believe they make good wages because they receive huge tips at the mercy of their clients. In contrast, in other cultures, this would be seen as shameful, as it is the responsibility of the owner of the restaurant (including government policies) to provide decent salaries for employees. Taken with a critical theories perspective, this issue may be regarded as a kind of exploitation by future researchers in global careers.

According to the contributors of this chapter, studying global careers in the US is not an easy task because it is quite complex. The contributors from Canada make the same claim and the reader is invited to return once again to the beginning of this book.

## References

Adler, N. J. (1984). Women in international management: Where are they? *California Management Review*, 26(4): 78–89.

Al Ariss, A. (2012). *Self-Initiated Expatriation: Individual, Organizational, and National Perspectives*. London: Routledge.

Altman, Y. & Baruch, Y. (2012). Global self-initiated corporate expatriate careers: A new era in international assignments? *Personnel Review*, 41: 233–255.

Altman, Y. & Shortland, S. (2008). Women and international assignments: Taking stock—A 25-year review. *Human Resource Management*, 47: 199–216.

Arthur, M. B., Hall, D. T. & Lawrence, B. S. (1989). *Handbook of Career Theory*. Cambridge: Cambridge University Press.

Bartlett, C. A. & Ghoshal, S. (1989). *Managing Across Borders. The Transnational Solution.* Boston, MA: Harvard Business Press.

Baruch, Y. (1995). Business globalization – the human resource management aspect. *Human Systems Management,* 14(4): 313–326.

Baruch, Y. (2002). No such thing as a global manager. *Business Horizons,* 45(1): 36–42.

Baruch, Y. & Altman, Y. (2002). Expatriation and repatriation in MNC: A taxonomy. *Human Resource Management,* 41(2): 239–259.

Baruch, Y., Dickmann, M., Altman, Y. & Bournois, F. (2013, in press). Exploring international work: Types and dimensions of global careers. *The International Journal of Human Resource Management.*

Black, J. S., Gregersen, H. B. & Mendenhall, M. E. (1992). *Global Assignments.* San Francisco, CA: Jossey-Bass.

Bozionelos, N. (2009). Expatriation outside the boundaries of the multinational corporation: A study with expatriate nurses in Saudi Arabia. *Human Resource Management,* 48: 1111–1134.

Braverman, H. (1974). *Labor and Monopoly Capital: The Degradation of Work in the Twentieth Century.* London: Monthly Review Press.

Briscoe, J. P., Hall, D. T. & Mayrhofer, W. (2012). *Careers Around the World: Individual and Contextual Perspectives.* New York: Routledge.

Castles, S. & Miller, M. J. (2003). *The Age of Migration.* 3rd Edition. New York: The Guilford Press.

Dickmann, M. & Baruch, Y. (2011). *Global Careers.* New York: Routledge.

Dickmann, M. & Harris, H. (2005). Developing career capital for global careers: The role of international assignments. *Journal of World Business,* 40: 399–408.

Gunz, H. P. & Peiperl, M. A. (Eds.) (2007). *Handbook of Career Studies.* Thousand Oaks, CA: Sage.

Habermas, J. (1974). *Theory and Practice,* trans. J. Viertal. London: Heinemann.

Hofstede, G. (1980). *Culture's Consequences: International Differences in Work Related Values.* Beverly Hills, CA: Sage.

Hofstede, G. (2001). *Culture's Consequences: Comparing Values, Behaviors, Institutions, and Organizations Across Nations.* Beverly Hills, CA: Sage.

Howe-Walsh, L. & Schyns, B. (2010). Self-initiated expatriation: Implications for HRM. *The International Journal of Human Resource Management,* 21: 260–273.

Hu, Y. S. (1992). Global or stateless corporations are national firms with international operations. *California Management Review,* 34(2): 107–126.

Korbin, S. J. (1994). Is there a relationship between a geocentric and multinational strategy? *Journal of International Business Studies,* 25(3): 493–511.

Levinson, D. (1978). *Seasons of a Man's Life.* New York: Knopf.

Mill, J. S. (1869). *The Subjection of Women.* Dover Thrift Editions.

Peiperl, M. A. & Jonsen, K. (2007). Global careers. In H. P. Gunz & M. A. Peiperl (Eds.), *Handbook of Career Studies* (pp. 350–372). Los Angeles, CA: Sage.

Reis, C. (2004). *Men Working as Managers in a European Multinational Company.* München und Mering, Germany: Rainer Hampp Verlag.

Reis, C. (2010). Women entrepreneurs in Portugal. In S. L. Fielden & M. J. Davidson (Eds.), *International Research Handbook on Successful Women Entrepreneurs.* Edward Elgar Publishers.

Reis, C. (2012). Listening to the material life in discursive practices, *Tamara Journal for Critical Organizational Inquiry,* Special issue on Materiality & Storytelling, 2.

Ronen, S. & Shenkar, O. (1985). Clustering countries on attitudinal dimensions: A review and synthesis. *Academy of Management Review*, 10: 435–454.

Schwartz, S. H. (1999). A theory of cultural values and some implications. *Applied Psychology. An International Review*, 48(1): 23–47.

Sullivan, S. E. & Baruch, Y. (2009). Advances in career theory and research: Critical review and agenda for future exploration. *Journal of Management*, 35(6): 1452–1571.

Tams, S. & Arthur, M. B. (2007). Studying careers across cultures: Distinguishing international, cross-cultural, and globalization perspectives. *Career Development International*, 12: 86–98.

Tharenou, P. (2009). Self-initiated international careers: Gender difference and career outcomes. In S. G. Baugh & S. E. Sullivan (Eds.), *Maintaining Energy, Focus and Options Over the Career: Research in Careers Volume 1* (pp. 197–226). Charlotte, NC: Information Age.

# 2

# THE SITUATION OF GLOBAL CAREERS IN CANADA

*Anthony R. Yue and Scott MacMillan,*
*Mount Saint Vincent University, Canada*

## Introduction

In this chapter, we focus upon an investigation of global careers in a Canadian context. Canada is the second largest country by landmass on Earth, and yet it has only slightly more than 34 million inhabitants. The history of immigration, proximity to the United States of America and linguistic diversity are all issues that make Canada an interesting place to consider when coming to grips with the idea of a global career. To this end, we provide a brief survey of global careers in Canada and offer two key high-profile stories of Canadian careers that illustrate some important aspects, which we are able to highlight through elements of a critical sensemaking approach. We conclude with some thoughts about Canadian global careers and also how such examinations may offer some practical implications regarding career management in a postmodern context.

## Global Careers in Canada

Canada is the second largest country by landmass on the face of the Earth, comprising 9,984,670 km$^2$ and with an estimated total population of 34,030,589 (CIA, 2011). Based upon data from the 2006 census in Canada, foreign-born individuals accounted for virtually 19.8% of the total population. Furthermore, the change in immigration rate into Canada between 2001 and 2006 was almost four times higher than that of those who were born in Canada (*The Daily*, 2007).

Language is an important aspect of demographic patterns in Canada. Again, based upon the 2006 census, 20.1% of the population spoke neither English nor French (the two official languages of the country) as first language. It was further estimated that the third most common language reported, Chinese, was spoken as a first language by an estimated 1,034,000 individuals (*The Daily*, 2007).

Naturally, migration occurs within the country as well. Migration patterns reported from the periods spanning 1971/1972–2008/2009 show net outflows from all provinces except Alberta, British Columbia, Ontario and Prince Edward Island (Migration, 2011). These longer-term patterns seem to have shifted somewhat, based upon the most recent data, which show that, in 2008/2009, Alberta, British Columbia, the Yukon Territory, Saskatchewan and Newfoundland and Labrador showed net positive interprovincial migration (Migration, 2011).

There are far fewer data available concerning Canadians who emigrate from the country. We do, however, have some information available from the United States. Based upon data acquired from the American Community Survey (ACS), conducted by the U.S. Census Bureau, Statistics Canada reports that, during the period between 2000 and 2006, the number of emigrants from Canada to the US decreased slightly and represents an estimated 34,000 individuals. These emigrants are characterized as being relatively young, well educated and more likely to be working in knowledge-economy-type specialized jobs (US Emigration, 2010).

With an absence of substantial information concerning emigration patterns, it might be useful to consider attitudes towards expatriate assignments. Wang and Bu (2004) examined the perceptions of 145 Canadian undergraduate business students concerning international careers. The authors examined these attitudes in the context of a post-9/11-terrorist-attacks context. Some findings include the fact that the majority of these students have thought about an international assignment, and that males (compared with females) cite career advancement as a statistically significant rationale for doing so. On the other hand, males are also significantly more likely to reject the idea of an international assignment, based upon disruption to existing routine/ties, as well as potential missed promotion opportunities when compared with their female colleagues. Especially salient to this chapter is that the same study also highlights how those students with multiple languages, who have foreign friends and who report having parents involved in international work are more likely to report wanting their first job assignment to be outside the country. This suggests that perhaps generational accounts of career navigation may be most salient (see Lyons, Schweitzer and Ng, 2009). Certainly, first-hand familiarity with other cultures and languages in the context of considering international work seems to matter.

## Regionality

The brutal colonization of Canada's first nations peoples, first by competing European empires and then by Canadians themselves, manifests itself today in a country that has incompletely harmonized linguistic, social and, indeed, even legal practices. Yet, as an outgrowth of federal government policies emerging from the late 1950s into the 1960s, Canadians will typically differentiate themselves from Americans through referring to their approach to population diversity and

immigration as 'a multicultural mosaic,' as opposed to an American 'melting pot' description; essentially, a sort of *vive la différence* belief in the strength of diversity.

Being a parliamentary democracy and member of the British Commonwealth of Nations, Canada has clear ties to the former British Empire, but that does not exclude the sizeable impact that the population of the French-influenced province of Quebec has upon the identity of the nation. Furthermore, the north of the country is in a period of flux, in that modest inroads have been made towards self-determination by the people of Nunavut, who are attempting to put in place structures that will allow some sort of autonomy, still within the federal umbrella of the country.

The nature of Canada being a country with profound regional differences, when combined with substantial historical and contemporary immigration patterns, leads to the natural definitional question: What is a Canadian? The answer seems to be related to a certain comfort with, or even expectation of, being able to agree about disagreeing. Likewise, uniformity of linguistic, legal and cultural expectations is not apparent.

## Postmodern Conditions

We now come to a conception of Canada as being a melange of those with historical, as well as very recent, immigration experiences. With a Quebec legal system based upon a Napoleonic Code foundation, much of the rest of the country with the hallmarks of British common law presumptions, and even a northern territory in the process of a controlled move towards native self-government, there is substantial fragmentation of the national identity. When combined with the inevitable Canadian comparisons with their US neighbours to the south, we see that this multicultural-mosaic descriptor may well be more apt than not. These are compelling reasons to see Canada as being both an example and an exemplar of a case to be made for a kaleidoscope interpretation of career.

## Structural, Cultural and Contextual Difficulties

Given the above discussion, we now come to the point where we might ask questions concerning the relevance of some typical and well-articulated career concepts to the understanding of the situation in Canada. When held up against the backdrop of a country where immigration has largely been the norm, and indeed is increasingly becoming so, we see clear implications for the workplace and thus for careers. The ageing of the 'boomer generation' and the comparatively low birth rate among Canadians highlight the fact that the average Canadian workplace will comprise a multicultural context (again, see Lyons et al., 2009). More so than even the structural and cultural difficulties that might impede a Canadian concept of a global career, we see sensemaking, as shaped by the political and cultural landscape, as being especially salient in how individuals understand

their career. Perhaps then, even more useful than the protean, boundaryless and related conceptualizations of career, we might best make use of the kaleidoscope model in the case of Canada.

## Global Moves

The notion of a kaleidoscope model of career (hereafter KCM) (see Mainiero and Sullivan, 2005, 2006; Sullivan and Baruch, 2009) is one that maintains the primacy of the individual with agency. However, it allows for the shifting emphasis and pattern of contextual weighting of the three constituent dimensions: authenticity, balance and challenge. The implicit recognition that individuals shift their career emphasis at different times, for a variety of reasons and subject to the context they find themselves in, is especially congruent with the sensemaking perspective. If we examine the seven key sensemaking properties, this becomes somewhat apparent. Clearly, the fact that sensemaking is grounded in identity construction relates well to all three dimensions of the KCM, as do the sensemaking properties of being enactive of sensible environments, being focused upon and by extracted cues. The fact that career is constructed over time through inevitable comparisons points to the sensemaking properties of being retrospective in nature and being ongoing, plus being based upon plausibility. Naturally, work is also a social enterprise, and so also does that particular sensemaking property seem in alignment. So, what makes the KCM any different from sensemaking, if its dimensions seem logically to map on to the seven properties of sensemaking? Simply put, the contextual factors that allow for this intersection are not only static benign forces that frame an individual's career decision-making. The role of agency and power within the KCM is largely individually focused, and the addition of a critical sensemaking perspective asks how power is relationally embedded within the context/individual dyad. In the case of Canada, there is a shifting (and perhaps contested) sense of the constitution of the workplace, work and value of a global career in a globalized world.

When the globalized world is at least somewhat represented in a national microcosm (as in the case of Canada), two key possibilities arise. The first is that a global career is desirable and a natural outcome of such a context, for instrumental and practical reasons. The second possibility is that there is no need to pursue a globalized career (at least in terms of relocation), when the national workplace is effectively globalized. Note that neither possibility is particularly xenophobic in nature.

To explore and further consider these possibilities, we will describe two high-profile examples of Canadians with documented global careers: Conrad Black and Michael Ignatieff. Through describing some salient features of these two public figures and how Canadians have engaged with their mutual global careers, we attempt to show how critical sensemaking and intersections with the KCM offer a nuanced way to consider global careers, particularly in a Canadian context.

## Stories of Global Careers

We have chosen two prominent Canadian examples of global careers, both with complex career trajectories and likewise less than stellar outcomes. Our choices reflect a number of reasons, but, specifically, it is instructive to consider cases whereby what one might assume to be valuable international experience becomes an interesting form of liability in the Canadian context. Such shocks to straightforward assumptions often lead to the opportunity to consider, for instance, the roles of power and context in such cases. This falls in line with our contention that at least some of the broad considerations in a critical sensemaking perspective are useful. To this end, we first describe the rise and fall of Conrad Black and his eventual exit from the stage as a Canadian. We follow this with a brief examination of Michael Ignatieff and his rise to power in Canada, which was shortly followed by an equally precipitous fall in popularity.

---

### Conrad Black—A Canadian Global Career in Exile

Conrad Black, a Canadian international media baron, was convicted of fraud on 13 July 2007 in a U.S. district court in Chicago. He is currently incarcerated in a Florida prison.

Black's fall from grace—from being a successful, international businessperson who divided his time between Toronto, London and New York to a convicted felon in the US—is a fascinating story. He was truly a citizen of the world—born in Canada, successful in the UK, the US and Canada—but gave up Canadian citizenship in order to accept a British peerage appointment and was then convicted in a U.S. court.

Conrad Black was born on 25 August 1944 in Montreal, Quebec. His father, George Black, was a self-made businessman. Black grew up in a privileged environment and attended the best of private schools. He had capitalist inclinations as a youth and started buying stocks at the age of eight, when he invested $60 in a share of General Motors.

He went to Thornton Hall, for an undergraduate degree, and then attended York University's Osgoode Hall School of Law, but eventually graduated in Law at Laval University (1970). He subsequently completed a Master of Arts in History at McGill University (1973).

Black began building his empire while in his 20s with the acquisition of a number of Canadian newspapers. After his father's death in 1976, he inherited a large percentage of Ravelston Corporation, which owned over 60% of Argus Corporation, a very successful holding company. He took control of Ravelston after the death of the company head, John McDougald, in 1978.

He then went on to parlay his wealth and ownership holdings into a newspaper empire, Hollinger International, owning London's *Daily Telegraph*, the *Chicago Sun-Times*, the *Jerusalem Post*, the Fairfax newspapers in Australia and the Southam newspapers in Canada. He became one of the wealthiest men in the world and, in 1990, was made an Officer of the Order of Canada. In 2003

and 2004, Black was named Canadian business and newsmaker of the year by the Canadian press and broadcast news. He authored four books and also wrote for the *National Post*, which he owned.

In 1999, Black became a British citizen and was offered a peerage appointment to the British House of Lords, initiated by Prime Minister Tony Blair. To do this, however, he had to give up Canadian citizenship, as Prime Minister Jean Chretien invoked the Nickle Resolution, which forbids Canadian citizens from accepting UK peerage appointments. Black challenged the Chretien government to no avail and, in 2001, chose to renounce his Canadian citizenship in order to become Lord Black of Crossharbour.

In 2003, with falling share prices, some questionable business dealings, and under pressure from the board, Black stepped down as CEO of Hollinger International. In 2004, a suit was launched by five Canadian investors against Black, his wife, Barbara Amiel, and his second in command at Hollinger, David Radler. At the same time, Black was the subject of an ongoing investigation by U.S. prosecutors, which, in 2005, resulted in charges of fraud, racketeering and obstruction of justice. After two years of legal wrangling and a lengthy trial, in 2007, Black received a six-and-a-half-year sentence. He began serving his sentence on 3 March 2008, at the Coleman Correctional Complex in Florida.

He appealed his conviction and was released on bail after serving 29 months. However, in June 2011, he was ordered to return to prison to finish his original sentence of 42 months. He was incarcerated in the Federal Correctional Institution in Miami and was released in May 2012. Prior to his release, Conrad Black had publicly stated that Canada was his home, and his plan was to return to Toronto after his sentence in the US was completed. At present, he resides in Canada on a temporary residence permit.

Compiled from: Black, 1995; Bower, 2006; Conrad Black Timeline; Conrad Black's legal travails; McNish & Stewart, 2004; Siklos, 2004; Wong, 2011.

## Michael Ignatieff—A Complicated Canadian Homecoming

Michael Ignatieff has worked and lived as a citizen of the world for much of his adult life. However, being a global citizen did not work in his favour (and, in fact, played an instrumental role in his failure) as a political leader in Canadian politics. He suffered a humiliating political defeat as leader of the Federal Liberal Party of Canada at the hands of the Conservatives, led by Stephen Harper.

Michael Ignatieff was born on 12 May 1947, in Toronto, Canada. His father was a diplomat, and Ignatieff grew up in a privileged environment, with ample opportunities. He attended the University of Toronto, Oxford University and Harvard University, where he completed a Ph.D. in History.

For the next 30 years, he worked at a variety of academic institutions, the University of British Columbia, Kings College, Cambridge, Oxford, the University of London, London School of Economics and the University of California, and as a public intellectual, authoring almost 20 books, and numerous journal articles and opinion pieces. In 2000, he accepted a position at Harvard University as head of the Carr Center for Human Rights Policy. During this time, he continued

to write and enhance his reputation as a scholar and public intellectual. Because he was absent from Canada for much of this time, writing and travelling extensively, one of the criticisms of him was that he wrote as an American and, in fact, that he became more an American than a Canadian. His political writings had much to do with this assessment, as he supported controversial U.S. foreign policy, such as the invasion of Iraq.

However, Ignatieff's academic life would be interrupted in 2005, when he was convinced to leave Harvard and return to Canada, to enter a very different career and an entirely new phase of life—that of the political arena and public service. He had a lot to lose, as, for Ignatieff, the objective from the beginning was to succeed the shortly retiring Jean Chretien as prime minister of Canada, and anything less would be considered a failure. If he became successful, he would have made the transition from global intellectual to leader of the one of the most admired and successful countries in the world.

He made his debut in Canadian politics in 2006, running as a member of parliament in the House of Commons in a Toronto-area riding. He had high name recognition and won his riding. In 2006, he then ran for the leadership of the Liberal party, challenging Stephane Dion. He lost, but challenged for the leadership a second time in 2008, after the Conservative party, led by Stephen Harper, defeated the Liberal government with Dion at the helm. He was officially endorsed as leader in 2009 and was quickly anointed the new saviour of the Liberal party. Over the next 3 years, he worked on building his credibility with the Canadian public. Polls seemed to suggest he had some success in changing his image, but it seemed that Canadians were still wary of the Harvard academic.

In 2011, Ignatieff forced parliament to be dissolved with a non-confidence vote, and a new election was called. In hindsight, this was a huge error in judgement on his part. The Liberal party had great ambitions to replace the Conservative government, and Ignatieff embarked on an energetic campaign that he (along with many other Canadians) expected would culminate with the election of the Liberal Party and Ignatieff becoming the new prime minister of Canada.

However, the problem of not living in Canada for many years led to the charge that he was not a 'real' Canadian. The Conservatives created some very effective attack ads emphasizing the theme, 'he didn't come back for you'. Many Canadians seemed to agree with this assessment of Ignatieff. He was accused of being a carpetbagger, only back in Canada to satisfy his personal ambitions and not for the good of the country, as he often eloquently claimed.

He was also criticized for his views on foreign intervention. He supported the Iraq war, which Canada sat out and with which the majority of Canadians did not agree. In Canadian politics, he argued for a more forceful global approach to Canada's foreign policy. As an MP, he voted to extend Canada's role in Afghanistan, again an unpopular position nationally.

He was also accused of being out of touch with regular Canadians, many perceiving him as an elitist academic. He was even accused of being too smart. His Ph.D. and vast global success did not endear him to many Canadians, as evidenced by the final vote results. Harper was as successful in portraying Ignatieff as an elitist as George Bush was with Al Gore. It's the old, which-one-

would-you-rather-have-a-beer-with question. And Ignatieff did not fare well with the answer. For that matter, neither did Gore.

He lost the Federal election on 3 March to Stephen Harper, who gained a majority in parliament for the first time. It was not only a loss for Ignatieff, who lost his own seat, but a complete devastation of the Liberal party, which won only 34 seats, finishing far behind the New Democrat Party. They lost official opposition status, and the party's prospects for the future are dim.

A week after the election, Ignatieff stepped down as leader of the Liberal party and left politics, probably for good, to return to academia. He is currently a professor at the University of Toronto. He went from respected scholar, public intellectual, global citizen and expected future prime minister of Canada to political pariah, in a very short time.

Compiled from: Ignatieff, 2009; Morgan, 2006; Smith, 2006; Smith, 2011; Valpy, 2011.

## Critical Perspectives on Global Careers

There is an embedded notion of the individual being the predominant factor in the selection and pursuit of differing career options. Indeed, this presumption is manifest in the ideas of the protean career model, as well as the concept of the boundaryless career (see Sullivan and Baruch, 2009: 1545–1548). In particular, the protean career perspective privileges the individual's attitudes, behaviours and preparations in terms of career and career choices. This is perhaps a natural presumption, and yet one that potentially has enormous implications for our understanding of global careers.

If we consider the individual-level decision-making regarding career choices (including location as one salient outcome), we come invariably to the contextual factors, which may influence not only the choices themselves, but also the framing of the range of choices. We might think of this as a certain type of bounded rationality, whereby both presumptions and the limitations in information set the stage for what range of choices an individual ascertains, including the choices related to career. Much of a bounded-rationality perspective is linked with the idea of a rational and utility-based analysis on the part of the individual. This is an important perspective, for it allows for discussion of career choices based upon heuristics such as the job/career/calling model (Bellah et al., 1985), for example. However, a critical account of careers demands something more: we must consider the role of context and power relations as they influence individual career choices.

The problematic of untangling a situated Canadian making career choices for his or herself is intriguing. This is for a multitude of reasons, but the recent history and composition of the country itself form a strong case for this contention. One might argue that Canada is, at least from a Eurocentric perspective, a comparatively young country, formed through a series of intersecting colonialist immigration policies. It also cannot be overstated that Canadians are dramatically influenced by the people, policies and media of their close neighbour, the United

States. As a consequence, the historic and topographical influences upon the present context, when applied to our discussion of global careers, have Canadians looking inward as much as outward.

In order to address the above considerations, we take a perspective upon global careers and Canada that might loosely be called a critical-sensemaking (Thurlow, 2010) approach. Through incorporating notions of power as relationally informing how individuals or groups of individuals perceive and enact choice regarding careers, we not only intend to write about the Canadian context, but also to illustrate how critical sensemaking is a useful form of case-study analysis. We will do this by characterizing Canada as being remarkably plurivocal and yet constrained by the same sense of identity that surrounds this idea of multiculturalism.

## The Critical-Sensemaking Approach

Sensemaking is an approach to organizational analysis that simultaneously assigns primacy to individuals, while at the same time illuminating the profound role that social context plays in how those same individuals navigate their social milieu. Weick (1995, 2001) articulates seven properties that contribute to how individuals make sense of their world. Briefly, this inexhaustive list of properties includes: being grounded in identity construction, being retrospective in nature, being enactive of sensible environments, being social, being ongoing, being focused on (and by) extracted cues, and being driven by plausibility, not accuracy (Weick, 1995: 17). Critical sensemaking is an effort to situate the sensemaking process within a contextual understanding that privileges power relations as they impact the more individual social psychological process understood through sensemaking. Consequently, there is value in taking a perspective that places emphasis upon both individuals and their context in a nuanced and intertwined manner.

Thurlow (2010: 258) describes how, in most case-analysis examples of critical sensemaking, a particular organizational shock is the starting point of the unravelling of features and processes by which the approach is harnessed. In our examination of the Canadian context of global careers, we instead start with a particular description of the Canadian context, which makes oblique references to a number of such shocks. This is owing to an economy of words and also because it is our belief that the aggregated and juxtaposed nature of these shocks is the main, salient feature of the Canadian context, in comparison with other possible sites of interest (be they national and geographic or not). As a consequence of these decisions, our perspective in this chapter may seem vaguely postcolonialist, yet our focus upon individual-level effects sits more comfortably within a critical sensemaking style of discussion and analysis.

The combination of both similarities and juxtapositions found in the above cases of Conrad Black and Michael Ignatieff is useful in beginning to tease out some salient features of the Canadian response to the very multicultural mosaic that forms a source of Canadian pride. For example, if Canada truly does see

itself as being multicultural and likewise recognizes that the US is the country's largest trading partner, then it stands to reason that someone with US experience would be seen as valuable in government. The fact that Ignatieff was criticized for, among other things, being sympathetic to US policy regarding Iraq is especially interesting when considered against a backdrop of somewhat similar policy that was being tacitly implemented in Canada. This highlights one way in which plausibility rather than accuracy (per Weick's sensemaking properties) can be observed. The duelling identity-construction moves of the federal election that went so poorly for Ignatieff and his political party show how the aspect of sensemaking that is enactive of sensible environments plays within the powerful sensegiving arena of political opponents. Stephen Harper and the Conservative party might be seen as being substantially closer in ideology to the Republicans in the US, and levying the charge that Ignatieff is more American than not, based upon his global career, creates a sensemaking environment where Ignatieff's very strength is seen as evidence of his lack of patriotism or connection to his country. Furthermore, the suggestion that he is a sort of overeducated dilettante by virtue of his background and work experience (when has being a professor at Harvard ever been seen as a liability?) plays a similar sensemaking card. If Canadians who live in the US are largely working in jobs that require specific expertise, then the fact that Ignatieff left implies that he is in fact part of an already discernable emigration trend and has contributed towards the country's brain drain.

If we move to the case of Conrad Black, we are able to discern a very particular juncture in terms of his identity as a Canadian. The very fact that Black was forced to renounce his Canadian citizenship in order to attain his peerage in the UK is fascinating enough. Even more intriguing is that it was the then prime minister, Jean Chretien, who forced the issue by invoking the Nickle Resolution. A French Canadian prime minister invoking legislation that prevents the attainment of a peerage appointment in the UK by a Canadian citizen highlights the historically constituted tensions that form Canada.

These examples, plus more that can be gleaned by the reader, offer illustrations of how historically constituted relations represent sedemented power relations that affect present conceptualization of what it is to be Canadian. These experienced, but largely unapprehended, sensemaking features profoundly shape how well received (or not) the global career is in Canada. This has broad implications, for, in a globalized world with great mobility of workers, jobs and cultures, we might argue that the multicultural-mosaic conception in Canada is, in fact, a reasonable postmodern template for what the larger global context will look like in the near future.

## Conclusions

The conceptions of the protean and boundaryless models of career development follow from the erosion of the idea of the employment-for-life model of organizational commitment to workers. In the wake of this erosion, ways of

understanding what individuals were doing to conceptualize their situation and then manage their careers were theorized. In the words of Gunz, Evans and Jalland:

> At present, the boundaryless career argument is eerily reminiscent of the quest for the 'one best way' that dominated management and organizational writing for the first half of this century. Boundaryless careers, goes the argument, are the way of the future, and the only question is learning how to live in a world of boundarylessness.
>
> (Gunz, Evans and Jalland, 2000: 30)

Interestingly, in an almost prescient manner, the same authors point to this chapter's present arguments when they paraphrase Weick himself:

> We followed this argument because of our belief that boundaries are to do with making sense of one's place in the world. Weick (1996) draws on the concept of strong and weak situations, and argues that when a situation weakens, people redraw boundaries to create a different strong situation.
>
> (Gunz et al., 2000: 29)

They follow with:

> There is no necessary shame in recognizing that there are boundaries that shape one's career, and there may be a great deal to be gained from understanding the forces that create these boundaries.
>
> (Gunz et al., 2000: 30)

Boundaries shift and morph, but a context without boundaries is no context at all. When Yue and Mills (2008) investigated the profound loss of a sensible environment in which to sensemake, they described a crisis that relates to the very conception of a self with a future—in short, one's very existence. On the other hand, when Yue and Helms Mills (2007) considered Hurricane Katrina through a sensemaking and postcolonialist lens, they were attempting to address how historical and power-laden discourses rendered unthinkable situations plausible through an ongoing neocolonialistic process. A loss of boundaries and context forces poignant sensemaking, and sensemaking is subject to shaping through very powerful aspects of context.

In this churn, we might usefully ask how to advise individuals what to do when making career decisions. The KCM becomes especially useful because, when it is combined with a critical sensemaking approach, we are able to discern the role that a variety of powerful presuppositions and discourses play in how we make sense of the context in which we operate. If we further extend the model through specifically interrogating the authenticity dimension of the KCM, we have a very real chance to empower individuals to consider issues of meaning, one's life and career in such power-laden contexts. There is a substantial body

of philosophy that examines the roles of choice and authenticity, and a growing body of literature that then goes on to apply such ethics of the self to the world of organizational analysis. In this regard, MacMillan's (2006, 2009; Macmillan and Mills, 2002) focus upon meaning, authenticity and existentialism as a move beyond the job/career/calling model of work (life) purpose is a philosophically grounded and pragmatic interrogation of the role of authenticity in career choices.

We have attempted to offer the argument that Canada is an interesting example through which to examine how power-laden sensemaking comes to manifest itself in a remarkably plurivocal and multicultural context. This manifestation has seemingly unanticipated and counterintuitive consequences for the individual seen as having a global career. If we are willing to consider Canada as a sort of prototypical postmodern state, then the applicability (or not) of certain career models becomes a useful starting point for considering how best to advise individuals about their own career choices. In a contextual environment that is so nuanced and shifting, the solidest touch point becomes the notion of authenticity. Fortunately, the heuristic of the KCM allows for empowered individuals to take into account the shifting foci of their needs and wants over time. In this manner, both a complex and morphing environment and also a simultaneous privileging of being authentic are practical adaptations for navigating a global career and its consequences.

## References

Bellah, R. N., Madsen, R., Sullivan, W. M., Swidler, A. and Tipton, S. (1985). *Habits of the Heart: Individualism and commitment in American life*. Berkeley, CA: University of California Press.

Black, C. (1995). Canada's continuing identity crisis, *Foreign Affairs*, 74(2): 99–115.

Bower, T. (2006). *Outrageous Fortune*. New York: HarperCollins.

CIA (2011). Retrieved from https://www.cia.gov/library/publications/the-world-factbook/geos/ca.html, 23 September 2011.

Conrad Black: Timeline, CBC News. Retrieved from www.cbc.ca/news/background/black_conrad/timeline.html, 15 September 2011.

Conrad Black's legal travails: A timeline. *National Post*. Retrieved from http://news.national post.com/2011/06/23/conrad-blacks-legal-travails-a-timeline/, 15 September 2011.

Gunz, H. P., Evans, M. G. and Jalland, R. M. (2000). Career boundaries in a 'boundaryless' world. In M. A. Peiperl, M. B. Arthur, R. Goffee and T. Morris (eds), *Career Frontiers: New Conceptions of Working Lives*. Oxford: Oxford University Press, and retrieved from http://faculty.fuqua.duke.edu/oswc/2000/papers/wednesday/GunzEvansJalland.pdf, 23 September 2011.

Ignatieff, M. (2009). *True Patriot Love: Four Generations in Search of Canada*. Toronto: Penguin Group.

Lyons, S., Schweitzer, L. and Ng, E. S. W. (2009). The shifting nature of careers in Canada: A framework for research, presented at the ASAC Conference, Niagara Falls, Ontario, and retrieved from http://ojs.acadiau.ca/index.php/ASAC/article/viewFile/595/504, 23 September 2011.

MacMillan, S. (2006). Existentialism, spirituality and work: Toward a paradigm of authenticity. Paper presented at the Academy of Management.

MacMillan, S. (2009). Towards an existential approach to the meaning of work. Unpublished Ph.D., Saint Mary's University, Halifax.

MacMillan, S. and Mills, A. (2002). Existentialism and management theory. Paper presented at the Atlantic Schools of Business.

McNish, J. and Stewart, S. (2004). *Wrong Way: The fall of Conrad Black*. Toronto: The Penguin Group.

Mainiero, L. A. and Sullivan, S. E. (2005). Kaleidoscope careers: An alternative explanation for the 'opt-out generation', *Academy of Management Executive*, 19: 106–123.

Mainiero, L. A. and Sullivan, S. E. (2006). *The Opt-Out Revolt: How people are creating kaleidoscope careers outside of companies*. New York: Davies-Black.

Migration (2011). Retrieved from www.statcan.gc.ca/pub/91-209-x/2011001/article/11514/tbl/tbl-eng.htm#t1www, 23 September 2011.

Morgan, M. C. (2006). Michael Ignatieff: Idealism and the challenge of the 'lesser evil', *International Journal*, 61(4): 971–985.

Siklos, R. (2004). *Shades of Black: Conrad Black – His rise and fall*. Toronto: McLelland & Stewart.

Smith, D. (2006). *Ignatieff's World: A Liberal leader for the 21st century?* Toronto: James Lorimer & Company.

Smith, J. M. (2011). Iggy Pops: The Michael Ignatieff experiment, *World Affairs Journal*, July/August.

Sullivan, S. E. and Baruch, Y. (2009). Advances in career theory and research: A critical review and agenda for future exploration, *Journal of Management*, 35(6): 1542–1571.

*The Daily*. (2007). Retrieved from www.statcan.gc.ca/daily-quotidien/071204/dq071204a-eng.htm, 23 September 2011.

Thurlow, A. (2010). Critical sensemaking. In A. J. Mills, G. Durepos and E. Wiebe (eds), *The Sage Encyclopedia of Case Study Research, Volume 1* (pp. 257–260). Thousand Oaks, CA: Sage Publications.

US Emigration (2010). Retrieved from www.statcan.gc.ca/pub/11-008-x/2010002/article/11287-eng.htm, 23 September 2011.

Valpy, M. (2011). U of T teaching job marks end of my life as a politician, Ignatieff says. *The Globe and Mail*, 5 May.

Wang, B. C. Y. and Bu, N. (2004). Attitudes towards international careers among male and female Canadian business students after 9–11, *Career Development International*, 9(7): 647–672.

Weick, K. E. (1995). *Sensemaking in Organizations*. Thousand Oaks, CA: Sage Publications.

Weick, K. E. (1996). Enactment and the boundaryless career: Organizing as we work. In M. B. Arthur and D. M. Rousseau (eds), *The Boundaryless Career: A new employment principle for a new organizational era*. Oxford: Oxford University Press.

Weick, K. E. (2001) *Making Sense of the Organization*. Malden, MA: Blackwell.

Wong, C. (2011). Conrad Black returns to prison in Miami. *The Globe and Mail*, 6 September 2011.

Yue, A. R. and Mills, A. J. (2008). Making sense out of bad faith: Sartre, Weick and existential sensemaking in organizational analysis, *Tamara Journal for Critical Organization Inquiry*, 7(1): 66–80.

Yue, A. R. and Helms Mills, J. (2007). A cacophony of voices: Postcolonialist sensemaking and Hurricane Katrina. Paper presentation and proceedings, Standing Conference on Organizational Symbolism (SCOS) XXV, Ljubljana, Slovenia, 1–4 July.

# 3

# GLOBAL CAREERS: PERSPECTIVES FROM THE UNITED KINGDOM

*Tracy Scurry, Newcastle University, UK,*
*John Blenkinsopp, Teesside University, UK, and*
*Amanda Hay, Nottingham Trent University, UK*

## Introduction

In this chapter, we examine global careers in the context of the United Kingdom (UK) by synthesising perspectives from a range of disciplines to explore the behaviour and experience of individual actors who are pursuing global careers, either in the UK or from the UK. The UK is a surprisingly underresearched context within the global-careers literature, despite being an obvious location from which to study global careers: modern notions of global careers, in particular the widespread use of expatriate managers, were in many ways prefigured by the development of Britain's civil service and military to manage its colonial possessions from the late eighteenth century onwards. This colonial past continues to influence the UK labour market, as levels of migration from former British colonies to the UK remain significant (Office for National Statistics, 2011a). However, enlargement of the European Union has led to growing numbers of migrants from the Accession 8 (A8) countries (Czech Republic, Estonia, Hungary, Latvia, Lithuania, Poland, Slovakia and Slovenia) (Pollard, Latorre and Sriskandarajah, 2008), with 2010 figures estimating over 500,000 Polish-born people residing in the UK, up from about 60,000 in 2001 (Office for National Statistics, 2011a). In recent decades, it has been immigration that has exercised the public imagination and been the focus of political debate. Census data show that the foreign-born population in the UK doubled from 2.1 million in 1951 to 4.8 million in 2001, and 2010 estimates suggest that this figure had risen to over 7 million (Office for National Statistics, 2011a). Although the pattern of significant immigration to the UK was previously counterbalanced by emigration, since the 1970s, the UK has generally seen net immigration, and immigration has exceeded emigration every single year since 1992 (Hatton, 2005; Office for National Statistics, 2011b).

The UK thus represents an especially fertile location for the study of global careers, and we begin by highlighting the complexity of what a global career might mean within the context of the UK, highlighting the diverse group of individuals who might be conceived to be enacting a global career in this country. Leading on from this, we highlight the peculiarities of the UK context, before considering the ways in which the reported experiences of career actors in this context often challenge modern notions of career. Such challenges are explored through a consideration of the complex patterns of movement in and out of the UK, which highlight the existence of diverse barriers to the realisation of a global career in this context. Throughout the chapter, we seek to pay particular attention to those who are frequently marginalised in the careers literature, proposing that further recognition and exploration of these groups are needed to open up possibilities for transformation and leverage the promise of the global career in the UK.

## Conceptualising global careers

The classic definition of career is the 'evolving sequence of a person's work experience over time' (Arthur, Hall and Lawrence, 1989), and the recent definition of global career proposed by Dickmann and Baruch simply appends the following phrase: 'when part of that sequence takes place in more than one country' (2011: 7). This simple adaptation serves to underline two important aspects of global careers – their defining characteristic is their crossing of national borders, and yet, in all other respects, they can be thought of simply as another form of career. This is useful in drawing attention to the surprisingly diverse range of individuals who can be conceived of as pursuing global careers – from illegal immigrants undertaking 'dirty jobs' in the informal economy to global superstars in the entertainment industry. The UK context reflects this range, but we identify four groups that seem to us to typify global careers in the UK context:

- professionals and managers coming to, or moving from, the UK to work in MNCs;
- self-initiated expatriates from the UK;
- self-initiated expatriates to the UK;
- illegal immigrants (or legal migrants working in the informal economy).

The first group seems likely to be the smallest, and yet research on this group dominates the careers and HRM literature, followed at some distance by studies of self-initiated expatriates moving from developed countries such as the UK to work in less developed countries. Given the emphasis on critical perspectives, we have chosen in this chapter to focus largely on the other two groups, partly because they have been largely neglected in the careers literature (although not necessarily in other literatures), and partly because individuals in these groups are often (but by no means always) marginalised and disadvantaged in the UK labour market.

Many dimensions are relevant to understanding the vast spectrum of meaning and experiences of global careers. As Bimrose and McNair (2011) highlight, economic migration is not a homogenous phenomenon and should be viewed as a wide continuum, from highly skilled professional migrants to low-skilled manual workers (perhaps illegal and undocumented). In order to further our understanding of global careers from a UK perspective, we have developed a conceptualisation of global careers that incorporates the formal and informal, the planned and unplanned, and the regular and irregular. In addition, we draw on Arnold's (1997) conceptualisation of career, incorporating employment-*related* positions, roles, activities and experiences to avoid a focus on employment alone, and acknowledge activities associated with global careers, such as training and education. Our analysis of global careers incorporates, but is not restricted to, the dimensions outlined in Table 3.1.

Using these dimensions as a framework for our discussion, we hope to broaden the conceptualisation of global careers and, in doing so, respond to the call for a wider perspective of global careers, beyond international assignments or interorganisational moves (Inkson and Thorn, 2010). The literature on self-initiated global careers can be seen as one response to this call (Al Ariss and Syed, 2011; Doherty, Dickmann and Mills, 2011; Inkson, Arthur, Pringle and Barry, 1997; Richardson, 2006; Richardson and McKenna, 2003; Thomas, Lazarova and Inkson, 2005), but exploration of global careers within the careers literature remains

**TABLE 3.1** Dimensions of global careers (adapted from Dickmann and Baruch, 2011)

| Dimension | Elements – key questions to consider |
| --- | --- |
| Originator | Was the move to work in another country initiated by the individual, an assignment given by the organisation, or the result of an interorganisational move? |
| Duration and frequency | How long has the individual worked in another country? How many times has the individual worked in another country? How many different countries? |
| Skill level | Is the individual highly skilled? Is s/he unskilled? Are his/her existing skills and qualifications recognised in different countries? |
| Connection to immigration | Is the employment connected to immigration? Or is it a short-term international assignment/experience? |
| Legality | Is the individual legally documented to work in another country? Is he/she irregular or illegal in terms of his/her employment status? Is he/she irregular or illegal in terms of the nature of the work he/she undertakes? |
| Formality | Is he/she formally employed? Is he/she employed in an informal/casual manner, e.g. seasonal work? |

almost entirely focused on those operating within the formal economy. Hugely important, yet largely neglected, forms of global career are being enacted by individuals operating outside the formal economy in terms of their own status (e.g. illegal immigrant) or the type of employment they undertake, which may be illegal in terms of nature (drugs, illegal activities) or form (cash in hand, off the books, no questions asked) (Vasta, 2011). Although these global careers have received limited attention within the field of careers (Marfleet and Blustein, 2011), they have been explored in other fields, notably migration research. We shall draw on this broader literature to inform our discussion, as this is a crucial aspect of global careers in the UK context, given high levels of immigration and the attention these have received in the political domain.

## UK Context Overview

The UK is the third largest economy in Europe, with an estimated labour-market participation rate of almost 50 per cent (Office for National Statistics, 2011c). In the past 50 years, the UK labour market has seen a number of changes, which include a growth in the size of the labour force, increased female participation in the labour market, a shift away from manufacturing to services, and periods of recession in every decade since the 1970s (Spence, 2011). As of June 2011, over 29 million people were employed in the UK, 6 million of these in the public sector, with non-UK-born workers accounting for 4.15 million of the workforce (Office for National Statistics, 2011c). Since the recession of 2008, unemployment has increased significantly, with 2.51 million people unemployed in the UK in June 2011. The number of unemployed people per vacancy has more than doubled, from 2.3 to 5.1, since March 2008 (Spence, 2011). Youth unemployment is a particular area for concern, with almost 21 per cent of economically active 16–24-year-olds unemployed (Office for National Statistics, 2011c). New graduates are also experiencing the highest level of unemployment for a decade, and, even among those in jobs, there is increasing evidence of underemployment (Scurry and Blenkinsopp, 2011; Spence, 2011).

**TABLE 3.2** UK labour market indicators (Office for National Statistics, 2011c)

| UK labour market statistics | Total |
| --- | --- |
| Employment rate | 70.5% |
| Unemployment rate | 7.9% |
| Public-sector employment | 20.7% |
| Part-time employment | 26.8% |
| Jobs in services | 84.4% |
| Jobs in manufacturing | 8.9% |
| Average working hours | 31.4 hours |
| Average weekly gross earnings (including bonuses) | £464.00 |

In spite of the state of the economy, rising levels of unemployment and changes to government policy that seek to reduce immigration, the number of immigrants to the UK remains high – an estimated 455,000 in 2010. A diverse range of individuals pursue global careers in the UK, ranging from highly skilled professionals to low or unskilled workers, from individuals who are here for the purpose of pursuing enhanced opportunities to those who have been forced to migrate as refugees seeking asylum. The UK continues to be an attractive destination for highly skilled professionals pursuing global careers, being consistently identified as one of the top three destinations for international assignments (Brookfield Global Relocation Services, 2011).

Limitations in the official data on emigration and immigration mean it is not always clear if people have migrated for the purpose of employment (economic/labour migration) or if they moved for other reasons (e.g. study) and chose to remain for employment. This lack of data makes it incredibly difficult to establish a sense of just how many individuals are enacting global careers in the UK and what these careers 'look like'. However, drawing on various data sources as proxy measures, we can infer that a large number of migrants participate in the UK labour market. For example, in the year to June 2011, over 158,000 work-related visas were issued in the UK (Office for National Statistics, 2011b). This level of immigration – and the debate surrounding it, particularly in relation to work and employment – makes the UK an interesting context for the examination of global careers.

In the following section, we review contemporary career models, to consider whether they are a good fit for the UK, focusing on the relevance (or otherwise) of concepts such as the boundaryless and protean career to the observed pattern of careers in the UK, at the individual, organisational and national levels.

## Contemporary Career Theory

Within contemporary careers research, considerable attention has been paid to the claimed emergence of new employment patterns, such as the boundaryless, protean and kaleidoscope careers (Arthur, 1994; Hall, 1996; Mainiero and Sullivan, 2005). The discourse around these 'contemporary careers' (Arthur, 2008) suggests that traditional boundaries (vertical, horizontal, geographical) are diminishing (DeFillippi and Arthur, 1996); that individuals are assuming more responsibility for their career development and management (Hall, 1996); and that subjective factors play an important role in an individual's career decisions and evaluation of career success (Mirvis and Hall, 1994). These new career concepts were developed mainly in the USA, and there has been growing debate about their relevance to different contexts – national, professional and generational (Khapova, Vinkenburg and Arnold, 2009; King, 2003). Despite this rhetoric of contemporary careers, career expectations in the UK appear to align with more traditional perspectives of career and employment (Guest and Conway, 2004).

Gerber, Wittekind, Grote, Conway and Guest (2009) found that British employees had low levels of orientation towards boundarylessness within their careers, yet displayed highly protean attitudes, with a focus on advancement and the future. This suggests that long-term employment and job security are prioritised over employability, and yet there is a desire and/or recognition of the need to take individual responsibility for career management. This orientation differed from the Swiss employees in their sample, and the authors argue this is owing to the cultural context of the UK. Zaleska and de Menezes (2007), studying six UK-based companies in different industries in 1997 and 2000, also found evidence that traditional career structures were not declining, but individuals were nevertheless taking more responsibility for defining careers. However, this evidence of greater personal ownership in careers is rather contradicted by research looking at career expectations of graduates in the UK, which shows most graduates still anticipate traditional career trajectories in single organisations, with an expectation of organisational career management (King, 2003; Pitcher and Purcell, 1998). This is surprising, given the significant changes that have occurred in the UK graduate labour market in recent years. Research findings have shown that access to a 'traditional' career is limited, and that labour-market outcomes are increasingly varied, with a higher chance of underemployment and unemployment (King, 2003; Scurry and Blenkinsopp, 2009). It is also contrary to arguments that suggest that younger generations, often referred to as 'millennials' or 'Generation Y', have embraced contemporary notions of career (Westerman and Yamamura, 2007).

The emphasis on the importance of individual agency and individuals' career capital is captured by the notion of the intelligent career. This concept was proposed by DeFillippi and Arthur (1996), who argue that individuals can develop career capital through accumulation of competencies – knowing why, knowing how and knowing whom. Carr, Inkson and Thorn (2005) draw on this framework in their consideration of boundaryless global careers. Arguing that there is need to consider more than the physical geographic mobility of global careers, they suggest that exploring career competencies provides insight into the dynamic

**TABLE 3.3** Career competencies in global careers (based on Carr, Inkson and Thorn, 2005)

| Intelligent career competencies | Relation to global careers |
| --- | --- |
| Knowing why | Motivation to pursue a global career<br>Personal values |
| Knowing how | Obtaining recognition (or not) of experiences and skills in different global contexts |
| Knowing whom | Integration and acceptance into networks<br>Development of personal reputation in new global context |

taxonomy of factors that underpin individuals' decisions to enact global careers and their experience of those careers. These factors are outlined in Table 3.3, and we return to them in considering the structural, cultural and contextual difficulties of global careers in the UK context.

## Global Careers as Talent Flow

Cappellen and Janssens (2005) argue that global careers are influenced by a range of intersecting factors within the individual, organisational and global environments. Factors identified as relevant to the UK context include career development, cultural and travel opportunities, economic gain, development of human capital, quality of life, political environment and family/social relationships. Moving away from traditional conceptions of migration as brain gain and brain drain, Carr et al. (2005) present global career moves in terms of talent flow. This overarching concept captures the dynamics of knowledge flow in the contemporary global economy – moving beyond notions of intelligence, scientific or technological, and incorporating a wider range of global movement, such as skills and competencies. Drawing upon this model, we examine global talent flow within the UK context, focusing on outflow and inflow.

### Outflow: Careers of UK Nationals in the Global Context

It is estimated that some 2.7 million British nationals emigrated from the UK between 1966 and 2005 (Sriskandarajah and Drew, 2006). Recent OECD data suggest that 3.4 million UK-born individuals reside in other OECD countries (Dumont and Lemaître, 2005), and, within popular culture, there are extensive references to 'Brits abroad'. Despite this, there is a scarcity of research that focuses on this group of migrants, reflecting a tendency for migration research to focus on low-skilled, economically disadvantaged individuals migrating to developed industrial contexts, as opposed to 'privileged' Europeans (Fechter and Walsh, 2010). Ironically, the trend in the careers literature is almost exactly the opposite.

Recent Office for National Statistics (ONS) data estimate that long-term emigration from the UK has declined from 427,000 in December 2008 to 336,000 in December 2010 (Office for National Statistics, 2011b). Although these data suggest that high numbers of UK nationals continue to emigrate from the UK to reside in other countries, they lack detail with regards to the duration and purpose of the stay, individuals' occupations and qualifications, and whether they return to their home country. Drawing on the International Passenger Survey (IPS), it is estimated that of the 336,000 leaving the UK in the year ending December 2010, 179,000 (53 per cent) were doing so for work-related reasons. Of this group 60 per cent were emigrating to a definite job (Office for National Statistics, 2011b). The figures therefore suggest that almost 50 per cent of those emigrating from the UK do so for purposes other than work, with growing numbers emigrating from the UK upon retirement (King, Warnes and Williams,

2000). It is difficult, therefore, to gain an accurate picture of the number of UK nationals who are working abroad, enacting global careers.

The idea of a cadre of international managers pursuing global careers, through a range of international assignments for multinational enterprises, has been a popular notion for many years. Often referred to as expatriates (colloquially and within the academic field), these individuals are typically employees of multinational enterprises and occupy a privileged position within the labour market, having guaranteed employment and organizational support (Collings, Doherty, Luethy and Osborn, 2011). Traditionally, international assignments were long term, but there has been growing use of alternative forms, including short-term, frequent-flyer or commuter assignments (Collings, Scullion and Morley, 2007). However, recent data indicate that long-term global assignments (of a year or more) are still the most common type (Brookfield Global Relocation Services, 2011). Writing in 2000, Forster argued there was little evidence from labour market data to suggest that this pattern was common in the UK. Although large numbers of UK-born individuals work overseas, the majority of these individuals are permanent migrants, as opposed to the international global manager as portrayed in the management-practitioner and academic literature. McKenna and Richardson (2007) highlight a similar issue in relation to self-initiated expatriates, who 'elect to go overseas independently' (Richardson, 2006: 469), rather than on international assignments for an employer, suggesting it is difficult to distinguish between those who are emigrating and those who intend to return home or move elsewhere. This is important, as individuals enacting careers associated with migration may have significantly different motivations and experiences.

Drawing on the intelligent-careers framework presented in Table 3.3 allows us to consider what drives individuals to undertake global assignments. Knowing-why competencies relate to personal meaning and motivation in relation to global careers, with individuals looking to fulfil intrinsic motives for challenge that reflect their global mindset by searching for international challenges or pursuing careers in different countries (Cappellen and Janssens, 2005). Baruch (2002) argues that a global mindset does not stem from demographic characteristics, or particular knowledge or experiences; rather, it comes from openness, awareness and appreciating the unknown. The idea of a 'global mindset' driving the pursuit of global careers may not, however, apply to UK nationals. Drawing on data collected from individuals in UK companies who had undertaken an international assignment, Forster (2000) found that very few were planning careers that would involve long periods of time away from the UK. Individuals who had accepted international assignments were often unwilling to relocate for a second time, with only 13 per cent indicating they would definitely accept further international assignments (Forster, 2000). By contrast, similar data collected from Finnish and Japanese samples found that individuals displayed a greater level of willingness to accept multiple international assignments (Suutari, 2003). If a global mindset is not necessarily the main driving force behind UK nationals' willingness to accept

global assignments, there is evidence that this mindset – personal desire for travel, adventure and cross-cultural experience – *is* a driver for self-initiated expatriation (Doherty, Dickmann and Mills, 2011; Richardson and McKenna, 2003). Research has also highlighted the importance of family considerations in making decisions (Richardson and McKenna, 2006). In a study of British and Indian scientists who were in the USA, Harvey (2011) found that over 50 per cent of participants had made their decision with family members.

## Inflow: Immigration in the UK Context

The UK has experienced high levels of immigration in the postwar period, at first predominantly from former colonies, and more recently from Central and Eastern Europe and the Middle East (Demireva, 2011). Determining levels of economic migration is challenging and relies on proxy measures, such as the issue of work-related visas and allocation of national insurance numbers to non-UK nationals. In the year to June 2011, there were 158,180 work-related visas issued, and, in the same period, over 700,000 non-UK nationals were allocated national insurance numbers, of which 187,000 were allocated to A8 nationals (Office for National Statistics, 2011b). These data provide an idea of the number of 'foreign-born' individuals currently residing in the UK, but we can only estimate the numbers that are enacting global careers. The IPS data suggest that 110,000 of those migrating to the UK between June 2010 and June 2011 were doing so for a definite job; this is the lowest since March 2004 (Office for National Statistics, 2011b).

Research on international assignments has typically focused on managers from Western countries working in less affluent countries, therefore neglecting the growing numbers of multinationals and expatriates from other countries coming to the UK (Lett and Smith, 2009). From the organisational perspective, the UK is seen as an attractive destination for foreign direct investment, owing to the size of, and access to, wider European markets and political stability (Jones and Wren, 2005). In addition, for some, the perceived familiarity and similarity with language, history and culture result in perceptions of lower psychic distance and are major drivers for foreign companies to locate in the UK (Fenwick, Edwards and Buckley, 2003). For individuals, a complex range of factors underpins acceptance of global assignments (Dickmann, Doherty, Mills and Brewster, 2008), which, for the UK, includes career development, increased living standards, opportunities for family and a different working environment to that of their country of origin (Lett and Smith, 2009). Some studies suggest, however, that for some the primary motivation is the organisation's need: in their study of Japanese expatriates in Britain, Nicholson and Imaizumi (1993) found that 73 per cent of the sample agreed that the purpose of the assignment was 'to meet a specific operational need', compared with only 59 per cent who agreed with the proposition that it was to advance their career. Dickmann and Mills (2010) highlight the need to incorporate

location as an influencing factor. Drawing on data from company-sent and self-initiated foreign professionals working in London, they propose that specific location factors can be as important as individual, family and country factors. This is particularly important for the UK, as there are pronounced variations between regions, in particular between London and the rest of the UK, with regards to multiculturalism, reputation as a place to do business, and attractiveness as a place to live. In addition, London's status as a 'global city' (Sassen, 1991) draws in people from around the world, and this has an impact on the UK as a whole. This is reflected in immigration data that show that London has the highest levels of work-related immigration in the UK (Office for National Statistics, 2011b). In relation to self-initiated expatriates, there is limited empirical research. A report into migration of academics from Africa, who can be viewed as highly skilled professionals, identified that higher wage levels, increased opportunities, working conditions and stable political environments were key 'pull' factors for coming to the UK (Nunn, 2005).

Thus far, we have used the term expatriate to refer to those leaving or coming to the UK, either self-initiated or initiated by an employing organisation, who are pursuing global careers. The term continues to pervade popular media and is highly visible within the discourse of international HRM and among 'expatriates' themselves. However, Fechter and Walsh (2010) argue that the term tends to be reserved for white, Western migrants and marks this out as a different form of migration. This is important to highlight in a discussion of the 'inflow' of talent to the UK, as the majority of migrants enacting global careers are not classified in these terms (Al Ariss, 2010). The term migrant worker is used to refer to both skilled and unskilled migrants and, therefore, covers a vast spectrum of groups and types of employment. For example, skilled migrants to the UK are a key element of the National Health Service (NHS) workforce, which has long been reliant on migrant labour, especially medical staff – as early as the 1950s, over 10 per cent of NHS doctors were overseas-trained (Bornat, Henry and Raghuram, 2011). In contrast, low-skilled migrants occupy low-wage occupations, often within agriculture, construction and hospitality (Anderson, Ruhs, Rugaly and Spencer, 2006). It is difficult to estimate the numbers of individuals within these groups. ONS data indicate marked differences between UK-born and migrant workers in terms of the industry and type of employment they enter. Those from A8 countries tend to work in sectors requiring lower levels of skills and training. Concentrated mainly in manufacturing, distribution, hotels and restaurants, over a third of this group works in 'elementary occupations' (Khan and Ker, 2009). Migrant workers make up large proportions of the workforce in certain sectors, such as tourism, which relies heavily on migrant workers (Baum, 2007), with 22 per cent of the workforce nationally born overseas, rising to 63 per cent in London (People 1st, 2011). Janta, Brown, Lugosi and Ladkin (2011a) identify that Central and Eastern European migrants, in particular Polish nationals, are the largest workforce groups within this sector.

In 2008, over 109,000 of the 171,940 registered migrants employed in hospitality were Polish (Janta, Ladkin, Brown and Lugosi, 2011b). Research in other sectors has also highlighted reliance on migrant workers, albeit with considerable regional variation – approximately 18 per cent of social care workers in the UK are migrants, reaching 50 per cent in London (Cangiano, Shutes, Spencer and Leeson, 2009). Growing numbers of migrants in the UK are seeking self-employment as an option; this has been a traditional route for Asian migrants, but 'new' migrant groups from EU10 and Eastern Europe are increasingly self-employed, particularly in construction (Demireva, 2011). Within the literature, the motivations ascribed to this group vary, but tend to align with those previously identified for other groups – higher earnings, opportunity to improve language skills, overseas experience and career development (Janta et al., 2011a, 2011b). Social networks have increasingly been identified as key to the motivation and facilitation of international migration, providing finance, accommodation and jobs. White and Ryan (2008) found that networks explained the destination of Polish migrants to the UK, linked to what Janta et al. (2011a: 4) call chain migration, where 'new members of family and others from migrants' social network are "pulled in" by those who have migrated before', illustrated by the ways in which social networks of Polish migrants in the tourism industry provided access to employment opportunities and emotional support.

So far, our discussions have focused on those coming to the UK in a formal and regular sense. We now turn to our considerations to those who are enacting illegal or 'irregular' global careers. Relatively neglected within the careers field, this phenomenon has been explored within the migration research – see Anderson and Ruhs (2010) for a discussion. It is estimated that there are over half a million irregular migrants in the UK, over 60 per cent of whom are in London (Finch and Cherti, 2011). Irregularity can apply to individuals who arrive in the UK as refugees seeking asylum, or individuals here in the pursuit of opportunities without the necessary legal status. Bloch, Sigona and Zetter (2011), drawing on data gathered from seventy-five undocumented workers without right of residence in the UK, found that reasons for migrating to the UK were a complex interplay of political and economic situations in the country of birth, and were driven by both individuals and their families. For the majority, migration to the UK was about economic survival for themselves and their families, although a minority of their respondents were seeking personal development through overseas experience. Marfleet and Blustein (2011) make a similar point, seeing economic survival as the main driver for the 'global career' of irregular migrants. Aside from the personal circumstances of this group, they argue that the types of job that they are able to enter do not offer opportunity for career development or progression. This raises questions about the appropriateness of existing career theories for exploring the global careers of such groups.

Those coming to the UK to study represent another very large group of migrants, with figures for June 2011 suggesting there were about 228,000

international students in the UK, of whom 78 per cent were from outside the EU (Office for National Statistics, 2011c), with China and India being especially important sources of students. Students would appear to be an important group to consider, and yet are largely neglected within the skilled-migration and global-career literatures (Harvey, 2011). They are especially important in the UK context, partly because of the very high numbers, but also because of the 'career premium' attached to education and experience gained in the UK, particularly by those from developing countries. Individuals who elect to further their education often do so with career development in mind – aiming to accumulate career capital through their qualifications and experiences (Simpson, 2000; Simpson, Sturges and Weight, 2010). Many students come to the UK on a temporary basis, intending to return to their home country after completing their programmes and potentially gaining some work experience (Baruch, Budhwar and Khatri, 2007), and they invest in this experience in the hope that time spent in the UK will provide them with opportunities for career development in the global arena. Such investments are underpinned with expectations for self-improvement, professional advancement, increased global mobility and enrichment from the foreign experience (Robinson, 2005; Simpson et al., 2010).

## Structural, Cultural and Contextual Difficulties Pursuing Global Careers in the UK Context

The importance of considering the cultural context was highlighted at an early stage in the development of the careers field, with Schein arguing that,

> Societal, occupational and organizational cultures influence the structure of the external career, prestige associated with given careers, the legitimacy of certain motives underlying careers, success criteria, the clarity of the career concept itself, and the importance attached to career versus family and self-development. How career occupants view their careers and the degree of variation in such views within given societies, occupations, and organizations is culturally patterned.
>
> (Schein, 1984: 71)

In spite of this call, these aspects have not been explored in depth within the careers field outside the USA (Khapova et al., 2009), and there is a need to explore the transfer and translation of career concepts from different cultures to the UK. We agree with Cohen, Arnold and O'Neill (2011) that there is a need to move beyond simply profiling countries in terms of cultural norms, and to explore the wider institutional and societal factors that influence the deployment and accumulation of career capital for different groups; see also Kats, Van Emmerik, Blenkinsopp and Khapova (2010). In addition, we acknowledge the call of Al Ariss and Syed (2011) to explore the agency of individuals in the context of

the structural and institutional influences. Within this section, we therefore incorporate these perspectives into our discussions of the difficulties encountered by those pursuing global careers in the UK context.

At the macro level, UK government immigration policies, alongside development of the European Union, have a significant impact on global careers. Although the effect varies for different groups, they can be far reaching and have implications for expectations and experiences. Migrants who arrive for purposes of asylum feel the effects most keenly, finding themselves in a state of limbo while their cases for asylum are considered, without access to the documents that provide them with 'permission' to live and work in the UK. Bloch et al. (2011) found some individuals had actively chosen irregular migration rather than enter the formal process of asylum, owing to the fear of being refused and deported. Both contexts drive some to enter the informal economy or to enter the formal economy through illegal means – what Vasta (2011: 187) refers to as the 'borrowing, renting and buying of identities'. Her research found this was both an act of resistance and accommodation to state control and exclusion. The migrants engaged in what she terms 'constructive subjectivity', whereby identity construction was a process of irregular formality – a way by which they could contribute to the host country and challenge their stigmatized position. In career terms, this can have constraints on individuals' ability to utilise their human capital, both now and in the future. In addition, transitions to formal employment can be difficult – both in terms of accounting for this period of time but also of how to display development if it has occurred. Bloch et al. (2011) highlight how attempts to regularise and formalise status are risky, as they make individuals 'visible'.

A different perspective on visas and government immigration policies comes from the work of Forstenlechner (2010), who found that intentions to remain for British self-initiated expatriates in Austria and the United Arab Emirates were influenced by perceptions of host country support (legal rights, discrimination and government interactions). Respondents in Austria reported higher levels of dissatisfaction, which, on the face of it, seems surprising, given its greater similarity to the UK, but may stem from a greater mismatch in expectations. Such issues, however, were seen to be counterbalanced by other factors, such as salary, reflecting the highly skilled, often privileged, positions that these individuals occupied within organisations. Migrant workers also experience issues related to the translation and adaptation of experience and educational credentials accumulated in countries of origin to a UK context. This raises questions regarding the transferability of migrants' career capital, highlighting that career capital accumulated in some countries has low levels of currency in the UK (Mayrhofer, Meyer, Iellatchitch and Schiffinger, 2004). Bimrose and McNair (2011) also acknowledge the difference between migrants with internationally recognised qualifications, often in highly skilled occupations, and those occupying lower-level jobs, as their qualifications are not recognised. For some highly skilled migrants, their qualifications are recognised, and yet a limited availability of positions results in

overrepresentation of skilled migrants in unskilled jobs (Demireva, 2011). In such circumstances, accepting lower-level positions is seen to be adequate in the short term, as career capital, development of language and experience in the host country can be accumulated to facilitate moves into jobs of the appropriate level (Anderson et al., 2006). Such issues raise debates related to the underemployment of migrants and notions of talent waste. This can lead to career frustration (Carr et al., 2005) and long-term wage disadvantage, in comparison with the native population, and within and between different migrant groups. Skill level, occupation, country of origin and ethnicity have all been found to affect the labour-market opportunities and trajectories of individuals (Bimrose and McNair, 2011; Demireva and Kesler, 2011) and are significant contributing factors to talent waste in the UK. This situation is arguably exacerbated by the practice of employing the majority of migrant workers in the UK on the basis of 'maximum hours for minimum wage' (MacKenzie and Ford, 2009: 156). Janta et al. (2011b) note that, although a high percentage of migrants have the potential to be developed in career terms, this is not a high priority for employers. This both reflects and perpetuates discrimination evident within the UK related to county of origin and ethnicity. Demireva and Kesler (2011) found that certain groups of migrants experienced higher levels of instability, in particular Turkish and EU10 (the 10 countries to join the EU in 2004 – the A8 plus Cyprus and Malta) immigrants, and were persistently disadvantaged in the labour market, with little chance of future improvement. Erel (2010) also found that Turkish migrants were affected by non-recognition of qualifications and racist labour-market structures.

Individuals coming to the UK often experience difficulties in adjusting to the culture, apparently because of assumptions of similarity made by individuals and organisations from Western countries. This can lead to adjustment difficulties, owing to a lack of preparation. The 2011 Global Relocation Trends Survey (Brookfield Global Relocation Services, 2011) identified that individuals on assignment in the UK face greater difficulties than in other European countries. This assumption of similarity may stem from stereotypes made on the basis of language. Caligiuri, Phillips, Lazarova, Tarique and Burgi (2001) found that expatriates who spoke the language of a host country tended to expect an 'easier experience' than those who did not. Fenwick, Edwards and Buckley (2003) found that perceived similarity or familiarity between Australia and Britain resulted in 'cultural over-confidence', particularly in relation to management style. In a similar vein, other research found that Swedish and Finnish expatriates in the UK experienced unanticipated difficulties in adjustment, owing to contrasting leadership styles between their country of origin and the UK (Brewster, 1993; Suutari and Brewster, 1998). Lett and Smith (2009) explored the experience of Polish expatriates in the UK and found that a number of UK-specific factors influenced individuals' adjustment. The individualism and associated autonomy of the UK context was welcomed; however, there was limited social interaction with host-country nationals (HCNs), as well as negative consequences of the UK's

culture of long hours. Conversely, a study of Japanese expatriates in the UK found that they experienced increased work–life balance, causing potential problems for repatriation in the future (Nicholson and Imaizumi, 1993).

Integration into the UK has been highlighted as an area where migrants of all levels experience some challenges. In a study of highly skilled expatriates from India and the USA, Varma, Pichler and Budhwar (2011) found that HCNs in the UK were more likely to include 'expatriates' in their in-groups, offering information and social support, if they perceived them to have similar values, often established from characteristics such as national origin, ethnicity and gender. Migration research has highlighted similar issues for those in lower-skilled positions, although it is suggested that location can play an important role (Dickmann and Mills, 2010). For example, Weishaar (2010) found that Polish migrants in Edinburgh tended to integrate successfully, perhaps as a result of the city having a diverse and international environment.

Within the UK, there are questions about the value of international experience in relation to careers. Ackers (2005) notes that the premium attached to international experience and working abroad (in the context of scientific research) is much higher in most EU member states than it is in the UK, partly explaining why so many EU researchers come to the UK, and comparatively few UK nationals leave. This is reflected in a study of UK expatriate academics that found that individuals were anxious about the impact of their expatriation on their future career (Richardson and Mallon, 2005).

## Stories of Global Careers

Researchers have questioned the extent to which the expectations of migrants seeking to further their careers in the UK are met (Currie, 2007; Robinson, 2005; Simpson et al., 2010) and claim that, although geographical boundaries are crossed, deeper boundaries remain. The stories below of international students studying on UK Master's programmes illustrate some of the structural and cultural barriers faced in developing the global career in the UK context.

The stories of Jie and Zahid suggest that the potential for study abroad to assist the development of a global career is not always realised. HCNs, whether they be other students, faculty or recruiters, seemingly struggle to respond to the diversity of the international student body in ways that value them and facilitate an enriched experience for all. However, there are many positive elements to the international student experience in the UK. Although the experience can often be challenging, a significant proportion of students have intentions to remain in the UK (Baruch et al., 2007), and, ultimately, the experience can result in profound learning (Griffiths, Winstanley and Gabriel, 2005; Simpson et al., 2010), which suggests that education offers real promise for the development of global careers in the UK. However, echoing calls from Tomlinson and Egan (2002), further research is needed to deepen our understanding of the dynamics

## Developing a Global Career through Education

Jie is an MBA student from China, who, like many other international students, found the learning experience was at times extremely frustrating and challenging. The differences evident in the UK programme resulted in 'learning shock' (Griffiths et al., 2005), which left her feeling isolated and lonely. Of course, language was a problem – the UK students and teachers often spoke far too quickly for her to keep up – but differences ran deeper than this. Group work, in particular, presented special challenges, as she struggled to cope with the high levels of group conflict, which stood in stark contrast to her preference for group harmony. In addition, Jie was perplexed by expectations of active contribution to class discussions and critique of presented material. Why was she being asked to do this? However, when Jie did attempt to share her experiences from the Chinese context, she felt these were undervalued, with others failing to see the world from her point of view.

Moreover, it is not just the learning experience that can be challenging. Zahid is a 24-year-old Master's in HRM student from Pakistan who illustrates the difficulties international students face in obtaining work experience in the UK. As part of his programme, Zahid was required to undertake a placement of 100 hours. This was one of the elements of the programme that had attracted him, and he was keen to use the placement to develop his CV. Zahid, like many of the other international students on his programme, had immense difficulty in securing a placement. He applied for all placements that were offered at the university and independently approached a large number of organisations. He eventually secured a placement with the local council for a project focused on encouraging diversity in the workforce. Zahid was also keen to secure further work experience after the completion of his course, but two years later he had still not obtained employment – despite having a Master's degree and work experience, Zahid was rarely making it to interview. He had taken some temporary agency positions, but these were mainly administrative roles for a few days at a time and failed to be the stepping-stone that he hoped. Zahid was keen to fulfil his ambition of obtaining work experience in the UK but was aware that his visa was coming to an end. He finally managed to obtain employment on a fixed-term contract with the local council with which he had undertaken his placement.

that arise from studying across cultural boundaries to leverage positive experiences of international students seeking to develop their careers in the UK.

The story of Awate, an asylum seeker from Eritrea, illustrates the often hidden struggles of immigrants in the UK, highlighting further the complexities of the global career as played out in the UK context.

This example illustrates the complex motivations that can lie behind the enactment of the career in the UK context. Although the prestige of the UK education system is a potential pull factor, it is the pressing dangers of his home country that push the individual to develop his career in another country, with

## Global Careers and Migration

Awate was born in 1971 to a well-off family in Asmara, the capital city of Eritrea. He went to the only university in the country and completed a degree in accountancy, obtaining a post with the Ministry of Finance after graduating and eventually progressing to a senior role. He was earning a decent salary, happily married with a son, and living in a property owned by his father. He had no plans to come to Britain beyond a faint possibility of coming to study for a year or two, stemming from the perception that Britain has the best education system in world. This linked to his career ambitions of becoming a university lecturer, a prestigious occupation in Eritrea.

His departure was triggered by the experience of war in his country, which led to persecution of minority ethnic and religious groups. Awate was a prominent lay preacher and, because he also worked for the government, he felt he was a target for arrest. In 1998, following a police raid on his house and the arrest of members of his church who were attending a bible study and prayer session, he paid an agent to take him out of the country to a safe country, not knowing where he would be taken. Unusually, he was flown directly to the UK, whereas the typical route for an Eritrean asylum seeker would be more treacherous – typically a land journey (often largely on foot) taking anything from 6 months to 2 years, at a cost of around £15,000, money that is borrowed and repaid as soon as possible.

Awate arrived in the UK in March 1999 and immediately claimed asylum at the airport. This was the start of a 7-year process, during which time Awate struggled to have his account accepted. He was repeatedly told by Home Office officials that Eritrea was a safe country, and that his account was contrary to this. Awate was given a work permit 6 months after arrival, which he now considers most fortunate. Policy has since changed, and asylum seekers are not permitted to work until granted refugee status, which can take many years. Had Awate not received the work permit, he is sure that he, like many other Eritreans, would have been forced into the 'black economy' and welfare cheating, because of the length of the asylum process. He acknowledges the detrimental effect that working in the illegal economy has had for other Eritrean migrants in the UK. They are not able to have savings in their name, nor do they accumulate any official work experience. In the 7 years awaiting a decision from the Home Office, Awate studied for an MBA and a PGCE (Post Graduate Certificate in Education) and, as he had a work permit, he was also able to work as a supply teacher for 4 years. In addition, he worked as a sessional interpreter for the NHS (GPs, dentists, opticians), Social Services, the Police and, ironically, for the Home Office and Immigration.

the UK being an attractive location for many reasons. Given the issues surrounding the legality of employment status in the UK, the career can be seen to unfold in a rather haphazard and fragmented way. The very real challenges of developing a career under precarious conditions highlight the marginalised complexities of immigrants pursuing careers in the UK context, as they battle difficult and lengthy legal processes.

## Critical Perspectives of Global Careers in the UK Context

In spite of the increasing rhetoric of careers without borders, our understanding of the majority of individuals that are enacting such careers in the UK context is limited.

It is surprising what we do not know, and also what we appear to ignore. Our discussions suggest that, despite figures that suggest a healthy circulation of global talent to and from the UK, especially in regards to the high levels of immigrants entering the country, the reality is often less positive, with an underutilisation of talent evident. Echoing calls from Tams and Arthur (2007: 96), who advocate 'bringing to light . . . less obvious and marginalised accounts of those groups that face greater barriers in adapting to a global economy', we argue that it is important to understand and reflect upon the lived experiences of those developing global careers, to illuminate the diverse and complex barriers that serve to limit the realisation of global talent residing in the UK.

While recognising that we need to avoid 'skewed notions of who migrants are' (Fechter and Walsh, 2010: 1198), we argue that, in the UK context, there is a particular need for further consideration of low-skilled, economically disadvantaged individuals, as current perspectives within the field of global careers are inadequate in capturing the dynamic interplay of structural and cultural barriers that influence the deployment and accumulation of career capital for migrant workers, as they negotiate their own identities and position within the UK context (Cohen et al., 2011). To date, research in the global-careers field has tended to study people most like 'us' – individuals who are professional and highly skilled – which neglects the rather different challenges that are faced by lower-skilled migrants that are so important in the UK context. Despite increased levels of globalisation, migrants are experiencing tighter regulations, requirements and restrictions, accompanied by an increasing importance placed on citizenship. Our discussions have highlighted how global careers are characterised by precariousness for some groups. This not only arises from their legal status and the nature of their employment, but is also evident in the extent to which individuals are able to deploy and develop their career capital.

Bourdieu (1986) argues that capital takes three forms: economic (financial assets), social (relationships, networks, memberships) and cultural (education, knowledge, skills). Given that social and cultural capital have been acknowledged as playing an important role in the occupational and social mobility of migrants (Al Ariss and Syed, 2011), we need to explore the barriers that individuals and groups face when attempting to mobilize their cultural and social capital in the UK context. Drawing on the Bourdieusian concept of the institutionalised state of cultural capital, Erel (2010) notes that, for many migrant workers, institutional cultural capital (for example, formal education qualifications) is not always 'transnationally valid', and, as a consequence, they face 'nationally based protectionism', whereby their qualifications are not formally recognised, or are negated by the lack of

experience in the local context. Social capital is argued to play an important role in the facilitation of migration; however, research indicates that this is often simplified in relation to migrants, arguing that migrants are not homogenous, and that experiences differ, with individuals and groups needing to negotiate and develop their social capital in different ways at different points in time (Ryan, Sales, Tilki and Siara, 2008). There is a need to explore how individuals and groups negotiate the value of their capital through '*position-taking*' (Bourdieu and Wacquant, 2007: 99, cited in Erel, 2010), and how this is influenced by gender, ethnicity, level of education and skill (Erel, 2010; Ryan et al., 2008).

However, that is not to suggest that individuals within this group are homogenous, nor are they simply passive recipients of the difficulties that we have outlined. Migration research has highlighted that migrants construct and negotiate their own identities and positions within this context (Bloch et al., 2011). We need to understand this in relation to the development of global careers, as this highlights how, 'the reality of the social world, including the self, is socially produced and therefore, open to transformation' (Alvesson and Willmott, 1992: 435). Consideration of the socially constructed nature of these situations also highlights the significance of exploring, not only the constructions of global careerists, but also the constructions of HCNs, who have a significant role to play in the unfolding of the global career. Study of the global career typically focuses on the perspectives of the global-career actor and his/her attempts to integrate into the UK. This marginalises the perspectives of UK nationals, which are needed to illuminate cultural and structural issues that act as barriers to the development of the global career.

## Conclusions

Throughout this consideration of global careers in the context of the UK, we have highlighted the complexity and diversity of experiences for individuals, organisations and societies. We have explored the diverse barriers, structural and cultural, that limit the realisation of the global careers for different groups within this context, and yet we have acknowledged the agency of individuals and groups. Our discussions have highlighted that certain groups are marginalised within the existing careers literature, in particular low-skilled workers and irregular migrants, both of which are important groups to consider in the context of the UK. We propose that further recognition and exploration of such groups are needed.

## References

Ackers, L. (2005). Moving people and knowledge: scientific mobility in the European Union, *International Migration*, 43(5): 99–131.

Al Ariss, A. (2010). Modes of engagement: migration, self-initiated expatriation, and career development, *Career Development International*, 15(4): 338–358.

Al Ariss, A. and Syed, J. (2011). Capital mobilization of skilled migrants: a relational perspective, *British Journal of Management*, 22: 286–304.

Alvesson, M. and Willmott, H. (1992). On the idea of emancipation in management and organization studies, *Academy of Management Review*, 17(3): 432–464.

Anderson, B. and Ruhs, M. (2010). Researching illegality and labour migration, *Population, Space and Place*, 16(3): 175–179.

Anderson, B., Ruhs, M., Rugaly, B. and Spencer, S. (2006). *Fair enough? Central and East European Migrants in Low-Wage Employment in the UK*. York: Joseph Rowntree Foundation.

Arnold, J. (1997). *Managing Careers into the 21st Century*. London: Paul Chapman.

Arthur, M. B. (1994). The boundaryless career, a new perspective for organizational inquiry, *Journal of Organizational Behaviour*, 15: 295–306.

Arthur, M. B. (2008). Examining contemporary careers: a call for interdisciplinary inquiry, *Human Relations*, 61: 163–186.

Arthur, M., Hall, D. and Lawrence, B. S. (1989). Generating new directions in career theory: the case for a transdisciplinary approach. In M. Arthur, D. Hall and B. S. Lawrence, *Handbook of Career Theory* (pp. 7–25). Cambridge: Cambridge University Press.

Baruch, Y. (2002). No such thing as a global manager, *Business Horizons*, 45(1): 36–42.

Baruch, Y., Budhwar, P. and Khatri, N. (2007). Brain drain, inclination to stay abroad after studies, *Journal of World Business*, 42: 99–112.

Baum, T. (2007). Human resources in tourism: still waiting for change, *Tourism Management*, 28(6): 1383–1399.

Bimrose, J. and McNair, S. (2011). Career support for migrants: transformation or adaptation?, *Journal of Vocational Behavior*, 78(3): 325–333.

Bloch, A. N., Sigona, N. and Zetter, R. (2011). Migration routes and strategies of young undocumented migrants in England, a qualitative perspective, *Ethnic and Racial Studies*, 34(8): 1286–1302.

Bornat, J., Henry, L. and Raghuram, P. (2011). The making of careers, the making of a discipline: luck and chance in migrant careers in geriatric medicine, *Journal of Vocational Behavior*, 78: 342–350.

Bourdieu, P. (1986). The forms of capital. In J. E. Richardson (ed.), *Handbook of Theory of Research for the Sociology of Education* (pp. 241–258). New York: Greenwood Press.

Bourdieu, P. and Wacquant, L. (2007). *An Invitation to Reflexive Sociology*. Cambridge: Polity.

Brewster, C. (1993). The paradox of adjustment: UK and Swedish expatriates in Sweden and the UK, *Human Resource Management Journal*, 4(1): 49–62.

Brookfield Global Relocation Services (2011). *Global Relocation Trends – 2011 Survey Report*. Brookfield Global Relocation Services.

Caligiuri, P., Phillips, J., Lazarova, M., Tarique, I. and Burgi, P. (2001). The theory of met expectations applied to expatriate adjustment, the role of cross-cultural training, *The International Journal of Human Resource Management*, 12(3): 357–372.

Cangiano, A., Shutes, I., Spencer, S. and Leeson, G. (2009). *Migrant Care Workers in Ageing Societies: research findings in the United Kingdom*. Oxford: Compas, University of Oxford.

Cappellen, T. and Janssens, M. (2005). Career paths of global managers: towards future research, *Journal of World Business*, 40(4): 348–360.

Carr, S. C., Inkson, K. and Thorn, K. (2005). From global careers to talent flow: reinterpreting brain drain, *Journal of World Business*, 40: 386–398.

Cohen, L., Arnold, J. and O'Neil, M. (2011). Migration: vocational perspectives on a complex and diverse transition, *Journal of Vocational Behavior*, 78: 321–324.

Collings, D. G., Doherty, N., Luethy, M. and Osborn, D. (2011). Understanding and supporting the career implications of international assignments, *Journal of Vocational Behavior*, 78: 361–371.

Collings, D. G., Scullion, H. and Morley, M. (2007). Changing patterns of global staffing in the multinational enterprise: challenges to the conventional expatriate assignment and emerging alternatives, *Journal of World Business*, 42: 198–213.

Currie, G. (2007). 'Beyond our imagination.' The voice of international students on the MBA, *Management Learning*, 38(5): 539–556.

DeFillippi, R. J. and Arthur, M. B. (1996). Boundaryless contexts and careers, a competency-based perspective. In M. B. Arthur and D. M. Rousseau (eds), *The Boundaryless Career* (pp. 116–131). New York: Oxford University Press.

Demireva, N. (2011). New migrants in the UK: employment patterns and occupational attainment, *Journal of Ethnic and Migration Studies*, 37(4): 637–655.

Demireva, N. and Kesler, C. (2011). The curse of inopportune transitions: the labour market behaviour of immigrants and natives in the UK, *International Journal of Comparative Sociology*, 52(4): 306–326.

Dickmann, M. and Baruch, Y. (2011). *Global Careers*. London: Routledge.

Dickmann, M. and Mills, T. (2010). The importance of intelligent career and location considerations: exploring the decision to go to London, *Personnel Review*, 39(1–2): 116–134.

Dickmann, M., Doherty, N., Mills, T. and Brewster, C. (2008). Why do they go? Individual and corporate perspectives on the factors influencing the deceivon to accept an internatiaonl assignment, *The International Journal of Human Resource Management*, 19(4): 731–751.

Doherty, N., Dickmann, M. and Mills, T. (2011). Exploring the motives of company-backed and self-initiated expatriates, *The International Journal of Human Resource Management*, 22(3): 595–611.

Dumont, J. C. and Lemaître, G. (2005). *Counting Immigrants and Expatriates in OECD Countries: A New Perspective*. OECD.

Erel, U. (2010). Migrating cultural capital, Bourdieu in migration studies, *Sociology*, 44(4): 642–660.

Fechter, A. M. and Walsh, K. (2010). Examining 'expatriate' continuities, postcolonial approaches to mobile professionals, *Journal of Ethnic and Migration Studies*, 36(8): 1197–1357.

Fenwick, M., Edwards, R. and Buckley, P. J. (2003). Is cultural similarity misleading? The experience of Australian manufacturers in Britain, *International Business Review*, 12: 297–309.

Finch, T. and Cherti, M. (2011). *No Easy Options: Irregular Immigration in the UK*. UK: Institute for Public Policy Research.

Forstenlechner, I. (2010). Exploring expatriates' behavioural reaction to institutional injustice on host country level, *Personnel Review*, 39(2): 178–194.

Forster, N. (2000). The myth of the international manager, *The International Journal of Human Resource Management*, 11(1): 126–142.

Gerber, M., Wittekind, A., Grote, G., Conway, N. and Guest, D. (2009). Generalizability of career orientations, a comparative study in Switzerland and Great Britain, *Journal of Occupational and Organizational Psychology*, 82: 779–801.

Griffiths, D. S., Winstanley, D. and Gabriel, Y. (2005). Learning shock. The trauma of return to formal learning, *Management Learning*, 36(3): 275–297.

Guest, D. and Conway, N. (2004). *Employee Well-being and the Psychological Contract*. London: CIPD.

Hall, D. T. (1996). Protean careers of the 21st century, *Academy of Management Executive*, 10: 8–18.

Harvey, W. S. (2011). British and Indian scientists moving to the United States, *Work and Occupations*, 38(1): 68–100.

Hatton, T. J. (2005). Explaining trends in UK immigration, *Journal of Population Economics*, 18: 719–740.

Inkson, K. and Thorn, K. (2010) Mobility and careers. In S. C. Carr (ed.), *The Psychology of Global Mobility* (pp. 259–278). New York: Springer.

Inkson, K., Arthur, M. B., Pringle, J. and Barry, S. (1997). Expatriate assignment versus overseas experience: international human resource development, *Journal of World Business*, 2: 351–368.

Janta, H., Brown, L., Lugosi, P. and Ladkin, A. (2011a). Migrant relationships and tourism employment, *Annals of Tourism Research*, 38(4): 1322–1343.

Janta, H., Ladkin, A., Brown, L. and Lugosi, P. (2011b). Employment experiences of Polish migrant workers in the UK hospitality sector, *Tourism Management*, 32: 1006–1019.

Jones, J. and Wren, C. (2005). *Foreign Direct Investment and the Regional Economy*. Aldershot: Ashgate.

Kats, M. S., Van Emmerik, I. J. H., Blenkinsopp, J. and Khapova, S. (2010). Exploring the associations of culture with careers and the mediating role of HR practices: a conceptual model, *Career Development International*, 15(4): 401–418.

Khan, K. and Ker, D. (2009). *Employment of Foreign Workers: Period of Arrival*. UK: Office for National Statistics.

Khapova, S. N., Vinkenburg, C. J. and Arnold, J. (2009). Careers research in Europe: identity and contribution, *Journal of Occupational and Organizational Psychology*, 82: 709–719.

King, Z. (2003). New or traditional careers? A study of UK graduates' preferences, *Human Resource Management Journal*, 13: 5–26.

King, R., Warnes, T. and Williams, A. (2000). *Sunset Lives: British Retirement Migration to the Mediterranean*. Oxford: Berg.

Lett, L. and Smith, M. (2009). East meets West, the case of Polish expatriates in the UK, *The International Journal of Human Resource Management*, 20(9): 1864–1878.

McKenna, S. and Richardson, J. (2007). The increasing complexity of the internationally mobile profession: issues for research and practice, *Cross Cultural Management: An International Journal*, 14(4): 307–320.

MacKenzie, R. and Forde, C. (2009). The rhetoric of the 'good worker' versus the realities of employers' use and the experiences of migrant workers, *Work, Employment and Society*, 23(1): 142–159.

Mainiero, L. and Sullivan, S. E. (2005). Kaleidoscope careers, an alternate explanation for the 'Opt-out' revolution, *Academy of Management Executive*, 19: 106–123.

Marfleet, P. and Blustein, D. L. (2011). Need not wanted: an interdisciplinary examination of the work-related challenges faced by irregular migrants, *Journal of Vocational Behavior*, 78: 381–389.

Mayrhofer, W., Meyer, M., Iellatchitch, A. and Schiffinger, M. (2004). Careers and human resource management – a European perspective, *Human Resource Management Review*, 17: 473–498.

Mirvis, P. H. and Hall, D. T. (1994). Psychological success and the boundaryless career, *Journal of Organizational Behaviour*, 15: 365–380.

Nicholson, N. and Imaizumi, A. (1993). The adjustment of Japanese expatriates to living and working in Britain, *British Journal of Management*, 4(2): 119–134.

Nunn, A. (2005). *The Brain Drain: Academic and Skilled Migration to the UK and its Impact on Africa*. Report to the AUT and NATFHE. Leeds: Policy Research Institute.

Office for National Statistics (2011a). Population by Country of Birth and Nationality Oct 2009 to Sep 2010. Retrieved from www.ons.gov.uk/ons/publications/re-reference-tables.html?edition=tcm%3A77-219289, 6 October 2011.

Office for National Statistics (2011b). Migration Statistics Quarterly Report August 2011. Retrieved from www.ons.gov.uk/ons/rel/migration1/migration-statistics-quarterly-report/august-2011/index.html, 6 October 2011.

Office for National Statistics (2011c). Labour Market Statistics September 2011. Retrieved from www.ons.gov.uk/ons/rel/lms/labour-market-statistics/september-2011/index.html, 6 October 2011.

People 1st (2011) Unravelling the Skills Spaghetti. Retrieved from www.people1st.co.uk/webfiles/Pdfs/Research/Unravellng%20the%20Skills%20Spaghetti%20.pdf, 10 October 2011.

Pitcher, J. and Purcell, K. (1998). Diverse expectations and access to opportunity, is there a graduate labour market?, *Higher Education Quarterly*, 52(2): 179–203.

Pollard, N., Latorre, M. and Sriskandarajah, D. (2008). *Floodgates or Turnstiles? Post EU Enlargement Migration Flows to (and From) the UK*. London: Institute for Public Policy Research.

Richardson, J. (2006). Self-directed expatriation: family matters, *Personnel Review*, 35(4): 469–486.

Richardson, J. and McKenna, S. (2003). International experiences and academic careers – what do academics have to say, *Personnel Review*, 32(6): 774–795.

Richardson, J. and McKenna, S. (2006). Exploring relationships with home and host countries: a study of self-directed expatriates, *Cross Cultural Management: An International Journal*, 13(1): 6–22.

Richardson, J. and Mallon, M. (2005). Self-directed expatriation: career interrupted?, *Journal of World Business*, 40: 409–420.

Robinson, S. (2005). Becoming international? Internationalisation and the MBA, a critical exploration of students' experiences from four MBA programmes. *4th International Critical Management Studies Conference*, Cambridge, 4–6 July.

Ryan, L., Sales, R., Tilki, M. and Siara, B. (2008). Social networks, social support and social capital, the experiences of recent Polish migrants in London, *Sociology*, 42(4): 672–690.

Sassen, S. (1991). *The Global City: New York, London, Tokyo*. Princeton, NJ: Princeton University Press.

Schein, E. (1984). Culture as an environmental context for careers, *Journal of Occupational Behaviour*, 5: 71–81.

Scurry, T. and Blenkinsopp, J. (2009). Failure to launch? Graduate underemployment and the subjective career. In: *2009 Academy of Management Annual Meeting*. Chicago, IL: Academy of Management.

Scurry, T. and Blenkinsopp, J. (2011). Under-employment among recent graduates: a review of the literature, *Personnel Review*, 40(5): 643–659.

Simpson, R. (2000). Winners and losers: who benefits most from the MBA?, *Management Learning*, 31(3): 331–351.

Simpson, R., Sturges, J. and Weight, P. (2010). Transient, unsettling and creative space: experiences of liminality through the accounts of Chinese students on a UK- based MBA, *Management Learning*, 41(1): 53–70.

Spence, A. (2011). *Labour Market*. Social Trends 41, UK: Office for National Statistics.

Sriskandarajah, D. and Drew, C. (2006). Mapping the scale and nature of British emigration. UK: Institute for Public Policy Research.

Suutari, V. (2003). Global managers, career orientation, career tracks, life-style implications and career commitment, *Journal of Managerial Psychology*, 18(3): 185–207.

Suutari, V. and Brewster, C. (1998). The adaptaion of expatriates in Europe – evidence from Finnish companies, *Personnel Review*, 27(2): 89–103.

Tams, S. and Arthur, M. B. (2007). Studying careers across cultures. Distinguishing international, cross-cultural and globalization perspectives, *Career Development International*, 12(1): 86–98.

Thomas, D. C., Lazarova, M. B. and Inkson, K. (2005). Global careers: new phenomenon or new perspectives?, *Journal of World Business*, 40: 340–347.

Tomlinson, F. and Egan, S. (2002). Organisational sensemaking in a culturally diverse setting: limits to the valuing diversity discourse, *Management Learning*, 33(1): 79–97.

Varma, A., Pichler, S. and Budhwar, P. (2011). The relationship between expatriate job level and host country national categorization: an investigation in the UK, *The International Journal of Human Resource Management*, 22(1): 103–120.

Vasta, E. (2011). Immigrants and the paper market, borrowing, renting and buying identities, *Ethnic and Racial Studies*, 34(2): 187–206.

Weishaar, H. B. (2010). You have to be flexible – coping among Polish migrant workers in Scotland, *Health and Place*, 16: 820–827.

Westerman, J. W. and Yamamura, J. H. (2007). Generational preferences for work environment fit: effects on employee outcomes, *Career Development International*, 12(2): 150–161.

White, A. and Ryan, L. (2008). Polish 'temporary' migration, the formation and significance of social networks, *Europe–Asia Studies*, 60(9): 1467–1502.

Zaleska, K. J. and de Menezes, L. M. (2007). Human resources development practices and their association with employee attitudes: between traditional and new careers, *Human Relations*, 60(7): 987–1018.

# 4

# IN AND FROM THE HEART OF EUROPE

## Global Careers and Austria

*Astrid Reichel, Christiane Erten-Buch,
Katharina Chudzikowski, and Wolfgang
Mayrhofer, WU Vienna (Vienna University
of Economics and Business), Austria*

## Introduction

In cultural terms, Austria is part of Western Europe (Schwartz, 2006) and, within Europe, belongs to the Germanic–culture cluster (Ronen and Shenkar, 1985), which is characterized by high levels of assertiveness, performance orientation and a desire for rules and regulations. Economically, Austria is well developed and enjoys a high standard of living. Geographically, it is located in the heart of Europe, sharing borders with eight different countries. This specific location, combined with a shared history with many of the neighbouring countries, is probably one of the most relevant factors shaping global careers in Austria. Its long tradition of migration continues, as new waves of immigrants, spurred by political events in the surrounding countries, settle in Austria. Most recently, the fall of the Iron Curtain in the early 1990s led to a strong influx of migrant workers and immigrants, particularly from Central and Eastern Europe. Not only did this event lead to an increased internationalization of the workforce, it also widened the horizon of Austrian employers and employees for careers beyond national borders. Combined with a high export-orientation, Austria provides a unique setting for examining the issues related to working internationally and pursuing a global career.

Using a Bourdieusian perspective as an organizing frame, focusing on career fields, career actors and career capitals (see Iellatchitch, Mayrhofer, and Meyer, 2003), this chapter addresses three issues. First, we will briefly present some basic country background and analyse the specifics of the Austrian context as a career field. Among other things, this allows for new forms of international assignment within all European countries. Second, we will identify five major

forms of global-career mobility that are relevant in the Austrian context: expatriation, international business travel, internationalization in reverse, global careers 'at home' and remigration. Following a description of each of these forms, we will present individual career histories that illustrate them. In a final step, we will critically look at current developments and assess their consequences.

## The Situation of Global Careers in Austria

### Basic Country Background

#### Economy

Austria is a well-developed market economy with a high standard of living. In 2010, it had a GDP per capita (purchasing power parity) of about $40,400. This number ranks ninth in the world according to the World Bank (World Bank, 2011b). Its economy features a large service sector (69.2 per cent of GDP), a sound industrial sector (29.3 per cent of GDP) and a small (1.5 per cent of GDP), but highly developed, agricultural sector. The global economic downturn in 2008 led to a recession and pushed the budget deficit to 3.5 per cent of GDP in 2009 and 4.7 per cent in 2010, from only about 1.3 per cent in 2008 (CIA Factbook, 2011). However, the unemployment rate was the lowest in the EU in the second half of 2011 (Eurostat, 2011b).

Geographical proximity and close historical and cultural ties to Germany and the Eastern European neighbours have enabled even small and medium-sized Austrian enterprises to achieve a high surplus in the balance of trade in the 1990s. From 2000 until today, foreign direct investment stocks in the neighbouring Eastern European countries (especially in Hungary and the Czech Republic (Altzinger, 1998)) have been growing constantly and considerably (Austrian National Bank, 2011).

#### Population

Austria is located in the centre of Europe, surrounded by Germany, Czech Republic, Slovakia, Slovenia, Hungary, Italy, Switzerland and Liechtenstein. Austria's population in 2011 was 8.39 million, and 4.1 million inhabitants are gainfully employed. This equals an employment rate of 71.7 per cent among 15–64-year-olds. In 2010, about 30 per cent of all employed had a non-standard work arrangement (18 per cent part-time, 12 per cent temporary work, fixed-term contracts and others). In recent decades, non-standard employment has increased significantly (Geisberger and Knittler, 2010; Statistik Austria, 2011a).

About 15 per cent of the population is under 15 years old; 23 per cent are 60 years old or older. Life expectancy for women is 83.2 years, and for men 77.7. The average number of children per woman is 1.39. The birth rate is 9.4 live

births per 1,000 inhabitants, and the death rate is 9.2 deaths per 1,000 inhabitants (Statistik Austria, 2011b). Austria's small, positive population growth rate is mainly due to migration. In 2010, 11 per cent of the Austrian population was foreign born. Including first- and second-generation migrants, the percentage reaches almost 19 per cent. Currently, the biggest groups with foreign citizenships are Germans, Serbs (with Montenegro and Kosovo), Bosnians and Turks. The biggest part of net migration is allotted to Germany. Over 60 per cent of new immigrants are from the twenty-seven EU countries (Bock-Schappelwein et al., 2009; Statistik Austria, 2011b). On the other hand, about 500,000 Austrian citizens are estimated to live abroad (in Germany (240,000), Switzerland (50,000), the US, UK, South Africa, Australia and Spain (Austrian Foreign Ministry, 2011a)).

Austria will face demographic challenges in the future. For 2050, prognoses estimate a population of 9.5 million people. The percentage of inhabitants over 60 years old is assumed to reach about 34 per cent (Statistik Austria, 2008). The ageing society is especially challenging, because Austria is a welfare state, with high expenditures on social welfare (€9,123 per inhabitant per year; the EU average is €6,521 per inhabitant per year) (Eurostat, 2011a). As the actual age of retirement is much lower than the official age of 65 years for men and 60 years for women (e.g. Austrian men, on average, retire more than six years before the official retirement age (ORF, 2012)), Austria already has the third highest expenditures for pensions in the European Union (Eurostat, 2011a).

## History

Settlement in the alpine region and the fertile plains of the Danube occurred as early as the Middle Paleolithic Era, about 200,000 years ago. The first record showing the name Austria, written as Ostarrîchi, dates back to 996. Austria's long history of migration and multi-ethnicity was mainly shaped by the Habsburgs, who were the ruling dynasty between 1246 and 1918 and who created an impressive multi-ethnic state ('Vielvölkerstaat'). In 1867, the Double Monarchy of Austria–Hungary was home to over 50 million people of different ethnic groups and the second largest political entity of Europe in terms of area (Kann, 1974). However, increasing national conflicts and the assassination of the Austrian successor to the throne led to World War I in 1914. The defeat of Austria and Germany meant the end of the Habsburg monarchy. After radical border adjustments, Austria was proclaimed a republic of about today's size (Johnson, 1989; Szabo and Reber, 2007).

This so-called First Republic provided the foundation of today's democracy. However, in 1933, unstable economic and political conditions led to a short civil war, resulting in a consolidation of power by Engelbert Dollfuss. Austria remained a weak and embattled autocracy until 1938, when Hitler incorporated Austria's territory into the German Reich (Szabo and Reber, 2007). Austria, as part of the German Reich, lost about 240,000 soldiers and 40,000 civilians in World War

II. More than 60,000 Austrian Jews were killed in the Holocaust. After the victory of the Allied Powers, Austria was revived as the so-called Second Republic but remained occupied by the Allied Armies until 1955 (Putzger, 1969).

In 1955, the Austrian State Treaty was signed, and Austria became an independent state with a long-term policy of active neutrality. Austria joined the United Nations in 1955 and the Council of Europe in 1956. In 1995, the country joined the EU and signed the Schengen Agreement. In 2002, the euro was introduced as the official currency (Szabo and Reber, 2007).

## Politics

Austria is a federal democratic republic embracing nine provinces. The national government consists of a president, whose functions are largely ceremonial, a cabinet headed by a chancellor and a bicameral legislature, the National Council ('*Nationalrat*'), with 183 representatives elected every four years, and the Federal Council ('*Bundesrat*'), representing the provinces and restricted to a review of legislation already passed by the National Council (Szabo and Reber, 2007).

Domestic politics are largely dominated by coalition governments between the two largest parties, the Social Democrats (SPÖ) and the conservative People's Party (ÖVP; (Johnson, 1989)). Currently, both parties form a so-called 'grand coalition' government, with the Freedom Party (FPÖ), the Greens and the Alliance for the Future of Austria (BZÖ) in opposition.

By means of the so-called system of '*Proporz*,' the dominance of the two large parties was, and still is, transferred to the institutional and economic environment. '*Proporz*' refers to a system in which the Social Democrats and the People's Party apportion their power in a manner equal to their party strength in elections when staffing positions in the public sector and nationalized industry. Thus, many of the economic leaders in Austria are directly or indirectly linked to and depend on the political system.

## Cultural Background

Austria is part of the Western European culture cluster, which emphasizes harmony, egalitarianism and intellectual autonomy more than any other world region. Inside this group of countries, it shows the most cultural similarities with Germany, Switzerland (Ronen and Shenkar, 1985) and, according to Gupta, Hanges and Dorfman (2002), also the Netherlands. The Germanic cluster is characterized by a tendency to standardization and rules, high levels of assertiveness and – compared with other Western European countries – gender inequality (Hofstede, 1980; Szabo, Brodbeck, Den Hartog, Reber, Weibler and Wunderer, 2002). Accordingly, Austria places a high value on avoiding uncertainty, as reflected in its desire for regulations. On the other hand, Austrians perceive assertiveness and gender inequality as being too high and they wish for much lower levels of both (Szabo and Reber, 2007).

Performance orientation is an important Austrian value. Although scores are already high, Austrians still wish for a higher level. At the same time, harmony and human orientation are very highly valued. These dimensions, however, are not perceived to be living up to the desired standards. By contrast, future orientation is high, but not seen as an important value (Szabo and Reber, 2007). Power distance is rather low (Hofstede, 1980; Trompenaars, 1993). Unequal distribution of power is reluctantly accepted. Although Austria can be classified into a Western European country cluster that is generally characterized by individualism, within Europe, Austria is seen as more of a collectivist than an individualistic country. Societal, organizational and institutional practices encourage and reward the collective distribution of resources and collective action (Szabo and Reber, 2007).

## Structural, Cultural and Contextual Difficulties and Opportunities in Austria

### Working Internationally in the Austrian Context: Career Field, its Rules and Main Actors

Borrowing from Bourdieu's field perspective (Iellatchitch et al., 2003), we will describe the Austrian context as a career field within which various career actors play according to specified rules of the field.

### Field Description of the Austrian Labour Market

Besides the political parties (especially the Social Democrats and the People's Party) and the government, representatives of employers (Chamber of Commerce), employees (Chamber of Labour), farmers (Chamber of Agriculture) and trade unions (organized under the umbrella association '*Gewerkschaftsbund*') are important actors in the Austrian labour market. Between and within these associations, the so-called '*Proporz*'-principle calls for a balanced power structure. The basic idea behind this principle is to avoid a concentration of too much power in the hands of single actors, in particular political parties or individuals linked to these parties.

The key actor groups mentioned above interact in the so-called social-partnership model. This system of economic and social cooperation at the national level is based on the principle of voluntarism and is carried out in an informal way. The general idea of the system is that the basic aims of economic and social policy can be better realized through cooperation than through confrontational means (Chamber of Labour, 2008a). This consensus model is based on a highly regulated system of labour law. For example, membership of employers and employees in their respective collective bodies (Chambers of Commerce, Labour and Agriculture) is obligatory, codetermination in large organizations is legally

mandated, and employee representatives are part of the supervisory board (Hammer, 1996). Austria is classified as a coordinated market economy. While stock-market capitalization is low, employment protection is prominent (Hall and Soskice, 2001). In a nutshell, employment in Austria is highly regulated and dominated by balances of power (between political parties, employers and employees, federal provinces), consensus politics and harmony.

## Organizations

One important actor group playing in the labour-market field described above is the group of organizations. Everybody conducting a trade, from sole proprietors to large subsidiaries or headquarters of MNCs, automatically becomes a member of the Chamber of Commerce when registering the trade. The Chamber represents the organization in the social partnership and in public discourse. About 300,000 organizations operate in Austria. The average size is nine employees. Only 42,000 employ ten or more people – in sum, 2.4 million people work for medium-sized and large organizations. In 2009, about 9,000 foreign-owned companies employing 500,000 people were located in Austria (Statistik Austria, 2012b).

Many of these MNCs want to attract expatriates for their Austrian subsidiaries. On the one hand, both employers and employees are challenged by a number of things, and in particular high rates of dues and taxes. For example, the marginal tax rate for an annual income greater than €50,000 is 50 per cent, and social insurance contributions are 18 per cent of gross income (Chamber of Labour, 2008b). On the other hand, however, living in Austria, especially in Vienna, is very attractive. In 2010 and 2011, Vienna ranked number one worldwide in the Mercer study on quality of living. The ranking is based on an index of issues particularly relevant for expatriates. It includes areas such as stability in international relations, political system, crime rate, health care, education, availability of consumer goods and housing, and quality of air and drinking water, but also the availability of various restaurants, cinemas, theatres and sports (Mercer, 2012). The wide variety of cultural opportunities is considered particularly attractive. Thus, Austria and its capital offer a bundle of very good incentives for expats to move in. Although data on the number of expats in Austria is not available, judging from the number of websites for expats in Vienna (including a service centre from the City of Vienna at www.expatcenter.at), this group seems to be highly relevant.

Compared with subsidiaries of foreign organizations in Austria, subsidiaries of Austrian companies abroad generated an even higher turnover (€238 billion vs. €186 billion). In more than 5,000 foreign subsidiaries in ninety-nine countries around the globe, 938,000 people are employed. Almost 40 per cent of those working for Austrian subsidiaries are located in a neighbouring country (Hungary, Slovenia, Italy, Liechtenstein, Switzerland, Germany, Czech Republic and Slovakia), 10 per cent in Romania and 4 per cent in Poland (Statistik Austria, 2012b). Among them are Austrian expatriates. Although exact figures are missing,

the total number of Austrian citizens living abroad is estimated to be 500,000. The majority are located in Germany (about 240,000), followed by Switzerland (50,000), the US, UK, South Africa, Australia and Spain (Austrian Foreign Ministry, 2011a). The high quality of living, with high stability and reliable social backup, may discourage Austrians from going abroad. However, the stable, highly regulated environment also has a limiting effect and encourages, in particular, highly motivated employees to sign on as expats. Especially in the former communist countries, there were, and partly still are, better opportunities to build something new, to start from scratch.

Owing to Austria's central geographical position, easy accessibility and strong economic ties with neighbouring and other EU countries, international business travel – also called flexpatriate arrangements – is a highly attractive alternative to expatriation. Flexpatriates (Demel, 2010) keep their centre of life in their home country and conduct short business trips abroad. In this way, employees can enjoy Austria's high living standard, while still having an international career. For employers, the costs associated with flexpatriation are normally much lower than those for an expatriate assignment. It thus facilitates cross-border cooperation and the establishment of foreign subsidiaries, even for small and medium-sized organizations, many of which took advantage of being a 'first mover' owing to geographical proximity and close historical and cultural ties with former communist countries (Altzinger, 1998).

Austria's capital, Vienna, is home to many leading international, inter-governmental organizations and one of the four headquarters of the United Nations, its only official seat within the EU. The Vienna International Centre (VIC) hosts major United Nations bodies: the International Atomic Energy Agency (IAEA), the United Nations Industrial Development Organization (UNIDO), the Preparatory Commission for the Comprehensive Nuclear-Test-Ban Treaty Organization (CTBTO) and the United Nations Office on Drugs and Crime (UNODC). In addition to the UN bodies, several other international organizations are based in Vienna, e.g. OSCE and OPEC. In total, Austria currently hosts around thirty international, intergovernmental organizations. For around 5,000 people, a quarter of them Austrian citizens (Austrian Foreign Ministry, 2011b), these organizations offer a very international work environment, with employees from more than 100 countries. The VIC in particular, also known as UNO City, is a global village that offers Austrians a sort of international career 'at home'. This is not only characterized by multinational teams and foreign working languages, but also by a specific set of rules for the organizations and their employees. Thus, the organizations are not represented by the Chamber of Commerce, and the employees are not subject to collective bargaining. Never-theless, intergovernmental organizations are a group of actors playing in the field of the Austrian labour market, and the stability provided by Austrian consensus policy is one of the reasons why intergovernmental organizations settle in Vienna in the first place.

## Employees

Individual employees, represented by and large by the Chamber of Labour and the Federation of Trade Unions, constitute the second group of key actors in the field. People aiming for an international career have many opportunities to follow such a career path embedded in organizations. However, a bigger group of individuals take the initiative to pursue an international career detached from any organizational context.

Highly relevant in terms of size is the group of employees with a migration background. Austria has a long tradition as an immigration country. During Habsburg times, Vienna, as the centre of the multi-ethnic empire, was home to many immigrants from countries within its ruling sphere. After World War II, it sheltered Sudeten Germans fleeing from Czechoslovakia and participants in the revolts in Hungary (1956) and the Prague Spring (1968). In the 1960s and early 1970s, a significant number of so-called guest workers were recruited from Yugoslavia and Turkey. At the end of the 1980s, 4 per cent of the Austrian population was foreign born. In the 1990s, immigration changed because of the civil war in former Yugoslavia (more than 100,000 refugees came to Austria) and the fall of the Iron Curtain (Payer, 2004). Immigrants from former communist countries were better educated than the guest workers. In addition, strong historical and cultural ties made it comparatively easy for citizens of the neighbouring countries to feel at home in Austria. The entry of several former communist countries into the European Union further facilitated moving to Austria, although, from 2004 to 2011, access to the European labour market was limited for eight former communist countries (European Parliament, 2011). Liberalization on 1 May 2011 meant that, in that year, an extra 20,000 people moved to Austria from these countries (Austrian Federal Ministry for Labour, Social Affairs and Consumer Protection, 2011).

Despite the centuries-long experience with a culturally diverse population, by and large immigration is perceived as more problematic than enriching. The diversity policy index that refers to the degree to which governments and other administrative bodies promote cultural diversity as a national goal is low in Austria (Podsiadlowski and Reichel, 2012). One important reason for this situation is the history of guest workers mainly from Turkey and former Yugoslavia. The majority of second- and third-generation migrants are the offspring of immigrants who intended only to come as guest workers for a few years. Neither the Austrian government and population nor the foreign workers themselves were prepared for a permanent move to Austria, including family reunification – which in fact happened (Payer, 2004). In many cases, the children and grandchildren of the low-skilled workers still achieve significantly lower levels of education than the Austrian average. Income in this group is lower and unemployment is higher than the Austrian mean (Statistik Austria, 2010). Their specific cultural capital is hardly valued in the field of the Austrian labour market. Even if grandchildren of former guest workers have reached higher education, they are still confronted

with prejudices. These conditions, plus economic growth demanding skilled employees, are reasons for second- and third-generation migrants to leave Austria for the home country of their parents or grandparents.

Geographic location and small size certainly influence cross-border movement. The large number of neighbouring countries encourages commuting. There is not only a commuter flow from the neighbours to Austria (about 100,000 people, see Huber and Ederer, 2011), but also about 60,000 Austrians (census 2001; Statistik Austria, 2011c) regularly commute abroad, especially to Switzerland and Germany. The proximity of many other countries and good transport connections render commuting an alternative international career. Strong historic, economic and cultural ties further encourage movement between Austria and numerous European countries. Moreover, it is comparatively easy for Austrian citizens to travel and live abroad. As citizens of the EU, Austrians enjoy freedom of settlement in all EU member states. Austria is also part of the Schengen area, which abolished checks at the Union's internal borders among the participating countries (European Commission Home Affairs, 2011).

The small size of the country results in limited jobs in certain areas. Very specific knowledge in, for example, aviation, aerospace or microchip production can be attained in Austria, but qualified positions are extremely rare. Although Austria does not generally suffer from brain drain to a great extent, there are certain areas, e.g. research, where highly qualified people are forced to emigrate in order to find an adequate position (Breinbauer, 2008). Also, adventurous entrepreneurial characters might feel forced to leave the country because of its small size and the comprehensive body of legislation, which does not stop at the founding of an enterprise. When starting a new business, the entrepreneur has to overcome a lot of bureaucratic and legal hurdles. A measure (sub-index of the ease-of-doing-business index) that compares time, number of procedures, cost and paid-in minimum capital requirements for opening up a business ranks Austria as 134 out of 183 (with number 183 being the most restrictive country; World Bank, 2011a). Also, professions and trade skills in Austria are protected by professional associations and the Chamber of Craft. Thus, working as a self-employed craftsperson is only allowed for people having completed a certain type of education defined by the respective chamber.

## The Relevance of Contemporary Career Concepts in Austria

### A Bourdieusian Perspective as Organizing Frame Focusing on Career Theory

In the described field, careers evolve. In the last decade, career research has focused on boundaryless and protean careers as basic concepts for the 'new career,' which was contrasted with, and predicted to displace, the traditional organizational career. New career concepts are mainly formulated on the following assumptions:

First, that the environment of organizations is highly variable (Castells, 2003), stimulating high mobility of careers (Baruch, 2003; Cascio, 2000). Second, that crossing organizational boundaries is beneficial for growth in career development and learning. Finally, these models promote a very agentic approach to careers for individuals, especially for career self-management (King, 2004), employability (Van Buren, 2003), mobility (Eby, Butts and Lockwood, 2003) etc. As the career patterns did not change as radically as expected, the predictions have more recently been recanted: 'We were wrong: the organizational career is alive and well' (Hall and Las Heras, 2009: 182).

In line with this insight, traditional organizational careers are the most important career patterns in Austria. Asked about their career aspirations, the graduates of 2010 from Austria's biggest business school very much favoured a traditional 'company-world' career over a 'chronic flexible' career. Compared with students who graduated in 2000 and 1990, the aspirations for an organizational career in the youngest cohort are strongest (Mayrhofer et al., 2011). Corresponding to the attitude of the young business-school graduates, one can also observe that job mobility has not increased dramatically in Austria (Chudzikowski, 2012).

Labour-market data show that, in recent decades, the share of employees in non-standard work has been increasing. However, this rise is mainly driven by an increase in part-time work. More than half of non-standard work is part time, i.e. a contractual working time of less than 40 hours per week. Part-time work is highly segregated – women make up almost 85 per cent of the total (Statistik Austria, 2012a). Structure, in the form of family obligations paired with deficient public child care, rather than agentic behaviour to improve one's employability, drives the decision for this type of atypical career (*dieStandard*, 2012).

Given the field description of the Austrian labour market and the prevailing cultural values, a preference for organizational careers and highly valued employment security does not come as a surprise. Even if careers involve crossing boundaries and working in one or more foreign countries, these global careers still mostly evolve within a company.

We have identified five main forms of global career especially relevant to the Austrian context: expatriation, flexpatriation, internationalization in reverse, global careers 'at home' and remigration. This selection covers a wide range of global careers, with differences concerning duration, the crossing of national boundaries and integration into particular organizations. Following a description of each of these forms, we present individual career histories to illustrate them further.

## Stories of Global Careers in Austria

### Expatriation

For a long time, expatriation was an opportunity for employees to work abroad. Mainly MNCs used expatriation assignments to send highly qualified personnel abroad for at least 1 year. In general, expatriation programmes are characterized

## A Story about Expatriation

Stefan:

- male, 55 years old, married, two children;
- expatriate/global manager, various long-term assignments with one company, electronic industries.

When Stefan first went abroad, he had an aspiration to enter a special career track, driven by the desire to do work that he considered difficult and interesting. Because Austria is a very small country, with restricted market potential, staying in his native country was not reasonable. Being stationed abroad was simply part of his career aspiration. After some years of being abroad, he had a 3-year stay in his home country, being responsible for marketing and sales for his company worldwide. The perceived provincial and often narrow-minded reactions of colleagues in his office, as well as slow decision-making, driven by the desire for compromise rather than wanting to be the best – and all this in a densely regulated environment – made him feel like a prisoner. His experiences in his home country and an offered opportunity were the drivers for his decision to go abroad again.

He described the unfolding of his career as rather spontaneous. He was offered the opportunity to go abroad and he took it. Then, there was another offer to go to another destination – again, it happened. Basically, it always started out with a very personal desire to change his environment. Everything else was mostly mechanics and logistics.

> When you think about the future sitting on the plane, you wonder if it was the right decision to leave. Upon arrival, there are lots of new things to explore, especially if you come from a small country that is characterized by a closed and conservative mentality. But then, there are extrinsic impacts that make you question your decision again – your wife gets sick, things on the job don't work out as you thought they would. No matter how much you prepare, or how often you do this, you just have to immerse yourself, and hope for the best.

Returning home was never really an option:

> You feel the success, the possibilities and the chances and you cannot think any more of a country like Austria. Even though it is said that the standard of living is high and Vienna holds a high position in rankings of quality of life, you do not want to change the international flair and the feeling of 'everything is possible if you make it possible'.

Concerning the consequences for private and social life he answered: 'you constantly leave social networks and you rebuild them again. Privately, there is this saying that "a family that moves together, stays together". It strengthens relationships with the family members that move with you, in particular your spouse.'

Concerning future career plans, he never had clear plans for his career; he just wanted to be the best in his field. When there were opportunities, he took them.

by an international assignment of between 1 and 5 years (Harris, Brewster and Erten, 2005). Expatriation is very costly for companies. Moreover, in the last few years, many organizations reported difficulties finding and motivating suitable people to undertake international assignments (Doherty and Dickmann, 2012). Thus, a trend towards reducing expatriation programmes can be observed (Erten, Schiffinger, Mayrhofer and Dunkel, 2006). As Austria's economy is dominated by small and medium-sized companies, the group of large MNCs able to offer expatriate programmes is limited in any case. However, for many of them, expatriation still is an essential part of their international expansion (OMV Group, 2010; Wienerberger, 2010).

## Flexpatriation

Changes in transportation and communication systems, organizational networks and the flexible intra-organizational coordination of global units, together with the high costs and risks associated with expatriation, challenge 'traditional' assignments. Alternative forms of assignment that do not last more than a year gain importance (Doherty, Dickmann and Mills, 2010). These short-term assignments are commonly labelled as frequent flyers, commuters and rotational assignments, business travellers or flexpatriate assignments (Demel and Mayrhofer, 2010; Dowling, Festing, and Engle, 2008; Harris et al., 2005) and are especially common within Europe. Flexpatriates split their time between home and the host country, regularly travelling between at least two countries. Thus, a career as a flexpatriate is characterized by changing workplaces across different cultural contexts, a flexible schedule of time and time zones, and high frequency of change in social relations and contacts with coworkers (Demel and Mayrhofer, 2010). For companies located in the centre of Europe (such as Austrian companies), flexpatriation is a viable alternative for running subsidiaries in surrounding countries. Owing to the lower costs compared with expatriation, flexpatriation can support the internationalization of small and medium-sized companies, which dominate Austria's economy.

## Internationalization in Reverse: Immigration

Migrants leave their home country and settle in a foreign country. This move can be forced (e.g. threat to life because of war) or voluntary (e.g. moving to a sunny place to enjoy retirement), with various nuances between these two ends of the scale; it can be (intended to be) temporary or permanent; and, when distinguishing the particular reasons for migration, a myriad of different migrant groups, ranging from highly skilled people looking for the best job offer to love migrants can be identified (King, 2002). As argued above, Austria has a long tradition as an immigration country. The two most recent, important 'waves of immigration' can be ascribed to the fall of the Iron Curtain and the civil war in

## A Story about Flexpatriation

Hermann:

- male, 32 years old, in partnership, no children;
- flexpatriate, construction industry.

When Hermann decided to work in the field of plant engineering, he was driven by two strong motivators: his love of working on technical solutions and the prospect of going abroad regularly. He perceived the restrictions of his small home country on exactly these two levels: (1) not enough potential if you are constantly in search of creating new value and finding new solutions; and (2) the narrowness of the environment (geographically, and the mentality of the people).

At the beginning, he was not really aware of the consequences of flexpatriation for an individual, especially in his personal life. However, once he had started and accustomed himself to the situation of regularly being abroad for a few weeks, he organized a framework that helped him to make this kind of professional life a comfortable one.

He said that coming from a country that is very regulated helps him to remain patient in all kinds of specific situation:

> Being a flexpat often means that you need licences for operations, for people you work with, equipment you bring with you, etc. Those things are not easy to get or you have to discuss it with workers/managers from the respective country in order to convince them of necessary amendments and short-term changes. In such situations a background mentality of a decision-making culture that is based on compromising and on 'social partnership' is a big advantage. Additionally, rather indirect communication styles have proven to be very helpful and suitable.

To continue this way of life means keeping a base in one of the world's countries with the highest quality of living, and at the same time being able to experience adventures. Is such a compromise feasible? 'As long as you are young, no problem.'

> To keep social networks is difficult if you are constantly absent from the birthday party of your best friends, even though you had been in town just one week before. In your private life you need a very independent and reliable partner for such a lifestyle.

Hermann wants to build production facilities for his company and then perhaps move on to becoming an expat. He will then see how to find a balance between his work and private life in view of enlarging his family.

# A Story about Immigration

Anna:

- female, 52 years old, married, two children;
- Croatian nurse employed in a hospital in Vienna.

In her youth, Anna had a strong desire to just leave Croatia, but she visualized her move to Austria differently. Her parents were very isolated after the war, and she remembers that her house was always locked. She was raised very rigorously, and she also felt isolated. That is why she aspired to leave the country after finishing school. 'I thought, I don't want to live here anymore, I feel so locked in and I decided to leave Croatia.' She said that her father didn't want to say goodbye to her because he felt ashamed; normally, in the 1970s, only poor people left the country and moved to Vienna. Her first contact in Vienna was her aunt, with whom she lived for 2 weeks, while being self-employed as a cleaning lady. Subsequently, she moved to a home for nurses next to the 'Poliklinik', a hospital in Vienna.

Retrospectively, it all happened very fast for her. At that time, there was a high demand for nurses. She already spoke German, because she had learned it at school for 8 years. Because she literally grew up with the German language, she had no problems entering the nursing school and rapidly adapted. In 1972, 2 years after starting employment, she was pregnant with her first child. At that time, one did not take prolonged maternity leave, because there was no social or financial support for mothers. Thus, she started work 2 months after giving birth. Otherwise, she would have lost her job. Fortunately, she was aided by a friend from nursing school, who could look after the baby because her husband had to work full time. At that time, she changed jobs to move to another hospital, because it paid more money, and she wanted a job-related change. She found the job because she knew someone who sponsored her.

Then she got pregnant with her second baby and she decided that she was no longer able to work night shifts. Because her husband and mother-in-law were unable to help her care for the second baby, they looked for another hospital where she could work without night duties. By chance, she found a job at a Catholic hospital. Since then, 26 years ago, she has worked for this hospital and has meanwhile been promoted to the position of nursing supervisor. Since the time Anna moved to Austria from Croatia, she wished to stay. Her attachment to Austria has, in the meantime, increased, because her two daughters and husband also live in Vienna. She came to Austria at the age of 20. She was not in a relationship at that time. She met her husband in Vienna some years later. For her, it was an easy decision to leave Croatia, because she could not have imagined staying there with no future prospects.

As to her future, she expects to stay in Austria with her family and to retire after at least 8 more years of working. She still loves her job and expresses her gratitude for having such a fortunate life.

former Yugoslavia in the 1990s. In addition to the guest workers arriving in the 1960s and 1970s, these flows of immigrants have been formative for Austria's society and labour market.

## Global Careers 'at Home'

Austria's perpetual neutrality, its central position in Europe, and Vienna's long tradition as a melting pot of people from different countries have encouraged many international, intergovernmental organizations to move to Vienna. An attractive infrastructure has been provided to host these organizations adequately. The good reputations of the intergovernmental organizations, combined with the high-end infrastructure, various fringe benefits and not least the international work environment, make careers in these organizations highly attractive. For example, more than 4,000 employees, from over 110 countries, work for the Vienna–based UN organizations. UN organizations also recruit some personnel from Austria, corresponding to a quota for each nationality. Although vertical career moves mostly require international assignments in the long run, for a limited number of Austrians, international, intergovernmental organizations offer global careers 'at home'.

---

### A Story about the Global Career 'at Home'

Gerald:

- male, 39 years old, single, no children;
- HR administrator, UNODC.

Gerald was always interested in different countries and cultures and wanted to go abroad. However, he never actually thought about working for the UN. He said that his career just unfolded this way and was unexpected, because the exam for the UN was difficult, and he never thought that he would pass.

After his studies in international business he worked for an Austrian telecommunications company in Vienna for 4 years. He always wanted to work for the EU, but, when he saw a United Nations job advertisement in the newspaper, he applied to participate in the UN national competitive exam. He passed the exam, and it took another 2 years to get a job with the UN. His first job was in New York, where he worked in the areas of human resources (HR), administration and finance. After 3 years, he went to Santiago de Chile for 1.5 years to work in a UN regional commission, and then he moved to Mexico City, where he first worked for the finance and procurement departments. Subsequently, he went back to the UN headquarters in New York and worked exclusively for the HR department. At that time, he knew that he wanted to go back to Vienna. After 3 years, there was a vacant position in Vienna that matched his profile perfectly, and so he returned to Vienna 2 months ago.

If you want a career at a supranational organization like the UN, they expect their employees to be mobile and to change their locations at least twice

within their careers, and preferably after three years if they want to advance within the organization.

Now that he has returned to Vienna, Gerald wants to 'grow into' his new position for the time being. Right now, he has no future plans because he has just come back to Austria. Whether he stays or leaves again depends on the job opportunities in Vienna and how his private life develops. 'You can only partly plan your career: be active but also take your time.'

He always wanted to come back to Austria once in his career. For him, his home culture and language were important motivators for his return, especially after staying in non-European cultures. For him, the social setting and culture are very important, and he expressed this with the words 'to feel at home'. Thus, his return to Vienna was mainly driven by the desire to live in his own culture. Also, the socio-cultural environment of Vienna offers culture (e.g. theatre), green parks and areas and a language he is familiar with: Austrian German. For him, the culture plays a formative role in his personal development.

> In general, when you are abroad the possibilities to care about your social networks at home are limited, especially when you have long distance flights to get back. If you are abroad for several years this gets more and more difficult.

He expressed the personal consequences of assignments in the following quote:

> You have to sacrifice in a way. You have to have roots, this can be your family or it is the country of your origin, your culture and friends. You have to care about your social network, which is based in Vienna in my case. In general I think you have to decide between career and family. It is impossible to have both.

Gerald returned from New York to be at home again because of culture and language. In general, he wants to stay in Austria; at least until he needs to change his job again . . .

## Remigration

As argued above, the influx of – what were intended to be 'guest' – workers from Turkey and former Yugoslavia very much shaped the image of immigrants in Austria. Most of the first-generation immigrants planned to go back to their home countries after earning enough money, but never did. Instead, a partly idealized image of their country of birth was passed on from generation to generation. Thus, although in terms of numbers the former guest workers, their wives, children and grandchildren are an important group in Austrian society, for many of them their grandparents' country of origin is still present in their consciousness. In addition, since the 1960s, the economic situation in Turkey and many former Yugoslavian countries has changed dramatically. Turkey today is a growth market that values well-educated remigrants highly.

## A Story about Remigration

Oguz:

- male, 25 years old, single, no children;
- remigration to Turkey, employed by a logistics company (headquarters in Vienna).

Oguz only recently decided to go back to Turkey, his home country. In fact, until this decision, Turkey did not exist as 'home country' in his mind. It was more of a holiday place he liked to visit. Being a third-generation Turk in Vienna, he always felt Austrian. His German is perfect, whereas his Turkish is just some sort of spoken language. However, the feeling of still not being accepted, as well as the perceived, strongly increasing racism and the exclusion he continuously faced helped him make the decision. The feeling of rejection was exacerbated by stories from his grandparents about how nice Austrians seemed to have been in the 1960s when they were called to come as workers. Such factors, along with the strong economic development in Turkey, formed the basis for the track he and many of his friends are now following, back 'home'.

After a solid education (Higher School of Engineering, Arts and Crafts), he joined a globally based group and followed a few sequences of vocational training. Compared with Austrian colleagues, he became known for not drinking alcohol and being reliable, ambitious and hard working. He was soon offered a job in Turkey facilitating a recently started-up operation in a difficult rural area, and he accepted the offer.

While preparing for this departure, he became aware of his strong Austrian identity. It was hard to work on a written command of Turkish, and after arrival he felt like a stranger. It was very hard in the beginning to realize that in fact he did not have a real 'home' country where he was accepted. However, being persevering, patient, and hard working helped him to create an identity.

Returning to Austria had been the plan when he left, but, once he got to know the different quality of life in Turkey, the excellent food, climate and the huge prospects the country and the economic development had to offer, staying in Turkey became a real option. Now, looking back, he can hardly imagine how he could have thought about a future in a country of 'mostly old people who talk about retirement all the time'.

His move to Turkey required that he build social networks. It was not easy, but, on the basis of so many experiences of exclusion, the challenge was manageable. For himself and his future family, he is looking forward to a variety of challenges.

Concerning future expectations about his career, he expressed the opinion that it depends on the money he can make. He is planning to apply for a Master's programme in order to pursue his career. In view of the very high tuition fees at Turkish universities (compared with the Austrian university system, which is free of charge), this may be hard, but he is convinced that he can also overcome this new challenge.

## A Critical Reflection of the Current Austrian Situation

From a critical perspective, as proposed by the concept of the editors of this book, which partly draws on, but is not limited to, ideas from critical-management studies (see Alvesson and Willmott, 2003; Collings and Wood, 2009; Linstead, 2004), a number of issues emerge when looking at working internationally in the Austrian context.

Research focusing on global careers in the Austrian context in the broadest sense is characterized by varying degrees of insight into different forms of working internationally. At one end of the continuum, a constant stream of research over several decades deals with the effects of immigration ('internationalization in reverse') on the individuals themselves, the organizations employing them and Austrian society as a whole (e.g. Aigner, 2008; Oberlechner and Hetfleisch, 2010). At the other end, some forms of international work remain largely unexplored. For example, there is little, if any, insight into the reasons why second- and third-generation migrants, some of them highly qualified, return to the country of their grandparents. Likewise, we do not know of any substantial research on those Austrian citizens who work internationally 'at home,' i.e. pursue a career in a local international environment, such as the UN organizations in Vienna. This lack of research is disconcerting on a number of accounts. First, it allows neither individuals, such as counsellors, nor organizational decision-makers, let alone policymakers, to base their decisions on a sound theoretical and empirical basis. This leaves collective and individual action open to ideological bias. For example, the general attitude or political stance towards migrants and their movement across national borders, rather than hard empirical data about their life and career goals, informs policies for supporting the integration of second- and third-generation migrants. Second, a lack of insight is also harmful for individual career planning. Even in better researched areas, such as expatriation, immigration or international business travel, it is personal experience, hearsay and the organizational or social-network grapevine that strongly influence individual decision-making. A richer picture would enable both individuals and supporting institutions, such as labour-market agencies or the Chamber of Labour, to base career-related individual action on a better foundation. Third, the knowledge deficit also allows no sound, critical discourse on a number of pressing issues, such as the effects of knowledge outflow due to self-initiated expatriation and remigration, the potential knowledge gain for Austrian companies, not only from MNCs but also from international organizations operating in the country, through a better knowledge interface between international organizations and the local context, or the best use of the inflowing talent through migration.

We also hardly see a critical angle in much of the career research coming from management. Whereas the issue of migration is not only broadly, but also critically, covered, there is little critical analysis of other forms of working internationally in the Austrian context. Questions hitherto largely unaddressed include: What effects do various forms of continuous cross-border mobility

('proximal flexpatriation') have on the individuals and their families in their personal and national identity, well-being, life satisfaction and cognitive-skill development? When individuals constantly move across national borders for their daily work, what does this mean for the local contexts in border regions in terms of the social fabric, culture and economic development? How does the dual role of an Austrian citizen living in Vienna and working in an extremely international environment such as the UN organizations affect his or her career, life plans and identity? How does the social fabric of organizations change owing to a high level of 'imported internationalization,' and what are the consequences for individuals and the organization? This list of questions could easily be extended.

From a Bourdieusian perspective, a number of critical issues emerge when we look at global careers in Austria. One topic is the changing role of relevant actors in the Austrian career field. Overall, the various forms of international working weaken the importance of actors operating at a national level. For example, if individuals build international networks through their activities across national and cultural borders, these networks at least partly replace more traditional professional networks, linked with established collective actors such as trade unions, chambers of commerce, political parties or associations based on ideological or religious beliefs such as Rotary Clubs or the '*Kartellverband*' (a conservative Austrian federation of current and former students). In this way, the power relations and rules in the career field are changing. At the same time, boundary-spanning activities make personal and working life more complex. This often leads to uncertainty, legal issues and conflict between employees and employers. This, in turn, increases the importance of protective associations such as trade unions.

In general, it is safe to say that the forms of international work addressed in this chapter are causing a process of change among the individual and collective career actors of Austria, as well as in the rules of the field. For example, in Vienna, about one third of the population has a migration background. It is also home to many flexpatriates. Compared with the 1960s, which were characterized by a much more homogenous population, there is now increasing diversity in countries of origin, languages and religions (e.g. the proportion of Catholics in Austria has dropped from 89 per cent in 1951 to 64.8 per cent in 2010; see ORF Religion, 2011; Statistik Austria, 2011b). All this has effects on numerous aspects of professional and private life. This includes individuals' career horizons, which now exceed national borders; the importance of foreign languages, always an integral part of Austrian education, but now becoming of paramount importance, with children in the kindergarten already taking the first steps in learning English; and culturally and religiously mixed working groups, even at the national level. Beyond that, the career-capital configurations valued in the field are also changing. For example, the need for international experience seems to be going beyond mere rhetoric and is becoming essential. In addition, internationally transferable education qualifications are becoming more important, thus facilitating international mobility. This trend is supported by the EU countries, which are

trying to adapt the Bologna process to three educational cycles: Bachelor, Master's, and Ph.D.

## Concluding Remarks

The changes in the field for the actors, their power relations, the rules of the field and the capital configuration of the individual career actors as a whole have created a situation 'in flux,' which is in stark contrast to the more stable, regulated situation that had characterized careers in Austria for a long time. For both research and practice, the changes offer ample opportunities to gain a better understanding of the new situation. Researchers should now assess the new developments critically in order to see their effects on power relations, personal and collective identities, and society.

## References

Aigner, P. (2008). *Migration and Politics: Leadership and Legitimacy in Austria*. Oxford, Vienna: Lang.

Altzinger, W. (1998). Austria's foreign direct investment in Central and Eastern Europe: 'supply based' or 'market driven'?, *Department of Economics Working Paper Series, 57*. Vienna: WU Vienna.

Alvesson, M. and Willmott, H. (2003). *Studying Management Critically*. London: Sage.

Austrian Federal Ministry for Labour, Social Affairs and Consumer Protection (2011). Liberalisierungseffekt im September 2011. Retrieved from www.dnet.at/elis/Tabellen/arbeitsmarkt/Liberalisierungseffekt.pdf, 13 November 2011.

Austrian Foreign Ministry (2011a). Auslandsoestereicher/innen (Daten & Fakten, Wo leben Oesterreicher/innen im Ausland?). Retrieved from www.statistik.at/web_de/statistiken/bevoelkerung/volkszaehlungen_registerzaehlungen/index.html, 12 November 2011.

Austrian Foreign Ministry. (2011b). International organizations. Retrieved from www.eu2006.at/en/Austria/International_Organisations/index.html?null, 3 November 2011.

Austrian National Bank (2011). Direct investment 2009, Austrian outward and inward direct investment at the end of 2009. Retrieved from www.oenb.at/en/img/shst_2009_direct_investment_2009_tcm16–240109.pdf, 12 November 2011.

Baruch, Y. (2003). Career systems in transition: A normative model for organizational career practices. *Personnel Review*, 32(1/2): 231–251.

Bock-Schappelwein, J., Bremberger, C., Hierlaender, R., Huber, P., Knittler, K., Berger, J., Hofer, H., Miess, M. and Strohner, L. (2009). Die oekonomischen Wirkungen der Immigration in Oesterreich 1989–2007, WiFo Publication.

Breinbauer, A. (2008). Long-term mobility of highly qualified/scientiests (Brain Drain) from Austria and Hungary – case study mathematicians. *SWS-Rundschau*, 48(2): 167–190.

Cascio, W. F. (2000). New workplaces. In J. M. Kummerow (Ed.), *New Directions in Career Planning and the Workplace*. Palo Alto, CA: Davies-Black.

Castells, M. (2003). *The Internet Galaxy: Reflections on the Internet, Business, and Society*. Oxford: Oxford University Press.

Chamber of Labour (2008a). The chamber of labour—an Austrian solution. Retrieved from www.ak-salzburg.at/pictures/d55/Mandarin.pdf, 20 November 2011.

Chamber of Labour (2008b). Lohnzettel. Retrieved from http://wien.arbeiterkammer.at/bilder/d91/ProjektLohnzettel.pdf, 20 November 2011.

Chudzikowski, K. (2012). Career transitions and career success in the 'new' career era. *Journal of Vocational Behavior*, 81(2): 298–306.

CIA Factbook (2011). Austria. Retrieved from www.cia.gov/library/publications/the-world-factbook/geos/au.html, 12 November 2011.

Collings, D. G. and Wood, G. (Eds.) (2009). *Human Resource Management. A Critical Approach*. London, New York: Routledge.

Demel, B. (2010). *Karrieren von Expatriates und Flexpatriates: eine qualitative Studie europaweit taetiger ManagerInnen aus Oesterreich*. München: Hampp.

Demel, B. and Mayrhofer, W. (2010). Frequent business travellers across Europe: Career aspirations and implications. *Thunderbird International Business Review*, 52(4): 301–311.

dieStandard (2012). Teilzeit ist 'Zwang und Wunsch'. Retrieved from http://diestandard.at/1329870139586/Kampagne-der-SPOe-Frauen-Teilzeit-ist-Zwang-und-Wunsch, 23 February 2011.

Doherty, N., Dickmann, M. and Mills, T. (2010). Mobility attitudes and behaviours among young Europeans. *Career Development International*, 15(4): 378–400.

Doherty, N. T. and Dickmann, M. (2012). Measuring the return on investment in international assignments: An action research approach. *The International Journal of Human Resource Management*, 23(16): 3434–3454.

Dowling, P. J., Festing, M. and Engle, A. D. (2008). *International Human Resource Management. Managing People in a Multinational Context*. London: Thomson.

Eby, L. T., Butts, M. and Lockwood, A. (2003). Predictors of success in the era of the boundaryless career. *Journal of Organizational Behavior*, 24(6): 689–708.

Erten, C., Schiffinger, M., Mayrhofer, W. and Dunkel, A. (2006). The use of foreign assignments and their relationship with economic success and business strategy: A comparative analysis of Northern, Southern and Eastern European countries. In M. J. Morley, N. Harety and D. G. Collings (Eds.), *New Directions in Expatriate Research* (pp. 39–63). Hampshire: Palgrave.

European Commission Home Affairs (2011). Schengen: Europe without internal borders. Retrieved from http://ec.europa.eu/home-affairs/policies/borders/borders_schengen_en.htm, 12 November 2011.

European Parliament (2011). Germany, Austria finally open to workers from new EU countries. Retrieved from www.europarl.europa.eu/en/headlines/content/20110504STO18667/html/Germany-Austria-finally-open-to-workers-from-new-EU-countries, 2 November 2011.

Eurostat (2011a). Annual national accounts. Retrieved from http://epp.eurostat.ec.europa.eu/portal/page/portal/national_accounts/data/main_tables, 12 November 2011.

Eurostat (2011b). Harmonised unemployment rate by gender – total. Retrieved from http://epp.eurostat.ec.europa.eu/tgm/table.do?tab=table&language=en&pcode=teilm020&tableSelection=1&plugin=1, 12 November 2011.

Geisberger, T. and Knittler, K. (2010). Niedrigloehne und atypische Beschaeftigung in Oesterreich. *Statistische Nachrichten*, (6): 448–461.

Gupta, V., Hanges, P. J. and Dorfman, P. W. (2002). Cultural clusters: Methodology and findings. *Journal of World Business*, 37(1): 11–15.

Hall, D. T. and Las Heras, M. (2009). Long live the organisational career. In A. Collin and W. Patton (Eds.), *Vocational Psychological and Organisational Perspectives on Career: Towards a Multidisciplinary Dialogue* (pp. 181–196). Rotterdam: Sense.

Hall, P. A. and Soskice, D. (2001). An introduction to varieties of capitalism. In P. A. Hall and D. Soskice (Eds.), *Varieties of Capitalism: The Institutional Foundation for Comparative Advantage*. Oxford: Oxford University Press.

Hammer, T. H. (1996). Industrial democracy. In M. Warner (Ed.), *International Encyclopedia of Business and Management*. London: Routledge.

Harris, H., Brewster, C. and Erten, C. (2005). Auslandseinsatz, aber wie? Klassisch oder alternative Formen: Neueste empirische Erkenntnisse aus Europa und den USA. In G. Stahl, W. Mayrhofer and T. M. Kühlmann (Eds.), *Internationales Personalmanagement: Neue Aufgaben, neue Lösungen*. München and Mering: Rainer Hampp Verlag.

Hofstede, G. (1980). *Culture's Consequences: International Differences in Work-Related Values*. Beverly Hills, CA: Sage.

Huber, P. and Ederer, S. (2011). FAMO—Fachkräftemonitoring: Regelmäßige Erhebung des Angebots und des Bedarfs an Fachkräften in der Grenzregion Ostösterreichs mit der Slowakei, FAMO II: Regionale und gesamtwirtschaftliche Entwicklung in Österreich und den neuen EU-Ländern, WiFo Publication.

Iellatchitch, A., Mayrhofer, W. and Meyer, M. (2003). Career fields: A small step towards a grand career theory? *The International Journal of Human Resource Management*, 14(5): 728–750.

Johnson, L. (1989). *Introducing Austria: A Short History*. Riverside, CA: Ariadne Press.

Kann, R. A. (1974). *The History of the Habsburg Empire 1526–1918*. Berkeley, CA: University of California Press.

King, R. (2002). Towards a new map of European migration. *International Journal of Population Geography*, 8: 89–106.

King, Z. (2004). Career self-management: Its nature, causes and consequences. *Journal of Vocational Behavior*, 65(1): 112–133.

Linstead, S. (2004). Managing culture. In S. Linstead, L. Fulop and S. Lilley (Eds.), *Management and Organization. A Critical Text*. New York: Palgrave.

Mayrhofer, W., Schiffinger, M., Chudzikowski, K., Demeter, P., Latzke, M., Loacker, B., Reichel, A., Schneidhofer, T. and Steyrer, J. (2011). Employability: Yes, but post-organisational!? A four-cohort study of business school graduates' changes in career aspirations 1970–2010, Academy of Management Meeting: 12–16 August, San Antonio.

Mercer (2012). Mercer's 2011 quality of living ranking highlights—global. Retrieved from www.mercer.com/qualityofliving, 5 July 2012.

Oberlechner, M. and Hetfleisch, G. (Eds.) (2010). *Integration, Rassismen und Weltwirtschaftskrise*. Vienna: Braumüller.

OMV Group (2010). Sustainability report, Social responsibility. Retrieved from www.omv.com/portal/01/com/!ut/p/c5/04_SB8K8xLLM9MSSzPy8xBz9CP0os3hzA0sTI2MDI0t3Jw9XA0_XAGdTp0BfIwNTc6B8pFm8gb-pRaCXo7ORq4G7p4evh6mxARQQ0O3nkZ-bqh-cmqdfkBtRDgAmDo5E/dl3/d3/L2dJQSEvUUt3QS9ZQnZ3Lz ZfNzA5NDIzMDI5R0JIRTBJRVBDNUJRTTIwTDQ!/, 20 December 2011.

ORF (2012). Gesetzliches Pensionsalter als Illusion. Retrieved from http://newsv1.orf.at/091015-43681/, 5 July 2012.

ORF Religion (2011). Austrittszahlen offiziell: Ueber 87.000 verlassen katholische Kirche. Retrieved from http://religion.orf.at/projekt03/news/1101/ne110111_austritte_fr.htm, 12 November 2011.

Payer, P. (2004). Gehen Sie an die Arbeit. Zur Geschichte der 'Gastarbeiter' in Wien 1964–1989. *Wiener Geschichtsblaetter*, (1): 1–19.

Podsiadlowski, A. and Reichel, A. (2012, forthcoming). Action programs for ethnic minorities: A question of corporate social responsibility? *Business & Society*.

Putzger, F. W. (1969). *Historischer Weltatlas.* Bielefeld: Velhagen & Klasing.

Ronen, S. and Shenkar, O. (1985). Clustering countries on attitudinal dimensions: A review and synthesis. *Academy of Management Review,* 10(3): 435–454.

Schwartz, S. H. (2006). A theory of cultural value orientations: Explication and applications. *Comparative Sociology,* 5: 136–182.

Statistik Austria (2008). Oesterreichs Bevoelkerung waechst und altert, Prognose 2050: 9,5 Mio. Einwohner. Retrieved from www.statistik.at/web_de/presse/033887, 20 November 2011.

Statistik Austria (2010). Migration und Integration. Zahlen, Fakten, Indikatoren. Retrieved from www.statistik.at/dynamic/wcmsprod/idcplg?IdcService=GET_NATIVE_FILE &dID=77473&dDocName=050010, 12 November 2011.

Statistik Austria (2011a). Arbeitskraefteerhebung 2010 – results of the microcensus. Retrieved from www.statistik.at/web_de/Redirect/index.htm?dDocName=052325, 20 November 2011.

Statistik Austria (2011b). Bevoelkerung. Retrieved from www.statistik.at/web_de/ statistiken/bevoelkerung/index.html, 2 November 2011.

Statistik Austria (2011c). Bevoelkerung (Volkszaehlung, Registerzaehlung). Retrieved from www.statistik.at/web_de/statistiken/bevoelkerung/volkszaehlungen_registerzaehlungen/ index.html, 2 November 2011.

Statistik Austria (2012a). Teilzeitarbeit, Teilzeitquote. Retrieved from www.statistik.at/ web_de/statistiken/arbeitsmarkt/arbeitszeit/teilzeitarbeit_teilzeitquote/062882.html, 5 July 2012.

Statistik Austria (2012b). Unternehmen, Arbeitsstätten. Retrieved from www.statistik.at/ web_de/statistiken/unternehmen_arbeitsstaetten/index.html, 5 July 2012.

Szabo, E. and Reber, G. (2007). Culture and leadership in Austria. In J. S. Chhokar, F. C. Brodbeck and R. J. House (Eds.), *Culture and Leadership Across the World* (pp. 109–146). Mahwah, NJ: Lawrence Erlbaum Associates.

Szabo, E., Brodbeck, F. C., Den Hartog, D. N., Reber, G., Weibler, J. and Wunderer, R. (2002). The Germanic Europe cluster: Where employees have a voice. *Journal of World Business,* 37(1): 55–68.

Trompenaars, F. (1993). *Riding the Waves of Culture: Understanding Cultural Diversity in Business.* San Francisco, CA: Jossey-Bass.

Van Buren, H. J. (2003). Boundaryless careers and employability obligations. *Business Ethics Quarterly,* 13(2): 131.

Wienerberger. (2010). Sustainability report. Retrieved from www.wienerberger.com/ sustainability, 20 December 2011.

World Bank (2011a). Doing business; measuring business regulations. Retrieved from www.doingbusiness.org/rankings, 12 November 2011.

World Bank (2011b). GDP per capita, ppp (current international $). Retrieved from http://search.worldbank.org/quickview?name=%3Cem%3EGDP%3C%2Fem%3E+%3 Cem%3Eper%3C%2Fem%3E+%3Cem%3Ecapita%3C%2Fem%3E%2C+%3Cem%3EP PP%3C%2Fem%3E+%28current+international+%24%29&id=NY.GDP.PCAP.PP.CD &type=Indicators&cube_no=2&qterm=GDP+per+capita+ppp, 12 November 2011.

# 5

# THE EMBODIMENT OF UNHEALTHY GLOBAL CAREERS AMONG SWEDISH PROFESSIONALS

*Anna Essén, Torkild Thanem and
Sara Värlander, Stockholm University School
of Business, Sweden*

## Introduction

In this chapter, we discuss global careers in the context of Swedish professionals. By introducing an embodied approach that goes beyond, and yet complements, established concepts in career studies, we investigate how Swedish professionals embody unhealthy global careers. We invoke two vignettes to substantiate this argument. In particular, these vignettes draw attention to the ways in which Swedish professionals in global firms deal with the physical and emotional stress and strain of global work and careers. This is based on interviews with employees from ten different firms and an observation study in one of the firms.

The chapter is structured as follows: In the first section, we provide a brief introduction to the Swedish context of global careers. In the second section, we discuss the notion of global work and careers by complementing extant concepts in career studies with what we call a critically embodied approach, to study the bodily practices and experiences of global workers. In the third section, we present the two vignettes mentioned above. In the fourth section, we then discuss these vignettes in relation to extant concepts in career studies and in relation to the embodied approach mentioned above. Whereas the former enables us to problematize the structural and cultural aspects of global careers among Swedish professionals, the latter enables us to problematize bodily aspects that are hitherto underresearched within the field of career studies. Finally, we discuss how these findings and concepts may inform critical engagements with global careers in future research.

## The Situation of Swedish Global Careers

Sweden is a small, Western country that does not score highly in mainstream global-career rankings. For instance, in a recent survey of international destinations for international assignments carried out by Brookfield Global Relocation Services (2011), Sweden came twenty-second – and last of the countries included. But, according to this same survey, relocating to Sweden was also not seen to pose particular hurdles or challenges compared with other countries. Hence, Sweden does not seem to stand out – positively or negatively – as a destination for internationals pursuing global careers. Nevertheless, it poses a rather adequate context for investigating how nationals manage global careers, and particularly the distance work and business travelling that typically come with global careers.

Although there are limited official statistics on distance work and business travelling among Swedes involved in global work specifically, a recent survey by the Swedish Transport Agency (2009) shows that 19 per cent of all international trips were business trips, and that 81.3 per cent of those trips were carried out by air travel. Over all, the survey showed that men travel more by air than women, and that well-paid, high-ranking professionals in the private and public sectors travel more by air than other socio-economic groups.

These statistics can be seen in relation to more general surveys of distance work and business travelling among Swedes, which include domestic as well as international journeys. According to Gustafson (2005), long-distance work-related travel by Swedish employees has increased significantly during the last few decades. The most recent survey from the Swedish Institute for Transport and Communications Analysis, in 2006, shows that, between 2003 and 2004, 11 per cent of the Swedish working population carried out distance work, the largest group being those aged between 35 and 44. Further, it shows that, on average, this part of the working population worked 6 days a month at a location other than their regular workplace; 16 per cent also worked while travelling to and from work and during longer business trips, and, on average, they worked 10 days per month while travelling.

Again, there are significant differences between men and women. Whereas married men and men living in registered partnerships travel for work more than do single men, married women travel less for work than do single women (Gustafson, 2006). Women also tend to reduce their work-related travel significantly when having children (ibid.). Furthermore, approximately 65 per cent of working women in Sweden rarely or never travel for work, whereas the corresponding figure for men is 42 per cent. Indeed, 35 per cent of working men engage in work-related travel every week or more, whereas 15 per cent of working women do so (Bergström Casinowsky, 2010).

In summary, work-related travel and global careers are unevenly distributed across gender, age and socio-economic groups. This is further confirmed by anecdotal evidence. The dozen or so times that we have been to the Scandinavian

Airlines business-class lounges at Stockholm Arlanda Airport, at London Heathrow Airport and at Newark Airport, we have encountered groups predominately consisting of middle-aged Swedish men busy dealing with emails, preparing presentations and reports, and engaging in telephone conversations with colleagues and clients. Perhaps not surprisingly, the overall picture that emerges of the Swedish-based global worker is therefore that of a well-paid, middle-aged, male business traveller, at the higher echelons of organizational life.

## The Relevance of Contemporary Career Concepts

Career theory and research describe a shift from linear careers, taking place within the context of stable organizational structures (e.g. Levinson, 1978), to non-linear and discontinuous career paths (Hall, 1996; Sullivan, 1999). Whereas traditional career concepts emphasize how individuals progress up organizational hierarchies in order to obtain greater extrinsic rewards, more recent concepts emphasize paths that are more strongly driven by intrinsic motivation (Sullivan and Baruch, 2009). In particular, the boundaryless-career model and the protean-career concept have been effectively mobilized in understanding non-linear careers. The protean careerist is self-directed and driven by intrinsic values (Hall, 1996). Similarly, the boundaryless careerist breaks with traditional organizational career arrangements and assumptions about organizational hierarchy and career advancement and pursues instead career opportunities that go beyond any single employer (Arthur and Rousseau, 1996). For example, boundaryless careerists may reject existing career opportunities for personal or family reasons. However, as boundaryless careers are driven by protean motives, the distinction between protean and boundaryless careers is not clear-cut.

### Global Careers and Technology

These non-linear career models have been associated with globalization and technological advancements. However, despite the possibilities that information technology ostensibly offers for coordinating global work without physical displacement, the state of affairs in contemporary multinational organizations shows that email, video-conference systems and other IT-based communication channels rarely eradicate the need for face-to-face meetings. Indeed, face-to-face meetings continue to be imperative in establishing and sustaining relationships (Kraut, Fussell, Brennan and Siegel, 2002; Schunn, Crowley and Okada, 2002), managing conflict (Maruping and Agarwal, 2004; Hinds and Mortensen, 2005), fostering trust (Oertig and Buegri, 2006), sharing knowledge and socializing individuals (Mortensen and Hinds, 2001). As expressed by one respondent in a previous study, 'collaboration remains a body contact sport' (Kiesler and Cummings, 2002: 57). Thus, the growth of global work and careers is related both to the new possibilities for remote work created by information and communication technology and to

the limited capacity of those same media in replacing face-to-face meetings for certain organizational tasks (DeFrank, Konopaske and Ivancevich, 2000). This, however, does not come without consequences, but implies more overtime and impaired job stability (Stalder, 2006), 'tons of travel' and 'physical and emotional wear and tear' (Orlikowski, 2002: 259, 260), as well as an individualization that increasingly leaves workers to themselves and leads to further alienation (Castells, 1997).

Although these studies testify to the challenges, complexity and partially embodied aspects of global work, little attention has been paid to the bodily practices and experiences of managers and professionals involved in global careers. Rather, global careers are often depicted as glamorous and disembodied. Indeed, a dominant image of global workplaces is that they are 'places lifted out of time and space, places where communication and innovation are free from the drag of local cultures and practices and untainted by power relations' and where 'new information and communication technologies make it possible and even necessary to reorganize firms into "global webs" and employees into global telecommuters' (O'Riain, 2000: 259). This suggests an unproblematic view of global careers, where people smoothly and effortlessly move back and forth between distant places and different time zones. Little is therefore known about how people with global careers experience and cope with time differences, long-haul travel and cultural difference. Let us now introduce an embodied phenomenological approach in order to explore how Swedish professionals experience and cope with their global work and careers.

## An Embodied Approach to Global Careers

According to Merleau-Ponty (1962), our experience and perception of the world are shaped by our bodily capabilities and bodily engagement with the world. Hence, cognition is rooted in its situated, material, physical context; there is no clear boundary between the cognitive, the bodily and the social; and the material and the immaterial are intertwined and mutually constitutive. What we perceive is thus reflected in the physical capacities of our bodies and influenced by the physical context in which we are situated. We always perceive the world from somewhere. Furthermore, all bodily acts are rooted in our prereflective intention to achieve 'maximum grip' and be in harmony with the environment. Through bodily performances, we acquire a capability to perceive, respond to and minimize tensions from such equilibrium states, without having to pay conscious attention. Indeed, with experience, our bodies accumulate a capability to become effortlessly immersed in physical contexts, receding into the background and becoming a medium of perception rather than an object of perception. In this view, consciousness is not a matter of 'I think' but of 'I can' (ibid.: 137).

Inspired by Merleau-Ponty, Bourdieu's (1990) notion of the habitus emphasizes the role of bodiliness and physical situatedness in human experience. A product

of structural conditions, the habitus ensures the active presence of past experiences in terms of embodied principles. These principles are deposited in individual bodies through perceptual schemas, thought and physical movement. Generating all the reasonable, common-sense behaviours that are possible within the limits of these regularities, the habitus makes our practices adequate for the situation and constant over time. In other words, the habitus constitutes our practical sense, which enables us to develop and experience a sense of familiarity with our surroundings.

This embodied practical sense cannot be attained by conscious effort but requires us to participate physically in the particular social field in which we find ourselves situated. This also means that the habitus is challenged when we find ourselves in unfamiliar environments. Indeed, '[individual] dispositions are ill-adjusted [. . .] when the environment they actually encounter is too different from the one to which they are objectively adjusted' (ibid.: 62). In such cases, dispositions are 'out-of-phase', because they are adjusted to conditions that no longer apply.

With Merleau-Ponty (1962), we assume that, in such situations, our bodies lack the accumulated capability to reduce tensions in prereflective ways. Instead, our bodies experience breakdowns and interruptions, which make us less directed to our surroundings and more directed towards ourselves, how we feel and what we do. Consequently, our bodily state becomes a passive object of perception rather than an active medium of perception. Furthermore, this means that physicality acquires a more salient role in our experience than had we been situated in familiar environments. For global workers, who often find themselves in new physical, cultural and social contexts, such breakdowns are commonly experienced. Merleau-Ponty's embodied phenomenology and Bourdieu's notion of habitus, therefore, enable us to examine how people with global careers experience and cope with such problems. In what follows, we will utilize this approach to examine how Swedish professionals experience and struggle to cope with the unhealthy habits that come with their global careers.

## Stories of Global Careers Among Swedish Professionals

The globalization of managerial and professional work puts increasing pressure on an increasing number of employees to manage the bodily strains that come with a global career. The following two composite vignettes (Ely, Vinz, Downing and Anzul, 1997; Spalding and Phillips, 2007) may serve to illustrate some of these strains and problems. The vignettes are composed from a broader empirical study where we interviewed and observed a number of Swedish professionals with global careers. All of the respondents worked as high-income, international consultants, and the two vignettes bring out typical experiences that were shared by several respondents.

# Global Careers and Unhealthy Lives I

I probably should be really lucky that I get to travel so much in my work. I mean, most people think that it's really glamorous even though it's not, and I'm so happy to see new places and being paid for it. But this has a price. Every time a new trip is coming up I feel bad for leaving my family, and I know that they'll miss me and that I can contribute less to all the household chores, which means that my wife is left to do all the housework for extended periods of time. And instead of being able to spend more time with my family before I leave, I often have to work late in order to finish things in the office. Otherwise my colleagues will chase me wherever I am in the world, and it's even worse to have to respond to emails and phone calls and try to coordinate work with the team back home when I'm away, since I'm often in another time zone. It's so much more challenging and requires even more effort and time.

My travel goes to all continents and there is often several hours of time difference. When I arrive at a new destination I always hope they've booked me into a nice hotel with a gym and a pool, but that's far from always the case. I understand that there are budgetary constraints, and most of the time it's only the expensive hotels that have those facilities. But having them really makes a difference to my stay. Staying healthy also involves trying to eat healthy, and that's a huge challenge when travelling. I try to avoid having the food on the plane since it's not particularly healthy. Instead I buy something at the airport if there's time, but that's not always the case either, and some airports don't even have healthy alternatives.

After a long flight I feel terrible. My skin feels dry, my stomach bloated and my hair dull. I really hate to see myself in that airplane bathroom mirror and sometimes I try hard to avoid looking at myself. The worst is of course if I have a business meeting on the same day that I arrive, and sometimes I don't even have time to go to the hotel and have a shower.

It's a lot of stress and adrenaline as you're always a bit nervous when meeting people you don't know that well, who on top of that are foreigners too, so you're afraid of making cultural blunders. I feel that I constantly have to think about how I behave, which is very demanding. I can never relax and just be myself. You become more aware of your body language, how you express yourself and so on.

After the meetings are over for the day and I'm back in my hotel room I usually have to continue working. Don't assume that I can take a bath in the nice hotel bathtub then! No, since I've been away from the office during the afternoon, I have to check my e-mails and deal with problems at the office back home. Sometimes I have to call people in Sweden, which is embarrassing, as I know they're at home by that time and not in the office. But if it's an urgent matter I have to, as I'll be occupied with my foreign colleagues the following day.

So actually, it's not very luxurious to travel. It's much harder work than staying at home and I can never enjoy the city where I am or have a nice evening out. Each minute has to be used for preparing or closing meetings. That's kind of stressful too. I want to do some sightseeing, but there's hardly ever time for that. I sometimes book fictive meetings in my calendar to get gaps in my schedule

and time to just relax. That can be a lifesaver, especially when coming home late at night and being expected to be in the office as usual at 9. To sum up, I'm constantly stressed and have bad conscience for not being a good husband, father, colleague and employee and for not being able to stay as healthy as I would like too.

## Global Careers and Unhealthy Lives II

I've travelled for work for five years now. In the beginning I saw it as a great opportunity to show my employer that I'm willing to do anything for my career and that work comes first. Now, I just feel tired of it. Last year I had almost one hundred travel days. I start to feel that my social life suffers, I have difficulties keeping in touch with friends, and I feel like an alien at my home office since I'm hardly ever there. I also have the feeling that my colleagues sometimes think that I'm not working that hard.

But it's a hard life! When I travel I don't have time to do much more than work. Sometimes I'm in a new country but I don't feel like I'm there. I sit with my laptop on my knee, communicating with my colleagues back home. I'm in a little bubble, working on my project. I take a taxi to the foreign office directly, and sometimes we order sandwiches to the room where we have the meeting. Then, we take a taxi to the airport and we're back in Sweden again. It's such a strange feeling. When I stay overnight I often have business dinners that I need to attend, so there's little spare time. And those business lunches and dinners, and the coffee breaks that we have, all that makes me eat quite unhealthy compared to when I'm at home. I eat cookies and drink lots of coffee, even though I actually don't really like any of it, and if food is served I always eat, to be polite or as a social thing.

I must also admit that I drink more when I'm abroad than when I'm at home. I think it's a way for me to relax, and also to fall asleep more easily. And it's more culturally accepted abroad. Also, it's a big part of the 'business man' culture. I start drinking already on the plane, not much, but a glass of wine or so with the food. And I always have a few drinks in the hotel bar during a stay. It's a way to kill the loneliness and to relax and sleep better. I'm lucky to be able to handle jetlag quite ok. It doesn't really affect me. I manage to sleep almost everywhere, but I quite often take sleeping pills and a few drinks when I arrive at the hotel.

I often have a bad conscience about my weight since I've gained a few kilos during the last few years. I should try to eat healthier when I travel. The bad food, the strange eating times and too much sitting down makes me constipated, but it's almost impossible to eat healthy when you must resort to restaurant food. I try to cut out the bad stuff, but I realize I'm still far away from eating as healthy as I do back home. And you need food and energy, to keep up with the fast pace and to stay alert in all the meetings. It doesn't make it better that I never have time to just unwind or exercise. I try to walk to the office sometimes, or jump out of the cab a few blocks earlier, just to get some sort of exercise.

In particular, these two vignettes draw attention to the bodily wear and tear experienced by Swedish professionals engaged in extensive, long-haul business travel. Before discussing this in further detail, we should point out two critical incidents that occurred while we generated data about this. One of our female respondents, who we can call Maria, decided to resign from all travel-related work. She explained to us that she simply could not bear all the travelling anymore and the consequences that it had for her health. In previous years, Maria had travelled an average of 85 days per year. Another respondent, who we can call Eric, had to cancel the first interview we had scheduled with him because he was suddenly suffering from burnout. Waking up one morning not knowing where he was, he later told us that he ended up being hospitalized in Moscow. Eric is now getting better, but he too has resigned from all work-related travel. In a way, we are not surprised by this. Indeed, this chapter partly sprung out of a severe migraine attack that one of us faced as he was co-organizing (along with one of the editors of this book) and speaking at a professional development workshop at the Academy of Management Meeting in Montreal in 2010, six time zones away from home.

In order to problematize the structural, cultural and bodily dimensions of global careers among Swedish professionals, we will now discuss our two vignettes in relation to key concepts in career studies and in relation to the embodied phenomenological approach outlined above.

## Swedish Professionals Managing and Embodying Global Careers

The aim of the present chapter was to explore how Swedish professionals experience and cope with some of the strains associated with global work and careers. Whereas the non-linear career models of the boundaryless and the protean careerist have been associated with globalization and technological advancements, our two vignettes from Swedes working as high-income, international consultants suggest that global work may reinforce traditional career paths and structures within organizational boundaries.

Although our respondents were careerists who invested much time and effort in their jobs, their motivation and career choices neither reflect the protean model nor the boundaryless model of careerism. Rather, we would argue that they were motivated by a mix of intrinsic and extrinsic factors. This is not to say that protean traits of careerism, such as the drive for personal learning, development and growth (Hall, 2004; Sullivan and Baruch, 2009), were not evident. However, as their jobs involved more global business travel than they preferred, the extensive business travel endured by our respondents was more strongly motivated by extrinsic factors than by intrinsic factors. The fulfilment of management and client expectations was more significant than the desire to 'be true to oneself' and balance work and non-work demands (see Mainiero and Sullivan, 2006). In other words, their practices of career management were more strongly shaped and driven by

organizational values and structures than by individual values and career concerns (see Sullivan and Baruch, 2009).

Further, the data underpinning our two vignettes were only in partial agreement with the boundaryless-career model. Certainly, the Swedish professionals we studied enacted a global career that transgressed national and regional geographical borders. But, whereas some respondents were able to make upward career moves by being recruited by client firms, most respondents contended with the psychological mobility and challenges (Mainiero and Sullivan, 2006) provided by the multinational assignments of their current employment. Hence, they crossed geographical, cultural and psychological borders, but without crossing organizational borders.

Multiple career paths were limited and were not readily available to Swedish professionals who wanted to stay within one and the same firm. Instead, they had to accept the extensive amount of global business travel, should they wish to have any prospect of moving upwards in the organizational hierarchy – or avoid being moved downwards for that matter. Indeed, respondents who refused the extensive travel typically ended up being assigned less prestigious positions, or they were pretty much forced to look for work elsewhere.

Hall, Gardner and Baugh (2008) claim that individuals become more self-directed in their careers, or choose lateral and even downwards career moves to fulfil personal needs. Similarly, Swedish women professionals who we interviewed seemed to cross organizational boundaries and choose different types of employer as a way to avoid the travelling and to better balance work concerns with broader life concerns. In line with previous findings (e.g. Gustafson, 2005; Kirchmeyer, 2002), this meant that they ended up prioritizing family life and personal health at the expense of their professional career. Conversely, our vignettes suggest that global careers produce unhealthy lives by cutting Swedish professionals off from the opportunity to enact healthy bodily habits.

## Structural and Cultural Constraints on the Embodiment of Healthy Global Careers Among Swedish Professionals

Structural and cultural constraints may be seen to have further effects on how Swedish professionals embody, experience and cope with global careers. Actualizing Merleau-Ponty's (1962) and Bourdieu's (1990) emphasis on body–environment equilibrium, our vignettes suggest that the negative experiences that our respondents had of global work were primarily an outcome of disharmony between body and environment. This does not mean that these Swedish professionals were merely passive objects, suffering from the strains and pains of their global careers. When feeling exhausted or wanting to exercise, they invented destructive as well as constructive tactics to restore harmony between their bodies and the environment. Specifically, they tried to avoid unhealthy foods

and snacks to avoid gaining more weight, but they also used alcohol in order to try and wind down, relax, sleep and cope with loneliness.

However, being in a different culture made it more difficult for them to enact constructive tactics than destructive tactics to restore body–environment harmony. Indeed, wishing to be polite to their overseas hosts, some of our respondents would eat even when they were not hungry and even if they regarded the food and beverages being served as unhealthy. Some of them also used alcohol more readily to cope with the strains of global business travel, because this was more culturally accepted abroad than in Sweden. Even though these tactics were aimed to deal with the unhealthy and painful aspects of global work, then, they also worked to create and reinforce feelings of pain and unwellness.

Further on, the habitus of our respondents was at odds with the environments they found themselves situated in when abroad. As their global careers often situated them in new and unfamiliar environments, they constantly experienced tensions and interruptions that their bodies were unable to cope with prereflectively. Incapable of embodying a practical sense adequate for the situation, and incapable of experiencing a sense of familiarity with the new surroundings, they worried about making cultural blunders and sought to be mindful about every social and physical movement they made. For others, their bodies made themselves felt through sensations of pain, suffering and unwellness (cf. Leder, 1990), or they made themselves seen: indeed, a number of our respondents were unhappy and uncomfortable with the grey, tired face they encountered each time they looked at themselves in the mirror. Consequently, their global careers made it difficult to restore harmony between body and environment. Rather than receding into their cultural and contextual background (that is, their habitus), to be taken for granted as the medium through which they sense and perceive the world, their bodies became the object of their own careful, worried attention.

In summary, then, our vignettes suggest that the global careers of Swedish professionals are shaped by structural and cultural factors, but also that these factors affect how Swedish professionals experience and embody global careers. Indeed, while the global careers explored here contrast with some of the predominant concepts in contemporary career studies (see Sullivan and Baruch, 2009), they are deeply associated with bodily problems and sensations that appear to exert much influence on employee satisfaction and effectiveness, health and well-being.

## Critical Perspectives

There is a tendency to romanticize nomadic life on the road, as if it offers a particular freedom and weightless life (Eyerman and Löfgren, 1995). This stereotypical image also seems to prevail around global business travel, as a sense of glamour is typically attributed to global careers, perhaps particularly by people who have not personally experienced it. In contrast, our vignettes of Swedish professionals have drawn attention to the bodily and emotional strains and

problems of global careers, as well as the structural and cultural constraints highlighted by extant research in the field of career studies. Although our findings are based on a study of Swedish professionals working in particular consultancy firms, we suspect that they have relevance for the understanding of global careers more broadly.

First, our findings problematize some of the predominant concepts in contemporary career studies by showing how global careers follow quite traditional career paths that are shaped by organizational values and constraints, rather than by intrinsic values and concerns. However, this does not lead us to propose a general relationship between globalization and traditional career paths. Instead, we would argue that the association between globalization and boundaryless careers needs to be further nuanced and problematized in future research, so as to acknowledge how global career paths may be interwoven and interchanged throughout an individual's career. These issues warrant further scholarly attention, particularly if we are to understand what career paths are available in different kinds of global firm and how different people experience and enact such career paths, depending on gender, age and other embodied diversity factors.

Second, our findings highlight an interesting relationship between globalization and embodiment hitherto underexplored in the literature on global careers and career studies more broadly. The more 'global' an organization and its career paths become, the more apparent embodiment seems to become. Hence, embodiment emerges as a strategically important issue in need of management. However, despite evidence from other firms that the health and bodies of global managers and professionals constitute an object of management, regulation and modification,[1] this was not evident in the firms we studied here. Indeed, the Swedish professionals in our two vignettes were pretty much left on their own to handle the physical strains caused by their global work and careers. None of them reported any advice or support from management regarding how to deal with the bodily and emotional strains and suffering caused by extensive global business travel. Although one might reasonably expect senior managers at such firms to be aware of the challenges involved (indeed, they have typically gone through the same amount of business travelling themselves when working at more junior levels), management support was absent. Instead, extensive travel was regarded as a normal part of the job, and the bodily problems and unhealthy side effects following from this were largely ignored, unacknowledged and trivialized.

Further, our findings raise an important question regarding the powers and limits of managerial responsibility. Although the management of employee health and well-being is a delicate issue, which might raise concerns of 'managerial colonialism', the context of global work and careers examined here points to a 'managerial absence', which also may be a problem.[2] Without trying to reconcile these conflicting concerns here, we would argue that further research is required to investigate if management can acknowledge and offer support to

help global workers cope with the bodily strains of global careers, without doing so in invasive ways.

Either way, this connects the challenges of global careers to central themes addressed in the burgeoning literature on embodiment in organization studies. As the bodies of professionals with global careers are primary media of experience, as well as objects of attention and intervention, we must bear in mind that the body is an active subject, central to the understanding of any human experience, rather than simply a passive object of human understanding.

From this, we would conclude that it is pertinent for the field of global-career studies to further investigate and scrutinize how global work and careers are embodied. This begs empirical questions about how work organizations seek to manage the health and bodies of their global managers and professionals, and how global managers and professionals deal with the ways in which organizations expect them to take care of their own health, while simultaneously making and managing their own global careers.

We would further urge the field to employ more clearly embodied methods than we have shown here to generate data about these aspects of global careers. In particular, this would require us to generate more deeply embodied data. Although this can be accomplished through conventional methods, such as interviews, observations and shadowing, embodying these methods requires us to pay more attention to the bodily appearance, body language and feelings displayed by the people that we interview, observe and shadow. It also requires us to reflect about our own embodied experiences throughout the research process (see Engelsrud, 2005; Knights and Thanem, 2011; Thanem and Knights, 2012).

Finally, we would encourage the field to explore embodied theories further in order to make sense of how people experience, enact and cope with their global careers. As we have sought to demonstrate in this chapter, Merleau-Ponty's (1962) embodied phenomenology and Bourdieu's (1990) sociology are good starting points in this respect. Merleau-Ponty provides a sophisticated conceptualization of the lived body as an active subject of experience and practice, capable of coping with the environment. Acknowledging this active nature of the body, Bourdieu helps us understand how the body is embedded in, and habituated by, social structures that make it able to handle familiar environments, but inept at dealing with unfamiliar environments. In particular, Merleau-Ponty's concepts have been fruitful in helping other areas in organization studies investigate bodily experience and practices in settings of work and organization (see e.g. Dale, 2001; Küpers, 2005).

We realize that the development and use of embodied methods and theories are not endeavours free from risks and problems (see, e.g., Engelsrud, 2005; Knights and Thanem, 2011; Thanem and Knights, 2012). However, we are confident that pursuing these endeavours is necessary if we are more appropriately to explore and understand the bodily practices, experiences and problems that seem to have such an important bearing on contemporary global careers.

## Notes

1. The so-called GM Diet, which the automobile giant General Motors prescribes to its global executives, may be a case in point here. Acknowledging the difficulties of combining an executive lifestyle of global work and business travel with a lean body weight, the main purpose of the GM Diet was to help General Motors' executives, in particular, to lose weight quickly. Whether or not the GM Diet facilitates good health, it does illustrate how certain employers seek to help employees handle some of the bodily strains associated with global careers.
2. Indeed, the stress experienced by the Swedish professionals we interviewed ought to be seen in relation to previous studies, which have found measurable connections between work stress and metabolic syndrome (Chandola, Brunner and Marmot, 2006) and between work stress and cardiovascular disease and mortality (Marmot, 2004).

## References

Arthur, M. B. and Rousseau, D. M. (1996). 'The boundaryless career as a new employment principle', in M. B. Arthur and D. M. Rousseau (eds) *The Boundaryless Career*, pp. 3–20. New York: Oxford University Press.

Bergström Casinowsky, G. (2010). 'Tjänsteresor i människors vardag – om rörlighet, närvaro och frånvaro', *Göteborg Studies in Sociology* 43. Department of Sociology, University of Gothenburg, Sweden.

Bourdieu, P. (1990). *The Logic of Practice*, trans. R. Nice. Stanford, CA: Stanford University Press.

Brookfield Global Relocation Services (2011) *Global Relocation Trends: 2011 Survey Report*. Retrieved from www.brookfieldgrs.com, 1 March 2012.

Castells, M. (1997). 'An introduction to the information age', *City* 7: 6–16.

Chandola, T., Brunner, E. and Marmot, M. (2006). 'Chronic stress at work and the metabolic syndrome: Prospective study', *British Medical Journal* 332: 521–525.

Dale, K. (2001). *Anatomising Organisation Theory*. Basingstoke: Macmillan.

DeFrank, R. S., Konopaske, R. and Ivancevich, J. M. (2000). 'Executive travel stress: Perils of the road warrior', *Academy of Management Executive* 14(2): 58–71.

Ely, M., Vinz, R., Downing, M. and Anzul, M. (1997). *On Writing Qualitative Research: Living By Words*. London: Falmer.

Engelsrud, G. (2005). 'The lived body as experience and perspective: Methodological challenges', *Qualitative Research* 5(3): 267–284.

Eyerman, R. and Löfgren, O. (1995). 'Romancing the road: Road movies and images of mobility', *Theory, Culture & Society* 12: 53–79.

Gustafson, P. (2005). 'Resor i arbetet. En kartläggning av svenskarnas tjänsteresor 1995–2001', *Forskningsrapport* 135, Sociologiska institutionen, Göteborgs universitet.

Gustafson, P. (2006). 'Work-related travel, gender and family obligations', *Work, Employment & Society* 20(3): 513–530.

Hall, D. T. (1996). 'Long live the career', in D. T. Hall (ed.) *The Career Is Dead – Long Live the Career*, pp. 1–12. San Francisco, CA: Jossey-Bass.

Hall, D. T. (2004). 'The protean career: A quarter-century journey', *Journal of Vocational Behavior* 65: 1–13.

Hall, D. T., Gardner, W. and Baugh, S. G. (2008). 'The questions we ask about authenticity and attainability: How do values and beliefs influence our career decisions?' Careers Division theme session panel discussion, Academy of Management, Anaheim, CA.

Hinds, P. J. and Mortensen, M. (2005). 'Understanding conflict in geographically distributed teams: The moderating effects of shared identity, shared context, and spontaneous communication', *Organization Science* 16: 290–307.

Kiesler, S. and Cummings, J. N. (2002). 'What do we know about proximity and distance in work groups? A legacy of research', in P. Hinds and S. Kiesler (eds) *Distributed Work*, pp. 56–80. Cambridge, MA: MIT Press.

Kirchmeyer, C. (2002). 'Gender differences in managerial careers: Yesterday, today, and tomorrow', *Journal of Business Ethics* 37: 5–24.

Knights, D. and Thanem, T. (2011). 'Gendered incorporations: Critically embodied reflections on the gender divide in organisation studies', *International Journal of Work, Organisation & Emotion* 4: 217–235.

Kraut, R. E., Fussell, S. R., Brennan, S. E. and Siegel, J. (2002). 'Understanding effects of proximity on collaboration: Implications for technologies to support remote collaborative work', in P. Hinds and S. Kiesler (eds) *Distributed Work*, pp. 137–162. Cambridge, MA: MIT Press.

Küpers, W. (2005). 'Phenomenology of embodied implicit and narrative knowing', *Journal of Knowledge Management* 9(6): 114–133.

Leder, D. (1990). *The Absent Body*. Chicago, IL: University of Chicago Press.

Levinson, D. J. (1978). *The Seasons of a Man's Life*. New York: Knopf.

Mainiero, L. A. and Sullivan, S. E. (2006). *The Opt-Out Revolt: How People Are Creating Kaleidoscope Careers Outside of Companies*. New York: Davies Black.

Marmot, M. (2004). *The Status Syndrome: How Social Standing Affects Our Health and Longevity*. London: Times Books.

Maruping, L. M. and Agarwal, R. (2004). 'Managing team interpersonal processes through technology: A task-technology fit perspective', *Journal of Applied Psychology*, 89: 975–990.

Merleau-Ponty, M. (1962). *Phenomenology of Perception*. London: Routledge.

Mortensen, M. and Hinds, P. J. (2001). 'Conflict and shared identity in geographically distributed teams', *International Journal of Conflict Management* 12: 212–238.

Oertig, M. and Buegri, T. (2006). 'The challenges of managing cross-cultural virtual project teams', *Team Performance Management* 12: 23–30.

O'Riain, S. O. (2000). 'Networking for a living. Irish software developers in the global workplace', in R. Baldoz, C. Koeber and P. Kraft (eds) *The Critical Study of Work: Labor, Technology, and Global Production*, pp. 258–282. Philadelphia, PA: Temple University Press.

Orlikowski, W. J. (2002). 'Knowing in practice: Enacting a collective capability in distributed organizing', *Organization Science* 13(3): 249–273.

Schunn, C., Crowley, K. and Okada, T. (2002). 'What makes collaborations across a distance succeed? The case of the cognitive science community', in P. Hinds and S. Kiesler (eds) *Distributed Work*, pp. 407–427. Cambridge, MA: MIT Press.

Spalding, N. J. and Phillips, T. (2007). 'Exploring the use of vignettes: From validity to trustworthiness', *Qualitative Health Research* 17: 954–962.

Stalder, F. (2006). *Manuel Castells: The Theory of the Network Society*. Cambridge: Polity Press.

Sullivan, S. E. (1999). 'The changing nature of careers: A review and research agenda', *Journal of Management* 25: 457–484.

Sullivan, S. E. and Baruch, Y. (2009). 'Advances in career theory and research: A critical review and agenda for future exploration', *Journal of Management* 35: 1542–1571.

Swedish Institute for Transport and Communications Analysis (2006). *KOM: The National Communications Survey* 32. Östersund.

Swedish Transport Agency (2009). *Aviation Trends: Statistics, Analysis and Information from the Swedish Transport Agency.* Norrköping.

Thanem, T. and Knights, D. (2012). 'Feeling and speaking through our gendered bodies: Embodied self-reflection and research practice in organisation studies', *International Journal of Work, Organisation & Emotion* 5: 91–108.

# 6

# GLOBAL MOVES FROM AND TO BRAZIL

*Alan P. Marcus, Towson University, USA*

## Introduction

Stephen Castles and Mark J. Miller have stated: "migration ranks as one of the most important factors in global change" (2003, p. 4). In this vein, the recent influx of immigrants to the United States over the past four decades, for example, has transformed ethnic and global landscapes significantly, as geographers have observed (e.g., Airriess & Miyares, 2007; Berry & Henderson, 2002; Frazier & Tettey-Fio, 2006; Kaplan & Li, 2006). Likewise, communities in places of origin (sending communities)[1] are affected, not only when family members or loved ones migrate, but also when migrants return home. In the case of Brazil, as migration processes shape important economic and sociocultural dimensions in receiving communities, they also affect sending communities in Brazil, transforming places on many levels (Siqueira, 2007). Consequently, transnational migration processes have transformed individual and community livelihoods, including careers.

The important dimensions of careers outlined in Sullivan and Baruch (2009) provide context for the protean career, where the "protean careerist is able to repackage his or her knowledge" (1545), and boundaryless careers, which involve various dimensions of mobility. Here, the word *place* provides a fundamental fulcrum (i.e., figurative and literal) toward understanding the economics of gender dynamics and cultural change—and for which I draw upon transnational theory (e.g., Basch, Schiller, & Blanc, 1995; Levitt, 2001, 2004, 2007; Margolis, 1994; Siqueira, 2007; Tsuda, 1999). Transnational theoretical approaches concentrate on the significance of migrants' ongoing ties and loyalties to their country of origin, and how they are generated and maintained through various spatial, sociocultural, and financial processes (Basch et al., 1995)—and are tied to the concepts outlined by Sullivan and Baruch (2009). They also challenge the

ways in which we have traditionally thought about borders, boundaries, and movement. In addition, I also draw on the literature on Brazilian migration processes, as an illustrative example of transnationalism (e.g., Almeida, 2003; Beserra, 2003; Goza, 1999; Margolis, 1994, 1995, 1998, 2006; Marrow 2003; Martes & Soares, 2006; Sales, 1998; Siqueira, 2007). Using the above theoretical frameworks, I discuss the following questions: How are returnee immigrants affected once they return to their sending communities in Brazil? How are women and men affected separately? Are they happy? How do social spaces change, and how are they experienced? What are the social implications for individuals, communities, and, in general, the global economy, taking into account those who are in a secondary role, trivialized, or marginalized? I use qualitative multi-methods (see Charmaz, 2006) to answer these questions, and also show how significant changes occur within a transnational optic.

Rather than focus on careers and migration processes at macro levels (structure, and aggregate levels), this study looks at the micro levels (process, individual and family experiences, decisions and actions). Therefore, this study should not be generalized for statistical purposes, as it is not about all Brazilian immigrants in the United States or returnees in Brazil. I also evaluated my positionality between the researched and the broader outcome of this study through *critical reflexivity*.[2] That is, I learned to emphasize critically the significance and the position of researcher in fieldwork, as I recognize advantages and disadvantages of the several perceived knowledge claims (e.g., gender, ethnicity, career, etc.) in relation to the researched.

I conducted fieldwork in four locations: Framingham, Massachusetts, USA, and Governador Valadares, in the state of Minas Gerais, Brazil—which are two older, well-established places of destination and origin, respectively (e.g., Almeida, 2003; Margolis, 1994; Sales, 1998; Siqueira, 2007)—and, Marietta, Georgia, USA, and Piracanjuba, in the state of Goiás, Brazil, two places that represent more recent, important "migration corridors." I wanted to evaluate cultural and socioeconomic interrelationships, particularly in two distinct U.S. regions of destination and origin, respectively. Results from my doctoral dissertation fieldwork research (Marcus, 2009a, 2009b, 2010, 2011a, 2011b, 2011c) were conducted between September 2006 and September 2007, when I completed a total of 273 informal and formal interviews using ethnographic techniques, including participant observation (see Hay, 2000; Hoggart, Lees, & Davies, 2002). During fieldwork research, I developed contacts through snowball sampling (see Margolis, 1994), which were helpful in establishing ties with U.S. immigrants' kinship/friendship contacts in Brazil. However, in this chapter, I use only a few selected interview excerpts from that project, which focus on returnees *in Brazil* in the form of several vignettes. I present and discuss striking case studies for this chapter, and weave them throughout, providing evidence to highlight the topic of careers upon returning to Brazil.

## The Situation of Global Careers in Brazil

After a 21-year military dictatorship, which began in 1964, Brazil held its first democratic elections in 1985. By the late 1980s, Brazil was experiencing a political environment fraught with corruption scandals, as well as a serious economic downturn, with inflation rates exceeding 1,000%. As a result, more than 1 million Brazilians left Brazil during that period—the so-called "lost decade" (Sales, 1998). Today, there are an estimated 2 million Brazilians living outside of Brazil (mostly in the United States, Japan, and throughout Europe), of which about 1.2 million reside in the United States, with the greatest three clusters in New York City (300,033), Boston (200,032), and Miami (150,018), respectively (Marcus, 2009a). As this chapter shows, the relevance and extent of contemporary Brazilian diasporas (e.g., Almeida, 2003; Beserra, 2003; Fritz, 2010; Goza, 1999; Margolis, 1994, 1995, 1998, 2006; Martes & Soares, 2006; Sales, 1998; Siqueira, 2007) reflect borderless careers at the individual, organizational, national, and transnational levels.

Brazilian immigrants differ from other Latin American immigrants to the United States on many levels: for example, linguistically (i.e., they are Portuguese-speakers; see Falconi & Mazzoti, 2007) and in terms of socioeconomic levels, educational and ethnic backgrounds, and social capital (Portes & Rumbaut, 1990; Williams, Steigenga, & Vasquez, 2009). The majority of Brazilian immigrants are not escaping dire poverty (they could hardly afford the US$15,000 fees to cross the U.S.–Mexican border unauthorized or the expensive airplane and transportation costs), nor are they political refugees seeking asylum (Margolis, 1994). Castles and Miller (2003) have pointed to the difference between *human trafficker* and *human smuggler*. The former will deceitfully entice a migrant, without his or her knowledge, to leave his or her country of origin, and the migrant will usually work under forced conditions, without consent, as a prostitute. The human smuggler will usually act as a travel "agent," with the migrant's knowledge and consent. Most Mexican immigrants, generally "rural laborers with low educational levels" (Portes & Hoffman, 2003, p. 71), differ from most Brazilian immigrants, who tend to have more social capital and tend to secure higher-paying jobs in the service sectors (Loret de Mola, Ribeiro, & Lizama, 2009).

Brazilian immigrants sent about US$6 billion in remittances back to Brazil in 2004, representing about 1% of the Brazilian gross domestic product (GDP); however, because most of these remittances were sent informally, the Brazilian Central Bank (*Banco Central*) officially registered only US$2.4 million in remittances for the same year (Marcus, 2011b; Martes & Soares, 2006). These transactions represent important examples of transnational exchange flows, linking communities across borders and driving the broader concept of transnationalism. For example, Brazilian immigrants send monthly financial remittances ranging from US$500 to US$1,000 back to their sending communities in Brazil (Siqueira, 2007). Entire communities have become dependent on these remittances. When

the U.S. dollar exchange rate decreases, economic ripple effects are felt throughout those sending communities, generating financial stagnation and resulting in a generalized local crisis (Moreira, 2007). Hence, transnational interactions affect careers and local economies *globally* and across formal borders, and, ultimately, and—in the vein of this book's core project, as well as its title—*without borders*.

Male returnees in Brazil, who once worked as plumbers, painters, or construction workers in the United States, and who are now surrounded by their Brazilian female family relatives (who are typically willing to do most household chores), are no longer willing to engage in what has been a traditionally perceived "immigrant career" abroad. They are also not willing to perform such jobs perceived as "menial" (be it in construction, house cleaning, or domestic work). Now, they would rather pay someone else to do those jobs, because returnee men are now the archetypal Brazilian "man of the house" when they return to Brazil. This individual and collective mindset among Brazilian returnee males has dramatically affected careers in sending communities. For example, in Governador Valadares, men who have not yet emigrated abroad experience a chronic local shortage of career opportunities, particularly in technical professions, mostly because most men either live abroad or stop going to school, expecting one day to emigrate abroad, work hard, and bring back enough money to build a house of their own (like their uncle, cousin, or father, for example).[3] Here, the contradictions of sociocultural norms are clear: what Brazilians were once willing to do—in terms of careers—during 4 or 6 years abroad, they will typically avoid doing (or refuse to do), once they return to Brazil. For example, Carlos, a local community activist, heads an organization in Governador Valadares partially financed by a Brazilian federal bank and by the Brazilian Workers' Union. Its goal is to protect workers by developing local sources of income, instead of having to rely entirely on immigrants' financial remittances. He explained that the local economic problems are magnified by the local "culture of migration," and the belief that Brazilians can only solve their problems with a "quick fix" of 6–8 years working abroad, saving money and returning "rich."

In light of the fact that most women are earning more than men financially and the changes involved in women's public behavior and activities perceived as acceptable to women in the United States—but once only granted to men in Brazil—the imbalance between immigrants' earned incomes helps exacerbate several predicaments faced by migrants' families when they return to Brazil. As Mara, age 47, a house-cleaning-business owner in Marietta, states: "here [Brazilian] men have to become kinder because they know that the woman has more monetary power whereas in Brazil he was *machista*." This quote provides a backdrop of Brazilian gender dynamics and careers as an important dimension among Brazilian returnees, as I discuss next.

## Women's Journey

Until recently, immigration studies tended to ignore women, or to portray them as mere passive followers of male immigrants. Today, women in some cases outnumber men, such as Southeast Asian (Castles & Miller, 2003) and Caribbean immigrants to the United States (Brettell & Hollifield, 1999). Castles and Miller have spoken in terms of the "feminization of migration" and how the awareness of women in migration studies has grown since the 1960s, as well as how women play a significant role in all types of migration (2003).

Brazilian immigrant women in the United States tend to experience increased social and economic empowerment and can earn as much as $8,000 monthly as house-cleaning-business owners; however, upon their return to Brazil, they are relegated to traditional female household cultural scripts (and, by proxy, to their cultural and physical spaces, financial dependency on their spouse) and much lower incomes when compared with their spouse. As my results show, they tend to be happier in the United States than their male counterparts—for a number of reasons, including change in career. Conversely, a sense of *emasculation* (Marcus, 2010) occurs for immigrant men, owing to the fact they are no longer able to "manage" or control power relations with their wives, daughters, or female loved ones, in the same way as they once did in Brazil. Furthermore, Brazilian immigrant men typically bring home lower financial earnings than their female counterparts, which adds to the feeling of *emasculation*, as "earning money" is very much a part of a *man's domain* (see Da Matta, 1985; Parker, 1991). In this case, Brazilian immigrant women become a salient dimension within broader discussions of power relations in the migration process. Brazilian women have become key actors in generating and maintaining social networks in both sending and receiving communities.

## Happiness in Brazil?

Although career theorists typically use terms such as "career satisfaction" and not "happiness" (as it is a highly ideological term), my survey is extracted from the disciplinary practises of geography, and I am thus transferring the data and elaborating the same ideas within career theory. I wanted to know if Brazilian immigrants and returnees were happy. I specifically use the term "happiness" here, as I used it in my survey instrument. Rather than using other terms, such as "satisfaction" or "self-fulfillment," the use of the term "happiness" implies economic as well as non-economic factors, and, in addition, it allowed me also to follow up with important, open-ended questions in my ethnographic interviews, so that the interviewee would explain to me what exactly he/she meant by "happiness." I found out that happiness levels were different for women and men when I interviewed them separately. For example, polar dynamics between men and women who I interviewed separately indicated fairly inverted levels of happiness. Brazilian immigrant women demonstrated higher levels of "happiness"

in the United States than in Brazil. On the other hand, their male counterparts were not as happy, despite having reached similar levels of socioeconomic empowerment, mainly in the construction sector.

In the past, most Brazilian immigrants belonged to middle or upper–middle socioeconomic backgrounds; however, recently, more Brazilians from the middle–lower socioeconomic levels are also emigrating. I wanted responses to focus on the way "happiness" was construed by the respondent as a multi-dimensional *experience* and *meaning*, relating to interviewees' perceptions of family, love, education, and economic and career dimensions. This interviewing process also provided me with an opportunity to follow up with open-ended questions, so the interviewees could explain to me what they really meant by "happiness."

In almost all cases, happiness meant a complex, layered articulation of economic factors (i.e., careers), as well as non-economic factors (e.g., love, family, feelings). Unhappiness levels[4] were clearly revealed among men in my survey; however, Brazilian women *in the United States* were happier (average 4.2) than men (average 3.3). Happiness levels *in Brazil* were slightly higher for men (4.25) than for women (4.15). The unhappiness levels, created by circumstances such as divorce, abuse, or a poignant event, were unraveled in fieldwork research through ethnographic techniques—otherwise, perhaps, they would have been absent had I only used a survey. Women had the same, relatively high happiness levels in both the receiving and sending communities (average 4.2 and 4.25, respectively). Men, however, were not as happy in the United States (3.3) and were slightly happier than women in Brazil (4.25).

Nonetheless, the ethnographic interviews showed slightly more intense unhappiness levels expressed by women in Brazil, and more intense happiness levels expressed in the United States.[5] Again, Barbara from Minas Gerais, the housecleaner in Marietta, says: "My husband's dream was to return to Brazil . . . so he could take his naps on the hammock and watch the townsfolk pass by. But the women like it here." The act of migrating becomes *socially seductive* and appealing for many Brazilian migrants in sending communities, which, again, was only magnified by the local political and social elites.

Although the great majority of male immigrants were married in receiving communities, 92% in Framingham and 64% in Marietta, this ratio was much smaller in sending communities, as half of the female returnees in Piracanjuba were single, and only one-fifth were married. Half the female returnees in Governador Valadares were married, and only 8% were single. The high percentage ratio of married male/female immigrants in receiving communities suggests the unfolding of five possibilities. First, men will claim they are married, even if this means an unofficial union to another woman, as is commonly done in Brazil. Second, those immigrants who are married, or remarried, will most likely remain in the United States, suggesting that married couples draw upon stronger network and financial resources that benefit their livelihoods and increase their possibilities for upward social and economic mobility and, by proxy,

their careers. Third, those who returned to Brazil have experienced family fragmentation and have since divorced or separated. Fourth, men will prefer to claim they are married, even if this is not true, only to avoid the stigma of being regarded suspiciously in the local community as a homosexual (which, in Brazilian society, is tantamount to complete failure to live up to the "male ideal"). Fifth, female immigrants and returnees have either separated from or divorced their spouses, owing to their newly found freedom and the social and economic empowerment attained or learned in the United States. Only sending communities included widows(ers). Their return to Brazil is most likely caused by strong family ties in Brazil and/or prolonged loneliness in receiving communities. The reason for the absence of widows(ers) in receiving communities is not known, except perhaps that those who were widowed at one point may have since remarried in the United States. These factors all contribute importantly to the broader understanding of careers in sending communities. I will discuss the particulars of career choices next.

## Careers and Returnees

In general, predominating careers in sending communities in Brazil (prior to when Brazilians migrate) reflect archetypal middle-class positions for those Brazilian emigrants, for example: salesperson, clerk, accountant, policeman, teacher, bank teller, journalist, and so forth. On the other hand, once they arrive in the United States, careers in the service sectors, such as house cleaning and construction, were the highest among Brazilian immigrants in receiving communities (Marcus, 2011c). Shifts in careers before and after migration shed light on the significance of socioeconomic spaces and livelihoods of Brazilian immigrants. I interviewed several Brazilian immigrants who were formerly teachers in Brazil, and they expressed their utter contempt for the remuneration and treatment of the career of teacher in Brazil (e.g., salary, pension funds, retirement, etc.), which helps to explain why so many left Brazil. Hence, the occupation of "teacher" (in Brazil) was among the highest in the United States. Many of those same former teachers are now working in the United States as construction workers or house cleaners (Marcus, 2011c).

At an immigrant center in Framingham,[6] the most sought-after jobs for Brazilian men were: "painting" (22%); "construction" (13%); "any" (10%); "landscaping" (9%); and "house cleaning" and "driver" (9%); in contrast, "housecleaning" was the most sought-after occupation for women (71%), followed by "babysitter" (6%), "any," and "teacher" (both 4%) (Marcus, 2011c, p. 72). Overall, I found that service-sector occupations were the most sought-after jobs on all application forms. Despite the fact that professions in Brazil such as *empregada* ("house cleaner") and *pedreiro* ("construction worker") carry strong, negative social stigma in that country, most Brazilian immigrants in the United States will still work in those service-sector jobs.

However, in a recent trend between 2005 and 2009, Brazilian immigrants have been leaving Massachusetts and returning to Brazil (or to the U.S. South—mostly to the Carolinas, Atlanta, or New Orleans) for a number of reasons. First, the recent real-estate-sector slump has seriously impacted the demand for construction work (for example, painting and roofing). Second, the increasingly unfavorable political and social climate, particularly acute soon after the U.S. terrorist attacks of September 11, 2001, and increased anti-foreigner/anti-immigrant sentiment have contributed to the decision to return to Brazil. One Brazilian Pentecostal pastor I interviewed in Framingham explained that, in the month of August 2007 alone, his church lost 14 Brazilian family members who returned to Brazil, and, between 2006 and 2007, his church had lost a total of 80 of its members, who had returned to Brazil.

Take, for example, Gil, who is 50 years old and has just returned to Brazil to build his own house, with money he had saved from working as a construction laborer over 4 years in Marietta. He explained his views about the bleak careers prospect upon return to Brazil: "if the immigrant comes back without money, he has to return and be a bricklayer, and will be considered a failure if he does not buy at least three apartments, if not he has no social status." Furthermore, when Brazilian immigrants decode new gender domains within receiving settlements, notions of what were once considered socially acceptable careers for men and women are suddenly inverted.

In general, Brazilian migrants implicitly acknowledge the significance of careers, as well as social and cultural capital gained by virtue of their migrating to the United States, as a step onto upward social mobility (perhaps also a figurative and literal step into "modernity"). Nonetheless, as Brazilian women gain financial and social empowerment as migrants, this is seen by most Brazilians as a manifestation of them *becoming more macho*. In Brazil, the pursuit of happiness as an outcome of socioeconomic empowerment would be, for the most part, seen as if women were the *transgressors* of prescribed Brazilian gender domains. Here, spatial processes—the literal and figurative spaces occupied by men and women— and careers are intrinsic to understanding the frictions brought on by change after immigrants return to Brazil who have experienced sociocultural differences in the United States.

## Critical Perspectives

Neo-classical theory asserts that migrants make rational economic choices to maximize their benefits by migrating and, therefore, will search for the best place to reside. However, Castles and Miller explain how, "macro-, meso-and micro-structures are intertwined in the migratory process, and there are no clear dividing lines between them, and that no single cause is ever sufficient to explain why people decide to leave one country and settle in another" (2003, p. 28). Immigrant activities and behaviors and immigrant labor-market success are multilayered and

## Vignettes from the Field

Barbara, age 53 and a Brazilian immigrant, is a house-cleaning-business owner in Marietta and she conveys that Brazilian women tend to gain social capital and a sense of value: "In Brazil house cleaning is a woman's job. Clients here in Atlanta talk straight to me, not my husband, who is now my assistant." In a powerful statement, she continued to explain her newfound economic and social freedom: "Imagine I am making $8,000 a month housecleaning! I tell my husband: 'now you are *my* employee and the check is in *my* name!'" These quotes clearly highlight the significance of financial earnings, inverted power relations in terms of gender dynamics, social capital, and women's sense of "self-worth" in the United States. Other Brazilian immigrant house-cleaning-business owners in Marietta and Framingham also described similar earnings (in the range of US$4,000–8,000 monthly revenues) and a sense of newly acquired social and financial empowerment.

Gisele, for example, age 49 and originally from Goiás, works as a realtor in Marietta, selling mostly residential apartments in Goiás to Brazilian immigrants living in Georgia from her office (aptly illustrating the applicability of transnational processes). She explained that Brazilian immigrant women are more independent than their counterpart males in the United States, who may not have the physical resistance for continual heavy manual labor, especially, for example, if they are over 40 years old. Men in this particular predicament often resort to working as house cleaners and usually as helpers for their wives, who own the house-cleaning business, because they are unable to find another job. Gisele told me, "you pay a helper $20 per house, and with four houses cleaned in three hours for $30 an hour, you can make $8,000 monthly." To summarize in Gisele's words: "women are the owners!" She concluded:

> I am not returning to Brazil. I have the opportunities here to work for another fifty years. Here I have professional satisfaction. I make between $50,000 and $60,000 yearly, and want to build a condominium and flip houses, refurbish them to re-sell.

Socioeconomic changes that occur after migration are often behind family fragmentation and changes in career. For example, Murtinho, a returnee now in Governador Valadares, used to earn between US$2,000 and US$3,000 a week as a painter in Massachusetts; at times, he would work for 48 hours with just a couple of hours sleep, and then he would sleep every other day. He wants to return to the United States to make those earnings again. When he and his wife returned to Brazil, they brought back with them a container filled with U.S. goods, including: a stainless-steel fridge, microwave, oven, toaster, a dining-room set, crystal set, chairs, and various paintings. Mirtes, his wife, suffered from depression when she returned to Brazil, was still unemployed, and complained about her husband (she hinted at marital problems too). Murtinho refused to do any of the domestic jobs inside their house, ones he would have done when they lived in Massachusetts, and, in addition, to submit to working as a construction worker or painter in Brazil was far too demeaning for Murtinho; instead, he would hire someone else to do it. Mirtes explains: "re-adaptation back into Brazil is harder than adaptation in the United States!"

complex. For example, labor-market success intersects with ethnic business clusters, and, in the case of Brazilians, Pentecostal Church members benefit from market outreach (Levitt, 2007) and outside social and market forces, *as well as* human and social-capital forces. Research results here show that Brazilian immigrants are not all making rational, market-player, economic decisions when they decide to migrate; rather, they are making a decision based on multiple, interrelated reasons, some of which are "hidden" or unknown factors (see Marcus 2009a, 2009b).

Another problematic that I will briefly touch upon here is that, according to the U.S. Census Bureau, Brazilian immigrants in the United States are not "Hispanic" or "Latino," because they are Portuguese-speakers (Marcus 2011c). In this case, Brazilian-immigrant identity in that "ethnic-obsessed" country becomes more transient and more obscure to trace and determine, and, more importantly, confused with the stereotypical Spanish-speaking identity. Brazilians who return to their home country live now in a country that is largely known for its socioeconomic conscriptions made upon on social class rather than "racial" or ethnic ones. It is also important to keep in mind that, since the mid nineteenth century, Massachusetts has long been a destination for Portuguese-speaking populations, such as the Portuguese, Azorean, and Cape Verdean communities, particularly in Fall River, New Bedford, Ludlow, and Somerville (Adler, 1972). This fact may also help explain why so many Brazilians initially gravitated to this state, as the language factor may have also facilitated the migration process. (About one in every six residents of Massachusetts speaks Portuguese, with the largest ongoing percentage of foreign-born Portuguese in the country; "MAPS": Massachusetts Alliance of Portuguese Speakers.) In this case, language occupies an important dimension in the decision-making factor, and also within inter-migrant relationships, particularly in places such as Massachusetts (i.e. "Spanish-speaking" versus "Portuguese-speaking" immigrant populations).

For those who return to Brazil, readaptation is generally difficult. For example, Wando, age 32, a returnee in Governador Valadares states: "It was not easy to get used to life back in Brazil. The readaptation was difficult . . . but you fall into reality." Dynamics within careers, family life, economic livelihoods, as well as differences in gender cultural scripts in Brazil, contribute to a sense of *uprootedness* and of transmigrant *in-betweeness*. Some returnees go back to the United States again, for another 4- or 6-year period, mostly with the intention to save enough money to eventually return to Brazil and purchase a house, an apartment, a car, or start a new business—or, as they call it: *Fazer a América* ("to make in it in America") (see Almeida, 2003, which also happens to be the title of her book). Conspicuous consumption among returnees in Brazil is a given. If a returnee does not engage in it, he or she will be perceived by the community as having failed in their migratory project. This type of consumption has driven local real-estate prices up noticeably, and, in this case, many returnees who believe they are well

informed about investments will often make poor choices and lose much of the money they saved while working abroad. Most of the conspicuous consumption coming from returnees has largely benefitted local political and social elites. In fact, I have argued (Marcus, 2010) that this "culture of migration" has been encouraged by the political and social elites in most sending communities in Brazil, as, for the most part, they are the ones who really benefit from the dissemination and "seduction" of out-migration (i.e., they are the direct benefactors of an artificial increase in local real-estate values or an increase in car sales, because they are mostly the owners of real estate and car dealerships). The mayor's office of Governador Valadares, for example, has inserted a plaque in a major city plaza, officially treating emigrants as "heroes." It reads: "The tribute to emigrants brings justice to the dignified work of these heroes for their contribution to the development of Governador Valadares." The unlikely date of the plaque inauguration, July 4 (U.S. Independence day), coincides with the city's official *Dia do Emigrante* ("Day of the Emigrant"). Some may claim that the ascription of "hero" in this case only perpetuates the lure of emigrating abroad, as well as sustaining the dependency on financial remittances for local developments and investments sent from emigrants abroad and increasing dividends from returnees' conspicuous consumption at the local level. This type of financial dependency and the "culture of migration" overshadow the social and economic upheavals at the local and regional levels in Brazil, as well as gender imbalance in careers and personal happiness, and particularly overshadow the chronic shortage of careers in small cities throughout Minas Gerais and Goiás.

## Notes

1. "Receiving communities" refers to places of destination, and "sending communities" refers to places of origin. Traditionally, the term "migrant" is commonly used for *internal migration* in the literature of migration studies; however, I use it here loosely in the context of international migration. I use the term "emigrant" to refer to those Brazilians who are *leaving* Brazil, and the term "immigrant" refers to those Brazilians who have *arrived* or who are already residing in the United States. I use the term "returnee" to refer to those Brazilian immigrants who have *returned* from the United States and who now reside in Brazil. Whenever I use the term "returnee," it will always be in the context of Brazilian immigrants who have returned to Brazil from the United States.
2. *Reflexivity* is defined by Hoggart et al. as follows: "The practice of reflecting upon and questioning the assumptions and statements of one's own research is termed 'reflexivity'" (2002, p. 24).
3. *Mourejar* in colonial Portuguese meant, "to work hard, like a Moor" at the time of the *Reconquista*, and the idea of manual labor as an undignified pursuit was deeply embedded in Brazilian consciousness and transferred its meaning into the New World.
4. I asked respondents to mark their "happiness levels" on a *Likert Scale* ranging from 0 to 5 (0 = unhappy, and 5 = very happy).
5. Responses that contributed to migration push factors among women included: unhappiness, abusive spouse, divorce, adventure seeking, boredom, miscarriage or death in the family, escape from family, or escape from spouse. On the other hand, responses

for pull factors included: social capital, cultural capital, fascination with the United States, curiosity, middle-class panacea, education, dignified livelihood, and the influence of Hollywood movies. This is what I call here the "seduction of the United States."

6. I analyzed 1,200 application forms, filled out by Brazilian immigrants between 1999 and 2006 at a Catholic center run by Brazilians in Framingham (Marcus, 2011c). From these forms, I selected, at random, a total of 400 application forms from 1999 to 2004 (40 women and 40 men for each year between 1999 and 2004), and a total of 800 application forms filled out in 2005 and 2006 (200 women and 200 men for each year). The total number of forms since 1997 is estimated at 20,000.

## References

Adler, J. P. (1972). *Ethnic Minorities in Cambridge. The Portuguese.* Summary edited by Eva H. Gemmill. Volume 1 (Summary). Community Development Program, Department of Planning, City of Cambridge, MA.

Airriess, C. A. & I. M. Miyares (Eds.) (2007). *Contemporary Ethnic Geographies in America.* Lanham, MD: Rowman and Littlefield.

Almeida, Z. M. de (2003). *Fazer a América: Inserção e Mobilidade do Imigrante Brasileiro em uma Economia de Base Étnica.* Minas Gerais, Brazil: Unileste Edições.

Basch, L., N. G. Schiller, & C. S. Blanc (1995). From immigrant to transmigrant: Theorizing transnational migration. *Anthropological Quarterly,* 6(1): 48–63.

Berry, K. A. & M. L. Henderson (Eds.) (2002). *Geographical Identities of Ethnic America.* Reno and Las Vegas, NV: University of Nevada Press.

Beserra, B. (2003). *Brazilian Immigrants in the United States: Cultural Imperialism and Social Class.* New York: LFB Scholarly Publishing LLC.

Brettell, C. B. & J. F. Hollifield (Eds.) (1999). *Migration Theory: Talking Across Disciplines.* New York: Routledge.

Castles, S. & M. J. Miller (2003). *The Age of Migration.* 3rd Edition. New York: The Guilford Press.

Charmaz, K. (2006). *Constructing Grounded Theory: A Practical Guide through Qualitative Analysis.* New York: Sage.

Da Matta, R. (1985). *A Casa e a Rua.* Rio de Janeiro, Brazil: Editora Brasiliense.

Falconi, J. & J. Mazzoti (Eds.) (2007). *The Other Latinos.* Harvard University David Rockefeller Center for Latin American Studies. Cambridge, MA: Harvard University Press.

Frazier, J. W. & E. L. Tettey-Fio (Eds.) (2006). *Race, Ethnicity, and Place in a Changing America.* Harpur College, New York, State University of New York at Binghamton: Global Academic Publishing.

Fritz, I. C. (2010). *Brazilian Immigration and the Quest for Identity (The New Americans: Recent Immigration and American Society).* New York: LFB Scholarly Publishing LLC.

Goza, F. (1999). Brazilian immigration to Ontario. *International Migration,* 37(4): 765–799.

Hay, I. (Ed.) (2000). *Qualitative Research Methods in Human Geography.* Oxford: Oxford University Press.

Hoggart, K., L. Lees, & A. Davies (2002). *Researching Human Geography.* London: Arnold.

Kaplan, D. H. & W. Li (Eds.) (2006). *Landscapes of the Ethnic Economy.* Rowman and Littlefield.

Levitt, P. (2001). *The Transnational Villagers.* Los Angeles and Berkeley, CA: University of California Press.

Levitt, P. (2004). Transnational migrants: When "home" means more than one country, *Migration Information Source*. Retrieved from www.migrationinformation.org/feature/display.cfm?ID=261, July 9, 2012.

Levitt, P. (2007). *God Needs No Passport. Immigrants and the Changing American Religious Landscape*. New York: The New Press.

Loret de Mola, P. F., L. Ribeiro & M. S. Lizama (2009). Brazilian and Mexican women: Interacting with God in Florida. In P. J. Williams, T. J. Steigenga, & M. Vasquez (Eds.), *A Place to Be: Brazilian, Guatemalan, and Mexican Immigrants in South Florida's New Destinations*, pp. 137–167. Piscataway, NJ: Rutgers University Press.

Marcus, A. P. (2009a). Brazilian immigration to the United States and the geographical imagination. *Geographical Review*, 99(4): 481–498.

Marcus, A. P. (2009b). (Re)creating places and spaces in two countries: Brazilian transnational migration processes. *Journal of Cultural Geography*, (26)2: 173–198.

Marcus, A. P. (2010). Back to Goiás and Minas Gerais: Returnees, geographical imaginations and its discontents. *Revista Tempo e Argumento*, 2(2): 121–134.

Marcus, A. P. (2011a). *Towards Rethinking Brazil: A Thematic and Regional Approach*. New Jersey: Wiley Select Custom, John Wiley & Sons.

Marcus, A. P. (2011b). Rethinking Brazil's place within Latin Americanist geography. *Journal of Latin American Geography*, 10(1): 129–147.

Marcus, A. P. (2011c). Experiencing ethnic economies. *Journal of Immigrant and Refugee Studies*, 9: 1–24.

Margolis, M. L. (1994). *Little Brazil: An Ethnography of Brazilian Immigrants in New York City*. Princeton, NJ: Princeton University.

Margolis, M. L. (1995). Brazilians and the 1990 United States Census: Immigrants, ethnicity, and the undercount. *Human Organization*, 54: 52–59.

Margolis, M. L. (1998). *An Invisible Minority: Brazilians in New York City*. New York: Simon and Schuster.

Margolis, M. L. (2006). Bibliography of Brazilian Emigration. BRASA (Brazilian American Studies Association). Retrieved from www.brasa.org, May 2009.

Marrow, H. B. (2003). To be or not to be (Hispanic or Latino): Brazilian racial and ethnic identity in the United States. *Ethnicities*, (3): 427–464.

Martes, A. C. B. & W. Soares (2006). Remessas de recursos dos imigrantes. *Estudos Avançados*, 20(57): 41–54.

Moreira, I. (2007). Dolar a R$2 gera crise em cidade de MG. In *Valor, Especial*, August 28, p. A16.

Parker, R. G. (1991). *Bodies, Pleasures, and Passions. Sexual Culture in Contemporary Brazil*. Boston, MA: Beacon Press.

Portes, A. & R. G. Rumbaut (1990). *Immigrant America: A Portrait*. Los Angeles and Berkeley, CA: University of California Press.

Portes, A. & K. Hoffman (2003). Latin American class structures: Their composition and change during the neoliberal era. *Latin American Review*, 38(1): 41–82.

Sales, T. (1998). *Brasileiros Longe de Casa*. São Paulo, Brazil: Editôra Cortez.

Siqueira, S. (2007). *Migrantes e Empreendedorismo na Microrregião de Governador Valadares: Sonhos e Frustrações no retorno* [Migrants and Entrerpreneurship in the Microregion of Governador Valadares: Dreams and Frustrations upon Return]. Governador Valadares, Minas Gerais, Brazil: Editora Univale.

Sullivan, S. E. & Y. Baruch (2009). Advances in career theory and research: A critical review and agenda for future exploration. *Journal of Management*, 35(6): 1543–1571.

Tsuda, T. (1999). The permanence of "temporary" migration: The "structural embeddedness" of Japanese–Brazilian immigrant workers in Japan. *The Journal of Asian Studies*, 58(3): 687–722.

Williams, P. J., T. J. Steigenga, & M. Vasquez (Eds.) (2009). *A Place to Be: Brazilian, Guatemalan, and Mexican Immigrants in South Florida's New Destinations*. Piscataway, NJ: Rutgers University Press.

# 7

# MAKING SENSE OF GLOBAL CAREERISM IN ARGENTINA

## The Structure, Culture, and Context

*Hugo Gaggiotti, Bristol Business School,*
*Faculty of Business and Law, University*
*of the West of England, UK*

## Introduction

This chapter begins with a short overview of the situation surrounding global careers in Argentina in relation to the social and historical roots of its engagement–disengagement, adjustment–readjustment, and integration–reintegration in the global markets (Black, Mendenhall, & Oddou, 1991). Throughout the chapter, I rely upon cases of individuals who were and are pursuing global careers in that country. I refer to them as "local global careerists," predominantly, but not exclusively, Argentineans, and "foreign global careerists," predominantly non-Argentineans.

The analysis begins with a brief contextualization of Argentina between 1870 and 2008. It follows with a section on the structural, cultural, and contextual difficulties and opportunities for global careers in Argentina, illustrated by the stories of two managers (one Argentinean and one British) who considered themselves to be "global managers." The chapter concludes with a discussion about the relevance of Argentina as a case for the study of global careerism and the appropriateness of a critical perspective for studying this topic.

As Dickmann and Baruch (2011) noted, "there is no clear definition about what a global career is, and it is unclear what is meant by a 'global firm' or a 'global organization'" (p. 6). Most streams of study on internationalization and globalization have taken either a general organizational perspective or a more specific perspective of the relationship between the manager and the organization within a global context, in an attempt to find a suitable definition for studying what is usually thought to be a problematic issue.

This chapter does not include a review of the huge literature devoted to internationalization and globalization, which is based primarily on national cases from North America and Europe. Rather, I focus only on (1) alternative research approaches addressing the structural, cultural, and contextual difficulties of global careers in Argentina that better explain these issues, and (2) the current research on global careerism, inspired by new paradigms that address organizing and social contexts. Structural, cultural, and contextual analysis of the Argentine case suggests that, in order to understand global careerism in that country fully, it is necessary to integrate immigration and emigration and to move beyond international assignments or formal work displacement. This is a crucial aspect of global careers in the Argentine context, but not because immigration and emigration are exceptional, nor because the issues have been featured in academia, the media, and political discourses, but because both are part of the ethos of Argentina as a nation state. Since 1949, Argentina has celebrated Immigrant's Day on September 4 every year. Article 5 of its National Constitution stipulates that, "foreigners enjoy within the territory of the Nation all the civil rights of citizens," and Article 25 encourages European immigration, with "no restriction, limit or burden with any tax whatsoever, the entry into the Argentine territory of foreigners who arrive for the purpose of tilling the soil, improving industries, and introducing and teaching arts and sciences" (Constitution of Argentina, 1853).

## The Situation of Global Careers in Argentina

Argentina is an underresearched context within the global-careers literature, despite being a historical case from which to study workforce global movements. The country has not been included as a case in comparative studies on career management, although other Latin American countries with less movement in their global workforce have been the subject of research (e.g., Briscoe, Hall, & Mayrhofer, 2012). Studies of Argentinean global careerists such as expatriates are few, as I discuss in various parts of this chapter. Immigration and emigration have been studied in greater detail, but primarily from sociohistorical and demographic perspectives.

Some authors (e.g. Bimrose & McNair, 2011) have suggested that anyone who emigrates or immigrates should be considered a global careerist. As I propose in greater detail later in this chapter, the historical Argentinean context would be a suitable case to support this position. Soon after the country's independence, members of the political and economic elite began to consider the global workforce as merely comprising immigrants—self-initiated global careerists with the right to live and work in Argentina—rather than indigenous people. Argentina has, in fact, a massive foreign population: its core political, economic, and intellectual elites are composed primarily of second- and third-generation immigrants.

The scarce literature on global careerism in contemporary Argentina unrelated to migration studies focuses on whether the development of a professional career is with a local or foreign multinational corporation (MNC), without distinguishing the nationality or the ethnic background of the global careerist. Immigration and emigration issues in Argentina currently receive less academic attention than these issues receive in most other countries, and what interest there is is predominantly related to Latin American immigrants from border countries. These issues are addressed solely by local academics, and then only among sociologists and sociohistorians who see it as a way of reflecting about themselves, their identity, and the roots of their "Argentineness." Because management and business scholars have shown no interest in immigration, emigration, and global careers in Argentina, I have had to draw on a broader literature to inform my discussion.

Osland and Osland (2005) have suggested that the more one is exposed to international experiences, the greater the development of one's global mindset. I argue later in this chapter that the idiosyncrasies of the Argentine case suggest that this global mindset would be less likely to develop among local, Argentinean global careerists than among foreign global careerists (those who are, or were, in Argentina, but are not originally from that country). Local global careerists usually consider themselves to be globally minded because of a strong mobility tradition; multiple origins; and intergenerational, internal, and external nomadic working and living experiences in the context of repetitive cycles of the huge expansion and contraction of Argentina's economy. Repetitive mobility tends to be associated with past immigrant practices, therefore, rather than with career experiences that could improve a global mindset (Gaggiotti, 2010).

The focus of this analysis is governed by my professional background, the specific characteristics of Argentina, and the years of research conducted on global workers in Argentina (mainly on cases of immigrants, emigrants, and local and foreign expatriates). I have therefore focused on, but not limited my analysis (adapted from Dickmann & Baruch, 2011) to, what I considered to be the most noteworthy dimensions of global careerism in Argentina: narratives of self-initiation (Suutari & Brewster, 2000) and employment versus self-employment, the multiple strategies that global careerists must adopt in order to justify the frequency of their global career, and the rhetoric of immigration/emigration in relation to professional and personal success.

## Structural, Cultural, and Contextual Difficulties and Opportunities for Global Careers in Argentina

The relationships between foreign global careerists, the global job market, and Argentina were caught in a moment of conflict during the last decade of the nineteenth century (Gaggiotti, 1999). The new careerist presented a dilemma to the political and economic elites of Argentina, who, up until then, had considered themselves able to manage a permanent, scattered, and sparse population. These "new careerists," however, presented an economic and cultural dilemma. On the one hand, the careerists were required to populate the country and provide a massive workforce—key issues for creating what was called a "national project"—basically, the creation of a "nation." On the other hand, the political and economic elites feared the possibility that such profound social and economic changes could undermine their foundations of power and distinctiveness.

The Republic of Argentina was in a situation similar to that of other "empty" countries, such as New Zealand, Australia, and Canada. All four had large areas devoted to settlement and integration and a great need for the integration and globalization of their economies—particularly commodities—in a competitive and growing international market.

Between 1870 and 1914, more than 6 million immigrants arrived in Argentina, and half of them settled permanently. By 1914, nearly one third of Argentina's population (29.8%) had been born abroad; nearly 80% of that group had immigrated from Italy or Spain. Beyond accommodating the sheer numbers of this great wave, the concern among the elite was primarily about the distribution of the new population. A country with a consolidated political territory of such vast proportions should encourage homogeneous distribution, particularly in the context of its explosive economic growth. However, almost 90% of the immigrants settled in urban centers, primarily around the capital city, Buenos Aires. By the turn of the century, the urban population of Argentina rose significantly: from 42.8% in 1895 to 57.3% in 1914 (in comparison, the urban population of the United States was 46.3% in 1910, and that of Great Britain was 55% in 1850). Between 1895 and 1914, the population of the city of Buenos Aires grew from 660,000 to 1,570,000 inhabitants. The annual population growth rate of Buenos Aires between 1904 and 1909 (5.8%) was, with the exception of Hamburg (6.1%), the highest in the Western world (Gaggiotti, 1999).

As happened in other major cities around the world, the densification of Buenos Aires was accompanied by social conflict and degradation. Many works focusing on this point have shown urban densification to favor disease, crime, and prostitution, and to be the cause of inequalities, overcrowding, and squalor (e.g. Guy, 1991).

In parallel with the conflicts experienced by the first generation of worker immigrants, however, immigration succeeded, especially in Buenos Aires and its suburbs, which had little or no local population. Immigration transformed the colonial urban world with an immigrant imagery that associated prosperity with urban/industrial development. Contrary to most of the writings on the economic historiography of the River Plate region, particularly the North American perspective, the immigrants who arrived in Argentina reorganized the space of Buenos Aires and gradually reconfigured the city for a decisive change. This was especially true for the Italians, with their strong, urban, Mediterranean behavioral patterns. Between 1880 and 1930, the immigrants had transformed Buenos Aires from a colonial town into an urban center—a network organized around the agro-export economy first, and industrial production and services later (Gaggiotti, 1989).

From the late nineteenth century, Argentina registered four distinct fluctuations in the workforce:

1. the period between 1870 and 1913, under the agro-export model of development, when foreign MNCs settled, local MNCs were born and expanded, and the global workforce migrated in and out of Argentina;
2. from 1914 to 1929, under import substitution industrialization;
3. between 1990 and 1998, during a period of privatization of national companies; and
4. the 2004–2008 period of contemporary global careerism.

For each of these waves, it is possible to identify a different profile of a global careerist (Table 7.1).

In this part of the chapter, I focus on the contemporary context of global careerism in Argentina: the period between 2004 and 2008–2009. In 2008, there were only 19 Argentine MNCs, with approximately US$19 billion in foreign assets. External sales of all these companies were close to US$21 billion, and they employed 42,400 people abroad. By 2007, Argentina was in 15th place among the emerging countries, based on its stock of foreign direct investment (FDI) abroad, but in 25th place in terms of flows, just below what are now referred to as the BRIC countries (Brazil, Russia, India, and China).

The Argentine expatriates I interviewed revealed that they had few options to work for a global corporation in their home country, forcing them to move to Buenos Aires and accept any international assignment they could find. Status and compensation were their basic motivations, but also, at the symbolic level, they believed that Buenos Aires provided them with their only opportunity to become global. As Benencia (2003) and Cacopardo, Maguid, & Martínez (2006) have suggested, this belief seems to be shared by other foreign global careerists—primarily immigrants from other countries, particularly those from the border countries of Argentina, who constitute the majority of contemporary newcomers. Global careerists in Argentina, past and recent immigrants, middle-level technicians, and managers justify their global careers by following an extended imaginary pattern: the idea that Argentina has organized and continues to organize its relations with the global world on a social, economic, and imaginary system centered on Buenos Aires (Gaggiotti, 2006a), a discourse shared by the local and foreign corporate and professional world.

The pay gap between senior management and clerical employees in Argentina is large. The spending power of Argentinean expatriates abroad is relatively low compared with expatriates who come from other countries in the region. Their reasons for leaving Argentina and accepting an international assignment are related, not to compensation, but to prestige, performance, and loyalty to their companies (Hay Group, 2009).

TABLE 7.1 Profiles of global careers as they relate to Argentina

| Period | 1870–1913 | | 1914–1929 | | 1990–1998 | | 2004–2008 | |
|---|---|---|---|---|---|---|---|---|
| Dimension | Foreign global careerists | Local global careerists | Foreign global careerists | Local global careerists | Foreign global careerists | Local global careerists | Foreign global careerists | Local global careerists |
| Self-initiation | Migrant workers to Argentina; self-initiated; basic farming; basic urban services | No local global careerists | Self-initiated/ British companies; European immigrants | No local global careerists | Non-self-initiation; European intermediate managers; Spanish MNCs | Non-self-initiation; born local MNCs branches abroad | Argentinean MNCs and non-MNCs; self-initiated migrant workers to Argentina | Argentinean MNCs and non-MNCs; self- and non-self-initiated |
| Frequency/ previous or post experience | No previous experience; two destinations | N/A | One or two other experiences | N/A | One or two other experiences | No previous experiences | One or two other experiences | No previous experiences |
| Skill level | Skilled for rural work and basic urban services | N/A | No; some with management skills | N/A | Basic management skills among the foreigners | Highly skilled | Basic management skills among the foreigners | Highly skilled |
| Immigra- tion/ emigration | Based exclusively on immigration | N/A | Sometimes long-term assignment | N/A | None connected with immigration; short-term assignment | Expatriate profile; 3 or more years' experience | Sometimes connected with immigration (border countries) | Long-term expatriates; self-initiated entrepeneurs |

| | | | | | | | | |
|---|---|---|---|---|---|---|---|---|
| **Legality** | Acquired legal status to work and live in the country | N/A | Acquired legal status to work and live in the country | N/A | Acquired legal status to work and live in the country | Acquired legal status to work and live abroad | Acquired legal status to work and live in the country (not for illegal workers for border countries) | Acquired legal status to work and live abroad |
| **Formality** | Formally employed | N/A | Formally employed | N/A | Formally employed | Formally employed | Illegal workers not formally employed/MNC workers formally employed | Formally employed or self-employed |
| **Location** | Buenos Aires | N/A | Buenos Aires city and Buenos Aires urban network | N/A | Buenos Aires | Europe and USA | Buenos Aires | Europe and USA |
| **Sources:** | Devoto, 2004; Gaggiotti, 1989; Gallo, 1984 | | Beyhaut, 1966; Cortés Conde, 2010; Lattes, 1973 | | Novick, 2007; Pellegrino, 2003 | | Benencia, 2003; Cacopardo et al., 2006; Cortés Conde, 2003; Gaggiotti, 1999, 2004; Kosacoff, 1999 | |

Argentinean managers expressed other reasons for moving to Buenos Aires and for moving abroad from there. The narratives of expatriates confirmed the central role of Buenos Aires in the imagination of anybody who wanted to consider a global career. Stories about their own expatriation were filled with references to the necessity of having a "*porteña* experience" (*porteño* or *porteña* is a name given to a citizen of Buenos Aires) and the "Buenos Aires rite of passage" in one of the international organizations located in that city (almost all of them are located there). Engineers, in particular, consider that, other than foreign corporations, only one local MNC—Tubworld[1]—could offer the opportunity for a truly global career.

At the beginning of World War II, almost all Argentine industrial activity was concentrated in Buenos Aires and its surrounding region. By 1960, the activities of all international companies were located in the capital of the republic (Chudnovsky & López, 1997). Later, local Argentine MNCs began settling their headquarters and main activities primarily in the Puerto Madero district of the city, where all the foreign MNCs were located. Of the 19 Argentine MNCs, 16 currently maintain their industrial activities exclusively in the city of Buenos Aires and its environs (Figure 7.1). This is despite the fact that foreign MNCs in Argentina differ from local MNCs in their evolution, the former having moved in and out of the country during the booms and collapses of the domestic market, and completely ceasing to invest during economic downturns (Lo Tártaro, 2011).

During the growth phase of 2004–2008, new international companies and established affiliates of foreign companies that serve as hosts in Argentina entered the local market. Foreign MNCs were dominated by European companies, particularly from Spain and the Netherlands, followed by MNCs from North America and South America, mostly commonly the United States, Brazil, and Chile.

An estimated 1,800 of these foreign host affiliates operate today in Argentina, and MNCs are active in a wide array of sectors and industries. Approximately 330 of the 500 largest national and international non-financial companies in Argentina in 2007 were foreign affiliates, providing approximately 405,000 jobs and accounting for US$121 billion in sales. Foreign affiliates also produced 84% of gross value added and 90% of the total profits of the 500 companies that year. These figures are evidence of the strong presence and successful operation of MNCs in the Argentine economy, and most of them have a long-term time horizon (Nofal, Nahon, & Fernández, 2010). The presence of MNCs is particularly relevant in the oil and gas, telecommunications, automotive, and agribusiness sectors, as reflected in the list of the 20 main foreign affiliates. Further analysis of this list reveals a high degree of concentration. In 2008, assets held in Argentina by these foreign affiliates represented 53% of the total FDI stock in Argentina, and their combined sales accounted for approximately 37% of total sales made by the 330 largest non-financial foreign affiliates (Nofal et al., 2010). They retain few global careerists among their local and foreign employees.

**FIGURE 7.1** Location of Argentinean MNCs

*Source*: Primer ranking de empresas multinacionales argentinas, 2009, p. 21

Argentina is a noteworthy case for the study of global careers, because of its paradoxical and extreme circumstances. It was one of the world's 10 wealthiest nations between 1880 and 1930; it has represented a fully integrated economy in the global market of commodities for almost 200 years; and, using GDP as the measure, it is currently the third largest economy in Latin America and has ranked among the top 30 economies of the world for the past 10 years (IMF, 2010;

World Bank, 2010). Between 1989 and 2002, it was also one of the preferred destinations for foreign investment and MNC relocation and expansion, and this situation, along with unrestricted practices for opening the country to foreign investment and any type of relocation, forced more than 82,000 local businesses to close. Argentina went into default in 2002, with 21% unemployment and more than 11 million people below the poverty line (Cortés Conde, 2003). One year later, however, the economy experienced a U-turn: between the second quarter of 2003 and 2011, the country managed to accumulate a GDP growth of 23% (IMF, 2010).

Despite the significant presence of MNCs in Argentina, the country has not become an attractive destination for professionals pursuing global careers, perhaps because of the fluctuating economy, lack of market restrictions, and constant changes in government economic policy. In fact, Sunkyu, Gentry, and Yong (2001) have listed Argentina as one of the least attractive destinations for the Asiatic global workforce. Research has demonstrated the difficulty of attracting mid-career foreigners, who are seldom interested in moving to Latin America or working in Argentine industries (Catalano, 2004). By the same token, local Argentinean professionals demonstrate little interest in pursuing a global career (Gaggiotti, 2004).

## Contemporary Career Concepts and Their Relevance for Global Careers in Argentina

Researchers in the area of international assignments have tried to define global careerism based on managerial performance (Kohonen, 2008) and on the transformational scenarios of the managerial and the organizational experiences (Adler & Gundersen, 2008; Harzing & Christensen, 2004), and by identifying reasons for internationalization—the transferring of knowledge, management development, and organization development, for example (Edström & Galbraith, 1977; Harzing, 2001). Some authors have suggested that global careerists should be considered a subtype of expatriate (Greenhaus, Callanan, & Godshalk, 2009), and have introduced such terms as "transnational entrepreneurs" (Brewster & Scullion, 1997; Connelly, 2010), "flexpatriates" (Mayerhofer, Hartmann, Michelitsch-Riedl, & Kollinger, 2004), "virtual internationalists" (Suutari & Brewster, 2009), "career expatriates" (Collings, Scullion, & Morley, 2007), and "international itinerants" (Banai & Harry, 2004) as descriptors. The literature on careerism that has mentioned the Argentinean case does not consider other forms of working mobility in and out of Argentina as a global career, despite the fact that career researchers seem to have tried to understand, at different analytic levels, what happens when individuals travel through any type of professional and work experience (Briscoe et al., 2012).

Global careerism in Argentina is engaged in the approach of traditional scholars and practitioners of human resources and the definition of practical guidelines for understanding international careers, their problems, their solutions, and the

"right ways of managing"—particularly the management of expatriates (Black & Gregersen, 1999). Although recent research on expatriation has been produced on the role of individuals and their careers (Collings & Scullion, 2006; Collings et al., 2007; Lazarova & Tarique, 2005; Richardson & McKenna, 2000, 2006), it is recognized that organizations still have a dominant role in signifying, manipulating, and ultimately deciding upon international careers (Baruch, 2006). It is, therefore, suggested that an official discourse, dominated by mainstream business schools and human resource practitioners, finally imposes the meaning of what a global manager should be and what should be studied: the management of the people involved in the relationship between headquarters and hosts. This is how global careerism is understood in foreign global corporations settled in Argentina, where a global career is considered almost a central–periphery relationship, from headquarters outside Argentina to a host in Argentina. The social implication is that global careerists are silenced, marginalized, and "expatriatized" by a dominant managerial discourse.

In contrast, my research suggests that human resource practitioners of local Argentinean MNCs are starting to recognize that other practices of global careerism do not emphasize a transfer from headquarters to business units abroad. Rather, they are beginning to stress the more general development of a varied group with high potential, coming from various parts of the corporation (Kamoche, 1997). This practice is reflected in the expatriates' narratives, but also in human resource departments in charge of the management of the workforce in local MNCs. These departments are beginning to enter into the politics of balancing the number of expatriates by country, and are avoiding the monopolistic practices of always sending expatriates from headquarters in Buenos Aires.

Some authors have preferred to explore the concept of global careerism in terms of the repetitive change of destinations and the multiplicity of roles and positions (Mäkelä & Suutari, 2009; Suutari, 2003). Literature that has considered global careerism in terms of repetitive international work experiences suggests that previous experiences abroad are critical to the development of a sense of global career. I was able to unearth no studies on repetitive global careers in Argentina, however.

Other approaches focus more on cultural and identity perspectives (Kohonen, 2004, 2007, 2008), in an attempt to avoid what has been called an "ethnocentric" bias (Briscoe et al., 2012, p. 6; Mayrhofer & Brewster, 1996). These approaches could provide a more interesting way of studying the Argentine case. Global careerists in Argentina are embedded in their environment and affected by material and immaterial forces that require them to interact. Contextual approaches, with representational and symbolic descriptions of global careers, by their own actors and with alternative methodologies, such as the narrative and discourse approach, could better illuminate the Argentinean case.

From a narrative approach, the frequency of assignments, origin of the career, and performance must all be analyzed, along with the ways in which those involved

in international careers refer to themselves as "repetitive global managers," to their firms as "global corporations," and to the place they work and live as a "global market" (Näsholm, 2011). Interest in narrative was and is focused on global careerism from such angles as collective sensemaking (Boje, 2001; Czarniawska, 2004, 2008; Weick, 1995), organizational story paradoxes (Martin, Feldman, Hatch, & Sitkin, 1983), identity construction (Brown, Stacey, & Nandhakumar, 2008; Coupland, 2008; Czarniawska, 2002), power relations (Mumby, 1991; Smith & Keyton, 2001), and organizational change (Dunford & Jones, 2000). Each focus could be a productive way of visiting and revisiting Argentine global careerism.

## Stories of the Global Careers of Argentina

The meaning of a career evolves; it is not static, and it follows, not only the tendency of the firms to become global, but also the changing nature of what is understood as globalization by organizations (Dickmann & Baruch, 2011). But how is the meaning of a global career organizationally and culturally constructed in Argentina? The literature on careerism has recognized that there are no systematic approaches that address the way individuals in different cultures across the globe view such basic issues as what constitutes a career start (Harpaz, Honig, & Coetsier, 2002) or career success (Khapova, Briscoe, & Dickmann, 2012). In fact, for some years it was considered that the meaning of a career could be constructed only at an organizational level (Van Maanen & Schein, 1977). In the following section, I illustrate some of the ways of constructing this meaning with short vignettes of Argentinean global careerists.

Pedro, a local global careerist, said that, "a global manager must be able to change his plans" (implicitly denying the participation of women in global careerism).

The line manager's response to Pedro was a common experience among global careerists from local MNCs that I interviewed: they were obliged to change, usually by doing the same thing they had done previously, but in a different, more complex way. In this sense, anyone could be global in an Argentinean global corporation, depending on company demands. The story of Pedro suggests the contextual influences of Pipearg and Tubworld Buenos Aires headquarters, but also Buenos Aires as the concrete choice of a place to start a global career in Argentina (Gaggiotti, 2006b).

The general tone of this story suggests that, in the end, an Argentinean-born global manager of a global corporation is someone who must accept the dominance of Buenos Aires, or, as in Pedro's case, someone who aspired to return to or to work at Buenos Aires headquarters. This is a distinctive cultural imaginary world that contextualizes all global careerists in Argentina, independent of their category. Immigrants and formally employed careerists share the idea that the place to develop a career in Argentina must be Buenos Aires, and it is probably necessary to return there and finish one's career there as well.

## An Argentine-born Global Careerist: The Case of Pedro

Pedro is an Argentine engineer who graduated from Universidad de Santa Fe. After graduation, he started working for Tubworld through the Tubworld Junior Professional Program. From the beginning of his academic career, he knew that he wanted to work for this company—"a dream," he told me, of any Argentinean engineer. His "life project," as he defined it, was to move to Buenos Aires and from there to the world. After 4 years with Pipearg (one of the companies under the umbrella of Tubworld) in Buenos Aires, he was offered a move to Veracruz, Mexico—with a no clear role, but with a fixed 3-year-term contract. At the end of the third year, his manager asked him to remain one more year, to "consolidate the global culture produced with the Mexicans." At the end of the fourth year, he was informed that the company would prefer not to repatriate him, but wanted to relocate him to Venezuela for 3 years. He accepted, but, during his second year, he was asked to move to Bergamo, Italy. The next year, he asked to be repatriated to Argentina, but instead received an offer to move to Japan. This time, family issues made it more difficult for him to accept the offer. Pedro also thought that his career prospects would be better at the Tubworld headquarters in Buenos Aires, where he could contribute to the company's expansion with his strong international experience. Although he considers himself a global manager, he is under the administration of the Department of Expatriates of Tubworld. Pedro suggested to his line manager the possibility not accepting the Japan relocation. The answer was: "A global manager of Tubworld must be able to change plans and be relocated according to the organization's needs or must be ready to leave the organization."

According to the stories of some of the local global careerists, an itinerant careerist who doesn't come back to Buenos Aires is usually considered in a negative light—as someone in limbo. Other local global careerists that I interviewed considered the itinerant to be a "monster." These stories are permeated by the idea that the global career is part of an organizational discourse that the corporation is responsible for creating and imposing. It is the company, not the careerist, that must create the idea of the global career. As I learned in the context of Latin American managers working in central Asia, "work is important, as long as one can decide where to go" (Gaggiotti, 2006b, p. 20).

Pedro refers to himself as a global careerist, despite the fact that, technically and administratively, he is considered an expatriate. In contrast, John, a foreign global careerist, considered himself to be a "hybrid"—someone who is considered within the organization to be an expatriate, but who considers himself to be a "non-professional expatriate." He is an itinerant with a boundaryless global career, sometimes self-initiated, a member of a growing group within the larger group of global careerists (Banai & Harry, 2004), but not common in Argentina.

## A Foreign Global Careerist: The Case of John

John is a British engineer working in Argentina. His father was a diplomat, and he saw a global career as being strongly linked to diplomatic service. As he said: "With my background, being brought up in a diplomatic family, living in different parts of the world, I had a lot of experience with cross-cultural issues. That has never been a problem for me." During our interview, he said that he thought,

> when many people use the word "expatriate" there's a lot of associations lingering with that, but they don't believe that that is really the case with global careers today. I don't think expatriation should be what it was 30 years ago, even if there is a natural association with that old way in the minds of most people. Normally you used to go where you were sent. You had an additional allowance for living in that country, and there are also additional conditions.

For him,

> it's something common across the world . . . It used to be that you would always get something on top. But now it's not necessarily the case. Especially when you have a country like Argentina, where the cost of living is much lower.

For him, the lifestyle of the global manager is changing, because the world has become more international; many more people are living outside their home country; there's much greater movement of people generally; and the need to work in different parts of the world is better accepted as part of the global career. For him, "everything's become more mobile. In my case, I was invited to join the company here in Argentina directly from London, where I was living. So it's not a standard expatriation, as I was not working for the company before." He had spent a gap year working in Australia after he left university, and he then moved to Japan to work for 3 years. After returning to the UK, he was hired by Pipearg to do something similar to what he had done in Japan. As he said:

> Not really on expatriate conditions but . . . So, in a certain sense, I have a lot more experience of working as a . . . I don't know how you would describe it, but as person who's not necessarily a professional expatriate but who is used to working in other cultures, in other organizations outside their home country.

He thinks that more and more, in the future, this is the direction things will go: "competition for the global talent." But it was only in 2000 that he decided he needed a change. Talking about his status, he said it was "a little bit ambiguous. It's not entirely clear. I don't fit the standards. Officially, I'm an employee of Pipearg with some expatriate conditions. It was crucial to me to work here in Buenos Aires."

## Global Careerism in Argentina: A Question of Roots and Power

It is recognized in the research on non-formalized or non-organizational global careerism in Argentina (self-initiated immigration, particularly from other Latin American countries) that the expectations of immigrants seeking to further their professional careers in Argentina are not being met (Martínez Pizarro & Villa, 2005).

As discussed previously, the centralization of local and foreign global corporations is related to Buenos Aires' industrial heritage and its economic—but also its symbolic—importance. The names of relevant actors and events in Buenos Aires' industrial heritage are manifested in official documents, chronicles, and narratives of the global careerists I studied during my fieldwork (Gaggiotti, 2010). This symbolic power of Buenos Aires' industrial heritage is rhetorically justified in the Argentinean historical context, but also in the headquarters and hosts of the local MNCs, with images, logos, posters, and commemorative plaques (Gaggiotti, 2012). Workers from border countries are also attracted to Buenos Aires' symbolic economic power (Parrado & Cerrutti, 2003).

"Argentineness" seems to be another issue to consider; there are few examples of global careerists with non-Argentine backgrounds who have risen to top leadership positions in local MNCs. As the cases demonstrated, some managers from foreign branches of local MNCs worried about accepting assignments in Argentina, because there did not appear to be any higher-level leadership opportunities abroad to which they could eventually return (Catalano, 2004).

The influence of Buenos Aires' industrial heritage on the symbolic construction of local global corporations is established, spread, and reproduced through the narratives of Argentinean expatriates. The expatriates of local global corporations, and particularly those not born in Buenos Aires, acknowledged and accepted this influence as a fact and a necessary step in their career. But the origins of local corporations are usually constructed as ancient stories of the European founders, not rooted in Buenos Aires. Local global careerists who complete part of their career in Buenos Aires are aware of their historical, social, and symbolic superiority, particularly when they move abroad to lead a takeover or a merger. The expatriates tried to make sense of the contradictions of the global power by relating localness, foreignness, and resistance. Some of the testimonies suggested disappointment among Argentinean global careerists who noticed, from a new position abroad, that coming from Buenos Aires, which was supposed to have granted them superiority, was, in fact, irrelevant.

## Critical Perspectives on Global Careers: Suggestions from the Argentine Case

I am unaware of any systematic studies of global or international careerism in Argentina from any of the main streams that have dominated the field. In this

section, I outline why I believe that some of the streams of the field, classical and alternative, could or could not benefit the study of the Argentine case.

In the late 1990s, two main streams of research began to focus on the extent to which cultural differences were beneficial in global integration processes and global careerism. One stream could best be described as outlining the positive factors associated with cultural differences, and the other stream as delineating the complexity of global careerism.

The cultural-differences stream underlined the key role that these differences played in producing synergy in every issue involving global integration (Marks & Mirvis, 1998). This literature suggested the benefits of a global manager whose ultimate desire is to be able to manage an effective integration, to attain the ability to integrate innumerable and diverse global business processes and phenomena into a unified comprehension, and to create a situation of unity in diversity. Along these lines, Harung, Heaton, and Alexander (1999) have underlined the importance of the global careerist in synthesizing the intellect and feelings into a Gestalt. This literature has not focused on the social-constructive nature of the global career from the actors' perspective. A reflection—at least a theoretical reflection—of the life experiences of those global careerists in Argentina could represent a good start in placing the country on the agenda of this academic area.

The second stream of research focused on the complexity of global careerism (Larsson & Finkelstein, 1999), particularly expatriation. These issues were tackled from the most visible aspects that intervene in the process: selection, especially selection based on the expatriate's functional and technical competences (Mendenhall, Dunbar, & Oddou, 1987; Tung, 1981, 1988); training (Oddou, 1998; Tarique & Caligiuri, 2004); relocation (Feldman & Tompson, 1993; Harvey, 1997); compensation (Chen, Choi, & Chi, 2002; Harvey, 1993); contractual conditions and repatriation (Black, 1992; Cox, 2004; Naumann, 1992); or personality in relation to the adjustment (Johnson, Kristof-Brown, Van Vianen, De Pater, & Klein, 2003; Wang, 2002).

I would argue that these perspectives could provide a fascinating angle for studying local and foreign corporations in Argentina and their relationship with their global workforce, but it would be equally appealing to understand Argentinean political discourses of public management on immigration and emigration. In other countries, these approaches tend to resort to the necessity of creating systems that guarantee internationalization, legality, adaptability, and resistance to rejection, segregation, discrimination, motivation, commitment, loyalty, and performance; that counteract the possibilities of failure, illegal immigration, and an undesirable foreign working force; and that minimize the high costs of efficient management. It should be of interest to determine if the same thing happens in the Argentinean case.

As a way of finding a "missing link" between managerialist–functionalist research and critical international human resource management research, some authors have suggested alternative approaches, from, for example, the different

meanings of careers (Legge, 1995) or from Foucauldian perspectives (Townley, 1994). Other authors have commented on the international human resource management discourse of global careerism from the point of view of identity production and regulation (Fournier & Grey, 2000), and yet others have studied the production of cultural identities in organizational contexts, considering the broader institutional/ideological contexts (Alvesson & Willmott, 1996; Willmot, 1997).

Besides this multinationality, global careerism involves power relations (Edström & Galbraith, 1977), as we saw in the stories of Pedro and John. As Peltonen (1999) suggests, the discourse on, for example, expatriates, revolves mainly around the role of international assignment as an organizational control mechanism by an elite of global managers. The implicit assumption in this approach has been that every expatriate goes from a powerful center to a periphery of a corporation or a "global market" and acts as the modern equivalent of a colonial governor. Thus, the global careerist moves to another country in order to "have the power" and, therefore, "is in power," whereas local individuals remain within the confines of their own limited territory and do not belong to the category of "global careerism" (Peltonen, 2004). This situation provides another perspective from which to study the Argentinean case.

Global careerism, especially expatriation, has been presented, not only as a complex administrative issue, but also as a management problem (Dowling & Welch, 2004). In the case of Argentina, this also appears to be the situation for past and contemporary immigrants (Cortés Conde, 2003). One way in which human resource management departments, mainstream management literature, and political decision-makers propose to solve this issue is via procedures and regulations: laws that would regulate age, language, culture, religion, and skills, and company regulations that would precisely define skills, duration of assignment, culture, and marital status. It is assumed that the companies that manage to handle international assignments effectively and efficiently, with a concrete procedure, will be able, not only to reduce their costs, but also to obtain benefits and positive results in their global strategy and market expansion. Countries could also benefit by attracting the workforce they need and rejecting the workers they do not need. This developmental view and standardization (Kohonen, 2005) focuses, not on the global careerists themselves, but on organizational needs. I would argue that, although no systematic research was conducted in Argentina, a similar understanding could be part of the contemporary rationale of Argentinean government regulations on immigrants and foreign workers, particularly those coming from Latin American countries bordering Argentina (Benencia, 2003; Cacopardo et al., 2006; Gaggiotti, 1999, 2004; Kosacoff, 1999).

There has been an attempt to consider global careerism as a significant and "problematic" issue that must be solved, not only by managers and political elites and "between business and society and between management and employees" (Peltonen, 1998, p. 882), but also by the actors themselves. Some authors have,

therefore, adopted a narrative and discursive perspective on career (Cochran, 1990). They have focused on global careerism, suggesting that the importance of being "global" and having a "global mindset" is an extended discourse in corporations (Kohonen, 2005; Larsen, 2004) and in contemporary capitalism, and that it is nevertheless unclear if it originates with the careerists themselves or is imposed on them by organizational or ideological discourses (Gaggiotti, 2010).

Accordingly, research on expatriation has shifted toward a perception of expatriates as playing an active role in their career decision-making, as if they really are in control (Lazarova & Tarique, 2005). The literature on global careers and expatriation suggests that individuals are becoming more proactive toward, and engaged in, transactional relationships when deciding about and discussing their own careers (Baruch, 2004). Cases of self-initiated international assignments have described how the individuals appear to be self-motivated when deciding to move abroad (cf. Collings et al., 2007; Richardson & McKenna, 2006). This literature emphasizes self-initiation (Suutari & Brewster, 2000) as a way of defining global careerism, as if self-convincing narratives of being global careerists were prerequisites to successful competitiveness in the global job market (Gowler & Legge, 1989). It is not clear if those self-narratives tend to reproduce existing power structures, ideologies, and identities (Mumby, 1991; Smith & Keyton, 2001). Using an analysis of case studies showing institutionalized and individual narratives of global workers, researchers who use the narrative approach to global careerism try to deconstruct the self-initiation argument by examining how, why, and with what effects different macro- and micro-level narratives are translated or drawn upon in specific contexts (O'Connor, 2002). It was suggested, for example, that self-convincing narratives of global careerism could be heavily promoted by organizational discourses, as companies generate a greater benefit in employing self-initiated global careerists than they do in employing expatriates; global careerists are cheaper, as they are employed under local conditions and on a temporary basis, with no home/host adjustment, extra repatriation costs, or risk of failure (Banai & Harry, 2004; McKenna & Richardson, 2007). In my research in local Argentinean MNCs, expatriates and itinerants did not assume a significant role in deciding their assignments, and they had no narrative on the issue.

A distinctive element of a narrative approach to global careerism is the way in which the notion of global career itself is constructed. This approach could serve to illuminate the Argentinean case. Global careerism is usually considered as a practical, professional, and/or living experience. The assumption is that global careerists and organizations are exclusively involved on a professional or an organizational praxis. Global careerism is always narrated and rhetorically justified, however, and present in all traditional discursive manifestations, such as small stories of changing jobs (Nicholson & West, 1989); grand narratives that give support to "the global workforce" (Boltanski & Chiapello, 2005); and accounts and texts of human resource management practitioners, public administrators, and experts (Alvesson & Kärreman, 2000); or "itinerant experts" (Amit, 2002; Barley & Kunda, 2004).

The narrative approach is not the only stance from which the managerial perspective on global careerism has been revisited. The concept of globalization itself has been reconsidered as an economic–financial type of rationalization to be related to the constantly changing ideals of neoliberalism (Harvey, 2007), similar to other rationalizations and the production of capitalist subjectivity (Foucault, 1988 [1977–1984]). Thus, factors such as "growth," "economies of scale," "globalization," "efficiency," and "shareholder value" (Vaara, 2000; Vaara, Tienari, & Laurila, 2006), as well as the concept of global careerism, have been revisited.

Some works tend to demonstrate that the complexity that forms the basis of international human resource management studies does not necessarily exist (Peltonen, 1998). Other literature has suggested that the discourse of the complexity is an epiphenomenon of the traditional culturalistic approaches. Some scholars suggest that literature usually fails to explain most of the elements of management internationalization, as is the case with what is usually considered "failure" in the expatriation of managers (Evans, Pucik, & Barsoux, 2002; Harzing & Christensen, 2004) or with companies that practice internationalization without resorting to expatriation (Bonache & Cerviño, 1997) or are based on self-initiated expatriates (Howe-Walsh & Schyns, 2010; Jokinen, Brewster, & Suutari, 2008). The authors of these works did not aspire to start a new methodological or theoretical trend, but merely aimed to point out a certain exhaustion in the classical approaches—that they had lost their power to convince.

The proponents of one such trend in global careerism have argued that the limitations of international human resource management and the literature that supports it reside in the fact that those approaches reproduce explanations and justifications that are part of a neocolonial discourse. Postcolonialists remark that neocolonial discourse, hidden under the rhetoric of globalization and multi-nationality, simplifies the complexity of the local and imposes uniformity on the symbolic relation of the expatriate with the organization (Peltonen, 1997, 1999)—even on the expatriates, particularly in their identity representations (Leonard, 2010). Basically, what has been noted is its lack of neutrality, its simplicity, and its unidimensional perspective—a perspective that was suggested to have been inherited from the colonial organization of the world. The few local Argentinean MNCs are now operating in different parts of the world, and their global workforce is recreating their identity from a dominant stand, imposing their power onto others, and following postcolonial imagery experienced as a colony rather than a metropoly. Similar cases of "reverse-colonialism" have been studied with Brazilian expatriates in Portugal (Morilha Muritiba, Nunes Muritiba, Galvão de Albuquerque, Bertoia, & Lawrence French, 2010) and Finns in Sweden (Peltonen, 1999). A development of the Argentine case could benefit from this approach, particularly in countries such as Spain, the USA, and the UK that had a "central–peripheral" relationship with Argentina at one time.

Scholars who adhere to these perspectives have trouble explaining the Argentinean case, because of their characterization of the global careerist as a subject with an identity split between country of origin and country of work, a subject that necessarily differs from others and is patronized by others; or a subject that imposes power on others, like a globalizing, imperial agent (Peltonen, 1999). The global careerist is like a tourist who travels the world in search of encounters with aliens, sometimes considered a visitor with good intentions, sometimes an invader. There is an idea that there must be differences between global careerists and others. In this respect, these perspectives still contain the notion of a necessary "cultural adjustment," a popular concept in the global-careers literature (see, for example, Selmer, 1998, 1999, 2002). My research suggests that, in the case of global careerists in Argentina, the difference between local and foreign does not always exist, as it does in other countries. The fact that almost all the presidents of Argentina in the past 100 years belonged to a second or third generation of immigrants, as did the economic elite of managers, founders, and owners of MNCs, could explain why this clear separation is not always similar to that of other countries. It suggests, in fact, that a more hybrid approach to global careerism is probably needed in order to study the Argentine case.

## Conclusions, Limitations, and Suggestions for Future Research

Over the past two decades, the literature on global careerism has been broadening to include European companies (Brewster & Harris, 1999; Peltonen, 1998; Sparrow, Brewster, & Harris, 2004), but Latin American countries remain underrepresented. Argentina is a case in point. This perspective has engendered a harsh critique of management scholars, some of them inspired by a postcolonial approach and North European cases (Peltonen, 1999). Most common changes and updating in the global-careerism literature have focused on the inclusion of non-American cases (mainly European and Asian countries) and on the addition of new variables of analysis (formality, legality, self initiating, repetition). But the case of Argentinean local corporations illuminates a different perspective on global careers: not the traditional Western–non-Western flux of managers and not a reverse colonial relationship. In the Argentinean permanent emigrant–immigrant context, the central–peripheral relationship is ambivalent. It depends upon power relations; the historical centralization of Buenos Aires; the context of mergers and acquisitions; and the imagery rhetorically justified to invent foundations, origins, and similarities, not necessarily decided because of a fixed "organizational location" (Bhabha, 1994).

The symbolic power of localization, based on the creation and recreation of an industrial heritage and the material and immaterial construction of the centralization of Buenos Aires, is an important facet of this context, if one is to consider global careerism in Argentina. Nevertheless, global careerists in that

country have included immigrants from the border countries who are studied in the literature on social movements, and expatriates of local and foreign MNCs are not discussed from these or other perspectives.

Narratives of the globalization of the world are evidenced in the stories of global careerists involved in the expansion of local Argentinean global corporations. A narrative of the globalization of the world helps the global careerists in Argentina to create a story that explains the double imposition of globalization on themselves and on others, giving sense to their own experiences.

The construction of the meaning of globalization in local Argentinean global corporations operates, not only in a prospective dimension that justifies the future of the career, but also in a retrospective dimension that helps to create a uniform and sometimes mythical past of a hierarchized place and country to emigrate to, in order to start or continue a professional career or a new life. Applying a narrative analysis to the rhetorical uses of the industrial heritage of Buenos Aires in global careerist narratives is not a critique of other ways of explaining global careerism in Argentina, but rather an explanation of the contextual situation of this social issue that affects emigrants, immigrants, expatriates, and any other global careerists.

The global careerists in Argentina reproduce the meaning of globalization of the world, because they can imagine their global career in context—not merely as the reaction of an administrative or political decision. Like other approaches to the narratives of global careerism (Fougere, 2005), the imagery of a global career emerges through their stories with no necessary connection to their positive or negative outcomes, repetitive destinations, cultural adjustment, or legal or illegal status, but with ways of dealing with power relations, status aspirations, their preferred location to live and work with their families, a concrete place— the city of Buenos Aires—and as a way of making sense of the decisions they made to move in or out of Argentina, sometimes just to start a new career abroad (Louis, 1980).

As the global is socially constructed, and its meaning is continuously changing, a longitudinal analysis that compares different stages of the narratives of global careers in Argentina could provide a better understanding of the way in which the global career is defined and redefined by its own actors, particularly for those not considered global careerists—people such as illegal immigrants or informally employed workers.

## Note

1. Pseudonyms have been used to protect the anonymity of the companies.

## References

Adler, J. & Gundersen, A. (2008). *International Dimensions of Organizational Behavior* (5th ed.). Mason, OH: Thomson South-Western.

Alvesson, M. & Kärreman, D. (2000). Varieties of discourse: On the study of organizations through discourse analysis. *Human Relations*, 53(9), 1125–1149.

Alvesson, M. & Willmott, H. (1996). *Making Sense of Management: A Critical Introduction.* London, Thousand Oaks, CA: Sage Publications.

Amit, V. (2002). "The moving expert": A study of mobile professionals in the Cayman Islands and North America. In N. Sorenson & K. Olwig, *Work and Migration: Live and Livelihoods in a Globalizing World.* London: Routledge.

Banai, M. & Harry, W. (2004). Boundaryless global careers—The international itinerants. *International Studies of Management and Organization,* 34, 96–120.

Barley, S. & Kunda, G. (2004). *Gurus, Hired Guns, and Warm Bodies: Itinerant Experts in a Knowledge Economy.* Princeton, NJ: Princeton University Press.

Baruch, Y. (2004). Transforming careers: From linear to multidirectional career paths—Organizational and individual perspectives. *Career Development International,* 9, 58–73.

Baruch, Y. (2006). Career development in organizations and beyond: Balancing traditional and contemporary viewpoints. *Human Resource Management Review,* 16, 125–138.

Benencia, R. (2003). La inmigración limítrofe. In F. Devoto, *Historia de la inmigración en la Argentina.* Buenos Aires: Sudamericana.

Beyhaut, G. (1966). Los inmigrantes en el sistema ocupacional argentino. In T. di Tella, G. Germani, & J. Graciarena, *Argentina, sociedad de masas.* Buenos Aires: Eudeba.

Bhabha, H. (1994). *The Location of Culture.* London, New York: Routledge.

Bimrose, J. & McNair, S. (2011). Career support for migrants: Transformation or adaptation? *Journal of Vocational Behavior,* 78(3), 321–392.

Black, J. (1992). Coming home: The relationship of expatriate expectations with repatriation adjustment and job performance. *Human Relations,* 45(2), 177–192.

Black, J. & Gregersen, H. (1999). The right way to manage expats. *Harvard Business Review,* 77(2), 52–63.

Black, J., Mendenhall, M., & Oddou, G. (1991). Toward a comprehensive model of international adjustment: An integration of multiple theoretical perspectives. *Academy of Management Review,* 16, 291–317.

Boje, D. (2001). *Narrative Methods for Organizational and Communication Research.* London: Sage Publications.

Boltanski, L. & Chiapello, E. (2005). *The New Spirit of Capitalism* (Gregory Elliott Trans.). London: Verso.

Bonache, J. & Cerviño, J. (1997). Global integration without expatriates. *Human Resource Management Journal,* 7, 89–100.

Brewster, C. & Harris, H. (1999). *International HRM: Contemporary Issues in Europe.* New York: Routledge.

Brewster, C. & Scullion, H. (1997). A review and an agenda for expatriate HRM. *Human Resource Management Journal,* 7(3), 32–41.

Briscoe, J., Hall, D. & Mayrhofer, W. (2012). *Careers around the World.* London: Routledge.

Brown, A., Stacey, P., & Nandhakumar, J. (2008). Making sense of sensemaking narratives. *Human Relations,* 61(8), 1035–1062.

Cacopardo, M., Maguid, A., & Martínez, R. (2006). La nueva emigración de latinoamericanos a España: el caso de los argentinos desde una perspectiva comparada. Proceedings from *II Congreso de la Asociación Latinoamericana de Población.* Guadalajara, Mexico.

Catalano, Ch. (2004). *Tenaris: Creating a Global Leader From an Emerging Market.* Case IB-60. Stanford, CA: Stanford Graduate School of Business.

Chen, C., Choi, J., & Chi, S. (2002). Making justice sense of local-expatriate compensation disparity: Mitigation by local referents, ideological explanations, and interpersonal

sensitivity in China–foreign joint ventures. *The Academy of Management Journal*, 45(4), 807–817.

Chudnovsky, D. & López, A. (1997). *Las estrategias de las empresas transnacionales en Argentina, Brasil y Uruguay en los años noventa.* Buenos Aires: CENIT.

Cochran, L. (1990). Narrative as a paradigm for career research. In R. Young & W. Borgen (Eds.), *Methodological Approaches to the Study of Career.* New York: Praeger.

Collings, D. & Scullion, H. (2006). Global staffing. In G. Stahl, K. Gunter, & I. Björkman (Eds.), *Handbook of Research on International Human Resource Management* (141–157). Cheltenham: Edward Elgar.

Collings, D., Scullion, H., & Morley, M. (2007). Changing patterns of global staffing in the multinational enterprise: Challenges to the conventional expatriate assignment and emerging alternatives. *Journal of World Business*, 42, 198–213.

Connelly, B. (2010). Transnational entrepreneurs, worldchanging entrepreneurs, and ambassadors: a typology of the new breed of expatriates. *International Entrepreneurship and Management Journal*, 6(1), 39–53.

Constitution of Argentina (1853). *Constitution of the Argentine Nation.* Retrieved from www.senado.gov.ar/web/interes/constitucion/english.php, 2 February 2012.

Cortés Conde, R. (2003). La crisis Argentina de 2001–2002. *Latin American Journal of Economics*, 40(121), 762–767.

Cortés Conde, R. (2010). The monetary and banking reforms during the 1930 depression in Argentina. Working Paper 98 of the Department of Economics of Universidad de San Andres, Buenos Aires.

Coupland, C. (2008). Identities and interviews. In A. Pullen, N. Beech, & D. Sims (Eds.), *Exploring Identity: Concepts and Methods.* Basingstoke: Palgrave-Macmillan.

Cox, J. (2004). The role of communication, technology, and cultural identity in repatriation adjustment. *International Journal of Intercultural Relations*, 28, 201–219.

Czarniawska, B. (2002). Identity lost or identity found? Celebration and lamentation over the postmodern view of identity in social science and fiction. In M. Schultz, M. Hatch, & M. Larsen (Eds.), *The Expressive Organization. Linking Identity, Reputation and the Corporate Brand* (271–283). Oxford: Oxford University Press.

Czarniawska, B. (2004). *Narratives in Social Science Research.* London: Sage.

Czarniawska, B. (2008). Alterity/identity interplay in image construction. In D. Barry & H. Hansen (Eds.), *The Sage Handbook of New Approaches in Management and Organization* (49–62). London: Sage.

Devoto, F. (2004). *Historia de la inmigracion en la Argentina.* Buenos Aires: Sudamericana.

Dickmann, M. & Baruch, Y. (2011). *Global Careers.* Oxford: Routledge.

Dowling, P. & Welch, D. (2004). *International Human Resource Management: Managing People in a Multinational Context* (4th ed.). Mason, OH: Thomson/South-Western.

Dunford, R. & Jones, D. (2000). Narrative in strategic change. *Human Relations*, 53(9), 1207–1226.

Edström, A. & Galbraith, J. (1977). Transfer of managers as a coordination and control strategy in multinational organizations. *Administrative Science Quarterly*, 22, 249–263.

Evans, P., Pucik, V., & Barsoux, J. (2002). *The Global Challenge: Frameworks for International Human Resource Management.* Boston, MA: McGraw-Hill.

Feldman, D. & Tompson, H. (1993). Expatriation, repatriation, and domestic geographical relocation: An empirical investigation of adjustment to new job assignments. *Journal of International Business Studies*, 24(3), 507–529.

Foucault, M. (1988 [1977–1984]). *Politics, Philosophy, Culture: Interviews and Other Writings.* L. Kritzman (Ed.). New York: Routledge.

Fougere, M. (2005). *Sensemaking in the Third Space. Essays on French–Finnish Bicultural Experiences in Organizations and Their Narratives.* Helsinki: Swedish School of Economics and Business Administration.

Fournier, V. & Grey, C. (2000). At the critical moment: Conditions and prospects for critical management studies. *Human Relations,* 53(1), 7–32.

Gaggiotti, H. (1989). *Características socioculturales y socioeconómicas de la migración externa e interna en el Territorio Nacional de La Pampa. El caso de General Acha, 1889–1899.* Santa Rosa: UNLPam. Facultad de Ciencias Humanas.

Gaggiotti, H. (1999). De la identidad urbana a la identidad corporativa: las formas de la pertenencia en el grupo Techint. *Scripta Nova,* 45(13). Retrieved from www.ub.edu/geocrit/sn-45-13.htm, 4 March 2012.

Gaggiotti, H. (2004). ¿Quienes quieren ser globales? Deslocalización, sentido del trabajo y resistencia a la globalización en los directivos de empresas mutinacionales españolas y latinoamericanas. *Scripta Nova,* 8, 170(5). Retrieved from www.ub.edu/geocrit/sn/sn-170-5.htm, 4 March 2012.

Gaggiotti, H. (2006a). *Un lugar en su sitio: narrativas y organizacion urbana en el espacio latinoamericano.* Sevilla: Doble JJ/Comunicación Social.

Gaggiotti, H. (2006b). Going from Spain and Latin America to Central Asia: Decision-making of expatriation and meaning of work. *Central Asia Business Journal,* 1(1), 8–22.

Gaggiotti, H. (2010). Official chronicles of corporate globalization and unofficial stories of international mobility: Resisting patronage of meanings? *Journal of Organizational Change Management,* 23(2), 157–165.

Gaggiotti, H. (2012, forthcoming). The rhetoric of synergy in a global corporation: Visual and oral narratives of mimesis and similarity. *Journal of Organizational Change Management.*

Gallo, E. (1984). *La Pampa gringa. La colonización agrícola en Santa Fe (1870–1895).* Buenos Aires: Sudamericana.

Gowler, D. & Legge, K. (1989). Rhetoric in bureaucratic careers: Managing the meaning of the management success. In M. Arthur, D. Hall, & B. Lawrence (Eds.), *Handbook of Career Theory.* Cambridge: Cambridge University Press.

Greenhaus, J., Callanan, G., & Godshalk, V. (2009). *Career Management.* London: Sage.

Guy, D. (1991). *Sex and Danger in Buenos Aires: Prostitution, Family and Nation in Argentina.* Lincoln, NE: University of Nebraska Press.

Harpaz, I., Honig, B., & Coetsier, P. (2002). A cross-cultural longitudinal analysis of the meaning of work and the socialization process of career starters. *Journal of World Business,* 37(4), 230–244.

Harung, H., Heaton, D., & Alexander, C. (1999). Evolution of organizations in the new millennium. *Leadership and Organization Development Journal,* 20(4), 198–207.

Harvey, D. (2007). *A Brief History of Neoliberalism.* Oxford: Oxford University Press.

Harvey, M. (1993). Empirical evidence of recurring international compensation problems. *Journal of International Business Studies,* 24(4), 785–799.

Harvey, M. (1997). Dual-career expatriates: Expectations, adjustment and satisfaction with international relocation. *Journal of International Business Studies,* 28(3), 627–658.

Harzing, A. (2001). An analysis of the functions of international managers in MNCs. *Employee Relations,* 23(6), 581–598.

Harzing, A. & Christensen, C. (2004). Expatriate failure: Time to abandon the concept? *Career Development International,* 9(7), 616–626.

Hay Group (2009). *The Global Management Pay Report*. Retrieved from www.haygroup. com/se/press/details.aspx?id=24594, 15 January 2012.

Howe-Walsh, L. & Schyns, B. (2010). Self-initiated expatriation: Implications for HRM. *The International Journal of Human Resource Management*, 21(2), 260–273.

IMF (2010). International Monetary Fund. 2010 Gross Domestic Product. Retrieved from www.imf.org/external/pubs/ft/weo/2010/02/weodata/index.aspx (accessed December 12, 2011).

Johnson, E., Kristof-Brown, A., Van Vianen, A., De Pater, I., & Klein, M. (2003). Expatriate social ties: Personality antecedents and consequences for adjustment. *International Journal of Selection and Assessment*, 11(4), 277–288.

Jokinen, T., Brewster, C., & Suutari, V. (2008). Career capital during international work experiences: Contrasting self-initiated expatriate experiences and assigned expatriation. *The International Journal of Human Resource Management*, 19(6), 979–998.

Kamoche, N. (1997). Knowledge creation and learning in international HRM. *The International Journal of Human Resource Management*, 8(3), 213–225.

Khapova, S., Briscoe, J., & Dickmann, M. (2012). Careers in cross-cultural perspective. In J. Briscoe, D. Hall, & W. Mayrhofer (2012). *Careers Around the World*. London: Routledge.

Kohonen, E. (2004). Learning through narratives about the impact of international assignments on identity. *International Studies of Management and Organizations*, 34(3), 27–45.

Kohonen, E. (2005). Developing global leaders through international assignments: An identity construction perspective. *Personnel Review*, 34(1), 22–36.

Kohonen, E. (2007). *Essays on the Consequences of International Assignments on Expatriates' Identity and Career Aspirations*. Ph.D. dissertation. Acta Wasensia 170, Vaasa, Finland: Vaasa University.

Kohonen, E. (2008). The impact of international assignments on expatriates' identity and career aspirations: Reflections upon re-entry. *Scandinavian Journal of Management*, 24, 320–329.

Kosacoff, B. (1999). *Las multinacionales argentinas: una nueva ola en los noventa*. Comisión Económica para América Latina y el Caribe. Documento de trabajo 83. Buenos Aires: United Nations.

Larsen, H. (2004). Global career as dual dependency between the organization and the individual. *Journal of Management Development*, 23(9), 860–869.

Larsson, R. & Finkelstein, S. (1999). Integrating strategic, organizational, and human resource perspectives on mergers and acquisitions: A case survey of synergy realization. *Organization Science*, 10(1), 1–26.

Lattes, A. (1973). Las migraciones en la Argentina entre mediados del siglo XIX y 1960. *Desarrollo Económico*, 12(48), 849–865.

Lazarova, M. & Tarique, I. (2005). Knowledge transfer upon repatriation. *Journal of World Business*, 40, 361–373.

Legge, K. (1995). *Human Resource Management: Rhetorics and Realities*. London: Macmillan.

Leonard, P. (2010). *Expatriate Identities in Postcolonial Organizations: Working Whiteness*. Surrey: Ashgate.

Lo Tártaro, D. (2011). *Distribución geográfica de las empresas en Argentina*. Buenos Aires: Instituto argentino para el desarrollo de las economías regionales (IADER).

Louis, M. (1980). Surprise and sense-making: What newcomers experience in entering unfamiliar organizational settings. *Administrative Science Quarterly*, 25(2), 226–251.

McKenna, S. & Richardson, J. (2007). The increasing complexity of the internationally mobile professional: Issues for research and practice. *Cross Cultural Management*, 14, 307–329.

Mäkelä, K. & Suutari, V. (2009). Global careers: A social capital paradox. *The International Journal of Human Resource Management*, 20(5), 992–1008.

Marks, M. & Mirvis, P. (1998). *Joining Forces*. San Francisco, CA: Jossey-Bass.

Martin, J., Feldman, M., Hatch, M., & Sitkin, S. (1983). The uniqueness paradox in organizational stories. *Administrative Science Quarterly*, 28, 438–453.

Martínez Pizarro, J. & Villa, M. (2005). *International Migration in Latin America and the Caribbean: A Summary View of Trends and Patterns*. United Nations Expert Group Meeting on International Migration and Development.

Mayerhofer, H., Hartmann, L., Michelitsch-Riedl, G., & Kollinger, I. (2004). Flexpatriate assignments: A neglected issue in global staffing. *The International Journal of Human Resource Management*, 15(8), 1371–1389.

Mayrhofer, W. & Brewster, C. (1996). In praise of ethnocentricity: Expatriate policies in European multinationals. *The International Executive*, 38(6), 749–778.

Mendenhall, M., Dunbar, E., & Oddou, G. (1987). Expatriate selection, training and career-pathing: A review and critique. *Human Resources Management*, 26(3), 331–345.

Morilha Muritiba, P., Nunes Muritiba, S., Galvão de Albuquerque, L., Bertoia, N., & Lawrence French, J. (2010). Estratégia internacional, distância cultural e políticas de gestão nas companhias internacionais brasileiras. *Revista de Globalización, Competitividad y Gobernabilidad*, 4(3), 24–37. Georgetown University/Universia. Retrieved from http://gcg.universia.net/pdfs_revistas/revista_23_1289812301548.pdf, 5 March 2012.

Mumby, D. (1991). Power and discourse in organization studies: Absence and the dialectic of control. *Discourse & Society*, 2(3), 313–332.

Näsholm, M. (2011). *Global Careerists' Identity Construction. A Narrative Study of Repeat Expatriates and International Itinerants*. Umeå: Umeå School of Business.

Naumann, E. (1992). A conceptual model of expatriate turnover. *Journal of International Business Studies*, 23(3), 499–531.

Nicholson, N. & West, M. (1989). Transitions, work histories, and careers. In M. Arthur, D. Hall, & B. Lawrence (Eds.), *Handbook of Career Theory*. Cambridge: Cambridge University Press.

Nofal, B., Nahon, C., & Fernández, C. (2010). Inward FDI in Argentina and its policy context. *Columbia FDI Profiles*. Vale Columbia Center on Sustainable International Investment.

Novick, S. (2007). Políticas y actores sociales ante la emigración de argentinos. In S. Novick (Ed.), *Sur-Norte. Estudios sobre la emigración reciente de argentinos*. Buenos Aires: Catálogos/Instituto de Investigaciones Gino Germani, UBA.

O'Connor, E. (2002). Storied business: Typology, intertextuality, and traffic in entre-preneurial narrative. *Journal of Business Communication*, 39(1), 36–54.

Oddou, G. (1998). *Managing Internationally: A Personal Journey*. Fort Worth, TX: Dryden Press.

Osland, J. & Osland, A. (2005). Expatriate paradoxes and cultural involvement. *International Studies of Management and Organizations*, (35), 93–116.

Parrado, E. & Cerrutti, M. (2003). Labor migration between developing countries: The case of Paraguay and Argentina. *International Migration Review*, 37(1), 101–132.

Pellegrino, A. (2003). Mano de obra calificada desde Argentina y Uruguay. Report del *Programa de Migraciones Internacionales*. Geneva: OIT.

Peltonen, T. (1997). Facing the rankings from the past: A tournament perspective on repatriate career mobility. *The International Journal of Human Resource Management*, 8(1), 106–123.

Peltonen, T. (1998). Narrative construction of expatriate experience and career cycle: Discursive patterns in Finnish stories of international career. *The International Journal of Human Resource Management*, 9(5), 875–892.

Peltonen, T. (1999). Colonialism, postcolonialism and the organization of the "local" self. Recursive identity narratives as tactical re-appropriations of the "half European" subjectivity. *Proceedings from CMS1*. Manchester: First International Critical Management Studies Conference.

Peltonen, T. (2004). La internacionalización de directivos como normalización y resistencia: expatriados, narrativas de carrera y teoría postcolonial. *e-Textos*. Programa de Altos Estudios Universitarios, 1(1), 1–25.

Primer Ranking de Empresas Multinacionales Argentinas (2009). Buenos Aires: ProsperAr-Agencia Nacional de Desarrollo de Inversiones and Vale Columbia Center.

Richardson, J. & McKenna, S. (2000). Metaphorical "types" and human resource management: Self-selecting expatriates. *Industrial and Commercial Training*, 32(6), 209–218.

Richardson, J. & McKenna, S. (2006). Exploring relationships with home and host countries—A study of self directed expatriates. *Cross Cultural Management: An International Journal*, 13(1), 6–22.

Selmer, J. (1998). Expatriation: Corporate policy, personal intentions and international adjustment. *The International Journal of Human Resource Management*, 9(6), 996–1007.

Selmer, J. (1999). Career issues and international adjustment of business expatriates. *Career Development International*, 4(2), 77–87.

Selmer, J. (2002). Practice makes perfect? International experience and expatriate adjustment. *Management International Review*, 42(1), 71–87.

Smith, F. & Keyton, J. (2001). Organizational storytelling: Metaphors for relational power and identity struggles. *Management Communication Quarterly*, 15, 149–182.

Sparrow, P., Brewster, C., & Harris, H. (2004). *Globalizing Human Resource Management* (1st ed.). New York: Routledge.

Sunkyu, J., Gentry, J., & Yong, J. (2001). Cultural adaptation of business expatriates in the host marketplace. *Journal of International Business Studies*, 32(2), 369–377.

Suutari, V. (2003). Global managers: Career orientation, career tracks, life-style implications and career commitment. *Journal of Managerial Psychology*, 18, 185–207.

Suutari, V. & Brewster, C. (2000). Making their own way: International experience through self-initiated foreign assignments. *Journal of World Business*, 35(4), 417–436.

Suutari, V. & Brewster, C. (2009). Beyond expatriation: Different forms of international employment. In P. Sparrow (Ed.), *Handbook of International Human Resource Management: Integrating People, Process and Context* (131–150). Chichester: John Wiley & Sons.

Tarique, I. & Caligiuri, P. (2004). Training and development of international staff. In A.-W. Harzing & J. Van Ruysseveldt (Eds.), *International HRM. Managing People Across Borders* (283–306). Newbury Park, CA: Sage.

Townley, B. (1994). *Reframing Human Resource Management: Power, Ethics and the Subject at Work*. Thousand Oaks, CA: Sage.

Tung, R. (1981). Selection and training of personnel overseas assignments. *Columbia Journal of World Business*, 16(1), 68–78.

Tung, R. (1988). *The New Expatriates: Managing Human Resources Abroad*. Cambridge, MA: Ballinger.

Vaara, E. (2000). Constructions of cultural differences in post-merger change processes: A sensemaking perspective on Finnish–Swedish cases. *Management*, 3(3), 81–110.

Vaara, E., Tienari, J., & Laurila, J. (2006). Pulp and paper fiction: On the discursive legitimation of global industrial restructuring. *Organization Studies*, 27, 789–809.

Van Maanen, J. & Schein, E. (1977). Improving the quality of work life: Career development. In J. Hackman & J. Suttle, *Improving Life at Work* (30–95). Santa Comina, CA: Goodyear.

Wang, X. (2002). Expatriate adjustment from a social network perspective: Theoretical examination and a conceptual model. *International Journal of Cross Cultural Management*, 2(3), 321–337.

Weick, K. (1995). *Sensemaking in Organizations*. Thousand Oaks, CA: Sage.

Willmot, H. (1997). Rethinking management and managerial work: Capitalism, control and subjectivity. *Human Relations*, 50, 1329–1359.

World Bank (2010). Gross Domestic Product 2010. Retrieved from http://siteresources. worldbank.org/DATASTATISTICS/Resources/GDP.pdf (accessed December 15, 2011).

# 8

# THE GLOBAL CAREERS OF AUSTRALIANS AND NEW ZEALANDERS

*Kerr Inkson, Universities of Auckland and Waikato, New Zealand, Yvonne McNulty, Shanghai University, China, and Kaye Thorn, Massey University, New Zealand*

## Introduction – and Some Examples

In this chapter, we focus on global careers as they apply to Australia (population 22.6 million) and New Zealand (population 4.2 million), developed countries whose culture, language and population have been shaped largely by those of the colonizing British, which they served originally as colonies, and later as dominions. The pressures of anti-colonialism and trade policies (particularly the UK's involvement in the European Union) have lessened historic ties, but the international careers of Australians and New Zealanders are nevertheless influenced by both history and geography – the latter particularly in terms of the geographical isolation of the two countries. The following vignette of a New Zealand global careerist is perhaps typical of young people from this region.

---

### The Globetrotter

Philip, a graduate computer programmer, left New Zealand in his early twenties, to undertake a period of travel around the world. At this stage, Philip wasn't confident enough to head for the usual European destinations normally favoured by New Zealanders, so he went to Australia, working as a contract programmer and travelling throughout the country. After a year, encouraged by friends in the UK, he went there, and worked in temporary jobs to earn money to fund travel around Europe. After a further year, he ventured to Africa, travelling throughout the continent. Nine months of 'roughing it' was sufficient to satisfy, for the moment, his travel urges, and he returned home to New Zealand. He wanted a change of career and studied to obtain a Master's degree in zoology.

On its completion, he was offered a job in Brisbane, Australia, as a fisheries officer. The opportunity to combine his skill sets in computing and fisheries management led to doctoral studies and a new career modelling fisheries stocks. A new job opportunity in the US resulted in a move, now with his wife and children, to San Diego. Three years later, Philip and his family transferred again to New Caledonia – a move partly determined by Philip's desire to be closer to family in Australia and New Zealand. At the time of writing, Philip's next move is being planned, and it will probably again be within Australia, to be near family while still taking advantage of the opportunities of an economy larger than those of both New Caledonia and New Zealand.

Philip's global career path has many characteristics typical of Australian and New Zealand international mobility. Philip self-initiates his international moves and is not involved in any long-term organizational career framework. Like many young people in Australia and New Zealand, he feels keenly his geographical isolation from the cosmopolitan cities and sophisticated cultures of Europe and America and seeks to travel to overcome the assumed deficit. His first move is within Australasia (a term sometimes used to describe the region that includes Australia, New Zealand and neighbouring Pacific Islands) and the second to the UK, a country with historical links and close cultural and language affinities with Australia and New Zealand, which global careerists often use as a launching pad for moving further abroad (Inkson and Myers, 2003). In his initial explorations, Philip 'travels light', taking temporary jobs to fund travel, and, driven less by a desire for career development than by a desire to experience novelty, moves to ever more exotic and culturally different locations. He also seeks periods in his home country and is able to fit in a major career transition there. The motives driving his career change over time, from exploration to career development, and then to family considerations. Through his travel and the work he does as he goes, he builds up a wider range of skills and networks on which to base a career, which may in the end remain 'global' in orientation.

Some of the different patterns of global career that are dominant in Australia and New Zealand are further illustrated in the careers of the three authors of this chapter, who are all of European origin. Their stories also show how global careers can affect career actors' children.

## The Authors' Global Careers

Kerr Inkson was born and educated in Scotland, but he and his Scottish wife emigrated to New Zealand – to a university job he had arranged ahead of travel – when they were young, on a planned three-year trip, and have made it their base ever since, while also spending substantial time abroad, particularly in the UK. Their son has remained in New Zealand, where he and his wife are bringing

up a family, and their daughter, a British citizen, took a trip to London in her mid twenties and has remained there for 14 years, pursuing a career with the BBC involving substantial international travel. London offers her career opportunities unobtainable in New Zealand.

Yvonne McNulty, a child of European immigrants to Australia, was born, raised and commenced her career there, first in naval telecommunications and then in various corporate roles. It was in Australia that she also met her Scottish-born husband. A year after their marriage, his career took them first to the United States, then Singapore, and now – 12 years later, with two overseas-born children in tow – on to Shanghai, China. During much of this time, Yvonne has been a 'trailing spouse' (see her website: www.thetrailingspouse.com), accompanying her husband as his career moved them to new cities, but in this time she also commenced a new career as an academic, completing a Ph.D. in 2010 on the management of expatriates. Yvonne's daughters are 'third culture kids':

> children who accompany their parents into another society [and] who, having spent a significant part of their adolescence years in cultures other than the culture of their parents, develop a sense of relationship to all of the cultures they have been exposed to while not claiming full ownership to any of them.
>
> (Selmer and Lam, 2004, p. 432)

With no immediate plans to return to Australia (their official home country) and no particular allegiance to any country – they hold multiple passports – this 'united nations' family embodies what it means to be global nomads.

Kaye Thorn is a New Zealander who has primarily stayed in New Zealand. Her mobility has been across occupations, from an economic analyst in the New Zealand Treasury, to an economic consultant, to an environmental tourism specialist and finally into academia. Her early international experience was atypical of Australasians as it involved studying (in Canada) rather than working. She travelled extensively around Canada before backpacking through Europe. She has recently completed a Ph.D., studying New Zealanders' disproportionate involvement in international careers. Her daughter, ironically, is one of those who plan to relocate permanently, as soon as she graduates, to the UK or France – countries she has never lived in, but with which she feels a natural affinity.

Between them, the three authors illustrate some of the key characteristics of global careers in their region: a willing mobility in pursuit of career; an ingrained wish to visit 'distant parts'; a mixture of self-initiation and organizational sponsorship determining locations; family concerns that frame and sometimes constrain travel; flexibility to make changes in occupation; long-term effects on the lives and careers of next-generation family members' own identity and careers; and, in their academic pursuits, a fascination with, and insiders' perspectives of, global careers.

This chapter examines the global mobility of Australians and New Zealanders, beginning with a brief summary of mobility into and out of the two countries

and the factors that influence that mobility. In two 'country case studies', the specifics of global careers in Australia and of Australians are then discussed, and then those of neighbouring New Zealand. The existing research on mobility to and from these countries is discussed, supplemented with exemplars of global careers. The chapter ends with the authors' perspectives on critical issues that need further consideration.

## Global Careers in Australia and New Zealand

Despite the predominance, in Australia and New Zealand, of Europeans such as the authors of this chapter, both countries still contain substantial groups of indigenous citizens (Australian Aborigines, New Zealand Maori). The neighbouring Pacific island states have mainly Polynesian populations, plus, in Fiji, many of Indian origin: these countries are small, and they survive economically through their substantial trading and labour-force relationships with Australia and New Zealand. The two countries have similar immigration policies, historical, language and cultural similarities, strong trade ties, close relationships and similar, mutually inclusive migration policies with free movement between them, so that, in some respects, they provide a single labour market in the Asia Pacific Economic Cooperation (APEC) region of the world (Hugo, Callister and Badkar, 2008). Australia is a major magnet for New Zealanders seeking to leave their small country, although it is a moot point whether the careers of those New Zealanders could be regarded as 'global'.

A major difference, however, is that per capita GDP is relatively low in the island states, moderate to high in New Zealand, and about 30 per cent higher in Australia than in New Zealand. The direction of mobility is therefore primarily from the island states to New Zealand and Australia, and from New Zealand to Australia. More recently, both Australia and New Zealand have experienced substantial changes in the ethnic make-up of their populations and workforces, owing to the influx of immigrants of Asian origin from China, Taiwan, Hong Kong, Vietnam, India and Pakistan, and migrants from Eastern Europe and the Middle East have also become more common.

## Factors Affecting Global Careers

Global careers are part of the history of Australia and New Zealand. Political and economic catastrophes, such as the eighteenth- and nineteenth-century Highland Clearances in Scotland and the Irish potato famine of the 1840s, precipitated the flight of many robust migrants into global careers, particularly to the USA and the English-speaking colonies of the British Empire, because the alternative, at home, was starvation. More recently, political and economic oppression and civil war in, for example, Sri Lanka, have resulted in many career actors relocating to seek better lives in Australia and New Zealand. Other flows of migrants are determined by the broad desires of people in many societies to improve their

economic, career or lifestyle situations, the changing willingness of Australia, New Zealand and other countries to accept newcomers, and the criteria they set for entry. However, which specific individuals migrate, and then 'go global', is detemined by the personal characteristics of individual career actors – not just their circumstances, age and gender, but personality factors such as openness to experience (Hudson and Inkson, 2007) and the motivational factor achievement motivation (Boneva and Frieze, 2001; Inkson et al., 2007; McClelland, 1953). Work by Suutari and Taka (2004) found, among their sample of Finnish expatriate employees, a new – and, in that particular sample, dominating, 'career anchor' – 'internationalism' to add to those identified earlier by Schein (1993). It would be interesting to test levels of this new career anchor among both natives in, and migrants to, geographically isolated states such as Australia and New Zealand.

At the same time, contextual factors are important in determining the directions and destinations taken by those undertaking global careers. For example, Western organizations such as those dominant in Australia and New Zealand emphasize division of labour, specialized accreditation of qualifications and status advancement based on merit, thereby creating clear structures along which career actors may seek to advance themselves; these may make Australia and New Zealand attractive to those whose career decisions are influenced by notions of upwardly mobile and meritocratic professional and organizational career paths. Also, although decisions on new destinations are often assumed to be driven by economic considerations, the fact that Australia is ranked second in the world in quality of life for expatriates (HSBC, 2010) and that five of the world's ten 'most liveable' cities are located in Australia and New Zealand – Adelaide, Auckland, Melbourne, Perth and Sydney (Business Travel Gulliver, 2010) – suggest a 'lifestyle' cachet for the region which may be influential in luring some migrant careerists, keeping Australians and New Zealanders at home and facilitating their return if they leave. Another important factor is likely to be local people's, particularly employers', real and reputed attitudes to incoming migrants, and other countries' acceptance of Australasians.

An important, potential, contextual influence on global careers is local culture, in this case Australasian culture. According to Thomas and Inkson (2007), culture is important to career theory because it helps to determine the economic, legal and political characteristics of a society, is largely invisible and therefore over-looked in its influence on individual behaviour, and acts as a legitimizing factor for the institutions that govern career practices and patterns, and for individual career actors' career attitudes, expectations and actions. Therefore, dominant Australian and New Zealand cultural characteristics are likely to have a substantial influence on the global careers of citizens, but those of the minority indigenous aboriginal and Maori cultures and the immigrant Polynesian peoples, who are collectivistic rather than individualistic, may provide different dynamics.

The fifty-two countries covered in Hofstede's (1980) classic description of international cultural variations enable us to understand something of the likely career attitudes and behaviour of Australians and New Zealanders, although both countries' cultural characteristics may have somewhat changed post Hofstede,

because of immigration from other cultures. In terms of the cultural dimensions identified by Hofstede, Australia and New Zealand are, unsurprisingly, similar both to each other and to three other English-speaking countries – the UK, USA and Canada (Hofstede, 1980). In sum, these countries are high on individualism (and therefore low on collectivism), low on power distance, moderate to low on uncertainty avoidance, and moderate to high on masculinity. The overall constellation of cultural characteristics might lead us to expect that Australian and New Zealand global careerists may pursue career directions relatively independently (e.g. giving below-average consideration to family or organizational ties); avoid countries and organizations with excessively steep bureaucratic hierarchies; take risks such as engaging in boundaryless career behaviour, improvising career opportunities and moving to new countries without certainty of a job; and adopt predominantly male definitions of career success (Gunz and Heslin, 2004). These career-development characteristics are certainly represented in local stereotypes of career behaviour, and there is some empirical evidence – in an in-depth study of a representative sample of New Zealanders' careers (Arthur, Inkson and Pringle, 1999) – to support them as well.

Recent developments in the economic, social, cultural and ethnic contexts in which Australians and New Zealanders conduct their careers in their own countries have led to an apparent diversification and increasing ambiguity in terms of career structures and trajectories. These changes have antecedents in the processes of globalization. For example, *boundaryless career theory* (Arthur and Rousseau, 1996; Sullivan and Baruch, 2009) is based on the view that societies progress from structured industrial states to flexible new economies in which boundaries – for example, those between organizations – are permeable, and career paths are less structured. As a number of writers have noted (Banai and Harry, 2004; Tung, 2008), the boundaryless-career principle can be extended to include the increasing permeability of *international* boundaries. International boundary crossing is initiated both by multinational companies, seeking to do business and to transfer staff across national boundaries, and by independent individual migrants. The latter cross national boundaries to escape political or ethnic oppression, to seek economically better conditions or simply to live internationally, experiencing different countries and cultures and perhaps becoming 'citizens of the world' rather than citizens of a specific country.

Individuals who are implicitly admired in the boundaryless-careers literature are those mobile professionals and managers who build and utilize their career competencies and generate economic value through transfer and cross-fertilization across boundaries (Inkson and Arthur, 2001). It is a short step to extend the definition of boundaryless careers to consider 'global boundaryless careers', which are practised by international itinerant 'professional managers who over their careers are employed for their ability, by at least two business organizations that are not related to each other, in at least two different foreign countries' (Banai and Harry, 2004, p. 100). Why the definition should be restricted to 'managers', however, is not clear.

These trends have dramatically impacted on the career paths and experiences of Australians and New Zealanders. This applies, moreover, to:

- those moving internationally within Australasia (e. g. from Fiji to Australia);
- Australians and New Zealanders developing global careers in other regions of the world;
- Australians and New Zealanders involved in 'boomerang' careers, in which they alternate between the home country and foreign parts (Thorn, 2010); and
- immigrant groups of 'new' Australians and New Zealanders, who enter the region in large numbers, change the ethnic and skill-based composition of the labour force, experience and try to solve problems of adjustment to their new societies, and may move on again in further global-career transitions.

Here, we will present evidence that these changes are not only symptomatic of changes in labour-force composition and career internationalization that are prevalent around much of the world, but that, in Australia and New Zealand, they take place at a more rapid rate and more extensively than the average, and are therefore worthy of special study.

Unusually large numbers of people move into, and from, Australia and New Zealand. For example, as we show below, over 1 million Australians and about 1 million New Zealanders live outside their home countries, giving global careers special significance in these countries. Further, although these global careers are a product of globalization, they are *not*, in our view, largely a product of the spread of the multinational, but rather of historical periods of colonization, selective immigration, mass immigration and substantial emigration, at different periods of the countries' histories. Most Australians and New Zealanders who travel elsewhere to live do so as *free agents*, heading abroad to sell their skills on the local labour markets of whichever region of the world they choose. A smaller group, particularly from Australia, head overseas as organizational expatriates, assigned to overseas jobs in their own organizations, but many of these subsequently become free agents on the international labour market (McNulty, Hutchings and de Cieri, 2012). Many from both groups soon, or eventually, return to build careers in their own countries (Tharenou and Caulfield, 2010), but others become permanent settlers in a new country, or global itinerants with no permanent allegiance.

In the meantime, members of the growing ethnic groups of Pacific islanders, South Africans, Eastern Europeans, Iranians, Indians, Chinese and other Asians seeking to build their careers in Australia and New Zealand make their way there, bringing their global careers and elements of their international and ethnic cultures into the host countries, thus creating a strong inflow and outflow of members of each society, and shifting balances of cultures, with associated challenges (Perrin and Dunn, 2007).

To assist understanding of the huge influence of global mobility on the ethnic diversity of, and the prevalence and character of global careers within, Australia

and New Zealand, we now present 'potted histories' of the global-careerist workforces of each.

## Global Careers: The Australia Case

For a long time, Australia has maintained one of the strongest flows of immigrants in the developed world. Census figures over the last decade show that at least half of all Australian residents were either born in another country or had a parent who was born in another country (Organization for Economic Co-operation and Development, 2007). Recent population-growth statistics attest to the importance of immigration to the local society and economy. In 2007, for example, 56 per cent of the annual population growth in Australia was attributable to net migration (Australian Bureau of Statistics, 2007), for good reasons. Projections of Australia's aged and working-age population reveal that, by 2031, more Australians will be aged over 65 than those actively engaged in the workforce (Australian Bureau of Statistics, 2003, 2004). Salt (2008) predicts that, by 2050, the net annual change in the population of Australia aged 15–64 will have declined by more than half, resulting in a shrinking labour pool. In other words, without increasing immigration still further, Australia will not be able to produce enough citizens to replace those retiring from the workforce.

In light of a declining fertility rate, it is not surprising that the Australian government, as it has done since the birth of the nation in 1788, has in recent years looked to immigration as a way to solve labour-market shortages, thereby boosting the number of international careerists in the country. Indeed, for the last half-century, the Australian government has maintained a very well-organized migration programme, attracting immigrants in various humanitarian and non-humanitarian categories (Birrell, Hawthorne and Richardson, 2006). The history and development of this programme are particularly interesting in terms of where Australia sources its immigrants, and why a significant shift in immigration policy has emerged over the past 60 years.

From its British colonization in the eighteenth century to the present day, the UK and Ireland have remained a major source of immigration to Australia. Prior to World War II, their citizens' European heritage, English-language abilities, 'white' Western-style affinity for Australian culture and strong familial ties were favoured characteristics. Postwar, the demand for immigrants grew larger, owing in part to a labour shortage in the burgeoning manufacturing sector, as well as perceived threats of invasion from the north. Operating on a 'populate or perish' mandate and facing a diminishing UK immigrant pool, the Australian government broke its almost exclusive focus on UK immigrants to accept over a quarter of a million 'displaced persons' from Eastern Europe. The relative success of permanently settling these new immigrants led, during the 1950s and 1960s, to an extension of Australia's immigration programme to other countries in Europe (e.g. Italy, Greece).

The rise of unemployment in the 1970s, along with the offshoring of manufacturing jobs, led to a second major shift in immigration policy: the move away from an exclusive 'white Australia' policy to include skilled economic migrants, those migrating for family reunion, and refugees and humanitarian migrants. There was also a mutual migration treaty with New Zealand. An important milestone during this period was the opening of Australia's borders for the first time to Asian immigrants and Indo-Chinese refugees, who, in the 1970s and 1980s, made up an increasingly large share of the new population.

In the 1980s, to facilitate the economically valuable addition of people with skills in demand in Australia, a points system was introduced that determined, according to skills shortages and a predetermined annual target set by the government, who should be allowed to settle. By the 1990s, a new type of visa was introduced to allow temporary residents from selected 'treaty' countries to visit Australia for up to one year, with provisions for subsequent permanent residency based on a skills assessment (Khoo, McDonald, Voigt-Graf and Hugo, 2007). During the 1990s, a regional migration programme was added to facilitate skilled immigration to designated economically lagging areas of the country: this category now accounts for one-fifth of immigrants in any given year (Hugo, 2008).

Today, Australia's migration programme attracts skilled and unskilled migrants from all corners of the globe, New Zealanders entering under the Trans-Tasman Travel Agreement, long-term visitors, and those who jump categories from temporary to permanent residence (Hugo et al., 2008). This contemporary policy illustrates a watershed change in Australian immigration policy over the past 30 years – a heavier focus on permanent, skilled/business migrants, who may improve national productivity, and the introduction of temporary migrants with the right to work, who may facilitate globalization and the acquisition of new skills, ideas and technology. For the individuals involved, both these emphases facilitate global careers.

So, what draws temporary migrants to work and live in Australia? Several reasons may be given. First, the country is economically attractive – a well-performing OECD member with a modern infrastructure, rich mineral wealth and a position in the OECD top tier in terms of per capita GDP. Owing to its primary resources and prudent financial policies, Australia weathered the ongoing economic crisis that originated in 2008 better than almost any country in the world. Australia is also a stable democracy, and its weather and lifestyle are attractive to many migrants and travellers (HSBC, 2010), although its isolation from cosmopolitan European and American centres may be a problem for some. Additionally, Australian employers are receptive to international labour recruitment, recognizing that people with specialized skills and knowledge are often in short supply (Khoo et al., 2007) and seeking to hire staff from overseas to overcome domestic shortages (Burke, 2011).

The Australian government is responsive to the changing demands of the global workforce in recognizing that temporary as well as permanent residents can play

a major role in addressing talent shortages. The last decade alone has seen a dramatic change in policy to support this agenda, with the introduction of three visa categories for temporary migrants: (1) the *Working Holiday Maker* allows individuals aged 18–30 from nineteen countries to work in Australia for up to 1 year, with an opportunity to extend their stay if they work in areas of labour shortage; (2) the *Temporary Business Entry Visa* enables long-term (4 year) and short-term (less than 1 year) skilled migrants to work in niche (but restricted) labour markets; and (3) the *Australia Student Visa* facilitates the temporary migration of up to eight categories of international student, by far the largest category of all temporary residents in Australia, three quarters of whom originate from five Asian countries – China, South Korea, India, Japan and Malaysia.

An additional policy change is the move towards *onshore migration*, where temporary migrants are able to change to permanent migrant status once in Australia, as a result of demonstrating success in the labour market over a number of years. In the period 2001–2006, onshore migration accounted for nearly 25 per cent of all permanent migrants to Australia, of whom nearly 32 per cent originated from Asia (Hugo et al., 2008). A large percentage of these newcomers are international students, who represent an increasingly significant proportion of skilled migrants.

## The Global Careers of Australians Abroad

Australians have a long and established history of working overseas, with approximately 1 million Australians (4.5 per cent of the total) currently living outside the country on a long-term basis (Fullilove and Flutter, 2004). Typically, young Australians take, or make, chances to go abroad and 'see the world' on a temporary basis, but then find that there are complex 'push-and-pull' factors that move some to become permanent emigrants, others to undertake multi-country global careers, and others again to return to Australia. As an example, what outcome would you predict for young Stacie?

---

### Balancing Conflicts in a Global Career

Stacie is an accounting graduate from Melbourne. On graduation, she started work with the local office of one of the 'big four' financial-services firms. From the start, she wanted a secondment overseas: she just wanted to travel and didn't care where to, but her boss was not supportive. After 3 years, she answered a general call from the London office for transferees, volunteering for the move, even though there was very limited financial support to relocate. The London office paid her airfare and put her on an 18-month contract. If she wanted to stay longer, she could negotiate that with the London office. A second contract would enable her to return to Melbourne if she wanted to, but it put her under no obligation to do so. In London, she acquired a UK-based boyfriend, who

worked in the same industry. So, Stacie has extended the London assignment by 6 months and is considering going on to a permanent UK contract, which would make the Australian contract null and void. Stacie feels torn, because her long-term plan is eventually to return to Melbourne for the lifestyle, but she also wants to retain the relationship with her boyfriend, whom she will likely marry. Plus, there are more travel opportunities from London than from Melbourne, which is what attracted her to the UK in the first place. Yet, her career prospects would be better in Australia – she would have prospects of promotion to partner if there, although more international experience would also help her. Like many global careerists, Stacie walks a fine line, balancing career aspirations, personal relationships and the desire for travel, while her status as a valued member of a multinational organization provides security and structure. Stacie's adaptable contract options are a nice example of an organization providing flexibility to indulge the changing needs of its valuable global careerists – but, in the longer term, such 'golden handcuffs' may also limit her opportunities.

For many middle-income families, the sending of young people on a 'gap year' as 'rite of passage travellers' (Fullilove and Flutter, 2004, p. 21) tends to carry a high degree of social cachet, not least because the entry of Australians' sons and daughters into the international labour market is often viewed as a sign of both personal and parental success. For slightly older Australians, the lure of higher remuneration in overseas markets remains a strong economic driver to pull 'gold collar workers' (p. 21) on to the international scene. The relative isolation and remoteness of Australia from the rest of the developed world (Committee for Economic Development of Australia, 2009), along with a local community whose culture supports much out-migration as a natural part of what it is to be 'Australian', mean we can begin to understand why Australia is suffering one of the worst periods of 'brain drain' in its young history.

Australia's brain-drain problem is exacerbated by the fact that expatriates who spend more than 5 years abroad become significantly less likely to return home (Hugo, 2002), a situation that prompted the Australian Senate to set up an inquiry in 2003 to examine the growing Australian expatriate community. Hugo (2006) concluded, in a recent study, that intention to return decreases with age: whereas 65 per cent of expatriates in the age group 30–34 intended to return to Australia, only 35 per cent in the 55–59 age group said they would do so. A stronger focus on cross-cultural training and policy improvements for departing Australian expatriates (Clegg and Gray, 2002; Hutchings, 2005) and a desire of Australian multinationals to use headquarters-based employees in overseas subsidiaries (Fee and Gray, 2011; Tharenou and Harvey, 2006) have apparently accelerated the trend of Australians having global careers.

The outflow of talent from Australia represents a net loss to the Australian economy on many levels, including the loss of taxable income, training, spending, investment and the reproduction of new citizens. Out-migration may be inevitable, but return migration is frequent, creating a 'rolling diaspora' (Fullilove

and Flutter, 2004, p. 20), or 'circular migration' (Skeldon, 2010, p. 22). The corresponding 'brain-drain' problems may not be how to prevent Australians from moving overseas, but rather how to get them back, in order to leverage their global careers on Australian soil, and how to attract appropriate new migrant talent to replace them.

## Global Careers: The New Zealand Case

New Zealand has a special interest in global careers, because so many New Zealanders and New Zealand residents are 'living' them – a much higher proportion, we believe, than almost anywhere in the world, including Australia. This is due in part to New Zealand's small size, island status, isolated location and highly developed education system.

Statistically, the proportion of New Zealand residents born overseas and the proportion of New Zealand-born people living and working overseas are far in excess of the 3 per cent figure provided by the International Organization for Migration (IOM, 2011) for the total proportion of the world's population living outside the country it was born in. Of nearly 4 million New Zealand residents registered in the most recent (2006) census, 23 per cent had been born outside the country. Although reliable statistics for the number of New Zealand-born people living abroad are harder to calculate, one estimate is of an identical figure of 23 per cent, or 850,000 individuals (Hugo, Rudd and Harris, 2003). In other words, New Zealanders exit their country at a high rate but are replaced by large numbers of returners and immigrants. In proportional terms, New Zealand's figures far outstrip Australia's, with nearly as many New Zealanders as Australians pursuing careers abroad, despite the much smaller size of their country.

The question of who stays, who leaves and who enters afresh is clearly a vital one for New Zealand's welfare. For example, New Zealanders are, on the whole, well educated and represent considerable human capital: the calculus of skills retained, skills lost overseas, skills New Zealanders develop abroad and bring back, and skills introduced by immigrants is of considerable national significance. The history and dynamics of migration, both to and from New Zealand, provide clues to the nature of the growing diversity of the workforce and the types of global career that New Zealanders pursue.

In essence, all New Zealanders are immigrants. The original Maori inhabitants of New Zealand are thought to have migrated from northern parts of Polynesia about a thousand years ago (Bedford, Ho and Lidgard, 2002). Their society, based on complex tribal systems, was much more collective than that of the British settlers who came to dominate them, after Captain James Cook's 'discovery' of New Zealand in 1772. So too were the societies of neighbouring Pacific islands, which were to become major sources of labour supply through immigration to New Zealand. The rapid absorption of the country by European colonialists, who brought the Maori guns to kill each other with, diseases from which to die, and legislation to steal their land (King, 2003), made life both more comfortable and

more monocultural for the immigrants. New immigrants were recruited almost exclusively from the UK, and racist policies, such as a poll tax on Chinese settlers that remained in force until the 1930s, preserved an ethnically narrow population. Labour shortages following World War II were a major concern, and the response of the New Zealand government was to develop a fully assisted migration scheme, targeting British citizens of 'European race and colour', with a preference for young, single people with industrial skills (Hutching, 1999). This scheme was later extended to the Netherlands to attract skilled workers. The labour demand continued through the 1960s and 1970s and eventually brought about the first challenges to the implicit 'white New Zealand' policy, by encouraging a rapid inflow of brown-skinned migrants from neighbouring South Pacific islands, such as Samoa, Tonga and Fiji – typically non-tertiary-educated people required for increasing numbers of unskilled and semi-skilled factory and service jobs.

By 1987, New Zealand had recognized that its economic future depended, not on historical ties with the UK (which had long since deserted its exclusive trading relationship with New Zealand for the wider benefits of being in the EU), nor on notions of racial purity, nor on brown-skinned immigrants slotted into simple jobs, but on a highly educated and skilled workforce of whatever ethnic and national origins could be found. The government passed an Immigration Act, including a points-based system that rated and ranked applicants from any country according to their qualifications, experience, personal characteristics and potential contribution to the national economy. New Zealand then admitted, in any given year, an appropriate ratio of applicants. The new policy has resulted in a rapid ethnic diversification of the national population, particularly a large influx of immigrants from China and other Asian countries that commenced in the 1990s and has continued unabated, although large numbers of white-skinned British and South African people continue to come as well. The increasing diversity of New Zealand is especially focused in Auckland, the largest city, where, in 2006, over 20 per cent of census participants stated a national identity identified as Asian (at least in part), with over 15 per cent as Pacific Island, and 12 per cent Maori.

How has New Zealand's new, post-1987 intake of migrants fared in terms of satisfaction and adjustment, and in employment and career terms? This must be considered in relation to immigrants' motives and aspirations in moving to the country, and here the evidence is limited. Research on immigration to New Zealand has focused on origin, empirical numbers and resettlement issues, but generally has not examined the motivation behind these people choosing New Zealand as a destination. Ip (2000) is one of the few exceptions, suggesting that Asian immigrants choose New Zealand to take advantage of the social and environmental resources of the country. Online sources promoting migration to New Zealand from other regions suggest the quality of life, beauty and ease of doing business (Mercer, 2011) are attractants, and the United Nations identifies New Zealand as the third best country in the world in which to live, based on health, education and income statistics (United Nations, 2010). Auckland has strong

appeal as the largest city, with a variety of employment and cultural-networking opportunities (Department of Labor, 2011). Anecdotal evidence, however, suggests that, for many potential migrants, especially from Asia, there may simply be a hierarchy of receiving countries, with the US ranked highly, and Australia and New Zealand further down the rankings.

There is also limited information about the redeployment of these immigrants. Apocryphal tales abound of medical specialists delivering junk mail around the cities. Oliver (2000), who interviewed forty-four professional migrants from China, Sri Lanka and Iraq, and also immigration officials and employers, revealed a distressing picture of migrants who had fled political oppression and economic deprivation: they were pleased with New Zealand as their chosen country, had established good links with their national and ethnic communities and intended to remain in New Zealand. But they had also faced major difficulties in their attempts to find suitable employment and were mostly employed below their level of skill. According to Oliver, 'many factors labeled as deficits in the migrants – lack of New Zealand experience, being overqualified, lack of fluent English – were in fact problems of attitude and discrimination amongst employers' (2000, p. 7). Other studies strongly suggest the charge of discrimination is justified (e.g. Wilson and Parker, 2007). A study by Tharmaseelan, Inkson and Carr (2010) of a sample of Sri Lankan immigrants in Auckland, a highly educated group who had been in New Zealand for an average of 6 years, showed that, in terms of occupational status, compared with their last job in Sri Lanka, 17 per cent had advanced in status, 25 per cent had the same status, and 58 per cent had declined in status, including 17 per cent who were unemployed. Such findings are not, of course, unique to New Zealand, but reflect a problem faced by many global careerists, especially when ethnic boundaries are crossed.

On the other hand, a recent longitudinal study by the New Zealand Department of Labor (2009) involved a survey of several thousand immigrants and showed 70 per cent of immigrants in employment and only 4 per cent looking for work, over half of them owning their own homes, and over 90 per cent satisfied or very satisfied with life in New Zealand. Such statistics, however, provide little information on the nature, part-time versus full-time status or level of employment outcomes in relation to skills, nor is there any breakdown by ethnicity.

## The Global Careers of New Zealanders Abroad

New Zealanders are renowned as a nation of travellers (Bedford, 2001). However, more than this, many display serial mobility, moving from country to country. In a survey of over 2,600 New Zealanders living and working abroad (Thorn, 2008), 15 per cent had moved between countries four or more times, and, of these, 58 per cent had not finished travelling, anticipating either a return to New Zealand or a move to another country in the next 5 years.

New Zealand's new, more liberal immigration policies have, in part, been responses to rising concerns about the loss of many New Zealanders, particularly those with good qualifications and skills, who have gone overseas in pursuit of better opportunities and have not returned. Here, the national institution known as the 'Big OE' (Overseas Experience) has played a part (Inkson and Myers, 2003). In the days of British domination, young, educated New Zealanders, recognizing that, although their country was pleasant to live in and prosperous, it was lacking in history, cultural depth, variety of experience and interesting career opportunities, would set off for a 'working holiday'. These sojourns were typically (because of historical ties, cultural similarity and the availability of 2-year 'working-holiday' visas) based in the UK, where the travellers would get whatever job they could, endeavour to 'see the world' and enjoy a culturally diverse and cosmopolitan lifestyle unavailable to them in their home country. Although there is evidence that those who returned to New Zealand brought gains in human capital with them (Inkson, Arthur, Pringle and Barry, 1997), there are also concerns within New Zealand about the many who find greater economic opportunities and more significant career challenges in the larger, even more prosperous, more diverse Western world. The Big OE has now become an established New Zealand cultural institution, with a significant proportion of the highly educated heading abroad shortly after graduation.

So, as in many other countries, in New Zealand 'brain drain' has become a preoccupation, particularly the loss of labour-force members to nearby Australia, which has low barriers to entry for New Zealanders, higher wages, a similar culture and language and (reputedly) better weather. The UK and the USA are also popular magnets for well-educated, ambitious New Zealanders: each offers higher salaries and wider career opportunities that cannot be matched locally. The statistics, however, would not support the view of a brain drain. Over the 10-year period to December 2010, New Zealand has experienced a net total influx of around 150,000 people, with only one of those years recording a net loss. Immigrants come from Australia (19 per cent of total arrivals in 2010), the UK (17 per cent) and, increasingly, from Asian countries, with India (8 per cent) and China (7 per cent) dominating this inflow. As the majority of new arrivals in New Zealand enter under the 'skilled-migrant' category, they bring their qualifications, skills and work experiences with them.

However, over this same period, nearly 540,000 New Zealand citizens have left the country, with only half of this number returning – a deficit of 270,000 or around 5 percent of the total population born in New Zealand. The trans-Tasman flow is significant for these citizens, with around 70 percent of departures heading for Australia. Other popular destinations include the UK, USA, and China.

The terminology of 'brain drain', however, is limiting, as it only considers a one-way flow. Recognizing this, Baruch, Budhwar and Khatri (2007) discuss the 'brain circulation' of students to a host country and home again. We, however, prefer the term 'talent flow' to discuss New Zealand's 'mobile-population' issues

(Carr, Inkson and Thorn, 2005), as 'talent' is wider than 'brain' (which is often used to refer to a restricted range of scientific occupations), and the term 'flow', like 'circulation', is less emotive than 'drain'. A Massey University study (Inkson et al., 2007) considered the global-career dynamics of New Zealanders abroad, using lists provided by local professional associations of their overseas members. Of the 2,200 New Zealanders who responded, more intended to return home than wanted to stay away, but many were undecided, and there were differences: the potential returners were more likely than the potentially permanent migrants to be in medical and social-service occupations, have high affiliation motivation and be interested in bringing up a family. In contrast, New Zealanders intending to remain overseas were more likely to be in financial and business occupations and had higher achievement motivation and greater interest in attaining their career goals. These differences no doubt reflect relative 'pull' factors in the different countries.

In the same study, both groups considered that the key attractions of returning to New Zealand were its natural environment, outdoors lifestyle and family-friendly ethos. The most common phrase New Zealanders use to praise their country is 'a great place to bring up children', and there is evidence that immigrants, too, perceive New Zealand to be a lower-stress environment than the one they have left (Meares, Ho, Peace and Spoonley, 2010; Oliver, 2000). However, the apparent bias of 'returners' to be high in affiliation rather than achievement motivation creates a problem in terms of the traditional view that achievement motivation is a primary driver of entrepreneurship and economic growth (McClelland, 1953). In the 1950s, New Zealand was the third-richest country in the world, as measured by per capita GDP; nowadays, its rank is in the high twenties. Is this connected with the drive – or lack of drive – of its citizens and its immigrants? Do global careers tend to deprive New Zealand of its most entrepreneurial people?

Against this backdrop, the vast diaspora of New Zealanders overseas nonetheless retains huge goodwill towards the country of origin (Gamlen, 2007; Larner, 2007), and it is recognized that developments in transport, telecommunications and information flows make it increasingly possible for them to contribute to their home country without actually living there. The Kiwi Expatriates Association (KEA) is a network of such people, tens of thousands strong, that only requires the right triggers for motivation to facilitate the strategic relocation of the skills these people have back to New Zealand, in a new, virtual segment of the workforce.

We also need to be aware that New Zealanders' Big OE is very much a white, middle-class institution, indicating that the samples in the studies cited above were probably monocultural, and that the resulting migration patterns are most likely a poor guide to future patterns. For example, when Maori New Zealanders travel abroad, it tends to be not to the UK and North America, but to Australia, where, according to one estimate, 120,000 Maori are resident, about a fifth of the number

in New Zealand (Hamer, 2007). It is apparent that finer-grained studies, with ethnic origin as a determining variable, would be of considerable value in understanding such migration patterns and the ways in which ethnicity, migration motivation and work opportunities balance themselves out within the country.

## Summary

To summarize research on global careers in Australia and New Zealand, we make two major points.

First, geographical isolation, in both historical and contemporary times, has played a major role in determining the extent of global careers. Tucked away in the South Pacific Ocean, over 24 hours' flight from central Europe, one can still, despite modern communications technology, feel disconnected from the rest of the world. New Zealand is very small, with few large organizations, and advancement often carries the prerequisite of a move to another country. Australia is a larger country and economy, providing more opportunities, but still far from the cosmopolitan cities of America and Europe. Because of this isolation, the topic of global careers is huge for New Zealand and highly pertinent for Australia.

The second factor is the influence of the Big OE on the global careers of both groups. Many people take time out from their career development to pursue cultural and travel opportunities in other parts of the world, typically the sophisticated, economically developed West, where their cultural background and command of English are valued. Once there, they often find career openings or romantic relationships that hold them there. Thereafter, all things are possible: permanent resettlement in the new country, return home, or on and on to more new countries. This is a group with big, and difficult, decisions to make, as their priorities and family cycle situations change; it is also a group that appears to be increasing in frequency and is therefore worthy of further study.

## *Critical Perspectives on Global Careers*

The picture we have painted of the global careers of Australians and New Zealanders, native and immigrant, is largely descriptive. We have shown the importance of geographical isolation, the Big OE phenomenon, and large-scale migration to 'make up the numbers'. We have shown that individual, familial, organizational, historical, legislative, cultural, economic, societal and other factors all impinge on careers. Such considerations are relevant to the decision-making and actions of many actors, including individual careerists and their families, organizations (especially multinational organizations), governments (for example, in immigration policy) and humankind in general. Such decisions include an individual's consideration of whether to stay offshore or return home, a company's decision whether to employ expatriates or locals in foreign locations, an immigration minister's policies regarding visas, and a society's ability to accept

global careerists into its mix. Such decisions are assisted if those concerned take a considered, reflective and critical view of what research tells us. What questions do our background in career studies and our research on global careers in Australia and New Zealand raise about the current conventional wisdom? And how do the answers to such questions direct future academic theory and research?

Here, we offer four areas for further critical exploration: the relative importance of corporate expatriation, self-initiated expatriation and permanent migration in influencing global careers; the notion of international career mobility as individual capital investment; the exploitation of marginal groups through global careers; and the role of migration criteria in determining global careers.

## 1 Global Career Development Through Corporate Expatriation, Self-initiated Migration and Permanent Migration

Fifteen years ago, based on a New Zealand study, the first author of this chapter and his colleagues offered a substantial critique of the literature on international careers (Inkson et al., 1997). The essence of their criticism was that the vast literature on international careers that had developed even by then was totally driven by an 'expatriate–assignment' model, which viewed international work as episodic and organizationally controlled. In their survey of local New Zealanders' careers, the authors found none that had ever contained a foreign company assignment, but many that included one or more lengthy, self-initiated spells, including employment, in foreign locations. They therefore suggested that the autonomous, self-propelled career, conducted without ongoing organizational sponsorship, might, in fact, be both more common than corporate expatriation, and a better analogue for a 'post-corporate' careers world (Peiperl and Baruch, 1997). Was it time to start studying seriously those whose careers were conducted, as it were, below any company's radar? Our current review has confirmed that, at least in Australia and New Zealand, notwithstanding the involvement of many Australians (such as 'Stacie' in one of our cases) in corporate international careers, the norm in our part of the world is for international careers to be self-directed. How has the academic community responded to this challenge?

The recent review of the field of global careers by Dickmann and Baruch (2011) indicates that the previous short-term and sometimes myopic preoccupation with the management of short-term foreign assignments has given way to a burgeoning research effort focusing on global careers in both their corporate and self-directed manifestations.

Self-initiated expatriation (SIE) is emerging as a growth research field. However, to date, there is no clear definition of what SIE incorporates. Doherty (2010), in a review of the extant SIE literature, identifies three key areas that are discussed: self-initiated mobility as part of a global talent flow; dispositions and typologies of self-initiated expatriates; and comparative studies of company expatriates versus self-initiated expatriates. Of more importance, perhaps, are the

gaps in our knowledge of SIEs – what motivates them to be mobile, how mobility impacts on their careers, whether they are a homogenenous group or if they vary across countries and cultures (Doherty, 2010).

The research agenda on SIE is therefore long, and current debate among researchers is focusing on the distinction between SIE and immigration. When does a person who has relocated to another country stop being an expatriate and become an immigrant? When does he or she stop having a global career and start having a national career in a new country? Dimensions such as length of time in the host country, citizenship, asset ownership, original motivation for mobility, level of interaction with host nationals and allegiance are being proposed as key differentiators. However, the debate is far from complete, with personal factors such as age, gender, life stage and relationships resulting in what might be termed accidental migrants – those who had every intention of returning to the home country, but who end up settled abroad permanently.

It is understandable that business-school academics have focused on corporate international careers: these are analogous to 'organizational' careers, international but conducted in apparently controllable settings, and potentially able to be within the corporate selection, development, compensation, career-path and other HRM systems. However, our evidence suggests that many, if not most, international career actors prefer to develop their careers in a different way, which means that organizations need to pay more attention to the external labour market, developing new, more flexible forms of engagement, including long-term but non-restrictive psychological contracts with international staff (Inkson and King, 2011).

In making this suggestion, however, we do offer a caveat. Emphasizing self-directed international careers takes us into the territory of the boundaryless career (Arthur and Rousseau, 1996) and the protean career (Hall, 1996), which, in our view, have over the years been romanticized by their proponents as opportunities for self-fulfilment, unfettered by petty restrictions (Inkson, Ganesh, Roper and Gunz, 2010). 'Boundaryless career' is a misnomer, because boundaries may be transcended without being abolished. It is time to start taking boundaries more seriously (Gunz, Peiperl and Tzabbar, 2007), and we note that the international boundaries that global-career actors face are typically daunting: draconian legislative restrictions on migration, the restrictive practices of local professional associations and other labour-market institutions, the fracturing of families, the barriers of cross-cultural unfamiliarity, the likelihood of ethnically based prejudice, to name but a few. Rather than assuming self-initiated global careers are all about the agency of the career actors who undertake them, we need to be serious about their structural constraints and study them in depth.

## 2 Global Careers as Capital and Investment

A second observation that we would offer from our deliberations is that the research we have reviewed seems to focus on the detail of individuals' moves and the

immediate purposes assumed to have been accomplished by their movement, rather than any longer-term or strategic consideration of the possible outcomes.

Elsewhere, we have found the concept of 'career capital' useful (Inkson and Arthur, 2001; Inkson and King, 2011). Careers require mutual investment, by individuals in the organizations they work for and by organizations in the individuals they employ. Each invests with the expectation of building capital (in the case of the individual, for example, motivation, expertise, networks). Yet we know little about capital accumulation through global careers, either for the individuals, the organizations or the societies involved. Boat people, whose rickety ships sink or who end up imprisoned in the supposedly free countries to which they headed, are merely the most spectacular examples of loss through failing to understand the probabilities of their investments bearing fruit.

McNulty, de Cieri and Hutchings (2009), having studied the return on investment (ROI) in corporate expatriation programmes for nearly a decade, view global careers – in their various forms, across both company-assigned and self-initiated arrangements – as central to both corporate and individual ROI outcomes.

Clearly, there are benefits to multinational corporations in attracting employees who pursue global careers: such employees typically have a global mindset, international experience, and cultural intelligence and other valuable traits. But the competitive advantage attained by employing global careerists may be short term rather than long term, as these employees move on to opportunities elsewhere. In the long term, an extensive, expensive corporate programme of expatriation may not yield good returns; alternatives, such as relying on local talent, may be much more cost effective. It is incumbent on international organizations to set up systems to monitor continually the ROI of their programmes.

For individuals, the benefits of a global career are potentially immense. In a study of Asia–Pacific expatriate careers, for example, McNulty et al. (2011) found that 87 per cent of expatriates perceived their marketability in the international labour market increased as a result of undertaking an international assignment. For many, however, a return to their home country did not seem a viable option, often – based on their belief that they had outlived their usefulness in these markets – being seen as a potential setback for their longer-term career prospects. These views obviously pose problems for policymakers and others interested in how best to recapture Australia's and New Zealand's 'lost talent'.

In considering ROI at other levels, there are benefits from global careers for governments, particularly those in developing nations (e.g. Thailand, Vietnam) or those markets where skilled talent may be in short supply (e.g. Singapore). The attraction and retention of foreign talent to these shores represent a win–win for those who choose to develop and extend their international experience (e.g. expatriates), as well as the governments that benefit long term from an increased transfer of knowledge. Additionally, there may be benefits to society as a whole wherever global careers are pursued: cultural diversity and tolerance, and inward

FDI to name a few. Again, it is imperative for government decision-makers to be informed by good research.

## 3 Global Careers and Exploitation

Australia and New Zealand are rich, Westernized countries. The Big OE and the ensuing glamorous career development in Europe or America are, by and large, privileges of middle-class, educated white citizens, many of whom report their most riveting and life-changing experiences when they go overseas as being their first encounters with the grinding poverty and dreadful squalor of under-developed countries (Inkson and Myers, 2003). Their optimistic tales of career self-development may conceal a different, more depressing set of career stories. Consider the following case.

---

### Global Careers for the Rich – and Poor

In a luxurious condominium in Singapore live three adults who are pursuing global careers, and three children who will almost inevitably have such a career. Michael and Debra are Australians, married to each other, and they own the condo they live in. Michael is an executive for a major American corporation, which has posted him for 4 years to its operations in Paris, then to Singapore to manage its Asia network. Debra is a 'trailing spouse', a well-educated American-born woman who gave up her career in public relations when her husband was posted abroad, to look after her family. Their son Tyler, ten, and twin daughters Charlotte and Sara, six, are 'third culture kids', having been born, respectively, in each country to which the family has relocated.

The sixth member of the household is Conceptione (Connie), the Filipina maid. Connie was educated as a preschool teacher in her own country and is married with two children, who live with her mother in the Philippines. Given her training, Connie helps with the education of Tyler and the twins, as well as doing much of the family's cooking, laundry and other chores. For this, in addition to her meals and a tiny room in the condo, Connie is paid US$400 a month, approximately 1 per cent of Michael's salary. She remits most of her earnings to her family in the Philippines. Connie has an official visa to be in Singapore, which enables her to be employed as long as Michael and Debra want her. If she can't find another job as a maid in Singapore, she will be deported back to the Philippines. She has been working full time in Singapore for nearly 15 years, with numerous expatriate families, but has no prospect – ever – of citizenship, because her work visa does not allow it.

Recently, Michael was asked by his company to transfer back to Australia. He still has wanderlust and would like to move somewhere more exotic, but Debra would like to resume her career, which would be easier in Australia. And they want to give Tyler a good, stable education as he heads into high school. It's a big decision for all of them. They haven't told Connie yet.

---

This story reminds us that what we think we know about global careers is derived largely from the domain of the advantaged – the educated and the employed, the well-heeled executive 'jet set' – but their careers are often made possible by the efforts of many other 'little people', who may not think of themselves as pursuing careers, but who are, many of them, like Connie, in an international labour market and in foreign settings. In our research, their voice, too, needs to be heard. Accounts of such careers draw attention to the parochialism of much conventional career theory and practice: for example, the assumption that individuals have *freedom* to cross international boundaries, the tendency to neglect the family issues of even individualized Western-style career actors, and the plight of refugees and low-skilled migrants, who think in terms not of 'career' but of 'survival'.

As far as Australia and New Zealand are concerned, even though they probably contribute more global careerists per head of population than any other developed country, it is still only a small proportion of the population that is able to access this opportunity. The disadvantaged of each country, particularly the Aboriginal people of Australia, are unlikely to have to face the decision of in which country it is best to pursue their global careers, or they may pursue such careers only as members of a casual, disposable, secondary workforce.

## 4 Global Careers and Migration Criteria

Because global careers involve ethnic mobility and population mixing and are framed by legislation in various societies that sanctions and/or restricts international mobility, they are inherently controversial and often grounds for intergroup hostility and discrimination.

In New Zealand, for example, local Maori academic Margaret Mutu has been quoted as recommending that her country's government restrict the number of white migrants arriving from countries such as South Africa, England and the United States, as they brought attitudes destructive to Maori, attitudes 'of white supremacy, that is fostered by the country' (*Sunday Star-Times*, 4 September 2011). At the other end of the spectrum, local economist Greg Clydesdale (2011, p. 114) argues that, because of the difficulties that non-white immigrants have in adapting to the dominant culture, migration policies should be 'ethno-centrically biased', favouring immigrants who are 'culturally compatible', i.e. predominantly white Europeans who speak English. However, such a view, apart from being apparently racist, appears to set the immediate accommodation of immigrants above the long-term benefits of ethnic diversity. A third view, the one reflected in the current immigration policies of both Australia and New Zealand, is that skill and expertise related to current economic conditions, and family welfare, are, and should continue to be, the key criteria for the two countries to consider when determining which global careers to encourage into the countries and which to discourage. In this view, short-term language and cross-cultural difficulties must

be resolved from within an increasingly multicultural society, rather than through restricting migration to culturally sympathetic or similar groups.

## Conclusion

The notion of writing a chapter about 'global careers in Australia and New Zealand' is, like that of global careers in any specific country or region of the world, inherently oxymoronic. We have tried to add insights on the issues faced by global careerists who identify Australasia as a region to which to travel, and those faced by Australians and New Zealanders when they embark on international moves, in careers that may become global. We have shown that the issues are especially relevant for Australia, and even more so for New Zealand. We have emphasized that the experiences of our countries' natives and immigrants in pursuing global careers appear to have far more to do with their individual agency and the policies pursued by their governments and other governments than to any policies or practices of international corporations. We look forward to a future where global careers will become even more vital to our two countries, and to completing further research to enable us better to understand them.

## References

Arthur, M. B., Inkson, K. and Pringle, J. K. (1999). *The New Careers: Individual Action and Economic Change.* London: Sage.

Arthur, M. and Rousseau, D. (Eds.) (1996). *The Boundaryless Career: A New Employment Principle for a New Organizational Era.* Boston, MA: Cambridge University Press.

Australian Bureau of Statistics (2003). Population projections Australia 2002–2101, Catalogue #3222.0, ABS, Canberra.

Australian Bureau of Statistics (2004). Australian demographic statistics, March Quarter 2004, Catalogue #3101.0, ABS, Canberra.

Australian Bureau of Statistics (2007). Australian Demographic Statistics, June Quarter 2007, Catalogue #3101.0, ABS, Canberra.

Banai, M. and Harry, W. (2004). Boundaryless global careers: The international itinerants. *International Studies of Management and Organization, 34*(3), 96–120.

Baruch, Y., Budhwar, P. S. and Khatri, N. (2007). Brain drain: Inclination to stay abroad after studies. *Journal of World Business, 42*(1), 99–112.

Bedford, R. (2001). 2001: Reflections on the spatial odysseys of New Zealanders. *New Zealand Geographer, 57*(1), 49–54.

Bedford, R., Ho, E. and Lidgard, J. (2002). International migration in New Zealand: Context, components and policy issues. In G. Carmichael and A. Dharmalingam (Eds.), *Populations of New Zealand and Australia at the Millennium* (pp. 39–68). Canberra: Australian Population Association.

Birrell, B., Hawthorne, L. and Richardson, S. (2006). *Evaluation of the General Skilled Migration Categories,* AGPS, Canberra.

Boneva, B. S. and Frieze, I. H. (2001). Toward a concept of a migrant personality. *Journal of Social Issues, 57*(3), 477–491.

Burke, K. (2011). Supply fails to satisfy skilled labor demand. *Sydney Morning Herald*, 26 July, p. 13.

Business Travel Gulliver (2010). It's Vancouver, again. *The Economist*, retrieved from www.economist.com/blogs/gulliver/2010/02/liveability_rankings, 3 September 2011.

Carr, S., Inkson, K. and Thorn, K. (2005). From global careers to talent flow: Reinterpreting 'brain drain'. *Journal of World Business*, *40*, 386–398.

Clegg, B. and Gray, S. (2002). Australian expatriates in Thailand: Some insights for expatriate management. *The International Journal of Human Resource Management*, *13*(4), 598–623.

Clydesdale, G. (2011). Valuation, diversity and cultural mis-match: Immigration in New Zealand. *Journal of Asia Business Studies*, *5*(1), 98–118.

Committee for Economic Development of Australia (2009). *Growth Report*. Melbourne: CEDA.

Department of Labor (2009). New faces, new futures: New Zealand. Findings from the longitudinal migration survey: New Zealand (LisNZ) – wave one. Wellington, NZ: IMSED Research. Retrieved from http://dol.govt.nz/publications/research/lisnz/, 21 August 2011.

Department of Labor (2011). Why Auckland? Advice and opportunity: A study of why migrants settle in Auckland. Wellington, NZ: New Zealand Department of Labor.

Dickmann, M. and Baruch, Y. (2011). *Global Careers*. London: Routledge.

Doherty, N. (2010). Self-initiated expatriates – Mavericks of the global milieu. Academy of Management, 6–10 August, Montreal, Canada.

Fee, A. and Gray, S. (2011). Fast-tracking expatriate development: The unique learning environments of international volunteer placements. *The International Journal of Human Resource Management*, *22*(3), 530–552.

Fullilove, M. and Flutter, C. (2004). *Diaspora: The World Wide Web of Australians*. Australia: Lowy Institute for International Policy.

Gamlen, A. (2007). Making hay while the sun shines: Envisioning New Zealand's state diaspora relations. *Policy Quarterly*, *3*(4), 12–21.

Gunz, H. P. and Heslin, P. (2004). Reconceptualizing career success. *Journal of Organizational Behavior*, *26*(2), 105–111.

Gunz, H. P., Peiperl, M. and Tzabbar, D. (2007). Boundaries in the study of career. In H. Gunz and M. Peiperl (Eds.), *Handbook of Career Studies* (pp. 471–494). Thousand Oaks, CA: Sage.

Hall, D. T. (1996). *The Career is Dead – Long Live the Career: A Relational Approach to Careers*. San Francisco, CA: Jossey-Bass.

Hamer, P. (2007). *Maori in Australia*. Wellington, NZ: Te Puni Kokiri and Griffith University.

Hofstede, G. (1980). *Cultural Consequences*. Beverly Hills, CA: Sage.

HSBC (2010). *The Expat Explorer's Guide: Expat Economics*. London: HSBC.

Hudson, S. and Inkson, K. (2007). Overseas development workers: 'Big Five' personality scores. *Journal of Pacific Rim Psychology*, *1*(1), 5–9.

Hugo, G. (2002). Emigration of skilled Australians: Patterns, trends and issues. Paper presented to the Conference of the Department of Immigration, Multiculturalism and Indigenous Affairs (Australia) on 'Migration: benefiting Australia', Australian Technology Park, Sydney, 7 May.

Hugo, G. (2006). An Australian diaspora? *International Migration*, *44*(1), 105–133.

Hugo, G. (2008). Australia's state specific and regional migration scheme: An assessment of its impact in South Australia. *Journal of International Migration and Integration*, March, 9, 1.

Hugo, G., Callister, P. and Badkar, J. (2008). Demographic change and international labor mobility in Australasia: Issues, policies and implications for co-operation. In G. Hugo and Y. Soogil (Eds.), *Labor Mobility in the Asia–Pacific Region* (pp. 131–170). Singapore: Institute of South East Asian Studies.

Hugo, G., Rudd, D. and Harris, K. (2003). Australia's diaspora: Its size, nature and policy implications. Canberra: Committee for Economic Development of Australia.

Hutching, M. (1999). *Long Journey for Sevenpence: An Oral History of Assisted Immigration to New Zealand from the United Kingdom, 1947–1975*. Victoria University Press.

Hutchings, K. (2005). Koalas in the land of the pandas: Reviewing Australian expatriates' China preparation. *The International Journal of Human Resource Management, 16*(4), 553–566.

Inkson, K. and Arthur, M. B. (2001). How to be a successful career capitalist. *Organizational Dynamics, 30*(1), 48–61.

Inkson, K., Arthur, M. B., Pringle, J. K. and Barry, S. (1997). Expatriate assignment versus overseas experience: Contrasting models of human resource development. *Journal of World Business, 32*(4), 351–368.

Inkson, K., Carr, S., Edwards, M., Hooks, J., Jackson, D., Thorn, K. and Allfree, N. (2007). The psychology of migration and talent flow: A New Zealand perspective. In I. Glendon, B. Thompson and B. Myors (Eds.), *Advances in Organizational Psychology* (pp. 301–321). Bowen Hills, QLD: Australian Academic Press.

Inkson, K. and King, Z. (2011). Contested terrain in careers: a psychological contract model. *Human Relations, 64*(1), 37–57.

Inkson, K. and Myers, B. (2003). 'The big O.E.': International travel and career development. *Career Development International, 8*(4), 170–181.

Inkson, K., Ganesh, S., Roper, J. and Gunz, H. (2010). *The Boundaryless Career: A Productive Concept that May Have Outlived its Usefulness*. Academy of Management, Montreal, August.

IOM (2011). About migration. Retrieved from www.iom.int/jahia/Jahia/about-migration/lang/en, 19 August 2011.

Ip, M. (2000). Beyond the 'settler' and 'astronaut' paradigms: A new approach to the study of the new Chinese immigrants to New Zealand. In M. Ip, S. Kang and S. Page (Eds.), *Migration and Travel Between Asia and New Zealand* (Vol. 1, pp. 3–17). Auckland, NZ: Asia-Pacific Migration Research Network.

Khoo, S.-E., McDonald, P., Voigt-Graf, C. and Hugo, G. (2007). A global labor market: Factors motivating the sponsorship and temporary migration of skilled workers to Australia. *The International Migration Review, 41*(2), 480–510.

King, M. (2003). *The Penguin History of New Zealand*. Wellington, NZ: Penguin Mass Market.

Larner, W. (2007). Expatriate experts and globalising governmentalities: The New Zealand diaspora strategy. *Transactions of the Institute of British Geographers, 32*(3), 331–345.

McClelland, D. C. (1953). *The Achieving Society*. New York: van Nostrand.

McNulty, Y., de Cieri, H. and Hutchings, K. (2009). Do global firms measure expatriate return on investment? An empirical examination of measures, barriers and variables influencing global staffing practices. *The International Journal of Human Resource Management, 20*(6), 1309–1326.

McNulty, Y., De Cieri, H. and Hutchings, K. (2012). Expatriate return on investment in the Asia Pacific: An empirical study of individual ROI versus corporate ROI. *Journal of World Business, 48*(2) [http://dx.doi.org/10.1016/j.jwb.2012.07.005].

Meares, C., Ho, E., Peace, R. and Spoonley, P. (2010). Bamboo networks: Chinese employers and employees in Auckland. Integration of Immigrants Programme Research Report No.1/2010. Albany: Massey University/University of Waikato.

Mercer (2011). *HR Atlas Asia Pacific*. Geneva: Mercer.

Oliver, P. (2000). Employment for professional migrants to New Zealand – barriers and opportunities. Wellington, NZ: Center for Operational Research and Evaluation.

Organization for Economic Co-operation and Development (2007). *International Migration Outlook*. Paris, France: OECD.

Peiperl, M. A. and Baruch, Y. (1997). Back to square zero: The post-corporate career. *Organizational Dynamics, 25*(4), 7–22.

Perrin, R.-L. and Dunn, K. M. (2007). Tracking the settlement of North African immigrants: Speculations on the social and cultural impacts of a newly arrived immigrant group. *Australian Geographer, 38*(2), 253–273.

Salt, B. (2008). *The Global Skills Convergence: Issues and Ideas for the Management of an International Workforce*. Switzerland: KPMG.

Schein, E. H. (1993). *Career Anchors: Discovering Your Real Values* (revised ed.). London: Pfeffer & Co.

Selmer, J. and Lam, H. (2004). 'Third culture kids': Future business expatriates? *Personnel Review, 33*(4), 430–445.

Skeldon, R. (2010). Managing migration for development: Is circular migration the answer? *The Whitehead Journal of Diplomacy and International Relations, 11*(1), 21–33.

Sullivan, S. E. and Baruch, Y. (2009). Advances in career theory and research: A critical review and agenda for future exploration. *Journal of Management, 35*(6), 1542–1571.

*Sunday Star-Times* (2011). Curb white immigrants: Academic, 4 September. Retrieved from www.stuff.co.nz/auckland/local-news/5561230/Curb-white-immigrants-academic, accessed 13 July 2012.

Suutari, V. and Taka, M. (2004). Career anchors of managers with global careers. *Career Development International, 23*(9), 833–847.

Tharenou, P. and Caulfield, N. (2010). Will I stay or will I go? Explaining repatriation by self-initiated expatriates. *Academy of Management Journal, 53*(5), 1009–1028.

Tharenou, P. and Harvey, M. (2006). Examining the overseas staffing options utilised by Australian headquartered multinational corporations. *The International Journal of Human Resource Management, 17*(6), 1095–1114.

Tharmaseelan, N., Inkson, K. and Carr, S. C. (2010). Migration and career success: Testing a time-sequenced model. *Career Development International, 15*(3), 218–238.

Thomas, D. C. and Inkson, K. (2007). Careers across cultures. In M. Peiperl and H. Gunz (Eds.), *Handbook of Career Studies* (pp. 451–470). Thousand Oaks, CA: Sage.

Thorn, K. (2008). Flight of the Kiwi: An exploration of motives and behaviours of self-initiated mobility. Doctor of Philosophy, Massey University, Auckland.

Thorn, K. (2010). Mobility patterns in international careers: Boomerang movers and global nomads. Paper presented at the European Group on Organizational Studies, Lisbon Portugal.

Tung, R. L. (2008). Brain circulation, diaspora, and international competitiveness. *European Management Journal, 26*(5), 298–304.

United Nations (2010). Human Development Report. Retrieved from http://hdr.undp.org/en/reports/global/hdr2010/chapters/en/, 18 August 2011.

Wilson, M. G. and Parker, P. (2007). The gap between immigration and employment: A policy-capturing analysis of ethnicity-driven selection biases. *New Zealand Journal of Employment Relations, 32*(1), 28–34.

# 9

# GLOBAL CAREERS IN PORTUGAL

*Susana Costa e Silva,*[1] *Catholic University of Portugal, Paulo Duarte, University of Beira Interior, Portugal, and Sílvia Ferraz, Unicer – Bebidas, SA, Portugal*

## Introduction

People have always moved from the place where they were born to different locations all over the world. In most cases, the main reason for this decision is the search for a better life. Portugal is no exception. Emigration has always been present in Portuguese society. More recently, with firms taking a leading role in business scenarios, a new approach to international mobility has started to gain relevance. In this chapter, we will focus on global careers in the Portuguese context. We will explore how Portuguese people have always been fascinated with travel to new destinations, meeting different cultures, and sharing knowledge. This ancient Portuguese travel practice is somehow the ancestor of today's global careers, where people move from one country to another, following a firm's international movements. People involved in these global working movements are known as expatriates, and they form the centerpiece of this chapter.

The viewpoints and perspectives expressed in this chapter are, of course, those of the authors and are rooted in a range of theoretical and empirical evidence taken from three main sources: (1) a review of the pertinent literature on expatriation and secondary data available on the emigration and expatriation phenomenon; (2) a survey of 133 Portuguese expatriates; and (3) 12 in-depth interviews given to company managers and employees involved in the expatriation process. Table 9.1 presents a summary of the profiles of the interviewees.

The information from the in-depth interviews was analyzed and has been incorporated into the text to support our theories and viewpoints about the role of expatriation in the development of global careers and the problems, benefits, and challenges associated with it, namely expatriates' satisfaction.

**TABLE 9.1** Profile of the interviewees

| | Name of company | Age | Gender | Country | Job |
|---|---|---|---|---|---|
| 1 | MTF | 35 | Male | Portugal | Administration |
| 2 | MTG | 58 | Male | Portugal | Administration |
| 3 | UC | 56 | Male | Mozambique | Country manager |
| 4 | HGT | 33 | Male | Mozambique | CEO |
| 5 | AMBX | 39 | Male | Netherlands | CFO |
| 6 | EFRUE | 43 | Male | Belgium | Representative of the Finance Ministry in the EU |
| 7 | CBG | 40 | Male | Serbia | CMO |
| 8 | JM | 39 | Male | Poland | CPO |
| 9 | EFC | 32 | Female | USA | Sales account manager |
| 10 | FF | 47 | Male | Argentina | CFO |
| 11 | AMR | 34 | Male | Denmark | Project manager |
| 12 | ALT | 33 | Female | Brazil | Project manager |

To ensure the readers' comprehension of the Portuguese tradition in global movements, we will begin this chapter with the country's historical, economic, and social backgrounds and current developments in the economy and labor market. Thus, in the following sections, an overview of the migration phenomenon in Portuguese society throughout the centuries will be presented, along with the current state of the global mobility of the Portuguese people. We will also discuss the challenges faced by all those engaged in expatriation processes and provide the results of a study addressing the satisfaction of Portuguese expatriates. Finally, the chapter concludes by presenting some critical perspectives on expatriation and global careers. We believe that this work will contribute to an improved school of thought on the intercultural mosaic portraying the current world scenario.

## The Situation of Global Careers in Portugal

Since its origins, emigration has been a very well documented topic and, in today's economic scenario, it has become an even more sensitive phenomenon, especially owing to the humanitarian perspective it involves. However, the focus of this chapter is different: it focuses on the phenomenon that involves the employees of an organization—employees who were initially hired to work in one country and were later assigned to work and live in a country other than the one where they were initially working and living, regardless of the duration of the expatriation experience. According to Freitas (2000), the process of expatriation is the transfer of a company worker based in one country to work for a subsidiary of the same company or group located in another country.

Portugal (see Table 9.2 for some figures) has always presented traits of an open economy, considering the amount of imports and exports in its GDP. The degree of openness of the Portuguese economy at the end of the 1990s oscillated between 35 and 37.5% of GDP and, in 2010,[2] was 38.2% and 31%, respectively, for imports and exports, but the financial crisis that reached Portugal in 2007–2008 produced significant consequences in terms of employment. In early 2012, the unemployment rate reached 14% among the general population and a disturbing 35.4% among youth. Many Portuguese firms became bankrupt, and many others underwent internal reorganization processes that led, in some cases, to labor insecurity. According to EuroFund data, in Portugal, 54% of the lost labor was due to bankruptcy that occurred after the crisis. Facing this harsh crisis, the firms that survived had almost no alternative other than to turn their hope to the external markets.

This is the reason internationalization has been referred to in all government speeches as a way out of the current crash. The main director of the Managerial Association for Innovation (translated), COTEC Portugal, advocated that firms should improve their competitiveness levels by crossing borders, adding that the solution for the problem lies in conquering markets worldwide.

The idea of Portuguese firms considering pursuing an internationalization strategy is not a new concept. However, it is expected that firms will pursue this type of strategy more pro-actively in the future, either through equity or non-equity joint ventures or the creation of sales or production subsidiaries, as the financial crisis of 2008 is still affecting the Portuguese economy severely, causing a wide range of domestic problems specifically related to the levels of public deficit in the economy, forcing companies to search for new opportunities in the global

**TABLE 9.2** Portugal in figures

| *Area* | *92,072 km²* |
|---|---|
| Population | 10.6 million |
| GDP | €158 billion |
| GDP by sector | Services: 74.5% |
| | Industry: 23% |
| | Agriculture: 2.6% |
| Unemployment rate | 14% (January 2012)* |
| Weekly average working time | 35.1 h |
| Structure of employment | Agriculture 11.2%; industry 28.2%; services 60.6% |
| Government deficit (2009) | €15.7 billion (9.3% of GDP) |
| Public debt | 82.1% of GDP |
| Foreign residents | 4.3% |

* According to www.ine.pt/ngt_server/attachfileu.jsp?look_parentBoui=135252337&att_display=n&att_download=y

*Sources*: Eurostat, Pordata, INE, Banco de Portugal

market. These entry modes involve more resource commitment and more risk than simple export, but they also involve greater levels of control over international operations, a scenario that did not take place beforehand, or took place to a lesser degree. Furthermore, many SMEs have started to develop active ways of seeking international opportunities, through both supply and demand operations.

This intensification of international moves has also been driven by contextual factors, such as ease of transport and communication making economies around the world more strongly intertwined. This has driven companies towards a competitive environment where the location to compete stopped being the domestic market and started being the so-called "global village." With the emergence of new marketplaces, firms seem to have no alternative other than to consider the worldwide market as their competition arena, definitively burying the concept of "domestic" market, only to be replaced by the concept of "international" market. Portuguese firms are also following this globalization tendency, and this is the main reason why most of them have been internationalized, in many cases, since their origins. In fact, Portugal has always been an open economy, and this has been shown, not only by the existence of many exporting firms in the country, but also by firms that are determined to grow internationally.

Portugal has indeed been trying to accomplish this. In the first three months of 2011, sales from outside Europe represented an increase of 15%. Thus, it is expected that internationalization, either through exports or through foreign direct investment, is now, more than ever, a top priority for firms, as a measure needed to face a difficult and shrinking domestic market. As the situation is similar in many other European countries, the journey of many firms in their internationalization process is taking them to some very different locations. Currently, a new group of countries, such as Brazil, Mozambique, and Angola, are high on the list of countries with increased potential for the international expansion of Portuguese companies. These new locations have also developed owing to the existence of certain cultural affinities, in some cases, resulting from past connections either with Portuguese-speaking African countries or Brazil.

The internationalization of Portuguese companies beyond simple export is rather a recent event. Even though international joint ventures (IJVs) are not that young (take the example of the IJV between Unilever and Jerónimo Martins, which is more than 80 years old), Portugal has few companies and brands that are globally known. We lack the Danish Lego, the Swedish Ikea, or the Finnish Nokia, to mention a number of companies from small countries. All these companies have been established on the world market for decades and are widely known and respected. Unfortunately, we do not find similar examples from the Portuguese industry. However, as the individual and collective experience of Portuguese companies increases, they are advancing into new markets and are employing more sophisticated modes. In some cases, companies began by

establishing offices in Spain, owing to the geographical proximity, and then moved into new markets, as was the case of Cimpor and Petrogal. Other companies decided on more distant locations, such as Poland (Jerónimo Martins), Morocco (Valouro), or Macau, China, and the United States (Efacec), to name but a few. This tendency was reinforced further by the latest economic developments on the Portuguese market that caused the growth opportunities within Portugal to diminish, as well as the maturity that some Portuguese firms have started to display, thus exhibiting competencies that the international market values. As a result, many firms are now creating subsidiaries overseas and, in some cases, they are also sending their employees to work at their new sites located all over the world.

An excellent example of the capability of the Portuguese to succeed in the global market is Portugal Telecom (PT). The Portuguese communications company currently has a dominant position in Africa, where the firm owns relevant stakes in different countries. Angola is one of its main markets, with PT owning 25% of Unitel, a cell-phone company with an estimated market share of 65%. This firm alone is responsible for 5.7 million clients and profits of €1.120 million. In Angola, the firm also has 40% of Multitel (data and ISP) and 55% of Elta (yellow and white pages). PT also owns stakes in other Portuguese-speaking countries. We are referring to: São Tomé and Principe and Cape Verde—with profits of €83 million—and Macau, East Timor, and Brazil. In Africa, the Portuguese group also has important positions in Namibia, where it reaches €124 million profits.

This is why, in many cases, it is said that Portuguese firms are rediscovering Africa and Brazil. The choice of these markets as receptors of the Portuguese internationalization process is also due to the fact that the crisis is affecting these countries less than other locations in Europe and the US, markets with which Portuguese firms had always exchanged business. So, these locations are now becoming the new place of employment for some Portuguese people.

## Portuguese Global Moves—A Long-Standing Tradition

Given the particular characteristics of the Portuguese people, for centuries going off on an adventure has been part of tradition. Portugal is a small country, with a total area of only 92,207 km², and yet Portugal benefits from an excellent geographical location, standing in a geo-strategic position between Europe, America, and Africa. Portugal is located at the very western extreme of Europe, and this has driven the desire of its people to broaden their minds and seek other cultures outside of Europe. Furthermore, the extreme location of the country has meant that other European locations have been considered almost as other countries, not part of the European continent. Therefore, for Portugal, its sharing a border with only one country has never held back its citizens. This geographical openness has turned into a cultural curiosity and has subsequently become part of Portuguese tradition. The beginning of Portugal's pioneering role in world exploration, usually termed Portuguese discoveries, may be traced back

to as far as 1279, when King Diniz set out to improve Portugal's emerging navy. The major improvements, however, were made after 1415, by Prince Henry the Navigator, who set Portugal on its course towards overseas expansion. The Portuguese were the first Europeans to visit Japan, arriving in 1543. This intangible cultural heritage has been passed on from generation to generation and is still alive in contemporary Portuguese culture.

There seems to be no doubt that the Portuguese people have always been curious about far-off, distant places, and this has driven some of them to move to different places, where, merely for the fun of it, or out of necessity, they have ended up settling. There are several ways of viewing this Portuguese characteristic of going abroad. On the one hand, there is the history of the migration movement that has always led people to be open-minded when it comes to the fulfillment of their professional interests. When job opportunities are not entirely satisfactory in a country, mainly owing to economic downturn, people take the risk of going abroad and looking for better opportunities in a foreign country. This has been a tendency in Portugal, demonstrated many times in its history.

The dispersion of the Portuguese people into the world is well known, following the discovery era and the expansion of trade in the fifteenth century; since this time, migration has become a historical constant. In the first half of the sixteeth century, the Portuguese people were spread throughout the different continents, representing about 10% of the population. In the mid eighteenth century, when the population of Portugal stood at 2.1 million, it is estimated that approximately 1.3 million Portuguese people were immigrants. With the advent of the industrial revolution, this exodus took on larger proportions, and it is estimated that, from 1855 to 1973, the overall level of emigration exceeded 4 million, which is more than any other Western European country. Initially, this movement was mainly to the US and to Brazil—it was characterized by migration to Brazil in the 1930s and to Europe, US, and Canada in the 1960s and 1970s.

After World War I, Portuguese emigration was predominantly to European countries. In the late 1950s, Portuguese emigration started to increase and follow labor-market demands toward new destinations in the expanding economies of Northern and Central Europe. By the late 1960s, an estimated 80% of Portuguese emigrants went to Europe. Many of these emigrants did so illegally, without the required documents, because the lure of Europe's prosperity was too strong to be resisted. During this period, France was the most popular destination. By the early 1970s, it was estimated that 8% of Portugal's population lived there. Between 1960 and 1970, more than 1.5 million Portuguese emigrated to take up jobs in low-wage, low-productivity sectors. Several factors contributed to this scenario, but the main reasons for this significant emigration movement were, in fact, the colonial war and political persecutions by the country's dictatorial regime that lasted from 1926 to 1974, combined with the deterioration of economic conditions (Morgado, 2011).

Portuguese emigration slowed in the mid 1970s. This was owing to two factors. The first was an economic crisis in Europe's major economies that led them to close their doors to foreigners in 1973, and the second factor was the Portuguese Revolution in April 1974, which brought down the dictatorship. The Revolution of 1974 resulted in the deterioration of economic and social conditions, which caused a slight rise of emigration in the late 1970s, but it never again reached the levels of the 1960s and early 1970s. During the 1980s, the rate of emigration slowed as the economy began to grow. Since then, emigration has been moderate, ranging between 12,000 and 17,000 a year in the 1980s. However, Portuguese emigration did not cease at this time, and even increased in the late 1980s and early 1990s. This movement, marked by some peaks in history, took place regularly, and at the time was mostly perpetrated by blue-collar workers. By the early 1990s, when Portugal was able to take advantage of the European Union's Schengen Agreement, which makes crossing European borders and European citizens' mobility much simpler, there was a reduction in emigration. In the late 1990s, the number of Portuguese residents in foreign countries highlights the size and importance of Portuguese emigration. There are currently about 4.6 million people of Portuguese origin living on the five continents, namely Europe (1,336,700), Africa (540,391), North America (1,015,300) South America (1,617,837), Central America (6,523), Asia (29,271), and Oceania (55,459).

During the 1990s, a change in the profile of emigrants was also evident, characterized by an increase in the proportion of females, rising skill levels, and the dominance of temporary migration to other EU member states. This trend has continued, and today we are able to witness a new emigration wave characterized by emigration flows of highly educated people who go abroad looking for professional opportunities that Portugal seems to be unable to provide. This latter trend has also been regarded as an opportunity to develop personal competencies, such as multiculturality and languages. Moreover, we have been able to see more young Portuguese following international trends, such as stylish fashion. There are more and more firms looking for internationally experienced people, and, therefore, according to the opinion of some interviewees, going abroad is no longer regarded as a secondary alternative to working in one's native country, but rather as an opportunity to gather knowledge, know-how, and competencies that are otherwise impossible to experience.

Indeed, we may say that globalization produces, among other things, increased international labor mobility. As more people are transferred from one place to another, it becomes more relevant to study the conditions associated with the global movement experience and expatriates' satisfaction. In fact, global labor mobility has become a very important topic in organizations, societies, and people's lives all around the world.

## Portuguese Global Moves Today

According to a recent International Assignments Survey (Mercer, 2010), expatriate employee numbers have grown greatly, and organizations see relevant value in expatriate assignments.

Working internationally can happen through a number of means, expatriation being only one of these ways. The concept of expatriation has been outlined by Stahl, Miller, and Tung (2002) or Cappellen and Janssens (2008) in different ways. One major distinction between the concepts has to do with the distinction between corporate-sponsored expatriation and self-initiated expatriation, depending on who initiates the process. Another key distinction relies on the time horizons, which can be radically different—usually a period between 6 months and 5 years. For example, Dickmann, Doherty, Mills, and Brewster (2008) found that the self-initiated foreign workers they examined had, on average, stayed 6 years in the host country. In the case of corporate expatriation, the length of stay can change from case to case and depends upon a variety of factors, both strategic and operational. However, the distinction is not always simple. Consequently, the plethora of expressions used in relation to people working abroad can be confusing, and this specific issue deserves more attention from researchers, who should agree on a set of objective criteria to assess the ambiguity surrounding these concepts. For the sake of the present study, we will consider expatriates as those employees sent by a firm that originally hired them to work and live in a different country.

Such studies devoted to this issue focus on expatriation costs and risks (Selmer, 1998), as well as presenting expatriation as a means to fulfill global careers, which are two important issues for both organizations and individuals (Larsen, 2004). For the expatriate, mobility to fulfill international assignments is only a stage in the development of a global career (Dickmann et al., 2008), as was confirmed by our interviews. In this perspective, which goes beyond the expatriation cycle itself (Harris, Brewster, & Sparrow 2003), repatriation is often not the end of the process, but just a transitional phase in the development of global careers. Some of our interviewees have jumped from one company to another, some even without coming back to Portugal.

From the firm's perspective, the expatriation motives can be divided into strategic and operational. The strategic reasons might include, among others, control and coordination objectives (Edstrom & Galbraith, 1977); knowledge creation, transfer, and use (Bonache & Zarraga-Oberty, 2008); and global leadership development (Gregersen, Morrison, & Black, 1998). Operational reasons might include filling open positions quickly, with a person in possession of the required qualifications, or in order to launch new businesses (Carpenter, Sanders, & Gregersen, 2001). These reasons were also identified among our interviewees, who stated that they favor the use of expatriates to fill higher-level management functions, whereas for other functions it was no longer so imperative.

For example, they consider that the person in charge should always be a Portuguese national, because it is a position of trust. The financial controller is usually a Portuguese national too. For more technical positions, it is common to hire local people, as the risks involved are smaller. Our findings for Portugal are consistent with a global relocation survey that found that the most common assignment objective was filling a skills gap (29%) (GMAC, 2008).

It is within this context that the expatriation phenomenon becomes important. Indeed, even when Portuguese firms have in their target market the resources necessary to develop their activities, it frequently occurs that, in the early stages of the process, they employ more expatriates than in the later stages of the internationalization process. Of course, there is a difference in the use of expatriates based on destination regions. Whereas Portuguese investments in Western Europe and North America tend to be based on the recruitment of nationals of these countries, in less developed economies, the employment of expatriates is more frequent, as it is more difficult to find people with the right skills and experience.

A more recent trend in Portugal is the decrease in corporate-sponsored expatriates. Although the Portuguese Labor Code (Law 07/2009 of February 12) provides companies with the possibility of assigning international positions to their employees, and the government has allowed the deduction of expatriate expenses to be increased by 120% for the 2011–2013 period, some companies still favor the direct hiring of workers by their company based on the country of destination. The choice depends largely on the tasks to be developed. For example, if the relationship with banks is important, it is better to work with an expatriate, but, if what is most important is the relationship with local councils, then in this instance it is preferable to work with locals.

The decision to employ expatriates or hire local people is a very important decision, one that managers of Portuguese firms actively considering the establishment of a unit in a different country have to take into account. The reality shows us that, in less developed countries, such as the ones that more recently seem to be the actual destiny of much Portuguese international investment, the preference is for expatriates. This is also true in the initial phases of the project, owing to the initial lack of knowledge about local resources and also owing to the need to be in charge of these operations. Expatriates carry with them know-how and the firm's values and beliefs, and this is very important when establishing and settling business abroad, at least during the initial period. Indeed, even though expatriation is expensive and requires special attention in terms of career management, the Portuguese managers interviewed recognize it as an important option to consider, given the higher product and firm knowledge displayed by expatriates and their loyalty to the firm. They are also more familiar with the culture of the firm and they allow higher levels of control from headquarters.

The choice of expatriation is supported, in general, by the need to further anchor the new company management models and values of the parent company, in particular through the creation of a direct control network and the diffusion

of knowledge. People going abroad as corporate-sponsored expatriates face less risk than those having to look for a job upon their arrival. Also, the organization of their personal lives (for example, accommodation, transport, etc.) is taken care of to some extent, if they have been specifically relocated by a company. Such people tend to display characteristics that Portuguese firms consider to be fundamental: they are motivated to work for the firm in a venue located in a different country.

The decision by Portuguese workers to accept an expatriation assignment is normally taken when it is considered that the time abroad is limited, the conditions to succeed abroad are in place, and a better position is likely on their return. In addition, Portuguese expatriates seem to value this as a professional and personal experience that is difficult to obtain in their own country. Thus, expatriation also seems to be important as a means of career development. According to Tomás (2009), expatriation is also a means of motivating and retaining talented workers, and it is no longer an option exclusive to firms that operate internationally, but is also an individual option for career development.

According to Tanure, Evans, and Pucik (2007), for human resource management (HRM), the biggest challenge in organizational instruments is the management of expatriation. This is particularly true in the early stages of a firm's internationalization process, where difficulties regarding adaptation to the new context may become an obstacle. As stated before, Portuguese people are, for historical reasons, well adapted and able to embrace global careers, as this is part of their culture, and they tend to possess specific characteristics that provide them with the ability easily and *successfully* to adapt to new cultures. Usually, Portuguese people do not have major problems with foreign languages or with the absence of Portuguese food. However, the selection of individuals with the appropriate profile for expatriation is not easy and imposes different requirements. It is necessary to find people with the right profile, where flexibility, empathy, and cultural and motivational characteristics seem to be critical factors in the selection. An expatriate with the adequate profile must have to be Portuguese in Portugal, Angolan in Angola, Brazilian in Brazil, and Polish in Poland, but always have a multinational vision.

Portuguese expatriates tend to value family support and comfort. An adequate school for children and a working position for the wife or husband are important decision factors, as the family provides very important support in the expatriation process. In the selection process, attention must also be given to the candidate's interests and personal development plans, as well as the structure of the candidate's family. When the expatriate's family also moves to the new destination, family size should also be taken into account, to provide them with adequate living conditions.

In order to facilitate integration, prior action should to be taken to familiarize the expatriate with the language and culture of the host country or region, as well as to provide him/her with training and the development of specific skills

that are critical in order to succeed. On the other hand, career management and rewards are also key factors to consider in the context of expatriation. Companies should ensure that they effectively evaluate and reward the results produced by the expatriate. A progressive career structure should also be defined that allows the expatriation period to be integrated successfully into both the career-development process of the individual and the organization.

The story of Nuno Nogueira illustrates the importance of the prior action taken by companies to facilitate the integration process and increase the satisfaction of the expatriate.

## A Global Employee: The Case of Nuno Nogueira

Nuno Nogueira was born in 1972 in the city of Porto, where he lived up to the age of 26. Nuno graduated in management and business administration in 1996. Three years later, he moved to Sines and got a position as manufacturing controller at Borealis, an Austrian–Norwegian–Emirate company. While holding that position, Nuno had the chance to learn about finance, performance management, and production processes. In 2000, the company moved him to the head office in Copenhagen, to become business unit controller. There, he learnt how a global manufacturing company is managed and how people from all over the world can work together.

As far as the expatriation experience in Copenhagen is concerned, Nuno considers it to have been very positive. He was welcomed to the town by a person from a company dedicated to the integration of foreigners that move to Copenhagen. This person accompanied Nuno during all the processes of integration, helped him with all bureaucratic matters, helped him to find accommodation, and even assisted him as he did his first shopping in a country where the language spoken is not easy . . . During this first experience abroad, Nuno considers himself to have grown a lot as a person. He also had the chance to improve his English, to travel around, and to meet other people from different cultures. As for the firm, he also enjoyed working in a big, multinational firm, which was very competitive and challenging. He was able to develop technical skills related to the area in which he was working. His responsibility in the firm increased as time went by. Borealis took care of Nuno's accommodation needs by providing him with a centrally located apartment, a car, and an interesting fringe-benefit package that included training, sauna, massages, and access to different sport practices. This was, according to Nuno, definitively a firm oriented to receive expatriates.

With regard to the professional experience, Nuno highlights the experience he gained professionally as well as as an individual. This international experience opened up new vistas to Nuno. After his return to Porto in 2004, he worked independently as a certified public accountant and professional trainer. Six years later, he was asked to go to Amorim Benelux in the Netherlands, where he is currently financial manager, in charge of the financial and logistics departments. The initial integration was smoother than in the previous case, because Denmark

and the Netherlands have some similarities. Amorim, a Portuguese firm, supported him with the initial integration but did not provide all the services previously provided by Borealis. However, he is not complaining, especially as his experience of living abroad is also enlarged now. In terms of assignments, Nuno says he has lots of responsibility, but also autonomy in his job.

Nuno, who considers himself a privileged man, currently lives with his wife and 1-year-old daughter, in Bergen op Zoom, a small town near Antwerp, that is centrally located, as are many cities in the Netherlands. He is trying to learn Dutch and developing new relationships, both with locals and with other foreigners also living in the Netherlands. He says that the Netherlands is an easy country that welcomes foreigners. It is very central and has direct flights to Portugal and other European countries. From where he lives, it is very easy to go to Paris, Brussels, Amsterdam, Frankfurt, or London. He can choose to go home for the weekend or visit these places. In the Netherlands, as in Denmark, the language is strange for foreigners, but, in both countries, the local people speak English fluently. In both countries, social equity is also well established, which is something that Nuno values. With regard to tolerance, pragmatism, and social courtesy, Nuno says that the two countries are different. Whereas the Dutch display great openness towards foreigners, the Danes tend to be more reserved. He speculates that it may be that the Dutch colonial experience made them more cosmopolitan. In any case, the largest difference, he says, is the comparison of both cultures with the Portuguese. He claims that, in Portugal, people are more into the use of titles, display great power distance, and don't have a positive view of their own country. Still, he misses his relatives and friends and has to overcome these feelings with the happiness of having his family living with him abroad, along with the working freedom that he has always valued.

The compensation needed in terms of human resources in the context of internationalization is also a sensitive issue, because of the increased costs arising for the company. In addition to other expenses, there are values that Portuguese companies usually accept in relation to salary that may double the salary in Portugal. For example, in Timor, Portuguese expatriates receive, as a rule, almost double the salary that they received in Portugal, mainly because of country risk and distance. Now, in Europe, an expatriate typically receives about 70% more. The increased compensation is not only necessary to ensure recognition of skills and results, but also the conditions for an adequate standard of living, regardless of the country where the expatriate is placed. The 70% increase in salary paid by Portuguese companies may seem a lot in countries such as Romania, but, in Bucharest, it is not such a significant increase, and, in cities such as London, some companies even provide expatriates with support for food and accommodation and even some pocket money.

A critical dimension in the management of expatriates has to do with the repatriation process. In some cases, an unsuccessful expatriation experience may

lead to an early return. Such situations might be the result of one or more components that were not properly managed, and, with some frequency, after returning, many employees leave the company. It is important that Portuguese companies plan the return carefully. Portuguese expatriates typically have high expectations concerning the repatriation process, but nowadays this is not the case, because companies no longer have the ability to integrate all the returning expatriates. That is, repatriation has begun to be a problem, and this has made Portuguese companies start to rethink their strategies for expatriation, in order to contain these negative feelings of frustration.

## Portuguese Expatriates in the World

The number of expatriates in the world seems to have doubled in the last 3 years, according to data from Mercer (2010). Mercer also conducted a study in Portugal that concluded that almost 80% of the firms that use expatriation are considering increasing the number of expatriates, and 50% of those firms are thinking of doing so in new locations.

There is also an additional motive to study this movement of people around the world, other than the strategic motives associated with the use of expatriates by firms that have an international scope. According to the consultancy company Mercer, in a survey conducted in 2008 of 94,000 expatriates worldwide (GMAC, 2008), it was possible to verify that expatriate numbers had doubled from 2005 to 2008. In addition, according to another study conducted by GMAC (Global Relocation Services) in 2011, one of the major trends identified is that expatriation figures are expected to maintain a growth rate of around 60% in 2011. The other trend points out that China and Brazil are expected to be the most important expatriation destinations.

An important finding from surveys conducted by GMAC (2008, 2011) is that the costs involved in expatriation and global careers are expected to decrease as a response to the current economic problems. This situation has also led individuals to broaden their horizons in terms of career development and to look beyond the boundaries of their native countries. It was also possible to observe that, in many cases, family resistance, family adjustment, and local country diffi-culties are the most commonly cited issues working as obstacles to expatriation.

Portugal is no exception, and research has shown that, as with other European countries, there has been an increased trend in the number of employees who are sent to work abroad. According to a study conducted by Mercer in Portugal, in 46% of the cases, the firms examined have fewer than 10 expatriates; however, around half of them are expecting to have a presence in new destinations in the next couple of years.

According to Mercer's (2009) latest study published on this subject, specifically for the Portuguese case, we can see that long-term expatriation (between 6 months and 5 years) is a common practice in 95% of national and multinational companies

located in Portugal, and short-term expatriation (2–6 months) stands at 71% (see Figure 9.1).

Regarding the destinations of Portuguese expatriates, Mercer's 2009 study indicates that, of the Portuguese companies (national and multinational) with expatriates, all of them have sent employees to work in Europe (100%), which is understandable in view of the proximity. The remaining major destinations for Portuguese expatriates are Latin America (48%) and Africa (43%), owing to cultural and linguistic affinities, and North America (43%) for historical reasons. In 2010, the percentage of Portuguese expatriates sent to Europe decreased to 78%, but, in contrast, expatriation to Africa has increased to 56%. There is also a significant percentage of expatriates in Asia, partly as a consequence of the Portuguese presence in Macau.

Next, we present the case of Tânia Fernandes, who can be considered a long-term expatriate, as she has lived and worked in the United States for 7 years.

Contrary to what happened in the past, where expatriation was primarily associated with positions of high responsibility—usually directors and general managers—currently, the process of international mobility is also available to employees with profiles associated with lower levels of responsibility. Expatriation processes are increasingly open to more junior employees, who are still in the early stages of their career. Mercer's (2009) survey suggests that the main motives

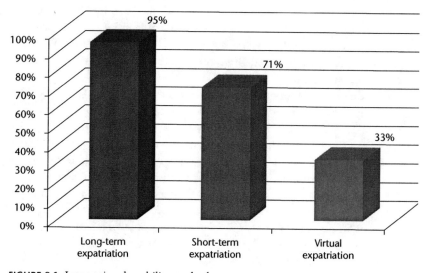

**FIGURE 9.1** International mobility outlook

Note: The sum of percentages exceeds 100%, as companies may have more than one motive for expatriation

*Source*: Adapted from Mercer (2009), International Assignments Survey Portugal; information available at: www.mercer.pt/articles/1361170 and accessed October 23, 2011

# A Global Employee: The Case of Tânia Fernandes

Tânia Fernandes is a 32-year-old Portuguese currently living in Savannah, where she has a position as sales account manager. Tânia was born in Braga, 50 km from Porto, the second largest city in Portugal, where Tânia completed her degree in international relations, economic and political branch, in 2000. In 2001, she started working in the marketing and sales back office at Efacec Energia for the Spain and Latin America market; in 2005, she joined marketing and sales, responsible for the North America market. Tânia started at Efacec when the company was already growing its internationalization strategy, and she was able to develop competencies at several levels, specifically in business development and in the contact with partners from all over the world. Efacec is a Portuguese group formed in 1948 and today is present in more than 65 countries, with over 4,500 employees and a turnover that exceeds €1 billion. The firm is active in several fields, from energy, engineering, and services to transport and logistics. After 8 years working at Efacec, Tânia had the opportunity to pursue an international career. She was offered the position of sales account manager with Efacec USA, Inc., where she moved to in January 2010.

Concerning her experience abroad, Tânia directly refers to how difficult it has been to be away from her relatives, and the fact that the US is a long way from Portugal. This makes visits very difficult, which, added to the fact that she lives alone, may create some emotional discomfort, as she says. This also means that she spends much more time working than she is expected to, because working is a compensation for isolation. However, with regard to integration, she says the fact that she already knew the US very well, as she had frequently traveled there, helped a lot. Obviously, a period of adaptation was necessary. Frequently traveling to a certain location is not the same thing as living effectively there. However, the adaptation was easy. Tânia was already able to speak the language fluently. Also, the company gave her important support.

Regarding the location, more specifically Savannah, there are no complaints—the place is developed, safe, and with all kinds of infrastructure and means. She refers to the fact that culturally there exist some differences between Americans from the South and those from elsewhere. She points out the accent and people's traditions. They are very affable too. The food, however, is not something that Tânia relishes that much . . . Referring to her social life, Tânia confesses that it revolves a lot around Efacec employees, especially the other expatriates. As the work involves a lot of traveling, Tânia has not been able to settle into too many new friendships. Traveling also has positive elements, and she names specifically the possibility of getting to know all the beautiful things that the US has to offer. She enjoys the country so much that, even on her holidays, she stays around to discover new places.

Professionally, the project that she embraced is very challenging. The start was complicated because she was involved in the creation of all the infrastructure from scratch. Also, there were some difficulties related to the specificity of the product that demanded people with lots of experience in all areas of the project. Dedication to work was crucial in the initial stages of the greenfield, and this made expatriates work harder than locals.

Weighing up her stay in the US so far, Tânia highlights the development that she has been able to use to assist her professional career. She has been able to develop many skills, both professional and personal. The workflow didn't get better, nor did her responsibilities. However, she now feels much more confident and autonomous in her decision-making. Tânia had high expectations regarding her future when she was invited by the firm to move to the US. She had to lower them, because she now admits to having faced more difficulties than she was expecting. She confesses that her expectations at the beginning were higher in terms of the recognition she was expecting to get from the firm. At present, she knows her mission is still to be in the US. However, she feels like she has to expand the periods spent in Portugal.

for expatriation are business development, the transfer of technology and know-how to local companies, and the professional growth of expatriates (see Figure 9.2).

International assignments are often associated with significant financial and non-financial benefits. For example, achieving a position at the same level as the one some professionals have in their global careers would be almost unthinkable in Portugal. In respect of financial benefits, according to Suutari (2003), differences in cost-of-living and taxation practices across countries can have a considerable

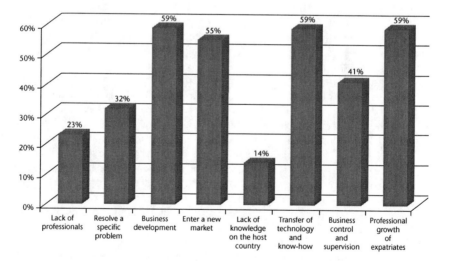

**FIGURE 9.2** Main motives for expatriation

Note: The sum of percentages exceeds 100%, as companies may have more than one motive for expatriation

Source: Adapted from Mercer (2009), International Assignments Survey Portugal; information available at: www.mercer.pt/articles/1361170 and accessed October 23, 2011

impact on the expatriate's standard of living. One of the primary factors taken into account by the prospective Portuguese expatriate is the extent to which his/her overall living situation will be affected by the specific assignment (McCallum & Olson, 2004). On the other hand, as stated before, the compensation in terms of human resources in the context of international mobility is a highly sensitive issue, as it should balance the cost-of-living differential and simultaneously compensate the impact of the change on the expatriate, his/her family, and friends, but also take into account the increased costs arising for the company. In fact, about 71% of Portuguese companies said that the greatest difficulty with expatriation processes was the costs involved (Mercer, 2010).

The majority of Portuguese companies with expatriate employees (67%) make adjustments in the fixed remuneration of the employee, taking into account the cost-of-living differential between the home country and city and the host country and city, in order to maintain the purchasing power of the employee (Mercer, 2009); however, only approximately half (48%) take into account the quality-of-life differential. Good expatriate *packages* come in many forms. The most common benefits associated with expatriation provided by Portuguese companies are company-sponsored accommodation, company car, and health and life insurance. Some also include in the package a retirement plan, child-education expenses, and extra support for all family members (Mercer, 2009).

Over the next two years, 47% of Portuguese companies expect to increase the number of expatriates sent to new destinations, and, furthermore, between 2008 and 2011, most companies have tended to increase the number of expatriate employees (79%). During this 3-year period, most of the companies (67%) questioned increased the number of expatriates, and 36% indicated that they intended to increase the number of female expatriates. It should be noted that, 5 years ago, only 22% of Portuguese companies had female expatriate employees, compared with 34% today (Mercer, 2010).

Considering the increased importance that expatriation and the development of global careers have gathered worldwide, and the different spheres of repercussion in societies and organizations and on individuals, it is evident that the topic of expatriates' satisfaction needs further research, as little is known about the satisfaction of Portuguese expatriates and what motivates them to accept an international assignment. The existing relevant literature on expatriation and satisfaction suggests that an expatriate's global satisfaction can be seen as the result of personal satisfaction, professional satisfaction, and satisfaction with the host country. Upon examining the research carried out in this area, it became evident that it is a multifaceted concept, with several dimensions. We conducted a survey of Portuguese expatriates to understand what generates their satisfaction. Based on 133 valid responses, we found that the major contributor to Portuguese expatriates' global satisfaction is professional satisfaction, followed by satisfaction with the host country. Personal satisfaction represents the lowest contribution.

The value of monetary compensation and its contribution toward professional satisfaction is an additional dimension of this phenomenon. McCallum and Olson (2004) indicate that financial incentives play a significant role in attracting individuals to international assignments. However, in our case, the interviewees' responses did not allow us to confirm this theory. In fact, several interviewees downplayed the importance of the monetary compensation for expatriation. They consider that monetary compensation is obviously important professionally, but is not the most important factor in their satisfaction. What seem to be determinants of their satisfaction are professional challenge and the perspectives of professional growth. For many Portuguese expatriates, monetary compensation is more a means than an end in itself.

## Structural, Cultural and Contextual Difficulties

Currently, there are not many job opportunities in Portugal similar to the ones that can be had in other countries. Within the context of the sovereign debt crisis in the euro area, the Portuguese economy projections published by the Portuguese Central Bank point to a contraction of the Portuguese economy in 2012, followed by a virtual stagnation in 2013. This contraction of economic activity, which has no precedent in the Portuguese economy, translates into a significant decline in domestic demand, both public and private, within a framework of adjustment of basic macro-economic imbalances.

As a member of the European Union, Portugal has a work system similar to other European countries, especially those in Southern Europe, both in terms of architecture and solutions. Moreover, the country's integration into the EU led to the inclusion of a number of European directives relating to labor relations, which are of common application within the European area.

With regard to the labor market, the Bank of Portugal's current projection points to a reduction in employment of 1.8% and 0.6%, respectively, in 2012 and 2013 (following a fall of 1.0% in 2011), which is the result of economic downturn. Unemployment is particularly acute among youth, and 40% of high-school graduates have no job. If they have a job, then they only earn about €1,000 per month. The average income in Portugal is €850, and 56% of 15–34-year-olds live with their parents.

According to the latest bulletin from the Bank of Portugal, in 2012, the magnitude of the employment contraction will be similar in both the public and private sectors, whereas, in 2013, it will be more intense in the public sector. In this way, the contribution of the work factor to the evolution of GDP should remain negative. In this context of adverse conditions, especially in the labor market, and in particular with a strong increase in unemployment, Portuguese families will face a reduction in real wages in the public and private sectors, being particularly tough in 2012. In this context of tough economic conditions, Portugal does not seem an attractive country to migrate to. Nevertheless, Portugal has

long been a top choice for workers and businessmen looking to live in mainland Europe. Despite the economic issues, it is a great place to live, owing to the great beaches, historic sites, wonderful food, friendly people, and lively culture.

In order to settle down, there are some formalities required. If the immigrant is from Europe, he/she has to take his/her passport to Portugal's immigration office, the *Serviço de Estrangeiros e Fronteiras* (SEF), and sign a statement that he/she is working or studying in the country. He/she will also be asked for bank statements, or some other proof that he/she can be self-supporting while living in Portugal. Once this process has been completed, immigrants are usually given a 5-year residency permit, which they can later trade for permanent residency. It is fairly easy to survive in Portugal just by speaking English, but social and professional opportunities will expand tenfold if the immigrant has another means of communicating with locals.

A significant development for foreign workers expatriated to Portugal was the approval of Decree Law 249/2009, dated September 23, 2009 (DL 249/2009), by the Portuguese government. This measure was designed to boost Portuguese tax competitiveness by establishing an attractive tax regime for expatriates. The basics of this Portuguese expatriate tax regime are as follows: A special expatriate tax regime (the non-habitual residents' regime) applies to inward expatriates who arrived in Portugal on or after January 1, 2009. Under the new regime, income related to work or services rendered in Portugal is subject to a flat rate of 20%. Other Portugal-sourced income is subject to the same taxation as income acquired by Portuguese residents. Foreign-sourced income is exempt in Portugal if, generally speaking, it is taxed or may be taxed in the source country. An expatriate, however, may elect to renounce the exemption (credit for foreign taxes will be given instead). The regime will be applied for 10 consecutive years to individuals who have not qualified as Portuguese residents in the 5 preceding tax years. Regarding the cost of living, there are a few price differences when compared with other EU countries. However, expats point to income tax, social security, fuel, and rent as the biggest living expenses in Portugal.

Still the financial weaknesses have stayed high, when economics dictates that they should have dropped, like incomes have. Shopping around is essential, as prices can vary by several euros within a block. Finally, the expatriate should think of the lifestyle that he/she will want to lead in Portugal and focus on learning the culture and making friends with locals, and he/she will soon be living like everyone else and feeling right at home.

## Critical Perspectives

The expatriation process begins with two main challenges: (1) Selecting people based on certain criteria that are pertinent to their performance in the host country; and (2) Choosing the best candidate who will be able to adjust most effectively to the new sociocultural environment. However, it is not merely a matter of

finding the right people. It encapsulates a process that needs to be carefully managed throughout. Indeed, it is true that the selection process often fails to consider factors such as the intercultural skills of the candidate and the willingness of the candidate's family to live in a foreign country.

However, performance during an expatriate mission is conditioned by an expatriate's characteristics and personal relationships. In addition, it also depends on his/her level of sociocultural adjustment to the host country. In fact, companies should invest more substantial efforts in assessing these factors. The selection of individuals with the appropriate profile for expatriation imposes requirements that go beyond the mastery of language or technical skills. Attributes such as a tolerance for ambiguity and uncertainty, cultural empathy, flexibility, and motivation are critical determinants for the selection. It is very important to define the profile very clearly from the start, because there are people who have the desired profile, but there are also others for whom the idea is not even feasible.

However, during this process, it is necessary to consider other issues, such as the interests and personal development plans and the core structure of the applicant's family. It was observed that some companies do not provide adequate support for training, or opportunities to become involved in local activities, to their employees who are sent abroad. If such measures are taken, it reduces the risk of failure of expatriated employees. The lack of company support was mentioned by some of our interviewees, in the same way that the complete support given by one firm to one of our interviewees was considered fundamental. Many Portuguese companies do not provide adequate support to expatriates. Within these companies, the expatriation process is not subject to any management support, which is a practice that deserves to be revised. According to Joly (1996), living abroad, especially in a culture very different to one's own, is an experience that might plunge an expatriate into some confusion. In the beginning, it is difficult to build a structure from scratch and, even worse, in a country that one does not know very well.

Career management and reward are also key factors to consider in the context of Portuguese expatriation. Career management is crucial for an employee's loyalty to the firm, and it should include preparation for the journey to the new country, the integration of the expatriate, and the preparations for his/her return. However, it seems as though more and more Portuguese companies are spending fewer resources on these types of activity, on the basis that it is part of the employee's task/responsibility to adjust to the environment and to absorb the costs associated with this. Some of them are also reducing the cost of expatriates, not just because they are able to find more qualified people in the host country, but also because there is a lack of jobs in Portugal, and people are willing to accept a position, regardless of its location.

In fact, for the same positions, earnings are comparatively smaller in Portugal than in other countries. If someone cannot find a job that is compatible with his/her qualifications in Portugal, he/she has to look for one abroad. Thus, they

may opt to apply for foreign jobs, competing with local people for a position. As this often involves qualified candidates, the challenge of securing a job outside of Portugal may be easier than securing one at home.

Regarding the repatriation process, it is clear that it is a critical dimension in the management of expatriates. Particularly critical are the cases of expatriation failure (early return), which are often the result of one or more components that were not properly managed. However, even in the case of a successful experience, the relationship with the firm is frequently ended following the repatriation experience. In fact, some expatriates interpret the end of their mission abroad as the end of their professional avenue. They do not envisage any further challenges within that particular career path and with that company and perceive it as the end of a cycle. Therefore, it is important that Portuguese companies prepare for an expatriate's return and plan it accordingly, anticipating such negative feelings of frustration. An employee who has returned from an expatriation experience will certainly have gained valuable knowledge that can be shared across the firm. Given the current economic conditions, many Portuguese firms can no longer absorb all the repatriates; at least, providing them with further progression in their career is not always an option. Furthermore, it is difficult to predict a position within the parent company 3, 4, or 5 years in advance. Each return should therefore be managed on a case-by-case basis. However, under normal circumstances, Portuguese companies should apply some rules: the rule is that the expatriated employee should be able to return to the same position that he/she held in the host country; there must be effective means, formal or informal, for the returnee to transmit acquired knowledge to other employees in the company; and the expatriate who returns must be given priority on the list of future expatriates to be sent to other countries, if the experience has been positive for him/her and profitable for the company.

The principal problem, and undoubtedly the most cited factor faced by Portuguese expatriates, concerns the provisions made for their families. The majority of our responses indicate that close proximity to their family is key for their satisfaction. Family support is crucial to the emotional balance of the expatriate and his/her professional performance. The satisfaction of the family is also considered very important for the satisfaction of the individual. This means that, in order to accommodate this specific issue, Portuguese firms have to spend additional money, which makes expatriation an even more expensive alternative.

Despite the importance placed on family, Portuguese expatriates are, in some cases, willing to sacrifice their family life to gain professional recognition and develop their careers. For most of them, professional career development takes priority. This specific aspect of their behavior could have an impact on future family and social values. Children raised in an environment where one of the parents is persistently away may develop emotional disorders. On the other hand, we have also verified that, in other cases, it is the strength of the family that helps some Portuguese expatriates to withstand the difficulties experienced during their

professional assignments. One interviewee specifically states that his being away allows his family members to have a better quality of life than if he were working in the home country. Another Portuguese expatriate interviewed said that the only reason he accepted such a heavy work load was because his family was very well integrated into society and this was the main reason why, at that moment, a return home or a change of country/town was out of the question.

## Conclusions

The interviews and the survey have uncovered a set of interesting issues on the reality of Portuguese expatriates, which deserve to be further analyzed. Expatriate satisfaction is one of these issues. We have realized that, despite the intention expressed by some firms to increase the number of expatriates, the truth is that many are currently weighing up the alternative situation of hiring people from the host country. Such employees would work directly for the subsidiary company, be paid in the local currency, according to local labor rules, and pay taxes in the host country. This way, even if the firm provides some initial support concerning integration, there is no further commitment in terms of the possible reintegration of the employee into the headquarters at the end of the contract. This shift is mainly because employees in Portugal, especially the most qualified ones, are now facing difficulties in securing a satisfactory position at home, and companies are also having to deal with the economic crisis and are looking for all possible means to cut costs. Therefore, regarding this issue, we understand that the future will bring a new wave of what can be labeled as "expatriates" —a combination of expatriates (employees who are introduced to the venue and the firm where they are going to work by a firm in their host country) and emigrants (employees who are not given any additional support by the firm, and where there is no further commitment in place with the mother firm, in the original country).

Concerning the managerial findings, it is important that firms assess if they are truly aware of the conditions that promote expatriate satisfaction, or if they are merely concerned about their own business performance. Some companies, judging by the statements obtained, do not provide an adequate level of support to expatriate employees, considering that such support goes beyond monetary assistance. Others do provide such support, and it is highly appreciated. Factors related to personal satisfaction need to go beyond organizational responsibilities, and the truth is that only the factors that contribute directly to company goals are prioritized. It would be useful if expatriation management policies were integrated into a company's corporate social responsibility reports. After all, these are also issues of social responsibility.

Furthermore, with regard to expatriates, some of them seem to be obsessed with the development of their professional career to such an extent that they are willing to sacrifice other aspects of their lives and the lives of their family.

Therefore, the question is, to what extent is it worth such a sacrifice, and for how long is it possible to sustain such a situation? Are they going to be absolutely overwhelmed after a certain period of time away from their families? It may be the case that, after a certain period of time away, under these conditions, expatriates no longer want to work for the firm and have to consider moving away. We were able to verify that, when families are not around, expatriates tend to work longer hours, occupying all their available time at work and therefore working towards securing a better position in their careers. This is a phenomenon that could spiral out of control and lead them to "burn out". This may be the reason behind the decision that some expatriates have made to move from a subsidiary company, to a multinational company, and then finally to a local firm. If this were the case, they would at least be provided with the same conditions as local employees, in particular their more moderate working hours.

In conclusion, our findings suggest that the global satisfaction of expatriates depends mostly on professional satisfaction, to a lesser degree on their level of satisfaction with the host country, and even less so on their personal satisfaction. Our interpretation of this interesting result is that many expatriates are prepared to sacrifice their personal interests to build a successful professional career that may provide them with some benefits in the future. Thus, it seems that Portuguese expatriates are more driven by the results the expatriation experience may allow them to attain in the future than with enjoying the journey that leads them there.

## Notes

1. Corresponding author.
2. Source: Outlook for the Portuguese Economy: 2011–2013, from the Bank of Portugal. Retrieved from www.bportugal.pt/en-US/EstudosEconomicos/Publicacoes/Boletim Economico/Publications/projecoes_e.pdf, accessed October 23, 2011.

## References

Bonache, J. and C. Zarraga-Oberty (2008). "Determinants of the success of international assignees as knowledge transferors: A theoretical framework." *The International Journal of Human Resource Management* 19(1): 1–18.

Cappellen, T. and M. M. Janssens (2008). "Global managers' career competencies." *Career Development International* 13(6): 514–537.

Carpenter, M., W. G. Sanders, and H. G. Gregersen (2001). "Bundling human capital with organizational context: The impact of international assignment experience on multinational firm performance and CEO pay." *Academy of Management Journal* 44(3): 493–511.

Dickmann, M., N. Doherty, T. Mills, and C. Brewster (2008). "Why do they go? Individual and corporate perspectives on the factors influencing the decision to accept an international assignment." *The International Journal of Human Resource Management* 19(4): 731–751.

Edstrom, A. and J. R. Galbraith (1977). "Transfer of managers as a coordination and control strategy in multinational organisations." *Administrative Science Quarterly* 22: 248–263.

Freitas, M. E. d. (2000). *Como vivem os executivos expatriados e suas famílias?* São Paulo: Núcleo de Pesquisas e Publicações - Fundação Getúlio Vargas.

GMAC (2008). Global relocation trends: 2008 survey report. Woodridge, IL: GMAC Global Relocation Services.

GMAC (2011). Global relocation trends: 2011 survey report. Woodridge, IL: GMAC Global Relocation Services.

Gregersen, H. B., A. J. Morrison, and S. S. Black (1998). "Developing leaders for the global frontier." *Sloan Management Review* 40(1): 21–33.

Harris, H., C. Brewster, and P. Sparrow (2003). *International Human Resource Management.* London: Chartered Institute of Personnel and Development.

Joly, A. (1996). Alteridade: Ser executivo no exterior. O *indivíduo na organização. Dimensões esquecidas.* J.-F. Chanlat. São Paulo: Atlas: 83–124.

Larsen, H. H. (2004). "Global career as dual dependency between the organisation and the individual." *Journal of Management Development* 29(9): 860–869.

McCallum, B. and D. Olson (2004). "Advising potential expatriate clients: A case study." *Journal of Financial Planning* 17(11): 72–79.

Mercer (2009). International assignments survey Portugal 2009. Lisbon: Mercer.

Mercer (2010). International assignments survey Portugal 2010. Lisbon: Mercer.

Morgado, F. I. (2011). "Tempo de exílio." *Latitudes* 11: 20–22.

Selmer, J. (1998). "Expatriation: Corporate policy, personal intentions and international adjustment." *The International Journal of Human Resource Management* 9(6): 996–1007.

Stahl, G. K., E. L. Miller, and R. L. Tung (2002). "Toward the boundaryless career: A closer look at the expatriate career concept and the perceived implications of an international assignment." *Journal of World Business* 37(3): 1–12.

Suutari, V. (2003). "Global managers: Career orientation, career tracks, life-style implications and career commitment." *Journal of Managerial Psychology* 18(3): 185–207.

Tanure, B., P. Evans, and V. Pucik (2007). *Gestão de pessoas no brasil: Virtudes e pecados capitais.* Rio de Janeiro: Elsevier.

Tomás, J. R. (2009). Expatriação em recém licenciados: Um trajecto profissional ambicionado ou aproveitado? Projecto de investigação sobre atitudes culturais e âncoras de carreira. *Secção de Psicologia dos Recursos Humanos, do Trabalho e das Organizações.* Lisbon: Universidade de Lisboa.

# 10

# GLOBAL CAREERS

## The Russian Experience

*Konstantin Korotov, European School of Management and Technology, Germany, Sheila M. Puffer, Northeastern University, USA, Daniel J. McCarthy, Northeastern University, USA, and Vlad Vaiman, Reykjavik University, Iceland*

## Introduction

This chapter deals with the Russian perspective on global careers by focusing on the unique Russian context, which is central to understanding the factors that advance or hinder the global careers of Russian employees. Given adverse country conditions for developing global careers, such as the highly hierarchical structures of Russian business and prevalent nepotism, many Russians choose to go abroad, on either a temporary or permanent basis, to commence their global careers. Those who stay in Russia, however, often prefer to work for Russian subsidiaries of Western multinationals, as most of them offer clear, merit-based career development paths, a benefit that may also lead to expatriation. The chapter also provides recommendations to Russian executives and policymakers on how to curb the current brain drain of top Russian talent.

The first section of the chapter provides an overview of global careers in Russia. Taking the concepts of boundaryless and protean careers as a point of departure, the authors note nine key career attributes (career definition; objective career; objective career success; subjective career; subjective career success; and three intelligent career investments of knowing why, how, and whom; as well as mobility) important to understanding changes in Russian career behaviors as the country shifted from a command-and-control to a market-based economy.

The second section examines the major factors influencing global careers for Russians and, illustrating with brief case studies, describes several career paths that these global careers may take. This section ends with an analysis of key career strategies, as well as major challenges that Russians have to overcome to initiate and develop their global careers.

The third section introduces critical perspectives on global careers in Russia, from the viewpoint of the country's institutions and organizations, and especially its HR policies and practices. The authors argue that two major challenges distinguish Russian companies from their Western counterparts. The first challenge relates to both the perceived low significance of human resource management (HRM) and the subsequent low level of investment in human resources, particularly in management development. The second challenge, which is also of critical importance to both local and foreign firms making sizeable investments in Russia, is motivating and retaining young, talented employees. Beyond these two challenges, another more recent critical perspective on global careers recognizes that Russians may find it increasingly more difficult to build global careers in the future, owing primarily to the diminishing prestige and quality of Russian tertiary education. The chapter ends with a more positive view, however, stating that, despite many challenges and obstacles for Russians trying to build their global careers, the situation may be improving somewhat, as the country becomes more involved in the global business arena.

## The Situation of Global Careers in Russia

Russia is a country that has undergone radical change in its socio-economic system, societal values, human identities, and the way people define themselves and the work they do. In the late 1980s and early 1990s, the country embarked on the precipitous route of developing a market economy, with the consequences affecting the way organizations function and people work. As a successor of the Soviet Union, Russia inherited a significant portion of former Soviet territory and natural resources, industrial facilities, research and education establishments, and a large portion of the USSR's population.

The population of Russia is about 142 million people, with approximately 73% living in urban areas (Rosstat, 2012). As of September 2011, 76.6 million economically active inhabitants were between the ages of 15 and 72, about 54% of the total population (Rosstat, 2011). The 2011 reported unemployment level was about 6.8% of the economically active population, down from 7.5% in 2010 (*CIA Factbook*, 2012). Russia has one of the highest literacy rates in the world, with over 99% of the population age 15 and above being able to read and write (*CIA Factbook*, 2012). This circumstance has led to Russia having a highly educated workforce. The OECD 2010 Country Statistical Profile for Russia reported that the percentage of the population aged 25–64 in 2007 that had attained tertiary education was 54.9. Tertiary entry rates in peer age groups in OECD countries averaged about 66% (OECD, 2010).

The Russian government generally does not provide reliable statistics on the number of Russians studying abroad, but, according to 2010 data from host countries and Russian organizations supporting candidates for study abroad, about 14,000 Russians were studying in the UK (Yudina, 2010). Those studying

in Germany numbered about 12,000 (Karbasova, 2010), with approximately 11,000 Russians studying in China (Yudina, 2010). Approximately 5,000 Russians were studying in the US, about 0.7% of the total number of foreign students in that country (IIE, 2010). France was hosting about 4,000, Canada around 3,000, and South Korea, Finland, and the Czech Republic approximately 1,100 each (Yudina, 2010).

## Relevance of Contemporary Career Concepts for Global Careers in Russia

Global careers can be seen as one manifestation of what others have called boundaryless careers and protean careers. A boundaryless career has been described as being "one of independence from, rather than dependence on, traditional organizational career arrangements" involving "opportunities that go beyond any single employer" (DeFillippi & Arthur, 1996: 116). Similarly, a protean career is one

> driven by the person, not the organization, and that will be reinvented by the person from time to time, as the person and the environment change. (This term is derived from the Greek god Proteus, who could change shape at will.)
>
> (Hall, 1996: 1)

A later work elaborated that,

> the protean careerist is able to rearrange and repackage his or her knowledge, skills, and abilities to meet the demands of a changing workplace as well as his or her need for self-fulfillment. The individual, not the organization, is in control of his or her career management and development.
>
> (Sullivan & Baruch, 2009: 4)

This is essentially the pattern that we have observed among Russians pursuing global careers.

It might be assumed that the 52,000 Russian students studying abroad would be excellent candidates to pursue global careers, as well as their predecessors and successors pursuing education in other countries. Their exposure to foreign cultures and institutions, possibly including private companies, would provide substantial background for pursuing that demanding path. Nine key career attributes typically found in the career research literature can be used to understand changes in Russian career behaviors as the country moved from a command to market-based economy (Khapova & Korotov, 2007). The choice of career attributes for that analysis was driven by their popularity and active use in the work of career scholars in the West (Arthur, Claman, & DeFillippi, 1995; Arthur, Hall, & Lawrence,

1989; Arthur, Khapova, & Wilderom, 2005; Barley, 1989; Baruch & Dickmann, 2011; DeFillippi & Arthur, 1996; Inkson & Arthur, 2001; Van Maanen, 1977). Khapova and Korotov (2007) continued the relatively thin stream of research on Russian careers (e.g., Bozrikova, Doctorova, & Lebedev, 1990; Jones, 1991; Kets de Vries, Shekshnia, Korotov, & Florent-Treacy, 2004; Michailova & Worm, 2003; Scorikov & Vondracek, 1993; Yakubovich, 2005). Their work also identified differences and dynamic changes in how the Western career-research concepts are viewed and perceived in Russia. The following nine concepts were analyzed: career definition, objective career, objective career success, subjective career, subjective career success, and three intelligent career investments of knowing why, how, and whom; as well as mobility.

One of the insights of this work was that the meaning ascribed to these concepts varied among chronologically different career-development periods in Russia: the Soviet period from the 1920s to the early 1990s, the transition years of 1990–2000 as a more market-based economy developed, and the current period since 2000. Interestingly, even the connotation of the term "career" has been changing. In Soviet times, for instance, the notion of careerism or anything related to proactive management of one's career was perceived as negative, because of the fear of standing out and the lack of meaningful opportunities for managing one's career. The meaning of the career concepts mentioned above are summarized for these three periods in Table 10.1 on p. 190 (Khapova & Korotov, 2007). However, currently and even earlier, the career concepts and career paths followed may also reflect differences in individuals and opportunities, such as relying upon parents' valuable connections, simply seeking money-making opportunities, and following a more traditional, Western-style career path.

As can be seen in Table 10.1, career concepts in Russia are still in flux. As a result, one can expect significant variance in attitudes and behaviors of career actors, managers, and HR professionals. There are certainly Russians who still expect a career to be provided to them, others who wait for the next opportunity that seems to be more attractive and seize it, and also people who take proactive steps in managing their careers. Only a few Russian career actors demonstrate career attitudes and engage in career behaviors that can be fully compatible with global careerists in other parts of the world.

Russians working towards building global careers are generally people who show career behaviours similar to those of individuals in other parts of the world. For most Russians, a global career is associated with the ability to find stable employment abroad and to remain employable outside of Russia. However, among those employed abroad, some return to Russia, often continuing to work there for a significant amount of time before returning to employment abroad. This is in contrast to students studying abroad, who often prefer to remain in the host country (*Economist*, 2011), similar to expatriates, including students, from many countries who prefer to remain abroad, essentially causing a brain drain for their

## A Global Academic Career Success

In 2010, the Nobel Prize in Physics was awarded to two Russian-born scientists, Konstantin Novoselov and Andre Geim, for their pioneering work on graphene, a material used in a large variety of industrial and consumer applications, from personal computers to solar cells to aerospace. Both physicists were educated in one of the premier Russian universities and both agree that their education was truly second to none in terms of its quality and worldwide recognition. Despite this, Konstantin and Andre emigrated from Russia some time ago and are now happily employed as professors at Manchester University in the UK, and their immediate plans do not include returning to their native country any time soon. The main reason behind their decision to leave and to remain abroad was the inability of Russian state-owned research institutes to provide adequate working conditions and clear career advancement opportunities for their top talent.

(Sources: Antonova, 2010; Podorvanyuk, 2010; Royal Swedish Academy of Sciences, 2010)

countries (Baruch, Budhwar, & Khatri, 2007). The desire of many Russian scientists to remain in the US working for high-technology companies has been seen as stemming from the corporate cultures and other organizational aspects of those companies. Such conditions have been viewed as providing respect for, and trust in, scientists, which is unusual for Russian organizations (Ataiants & Olimpieva, 2011). The same favorable conditions can also be found in Western universities, a vivid example being described in the box above, regarding two Nobel Prize-winning Russian scientists who chose to remain in the UK rather than return to Russia.

Regardless of whether global careerists choose to remain abroad or return to Russia, an important feature of a global career is one's perceived employability outside of the home country. Also, a relatively limited number of people may be located in Russia but work globally, in virtual teams or on a project basis. Although, in the past, this pattern was noticeable primarily among musicians, singers, and artists, such opportunities are now available for some highly qualified professionals, such as management consultants, IT specialists, educators, and salespeople.

The changes in Russia's socio-economic system and the relatively rapid pace of economic development enjoyed by the country since the early 2000s have also created positive conditions for career entrepreneurship (Korotov, Khapova, & Arthur, 2011). That term refers to taking career steps that may seem unconventional from the perspective of age, level of experience, or cultural or socio-economic background, with career entrepreneurs essentially pursuing opportunities beyond the resources they controlled at the time. Two examples of such risk takers are provided in the following boxes.

**TABLE 10.1** Meanings of career attributes in Russia over time

| Definitions | Soviet times (1920–1990) | Market transition period (1990–2000) | Currently (since 2000) |
|---|---|---|---|
| Career definition | A sequence of positions occupied by a person during his or her life, as well as the mechanisms of survival in occupational and social structures | A collection of steps and activities aimed at increasing one's earning opportunities | A sequence of choices and decisions in selecting one's work activities and career-development opportunities |
| Objective career | Degree of employee's contribution to the attainment of collective goals, as assessed by the authorities | Attaining material wealth through increased earning opportunities. Gaining new status symbols associated with work-related activities and progression | Progressing in accordance with one's set of expectations and career choices made |
| Subjective career | Associated with the content or prestige of work for some occupations (e.g., arts, research, military), or with availability of free time and opportunity to pursue other interests. In other occupations, stability and lack of need to worry about getting employment | Tied to opportunities to pursue a new lifestyle and also pursue further growth | Associated with the feeling of importance, meaning, intellectual challenge, and opportunities for further growth |
| Objective career success | Rewarding with acceptance by authorities, status, salary, and responsibility | Material rewards, work-related perks | Material rewards, employability, freedom to choose |

| | | | |
|---|---|---|---|
| Subjective career success | Following, at least partially, one's passion, regardless of the administrative or ideological barriers | Lifestyle opportunities, perception of future growth opportunities | Perceived rightfulness of choices made |
| Knowing—why | Diffused vocational identity and external locus of control | Search for a number of options; development of multiple possible selves | Development of a marketable professional identity |
| Knowing—how | Job-related skills and knowledge development. Mastery of Communist Party parlance and rules of the game | Job-search skills. Mastery of business language vocabulary. Quick learning of new business skills | Leadership skills, management skills at international level. Recognition, and mastering networking and personal marketing skills |
| Knowing—whom | Prevalence of informal support systems: relatives and friends | Development of formal and informal networks (e.g., executive search and placement agencies) | Increasing countrywide or global visibility. Development of multiple networks of contacts with various stakeholders |
| Mobility | Low geographical (including international), sectoral, and occupational-skill mobility | Increased level of geographical mobility (towards Moscow, St Petersburg, other large cities, and abroad); high level of sectoral and occupational-skill mobility. Early signs of movement from multinational to local employers | Growing geographical mobility towards and away from traditional centers; increasing international mobility. Decreasing sectoral and occupational-skill mobility. Increasing mobility from multinational to local employers |

*Source:* Khapova, S. N. & Korotov, K. (2007)

## Career Entrepreneurship: Doing What Others Don't Dare

Hakop is the marketing director of creativity at a global luxury-goods company. In the late 1990s and early 2000s, the small number of Russians pursuing self-initiated (as opposed to company- or government-sponsored) MBA degrees abroad were generally seeking jobs in banking or consulting, choosing primarily the UK or the US as a destination for career pursuit. In contrast, Hakop chose to specialize in marketing and begin his post-MBA work in France, despite that country's significantly higher barriers for obtaining work and residence permits for Russians. Hakop later returned to Russia and immediately enjoyed a significant career advantage owing to the limited supply of marketers with Western education and experience. He achieved outstanding job results. Importantly, however, obtaining a high level of responsibility for marketing in Russia, and later in Central and Eastern Europe, allowed him to use his talent without waiting for such an opportunity to be given to him. He also gained visibility in Russia and, importantly, inside the global organization where he worked. His career entrepreneurship meant that he found an opportunity to demonstrate his skills and motivation, without waiting for years for such an opportunity to materialize, displaying his propensity for taking risks to advance his global career.

(Source: Khapova & Korotov, 2007)

## Career Entrepreneurship: Engaging Connections

A second example of career entrepreneurship, encountered in our consulting practice, is that of Lina, a Russian in her early 40s. When she was at the university, she took an optional course in Hungarian. She liked the language, but initially didn't see any particular use for it. However, through her university teachers, she had found temporary jobs interpreting for Hungarian writers visiting the Soviet Union. One of them was Árpád Göncz, a famous Hungarian writer who had been imprisoned after protesting against the 1956 Soviet invasion. Lina helped Göncz as his interpreter during his visit to Latvia, where a play of his was staged. Lina became enthusiastic about his play and translated it into Russian and got it published. Less than a year later, Árpád Göncz became the president of Hungary. Lina, who was taking a semester-long course in Hungary to improve her language further, contacted the president. As a result of that contact, she obtained a teaching position in a Hungarian university and stayed in the country for several more years, before marrying a Russian diplomat and eventually moving on with her husband. She too displayed the risk-taking propensity of an entrepreneur and utilized it to enhance her career.

## Structural, Cultural and Contextual Opportunities and Difficulties of Global Careers in Russia

A typical way for a Russian to prepare for a global career is through education. A Russian may go abroad to study and, upon graduation, find a job outside Russia. He or she may then follow a traditional developmental path in the organization, and, at some point, may be given an assignment outside the country where s/he

was originally hired. A traditional expatriate career path, with its opportunities and risks, then ensues. If the person is successful, the succession to a global role or development of global employability typically follows. Global companies with significant interests in Russia may hire Russian graduates of international or local business schools outside Russia, give them a developmental position at headquarters or in a large operating unit, and work on preparing that person for a later move to Russia to occupy a position of significant responsibility. Some individuals who start their careers in Russia may eventually grow into a regional-level position, usually in countries of the Commonwealth of Independent States and/or Eastern Europe. An example of this path is described in the following box.

---

## From Experience Outside Russia to a General Management Position Back Home

Boris graduated from the chemistry department of Moscow State University and then went to complete his Ph.D. in life sciences in the US. Working towards his degree in California, he met with a number of local entrepreneurs and fell in love with the idea of life sciences as a business. He reinforced his scientific training with selected classes from a local business school and, upon graduation, without much hesitation left academia and went to work for one of the start-ups, specializing in the business rather than research side of the company. Enjoying success in his sales work, he decided to deepen his business acumen and went on for an MBA degree. Upon completion, he was quickly hired for a global staff role by a life-sciences giant, where his current position is viewed as a stepping stone to a general management position in Russia or the CIS region.

---

Another common path for growing into a global career is to start in a Russian subsidiary of a global corporation, achieve success, be included in a high-potential talent pool, spend a couple of years abroad as part of a developmental expatriate assignment, then return to Russia or go to a third country, and eventually be considered for another international position. Two such examples are provided in the boxes.

---

## From Experience in Russia to Globetrotter Career (1)

Maria is a global HR executive for a multinational, fast-moving consumer-goods (FMCG) company. She started her career in the HR department of the Russian subsidiary of a global technology company. Relatively soon she was invited to join the Russian operations of her current employer, where, owing to the rapid expansion of operations, she had a chance to grow quickly into a high-level role in the HR organization. She was then sent to Western Europe to work in the company's headquarters, where she developed the social capital for further career growth before returning to Russia for a short stint. Her next move was to Central Asia, where she became a country HR director, followed by a series of assignments in Southeast Asia, where she consistently filled the role of country HR director. Currently, she is back in Western Europe in charge of HR for a large region.

---

## From Experience in Russia to Globetrotter Career (2)

A similar career pattern is found in Ivan's experience. He is currently the head of marketing for his organization's operations in a large Asian country. Prior to that, he was marketing director in a CIS country, the job he rose to after having been in a second-level marketing role in Russia. He also gained experience in headquarters, as well as a developmental assignment in a small Central European country. Ivan, who had been trained as an aviation engineer, started his employment as a sales representative for the FMCG company for which he still works, and he has moved through the ranks to the level of a global executive.

---

Still another, although less frequent, opportunity for development of a global career may be associated with moving into shared services of a global organization with operations in Russia, after having worked at the local level, or working as part of a globally distributed team. For example, a company may establish a virtual structure, with employees who are physically located around the globe, and an employee may get involved in a worldwide or regional project while being located in Russia.

---

## International Career with Permanent Base in Moscow

Diana is part of the Europe, Middle East, and Africa (EMEA) talent-management team for a global professional-services firm. She has always been employed by the same organization, but her roles have evolved over time. She started in administrative support, but eventually moved to HR. The firm then sent her to work in the US, followed by a move to Southern Europe. She finally got back to Russia, which suited her family needs. However, her work not only deals with Russia, but she is also involved in helping the firm source talent for various countries of the EMEA region. Although very successful in pursuing her global career, Diana is on the road a lot, and, when in Moscow, she spends much of her time on the phone.

---

Finally, with Russian companies acquiring significant presences abroad, another channel has emerged for Russians to pursue global careers. That path involves working for the overseas operations of such companies, with the potential to make an eventual move to another overseas operation of the Russian firm, or to move to another company. This category of Russian career actors is relatively unknown to researchers, as access to such people and to the operations of Russian companies overseas is rather limited. An example, however, is described in the box.

## Global Career as a Result of Company Expansion Beyond Russia

Sergey has worked for a Russian natural-resources company that eventually formed a joint venture (JV) with a global organization. As one of the, at the time few, English-speakers in the Russian part of the JV, Sergey was selected to go to the JV headquarters to work on Russia-related projects. Eventually, he was recruited by another Russian natural-resources giant that was expanding its presence in Europe and needed staff there who would be able to act as a bridge between the Russian owners and the local operations of the company.

A more specialized category of global careerist consists of those of exceptional talent. These include artists, musicians, opera singers, ballet dancers, scientists, writers, athletes, academics, and fashion models. There are quite a few Russians in this category, some living in Russia, while others choose to live abroad permanently or become globally mobile. This category of career actor is not significantly different from other global careerists who work in businesses in many different countries.

One of the least explored categories is a group of career actors who choose global career paths by being recruited in Russia for work overseas. This category includes Russians working as crew on commercial vessels, pilots, flight attendants, hotel, resort, and cruise ships personnel, and nurses. Such individuals are typically recruited via private recruitment agencies or directly by employers who run ad hoc recruitment activities.

There are no reliable statistics on the number of Russians working abroad. The country has a system of mandatory registration of citizens at the place of their residence, and, when citizens go abroad for work and keep their Russian citizenship, they very often remain registered at the place of their latest residence. Even Russians who obtain a second citizenship in countries where it is explicitly allowed, or at least not prohibited, often prefer to keep their Russian residence registration, as it allows them to move with more ease through the vicissitudes of bureaucracy when they need something back in their home country. Moreover, they do not get registered with the Russian embassies as Russian citizens living outside Russia. As a result, statistical data are complicated to obtain and are generally not reliable. However, one source that might be helpful is a Moscow Higher School of Economics database of appointments and resignations for more than 1,800 career moves by senior executives in Russia, from 1999 to 2004 (Shekshnia, 2008).

One of the challenges for Russians embarking on a global-career path is the relative difficulty of obtaining work visas, authorizations for work, and residence permits. Companies seeking to employ Russians outside Russia have to go through a considerable amount of red tape, and often encounter delays in

processing work permits and visas. Additional legal and administrative fees are also a nuisance for employers. Also, with the recent tightening of work authorization for foreigners in many countries, it has become more difficult for Russians to obtain work permits when making their first move to employment abroad, or if they want to move from their foreign student status to worker status.

Returning home after working overseas is not unusual for many Russians. The move may be related to attractive career opportunities in some occupations or business sectors, and quicker advancement than was available in more developed Western countries (e.g., Kets de Vries et al., 2004; Korotov, 2008; Korotov et al., 2011). Significant earning opportunities are also an important inducement, with salaries for top managers in Russia having reached significant levels in recent years (Berezanskaya, 2011). Also, since the early 2000s, Russia has had a flat personal income tax rate of only 13%, making the disposable income of highly qualified managers quite attractive. However, the cost of living in Russia has been rising consistently.

A relatively common strategy used by Russians developing global careers is to obtain a second citizenship or, at least, obtain permanent residency in the US or Europe, and then return to work in Russia. Some pursue global careers by commuting between Moscow, where they work, and such cities as London, Paris, Riga, Prague, or Berlin, where they and their families reside. In informal interviews and personal discussions with such individuals, the authors have learned that such arrangements serve as psychological insurance for these career actors. Many such individuals believe that having a second citizenship or permanent residence outside Russia protects them from career risks associated with possible turmoil in Russia and/or foreign countries, increases their ability to act more independently and assertively at work, provides higher assurance of their children's future, and may offer some social-security guarantees that are perceived as insufficient or lacking in Russia.

Some individuals may choose to pursue opportunities in Russia as a conscious choice, to add that experience to their career portfolios. Such assignments can also serve as opportunities to develop networks in Russia that may be helpful in the future, and be valuable visibility enhancers, particularly in companies that expect to or currently enjoy significant growth in the Russian market. In some cases, the choice of returning to Russia for a period of time was related to important periods in one's personal life situation, such as the need to care for elderly parents.

At a 2010 roundtable of Russian executives who have succeeded as global managers, it was emphasized that the features contributing to the success of those Russians who manage to build a global career are entrepreneurial qualities, high intellect, good technical skills, the ability to analyze risks, results orientation, and the ability to learn quickly (Falaleev, 2010). The last characteristic may be particularly important, as development of a global career requires doing things differently from past experiences, and differently from those Russians choosing to build a more traditional career reflecting aspects of the Soviet career-

development path (Khapova & Korotov, 2007). Top global executives who come from Russia agree, among other things, that most Russians still need to learn more in order to qualify as global managers. Areas of need are the ability to work with subordinates, the ability to express one's thoughts clearly, thinking in context, the ability to make decisions, openness to other people's experiences, management of intercultural staff members, adaptability, teamwork, and planning (Falaleev, 2010).

It is also essential for Russians to learn about management and leadership, and to experiment with incorporation of the newly learned concepts in their behavior (Korotov, 2010). The latter may be particularly important for Russians in the context of what Hall (2002) calls "a metacompetency of identity learning," a foundation for acquiring the skills and abilities necessary for further success. He defines identity learning as "the ability to gather self-related feedback, to form accurate self-perceptions, and to change one's self-concept as appropriate" (Hall, 2002: 161). Hall describes identity learning as the ability to engage in self-assessment; seek and make sense of feedback; explore personal values; engage in and model a variety of professional development activities; reward involvement of others in developmental activities; be open to diverse activities and seek opportunities to build relationships with diverse people; and demonstrate a willingness to modify self-perceptions as situations change.

## A Critical Perspective

Global careers must be considered, not only in the context of a specific country, but also within that country's institutions, organizations, and specifically its human resources policies and practices. Two major challenges seem to distinguish nearly all Russian companies from their Western counterparts with respect to global-career issues. The first challenge concerns both the perceived importance of HRM and the ensuing level of investment in human resources, particularly in management development, which are significantly higher in the West. The second challenge, which is also of critical importance to local employers as well as foreign firms making significant investments in Russia, is motivating and retaining a young, talented workforce (Vaiman & Holden, 2011).

Regarding the first issue, some experts contend that employee development may even be of greater importance in Russia than in the West (Fey & Björkman, 2001; Kasperskaya, Kuznetsova, Sverdlov, Fey, & Schvachman, 2010). The reason is that many Russian employees and managers lack basic business knowledge and skills, mostly owing to the absence of Western-style business education in the Soviet Union and the relative youth of the market-oriented business culture in Russia. Still, workforce development should be considered an essential source of competitive advantage (Fey, 2008; Fey & Shekshnia, 2011; Puffer & McCarthy, 2011; Shekshnia, McCarthy, & Puffer, 2007). Some experts suggest that Russian companies' awareness of their own professional limitations

and continuing financial and economic dependency on their Western counterparts have forced them to engage in intense competition for knowledge and skills (Michailova & Jormanainen, 2011). This competition, however, has not yet materialized into specific actions aimed at rigorous and meaningful employee development in many Russian organizations.

Most private Russian companies are still owned and managed by their founders, who are unlikely to leave their positions and make way for the new generation outside of the owner's inner circle, a conundrum that creates career dynamics that are both challenging and frustrating for young, talented employees (Shekshnia, 2008). Realizing that there are no career-growth or professional-development opportunities in the current company, young talents look for better opportunities elsewhere and often begin pursuing global opportunities. Some leave Russia altogether, perpetuating what has been seen as significant brain drain. Those who stay measure their loyalty and commitment exclusively by the amount of compensation they receive (Falaleev, 2010).

While most young, talented employees are unable to develop their potential, on the other side of the equation, many managers are not eager to develop their employees. This negative attitude towards development on the part of Russian managers may be explained partly by their organizational myopia, a short-term orientation (McCarthy, Puffer, May, Ledgerwood, & Stewart, 2008). When a company hires an employee, especially in a managerial capacity, the individual is placed in a job that requires current expertise, and normally little, if any, consideration is given to the set of skills and abilities these managers should develop to be more useful to the company in the future. For the same reason, organizational myopia, most employers in Russia have little patience to develop star players, because they see stars as being needed now, and not in the future. In short, it appears to be problematic for Russian companies to view HRM issues as being strategic. A senior partner of McKinsey and Co. Russia admitted that she did not know of a company in today's Russia that would have its own system of attraction, motivation, and development of specialists over the 5–7-year time horizon (Falaleev, 2010).

In contrast, Russian employees working for Western companies experience markedly different treatment than those employed by Russian organizations. Western companies tend to offer relatively clear career-growth and -development prospects to their top talent. Some experts feel, however, that the overall situation is changing in a positive direction, as many organizations, including Russian companies, are coming to understand the importance of management quality. The growth of Western-style business education in Russia is clearly playing an important role in these positive trends (Michailova & Jormanainen, 2011).

The second issue affecting the development of global careerists is the motivation and retention of key employees. Although the strategies and techniques utilized by Russian companies are often not so different from those of their Western counterparts, some specific local practices prevail. For example, unlike their Western counterparts, many Russian employees expect quick promotions, but

such situations may cause negative reactions on the part of long-term staff, which in turn may lead to serious internal conflicts (Holden & Vaiman, 2012). Still, experts note that many Western-style retention strategies have proven to be viable in Russia, among the most successful of which are such essential components of a meaningful retention system as establishing a strong corporate culture of openness and fairness; offering possibilities to try different career directions within the organization; providing clear career paths and mentoring programs; providing the possibility to work abroad; flexible work schedules; and performance-based rewards, all creating and maintaining a healthy work environment (Falaleev, 2010).

If they are to become involved with global careers, Russian managers will have to be motivated to do so, and clearly some have been so motivated. Often, however, that motivation is self-motivation rather than being initiated by their organizations, perhaps with the exception of Western-firm subsidiaries. Many experts agree that top Russian professionals are not motivated solely by the size of their compensation packages, and that senior managers can use many other measures to motivate and retain key employees. Among the most successful measures are helping employees reach their professional goals; giving them more job autonomy; establishing more flexible organizational structures where talent can emerge, endure, and prosper; maintaining a close, trusted relationship with superiors; and creating an atmosphere of transparency and mutual support. In short, if they are to be motivated and stay with their current organizations, Russian employees should have the possibility of career and professional growth, as well as new and increasingly challenging responsibilities and collaboration with other talented people, and they should be exposed to meaningful leadership development programs (Falaleev, 2010). All of these enlightened human resources practices are also crucial to the development necessary to pursue global careers within or outside Russia.

A further critical perspective on global careers in the Russian context suggests that career actors may find it more difficult to build a global career in the future. For example, one of the advantages attributed to Russians has been their perceived high level of education. Despite the statistical data suggesting that the country has one of the highest student populations in the world, however, and the fact that the notion of Russia as a highly educated nation continues to be cultivated by both Russians and people studying in Russia, the actual situation may not be so positive. Thus, some current observers of the Russian educational system suggest that having the highest number of university students per thousand inhabitants in the world (similar to the data for Kazakstan) is due to low entrance barriers to higher education and the willingness of many lesser universities to accept students with mediocre high-school achievements (Panov, 2011).

The prevailing positive reputation of Russian education in the West, then, may be based on a perception related to former achievements of the Soviet Union, such as pioneering space exploration, significant breakthroughs in physics and mathematics, and achievements in other fields of basic science. It may be noted that perception of the high quality of Russian education may also be supported

by the successes of Russians studying in foreign universities, particularly at the Masters or Ph.D. levels, and also the visibility of successful Russians who have managed to build successful careers outside their home country. Furthermore, despite the large number of individuals entering universities in Russia and the success of some Russians in the global academic and professional worlds, the notion of the quality of Russian education can be challenged on the basis of the recent OECD Program for International Student Assessments (PISA) results. The 2009 PISA results suggest that the reading competencies of Russian 15-year-olds are below the OECD average, putting Russia in 41st–43rd position among the 65 countries included in the study. More surprisingly, results in mathematics had Russia in 38th–40th place. Although there has been an improvement in the reading results for Russia in comparison with earlier PISA studies, outcomes in mathematics stayed at the same level. Also, in science, Russia, ranking 39th, was placed lower than the OECD average (OECD, 2010). It is worrisome, then, that this declining status of secondary-school education may eventually have an impact on the development of the country's workforce, its capacity to compete globally, and its ability to foster global careers.

Other critical points that deserve attention in assessing Russia's situation include the reality that learning to be responsible for one's career is still new to many Russian managers and employees (Korotov, 2005), and the cultural mythology surrounding the role of the strong and all-knowing leader (Shekshnia, Puffer, & McCarthy, 2009) can impede subordinates from developing their own careers, if their activities for self-advancement appear to threaten their superiors. A related cultural tradition is subordinates' expectation that leaders should take responsibility for all decisions and outcomes, rather than delegating to others (May, Puffer, & McCarthy, 2005). Additionally, not all Russians pursuing advancement in their careers, particularly globally, realize the personal and professional costs associated with moving ahead in the organizational hierarchy (Korotov, 2009). Once they understand those costs and risks, they might opt for a less demanding career path. Additionally, as noted earlier, Russian managers are often impatient with the speed of career progression and moving ahead in the organizational hierarchy (Korotov, 2008). The expectation of rapid career advancement arose from fast promotions and job hopping in response to the dire lack of domestic managerial and professional talent, as the country developed toward a market economy during the last two decades. These characteristics and expectations may have been, and may still be, appropriate for domestic careers in Russia, but not for developing global careers.

## Conclusion

The concepts of boundaryless and protean careers appear to be quite relevant for understanding why and how many Russians are interested in pursuing global careers, just as they are for those in other countries with similar ambitions. Nevertheless, an understanding of the unique Russian context is crucial for

examining the specific factors that encourage or impede that career path for Russians, whether within or outside Russia. Because of the relatively unfavorable country conditions for developing and pursuing a global career within Russia, many globally oriented careerists opt to go abroad for education and to initiate their global careers, at times returning to Russia, but often remaining abroad. Paramount among these conditions is the extremely hierarchical structure of Russian business, which impedes talented individuals from fully developing their potential in Russian organizations. Specifically, employees of typical Russian companies need to be highly deferential to their superiors and become members of their inner circle to succeed, a condition that is unacceptable to many highly talented professionals. Thus, many Russians opt to work for Russian subsidiaries of multinational companies that have clear career paths based on merit. A basic reason for not returning to Russia concerns the administrative and bureaucratic difficulties of leaving the country initially, and the desire to avoid a repetition of those difficulties upon repatriation. All of these circumstances should send signals to Russian government policymakers and the executives of Russian companies that human resources policies, including managerial selection and development, such as clear, merit-based paths to global careers, must be adopted if the current brain drain of top Russian talent is to be stemmed.

In spite of the many obstacles described above, to present a more complete perspective on the potential for developing global careers on the part of Russians, it is useful to examine recent positive developments that have taken place that may help more Russian nationals to pursue global careers. For instance, the federal government has invested heavily in innovation initiatives by making institutional change a priority, while building an infrastructure to support innovation (McCarthy, Puffer, Graham, & Satinsky, 2012). One of the results of such investment in institutional changes could be a lessening of the brain drain that has been occurring, with many mobile Russians leaving the country over the past two decades to pursue their careers. Regional governments have also developed their own programs with the same objective. Perhaps most importantly, numerous multinationals, particularly in the high-technology sector, including Microsoft, Intel, Boeing, and Cisco, have been involved in the country for some time and have pledged further investment and involvement supporting governmental innovation initiatives. These are in addition to numerous other companies, particularly from Europe, that have established operations to capitalize on the growing Russian consumer and business markets. In a similar vein, AMBAR, an association founded in California's Silicon Valley in 2002 by Russian émigrés, is a network of high-technology professionals that supports the development of businesses in Russia. That organization and many of the international companies mentioned earlier may provide a springboard for Russian managers and other professionals to pursue global careers. As a result, in spite of many difficulties and barriers for Russians building a global career, the situation may well be improving, as the country becomes more involved in the global business arena.

## References

Antonova, M. (2010, October 5). Nobel Prize win exposes Russia's brain drain losses. Retrieved from www.physorg.com/news205500597.html, April 2012.

Arthur, M. B., Claman, P. H., & DeFillippi, R. J. (1995). Intelligent enterprise, intelligent careers. *Academy of Management Executive*, 9(4), 7–20.

Arthur, M. B., Hall, D. T., & Lawrence, B. S. (Eds.) (1989). *Handbook of Career Theory*. New York: Cambridge University Press.

Arthur, M. B., Khapova, S. N., & Wilderom, C. P. M. (2005). Career success in a boundaryless career world. *Journal of Organizational Behavior*, 26(2), 177–202.

Ataiants, J. & Olimpieva, I. (2011). The Russian diaspora in the USA: Russian emigrants in the corporate culture of American high-tech firms. *Russian Analytical Digest*, 107, (January 27), 5–8.

Barley, S. R. (1989). Careers, identities, and institutions: The legacy of the Chicago School of Sociology. In Arthur, M. B., Hall, D. T., & Lawrence, B. S. (Eds.), *Handbook of Career Theory* (pp. 41–65). New York: Cambridge University Press.

Baruch, Y. & Dickmann, M. (2011). *Global Careers*. London: Routledge.

Baruch, Y., Budhwar, P., & Khatri, N. (2007). Brain drain, inclination to stay abroad after studies. *Journal of World Business*, 42, 99–112.

Berezanskaya, E. (2011). Reiting zarplat rukovoditelei [Rating of salaries of top managers]. *Forbes Russia*. Retrieved from www.forbes.ru/rating/karera-package/rynok-truda/76523-reiting-zarplat-rukovoditelei-2011, April 2012.

Bozrikova, L. V., Doctorova, L. D., & Lebedev, P. N. (1990). At the apex of the managerial pyramid. *Soviet Sociology*, 29(6), 28–38.

*CIA Factbook* (2012, February 3). Retrieved from https://www.cia.gov/library/publications/the-world-factbook/geos/rs.html, April 2012.

DeFillippi, R. J. & Arthur, M. B. (1996). Boundaryless contexts and careers: A competency-based perspective. In Arthur, M.B. & Rousseau, D. M. (Eds.), *The Boundaryless Career* (pp. 116–132). New York: Oxford University Press.

*Economist* (no byline) (2011). The mood of Russia, time to shove off: The Soviet Union was undermined by stagnation and a sense of hopelessness. Is the same thing happening again? *Economist*, 400(8750), 27–30.

Falaleev, D. (2010). Upravlyaem po-vzroslomu [Managing like adults]. *Harvard Business Review Russia*, 55(1–2), 51–57.

Fey, C. (2008). Overcoming a leader's greatest challenge: Involving employees in firms in Russia. *Organizational Dynamics*, 37(3), 254–265.

Fey, C. & Björkman, I. (2001). The effect of human resource management practices on MNC subsidiary performance in Russia. *Journal of International Business Studies*, 32(1), 59.

Fey, C. & Shekshnia, S. (2011). The key commandments for doing business in Russia. *Organizational Dynamics*, 40(1) (January–March), 57–66.

Hall, D. T. (1996). Protean careers of the 21st century. *Academy of Management Executive*, 10(4), 8–16.

Hall, D. T. (2002). *Careers In and Out of Organizations*. Thousand Oaks, CA: Sage.

Holden, N. J. & Vaiman, V. (2012). Talent management in Russia: Troubled past, thorny present, uncertain future. Manuscript under review.

IIE (2010). Top 25 Places of Origin of International Students, 2008/09–2009/10. Open doors report on international educational exchange. Institute of International Education.

Inkson, K. & Arthur, M. (2001). How to be a successful career capitalist. *Organizational Dynamics*, 30(1), 48–61.

Jones, A. (1991). *Professions and the State, Expertise, and Autonomy in the Soviet Union and Eastern Europe*. Philadelphia, PA: Temple University Press.

Karbasova, N. (2010). Russische Studenten: Der Drang nach Westen [Russian students: The drive to the West]. *Medienblick Bonn*. Retrieved from http://medienblick-bonn. de/uniblick/studium/russische-studenten, April 2012.

Kasperskaya, N., Kuznetsova, I., Sverdlov, D., Fey, C., & Schvachman, I. (2010). Uderzhat' Luchshikh [Retain the best]. *Harvard Business Review Russia*, 9(61), 61–70.

Kets de Vries, M., Shekshnia, S., Korotov, K., & Florent-Treacy, E. (Eds.) (2004). *The New Russian Business Leaders*. New Horizons in Leadership Studies Series. Cheltenham: Edward Elgar.

Khapova, S. N. & Korotov, K. (2007). Dynamics of Western career attributes in the Russian context. *Career Development International*, 12(1), 68–85.

Korotov, K. (2005). Otvestvenny za karieru [Taking responsibility for one's career]. *Harvard Business Review Russia*, 10(12), 18.

Korotov, K. (2008). Citius, Altius, Fortius: Challenges of accelerated development of leadership talent in the Russian context. *Organizational Dynamics*, 37(3), 277–287.

Korotov, K. (2009). Liderstvo: Izderzhki professii [Leadership: The cost of the profession]. *Harvard Business Review Russia*, 12(54), 24.

Korotov, K. (2010). Mnenie eksperta (Expert opinion). *Harvard Business Review Russia*, 55(57), 1–2.

Korotov, K., Khapova, S. N., & Arthur, M. B. (2011). Career entrepreneurship. *Organizational Dynamics*, 40(2), 127–135.

McCarthy, D. J., Puffer, S. M., Graham, L. R., & Satinsky, D. M. (2012). Emerging innovation in an emerging economy: Can institutional reforms help Russia break through its historical barriers? Manuscript under review, Northeastern University.

McCarthy, D. J., Puffer, S. M., May, R. C., Ledgerwood, D. E., & Stewart, W. H., Jr. (2008). Overcoming resistance to change in Russian organizations: The legacy of transactional leadership. *Organizational Dynamics*, 37(3), 221–235.

May, R. C., Puffer, S. M., & McCarthy, D. J. (2005). Transferring management knowledge to Russia: A culturally-based approach. *The Academy of Management Executive*, 19(2), 24–35.

Michailova, S. & Jormanainen, I. (2011). Position paper: Knowledge transfer between Russian and Western firms. Whose absorptive capacity is it? *Critical Perspectives on International Business*, 7(3), 250–270.

Michailova, S. & Worm, V. (2003). Personal networking in Russia and China: Blat and Guanxi. *European Management Journal*, 21(4), 509–519.

OECD (2010). PISA 2009 Results: What students know and can do—Student performance in reading. *Mathematics and Science (Volume I)*. OECD.

Panov, A. (2011). Ne mozhem uchit' vsekh, znachit, budem uchit' luchshikh [If we can't teach everyone, we shall teach the best]. *Vedomosti*. Retrieved from www.vedomosti.ru/opinion/news/1404378/razvivat_elitnoe_obrazovanie, April 2012.

Podorvanyuk, N. (2010, October 6). The prize is 20% Russian, *Gazeta.ru*. Retrieved from www.gazeta.ru/science/2010/10/06_a_3426173.shtml, April 2012.

Puffer, S. M. & McCarthy, D. J. (2011). Two decades of Russian business and management research: An institutional theory perspective. *Academy of Management Perspectives*, 25(2), 21–36.

Rosstat (2011). Zanyatost i bezrabotitsa v Rossiyskoy Federatsii v sentyabre 2011 goda [Employment and unemployment in the Russian Federation in September 2011]. *Federal State Statistics Service*. Retrieved from www.gks.ru, April 2012.

Rosstat (2012). Russian population census. Retrieved from gks.ru/wps/wcm/connect/rosstat/rosstatsite/main/, April 2012.

Royal Swedish Academy of Sciences (2010, October 5). Press release. Retrieved from www.nobelprize.org, April 2012.

Scorikov, V. & Vondracek, F. W. (1993). Career development in the Commonwealth of Independent States. *The Career Development Quarterly*, 41, 314–329.

Shekshnia, S. (2008). CEO-founder succession: The Russian paradox. *European Journal of International Management*, 2(1), 39–55.

Shekshnia, S. V., McCarthy, D. J., & Puffer, S. M. (2007). Leadership development in Russia. In T. Lidokhover (Ed.), *Human Resources Management in Russia* (pp. 43–64). Aldershot, UK: Ashgate.

Shekshnia, S. V., Puffer, S. M., & McCarthy, D. J. (2009). Cultural mythology and global leadership in Russia. In E. H. Kessler and D. J. Wong-MingJi (Eds.), *Cultural Mythology and Leadership* (pp. 325–342). Cheltenham, UK, and Northampton, MA: Edward Elgar.

Sullivan, S. E. & Baruch, Y. (2009). Advances in career theory and research: A critical review and agenda for future exploration. *Journal of Management*, 35(6), 1542–1571.

Vaiman, V. & Holden, N. (2011). Talent management in Central and Eastern Europe: Challenges and trends. In D. Collings & H. Scullion (Eds.), *Global Talent Management*. London: Routledge.

Van Maanen, J. (Ed.) (1977). *Organizational Careers: Some New Perspectives*. New York: Wiley.

Yakubovich, V. (2005). Weak ties, information, and influence: How workers find jobs in a local Russian labor market. *American Sociological Review*, 70, 408–421.

Yudina, P. (2010). Obuchenie za rubezhom: Populyarnye napravlenia [Studying abroad: Popular destinations]. Retrieved from www.ucheba.ru/abroad-article/12626.html, April 2012.

# 11

# GLOBAL CAREERS IN HUNGARY

*Irén Gyökér and Henrietta Finna, Budapest University of Technology and Economics, Hungary*

## Introduction

In this chapter, we focus on the global careers of Hungarians, which are strongly shaped by the unique culture, language, and political transitions of the past decades. The global careers of Hungarians, while strongly influenced by economic and historical developments, are also affected by the characteristics of the people and the domestic labor market, and by emigration and immigration issues. Compared with other, neighboring countries, the level of migration in Hungary is relatively low, although it has increased over the last few years. Upon taking a closer look, we find that the global careers of Hungarians take two major, distinctively different forms: self-initiated expatriation and the global careers initiated by major multinational players that support Hungarian employees in developing their knowledge and skills in another business unit, in a different country, within the same organization.

Hungary's primary interest would be to provide opportunities for spending time abroad for a wide range of the population, in order to obtain international exposure, experience, and best practices, which, in return, could contribute to the nation's economic growth and give Hungarians a more competitive presence on the international market. For individuals, having a global career is a great challenge, but, at the same time, it provides enduring benefits for their future career. Highly qualified young people who have a global career and have gained experience and new competencies abroad have incentives to stay longer in their host country or not even to return to the home country, which, from a human-capital perspective, may negatively affect Hungary in the long run. Therefore, in this chapter, we pay special attention to this group that is considered to be a strategic asset for the country.

At the end of the chapter, we also take a look at the future challenges posed by immigrants coming to Hungary, and the types of issue and challenge that their assimilation and integration raise nowadays.

## The Situation of Global Careers in Hungary

In order to understand the willingness of Hungarians to build international careers, we have to take a look at the factors influencing people's behavior towards global careers.

### The Peculiarities of Migration in Hungary in the Past 130 Years

The general tendency that populations move from the poorer regions to those areas offering more job opportunities and a higher living standard also applies to Hungary. Owing to its history and its geographical position, Hungary has served as a transit country on several occasions during earlier periods of migration. From the last third of the nineteenth century, however, migration on various scales in different historical periods has been the general tendency, and remains the case even in the twenty-first century. Six main phases of emigration and immigration can be distinguished (see Table 11.1 below), with the typical direction of transnational migration and the estimated number of those involved.

The first mass emigration started in the last quarter of the nineteenth century, and the destination was typically North America. Nearly one and a half million

**TABLE 11.1** Migration data of Hungary in the past 130 years

| Period | Direction | Number of immigrants and emigrants (people) |
|---|---|---|
| End of 19th century–World War I (1880–1915) | Leaving | 1.5 million |
| Between the two world wars (1918–1945) | Leaving | 80,000–90,000 |
| | Entering | 250,000 |
| After World War II (1945–1956) | Leaving | 280,000 (other nationalities) |
| | | 200,000 (Hungarian nationality) |
| | Entering | 300,000 |
| Revolution in 1956 (1956) | Leaving | 200,000 |
| Period up to the system change (1956–1989) | Leaving | 150,000 |
| | Entering | 50,000 (other nationalities) |
| Period after the transition (1990–2010) | Leaving | 550,000 |
| | Entering | 150,000–200,000 (other nationalities) |

*Sources*: Yearbooks on Demographics ed. by Office of Immigration and Nationality; Hungarian Central Statistical Office; Hungarian Central Statistical Office Historical Statistical Timelines; Office of the United Nations High Commissioner for Refugees; Berencsi and Sik (1995). Calculated and edited by the authors

Hungarians left before World War I—mainly for economic reasons, because of the threat of sinking into poverty and the hope of striking it rich in America. The majority of emigrants came from regions outside Budapest; often, whole families or even whole villages left. They considered emigration just a temporary solution, but yet only a quarter of them returned.

As a result of World War I, emigration was replaced by immigration, when a great number of ethnic Hungarians (approximately 3 million, of which 2.4 are still living there)—left beyond the borders of the countries reshaped by the Trianon Treaty—arrived in the territory of the new Hungary. Most came through forced resettlements, but many were refugees. Emigration in this period was not significant (a few thousand people left, mainly for political reasons). The world economic crisis, however, gave a new impetus to the wave of emigration, but this time the chosen country was different. Because of the stricter immigration quotas, instead of the USA, the destination of choice was first Canada and then South America. However, the real change was brought about by the emigrants' social composition: the proportion of highly qualified professional Hungarians leaving the country (one-fifth of the emigrants) was steadily growing.

During World War II, Hungary experienced a dramatic loss of its population and its human capital: 6.49% of the population—about 900,000 people—died, of which 350,000 were military forces. From 800,000 Hungarian Jewish citizens living in the region, a section of the population that was highly educated, some 500,000 people had been deported (200,000 from the country's recent territory). The total number of Hungarian Jewish victims amounted to 410,000–460,000 people (Kollega Tarsoly, 1996).

In the postwar period, another significant wave of migration occurred, this time in two directions. While many people belonging to the German and Slovakian ethnic groups and a huge number of Hungarians left, an even larger number of Hungarian immigrants from Czechoslovakia, Transylvania, Yugoslavia, and the Soviet Union settled in Hungary. Among the 200,000 Hungarian emigrants, a further 51,230[1] Jews left the country for Israel (20,000) and other countries. The large-scale emigration during the postwar years—involving war refugees, dishonored groups, and those wanting to escape the impending Soviet-type takeover—was ended by the strict measures of the communist era and by the "Iron Curtain." From that time, leaving the country was a criminal act (Borbándi, 2006).

Another great loss was inflicted on Hungary when several hundred thousand people left the country because of the 1956 revolution. The proportion of professionals and skilled workers leaving was much higher than before. The fact that 90% of the refugees were younger than 40 had an unfavorable effect on the country's age pyramid. This wave of emigration, however, did not last long, as the borders were soon closed again.

In the subsequent period (1956–1989)—right up to the introduction of the new political system—leaving the country was an act of opposing the existing

political system, and those who decided to "defect" had to face serious consequences. Despite this, about 10,000 Hungarians emigrated each year, according to estimations based on related statistics from the host countries. As a result of the strictly controlled borders, the Iron Curtain, Hungary isolated itself from host and transit countries almost completely. The only people who arrived in Hungary were those employed temporarily through a structured scheme. They came from socialist countries, from Vietnam, Cuba, Mongolia, and Poland, for example, and students came especially from East Germany and the Soviet Union.

After the transition in 1989, as a result of the radical political and social changes in Eastern Europe, both the nature and the scale of emigration and immigration involving Hungary have changed dramatically. The country is equally characterized by a growing tendency for emigration and by the problems caused by immigration. While many Hungarians go abroad, attracted by Western countries (which have been especially appealing since Hungary's European Union (EU) accession), some foreigners also heading to the West use Hungary as a transit country and, eventually, also as a host country, a place where they can gather experience. As a result, 15,000–20,000 immigrants arrive each year, and at least the same or even higher numbers of Hungarians leave the country.[2] The daily mobility at the Hungarian–Austrian border, involving as many as 10,000–15,000 commuting Hungarians, deserves special attention (earlier illegal work is now being replaced by legal jobs) (Juhász, Csikvari, Szaitz, & Makara, 2006).

## Historical and Economic Factors of Hungary Influencing Global Carriers

Hungary is a relatively small, landlocked country, located in the Carpathian basin in Central and Eastern Europe (CEE), bordered by Austria, Croatia, Serbia, Romania, Slovakia, Slovenia, and Ukraine. Hungary's strategic location links Western Europe and the Balkan peninsula, and Ukraine and the Mediterranean basin. Its population today is nearly 10 million people, the vast majority of whom are Hungarian (96%). According to the latest population census (2002),[3] 4% of the population declared themselves to belong to a national or ethnic minority, most of them to the Hungarian-speaking Romany community.

Over the centuries, Hungarians have learnt to adapt to increasingly difficult, ever-changing conditions; they have also learnt to co-exist with other nations, as migration has become a routine part of daily life. The ancient Hungarians, a nomadic people, had migrated towards the West from the Asian regions. Hungary became a Christian kingdom in 1000 AD, under the kingship of Stephen. For decades, Hungary served as a bulwark against Ottoman Turkish expansion in Europe, while Central Hungary was ruled by the Turkish Empire for 150 years. The kingdom afterwards became part of the polyglot Austro-Hungarian Empire, which collapsed during World War I. As a consequence of the two world wars in the twentieth century, when Hungary allied itself with Austria and Germany,

two thirds of its lands were detached from its territory, with some 3 million Hungarians left beyond its new borders. The country fell under communist rule following World War II. In 1956, a revolt was met with a massive military intervention by Moscow. In 1968, Hungary began liberalizing its economy, introducing so-called goulash communism, characterized by strong political and economic affiliations with Soviet bloc countries. Hungary held its first multi-party elections in 1990 and initiated a free market economy that same year.

Hungary's economy is a medium-sized, structurally, politically, and institutionally open economy that is part of the EU's single market. It experienced market liberalization in the early 1990s as part of the transition from a socialist economy to a market economy. Declining exports, reduced domestic consumption, and fixed asset accumulation hit Hungary hard during the 2008 financial and economic crisis, resulting in a severe recession of −6.4%, one of the worst economic contractions in its history.

By 2010, the country's population had shrunk to a little less than 10 million people; 6.77 million belong to the 15–64-year working-age group. Over the last two decades, economic activity (66%) and the employment rate (55.4%) have been lower than the European average.[4] Its unemployment rate of 11% is consistent with the European average, but is perceived as much too high by Hungarians, to whom unemployment was an unknown concept for half a century. Compared with international standards, the economically inactive population is unusually high, representing a significant obstacle to the development of the national economy and also to those concerned with their own individual welfare. The reasons are heterogeneous. On the one hand, they can be linked to those decades under the communist regime when the labor market was characterized by full employment, and where individual competitiveness was not required. On the other hand, the socioeconomic changes attached to the liberalization of the economy and free-market processes, e.g., closing entire industries and downsizing, resulted in higher working inactivity (Adler, 2008). The different regions within the country show different conditions. Data from the Central region and West Transdanubian region are much more favorable, whereas serious inactivity problems are emerging in the northern regions of Hungary. These conditions will have an effect on migration in and outside of the country.

As in other EU countries, the aging population is generating major challenges in Hungary. The shrinking population—with a significant birthrate decline over the last 35 years—is leading to a decreasing number of young people of working age. This number is further reduced by higher-than-average migration in the group of 24–34-year-old Hungarians.

Based on the estimates of the Hungarian Central Statistical Office, 2% of the population, i.e., 5% of the working-age population is—for shorter or longer periods of time—employed outside of Hungary. According to the same statistics, the number of Hungarians who are of working age and employed abroad is increasing.

## Structural, Cultural and Contextual Opportunities and Difficulties for Global Careers in Hungary

Following the 1989 political and economic transition, migration was influenced by personal preferences and economical rationalism for the most part, which led individuals to global careers (Hárs, 2001, 2008). It wasn't until Hungary joined the EU in 2004 that the structural, legal, and other obstacles impeding global careers for Hungarians diminished. These obstacles were not completely eliminated until 2007, when restrictions relating to labor–market protection were removed by the EU15 countries. As these restrictive regulations slowly fade in Europe, the free movement of people within EU countries is possible.

Globalization and the increasing number of multinational companies operating in Hungary have also affected migration. HR policy in a number of international companies specifically requires transnational career changes every, say, 2 years. This practice provides an opportunity for many Hungarians to make a global career.

With regard to the legal side of migration, except for some special cases, there are no restrictions on leaving Hungary. The relevant passage of the Hungarian Constitution (based on Article 58 of Act XXXI of 1989) declares that everyone is free to leave, and there is no obligation to inform the authorities (Karoliny & Mohay, 2009). Consequently, there are no official statistical data on migration available, only research data and estimates.

Some factors that can be considered typical of self-initiated global careers of Hungarians emerge from the following stories, in the boxes.

---

### Global Entrant with Family Sponsorship

Péter C. is a successful, young (36-year-old) manager. In 1992, at the age of 17, his father offered him a study trip abroad. He spent 10 months in America, where he went to school and stayed with American families. According to Péter, the only advantage of this experience was that he gained a good command of the English language. After returning home, he graduated from the College of Finance and Accountancy. Instead of taking positions in auditing or accountancy, he started his career in marketing, working for different companies at mid- and senior-management level, and in executive positions. His desire for new and challenging tasks coincided with the option of working abroad, when he was tempted from an executive position at a major company to move to Microsoft. As head of a business unit, he had the opportunity to establish a closer relationship with the sister company in Ireland and, as a consequence, was offered a job by Microsoft Dublin. Recently, because of family reasons, he moved back to Hungary (his wife was expecting twins). Thanks to the company's flexible policy, he is now able to do his work partly in Hungary and partly in Ireland. Regarding his future career, he is planning to work abroad, but does not intend to leave Hungary forever.

---

Péter's career path is a good example of family influence, which plays an important role in facilitating an international career for Hungarians. Spending time abroad at a young age is an ideal opportunity for people to develop their language

skills and intercultural competences. Such skills will later significantly enhance flexibility, integration, and openness towards global careers, without leading necessarily to final emigration.

---

## The "Sportstrotter"

Gergely M.—a 34-year-old sport director of the International Triathlon Union (ITU)—was involved in organizing triathlon competitions in his home town. Successful in these projects, he joined international triathlon events. At the age of 20, while he was still a university student, he became the director of an international competition organized in Hungary; as a result of his remarkable activities, he was acknowledged as a triathlon expert. In the following years, he was invited to serve as a competition judge and technical supervisor. Two years after joining the Technical Committee of the Triathlon Federation in 2000, he became an elected member of the executive board of the European Triathlon Union. Working as a volunteer, he managed to stabilize the union's operations and finances. In 2003 (at the last moment before the event), the international federation requested him to accept the position of triathlon competition manager at the Athens Olympics. In a completely foreign environment, with a team comprising local people, and starting from scratch, he managed successfully to carry out the task. For Gergely, this was the most difficult and most enlightening period of his career. He resigned from the post of European Triathlon Union secretary general in 2009 to take up the position of sport director at the ITU in Switzerland. He is consciously building his international career and is not ruling out a return to Hungary.

---

Gergely's global career was triggered by his professional expertise and the fact that his volunteering activities became international. He gained experience in a global operation while working as the representative of a Hungarian organization. His global career was guided by his commitment and not by his intention to migrate. When contemplating his future, he focuses on processes, tasks, and venues of operation, rather than focusing on countries in which he would like to live.

---

## A Former Exchange Student

Katalin H. is an entrepreneur and coach living in Switzerland. In 1993, while a student at a Hungarian university, she applied to continue her studies for a term in a higher-education institution in Heidelberg. As her language skills were very poor, she was uncertain in many areas and was also in a difficult financial situation. She returned after a year, but she was still attracted to studying abroad and managed to go back to Germany on a student grant. During her stay, she also had the opportunity to participate in a Swiss teacher-training program. This was a turning point in her life: while looking for work after graduation, she was contacted from Switzerland, thanks to her earlier connections. She worked as an assistant and coach in planning and developing educational programs until her contract expired. She married and settled down in Switzerland, where she established her own successful coaching company. Even though she has established a similar enterprise in Hungary, she is not planning to move back; she already feels Swiss.

---

Katalin's career started while at university, when she spent a term abroad. For her, the opportunity for student mobility in higher education opened the path to emigrate, and she became a successful entrepreneur in a new country she chose for herself. Mobility programs in higher education play an important role in preparing young professionals for global mobility. The additional knowledge and skills Katalin gained abroad will hopefully be utilized in her domestic enterprise and so enhance the Hungarian economy, even though Katalin herself will remain in Switzerland.

In the past 5–10 years, because of economic difficulties, migration from Hungary has impacted specific groups of jobs and professions; the country is under serious threat of losing certain contingents of specialists. As an example, the biggest and most urgent problem concerns the retention of doctors and resident doctors, as well as specialist nurses and other health-care professionals in Hungary. Owing to low compensation and poor working conditions in the Hungarian health-care sector in comparison with developed European countries, increasingly high numbers of health-care specialists plan to work abroad. From July 2010 to May 2011, almost 1,500 young health-care professionals applied for the official certificate that would enable them to seek a job outside of Hungary. This high migration potential is a warning sign. It may cause serious problems, as the labor shortage in Hungarian hospitals is already more than 10% at the moment: the equivalent of one and a half times the number of medical students that graduate in a year. The situation in the health-care sector is also aggravated by the unfavorable age structure of family doctors. Those nearing retirement age represent a high percentage, especially in disadvantaged regions outside Budapest. Moreover, 20–30% of new medical graduates in a given year do not seek employment in their profession, choosing instead to embark on a new career (Eke, Girasek, & Szócska, 2008; MTI, 2011).

Studying the drivers of migration can provide important information, not just for researchers, but also for politicians and other decision-makers.

## The Migration Potential and Actual Migration of Hungarians Towards EU Countries

After Hungary joined the EU, the free movement of people became a real option. There have been several studies researching migration in the European region, and there are some findings that are important to the future development of global careers. When studying migration, one needs to make a distinction between migration potential (the intention of taking up a job abroad) and actual migration. Although migration potential always exceeds actual migration, overall it shows a similar pattern to the actual migration of Hungary, and so it is a phenomenon that it is worthwhile to study.

Since the transition in 1989, Hungarians' willingness to seek employment abroad and to emigrate has increased continuously, with the only exception in

2006. Although the intention to work abroad in the short term fluctuates more than the long-term intention, the willingness to emigrate is more predictable in both cases. By 2010, the host countries had changed: Austria regained its old status for short-term employment, whereas, in their long-term plans, more and more Hungarians began to consider Ireland as a destination. For those planning to emigrate, the USA has become popular again. At the same time, German-speaking areas are no longer as appealing for emigrants as they were previously (Sik, 2010).

Research by Hárs (2011) on the topic shows the accumulated migration potential (see Figure 11.1), i.e. over different years. The chart presents the rate of those in the population who have at least once mentioned their intention to go abroad for one of the three time periods (short term, long term, and emigration) and thus belong to the potential target group in the field of working abroad.

We use a wider approach to migration, which, besides a permanent stay abroad, also includes intermittent periods of working abroad alternating with periods of returning home (circular migration). A growing number of experts studying the issue tend to accept migration models suggesting shorter periods and reflecting what we actually experience as a growing tendency (McLoughlin & Münz, 2011). Moreover, that kind of international migration (and also daily commuting) is more characteristic of Hungary, and so it is important to include these employees in

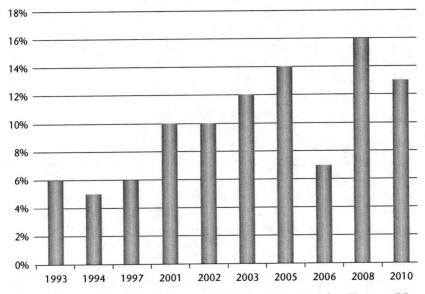

**FIGURE 11.1** The development of accumulated migration potential in Hungary (%), 1993–2010

*Source*: Based on Hárs, 2011

the migration labor market (Kincses & Rédei, 2009). Taking all these into consideration, as well as data that can be estimated on the basis of different statistics, indicates that 2% of the country's population is involved—in the shorter or longer term—in employment in the EU (i.e., about 5% of Hungarians of employment age).[5]

Hárs (2011) shows that there are three typical destinations for Hungarians in the EU: Germany, Austria, and the United Kingdom. The great majority of commuters from Hungary to Austria come from western Hungary. Further away from the Austrian border, Germany becomes the most attractive destination country. Groups of migrants from the eastern part of Hungary choose the new host countries: a great number leave for the United Kingdom, for example. The majority of migrant employees leave from Budapest or its surroundings. The destination countries chosen by them, however, are much more heterogeneous.

The nature, duration, and result of employment often show differences, depending on the host country. In Germany, it usually means long-term employment and moving to the country for a longer period (often permanently). In the case of employees in Austria and the United Kingdom—and also in the other EU15 states—it is more typical to have shorter periods of employment, then return to Hungary, and go back again to the destination country on several occasions, trying to stay in closer contact with the family (circular migration).

As for coming back, although Austria is a stable host country, the crisis-induced peculiarities in the labor market of the United Kingdom, an attractive migration location until the recent past, have led to the return of a great number of Hungarians. Similar phenomena have occurred in Germany, a traditional destination for Hungarian migrants.

In the three most popular host countries, the nature of the work also has different characteristics. Migrants are usually skilled workers (with specialized vocational training), but the number of employees with secondary-school education is also growing fast. The rate of Hungarian migrants with higher education is rising, which is especially typical in the United Kingdom.

The quality of the positions taken, however, does not match the competency level everywhere: although, in Germany and Austria, mainly skilled workers from Hungary performing skilled or semi-skilled work are employed in industrial and construction jobs, in the United Kingdom, the rate of—often highly qualified—people employed in unskilled work or in services is significant, and the rate of people performing highly qualified work is low everywhere. Among those returning to Hungary, the rate of people who were employed in unskilled work is significant, which may suggest that uncertainty is greater in jobs where no qualifications are required; however, these employees choose a strategy leading to a circular lifestyle. Those doing non-physical work are more likely to become resident migrants working abroad permanently.

As for the age of Hungarian citizens living abroad, they are in the most productive period of their working lives, and the trends suggest that the average

age is decreasing. Most emigrants belong to the 25–34 age group[6] (which comprises 30–45% of the Hungarian population of the hosting European countries). The 35–44 age group follows them, and the two age groups together amount to as much as 80% of the Hungarian population of the hosting country. There is no considerable gender difference: the proportion of men and women is balanced in most countries. It should be noted, however, that the rate of women returning to Hungary is higher; longer stays abroad are more typical for men.

## The Emigration of Highly Qualified Hungarians

Hungary is a small nation, but, if we consider the concentration of its mental capacity, it can be considered a major power—as Albert Szent-Györgyi once said. When we think of our Nobel Prize-winning scientists in absolute numbers, we outrank countries with big populations, such as China, Japan, Australia, or India. If, however, we compare the number of Nobel Laureates to the territory or population of the countries, then we are ahead of more developed countries (e.g., the USA). Specialist scholars such as Albert Szent-Györgyi, Imre Kertész, Jenő Wigner, Dénes Gábor, György Hevesy, Fülöp Lénárd, György Békésy, György Oláh, and János Harsányi, however, could only find what they were looking for abroad. Unfortunately, there is still this tendency. The great Hungarian minds working in research and development all migrate to the West; in Hungary, the financial conditions and infrastructure that could provide the necessary background for successful research are still missing.

According to educational policy, improving Hungary's competitiveness requires an increased number and a greater variety of opportunities that can help individuals develop their intercultural skills, as well as solutions, mechanisms, and incentives that support the exploitation of increased knowledge in Hungary. However, it also creates the danger of a brain drain.

Kónya's (2011) research based on the Global Employee Commitment Report 2011 confirmed that the willingness of highly qualified Hungarian employees to take up jobs abroad is higher than average. According to the survey, with regard to willingness to work and move abroad, Hungary is 7th out of 17 countries surveyed. A quarter of those participating in the survey would immediately leave their jobs, and a further 30% would leave their jobs within a year for an attractive job opportunity abroad, which is remarkably high compared with the size of the Hungarian working-age group.

Two distinct factors have a significant influence on mobility in Hungary, according to this research. One of them includes individual characteristics such as age and qualifications. The degree of mobility is highest among people under 30 and those who are graduates of higher-education institutions. Working for a multinational company can also increase the likelihood of migration. The majority of people with intentions to move abroad have 2 years of work experience and work for companies that have affiliates or subsidiaries in at least 10 other countries.

The migration of individuals with higher education may be characterized by the following features:

- Emigration level was constant between the year of transition, 1989, and the year of the EU accession, 2004, and thereafter, but, in these two particular years, there was a striking increase in the number of those leaving Hungary.
- It is not unusual that some Hungarian migrants have legal or economic degrees. Most migrants, however, have science degrees; every fourth graduate in this discipline migrates to a different country sooner or later.
- The main motives behind migration include increased income levels, higher levels of professional development, and a more balanced sociopolitical and economic climate. Returning is seriously impeded by the mere fact that the higher living standards experienced abroad cannot be achieved at home. Hungarians living abroad also report higher levels of job satisfaction.
- A third of the highly qualified migrants don't plan to return to Hungary, and another third plan to return after spending at least a decade abroad. The remaining third are uncertain about their plans (Csanády & Személyi, 2008).

The willingness of professional employees to migrate might be enhanced by student mobility during their university years (as the case of Katalin indicates). Research among students shows the growing popularity both of studying abroad and of starting a career abroad immediately after graduation (Langerné Rédei, 2009).

Although there are some extensive surveys in EU countries and in Hungary on student mobility (e.g., Eurostudent, BwSE, CHEERS surveys, Youth), there are only very few studies that analyze the impact of studying abroad on global careers in the Hungarian context.

The Graduate Survey carried out in 2010 is a significant study in the field. The results and lessons of that survey can be summarized as follows:

1. The level of mobility willingness is high (58% of the respondents are planning to work abroad, and 36% are planning to participate in education abroad), but this—just like in the case of other age groups—is combined with a low actual mobility. Only 6% of those surveyed gathered experiences abroad during their studies, and the rate of students participating in such programs on more than one occasion is even lower (1%).
2. Students mainly participate in shorter programs (78% spent 6 months or fewer abroad); typical destination countries are Germany and France, influenced by existent student-mobility programs and not by the respondents' choice.
3. Within the framework of state-funded higher education, 87% of mobile students study in full-time courses, and mostly in the capital (65% of these graduates studied in higher-education institutions in Budapest). Looking at the breakdown of the various disciplines, the dominance of economics and the humanities is obvious.

4.  Mobility during one's studies can lead to employment in positions that are international in focus or require intercultural and language skills. Obtaining work experience during the years of studying abroad also enhances individuals' later willingness to move abroad (Kasza, 2010).
5.  Women and men have equal opportunities to join the mobility programs.

There are several factors influencing the willingness of Hungarian students to study abroad. Some of these are:

*   socioeconomic background—children of parents with a degree in higher education are more likely to participate in courses abroad;
*   the family's financial situation—mainly children of relatively wealthy people can afford to study abroad;
*   the quality of secondary education—the rate of students graduating from more prestigious secondary schools, especially from 6- or 8-year grammar schools, is higher among those who participate in international programs.

The greatest barriers to spending study time abroad are:

*   lack of language skills;
*   financial uncertainty.

Therefore, students facing these barriers are less likely to have the opportunity to study abroad (Rédei, 2007).

Educated individuals tend to define the economic potential of a country; therefore, the particularly valuable human resources need special attention (Gyökér, 2004). Migration of highly qualified employees with a university or college degree in certain areas (such as engineering) is a growing problem in Hungary, especially because many of these people have no plans ever to return to Hungary. The brain-drain question is further aggravated by the fact that, in Hungary, there is a great shortage of high-potential, talented, qualified employees in those sectors, areas, and professions where migration levels tend to be higher than average, such as health care, higher education, engineering, and construction.

## The Relevance of Contemporary Career Concepts for Hungarian Global Careers

While observing the particularities related to global careers in Hungary, we have identified several lessons and questions that may open avenues for future research. This section gives a short overview of these issues.

Research suggests that, since the transition in 1989, the willingness to migrate has been growing, although the rate of actual migration is lower compared with the other Eastern European countries. Based on studies analyzing the global

movement of Hungarian employees, it can be concluded that Hungarians are equally involved in short-, mid-, and long-term migration (temporary employment, a career digression for several years, and emigration) (Buják, 2011). There are two potential explanations for this low migration rate: according to the first one, the favorable social-protection system may have prevented significant migration in the years after the political system changed. The second argues that the uniqueness of the language and the cultural characteristics, such as the tendency to avoid uncertainty and the deep-rooted need for stability, represent real barriers to migration.

If we examine the organizational environment, a critical factor in global careers, it is clear that organizational features (hierarchy, culture, human resources strategy, etc.) play a key role in providing appropriate conditions for employees' career aspirations (Cheramie, Sturman, & Walsh, 2007; Creed & Hood, 2009). The distinctive features of the Hungarian context (the growing presence of multinational organizations, the continuous shift from industrial activities to service industries, and, at the same time, the trend of flat organizations) have resulted in a growing number of motivational opportunities for Hungarian employees to build their global careers. The integration of individual and company needs, a two-way approach in managing careers, emerged in the early 1990s. In the past 20 years, it has become a standard requirement of the Hungarian job market. Best practices in managing career expectations and providing global-career opportunities have been spread mostly by the multinational companies present in Hungary. In certain areas, however, (e.g., in public-sector organizations), the possibility of building a global career has not yet been realized.

A successful career path generally means a position with greater responsibilities, tasks that are more complex and increasingly valued, a higher status and/or greater financial and moral appreciation by the organization (Dickmann & Baruch, 2010). There are two major types of career path: a specialized career in a specific area or promotion to higher managerial levels (Bérces & Hegyi, 2001). Therefore, upward mobility not only means promotion to a different level within the formal hierarchy of the organization, it also includes progress in the specialist's career path and promotion to an expanded and more valuable job, demanding more knowledge (Hamori & Kakarika, 2009). It has been shown that global careers provide opportunities for both (Gyökér & Finna, 2011). Horizontal changes through rotation, i.e. working in the same job in a different business unit or different geographical region, can be seen as an advancement and a successful career path if, in the new area, the status, prestige, and income are higher than before.

An individual's personality basically defines his/her career aspirations and also the way in which he/she exploits opportunities. On the basis of the traditional definition of career, employees can be strongly or moderately career-oriented (Koncz, 2002). Career opportunities for moderately career-oriented people will narrow continuously as organizations have a growing preference for those employees who take full responsibility for their own individual career

development, and who are easily moveable and open to change. The notion that a successful career requires a high degree of flexibility and mobility, and also greatly depends on personality traits, is increasingly accepted in Hungary (Koncz, 2003). Career aspirations are, of course, to a large extent defined by the individual's capabilities, interests, motivation, and personality, where the latter is related to all the former factors. In the context of the career-path model of Dessler (2006), the group of Hungarians between the ages of 24 and 44 can be characterized as building global careers, both in the trial and in the stabilization sub-stages of their experiences, depending on the type of motivation that is behind the decision to take up a job abroad. We can talk about a career change in the global career of Hungarians (between the ages of 25 and 44) in the context of the establishment stage of Super's Theory of Vocational Choice (Super, 1986), as, in this period, the necessary flexibility and adaptability are most likely to be present in the employees' competences. In the maintenance stage of the same model (ages 44–64), building a global career on one's own initiative is fairly unusual; people may sometimes be posted abroad by their organization, but the direction of the learning objective is reversed, and it is much more typical that employees take their specialist knowledge to the subsidiary in the foreign country.

Using Holland's (1966) orientation model, we can say that Hungarian cultural characteristics may also explain the fact that Hungarians do not build their global careers in an uninterrupted process; rather, they follow a cyclical pattern. Because of their high tendency to avoid uncertainty, Hungarians can be characterized in this context by conventional orientation. They prefer well-structured, clearly set out rules and controlled work processes: quite the opposite of Holland's enterprising orientation required to build a global career. People in this category are committed to continuous renewal and experimentation; they are willing to take risks; they enjoy competition; they have good skills in influencing others; and they enjoy power. All these skills are in line with most companies' expectations of managerial and executive positions.

Again, as a consequence of the cultural characteristics, the need for stability/security (both organizational and geographical)—one of the anchors in Schein's career model (1996)—is the most important factor for Hungarians when choosing a workplace and a career. Therefore, although they have a willingness to migrate, they rarely take up jobs abroad. If, however, they do take up a job abroad, the technical/functional competence anchor and the autonomy/independence anchor can be linked to their global career. At the same time, it is becoming increasingly typical that a new anchor—international experiences—also means considerable added value for employees.

These tendencies began after the system change in 1989; realistic opportunities arrived after Hungary's EU accession in 2004. While researching the subject, we should also consider the theories describing and explaining career-related behavior changes: the boundaryless (Arthur, Khapova, & Wilderom, 2005; Arthur & Rousseau, 1996; Baruch, 2009) and the variable (Hall, 1996) career approach, in

addition to the ideas of the integrated model of career change (Rhodes & Doering, 1983). Careers with no boundaries for Hungarians follow three major patterns (Bokor, Fertetics, Hidegh, & Váradi Szabó, 2010):

1. those who choose the world of multinational companies;
2. senior managers leaving the world of multinational companies; and
3. job hoppers.

The first and last groups of individuals are the potential global-career builders, but their different levels of awareness and self-consciousness will influence their career changes. Accidental events play a bigger part in the case of job hoppers than in the case of those who choose the world of multinationals when building a global career.

If we define international careers as career changes, then we should also note a phenomenon indicating a transformation in the mindset of Hungarian employees (Bokor et al., 2010). To Hungarian citizens in the last century, migration to a foreign country meant mainly a career change related to "leaving something behind"; employees mainly left companies and the country to distance themselves from the feeling of being stuck or of lacking something (see the history of migration above).

Global careers over the last 15–20 years have mainly been characterized by career patterns related to "searching" (employees are deliberately looking for something different because of their desires and goals of self-realization) or "moving on" (embracing new challenges, new opportunities, and better chances).

It is also important to distinguish between the behavioral patterns of blue- and white-collar workers: while workers doing physical activities show the characteristics of Bezanson's (2003) maneuverings (planned, deliberate navigation), professional Hungarians are typically more adventurous (the general direction is set, but there are less deliberate control and planning); thus, in the latter group, the proportion of those who are flexible, adaptable, and open to risk is higher.

## Critical Perspectives on Global Careers in Hungary

Hungarian emigration, compared with other CEE countries in the region, is at a lower level. The reason is Hungarians' strong need for stability and security. The poor command of foreign languages and structural and legal barriers that used to pose serious problems in the earlier years are now gradually disappearing. As the trends show, the rate of emigration is undoubtedly on the rise. Unless Hungary's economic situation improves, further increase is predicted. This forecast is supported by all the research dealing with the migration potential of Hungarians, as actual migration is in line with the migration potential that is high overall in the region. If the economy were to stabilize or start growing, the level

of migration most likely would become constant, as, within the characteristic settings of Hungarians, the need for stability and security is the highest.

Looking at the structure and characteristics of the migrant population in Hungary, there are several points worth highlighting, in terms of how critical migration may become to the Hungarian labor market and economy. Migration affects mainly the younger, highly qualified generation. The members of the age groups 25–34 and 35–44 are the most willing to build global careers. An increasing rate of migration will further decrease the size of the active working population, which also decreases owing to demographic trends. This will lead to real challenges in maintaining decent social-security and pension systems in Hungary. Among the migrants, a significant proportion are highly educated people, who leave the country either for an interim period of time or for longer periods of time (over 10 years). Based on the research, we find that these highly educated people tend to spend a longer time abroad than average, and at least 30% of them are considering becoming residents of the host country. This type of brain drain, mid to long term, may significantly influence Hungary's human capital negatively.

Among blue-collar migrants, one remarkable factor is that there are specific occupational groups, e.g., construction specialists or butchers, that are overly exposed to migration. Those migrating from these jobs to other countries will create significant skills shortages in the Hungarian labor market. We also notice that blue-collar migrants are characterized by circular migration or commuting back and forth. The reason for this is mainly because the host countries, most of the time, offer them either project-based jobs or limited-time assignments. At the same time, these "migrants" do not want completely to leave their own country, namely Hungary, where in most cases they leave the family behind. Most of these migrants will return, as soon as they find an appropriate job opportunity with an acceptable salary in Hungary.

Based on trends in the past decade, the favored destination countries of Hungarian emigrants searching for global careers are the economically more developed European countries. This tendency is expected to become stronger under the current circumstances. One reason for this is the geographical closeness, which allows emigrants to return home easily. Another reason for choosing the so-called economically more developed neighboring countries is that countries such as Germany or Austria are characterized by historical and economic ties to Hungary, and in the future will still rely pretty heavily on Hungarian jobseekers and professionals to fill their local labor needs. We must note that the Hungarian migrants have significantly better compensation in these host countries, while their working environment and appreciation are also more satisfying than they would be in the same work and position in Hungary. This is true for both blue-collar and white-collar workers. There are regions in Germany, for instance, where special policy programs are developed and supported by financial aid to attract back German compatriots living in the USA, and to replace German fellows with Eastern European fellows. There is a real danger of losing valuable human

resource capacity in Hungary in certain industries and professions where the tendency to emigrate is higher, for example health care and engineering.

Overall, the present situation is marked by (a) the emigration of Hungarian professionals to the West, which reinforces the brain-drain phenomenon, and (b) by the immigration of mainly Hungarian nationalities from neighboring Eastern European countries, which in fact can be considered inner migration.

The integration of these Hungarians, however, has not yet been achieved. As a result, Hungary is facing a double challenge: how to retain talent and attract back young Hungarians living abroad, and how to integrate Hungarian immigrants from neighboring countries.

Young, educated employees belong to the Y generation; for them, variety in several different jobs and workplaces is required and represents added value in building a fulfilling career, rather than being committed to one workplace over a longer period of time. As for preventing the loss of human capital, once we recognize that these young people cannot be forced to stay at home, it would be much more important to motivate them to assemble different experiences abroad before they return home. The negative effects of brain drain can be reduced if we find ways to encourage young people to gain global experiences and offer trade-offs for returning (Groizard & Llull, 2006; Stark, Helmenstein, & Prskawetz, 1997).

Brain exchange, for example (where the sending country is also a host country), or brain circulation (the population posted or migrating abroad leaves the country only for a limited period in order to gather experience) would be desirable solutions for Hungary. The results of research on emigrating professionals (Csanády, Kmetty, Kucsera, Személyi, & Tarján, 2008) clearly suggest that, although young people are mainly motivated by higher wages, in order to work in Hungary, a higher wage in itself is not enough. If we want people to stay here or to return, we will need changes in education and in policy; higher than current living standards; and changes in attitudes in the whole society.

International experience has shown, so far, that the migration of qualified people never stops entirely; the objective can only be to keep this within desirable limits. As long as there are no favorable domestic circumstances that automatically facilitate a decrease in the number of emigrants and an increase in the number of people returning home, it is vital to keep in close contact with those working abroad. A diaspora policy already has its well-functioning tools abroad, and these tools promote the development of the economy of the home country. However, this practice has still got a long way to go in Hungary.

Another aspect of the topic of global careers in Hungary is the situation of immigrants. It is time for Hungary to prepare for an increase in the problems caused by international migration; it is time for the country to prepare to address these. The situation of migrants arriving in Hungary is typically chaotic, given the fact that, for a long time, Hungary's role was that of the sender. It is difficult for foreigners arriving in Hungary to find a job (unemployment is high among

Hungarians, and no improvement is expected in the near future) (Gödri, 2008, 2010). In addition, settling down and getting a work permit are bureaucratic, complicated procedures.

Among other factors, the uniqueness of the language and the characteristics of the culture ensure that immigrants have great difficulties in integrating, apart from those arriving from neighboring countries, as their value systems and behaviors are similar to those of Hungarians, but even this is not fully resolved (Juhász, 2000).

At this point in time, we should consider that Hungarian immigration policy couldn't resolve the question that is formulated in Tóth's (2002) research as follows: What better serves the interests of the Hungarian state: Satisfying the needs of many different areas of the Hungarian labor market in the short term and improving the several-decades-long negative demographic indicators by attracting Hungarians from neighboring countries? Or is it better—according to considerations based on national policy—to support Hungarians living in neighboring countries to stay home and to develop and expand in the country where they were born.

Another important criterion, which should not be neglected, is the "migration tolerance" level of the host country, namely of Hungary. How does Hungarian society relate to immigrants? Presenting this question is of vital importance, as the proportion of foreigners living in Hungary is projected to be approximately 10% of the total population by 2020. The Hungarian situation requires the government to act immediately to create programs regarding migration and national policy, as at present both are missing.

## Summary

Studying the Hungarian situation, we find—on the basis of primary and secondary research—that there are no specific career models or special career patterns for global careers, although there are certain factors that may encourage Hungarians to build a career abroad.

Compared with other CEE countries in the region, Hungarian emigration is at a lower level; however, the tendency and the rate of emigration are undoubtedly increasing, affecting mainly the younger, highly qualified generation. Members of this group are the most willing to build global careers. Barriers that used to pose serious problems, such as a poor command of foreign languages, a lack of flexibility, and a lack of openness and adaptability are gradually disappearing and no longer prevent young professionals from building a global career (Finna, 2008). However, there is a real danger of losing valuable human resource capacity in Hungary in certain industries and professions, where the tendency for emigration is higher—for example, health care, education, and engineering.

According to young professionals whom we interviewed regarding difficulties in forging international careers, Hungarians have a twofold disadvantage.

One is—in comparison with other CEE employees—the uniqueness of the Hungarian language. A second important problem is that host countries have certain prejudices or mistrust against those who come from former Eastern Bloc countries. These make it exponentially difficult for Hungarians to be equally, justly, and impartially valued on the global career market. In addition, the lack of a thorough understanding of democracy and the "rules" and practices of capitalism, including full comprehension of a free-market economy, represents another set of genuine challenges for Hungarians trying to adapt and adjust to the global career market.

Hungary has a great responsibility and duty to prevent the final emigration of those who are irreplaceable; the government should be offering ways for talented Hungarians living abroad to return. In order for Hungary to increase its competitiveness, the objective should be to attract the highly qualified emigrants back to Hungary, or to provide those who are planning to build international careers with such provisions that will motivate them—after a shorter or longer stay abroad—to return to Hungary. This leads to new requirements, both in the field of education (within the education system, preparing people to become global citizens and developing their adaptability, but being responsible towards the development of their home country) and in management theory and practice (fine-tuning posting practices and relevant HR systems), and makes it necessary for the different players to change their way of thinking.

## Notes

1. Data from the Jewish Wold Congress.
2. The number of Hungarian citizens registered as immigrants in European states each year is between 20,000 and 28,000 (in 2007, it was more than 34,000). This is obviously the minimum number of emigrants, as, in some countries, there is a lack of data, and Hungarian citizens have also left for other continents (Gödri, 2010).
3. Preliminary results of the 2011 census are expected in spring 2012.
4. Data from 2010.
5. Without exact data, defining the rate of Hungarian migrants is only possible with estimated numbers based on data taken from official data collections, censuses, and the mirror statistics (data sources of hosting countries).
6. The decreasing age of Hungarian employees in the United Kingdom is conspicuous. There are hardly any people in the Hungarian population here older than the age group 25–34, which creates a new migration pattern.

## References

Adler, J. (2008). Motivation of working age inactive population, reasons for non-appearance in the labor market. *National Public Employment Foundation*, Conference paper, Budapest.

Arthur, M. B., Khapova, S. N., & Wilderom, C. P. M. (2005). Career success in a boundaryless career world. *Journal of Organizational Behavior*, 26: 177–202.

Arthur, M. B. & Rousseau, D. M. (1996). *The Boundaryless Career: A New Employment Principle for a New Organizational Era*. New York: Oxford University Press.

Baruch, Y. (2009). Career planning and management interventions from the organisational perspective. In Collin, A. & Patton, W. (Eds.), *Vocational Psychological and Organisational Perspectives on Career, Towards a Multidisciplinary Dialogue* (131–146). Amsterdam: Sense.

Bérces, R. & Hegyi, Z. (2001). TQM and organizational development. *Periodica Polytechnica—Social and Management Sciences*, 9(2): 117–126.

Berencsi, Zs. & Sik, E. (1995). Intentions to emigrate and to work abroad in Hungary in 1993–1994. In Fullerton, M., Sik, E., & Tóth, J. (Eds.), *Refugees and Migrants: Hungary at a Crossroads* (129–140). Budapest: MTA PTI.

Bezanson, L. (2003). Career development: Policy, proof and purpose. *Careers Education and Guidance*, October: 5–10.

Bokor, A., Fertetics, M., Hidegh, A. L., & Váradi Szabó, Zs. (2010). Career changers in Hungary—life stages and career changes, VII. *International Conference of Miskolc University GTK*. Conference paper, Miskolc.

Borbándi, Gy. (2006). Biography of Hungarian emigration, 1945–1985. Retrieved from mek.oszk.hu/03400/03472/03472.pdf, 8 May 2011.

Buják, A. (2011). Hungarian migrant. Retrieved from www.168ora.hu/itthon/migracio-kulfoldi-munkavallalas-kivandorlas-felmeres-tarki-78213.html, 11 March 2011.

Cheramie, R. A., Sturman, M. C., & Walsh, K. (2007). Executive career management: Switching organizations and the boundaryless career. *Journal of Vocational Behavior*, 71: 359–374.

Creed, P. & Hood, M. (2009). Career development, planning, and management from the organisational perspective. In Collin, A. & Patton, W. (Eds.), *Vocational Psychological and Organisational Perspectives on Career, Towards a Multidisciplinary Dialogue* (41–62). Amsterdam: Sense.

Csanády, M. & Személyi, L. (2008). Brain drain—Close-up about Hungarian people with higher education. Retrieved from www.szazadveg.hu/files/kiadoarchivum/szemelyi41.pdf, 10 July 2011.

Csanády, M. T., Kmetty, Z., Kucsera, T., Személyi, L., & Tarján, G. (2008). The Hungarian highly qualified migrants after the transition. *Hungarian Science*, (5). Retrieved from www.matud.iif.hu/08maj/11.html

Dessler, G. (2006). *Human Resource Management*. New York: Prentice Hall.

Dickmann, M. & Baruch, Y. (2010). *Global Careers*. London and New York: Routledge Taylor & Francis Group.

Eke, E., Girasek, E., & Szócska, M. (2008). Examination of Hungarian resident's labor market purposes, migration and career motivation. Final Study. *National Public Employment Foundation* OFA/7341/0032. 5–33.

Finna, H. (2008). Atypical employment forms enabling labor market flexibility among Hungarian small and medium-sized enterprises. Doctoral dissertation. Retrieved from database of Budapest University of Technology and Economics: www.omikk.bme.hu/collections/phd/Gazdasag_es_Tarsadalomtudomanyi_Kar/2008/Finna_Henrietta/ertekezes.pdf, 14 March 2011.

Gödri, I. (2008). Migration in the web of relations—Role of social networks and network capital in immigration to Hungary at the end of the millennium. Ph.D. dissertation. Retrieved from http://doktori.tatk.elte.hu.2009_Godri.pdf, 23 June 2011.

Gödri I. (2010). Migration deficit in Hungary in the last decade—How much are we actually?. *KorFa Online Population News*, 2010 (3). Retrieved from www.demografia.hu/letoltes/kiadvanyok/Korfak/KorFa%20online_2010_3.pdf, 30 March 2011.

Groizard, J. L. & Llull, J. (2006). Skilled migration and growth. Testing brain drain and brain gain theories, *DEA Working Papers*, *20*, Universitat de les Illes Balears, Departament d'Economía Aplicada.

Gyökér, I. (2004). Companies' intellectual capital—uncountable assets. *Harvard Business-manager*, Hungarian edition, 6(6): 48–59.

Gyökér, I. & Finna, H. (2011). Hungarians on global career path. *Information Society*, 11(1): 203–207.

Hall, D. T. (1996). Protean careers of the 21st century. *Academy of Management Executive*, 10(4): 8–16.

Hamori, M. & Kakarika, M. (2009). External labor market strategy and career success: CEO careers in Europe and the United States. *Human Resources Management*, 48(3): 355–378.

Hárs, Á. (2001). Hungarian emigration and immigration perspectives—some economic considerations. Retrieved from http://sites.uclouvain.be/aiece/publications/regular/medium/hungarian_emigr_10_2001.pdf, 10 March 2011.

Hárs, Á. (2008). Enlargement and disappointment—Hungarian labor market and migration. In *Social report 2008*. TÁRKI.

Hárs, Á. (2011). Hungarians' labor migration. Kopint-Tárki, EURES Emigration Working paper, Budapest.

Holland, J. L. (1966). *The Psychology of Vocational Choice*. Waltham, MA: Blaisdell.

Juhász, J. (2000). Migrant trafficking in Hungary. In *Migrant Trafficking and Human Smuggling in Europe: A Review of the Evidence with Case Studies from Hungary, Poland and Ukraine*. Geneva: International Organization for Migration.

Juhász, J., Csikvari, J., Szaitz, M., & Makara, P. (2006). Migration and irregular work in Europe (MIGIWE). Hungarian Scientific Academy, Panta Rhei Social Research Inc. Hungarian Central Statistical Office, OFA/5341/2.

Karoliny, E. & Mohay, Á. (2009). Legal framework of international migration. Retrieved from www.ittvagyunk.eu/application/essay/37_1.pdf, 8 June 2011.

Kasza, G. (2010). Helyzetkép a nemzetközi hallgatói mobilitásról. In Educatio Kht. (Eds.) *Tracking Graduates' Careers IV. Fresh Graduates 2010*. Budapest. Retrieved from www.felvi.hu/pub_bin/dload/DPR/dprfuzet4/DPRfuzet4_teljes.pdf, 19 May 2011.

Kincses, Á. & Rédei, M. (2009). Hungary at crossroads. *Romanian Journal of European Studies*, 7–8: 23–41.

Kollega Tarsoly, I. (Ed.) (1996). *Hungary in the XX Century*. Volume 1 (339–398). Szekszárd: Babits.

Koncz, K. (2002). *Career Management* (84–92). Budapest: Aula.

Koncz, K. (2003). Walk of life and career management at the workplace. I–II. Retrieved from www.mfor.hu/cikkek/Eletpalya_es_munkahelyi_karriermenedzsment.html, 9 April 2011.

Kónya, J. (2011). International brain-drain: Employees are looking for better jobs abroad. *Global Employee Commitment Report 2011*. GFK Hungária. Retrieved from www.gfk.hu/imperia/md/content/gfk_hungaria/pdf/press_2011/press_hun/press_2011_06_22_h.pdf, 13 August 2011.

Langerné Rédei, M. (2009). Student migration and the labor market. In Illés, S. (Ed.) *In Attraction of Hungary* (67–129). Retrieved from www.demografia.hu/letoltes/kiadvanyok/Kutjelek/Kutjel85_nyomdaba_vegleges.pdf, 27 August 2011.

McLoughlin, S. & Münz, R. (2011). Temporary and circular migration: Opportunities and challenges. Working Paper No. 35. European Migration and Diversity, Europe's Political Economy Programs.

MTI (2011). There can be deficiency of fresh specialists in the next few years. *Heti Világgazdaság Online*. Retrieved from hvg.hu/itthon/20111013_szakorvos_kepzes_ hiany, 19 April 2011.

Rédei, M. (2007). The Hungarian migration regime: From talent loss to talent attraction. *Geographical Forum—Geographical Studies and Environment Protection Research*, 6: 124–145.

Rhodes, S. R. & Doering, M. (1983). An integrated model of career motivation. *Academy of Management Review*, 8: 631–639.

Schein, E. H. (1996). Career anchors revisited: Implications for career development of 21st Century. *The Academy of Management Executive*, 10: 80–90.

Sik, E. (2010). Migration potential. *Tranzit Online*. Retrieved from www.tranzitonline. eu/cikkek/migracios-potencial, 6 April 2011.

Stark, O., Helmenstein, C., & Prskawetz, A. (1997). A brain gain with a brain drain. *Economics Letters*, Elsevier 55(2): 227–234.

Super, D. E. (1986). Life career roles. In Hall, D. T. (Ed.), *Career Development in Organizations*. San Fransisco, CA: Jossey-Bass.

Tóth, P. P. (2002). International migration—Hungary (1990–2000), Hungarian Central Statistical Office, Demographic Research Institute. Budapest: 2–11.

# 12

# GLOBAL CAREERS WITHIN AND OUTSIDE AN EMERGING COUNTRY

## The Case of Turkey

*Burak Koyuncu, Rouen Business School, France, and Julia Richardson, York University, Canada*

## Introduction

This chapter considers global careers within and outside Turkey. First, it explores the careers of Turkish nationals, with a specific focus on their desire for, and experiences of, pursuing global careers *outside* of Turkey and their views of repatriation. Second, it explores the career experiences of expatriates *in* Turkey. In doing so, it provides an understanding of global careers where Turkey is either the "home" country or the "host" country. At the end of the chapter, we will introduce a more critical perspective of global careers in Turkey and discuss the implications for policymakers and individual "global careerists." In order to ensure that the chapter is appropriately contextualized, however, we will begin with a discussion of Turkey's current economy and labor market.

## Global Careers in Turkey

Despite the current global financial crisis (GFC), the Turkish economy has shown consistent strength, with 11% growth in the first quarter of 2011 (*The Economist*, 2011a; Turkish Statistical Institute, 2011). Indeed, according to the OECD, Turkey is expected to be the fastest growing economy of the OECD members during the period 2011–2017, with a predicted growth rate of 6.7%.

As an emerging economy, Turkey has a relatively young population, with a median age of 29.2 years (see Box 12.1). Indeed, compared with EU countries, it has the largest ratio of youth population to overall population. Although it has the longest working hours in Europe, it also has the lowest number of sick days per employee—53.2 hours worked per week and an annual average of 4.6 sick

---

**Box 12.1** Turkey: Country Profile[1]

- Population: 75.8 million
- Median age: 29.2 (2010)
- Labor force: 25.9 million (October 2010)
- Unemployment rate: 9.4% (May 2011)
- GDP: $735billion
- Average annual growth in real GDP (2003–2008): 6%
- Structure of employment: Agriculture 26%, industry 26%, services 48%

---

days per employee (ISPAT, 2011). Where education is concerned, although the adult literacy rate (88.7%) compares reasonably favorably with other developing economies (notably the BRIC countries—Brazil, Russia, India, and China), there is still some way to go before it matches those of developed countries. However, investment in literacy continues to grow, with 3.7% of GDP spent on education, which also compares favorably with the BRIC countries. Although there is room for further economic development, employment and business opportunities in Turkey are growing for Turkish nationals and for foreign direct investment. According to government websites, for example, the increase in labor productivity and the decrease in real unit wage have provided a perfect setting for multinationals to expand in Turkey (ISPAT, 2011).

In addition to economic changes, Turkey's sociocultural environment has undergone considerable change. Recent research has reported that Turkey is now somewhat "less collectivistic (e.g. Goregenli, 1997; Aycan et al., 2000), less hierarchical (Aycan et al., 2000), and less uncertainty avoiding (e.g. Kabasakal & Bodur, 1998)" (Aycan, 2001, p. 253) than Hofstede (1980) has suggested. Although the shift away from collectivism towards more individualism has been emphasized by several studies (e.g., Karakitapoğlu Aygün, 2004; Karakitapoğlu Aygün & Imamoğlu, 2002), some caution is necessary. According to Fullagar, Sumer, Sverke, and Slick (2003), for example, "the nature of individualism [in Turkey] is quite different from that observed in most Western countries in that it is accompanied by deep-seated traditional values related to being a member of an ingroup" (p. 103). That is to say, social relationships and responsibilities are still very important in Turkish culture and play a dominant role in work and non-work life (Karakitapoğlu Aygün, 2004). Perhaps a better description of the role of relationships in contemporary Turkish organizations is that they are a hybrid of collectivism and individualism (Gopalan, Kavas, & Nelson, 2005).

Focusing specifically on employment opportunities and experiences, as noted in Box 12.1, just under half of the population is employed in the services sector, with a quarter in each of industry and agriculture. Although the average manager's salary is lower than that of their Western-European/American counterpart, salary levels in Turkey have moved closer to the European average. Moreover,

individual income tax (between 15 and 35%) is lower than that of many European countries. These changes, as well as the relatively low cost of living in Turkey compared with other European countries, are expected to have an impact on Turkey's ability to retain and attract workers.

## Structural, Cultural, and Contextual Opportunities and Challenges

Turning now to career opportunities, a comparative study of MBA students in Turkey, Britain, and Israel reported significantly greater perceptions of "free choice" among Turkish nationals (Özbilgin, Kusku, & Erdogmus, 2005). According to the study's findings, Turkish respondents believed that they have a relatively "free choice" when making their career decisions. Although they acknowledged the potential influence of acquaintances, friends, and/or family, they believed that their choices were primarily determined by their own needs for professional development (Özbilgin et al., 2005). Aycan and Fikret-Pasa (2003) reported similar findings, where individual concerns about professional and personal development had the greatest impact on career decisions. A more recent study of 18,800 Turkish professionals by Kariyer.net—one of the largest HR and career websites in Turkey—reflected similar findings (see Box 12.2). These findings also suggest that the work values of young Turkish professionals are similar

---

### Box 12.2 Survey Findings

- The most important thing for me when selecting the firm I will work at is:
  - development opportunities (40%);
  - compensation and benefits (33%);
  - leading firm in the industry (11%);
  - socially responsible firm (8%);
  - location (4%);
  - multinational firm (3%);
  - flexible/less strict work environment (1%).
- The meaning of work for me is:
  - a means to gain professional advancement and self-development (52%);
  - an important part of my life (30%);
  - a means to earn a living (10%);
  - a means to gain status (7%).
- My biggest fear related to my work life is:
  - working in an unfair environment (55%);
  - working with a team that I don't feel comfortable with (19%);
  - being in an unethical environment (13%);
  - working with a bad/wrong boss (8%);
  - not receiving the compensation I deserve (4%).

Source: Kariyer.net Survey, 2011

to those of young professionals (generation Y) from some Western countries (Meier & Crocker, 2010; Twenge, Campbell, Hoffman, & Lance, 2010).

These findings reflect the sense of "agency" that permeates contemporary discourse about careers as boundaryless and/or protean (Sullivan & Baruch, 2009). However, other studies have emphasized the influence of contextual and structural factors on careers in Turkey. One study of more than 1,500 graduates, for example, reported that, "father's income, self-employment status and social security status are important factors influencing an individual in choosing a riskier career such as business over a less risky one such as education or health" (Caner & Okten, 2010, p. 1060). Of course, parental status and education have been closely linked to career opportunities in many other countries (Johnson & Mortimer, 2002). The point here, however, is that, where Turkey is concerned, structural and institutional factors seem to have some influence on career trajectories. Indeed, according to the Kariyer.net Survey, introduced above, 58% of participants thought that they had control over which firm they work for, whereas 42% stated that they did *not*, owing to labor-market conditions. This clearly suggests that, although career choices in Turkey may be in part influenced by individual choice, those choices take place within societal and institutional structures, thus emphasizing the "Janus face" of careers as both individually and socially determined.

Exploring the theme of career choice in Turkey further, Tanova, Karatas-Özkan, and Inal (2008) found that education and training, knowledge of the labor market, love of the career, and promotion, training and development opportunities had a significantly stronger influence on Turkish women's career choice than on their male counterparts'. This difference may stem from broader perceptions of gender roles, where men are still seen as the "bread-winners" of the family and women as bearing greater responsibility for child rearing (Guney, Gohar, Akinci, & Akinci, 2006). Thus, women's career choices may focus more on self-/professional development rather than on opportunities to augment income and/or employment security.

Extending our exploration of women's participation in the Turkish labor market, according to *The Economist*, Turkey is third in the World Economic Forum's ranking of countries by the proportion of women CEOs (*The Economist*, 2011b). Other studies have reported similar findings where an increasing number of women occupy senior managerial and professional positions (see, for example, Aycan, 2001; Kabasakal, Aycan, & Karakaş, 2004). A comparative study of female professors in Australia and Turkey (Ozkanli & White, 2008) also reported that,

> there are clearly historical, social and economic factors, together with government regulations in relation to selection and promotion in academic employment, that explain the impressive performance of senior academic women in Turkey, which has a higher representation of female professors than most other countries.

(pp. 59–60)

Even in male-dominated occupations, women have made some headway. For instance, Katrinli, Gunay, Erdener Acar, and Zengin Karaibrahimoglu (2010) found that, although accounting is seen as a "male" profession, female accountants are viewed positively and widely recognized for their high levels of competency. However, despite the relatively high proportion of women in senior management positions compared with some other countries, "decision-making positions" in Turkey are still male-dominated (Fullagar et al., 2003). Similarly, political participation in Turkey is relatively low, where fewer than 10% of parliamentary seats are occupied by women (United Nations Development Programme, 2008). While some Turkish women have gained access to corporate-management positions and the concomitant earning power, there is still much room for progress—particularly in rural communities, where women's employment opportunities are much more restricted (Sinangil & Ones, 2003). Moreover, according to some studies, cultural conflict persists about the role of women and, especially, "between the modernization of women's roles and traditional values that promote segregation of gender roles" (Fullagar et al., 2003, p. 103). Therefore, despite positive comparisons with developed countries (Özbilgin & Healy, 2004), societal values in Turkey still create a barrier to women's career advancement (Aycan, 2004; Ozkanli & White, 2008).

We turn now to the concept of global careers, focusing first on Turkey as the *home* country *from* which Turkish nationals pursue global careers and *to* which they may (or may not) return.

## Global Moves of Turkish Professionals

During the 1960s, many Turkish professionals left Turkey, owing to political instability and ongoing economic crisis. The movement of highly skilled individuals from Turkey to other countries (mostly Europe or the USA) has continued, whether in the form of expatriation or immigration (Tansel & Gungor, 2003). Although the recent growth of the Turkish economy and the GFC may have slowed this trend, many Turkish professionals are still opting to pursue global careers, albeit on a more limited time scale.

Exploring the decision to pursue a career outside of Turkey, Tansel and Gungor (2003) conducted a study with 1,170 Turkish students living abroad. When asked about their motivation to go abroad, roughly one quarter cited the "prestige" of studying abroad, which points to international experience as a means of achieving some form of positive social recognition or reward. Other "pull" factors (Baruch, 1995) were also identified, such as opportunities to experience a different/better lifestyle, acquire a new language, and to be with a spouse living overseas, among others. "Push" factors included insufficient facilities and/or educational programs, demand for international experience in some Turkish universities, and limited educational opportunities for children in Turkey (Tansel & Gungor, 2003). Interestingly, a more recent study of business professionals pursuing careers

outside of Turkey, by the same authors, found similar themes (Gungor & Tansel, 2008). Taken together, these findings suggest a fairly widespread perception that both educational and work experiences gained outside of Turkey are "valuable" career assets. Indeed, there was general consensus that international experience would add to personal and professional development.

Thus far, we have considered the decision to pursue a global career as an individually driven endeavor—what some authors have called "self-initiated expatriation" (Richardson, McBey, & McKenna, 2008). Global careers may also be initiated by organizations, where employees are "sent" overseas as part of an international assignment (Doherty, Dickmann, & Mills, 2011). Research has identified multiple, complex, and dynamic reasons why national and international organizations send their employees overseas (Jokinen, 2010; Pattie, White, & Tansky, 2010) and why those employees accept such assignments. First, they may see them as an opportunity for personal and professional development (see Box 12.3, for an example). Indeed, an extensive body of research suggests that an overseas assignment helps professionals develop and acquire cultural and managerial skills (see, for example, Cappellen & Janssens, 2008; Dickmann & Harris, 2005; Jokinen, 2010; Suutari & Makela, 2007). Second, with fairly widespread agreement that international experience is now a prerequisite for top positions in large companies (Hamori & Koyuncu, 2011), many employees are realizing the need to take part in overseas assignments. Moreover, companies that send their employees abroad strengthen their organizational brand, even if it is costly. Third, according to some scholars, it is almost impossible for leaders fully to comprehend global challenges and customer expectations without moving from the headquarters (Bingham, Felin, & Black, 2000). Fourth, employees with international experience also provide other performance benefits to their employers. For instance, some studies have suggested that the international experience of top executives positively relates to the degree of international diversification of large-sized firms (e.g., Herrmann & Datta, 2005). Box 12.3 provides a useful example of a Turkish business professional's experiences as an international assignee. We will also explore this issue further, in the *Critical Perspectives* section at the end of this chapter.

In addition to corporate business executives being sent overseas by their employers, some governmental and academic institutions in Turkey send their employees abroad for training and development purposes. So, for example, the international sabbatical is a regular feature of many academic careers, where professors work overseas for a limited period of time in order to expand their international collaborative networks and research opportunities, among other things. Indeed, as we will discuss below, Turkish academic institutions regularly encourage scholars to go overseas in order to enhance their academic profiles and to keep up with the global trends towards the internationalization of higher education.

---

### Box 12.3 A Global Employee: The Case of Murat Candan

Murat Candan is a 29-year-old management consultant working in the Istanbul office of a multinational company (MNC). After several internships with MNCs and graduating from a prestigious Turkish university, he was delighted to find a position in a company operating in several different countries. He was even more delighted when, soon after starting at the company, his manager asked him to go on a 1-year international assignment. Given his propensity towards international travel and interest in global business, he didn't think twice before accepting the offer! Nor was he disappointed, as the assignment expanded his professional development and intercultural skills beyond anything that he might have imagined. After repatriation, he worked on several smaller international projects (for which he needed to travel frequently) that added further to his cross-cultural skills. However, despite his rapid career advancement, some aspects of his job bothered him, predominantly the working hours and salary. An average week for him meant at least 60 hours of work. In fact, if he was honest, he had had almost no life outside work since he first started with the company. Although his salary was reasonable, he knew that former colleagues were making about 50% more than him in other international companies, even though they worked fewer hours. Although he enjoyed the international travel, the long periods away from home were also starting to weigh on him, even though he knew that they

---

### Repatriation—When Turkish Nationals Come Home

After going abroad to study or gain international work experience, Turkish nationals may decide to return home or stay on in the host country for a longer or indeterminate period. Tansel and Gungor (2003), for example, reported that, although 53% of Turkish students studying abroad had *initially* intended to return to Turkey after completing their studies, once they had finished, only 13.5% said that they would be likely to do so (a very low ratio in comparison with other studies; c.f. Baruch, Budhwar, & Khatri, 2007). In terms of their satisfaction with life abroad, the majority stated that the *academic life* in their host country was better than what they might have had in Turkey. However, when it came to their *social life* in the host country, only 19% thought it was better than in Turkey. On the other hand, about 70% indicated that they had a better *quality of life* in Turkey (Tansel & Gungor, 2003). This finding seems to suggest that, even though the quality of life might have had some influence on the decision to repatriate, academic and professional factors were more of a priority, and so they decided to stay on in the host country.

Another study of self-initiated expatriate Turkish professionals (Gungor & Tansel, 2008) found that, although 50% had *initially* intended to return to Turkey, at the time of the study only 25% intended to do so. Those who still

intended to return drew on a number of reasons: they had reached their career/study goals (70.9%); they missed their families (60.8%); it would be better for their children's education (22.7%); they wanted to take advantage of job opportunities in Turkey (11.9%); they felt unsafe in their host country (7.6%); or they had to return to Turkey for military service (16.3%) or academic service (14.6%)[2] (Tansel & Gungor, 2003). This last reason reflects two very specific institutional influences (military- and academic-service obligations), which, although not unique to Turkey, are very much a part of the national context. We will explore each of these influences in more detail later in the chapter. Next, however, we turn to reported reasons for *not* returning to Turkey.

The two studies described above also reported important themes about Turkish expatriates' reasons for *not* wanting to return to Turkey. Among those who were reluctant to return, economic and political instability and a relatively high unemployment rate at the time of the study were dominant concerns. Some also expressed concerns about what were loosely described as "bureaucracy" and "unsatisfactory" income levels in Turkey, compared with those of their host country. Limited career-advancement opportunities in some occupations and dissatisfaction with the social/cultural life in Turkey were also cited as reasons *not* to return (Gungor & Tansel, 2008). Just as some students and professionals cited military- and academic-service obligations for why they were returning to Turkey, others cited those same reasons for *not* intending to return or delaying their return.

Focusing first on the theme of military service, all Turkish citizens with university degrees are required to complete either 6 months or 12 months of military service. Because of the time spent out of the labor market, many people see this service requirement as a career break (Tansel & Gungor, 2003). According to Turkish law, provided they pay a specified fee (€5,112 as of October 2011), individuals working abroad for 3 years or more can serve a 21-day military service, instead of the long-term obligation. Some of the students who were studying abroad stayed on in their host country until they had been away for the required 3 years specifically because it meant that they would be entitled to the short-term military service. Some professionals who were reluctant to return to Turkey also cited military-service obligations (Gungor & Tansel, 2008; Tansel & Gungor, 2003).

We turn now to the second form of "service obligation," academic service, which was also cited as a reason either to return or to delay returning. Reflecting broader global trends towards the internationalization of higher education (Altbach, 2004; Selmer & Lauring, 2010), the higher-education system in Turkey is characterized by policies seeking to increase the number of Turkish academics trained abroad. Initiatives have been introduced and implemented that provide financial support for academics who want to study abroad. In return for this support, they must agree to return to Turkey and work in a preselected state university for a specified number of years. As noted above, some professionals in Tansel and Gungor's (2003) study were returning to Turkey specifically in order

to *fulfill* their academic-service obligations. Others, however, were delaying their return specifically in order to *avoid* such obligations.

What we observe here, therefore, is that academic service (like military service) operates as both a driver to repatriation and as a reason for delaying repatriation. It is also notable that one of the key reasons for academic professionals *not* wanting to return to fulfill this obligation was a perceived lack of research support in Turkey, which many felt might impede their professional development. Indeed, Tansel and Gungor (2003) reported that most of the recipients of such scholarships chose to reimburse the government in order to extend their period abroad, rather than return to work in a state university. Despite this trend, however, it is notable that, during the last decade, the number of private universities operating in Turkey has increased. By 2011, for example, there were reported to be 62 private and 103 state universities (YOK, 2011). Although only 5% of students are enrolled in these private institutions, they are widely understood to provide better research facilities, laboratories, and support for scholarly work (Atakan & Eker, 2007). They are also increasingly attractive to Turkish academics working abroad, who are considering whether they want to repatriate.

Having explored the experiences of Turkish nationals pursuing global careers *outside* of Turkey, we turn now to expatriates from elsewhere pursuing global careers *within* Turkey.

## Expatriates Pursuing Global Careers in Turkey

With its strategic international location and expanding economy, Turkey is an increasingly attractive location for MNCs, nongovernmental organizations, and other international institutions (Vardar, 2011). It offers designated tax benefits and incentives for MNCs, such as a corporate income tax of 20%, which is lower than, or comparable with, other countries in the region (Celikkaya, 2010), as well as other tax incentives in the form of partial/total exemption from corporate income tax for corporations operating in specific industries or geographical areas (ISPAT, 2011). Other policies and laws supporting research and development and/or innovation have also been introduced to attract and support MNC activities. It is not surprising, therefore, that many global companies, such as Honda, Vodafone, Mercedes, and Bosch, have plans to increase their workforce in Turkey or to move their regional headquarters there (ISPAT, 2011).

As opportunities and incentives for MNCs to operate in Turkey increase, so, we might assume, do the incentives for foreign nationals to pursue global careers there—be it through a corporate assignment or self-initiated expatriation. With its growing economy and increasing political stability, Turkey may be an attractive location in which to enhance one's *global*-career capital (Jokinen, 2010). It also offers opportunities for business development, as well as enhancing one's cultural competencies, i.e., rather than moving to a more developed country with saturated markets. Indeed, in a study of Finnish corporate assignees (Jokinen, 2010),

some managers indicated that setting up business ventures from scratch, as might be the case in developing countries, was a particularly important learning experience.

Although moving to a developing country may offer important opportunities for enhancing one's global-career competencies, it can also present considerable professional and personal challenges (Richardson & Mallon, 2005). Foreign nationals (be they immigrants, self-initiated expatriates, or corporate assignees) in Turkey may face particular challenges accessing work permits and visas. With a relatively young working population and the expansion of higher education, Turkey has no shortage of qualified professionals. Indeed, according to government statistics, there are roughly 500,000 graduates from Turkish universities each year (ISPAT, 2011). It is not surprising, therefore, that the Ministry of Labor is reluctant to issue work permits to foreign nationals (*KPMG Careers Magazine*, 2010). Moreover, although English is widely spoken, linguistic competency in Turkish is essential, unless one is working in an MNC—although even then some basic competency might still be required. Other factors such as "cultural distance" and religious mores and values present further challenges to foreign nationals, particularly in the more rural areas.

Despite the challenges noted above, Turkey's growing economy and moves towards globalizing its business environment have increased the demand for professionals with international experience (notably foreign nationals) who can help Turkish companies access the international business marketplace. Indeed, an understanding of global markets and knowledge of different cultures or languages have become some of the most sought-after skills among companies in Turkey. For instance, KPMG provides an example of how some companies specifically hire foreigners for their Turkish subsidiaries in order to facilitate international business connections. The company has a *Japanese desk*, where they hire a Japanese assignee (a senior manager), who "handles day-to-day communication in Japanese with clients [Japanese multinationals] who are currently operating or considering investing in Turkey, and coordinates with experienced Turkish professionals" (KPMG website, 2011).

## Female Expatriates in Turkey

Given the increasing number of women pursuing global careers (Tharenou, 2010), it is important to reflect on the extent to which Turkey might be an attractive location for women considering either self-initiated expatriation or a corporate assignment. We might also consider whether widespread perceptions of it being a male-dominated, patriarchal, and Islamic country might impact on organizational decisions about whether women should be "sent" to Turkey. Indeed, some scholars have reported that gender-based selection decisions for expatriate assignments are quite common, despite empirical evidence that there are usually no performance differences between male and female expatriates (Sinangil & Ones, 2003). These

findings, together with other comparative studies that show the situation of women in Turkish business life (e.g., Napier & Taylor, 2002; Ozkanli & White, 2008), suggest that female expatriates in Turkey are unlikely to encounter more problems than their male counterparts. Indeed, Taylor and Napier argue that, "in general, if properly prepared, a woman professional should have no great difficulty in working successfully in Turkey, and can be just as successful if not more so than a foreign man" (2001, p. 359). However, other studies have reported that female expatriates working in male-dominated industries such as agriculture may face more challenges than their male counterparts, particularly if they are working in rural locations and/or have to work with Turkish nationals from such locations (Gopalan et al., 2005; Karakitapoğlu Aygün, 2004). There has also been some suggestion that single female expatriates may face more challenges than single male expatriates or married women, because social life usually revolves around the family, and there are more options for married couples than single professionals (Gopalan et al., 2005; Taylor & Napier, 2001).

## Expatriate Adjustment

There is a relative paucity of recent studies on expatriate adjustment in Turkey. Thus, while acknowledging that things are likely to have changed since that time, we draw here on a study of 78 expatriates conducted in 1999. Drawing on a sample of 78 expatriate managers, then, Yavas and Bodur (1999) examined their adjustment in four dimensions: (1) adjustment to amenities/facilities; (2) adjustment to work; (3) adjustment to everyday living; and (4) adjustment to social life and interactions with locals outside work. This study found that adjusting to amenities/facilities (which included adjustment to physical facilities such as housing, recreational areas, medical facilities, etc.) was most challenging. However, as might be expected, this was less of a concern for expatriates with company-provided housing, assistance with schooling for their children, or medical facilities. Interviewees also reported some difficulty adjusting to social life and interactions with Turkish nationals outside their work. In a more recent study, Richardson (2008) reported similar findings, where self-initiated expatriate academics in Turkey were more likely to live "on campus" with other expatriates than within local communities, precisely because of challenges relating to the "cultural distance" and linguistic competency (or lack thereof).

Yavas and Bodur (1999) also reported that married managers (especially those with children) had higher levels of interaction with locals. Richardson (2008) also found that single female SIE academics had fewer friendships with Turkish nationals than their single male counterparts. Taylor and Napier (2001) reported similar findings, where single expatriates (particularly women) faced more challenges in their social interactions with locals, as well as in their adjustment to everyday living. In terms of their adjustment to work, the nationality of the people they supervised did not have any influence, but the nationality of their

immediate boss did. Those managers who were managed by other expatriates had higher levels of work adjustment (Yavas & Bodur, 1999). Taken together, these findings seem to suggest that, whereas expatriates do not appear to face insurmountable problems—i.e., reporting some level of adjustment—their ability to adjust is more nuanced and related closely to whom they are working with/for, the extent of corporate support, and their marital status, among other things.

In addition to the amount of corporate support and previous expatriate experience, noted above, another earlier study (Culpan & Culpan, 1993) found that nationality also had an impact on adjustment. Comparing American and European expatriates' adjustment in Turkey, this study reported that, "European managers considered local work environments to be more similar to their own home work environments than the American managers did. Americans, however, viewed the local culture in general as unfamiliar but the work environment less so" (Culpan & Culpan, 1993, p. 439). This finding reflects the dominance of American business practices and American-type (US-oriented) college education in Turkey. It might also be explained by the impact of US multinationals on the business enterprise system. With increasing levels of globalization and a high number of very large multinational firms from the US, in most parts of the world, there is a convergence to the US system in business.

## Critical Perspectives on Global Careers in Turkey

Where individual career actors are concerned, our discussion thus far has clearly suggested that, with its growing economy and expanding labor market, Turkey may be an attractive place in which to pursue a global career. Indeed, whether one is a corporate assignee or a self-initiated expatriate, it appears that Turkey has much to offer, both in terms of short- or long-term marketability. However, despite these putative opportunities, there is some need for caution. Like all forms of international mobility, pursuing a global career within Turkey or from Turkey (or indeed elsewhere) invariably brings with it both risks and opportunities (Richardson & Zikic, 2007). A key point here is that, just as some Turkish nationals pursuing global careers outside of Turkey are likely to encounter difficulties, so too might those pursuing global careers within Turkey. As we have suggested, despite its economic and social development, recent studies of corporate assignees and SIE academics (Richardson, 2008; Tayler & Napier, 2001) have reported the same problems of adjustment and integration with local communities as earlier studies (Yavas & Bodur, 1999). This clearly suggests that, despite the relatively positive discourse about the value of pursuing global careers, for the individual, the organization, and the nation, they are not for everyone. It also suggests that, although economic and social development may enhance a country's reputation and attractiveness as a location in which to pursue one's global career, they are by no means a guarantee of a "smooth ride." Moreover, it is clear that economic expansion and increasing job opportunities are not enough to keep some Turkish

nationals at home, in a context where international experience is an increasingly important career "commodity." In order to illustrate these cautionary notes, we turn next to two of the specific challenges of pursuing a global career in Turkey.

## Instrumentalism in Global Careers

Earlier in this chapter, we spent some time discussing the instrumentalist approach taken by Turkish organizations and the Turkish government regarding international assignments. We made a particular point of showing how they might benefit from sending employees overseas and how those employees would add to organizational performance by expanding institutional knowledge of global business practices. Similarly, Turkish nationals sent on such assignments may well benefit in terms of their own marketability, in both the national and international job marketplace. However, such assignments may also come at a "cost." The case of Murat Candan, described in Box 12.3, provides us with an example of the way in which corporate assignments in Turkey might work. We see how his company is "grooming" him for a senior-management position by first sending him on an overseas assignment, followed by several smaller projects requiring international travel. We can also see, however, that, although the assignments and travel experiences are adding to his professional and personal development, they come at the cost of his personal life. This reminds us that, despite the potential value of global careers for individual professional and personal development, they are also characterized by certain challenges. Should corporations try to mitigate these challenges, if they want to help their employees develop their global skills? Or should they expect their employees to sacrifice their personal lives, etc., in return for the assignment experience they provide?

Continuing this theme further, but this time focusing specifically on academia, earlier in this chapter we reported how the Turkish government provides academics with financial support in order to gain international experience. As we discussed, the primary objective here is very much like that of the Turkish firm, where the government is seeking to enhance the credibility and standing of its higher-education system in the global marketplace. In return for the government's financial sponsorship, the individual academic must agree to return to Turkey for a specified period of time and fulfill certain professional obligations. Again, although such practices have the potential to make a valuable contribution to academics' careers, as well as to the Turkish higher-education system more generally, we must not overlook the challenge to academic freedom. Whereas this form of obligation is relatively commonplace in the corporate sector, as might be the case with a corporate-sponsored study on MBA programs etc., academia presents a different case. The idea of an obligation to specific duties seems, at least to us, somewhat at odds with the broader concept of academic freedom and international mobility that characterizes most academic careers. Having said that, we acknowledge that the provision of financial support during an overseas

sojourn merits some form of reciprocation. A middle way, therefore, might be to provide the respective scholar with a range of options in terms of the universities he/she can work in upon return to Turkey. Alternatively, some arrangement might be made that allows scholars to repay their funding. Of course, the extent to which any of these suggestions are effective may well depend on individual situations and career aspirations, as well as on contextual and institutional requirements.

## Career Opportunities for Women

Our discussion above suggested that Turkey provides a relatively positive environment for women's career experiences and potential career advancement, whether they are Turkish nationals or expatriates. Although this is clearly encouraging, our review of the literature suggests that there is still room for improvement. First, we noted that the political participation of women in Turkey is still very low, and most decision-making positions (especially those at the top of organizational hierarchies) are still occupied by men (Fullagar et al. 2003; United Nations Development Programme, 2008). That men continue to dominate decision-making positions is important, because of the concomitant implications for access to power and influence in political, business, and social contexts, to name but a few. Despite the relatively high ratio of women to be found across different occupations and senior organizational positions (in comparison with many developed countries), their limited political participation still raises questions about their overall access to power and influence more generally. It also raises questions about their ability to engage in, and perhaps even benefit directly from, contemporary changes in the country as a whole. In this respect, in as much as Turkish women appear to have extensive career opportunities, as Aycan (2004) suggests, certain societal values still create a barrier to their career advancement. The extent to which such barriers apply to expatriate women working in Turkey is, according to Taylor and Napier (2001), less of a concern. However, we also recommend some caution here, and further studies exploring the experiences of both national and expatriate women are necessary in order to paint a more detailed picture of their career experiences. Indeed, further studies specifically exploring the experiences of women in what is now a *growing* economic environment would be especially welcome.

## Conclusion

This chapter began by examining what we might call the "career climate" of Turkey—that is to say, its economy and labor market. We drew specific attention to the relative strength of the Turkish economy compared with other countries impacted by the GFC, particularly those in the eurozone. Although studies reporting "push and pull" factors are important and informative, they must be

understood within the context of *when* they were carried out. The recent GFC and financial problems in the eurozone have had a significant influence on international mobility, and specifically immigration trends. One recent report, for example, has suggested that immigration into developed countries is now *decreasing*, with more immigrants moving to developing countries or not moving at all (*The Economist*, 2011c). Therefore, with its consistent economic growth, it is perhaps not surprising that there has been an increase in the number of Turkish nationals *returning* to Turkey from abroad. Indeed, according to a recent newspaper report (Yinanc, 2011), between 2008 and 2009, approximately 190,000 Turkish nationals returned to Turkey from Germany.

However much these changing structural and institutional influences might impact on the decision to pursue a global career outside of Turkey, we should also recognize that individuals may immigrate/expatriate *regardless* of domestic labor-market opportunities. One might well argue that, in a context where international experience has an increasing value, individuals would be well advised to gain such experience, precisely in order to augment their marketability.

Although the prospect of home-country nationals moving overseas has given rise to concern among some governments about brain drain, the development of the Turkish economy and concomitant influx of MNCs and foreign nationals provide a clear example of what Inkson et al. (2004) have called "brain circulation." In other words, as much as Turkish nationals are continuing to expatriate/immigrate, so other nationals are coming/being sent to Turkey, and for exactly the same reasons—i.e., professional and personal development. Our decision to address Turkish nationals pursuing global careers outside of Turkey and foreign nationals pursuing global careers within Turkey has provided a prima facie example of a country characterized by brain circulation. Put another way, it has identified global careers as the *means* through which brain circulation to and from Turkey takes place. The main issue here, we believe, is that, rather than seeing Turkish nationals pursuing global careers as detrimental to national well-being, taking a long-term, broader approach enables us to appreciate the global dynamics of brain circulation. Although some may not repatriate, or may be reluctant to do so, others may well return, bringing with them their international experience. Moreover, the influx of foreign nationals should also be taken into consideration as another important dimension of the overall Turkish labor market. Therefore, just as Turkish companies encourage their employees to take up international assignments, and just as foreign companies send their employees to Turkey, we contend that the Turkish government should continue to encourage its nationals to gain overseas experience. In addition, Turkish professionals that live abroad continue to give support to development practices in Turkey (e.g., through cooperative projects, establishment of networks, forums, and consultancy services to Turkish companies; Gökbayrak, 2011). As there are potential positive externalities of skilled labor immigration from Turkey, the Turkish government should develop policies that support this "brain drain to brain gain" approach as well (Gökbayrak, 2011).

## Notes

1. *The Economist's Pocket World in Figures*, 2011 edition, Profile Books; data from the Turkish Statistical Institute, TurkStat, and ISPAT: taken from www.invest.gov.tr
2. Some academics and students who had gone overseas had signed "bonds" agreeing to return to their host institutions or to Turkey after their international experience.

## References

Altbach, P. G. (2004). Globalization and the university: Myths and realities in an unequal world. *Tertiary Education and Management*, 10(1), 3–25.

Atakan, M. G. S. & Eker, T. (2007). Corporate identity of a socially responsible university—A case from the Turkish higher education sector. *Journal of Business Ethics*, 76(1), 55–68.

Aycan, Z. (2001). Human resource management in Turkey—Current issues and future challenges. *International Journal of Manpower*, 22(3), 252–260.

Aycan, Z. (2004). Key success factors for women in management in Turkey. *Applied Psychology: An International Review*, 53(3), 453–477.

Aycan, Z. & Fikret-Pasa, S. (2003). Career choices, job selection criteria, and leadership preferences in a transitional nation. The case of Turkey. *Journal of Career Development*, 30(2), 129–144.

Aycan, Z., Kanungo, R. N., Mendonca, M., Yu, K., Deller, J., Stahl, G., & Khursid, A. (2000). Impact of culture on human resource management practices: A ten country comparison. *Applied Psychology: An International Review*, 49(1), 192–220.

Baruch, Y. (1995) Business globalization—The human resource management aspect. *Human Systems Management*, 14(4), 313–326.

Baruch, Y., Budhwar, P., & Khatri, N. (2007). Brain drain: Inclination to stay abroad after studies. *Journal of World Business*, 42, 99–112.

Bingham, C. B., Felin, T., & Black, J. S. (2000). An interview with John Pepper: What it takes to be a global leader. *Human Resource Management*, 39(2&3), 287–292.

Caner, A. & Okten, C. (2010). Risk and career choice: Evidence from Turkey. *Economics of Education Review*, 29(6), 1060–1075.

Cappellen, T. & Janssens, M. (2008). Global managers' career competencies. *Career Development International*, 13, 514–537.

Celikkaya, A. (2010). Dual income tax: A reform option for personal income tax in Turkey. *Business and Economic Horizons*, 3(3), 47–57.

Culpan, R. & Culpan, O. (1993). American and European expatriate managers: An empirical investigation. *The International Executive*, 35(5), 431–444.

Dickmann, M. & Harris, H. (2005). Developing career capital for global careers: The role of international assignments. *Journal of World Business*, 40(4), 399–408.

Doherty, N., Dickmann, M., & Mills, T. (2011). Exploring the motives of company-backed and self-initiated expatriates. *The International Journal of Human Resource Management*, 22(3), 595–611.

Fullagar, J. F., Sumer, H. C., Sverke, M., & Slick, R. (2003). Managerial sex-role stereotyping: A cross-cultural analysis. *International Journal of Cross Cultural Management*, 3(1), 93–106.

Gökbayrak, S. (2011). Skilled labour migration and positive externality: The case of Turkish engineers working abroad. *International Migration*. DOI: 10.1111/j.1468–2435.2009. 00520.x

Gopalan, S., Kavas, A., & Nelson, R. (2005). Gaining a perspective on Turkish value orientations: Implications for expatriate managers. *Journal of International Business Research*, 4(2), 43–56.

Goregenli, M. (1997). Individualist–collectivist tendencies in a Turkish sample. *Journal of Cross-Cultural Psychology*, 28(6), 787–794.

Guney, S., Gohar, R., Akinci, S., & Akinci, M. (2006). Attitudes towards women managers in Turkey and Pakistan. *Journal of International Women's Studies*, 8(1), 194–211.

Gungor, N. D. & Tansel, A. (2008). Brain drain from Turkey: The case of professionals abroad. *International Journal of Manpower*, 29(4), 323–347.

Hamori, M. & Koyuncu, B. (2011). Career advancement in large organizations in Europe and the United States: Do international assignments add value? *The International Journal of Human Resource Management*, 22(4), 843–862.

Herrmann, P. & Datta, D. K. (2005). Relationships between top management team characteristics and international diversification: An empirical investigation. *British Journal of Management*, 16, 69–78.

Hofstede, G. (1980). *Culture's Consequences: International Differences in Work-Related Values*. Beverly Hills, CA: Sage.

Inkson, K., Carr, S. C., Edwards, M., Hooks, J., Jackson, D., Thorn, K., & Allfree, N. (2004). From brain drain to talent flow: Views of expatriate Kiwis. *University of Auckland Business Review*, 6, 7–26.

ISPAT (2011). *Invest in Turkey*. Retrieved from www.invest.gov.tr, 26 August 2011.

Johnson, M. K. & Mortimer, J. T. (2002). Career choice and development from a socio-logical perspective. In D. Brown (Ed.), *Career Choice and Development* (4th ed., pp. 37–81). San Francisco, CA: Jossey-Bass.

Jokinen, T. (2010). Develoment of career capital through international assignments and its transferability to new contexts. *Thunderbird International Business Review*, 52(4), 325–336.

Kabasakal, H., Aycan, Z., & Karakaş, F. (2004). Women in management in Turkey. In M. J. Davidson & R. Burke (Eds.), *Women in Management Worldwide: Progress and Prospects* (pp. 273–293). UK: Ashgate.

Kabasakal, H. & Bodur, M. (1988). *Leadership, Values and Institutions: The Case of Turkey*. Research paper, Bogazici University, Istanbul.

Karakitapoğlu Aygün, Z. (2004). Self, identity, and emotional well-being among Turkish university students. *Journal of Psychology*, 138(5), 457–478.

Karakitapoğlu Aygün, Z. & Imamoğlu, E. O. (2002). Value domains of Turkish adults and university students. *Journal of Social Psychology*, 142, 333–351.

Kariyer.net Survey (2011). *What do Generation Yers think about the work life?* Presented at the 2nd Generation Y in Business Life Summit. HR Dergi, Istanbul.

Katrinli, A., Gunay, G., Erdener Acar, E., & Zengin Karaibrahimoglu, Y. (2010). Gender stereotyping in the accounting profession in Turkey. *Journal of Modern Accounting and Auditing*, 6(4), 15–25.

*KPMG Careers Magazine* (2010, January). *Spotlight on Turkey*. Retrieved from www. kpmg.com/Global/en/JoinUs/CareerNews/GlobalCareers/PublishingImages/Careers MagazineJan10/locationspotlight/working-cultures-turkey.html, September 4, 2011 (no longer available).

KPMG website (www.KPMG.com) (2011, August 7, *News and Events*). *KPMG Turkey Japanese Desk*. Retrieved from www.kpmg.com/TR/en/IssuesAndInsights/news-and-events/Pages/KPMG-Turkey-Japanese-Desk.aspxwww, 26 August 2011.

Meier, J. & Crocker, M. (2010). Generation Y in the workforce: Managerial challenges. *The Journal of Human Resource and Adult Learning*, 6(1), 68–78.

Napier, N. & Taylor, S. (2002). Experiences of women professionals abroad: Comparisons across Japan, China and Turkey. *The International Journal of Human Resource Management*, 13(5), 837–851.

Özbilgin, M., Kusku, F., & Erdogmus, N. (2005). Explaining influences on career "choice": The case of MBA students in comparative perspective. *The International Journal of Human Resource Management*, 16(11), 2000–2028.

Özbilgin, M. & Healy, G. (2004). The gendered nature of career development of university professors: The case of Turkey. *Journal of Vocational Behavior*, 64(2), 358–371.

Ozkanli, O. & White, K. (2008). Leadership and strategic choices: Female professors in Australia and Turkey. *Journal of Higher Education Policy and Management*, 30(1), 53–63.

Pattie, M., White, M. M., & Tansky, J. (2010). The homecoming: A review of support practices for repatriates. *Career Development International*, 15(4), 359–377.

Richardson, J. (2008). *The Independent Expatriate: Academics Abroad*. Saarbrucken, Germany: VDM.

Richardson, J. & Mallon, M. (2005). Career interrupted? The case of the self-directed expatriate. *Journal of World Business*, 40, 409–420.

Richardson, J. & Zikic, J. (2007) The darker side of international academic careers. *Career Development International*, 12(2), 164–186.

Richardson, J., McBey, K., & McKenna, S. D. (2008). Integrating realistic job previews and realistic living conditions previews: Realistic recruitment for internationally mobile knowledge workers. *Personnel Review*, 37(5), 490–508.

Selmer, J. & Lauring, J. (2010). Self-initiated academic expatriates: Inherent demographics and reasons to expatriate. *European Management Review*, 7, 169–179.

Sinangil, H. K. & Ones, D. S. (2003). Gender differences in expatriate job performance. *Applied Psychology: An International Review*, 52(3), 461–475.

Sullivan, S. E. & Baruch, Y. (2009). Advances in career theory and research: A critical review and agenda for future exploration. *Journal of Management*, 35(6), 1542–1571.

Suutari, V. & Makela, K. (2007). The career capital of managers with global careers. *Journal of Managerial Psychology*, 22, 628–648.

Tanova, C., Karatas-Özkan, M., & Inal, G. (2008). The process of choosing a management career: Evaluation of gender and contextual dynamics in a comparative study of six countries: Hungary, Israel, North Cyprus, Turkey, UK and the USA. *Career Development International*, 13(4), 291–305.

Tansel, A. & Gungor, N. D. (2003). "Brain drain" from Turkey: Survey evidence of student non-return. *Career Development International*, 8(2), 52–69.

Taylor, S. & Napier, N. K. (2001). An American woman in Turkey: Adventures unexpected and knowledge unplanned. *Human Resource Management*, 40(4), 347–364.

Tharenou, P. (2010). Women's self-initiated expatriation as a career option and its ethical issues. *Journal of Business Ethics*, 95(1), 73–88.

*The Economist* (2011a). *Pocket World in Figures*, 2011 ed. Profile Books.

*The Economist* (2011b). The daughter also rises. August 27. Retrieved from www.economist.com/node/21526872, 2 October 2011.

*The Economist* (2011c). Migration after the crash: Moving out, on and back. August 27. Retrieved from www.economist.com/node/21526777, 2 October 2011.

Turkish Statistical Institute (2011). IMF World Economic Outlook April 2011. Retrieved from www.invest.gov.tr, 26 August 2011.

Twenge, J. M., Campbell, S. M., Hoffman, B. R., & Lance, C. E. (2010). Generational differences in work values: Leisure and extrinsic values increasing, social and intrinsic values decreasing. *Journal of Management*, 36(5), 1117–1142.

United Nations Development Programme (2008). *Turkey 2008: Human Development Report*. Ankara: UNDP.

Vardar, M. F. (2011). Factors of investment decision for multinational corporations: The case of Turkey. *The Journal of Turkish Weekly*, October 19, 2011.

Yavas, U. & Bodur, M. (1999). Correlates of adjustment: A study of expatriate managers in an emerging country. *Management Decision*, 37(3), 267–278.

Yinanc, B. (2011). After Norway, Turks in Germany on thin ice. *Hurriyet Daily News*, August 5, Istanbul.

YOK (2011). The Council of Higher Education. Retrieved from www.yok.gov.tr/content/view/527/222/, 17 October 2011.

# 13

# GLOBAL CAREERS IN CHINA

*Victor P. Lau, Hang Seng Management College, Hong Kong, Yu-Shan Hsu, University of Wisconsin-Milwaukee, USA, and Margaret A. Shaffer, University of Wisconsin-Milwaukee, USA*

## Introduction

As China has become a major player on the global stage (Davidson, 1987; Picht, 2011), more and more people in China have careers that span geographical and cultural boundaries. Similarly, with increased foreign investment into China, more and more foreigners are working in China. According to the Ministry of Human Resources and Social Security of the People's Republic of China (2011), the total number of expatriates legally working in China had reached 231,700 by the end of 2010. Although researchers have considered the influence of globalization on China in terms of human resource management (e.g., Ahlstrom, Foley, Young, & Chan, 2005), the impact of globalization on the global careers of indigenous Chinese and expatriates in China has not been fully examined. Therefore, the purpose of this chapter is to review the evolution of global careers in China within the context of various forces of globalization. We first define global career, noting that talent shortage is a persistent and pervasive phenomenon in China, and that government interventions are attempting to prevent the associated brain-drain issue. Second, we discuss contemporary career concepts and how they are relevant to the Chinese context. Third, to understand better how contextual factors influence global careers in China, we describe some of the political, economic, technological, sociocultural, and legal/labor changes that characterize contemporary China. Fourth, we introduce two new concepts, globalization shock and globalization adjustment, and explore how these challenges affect people in the development of their global careers. Fifth, we provide two stories to illustrate how such challenges have or have not been overcome. Finally, we adopt a critical lens to evaluate the influences of globalization on global careers in China at individual, organizational, and societal levels.

## The Situation of Global Careers in China

### Defining a Global Career

Before we examine the situation of global careers in China, we define what a global career is. Researchers have generally acknowledged the ambiguous nature of definitions of global careers (Dickmann & Baruch, 2011; Thomas, Lazarova, & Inkson, 2005). Dickmann and Baruch (2011) viewed a global career as an evolving sequence of a person's work experience over time, when part of the sequence takes place in more than one country. This line of thought is more comparable with a traditional perspective of a global career, which is largely limited to understanding issues surrounding expatriate managers designated by multinational corporations (MNCs) and viewing an overseas assignment as a temporary difficulty imposed on the logic of organizational careers (Thomas et al., 2005). However, this perspective is subject to challenges by contemporary career concepts and in the context of globalization. First, contemporary career concepts, such as boundaryless or protean careers, emphasize internal careers, a more subjective sense of where people are going in their work lives, rather than external careers, dominated by the traditional view of an upward progression within organizations. Therefore, individuals recognize that overseas assignments may not necessarily have a positive effect on their external careers, but they still choose them just because they view them as a fulfillment of their internal careers and personal growth (Stahl, Miller, & Tung, 2002; Thomas et al., 2005). Second, in the context of globalization, individuals may experience (or suffer from) their "global careers" in global organizations or MNCs without this having to take place in another country. For example, during the past 20 odd years, China has rapidly gone through the globalization process. A large number of global organizations, operating in different entry modes, such as franchising, strategic alliances, or joint ventures, have been set up in China. Local employees may thus experience "culture shock" and "cultural adjustment" in these global organizations as well. As such, we adopt a broader perspective and define a global career as *an evolving sequence of a person's objective or subjective work experience over time, when part of the sequence takes place in the context of globalization.*

### Talent Shortage and Global Moves in China

As China has been playing a major role in the global economy, the inflow of foreign investment to China and the outflow of Chinese firms and talents overseas (Accenture, 2005) are expected to continue to prevail. Accordingly, there is a growing demand for "cosmopolitans," those who are globally minded, managerially and technologically knowledgeable, and competent in meeting global standards (Kanter, 1995). This relentless demand for cosmopolitans has generated a situation of *"the shortage among plenty."* Consequently, although China is the most populous nation in the world, there is a critical shortage of

human talent to meet China's dual objective of pursuing continued economic prosperity at home and success abroad (Farrell & Grant, 2005).

One of the reasons for the talent shortage stems from the legacy of the state-owned enterprise (SOE). Before the open-door policy in the 1980s, SOEs were the industrial backbone of China's economy. With the state taking responsibility for all profits and losses, there was no incentive for managers and employees to assume risk. According to Jeff Barnes, chief learning officer at General Electric, China, "*Chinese talent is first-generation. They don't have role models. Their parents worked for state-owned companies*" (*The Economist*, 2005). Furthermore, during the Cultural Revolution from 1966 to 1976, education and management development were severely disrupted. Because capitalism was deemed evil in that tumultuous decade (Tung, 2007), an entire generation of educated managers was lost.

Another reason leading to the brain drain and talent shortage in China is the large number of Chinese pursuing advanced education abroad. In the early 1990s, the Chinese government started to understand that, in order to improve science and technology in China, it was necessary to let people go abroad freely and then compete for them in the international marketplace by creating a favorable domestic environment that would attract them to return home. As such, liberalization of China's policy on traveling overseas, for studies as well as work, has led to a massive increase in the number of people going abroad (Zweig, 2006). However, upon graduation in disciplines that are in high demand, such as information technology and computer science, many Chinese-born students choose to remain in their adoptive countries to enjoy higher salaries and living standards. According to China News Service (2011), China has sent 1.92 million students and scholars to foreign countries for further studies in various fields since 1978, but, to the concern of the government, only about 630,000 of them (less than one third) have returned to China. The rate was even lower for those who graduated with doctorate degrees in science and engineering in the United States. According to Finn (2005), the stay rates were 90% for recipients of doctorate degrees in science and engineering from China. With such a high degree of brain drain, China has undoubtedly lost competitive strength in its rapid development (China News Service, 2011). Accordingly, China is zealous to attract these expatriates to return (Tung, 2007). Many of these diaspora members are highly educated and experienced in global business. Combined with their knowledge of Chinese language and culture, they could be an invaluable resource to either MNCs in China or China's outward foreign direct investments (Tung, 2007). However, because most returnees have obtained foreign citizenship, an estimated one-half of returnees have left again (Devoretz, Ma, & Zhang, 2002; Teferra, 2004). Thus, perhaps the term "brain circulation" or "triangular human capital flows" would be more appropriate to characterize this phenomenon whereby human talent leaves, then returns, and then leaves again (Teferra, 2004). This concept of brain circulation is consistent with the emerging trend towards boundaryless careers (Tung, 2007).

## Governmental Strategies to Reverse Brain Drain in China

The Chinese government has struggled to resolve the problems of talent short-ages and global moves in and out of China. Li Yuanchao, who is a member of the Political Bureau of the Communist Party of China Central Committee (CPCCC), member of the Secretariat of the CPCCC, and head of the Organization Department of the CPCCC, is the most senior officer handling the brain-drain issues in China. In the High-Level Overseas Talents Seminar held in Guangzhou in December 2011, Li explicitly highlighted that, even though China is a populous country, the highest-level talents and experts have been scarce in China. According to Li, the introduction of talented, senior people from overseas is an urgent requirement to establish an innovative, national personnel system, and more and more organizations in China need skilled people with international training and background (China News Service, 2011). According to statistics from the Ministry of Education, China now has about 200,000 overseas graduates who have stayed abroad to work for well-known international companies, universities, and research institutions (*China News*, 2011). To attract overseas talents and returnees to reverse China's brain drain, the Department of Organization of the CPCCC initiated a national-level program called the "Thousand Talents Program" in 2008. The program aims to bring top overseas talents back to China to contribute to the country's economy. More specifically, the program aims to recruit at least 2,000 of the highest-level over-seas talents in 5–10 years, to facilitate breakthroughs in key technologies, develop the high-tech industry, and to foster the emerging disciplines of innovation and entrepreneurship (China News Service, 2011). Selection into the program is not only a synonym of glory, but it is also a means of support and connection with the Chinese government. Successful applicants will be given a one-off, tax-free signing bonus of 1 million Chinese yuan (about US$158,662, as of January 2012), among many other benefits and entrepreneurial opportunities. With such favorable policies, as of August 2011, a total of 6,200 overseas scholars and experts have applied to join the program, and about 1,500 have been selected (China News Service, 2011).

## The Relevance of Contemporary Career Concepts

In conjunction with the emergence of MNCs operating in China with foreign investments, such as Sino-foreign joint ventures and wholly foreign-owned firms (Davidson, 1987), there has been an influx of Western management theories and contemporary career concepts to China as well. However, whether contemporary career concepts are relevant to China is subject to verification. In this section, we review some of these concepts and discuss the relevance of these concepts to careers in China.

## Contemporary Career Concepts

In the past, a career used to be confined to paid employment or a single organization, but contemporary concepts of careers have moved from a career played out within an organization to the career actors themselves (Wong, 2007). One characteristic of contemporary career concepts is that people's career choices have become more diverse and self-directed. Career choice refers to the selection of a role through which individuals implement their own identity and represent their own life work (Merrick, 1995). The notion of choice implies that people can make decisions at their own discretion. As such, an individual's career choice is anchored by his/her self-perceived talents, motives, and values that guide, constrain, and integrate his/her career (Schein, 1978). For example, some men and women take a break from the workforce to become the primary caregiver for children or elderly relatives. These individuals use this time purposefully to further their education or gain valuable skills through volunteer work, in order to build their résumé and ease their reentry to the workforce (Belkin, 2008; Sullivan & Baruch, 2009). Others have become more self-directed in their careers, self-initiating international careers (Tharenou, 2009) or choosing lateral, or even downward, job moves to fulfill personal needs (Hall, Gardner, & Baugh, 2008). Contemporary careers with these characteristics have also been conceptualized as boundaryless and protean careers.

Boundaryless and protean careers are two contemporary career concepts that manifest diverse and self-directed career choices. People involved in a boundaryless career are independent from, rather than dependent on, traditional organizational career arrangements (Arthur & Rousseau, 1996). The meanings of a boundaryless career are diverse, such as the careers of individuals who move across the boundaries of separate employers, those who reject existing career opportunities for personal or family reasons, or those who may perceive a boundaryless future regardless of structural constraints (Arthur & Rousseau, 1996). The development of a boundaryless career is a reflection of contemporary organizational environments that have become more and more uncertain and volatile. The impact of globalization, along with such organizational vocabularies as restructuring, downsizing, and layoff, has reduced opportunities for career advancement in large organizations, making a boundaryless career an increasingly attractive alternative (Lau, Shaffer, & Au, 2007; Wong, 2007).

A protean career is a similar career concept advocated by Hall (1976, 1996). The term protean is from Proteus, a Greek god who can change shape at will. A protean career is a process that the person, not the organization, manages. The protean person's own career choices and search for self-fulfillment are the unifying or integrative elements in his or her life. The criterion of success is internal (psychological success) rather than external (objective success) (Hall, 1976, 1996). People's career choices are increasingly driven more by their own desires than by organizational career-management practices (Sullivan & Baruch, 2009).

Thus, individuals now have a higher degree of self-control and freedom to choose their own careers and life patterns (Hall, 2002).

## Relevance to Careers in China

Although contemporary career concepts have been influential across various national boundaries, several alternative "boundaries" or obstacles to boundaryless and protean careers exist. These include, but are not limited to, cultural differences, gender discrimination, and individual competencies. Although boundaries in general have become permeable, the ease of passage between boundaries is not the same for all individuals, organizations, and nations (Sullivan & Arthur, 2006), which may help explain why numerous studies have still reported that individuals in their samples exhibited a more traditional career path (Sullivan & Baruch, 2009). In general, contemporary career concepts substantially clash with traditional Confucian culture in China. However, in the context of globalization, the sociocultural environment has become more dynamic. Accordingly, the relevance of contemporary career concepts to the local career system has become versatile as well. In the following, we discuss these social phenomena from traditional to contemporary perspectives in turn.

From a sociocultural perspective, Chinese people's career choices, for the most part, have been influenced by Confucian values. One central feature of Confucian values is parents' absolute authority (Ho, 1996), legitimizing parents' rights to bring up their children exactly according to their dictates. Chinese parents often have high expectations of their children's education, seeing it as an avenue to getting a good job and thus gracing the family and ancestors with pride and success (Ho, 1996; Wong & Slater, 2002; Wu, 1996). As a result, Confucian values tend to undermine Chinese people's motivation and opportunities to make career choices on their own.

Even though China has undergone many environmental changes, recent research shows that Chinese families continue to influence children's career choices, at least to a certain extent (Leung, Hou, Gati, & Li, 2011). Moreover, occupational inheritance (or *dingti*) is also a familial factor affecting Chinese people's career choices. The term *dingti* means that, when individuals retire, they should relinquish their jobs in favor of their sons or daughters (Williams, 2009). In a family business, parents may show a strong desire to pass on their business to their children (Wong & Slater, 2002) to ensure the continuity of the prosperity of the family business and career success of descendants. In an SOE, it is also popular that, when a worker retires, he or she may recommend a close relative for the job (Wong, White, & Gui, 2004). Even though *dingti* was formally cancelled in 1986, the practice has continued to exist in China (Warner, 1996). The prevalence of *dingti* implies that Chinese people often lack autonomy in making their own career choices: family members or those who have *guanxi* (relationship) often make career arrangements. Indeed, in a study (Chudzikowski et al., 2009) comparing causes of career

transitions across Austria, Serbia, Spain, USA, and China, external causes such as organizational destructuring, routine reassignment or transfer, and even government policy are much more emphasized in China than internal causes such as the desire for something new.

Before China's economic reform, the "iron rice bowl" policy allocated jobs for young Chinese workers after they left school. Traditional "personnel" management, especially in state-owned firms, has been characterized by high job security and low job mobility. Essentially, employees relinquished job mobility in exchange for job security and "cradle-to-grave" welfare coverage. Nowadays, many foreign firms hire or work with local Chinese employees, including people laid off from SOEs and surplus rural laborers, who have had little exposure to a market economy (Panitchpakdi & Clifford, 2002). Despite globalization and the environmental changes it has generated, many people in China still tend to retain a traditional mentality and traditional practices with regard to their career choices (Wong, 2007). These structural (political and economic) constraints, as well as the sociocultural conditions (parents' absolute authority and the practice of *dingti*), have substantially hindered Chinese people from embracing contemporary career concepts and choosing freely the careers they may really wish to develop.

## Structural, Cultural, and Contextual Issues in China

In this section, we explore the structural, cultural, and contextual issues in China and how these contribute to both the difficulties and opportunities encountered by people in the development of their global careers in China. We first examine the structural issues in China by describing some of the changes triggered by the economic reforms initiated by Deng Xiaoping's open-door policy to the West in the 1980s. In particular, we review the dynamic characteristics of the political, economic, technological, sociocultural, and legal/labor environments in China. Then, we examine the cultural issues in China by introducing two new concepts developed in this chapter, namely globalization shock and globalization adjustment, and propose that these conditions may affect those who develop global careers in China. Finally, we examine these contextual issues in an in-depth approach by introducing two contrasting case studies.

### China's Changing Political and Economic Environments

The People's Republic of China, a political regime modeled on the Soviet Union, was established in 1949 as a single-party country, where the Communist Party of China formed the government, and no other parties were permitted to run candidates for election. Two political changes have been particularly influential on Chinese culture. The first change was China's move from a planned to a market-oriented system. When China first opened its economy in 1978, its reform goal was to shift from a planned economy to an ill-defined, "socialist market

economy." The second change was China's entry into the World Trade Organization (WTO), which symbolized its attempt to comply with the rules of the game in the international arena and its willingness to be restricted by international trade rules (Panitchpakdi & Clifford, 2002). These changes resulted in a tremendous economic boost that has spanned three decades and has positioned China as a major global player. Evidence of this is the fact that China became the world's largest exporter in 2010 (Picht, 2011). China's economic prosperity has generally improved the living standards and quality of life for many Chinese people, especially the growing middle class. However, economic inequality has also grown in magnitude (Chen, 2007), and the potential for social instability has come to the attention of the Chinese government (*China Daily*, 2007). This economic inequality has resulted in perceptions of injustice, grievances against social phenomena, and a mistrust of Confucian ideology and traditional Chinese culture (*The Economist*, 2007).

## China's Changing Technological Environment

Just as China's economic environment has evolved, so has its technological infrastructure. The number of domestic Internet service providers has been rapidly increasing in China, and many foreign companies have made inroads into China's lucrative information technology market (Lacharite, 2002). However, as the large influx of information clashes with the political ideology and governmental control of the one-party nation, the government has attempted to censor and regulate the Internet. Currently, China blocks access to Facebook and heavily censors the rest of the Internet (Bussey, 2011). Despite China's desperate attempts to control the Internet process and content, the flow of "illegal" and "undesirable" information continues to bypass its primitive regulatory system (Lacharite, 2002). The never-ending influx of global information and new knowledge inevitably influences both political ideology and traditional Chinese culture.

## China's Changing Sociocultural Environment

Concurrent with political, economic, and technological changes, China's sociocultural environment has also evolved. The first change has to do with Chinese values. The increasingly diverse contemporary ideologies have challenged both traditional Chinese culture (e.g., Confucian teaching of being humble) and communist ideology (e.g., altruistic dedication to society). Legalism, another major traditional Chinese philosophy, also suggests that people abide by the laws without fully understanding the reason for compliance (Chinese Law, n.d.). As the result of increased interactions with other cultures and values in the global village (McLuhan, 1960), traditional Chinese values have been moderated, if not abandoned.

The second change is that Chinese people have begun to quest for human rights. Their desire for human rights and democracy remains strong, despite heavy censorship and brutal repression by the Chinese government. In addition, China's ever-increasing population of Internet citizens understands how to take advantage of the Internet to form pro-democratic discussion groups, express religious convictions, and communicate in secrecy. These events provide support for the shift from a traditional Chinese culture characterized by submissiveness to authority and apathy towards a culture that is global, humanistic, and democratic in its orientation (Yee, Liu, & Ngo, 1993).

The third change is Chinese society's awareness of the importance of corporate social responsibility. Myopic vision has led enterprises in China to undermine the environment and cheat customers for short-term gains. For example, the toxic milk powder from Sanlu Group caused the deaths, or serious illnesses related to urinary ailments such as kidney stones, of thousands of infants who were given formulas contaminated with melamine. Incidents such as this have generated great concern about the importance of corporate social responsibility in society (Chen, 2009; Xu & Yang, 2010).

## China's Changing Legal/Labor Environment

China's move to a free-market system in the 1980s encouraged millions of young workers to labor for low wages, creating a competitive advantage for China through low-cost exports. Foreign investment then poured into China (Barboza, 2006). After China's accession to the WTO in 2001, international bodies such as the WTO and the International Labor Organization (ILO) have closely monitored China's adherence to established trade regulations and labor standards. By the end of May 2003, China had ratified 23 ILO conventions, at least on paper, some of which were related to fundamental rights (no. 100 on discrimination; nos. 138 and 182 on child labor) (Lin, 2002). Recently, China has planned to adopt a new law that seeks to crack down on sweatshops and protect workers' rights by giving labor unions real power (Barboza, 2006). Despite China's effort to reform its legal system, including labor regulations, the success of implementing relevant changes is still in doubt. Social issues such as corruption (Lin, 1997), piracy of intellectual property (General Accounting Office, 2002), and inconsistent enforcement of administrative regulations (China Law Committee of the American Bar Association, 2002) continue to be significant obstacles to the establishment of a functional system of legal rule.

## Culture Shock and Globalization Shock

In this section, we introduce two new concepts that we believe represent cultural issues directly associated with global careers in China. In the previous section, when we reviewed the situation of global careers in China, we identified two

main categories of career actor in China. The first category includes the high-level overseas talent and returnees (or potential returnees). The second category contains local employees who develop their "global careers" in multinational organizations in China. We argue that both categories of Chinese career actor are subject to new challenges and opportunities, with globalization shocks and adjustments a logical consequence under the cross-cultural impact of globalization.

According to anxiety/uncertainty management (AUM) theory (Gudykunst, 1995), anxiety and uncertainty are central elements influencing the effectiveness of intergroup interactions. When two strangers get together, given their lack of knowledge of each other, anxiety and uncertainty levels are likely to be high, thus preventing effective interactions. In the context of global careers, when expatriates first interact with a foreign environment, given the lack of knowledge about the environment, they are likely to experience culture shock, which is precipitated by the anxiety that results from losing familiar signs and symbols of social intercourse (Oberg, 1960). Some possible symptoms of culture shock include excessive fear of being cheated or robbed, or a terrible longing to be back home. People may react to the frustrations associated with this in several ways. They may reject the environment that causes the discomfort. They may also find that the home environment becomes tremendously important—all the difficulties and problems are forgotten, and only the good things back home are remembered (Oberg, 1960).

We think that the acceleration of globalization will inflate people's culture shock, especially for those who are incapable of adjusting to the impact of globalization. We call this phenomenon *globalization shock*, and we define it as a sudden, and sometimes an extension of, anxiety that results from the loss of the familiar signs and symbols of social interaction, which arises from the impact of globalization. Unlike culture shock, which is generally experienced by foreigners working and living in another country, globalization shock affects both expatriates and indigenous employees.

## Cultural Adjustment and Globalization Adjustment

Adjustment refers to "the degree of a person's psychological comfort with various aspects of a new setting" (Black & Gregersen, 1991, p. 498). As empirical evidence has shown that the cultural adjustment of expatriates is a significant predictor of work attitudes, such as job and nonwork satisfaction (Shaffer & Harrison, 1998), and work outcomes, such as withdrawal cognitions, intentions to return early, and performance (Gong & Fan, 2006; Takeuchi, Yun, & Tesluk, 2002), the importance of people's comfort in an unfamiliar environment should not be overlooked.

In the era of globalization, adjustment may not only be a challenge for expatriates working in China, but it may also be an issue for Chinese locals, because of the complex interplay between indigenous cultural and globalization forces.

We call this phenomenon *globalization adjustment*, defined as the degree of a person's psychological comfort with various aspects of changes associated with the impact of globalization. We argue that all people involved in global careers, including expatriates and locals, working in both host and home countries, are subject to globalization adjustment.

## Globalization Shock and Globalization Adjustment of Expatriates

We believe that expatriates' experience of culture shock and adjustment in contemporary China is twofold. On the one hand, the anxiety that expatriates experience comes from cultural differences between host and home countries. On the other hand, expatriates' anxiety may come from the complex interplay between Chinese indigenous culture and globalization forces, leading to stereotyped or inaccurate perceptions of the so-called "Chinese culture" and causing difficulties in adjustment.

First, expatriates may experience culture shock and adjustment in China, a country that is distinctly different from most other countries and that is an especially challenging destination for Western business expatriates. Selmer (2005) argued that Western expatriates have to adjust to a fundamentally different cultural and social context than their own. In the venture-capital market, for example, Western investors face culture shock because, in the West, profit maximization, efficiency, and public information disclosure are important factors for investors, but, in China, personal relationships, networking, and harmony are more important (Pukthuanthong & Walker, 2007).

Second, expatriates' experience of culture shock in contemporary China may be intensified by their perceptual gaps between stereotypical Chinese culture and the "real" culture that has been shaped by globalization forces. Before engaging in any expatriate travels to China, these individuals will probably strive to learn more about Chinese culture. For example, expatriates-to-be may be told not to eat all the food served to them at a meal, because Chinese hosts may perceive that they have not provided enough food for the guests (International Business Etiquette and Manners, n.d.). Unfortunately, these are often stereotypes of traditional Chinese culture. The cultural etiquette of leftover food is changing, as Chinese people have increasingly gained insights into the need for environmental protection within the global village. An inability of expatriates to adjust to the new, and changing, environment is costly in terms of employment expenses, poor management, and poor productivity (Kaye & Taylor, 1997). Therefore, when organizations design predeparture training for expatriates assigned to China, the "real" contemporary Chinese culture should be taken into account, to reduce the potential globalization shock that may adversely affect expatriates' globalization adjustment and their career development.

## Globalization Shock and Globalization Adjustment of Locals

Globalization may represent a double-edged sword to people's careers around the world, as it brings both pros and cons to careers. However, it might be especially relevant to China, as it used to be a government-dominated country, and was not very open to external influences on its economy. Thus, when globalization took center stage in China, it may have been relatively more influential on Chinese locals, as they may not have experienced such an influx of external influences on their life and careers before. Thus, we elaborate on the advantages and disadvantages of globalization in the Chinese context.

As to the pros, globalization has provided a great deal of global career opportunities for Chinese locals. Opportunities for them to take on expatriate assignments have been increasing, as more Chinese companies have become multinational corporations (Wood & El Mansour, 2010), and more and more expatriate students from China have embarked on lifetime careers in foreign countries (Tung, 2007). As to the cons, globalization shock and globalization adjustment can be terrible ordeals for Chinese locals, especially for those who are in secondary roles, trivialized, or marginalized. China has been recognized as the "factory of the world," and numerous multinational corporations have set up factories in China to take advantage of the low operating costs. However, the exploitation of the well-being of Chinese locals has posed ethical challenges. Despite great domestic pressures to reform the labor laws in China, the vast majority of firms continue to breach labor contracts and wage regulations, with some firms underpaying, or neglecting to pay, their employees. With the lack of remedies for such unfairness, the victimized Chinese locals may adopt radical means of retaliation, such as protests or even uprisings (Cooney, 2006).

In sum, there are pros and cons of globalization with regard to its impact on the global careers of people working in China. We encourage policymakers and organizations to strike a balance between the benefits and potential damage brought about by globalization, and to help locals absorb the shocks of globalization and adjust to its realities. Although the double-edged-sword effect might be relevant to people's careers around the world, we believe it is especially significant for Chinese locals.

## Contrasting Stories of Global Careers in China

To exemplify the complexities of the contextual issues, both opportunities and challenges, encountered by people in the development of global careers, we describe two contrasting case studies that have recently occurred in China. The individuals in these cases represent distinctly different backgrounds and situations, and yet, in both cases, they were directly affected by environmental changes in China and the forces of globalization. The consequences of their stories are, however, very different.

## A Global Icon from China—Yao Ming

> One day when my career as a professional basketball player ends, it would
> be a comma, not a full stop . . .
>
> (Yao Ming)

Yao Ming is a retired Chinese basketball player who last played for the Houston
Rockets of the National Basketball Association (NBA). As of the 2010–2011 season,
he was the tallest player (2.29 meters) in the NBA. Born in Shanghai in 1980,
he started playing for the Shanghai Sharks in 1997. He was selected by the
Houston Rockets in the 2002 NBA draft, and he retired from the NBA after foot
and ankle fractures in 2011. With an average of 19 points and 9.2 rebounds per
game, Yao was praised by Shaquille O'Neal, another retired NBA superstar, who
said that he could have been one of the top five players of the game if he had
not had those injuries. Currently, he works with the Shanghai Sharks, the team
he played with early in his career and which he bought in 2009 (*Bloomberg News*,
2011; Yao Ming, n.d.; Johnson, 2011).

Yao's career is definitely boundaryless and protean, not only because his career
as a basketball player transcended national and cultural boundaries, but also
because he made his own career choices and searched for self-fulfillment in the
process. Being the fifth-highest-paid non-US athlete in the world (with an annual
income of US$36 million), Yao is not just an icon in China, but a global icon
and ambassador for athletics. For example, he carried China's flag in the Olympic
opening ceremonies in 2004 and 2008. He also had sponsorships with companies
including Nike, Reebok, Pepsi, Coca-Cola, T-Mobile, Apple, Visa, and McDonald's
(*Bloomberg News*, 2011; Yao Ming, n.d.; Johnson, 2011). Yao has also developed
an entrepreneurial career. For example, he has opened Yao Restaurants in
Houston and Shanghai, and he has invested in a satellite-positioning-services
provider and a Chinese music website. Nevertheless, he has also participated in
many nonprofit or charitable activities, including taking an active role in the
"Basketball without Borders" program, donating US$2 million to the victims of
China's Sichuan province earthquake, and advocating against AIDS discrimination
in China (*Bloomberg News*, 2011). Just like other expatriates, Yao also experienced
culture shock in his global career. Considering the secluded environment he came
from, and the sudden exposure to demanding and relentless media, it was
certainly a tough transition. Fortunately, he was a quick learner and adjusted
fast to the unfamiliar community (Joshi, 2009).

Yao certainly has his own core competencies in basketball playing, as well as
other competitive advantages, but we believe that his success can be largely
attributed to his ability to take advantage of environmental changes and
overcome the associated globalization shock and adjustment. Yao's success in
his global career has greatly benefited from China's political, economic, and
cultural changes and, in particular, the acceleration of globalization. Before its
political and economic reforms, China was behind what was known as the
"Bamboo Curtain" during the cold war. During the Cultural Revolution from 1966
to 1976, the Chinese government even put its section of the curtain under a
lock-down of sorts, forbidding entry into, or passage out of, the country without

explicit permission from the Chinese government. It was not politically or culturally correct, and was thus unfeasible, to have any physical or ideological exchanges with the "American Imperialists." However, globalization changed things. Individuals, including athletes such as Yao, who possess force of will and power of personality have the opportunity to transcend national boundaries and become mythical figures to people all over the globe. Increasingly, these superstars have also become money and marketing facilitators. Thus, Yao has also become the epicenter of a campaign by American brands to win the hearts, minds, and pocketbooks of 1.3 billion potential consumers in China's red-hot economy (*BusinessWeek*, 2004).

If the story of Yao Ming represents the potential of Chinese people to capitalize on the opportunities of globalization in China, the story of Foxconn Technology Group represents the dark side of the impact of globalization on local workers in China.

## Globalization Shock in China—the Case of Foxconn

A string of suicides at a factory in China owned by Taiwan firm Foxconn has highlighted what some say is a stressful working environment for migrant workers.

*(BBC News)*

Most people had probably not heard of Foxconn Technology Group until the firm became well known (or notorious) when 18 Foxconn employees attempted suicide and 14 died at the plant in Shenzhen between January and November 2010 (Foxconn Suicides, n.d.). Benefiting from China's political and economic reforms and the concurrent global-business opportunities, Foxconn, which manufactures electronic products, including the iPhone for Apple and computers for Hewlett Packard, became the largest private-owned enterprise in China. Foxconn employs about 1 million people, nearly half of whom work at the plant in Shenzhen, which is one of China's Special Economic Zones established by Deng Xiaoping. Foxconn's output accounts for nearly 40% of the world's consumer-electronics industry (Chung, 2010).

Over the past three decades, China's economic development has flourished, and millions of workers have migrated from the poor, rural, western provinces of China to Shenzhen, gambling on a chance to have new careers in factories such as Foxconn's as a way to improve their lives and the lives of their families back home. However, because of the global hunger for low-cost electronics, Foxconn workers were exposed to the negative aspects of the double-edged sword of globalization. Through interviews on international and local media, Foxconn's workers complained that they did 100 hours of overtime per month and did not even talk to the people working next to them. They claimed that coworkers did not have much time to communicate with each other, and they

felt lonely. The security at Foxconn was extremely tight: they had to surrender their passports to the guards, and bags were searched at the main gate. They could not find happiness and freedom, and they felt that the factory was just like a jail (*BBC News*, 2010).

The media also reported Foxconn's defenses against workers' accusations. A spokesperson for Foxconn quoted a study by a psychologist, who was invited by the company to review the suicides at its Shenzhen plant. According to the psychologist's report, the suicide rate among Foxconn employees was about 2 or 3 per 100,000, which was similar to the rate among college students in China. The spokesperson also cited statistics from the WHO that the suicide rate in China was 13.0 per 100,000 males and 14.8 per 100,000 females in 1999 (Chung, 2010). A factory manager for an electronics company in southern China commented that, while the rates of pay seemed a pittance to local employees in the West, they were in line with the local living standard. "Working 60 hours a week is hard, [but] I myself used to do more than 70 hours in a UK factory before," said the factory manager (*BBC News*, 2010). These arguments, with appealing data, however, did not help tone down the adversities experienced by local workers. As China opens up and its environments change, local workers are increasingly exposed to Western ideals of consumerism and freedom, especially in the Special Economic Zones. The days of toiling for hours for basic pay and being happy are long gone (*BBC News*, 2010). When the workers see (or assume) the beautiful new world outside, and yet perceive that they are treated as if a prisoner, globalization shock and depression are likely to occur. It is hard for them to adjust to the forces of globalization. Of course, the beautiful new world outside China is certainly a mirage. Although there have been high-level returnees back to China, the reality of the outside world in most Chinese people's minds is still veiled to a certain degree. It is human nature to long for freedom when one lacks it. That is why they idealize the Western world. For example, those who are rich or in power would send their children to be brought up in the West and expect that they could gain citizenship in the host countries. However, the rapid changes of environments due to globalization help to crystallize such a mirage.

## Critical Perspectives of Global Careers in China

In this section, we use a critical lens to evaluate the influences of globalization on global careers in China at individual, organizational, and societal levels.

At the individual level, with more foreign investment coming to China, more expatriates may be posted to China. This creates opportunities for Chinese locals to gain an understanding regarding how different it is for foreign-owned businesses, relative to SOEs, to operate in China. However, given that expatriates generally take the top management positions in their organizations, it is possible that there is a glass ceiling for Chinese locals. Regardless of how talented or how hard working they are, they may not move up the hierarchy of the organization, just because they work for a foreign company. As for the blue-collar Chinese

locals, their well-being has generally been neglected. However, as illustrated by the Foxconn case, more attention needs to be paid to them, as, in the long run, low safety and morale levels among the rank and file will ultimately influence the quality of the products and, therefore, the reputation of a business.

At the organizational level, it is important for organizations to strike a balance between local Chinese culture and the foreign culture, so that the organizational culture does not have a liability of foreignness that prevents the local Chinese from embracing the organization's culture. As mentioned previously, even though contemporary career concepts focus on individuals taking more control of their careers, the dominant influence of traditional Chinese culture emphasizes fulfilling expectations from authority, such as parents. Thus, organizations that wish to implement Westernized career-management concepts for their Chinese employees may need to consider the contextual factors. The challenges of blue-collar Chinese locals also warrant organizations considering their corporate social responsibility. Even though business might thrive owing to the low operating costs in China, as a responsible corporation, the welfare of all shareholders should be taken care of so the firm can thrive in the long run.

At the societal level, given that Chinese locals have more and more contact with people coming from other parts of the world, such as expatriates, self-initiated expatriates, or immigrants, the question of the preservation or evolution of Chinese culture is intriguing. Moreover, as brain-drain and talent-shortage issues continue to plague China, the effectiveness of government policies to encourage talented people who are educated aboard to come back to China is questionable. The sweatshop issue of Chinese locals also has implications at the societal level. Even though the Chinese government may now enjoy financial benefits brought by foreign business, this is at the cost of the welfare of Chinese people. Policymakers should therefore establish and reinforce labor laws and regulations to protect the welfare of their people.

## Conclusions

In this chapter, we reviewed global careers in China and discussed how globalization has brought about changes in the political, economic, technical, sociocultural and legal/labor environments of China, contributing to the globalization shock and adjustment of both expatriates and Chinese locals. To exemplify the situations of contemporary career concepts and the opportunities and difficulties encountered by people in the development of global careers, we described two contrasting cases that recently occurred in China, the NBA superstar Yao Ming and Foxconn's local workers. These career actors were all affected by the environmental changes in China and the impact of globalization, but the consequences of their stories were extremely different. Finally, we adopted a critical perspective to evaluate influences of globalization on global careers in China at individual, organizational, and societal levels. There is a need

for organizations and policymakers in China to understand that globalization has both positive and negative implications for global careers.

## References

Accenture (2005). China spreads its wings—Chinese companies go global. Retrieved from www.accenture.com, September 5, 2011.

Ahlstrom, D., Foley, S., Young, M. N., & Chan, E. S. (2005). Human resource strategies in post-WTO China. *Thunderbird International Business Review, 47*(3), 263–285.

Arthur, M. B. & Rousseau, D. M. (1996). The boundaryless career as a new employment principle. In M. B. Arthur & D. M. Rousseau (Eds.), *The Boundaryless Career.* New York: Oxford University Press.

Barboza, D. (2006). China drafts law to empower unions and end labor abuse. *The New York Times.* Retrieved from www.nytimes.com/2006/10/13/business/worldbusiness/13sweat.html?pagewanted=all, October 30, 2011.

*BBC News* (2010). Foxconn suicides: Workers feel quite lonely. *BBC News Asia–Pacific.* May 28. Retrieved from www.bbc.co.uk/news/10182824, October 30, 2011.

Belkin, L. (2008). Why dad's resume lists car pool. *New York Times.* Retrieved from www.nytimes.com, January 26, 2012.

Black, J. S. & Gregersen, H. B. (1991). Antecedents to cross-cultural adjustment for expatriates in Pacific rim assignments. *Human Relations, 44,* 497–515.

*Bloomberg News* (2011). Yao Ming retires from NBA after leg injuries cut short career. July 20. Retrieved from www.bloomberg.com/news/2011-07-20/china-s-yao-ming-retires-from-nba-after-foot-ankle-injuries-1-.html, October 30, 2011.

*BusinessWeek* (2004). *Wow! Yao!* October 25. Retrieved from www.businessweek.com/magazine/content/04_43/b3905010.htm, October 30, 2011.

Bussey, J. (2011). Facebook's test in China: What price free speech? *The Wall Street Journal.* June 10. Retrieved from online.wsj.com/article/SB10001424052702304778304576375810359779964.html, September 5, 2011.

Chen, J. (2007). Country's wealth divide past warning level. *China Daily.* May 12. Retrieved from www.chinadaily.com.cn/china/2010-05/12/content_9837073.htm, September 5, 2011.

Chen, S. (2009). Sham or shame: Rethinking China's milk powder scandal from a legal perspective. *Journal of Risk Research, 12,* 725–747.

*China Daily* (2007). Harmonious society. September 29. Retrieved from http://english.peopledaily.com.cn/90002/92169/92211/6274603.html, September 5, 2011.

China Law Committee of the American Bar Association (2002). Written comments on rule of law issues related to the People's Republic of China's accession to the World Trade Organization. Washington DC: United States Trade Representative.

*China News* (2011). To temptation: Secret of China's highest level talent plan. Retrieved from www.flyxin.com/477, January 26, 2012.

China News Service (2011). State plan to attract talent, halt brain drain. Retrieved from www.ecns.cn/in-depth/2011/11-23/4058.shtml

Chinese Law (n.d.). *Wikipedia.* Retrieved August 19, 2011, from en.wikipedia.org/wiki/Chinese_law

Chudzikowski, K., Demel, B., Mayrhofer, W., Brisco, J. P., Unite, J., Milikic, B. B., Hall, D. T., Heras, M. L., Shen, Y., & Zikic, J. (2009). Career transitions and their causes: A country-comparative perspective. *Journal of Occupational and Organizational Psychology, 82,* 825–849.

Chung, O. (2010). Foxconn suicide toll mounts. *Asia Times Online*. May 22. Retrieved from www.atimes.com/atimes/China_Business/LE22Cb01.html, October 30, 2011.

Cooney, S. (2006). Making Chinese labor law work: The prospects for regulatory innovation in the people's republic of China. *Fordham International Law Journal, 30*(4), 1050–1097.

Davidson, W. H. (1987). Creating and managing joint ventures in China. *California Management Review, 29*(4), 77–94.

Devoretz, D. J., Ma, Z., & Zhang, K. (2002). Triangular human capital flows: Some empirical evidence from Hong Kong and Canada. Working Paper Series 02–17, Research on Immigration and Integration in the Metropolis, Vancouver, Canada.

Dickmann, M. & Baruch, Y. (2011). *Global Careers*. New York: Routledge.

Farrell, D. & Grant, A. J. (2005). China's looming talent shortage. *McKinsey Quarterly*. Retrieved from www.mckinseyquarterly.com, October 30, 2011.

Finn, M. G. (2005). Stay rates of foreign doctorate recipients from U.S. universities, 2003. Retrieved from orise.orau.gov/files/sep/stay-rates-foreign-doctorate-recipients-2003. pdf, January 26, 2012.

Foxconn Suicides (n.d.). *Wikipedia*. Retrieved October 7, 2011, from en.wikipedia.org/wiki/Foxconn_suicides

General Accounting Office (2002). *World Trade Organization: Analysis of China's Commitments to Other Members*. Washington DC: General Accounting Office.

Gong, Y. & Fan, J. (2006). Longitudinal examination of the role of goal orientation in cross-cultural adjustment. *Journal of Applied Psychology, 91*, 176–184.

Gudykunst, W. B. (1995). Anxiety/uncertainty management (AUM) theory: Current status. In R.Wiseman (Ed.), *Intercultural Communication Theory* (pp. 8–58). Thousand Oaks, CA: Sage.

Hall, D. T. (1976). *Career in Organizations*. Pacific Palisades, CA: Goodyear.

Hall, D. T. (1996). *The Career is Dead—Long Live the Career: A Relational Approach to Careers*. San Francisco, CA: Jossey-Bass Business and Management Series.

Hall, D. T. (2002). *Careers In and Out of the Organization*. Thousand Oaks, CA: Sage.

Hall, D. T., Gardner, W., & Baugh, S. G. (2008). The questions we ask about authenticity and attainability: How do values and beliefs influence our career decisions? Career division theme session panel discussion presented at the Academy of Management, Anaheim, CA.

Ho, D. Y. F. (1996). Filial peity and its psychological consequences. In M. Bond (Ed.), *The Handbook of Chinese Psychology* (pp. 155–165). Hong Kong: Oxford University Press.

International Business Etiquette and Manners (n.d.). China. Retrieved August 30, 2011, from www.cyborlink.com/besite/china.htm

Johnson, J. (2011). The rise and fall of Yao Ming. *Bleacher Report*. February 28. Retrieved from bleacherreport.com/articles/222892-the-rise-fall-of-yao-ming, October 30, 2011.

Joshi, H. (2009). Foxconn suicide toll mounts. *Asia Times Online*. July 23. Retrieved from www.atimes.com/atimes/China_Business/LE22Cb01.html, October 30, 2011.

Kanter, R. M. (1995). *World Class: Thriving Locally in the Global Economy*. New York: Simon and Schuster.

Kaye, M. & Taylor, W. G. K. (1997). Expatriate culture shock in China: A study in the Beijing hotel industry. *Journal of Managerial Psychology, 12*, 496–510.

Lacharite, J. (2002). Electronic decentralization in China: A critical analysis of Internet filtering policies in the People's Republic of China. *Australian Journal of Political Science, 37*, 333–346.

Lau, V. P., Shaffer, M. A., & Au, K. (2007). Entrepreneurial career success from a Chinese perspective: Conceptualization, operationalization, and validation. *Journal of International Business Studies, 38*(1), 126–146.

Leung, S. A., Hou, Z. J., Gati, I., & Li, X. (2011). Effects of parental expectations and cultural-values orientation on career decision-making difficulties of Chinese University students. *Journal of Vocational Behavior, 78*, 11–20.

Lin, Y. L. (2002). Guoji laogong biaozhun yu jingji quanqo hua (International labour standard and economic globalisation). Paper presented at the Conference on the Influence of China's WTO Accession on Labor Relations, Beijing, October 15–16.

Lin, Z. (1997). *Quanli Fubai Yu Quanli Zhiyue (Corruption of Power and Limitations on Power)*. Beijing: Law Publishers.

McLuhan, M. (1960). *Exploration in Communication*. Boston, MA: Beacon Press.

Merrick, E. N. (1995). Adolescent childbearing as career "choice": Perspective from an ecological context. *Journal of Counseling and Development, 73*, 288–295.

Ministry of Human Resources and Social Security of the People's Republic of China (2011). Official statistical report of human resources and social security in 2010. Retrieved from www.mohrss.gov.cn/page.do?pa=40288020240500280124088 2b84702d7&guid=e60c0e f72ddd4e8eb968ac5f11900f59&og=8a81f0842d0d556d012d111392900038, January 26, 2012.

Oberg, K. (1960). Cultural shock: Adjustment to new cultural environments. *Practical Anthropology, 7*, 177–182.

Panitchpakdi, S. & Clifford, M. L. (2002). *China and the WTO: Changing China, Changing World Trade*. Singapore: J. Wiley & Sons (Asia).

Picht, J. (2011, January 19). China: A giant, but with feet of clay. *The Washington Times*. Retrieved from http://communities.washingtontimes.com/neighborhood/stimulus/2011/jan/19/china-giant-feet-clay, September 5, 2011.

Pukthuanthong, K. & Walker, T. (2007). Venture capital in China: A culture shock for Western investors. *Management Decision, 45*, 708–731.

Schein, E. H. (1978). *Career Dynamics: Matching Individual and Organizational Needs*. Reading, MA: Addison-Wesley.

Selmer, J. (2005). Cross-cultural training and expatriate adjustment in China: Western joint venture managers. *Personnel Review, 34*, 68–84.

Shaffer, M. A. & Harrison, D. A. (1998). Expatriates' psychological withdrawal from international assignments: Work, nonwork, and family influences. *Personnel Psychology, 51*, 87–118.

Stahl, G. K., Miller, E. L., & Tung, R. L. (2002). Toward a boundaryless career: A closer look at the expatriate career concept and the perceived implications of an international assignment. *Journal of World Business, 37*, 216–227.

Sullivan, S. E. & Arthur, M. B. (2006). The evolution of the boundaryless career concept: Examining physical and psychological mobility. *Journal of Vocational Behavior, 69*, 19–29.

Sullivan, S. E. & Baruch, Y. (2009). Advances in career theory and research: A critical review and agenda for future exploration. *Journal of Management, 35*, 1542–1571.

Takeuchi, R., Yun, S., & Tesluk, P. E. (2002). An examination of crossover and spillover effects of spousal and expatriate cross-cultural adjustment on expatriate outcomes. *Journal of Applied Psychology, 87*, 655–666.

Teferra, D. (2004). Brain circulation: Unparalleled opportunities, underlying challenges and outmoded presumptions. Paper presented at the Symposium on International Labor

and Academic Mobility: Emerging Trends and Implications for Public Policy. October 21–22. Toronto, Canada: World Education Services.

Tharenou, P. (2009). Self-initiated international careers: Gender difference and career outcomes. In S. G. Baugh & S. E. Sullivan (Eds.), *Maintaining Energy, Focus and Options Over the Career: Research in Careers* (pp. 197–226). Charlotte, NC: Information Age.

*The Economist* (2005). China's people problem. *The Economist.* April 14. Retrieved from www.economist.com/business/displayStory.cfm?story_id=3868539, September 5, 2011.

*The Economist* (2007). Confucius makes a comeback: You can't keep a good sage down. *The Economist.* May 17. Retrieved from www.economist.com/node/9202957, September 5, 2011.

Thomas, D. C., Lazarova, M. B., & Inkson, K. (2005). Global careers: New phenomenon or new perspectives? *Journal of World Business, 40,* 340–347.

Tung, R. L. (2007). The human resource challenge to outward foreign direct investment aspirations from emerging economies: The case of China. *The International Journal of Human Resource Management, 18*(5), 868–889.

Warner, M. (1996). Chinese enterprise reform, human resources and the 1994 Labour Law. *The International Journal of Human Resource Management, 7*(4), 779–796.

Williams, A. (2009). *Contemporary Issues Shaping China's Civil Aviation Policy: Balancing International with Domestic Priorities.* Burlington, VT: Ashgate.

Wong, A. L. Y. (2007). Making career choice: A study of Chinese managers. *Human Relations, 60*(8), 1211–1233.

Wong, A. L. Y. & Slater, J. R. (2002). Executive development in China: Is there any in a Western sense? *The International Journal of Human Resource Management, 13,* 338–360.

Wong, L., White, L., & Gui, S. (2004). *Social Policy Reform in Hong Kong and Shanghai: A Tale of Two Cities.* Armonk, NY: M. E. Sharpe.

Wood, E. D. & El Mansour, B. (2010). Integrative literature review: Performance interventions that assist Chinese expatriates' adjustment and performance: Toward a conceptual approach. *Human Resource Development Review, 9*(2), 194–218.

Wu, D. (1996). Chinese children socialization. In M. Bond (Ed.), *Handbook of Chinese Psychology* (pp. 143–152). Hong Kong: Oxford University Press.

Xu, S. & Yang, R. (2010). Indigenous characteristics of Chinese corporate social responsibility. *Journal of Business Ethics, 93,* 321–333.

Yao Ming (n.d.). *Wikipedia.* Retrieved October 4, 2011, from en.wikipedia.org/wiki/Yao_Ming

Yee, H. S., Liu, B. L., & Ngo, T. W. (1993). Macau's mass political culture. *Asian Journal of Public Administration, 15,* 177–200.

Zweig, D. (2006). Competing for talent: China's strategies to reverse the brain drain. *International Labour Review, 145*(1–2), 65–89.

# 14

# GLOBAL CAREERS FROM A JAPANESE PERSPECTIVE

*Mami Taniguchi and Chikae Naito,*
*Waseda University, Japan*

## Introduction

In this chapter, we examine change and continuity in global careers in Japan by considering the effects of cultural, economic, and social backgrounds on global careers. To begin with, we consider the situation and current changes in global careers in Japan. Then we focus on expatriates, foreigners working within Japan, and third-country nationals working for Japanese multinational companies as global careers. We examine the challenges they are facing by showing case studies. Finally, we discuss change and continuity in global careers in Japan and draw some implications about the future development of global careers for individuals and Japanese companies.

## The Situation of Global Careers in Japan

Global careers and global work experiences have been underestimated among Japanese companies. Although work experiences abroad could be advantageous to a company employee's career, such experiences abroad were not essential for promotion for many Japanese companies, as they practiced an ethnocentric business model. According to Perlmutter, a company headquarters has one of three orientations toward subsidiaries in an international enterprise: an ethnocentric, a polycentric, or a geocentric orientation (Perlmutter, 1969). Companies with an ethnocentric attitude primarily reflect the home-country view. Utilizing global-integration and local-responsiveness axes, Bartlett and Ghoshal (1989) studied major multinational companies and classified Japanese companies as headquarters-centered "global companies." Japanese companies located most of their core functions within the headquarters in Japan. Overseas subsidiaries had low levels of power and authority in corporate decision-making, as they largely

served a periphery or a supportive function. Thus, Japanese companies were ethnocentric in nature (Bartlett and Yoshihara, 1988).

From the late 1970s to the early 1980s, Japanese manufacturers expanded businesses overseas. However, the career planning for Japanese company employees was mainly within domestic rotations, and an overseas work assignment, therefore, was regarded as a peripheral, unconventional career pattern. As IT infrastructures were still poor at that time, Japanese employees overseas often experienced breakdowns in communication with their domestic human social networks. Moreover, Japanese companies create tacit knowledge by shared experiences (Nonaka and Takeuchi, 1995). In addition, trust is created through shared experiences (Manabe, 2002; Yamagishi and Yamagishi, 1994). Thus, an extended absence from the domestic human network in Japan—that is, an appointment to an overseas assignment—posed an impediment for an individual's career progress, as internal human relationships enabled employees to gain power and influence within the domestic headquarters in the course of their employment tenure.

## Changes in Competencies for Promotion in Japan

A number of factors explain the rise of Japanese expatriates and foreign recruitment over the years. Three main factors are presented here. First, the current rising yen increases labor costs in the domestic labor markets. As Japan is based on secondary industries, under the circumstances, manufacturing overseas is more reasonable than domestic production, utilizing a host-country labor force in overseas subsidiaries as labor markets. Moreover, it is more efficient for them to manufacture with counterparty companies in the supply chain than self-manufacture. Second, secondary domestic markets are shrinking because of the declining birthrate and an aging population in Japan. Therefore, companies in Japan have had to shift their business from the domestic arena to overseas. Finally, increasing interdependence with overseas operations enhances globalization of human resources in management—not only for expatriates but also for foreigners working in Japanese companies. As a consequence of these factors, Japanese companies are encouraged to change to be truly global companies, with internationalization at their headquarters in Japan.

## Demographic Change

Foreign labor working for Japanese companies is increasing. According to research carried out by the Exploratory Committee of the Index of Internationalization (Kokusaika shihyou kentou iin kai, 2009), the number of highly skilled foreigners entering Japan in 2003 was 22,728; it was 23,998 in 2004; 26,088 in 2005; 33,132 in 2006; and 39,020 in 2007. We see active recruitment of international students among major Japanese companies. The recruitment number

is small by comparison with Japanese new graduates, but this has recently become the general trend. Moreover, there is a tendency to promote third-country nationals among major Japanese multinational companies.

The number of Japanese expatriates is growing owing to the expansion of business overseas. According to the Ministry of Foreign Affairs of Japan (1997–2010), the number of expatriates from Japan was approximately 150,000 in 1997, but it grew to around 230,000 between 2003 and 2010. To complement the growth of Japanese expatriates, Japanese companies began to develop the global careers of expatriates.

After the lost decade in the 1990s, a global career has become regarded as a critical experience to acquire the key competencies for promotions. Owing to the appreciation of the yen and an aging population, combined with the diminishing birthrate in Japan, Japanese companies began to shift their core business overseas. These changes are good news for employees who work in companies abroad and reflect a global career path. In this respect, a global career becomes an asset, not only for the organization, but also for individuals.

## Conceptualization of Global Career

A career is defined as "the individually perceived sequence of attitudes and behaviors associated with work-related experiences and activities over the span of the person's life" (D. T. Hall, 1976), or a "sequence of positions occupied by a person during the course of a lifetime" (Super, 1980). In the broad sense, a global company includes "import and export of commodities and manufactured goods"; "investment of capital in manufacturing, extractive, agricultural, transportation and communication assets; supervision of employees in different countries"; and "investment in international services like banking, advertising, tourism, retailing and construction; transaction involving copyrights, patents, trademarks and process technology" (Taggart and McDermott, 1993, p. 4). In the narrow sense, a global company has the key strategic capability of "building cost advantages through centralized global-scale operations" (Bartlett and Ghoshal, 1989, p. 15) and is "an organization that attempts to standardize operations worldwide in all functional areas" (Ball and McCulloch, 1996, p. 8).

Peiperl and Jonsen (2007) describe a global career as, "a career that takes place in more than one region of the world, either sequentially or concurrently"(Peiperl and Jonsen, 2007, p. 351). However, other perspectives exist. One such perspective is that moving just across the border means an "international" career, and passing between more than two countries means a "global" career. Here, however, for the sake of convenience, we define a global career as inclusive of an international career. Rather, we define global careers as careers across borders, such as expatriates, foreigners working within Japan, and third-country nationals working for Japanese multinational companies.

## The Relevance of Contemporary Career Concepts for Global Careers in Japan

In this section, we examine change and continuity in Japanese global careers. There have been legal changes in employment before and after the 2000s. The revision of the Worker Dispatch Law led to the hiring of a large number of contingent workers. Furthermore, changes in governance structures, such as a revision of the Companies Act, made people believe that the clarification of roles and authorities, separation of top management and operational management, and transparency of management were important.

These environmental changes encouraged a transformation of Japanese personnel practices and changes from tacit into explicit features.

After the collapse of the bubble economy, in the late 1990s and the early 2000s, a number of Japanese companies tried to restructure their organizations. The Japanese career-management system became one of the targets for the radical organizational restructuring.

Recruitment and layoff policies and practices have changed from a lifetime-employment system to a "boundaryless career" (Arthur, 1994; Arthur and Rousseau, 1996). A boundaryless career is "the antonym of a 'bounded' or 'organizational' career" and "the most prominent is when a career, like the stereotypical Silicon Valley career, moves across the boundaries of separate employers" (Arthur, 1994, p. 296), and people who have boundaryless careers move with portable skills (Greenhaus, Callanan, and DiRenzo, 2008). In the past, sharing experiences and places were important for performance and trust in a global career in Japan. Now, however, a boundaryless career has greater significance, because it is useful to have the different points of view generated from diverse employees in a company to solve problems. Not only expatriates of internal promotion but also mid-career employees have become an important human resource for Japanese companies. The external labor market grew as a result of frequent mid-career employment, which creates the chance to employ people with global careers. Still, human resource development requires much time to foster, and this is the biggest challenge for the use of mid-career workers among Japanese companies previously known for ethnocentric business practices. Just when they directed their attention to external markets, Japanese external labor markets became flexible after the collapse of the bubble economy. The number of mid-career employees increased in the external labor market after large-scale layoffs and early retirement from major Japanese companies. Boundaryless careers promoted employment and the utilization of people with global careers within companies.

Additionally, companies tend to hire contingent workers, instead of new graduates, because of the legal-system reform concerning temporary workers' law. Companies have been encouraged to minimize the costs of human resources development and pay for permanent employees.

Japanese companies changed their personnel-evaluation and promotion systems from seniority-based pay to performance-based pay. Although the seniority-based-pay system was useful for gaining the power of influence within the domestic company network, it became inconsistent with the competencies essential for corporate globalization. Investments to develop the power of influence within the company, that is, human networks, often brought some constraints in radical organizational restructuring.

Japanese companies tend to develop human resources in the short term, and they select and assign high-potential employees at their earlier career stage. By comparison with Western global companies, Japanese companies regard it as a problem that Japanese executives are too old to tolerate a difficult global assignment. Young top executives are seen as the symbol of organizational renewal. Nowadays, Japanese companies have some challenges when it comes to global competitiveness, such as falling behind in global talent development. According to an IMD study (IMD World Competitiveness Center, 2008), in the ranking of how many "foreign high-skilled people are attracted to your country's business environment," Japan ranked at 42 among 55 countries. For language skill, it is ranked at 55 of the 57 countries included in the study. Managers' international experience is ranked at 52 among the 57 countries.

Japan lags behind in global talent development for the following reasons: (1) Japanese is not a universal language; (2) there is an adequate domestic market in Japan, which leads to a tendency for young people to stay in Japan; and (3) as an island country, Japan has not been susceptible to invasion.

## Exploration of the Structural, Cultural, and Contextual Difficulties and Opportunities in Japanese Global Careers

Although Japanese companies are changing their attitude toward global career development, there are still some challenges. In this section, we examine how global careers in Japanese companies are changing, and how the Japanese economic, political, cultural, and social backgrounds affect the development of global careers in Japanese companies through three research questions:

1. How have Japanese employees who have backgrounds as expatriates, as well as mid-career employees who have an overseas MBA, been treated in Japanese companies? Although they used to be treated as peripheral employees, how are they being valued recently?

2. How have foreigners working for Japanese companies been treated in Japanese companies? Recently, Japanese companies have been aggressively employing foreign new graduates. There are some changes compared with the past.

3. How can Japanese companies retain third-country nationals working for Japanese companies? Japanese companies are weak in supporting the global

careers of third–country nationals in comparison with the multinational companies in Japan.

## Expatriates from Japanese Companies

Table 14.1 shows the efforts of major Japanese companies to send more employees overseas. They assign global rotations to employees as a part of their strategies.

For instance, ITOCHU Corporation (ITOCHU Corporation Website, n.d.), a leading trading company with over 130 overseas bases in 67 countries, conducts various types of training program for developing global careers, by position and job class. Moreover, all new graduates are dispatched overseas for 4–5 months to acquire global perspectives and to improve language skills within the first 4 years. In the past, there have been some problems, as below, with Japanese companies in terms of support and evaluation of expatriates' careers.

The following case illustrates features of expatriates from typical Japanese companies.

---

### The Case of Japanese Expatriates

Kazutoshi works for a large Japanese electronics company, which has over 100,000 workers all over the world and markets its products worldwide. He had been in China for 5 years as an expatriate to a local subsidiary as a sales manager. The local subsidiary had 1,000 workers at that time.

### Psychological Contracts

He didn't feel any image gap between the image of the career after repatriation and the reality. Many sales workers in his company repeat the cycle of job rotations in Japan and overseas. He was assigned to the expected section with promotion and he was satisfied with the personnel transfer. Currently, salaries for employees of his company reflect a traditional seniority-based pay scale, and workers are aware that it is protected.

Moreover, he didn't suffer from cultural differences. At the overseas subsidiaries of his company, almost all the staff spoke Japanese fluently. Therefore, expatriates from Japan didn't have to speak Chinese in business. Business partners are also Japanese companies. A language facility is not required in the case of his company.

### Top Management's Commitment to a Global Career

As the domestic market shrank, the company shifted its core from domestic to overseas. The career pattern also changed, from domestic to overseas rotation. Since 2004, the new president has begun to focus more on global careers than the former president did. Now, experiences overseas are seen as important for promotion in his company. Thus, the perception of top management strongly affects the company's policy related to global careers.

**TABLE 14.1** Practices for developing global careers among Japanese companies, based on *Nihon keizai shinbun* (October 15, 2011) and the companies' websites

| Company name | Category of business | Consolidated number of employees | Practice |
|---|---|---|---|
| Hitachi, Ltd. | Consumer electronics | 361,745 | Increase the volume of overseas training in 2011–2012 from 200 to 2,000, ten times the previous 2 years |
| Sony Corporation | Consumer electronics | 168,200 | By 2013, dispatch 100 young employees in their 20s every year and increase the number of employees with TOEIC score over 730 to 5,000 |
| Toyota Motor Corporation | Automobiles | 317,716 | Provide potential recruits for 2012 with training programs, studying abroad for 6 months before joining Toyota |
| Mitsubishi International Corporation | Trading companies & distributors trading company | 58,470 | All workers in their 20s mandated to experience life abroad from 2011 |
| ITOCHU Corporation | Trading companies & distributors | 4,284 | Expatriate all employees overseas within 4 years of joining the company |
| Takeda Pharmaceutical Company Limited | Pharmaceutical | 18,498 | Reduce age of young workers who are on loan to another company from average of 37.5-years-old to late 20s |

In this case, there are psychological contracts (Rousseau, 1995) between the company and workers concerning payment and the promotion system, which could contribute to maintaining workers' reliability and retaining workers.

Macklon (1991) highlighted that Japanese expatriates don't speak English, through her interviews with English workers working for Japanese companies. This is one of the features of expatriates from Japanese companies. They hire Japanese-speaking staff for local offices in order not to bother expatriates with communication problems. It is useful for Japanese expatriates' early adjustment, but it creates the problem of hindering the utilization of the local country's staff. Ohbuchi and Takahashi (1994) demonstrated that the Japanese tend to avoid conflict to preserve relationships and hold a perception of shared responsibility, through the survey about Japanese and American students.

Meanwhile, some expatriates from Japanese companies are facing challenges. The following examples reflect these challenges.

## Repatriation Problems for the Organization and Individuals

Hideki works for a Japanese advertising company. He had been in France as a manager for several years. However, as his job disappeared, he was forced to repatriate. It depends on the circumstances of the account whether expatriates will come back or stay. Overseas experience is not especially valued for promotion in his company.

Many companies don't value employees' experiences of international assignment, as studied by Black, Gregersen, Mendenhall, and Stroh (1999), and repatriates often face problems.

## Gap Between Headquarters and Overseas Subsidiaries

After being repatriated to Japan, he was assigned routine work, and he suffered with the adjustment to the differences between the headquarters and the overseas subsidiary, such as the decision-making system or discretionary power. He was not satisfied with his job in Japan and required a long time to adjust. He could not expect the company to offer support for his adjustment. In terms of his company's culture, most employees believed that the adjustment was up to them. Moreover, he felt his career overseas was not appreciated by the company. In his company, a global career is not consistent. The careers of expatriates are not clear, and whether or when they will repatriate depends on the environment. Once expatriates have gone to an overseas branch, they usually never come back to Japan, unless their accounts diminish or decline. He felt that a global career was not valued by the company.

Black et al. (1999) showed that more than half their interviewees, expatriate managers, said that both autonomy and authority declined after repatriation to

their home countries. Lower levels of satisfaction with company support and poorer career-advancement opportunities within the company can be predictors of turnover intentions. Japanese companies have to care about expatriates more (Stahl, Chua, Caligiuri, Cerdin, and Taniguchi, 2009). However, there are some changes favoring a global career in his company.

### New Initiative for Global Leader

In his company, business expertise was seen as the primary element in expatriation, and the expatriation was accompanied by a move of the account to overseas, for which a global career had not been planned to be developed by design. Currently, the perception of a global career is changing from a sense of crisis about the absence of successors in the overseas branch. To develop young account managers who can work in global settings, a new program for young employees has been implemented to foster global account managers.

Colleagues see the members joining the global program as the "right people," who have adequate language skills and are good at their jobs. Trainees are selected through an open application system. Employees can apply for it without permission from their superiors.

The system guarantees outgoing career development through the open application system. Outgoing career development is essential for developing global leaders. Black, Morrison, and Gregersen (1999) positioned "travel" as one of the strategies for global leadership development.

### Foreigners Working for Japanese Companies

In the late 1980s to early 1990s, Japanese companies, especially small businesses, faced serious labor shortages at the peak of the economic bubble. Although Japanese government policy has intended to increase the number of highly skilled foreigners and decrease unskilled foreign laborers, in fact medium and small-sized businesses hired unskilled foreign people as cheap labor.

Currently, in the context of a falling population and the globalization of markets, there are trends of aggressive employment of foreign, highly skilled people by Japanese companies overall. According to research by the Japan Productivity Center (2011), a number of Japanese companies want to employ foreign workers.

This trend is reflected in the increasing number of foreign new graduates, as shown in Table 14.2, where Japanese companies are promoting to hire non-Japanese employees.

Lawson, Inc., the leading convenience-store chain, has aggressively hired foreign workers since 2008. Lawson offers some types of career opportunity for foreigners. It promotes a diverse labor force. After the training of new graduates, they are assigned to a directly managed store as a manager, where they work as store managers or store support supervisors. Then, they are promoted to the

**TABLE 14.2** Practices of Japanese companies promoting employment of foreign new graduates based on Recruit Shingaku Soken (2011). The numbers of employees are based on the companies' websites

| Company name | Category of business | Consolidated number of employees | Practice for foreign new graduates' employment |
|---|---|---|---|
| Aeon Co., Ltd. | Hypermarkets & super centers | 76,061 | Year-round recruitment regardless of age, sex, race. Planning to employ more than 10,000 globally oriented people for 3 years, and over 2,000 employees, twice as many as in usual years, in 2011 |
| NTT Communications Corporation | Integrated telecommunication services | 8,250 | Employed 10 foreign new graduates in 2011 and plans to employ 20, 10% of overall new graduates |
| NTT DoCoMo, Inc. | Wireless telecommunication services | 23,671 | 11 of 241 new graduates are foreigners |
| Sony Corporation | Consumer electronics | 168,200 | Employed 32 people among undergraduates in China and India and foreign students, and plans to employ 30% of new graduates among foreigners in 2013 |
| Takeda Pharmaceutical Company Limited | Pharmaceutical | 18,498 | 10% of 200 new graduates are foreigners, as global employment |
| Toshiba Corporation | Consumer electronics | 202,638 | Global employment in Asia since 2006, employing 30 people every year |
| Panasonic Corporation | Consumer electronics | 366,937 | Local recruitment within overseas subsidiaries, controlled by headquarters since 2004. 1,100 people, 80% of employees in 2012, are foreigners |
| FAST RETAILING CO., LTD. | Apparel, accessories & luxury goods | 14,612 | Planning to recruit over 80% of new graduates among foreign students in 2013 |
| Yamato Transport Co., Ltd. | Trucking | 139,320 | 20% of new graduates were foreign students in 2011. Global employment in 2012, regardless of nationality |
| Rakuten, Inc. | Internet software & services | 7,119 | English as its official language by the end of fiscal year 2012; 30% of new graduates each year will be foreign |
| Lawson, Inc. | General merchandise stores | 5,703 | 30% of new graduates will be foreign |

Note: Categories of business are based on GICS classification

level of supervisor in charge of store management if they pass the examination. Regularly, one supervisor is responsible for nine stores. In the upper management levels, branch managers manage 10–15 store supervisors. The reward and promotion system is clear. All employees receive equal monthly pay with respect to each part, plus a performance-related bonus.

Lawson develops various types of retail store as a differentiating strategy. One of them is Natural Lawson, which deals with health-conscious food products and targets mainly young women. Such a new type of store is also the employment basis for diverse people, including women and foreigners, where they can be active and develop their personalities in the business.

The following article indicates some challenges in the utilization of foreign employees in Japanese companies, as it illustrates a socialization problem experienced by foreigners.

---

## Socialization Problems for Foreign Employees

Some foreign employees cannot assimilate into the culture of Japanese companies. Conflicts often occur between supervisors without overseas experience and foreign employees. According to a newspaper article (*Nihon keizai shinbun*, 2012), some foreign employees working in Japan experience problems:

> A foreign employee entered a Japanese manufacturing company after studying in Japan. Although he was employed as "global recruitment," he felt that "that wasn't the deal." What to do to get promoted was ambiguous. No one told him when he could move to a foreign department. Personnel just said, "It depends on you." He finally gave up asking any more.
>
> Others said,"the speed of decision making is too slow to survive in a global environment in Japan," and "I wonder why all employees can equally receive bonus payments despite a merit-based system."
>
> The vague standards of Japanese companies can confuse foreign employees. It can lead to their turnover. Foreign employees sometimes feel that wasn't the deal. They recognize themselves as workforces in foreign business. "Japanese people tend to avoid unprecedented steps. They place more value not on outcome but process."
>
> A woman from China working for Japanese companies was often asked to do "language-related tasks," which she was not in charge of. Although she worked efficiently and reduced overtime work, her supervisor said that she did not work passionately.
>
> (*Nihon keizai shinbun*, January 18, 2012;
> translated into English by the authors)

According to the article, some foreign workers struggle with assimilation with other Japanese employees. E. T. Hall (1976) pointed out that Japan has "high-context" culture, in which "indirection" is regarded as polite, and people can understand what they want to say without saying it with words to each other, in contrast to American "low-context" culture. It is also called "A and UN breathing." It is one aspect of Japanese culture. However, when global companies employ multinational employees, it is unreasonable to force them to assimilate into such a culture.

The following case shows features of foreign workers in Japanese companies.

---

### Social Background in Japanese Companies

Keisuke works for a Japanese trading company, where there are some foreign employees among his colleagues at the headquarters in Japan. All of them speak Japanese fluently and were educated in Japan. They are well assimilated into Japanese culture and society. Some of them fit into the administrative position, and they can understand Japan's basic principles and real motives, which are called "Honne and Tatemae" in Japanese. Others leave because they cannot adjust to Japanese culture.

### New Program to Enhance Foreign Employees' Commitment

His company's sales department set up an original leadership program to foster young foreign staff as leaders. Participants among overseas staff are invited to the headquarters for 1 or 2 years, with their families. Because this program is business-oriented, the sales department covers the cost of the program, instead of the personnel department.

In this case, only those who could adjust to Japanese culture remained with his company. The company offers the program to foreign workers to enhance their commitment to the company. In fact, it is not rare to invite employees from foreign subsidiaries to enhance their commitment. Many multinational companies in Japan have worked on prevailing companies' codes of conduct or organizational culture for their foreign employees, which led to the key performance indicator. There are ways to manage people of diverse nationalities, such as sharing a goal, and, since the late 1990s, Japanese multinational companies have made long-term efforts to penetrate organizational culture in the sense of a longitudinal goal. Kitai and Tanaka (2009) reported that the penetration degree of organizational business creeds was positively related to employees' job satisfaction and commitment in Japanese companies, through their quantitative survey. By contrast, in the USA, David (1989) indicated that whether companies had a mission statement was not related to higher performance, through a survey of the CEOs of all the *Business Week 1000* companies.

---

### Global MBA Holders' in Japanese Companies

Although many Japanese make the effort to obtain an MBA through studying abroad, they are facing some challenges, as the following article shows.

## Japanese Companies Couldn't Grasp the Meaning of "Global Careers"

According to Diamond online (2012; translated into English by the authors), the website of the Japanese economics magazine, Japanese MBA holders are suspicious about whether Japanese companies have a clear definition of a global career or evaluate their careers and abilities properly.

"Some of them evaluate just my language skill. They don't value my MBA degree, mindset, and communication skill." "The experience of an overseas experience is not seen as important. Japanese companies may evaluate only the experience 'staying in foreign countries'."

"What ability do they want to hire? When a Japanese firm employs a person who has experienced study abroad, what kind of people do they want? They seem not to understand the meaning of 'global'."

As demonstrated in the research by the Japan Productivity Center (2011), 72% of respondent companies don't define the competencies for the companies, that is, what is a "global person" for the companies. Japanese companies have to make a clearer definition of the global person they require. From the employees' perspective, they could not understand what is expected. Ambiguity of role and authority is one of the characteristics of Japanese companies. Clear roles and definitions contribute to smooth collaboration as a team. Furthermore, the existence of long-term employment led to the custom of not clearly mentioning future careers, avoiding clear contracts in Japan.

## Problem With Evaluation by Personnel

"There are a lot of personnel who don't have the experience on the site. Many of them only send messages from the policy directed from abstract needs and the direction by management side from the top down. 'What kind of person is really needed' is not understood well." "Truly global companies offer the employee training and experiences in an overseas branch office, and employ global talent among people in mid-careers. We should ascertain whether it is such a company or not before we join it."

Moreover, some people complain that their abilities are not correctly evaluated in Japanese companies. "I think that coworkers do not understand the quality, even if an experienced person who has gone abroad to study writes the document in English." "Consequentially, it is related to the evaluation of work. People who only speak English and who can communicate well in English are treated all the same."

We can see the problem that the companies only employ people with global careers, and never change the human resource management practice, or are slow to change. Consequently, employees who have global careers are not evaluated. According to Demel et al. (2009) and Taniguchi (2011), objective criteria of career success are largely emphasized in Japan. Recognition, achievement, and performing one's role are consistent with an income or hierarchical advancement that is visible and "objectively" measureable. To attract and engage people with global careers, human resource management and practices need to be changed.

## Third-Country Nationals in Japan

Japanese companies have a small number of third-country nationals (Shiraki, 1995). Until now, they were not treated as possessing a high potential in Japan, and they were considered as non-essential, peripheral employees. Japanese companies recently began to take them on succession planning, to set them as a benchmark of better global-career management. There is a trend of hiring third-country nationals as top management of an overseas subsidiary. Although one famous Japanese manufacturer intended to transfer an English person as the head of its overseas subsidiary, he returned to his country as the result of a huge compensation deal and salary from other competing global companies. We give an example of support by multinational companies in Japan to utilize the global careers of third-country nationals to help Japanese companies.

---

### Career Development for Third-Country Nationals

Kenji is a corporate officer of the Japanese branch of a multinational pharmaceutical company. His company employs a number of third-country nationals. Their career paths are clear. For example, an English person who was a president in a U.S. branch made his career through his expatriation to Korea, Japan, and the US. He knew his expatriation was a part of his career development. Moreover, he was assigned a mentor, with whom he could be counseled about his own career. Through such an informal mentoring system by the company, he could keep a network with headquarters. Every employee understands the importance of mentoring. Kenji also contacted the president as an informal mentor. A mentoring system greatly helps employees to transfer across borders.

Stahl et al. (2009) refer to the importance of formal or informal mentoring. It can reduce career uncertainty for individuals. "From the individual's perspective, this significantly reduces the amount of career uncertainty and career risk associated with an international assignment" (Stahl et al., 2009, p. 95).

---

## Critical Perspectives on Global Careers for Japan

Only recently have Japanese companies shifted to globalize their business and their employees. To be truly global companies, there is so much to do. As we have shown in this chapter, the mindsets toward global careers in Japan are changing. However, some challenges still exist. One of the significant barriers to taking advantage of talents with a global career in Japan that we have not discussed in this chapter is rooted in a matter of the language. As Japanese is not a global common language, Japanese companies have lagged in the recruitment, retention, and development of global talents, compared with Western countries.

Additionally, to take full advantage of talents with global careers, not only companies but also the Japanese government and educational institutions need to take initiatives through a systematic approach. The Japanese government has to work on the issue of immigration policy, which supports the global career, and also fundamentally overhaul the curricula for compulsory education to emphasize language education.

## Conclusion

In this chapter, we have examined change and continuity in global careers in Japan by considering the effects of cultural, economic, and social backgrounds on global careers. Although economic and political backgrounds can be changed radically, cultural and social backgrounds take quite a few years to change.

We draw some implications with regard to developing global careers in Japan. Schein (1978) pointed out that a matching process between organizations and individuals is important for career development. The matching process between individuals and organizations includes the effects of psychological contracts (Rousseau, 1995) and commitments (Meyer and Allen, 1991). It is important for organizations to understand features and challenges in the framework of a career-management system. It is essential to maintain employees' commitment and motivation from a long-range standpoint of career development.

The same is true for global careers. It is necessary to match both organizational needs and individual needs at each stage of organization planning and individual career stage.

To utilize talents with global careers effectively, companies need to appreciate diversity, change the former human resource management practices, such as a personal evaluation that values diversity, and change the mindsets of employees who are not global-career-oriented from a monocultural to a multicultural way of thinking.

Changes to personal appraisal policies and practices are especially important to value global careers and to recruit and retain talents with global careers. In Japan's "monocultural" society, developing global careers is associated with the difficulty of accepting people with diverse nationalities and backgrounds.

We examined the situation of foreign employees in Japan facing multiple barriers of socialization, and Japanese who feel underappreciated with regard to their global career. Without exhibiting passive behavior, and assuming the slow change of organizations, individuals also need to become change agents themselves, leverage their own strengths, and think about where to utilize them, actively taking advantage of self-directed career practices, such as job posting in their companies.

If individuals do not have enough information about their company's practices, as they are outsiders, they have to find a way to get access to such information by themselves.

Greenhaus, Callanan, and Godshalk (2010) insisted that,

> career exploration is the collection and analysis of information regarding oneself and the environment that foster management process. Most people need to gather information so they can become more keenly aware of their own values, interests, and abilities, as well as the opportunities and obstacles in their environment.
>
> (Greenhaus, Callanan, & Godshalk, 2010, p. 49)

We suggest that individuals constantly develop global skills, networks, and career goals to survive an uncertain business world. Individuals need to take time to self-reflect by asking "knowing what," "knowing whom," and "knowing why" (Arthur, Claman, DeFillippi, & Adams, 1995).

Leading Japanese companies that made radical organizational transformations have shown successful results since 2000, compared with other companies without any changes. Also, there are certain amounts of evidence that successful Japanese companies have been led by a CEO with a global career, especially after the collapse of the bubble economy. Global-career experiences bring organizations different perspectives and allow fundamental changes to adjust to environmental changes.

## References

Arthur, M. B. (1994). The boundaryless career: A new perspective for organizational inquiry. *Journal of Organizational Behavior*, 15, 295–306.

Arthur, M. B., Claman, P. H., DeFillippi, R. J., & Adams, J. (1995). Intelligent enterprise, intelligent careers [and executive commentary]. *The Academy of Management Executive (1993–2005)*, 9(4), 7–22.

Arthur, M. B. & Rousseau, D. M. (1996). *The Boundaryless Career: A New Employment Principle for a New Organizational Era*. New York: Oxford University Press.

Ball, D. A. & McCulloch, W. H. (1996). *International Business: The Challenge of Global Competition* (6th ed.). Chicago, IL: Irwin.

Bartlett, C. A. & Ghoshal, S. (1989). *Managing Across Borders: The Transnational Solution*. Boston, MA: Harvard Business School Press.

Bartlett, C. A. & Yoshihara, H. (1988). New challenges for Japanese multinationals: Is organizational adaptation their achilles heel? *Human Resource Management*, 27, 19–43.

Black, J. S., Gregersen, H. B., Mendenhall, M. E., & Stroh, L. K. (1999). *Globalizing People Through International Assignments*. Reading, MA: Addison-Wesley.

Black, J. S., Morrison, A. J., & Gregersen, H. B. (1999). *Global Explorers: The Next Generations of Leaders*. New York: Routledge.

David, F. R. (1989). How companies define their mission. *Long Range Planning*, 22(1), 90–97.

Demel, B., Yan, S., Hall, D. T., Mayrhofer, W., Chudzikowski, K., Unite, J., Briscoe, J., Abdul Ghani, R., Bogicevic Milikic, B., Colorado, O., Fei, Z., Las Heras, M., Ogliastri, E., Pazy, A., Poon, J., Shefer, D., Taniguchi, M., & Zikic, J. (2009). Cracking the fortune cookies: Influencing factors in career success across 11 countries. Paper presented at Academy of Management Annual Meeting, August 2009.

Diamond online (2012). Amerika daigakuin ryugaku keikensha honne zadankai (jou),(ge). (Honest symposium by people experienced studying at universities in U.S. part 1, part 2), online article (in Japanese). December 8 and 15. Retrieved from http://diamond.jp/articles/-/15169 and http://diamond.jp/articles/-/15294. Accessed February 28, 2012.

Greenhaus, J. H., Callanan, G. A., & DiRenzo, M. (2008). A boundaryless perspective on careers, in J. Barling & C. L. Cooper (Eds.), *The Sage Handbook of Organizational Behavior: Volume 1, Micro Approaches* (pp. 277–299). London: Sage Publications.

Greenhaus, J. H., Callanan, G. A., & Godshalk, V. M. (2010). *Career Management* (4th ed.). Thousand Oaks, CA: Sage Publications.

Hall, D. T. (1976). *Careers in Organizations*. Santa Monica, CA: Goodyear.

Hall, E. T. (1976). *Beyond Culture*. Garden City, NY: Anchor Books, Doubleday.

IMD World Competitiveness Center (2008). *World Competitiveness Yearbook 2008*. IMD World Competitiveness Center.

ITOCHU Corporation Website (n.d.). Human resource development supporting the "seeking of new opportunities". Retrieved from www.itochu.co.jp/en/csr/employee/development. Accessed February 28, 2012.

Japan Productivity Center (2011). *Keizai sangyou shou itaku jigyou, heisei 22 nendo sougou chousa kenkyu tou itaku jigyou, kigyou no jinzai manejimento no kokusaika ni kansuru chousa* (Commissioned by the Ministry of Economy, Trade and Industry. 2010 year total research on internationalization of companies' human resource management) (in Japanese). Retrieved from www.meti.go.jp/policy/economy/jinzai/sangakujinnzai_ps/pdf/shihyo-report2010.pdf. Accessed February 28, 2012.

Kitai, A. & Tanaka, M. (2009). A quantitative analysis of penetration degree of organizational business creed: Embodiment and internalization (in Japanese). *Keiei Kyouiku Kenkyu (Management Development)*, 12(2), 49–58.

Kokusaika shihyou kentou iin kai (Exploratory Committee of the Index of Internationalization) (2009), Kokusaika shihyou houkokusho, (Report on the index of internationalization) (In Japanese). Retrieved from www.meti.go.jp/policy/economy/jinzai/kokusaika-sihyo/kokusaika _houkokusho_honbun.pdf (in Japanese). Accessed February 28, 2012.

Macklon, C. (1991). *Nihonjin no bosu: zai-ei nihon kigyou ni hataraku igirisujin no me* (Japanese boss: English worker) (in Japanese). Tokyo: Soshisha.

Manabe, S. (2002). Kigyou kan shinrai no kouchiku: TOYOTA no kesu (Building interfirm trust: the Toyota case) (in Japanese). Research Institute for Economics and Business Administration, Kobe University, Discussion paper, Series No. J42.

Meyer, J. P. & Allen, N. J. (1991). A three-component conceptualization of organizational commitment: Some methodological considerations. *Human Resource Management Review*, 1, 61–98.

Ministry of Foreign Affairs of Japan (1997–2010). Annual report of statistics on Japanese nationals overseas (in Japanese). Retrieved from www.mofa.go.jp/mofaj/toko/tokei/hojin/index.html. Accessed February 28, 2012.

*Nihon keizai shinbun* (2011). Hitachi, wakate 2000 nin o kaigai e. 3 bun no 2 o shinkukoku haken. Rainendo made. (Hitachi send young 2000 people to overseas, two-thirds of them to developing countries until next year) (in Japanese). October 15, morning, p. 12.

*Nihon keizai shinbun* (2012). Gaikokujin shain no honne "koko ga hen, nihon no kaisya" a-un no bunka, mou genkai (Foreign employees' honest opinion "That is strange about Japanese company", I have had it up to here, A and UN breathing culture) (in Japanese).

Online article. January 18. Retrieved from www.nikkei.com/life/living/article/
g=96958A90889DE1EAE2E5E3E6E0E2E3E5E2E3E0E2E3E08588EAE2E2;p=9694
E3E1E2EBE0E2E3E3E6E0E6E4. Accessed February 28, 2012.

Nonaka, I. & Takeuchi, H. (1995). *The Knowledge-Creating Company: How Japanese Companies Create the Dynamics of Innovation*. New York: Oxford University Press.

Ohbuchi, K. & Takahashi, Y. (1994). Cultural styles of conflict management in Japanese and Americans: Passivity, covertness, and effectiveness of strategies. *Journal of Applied Social Psychology*, 24(15), 1345–1366.

Peiperl, M. & Jonsen, K. (2007). Global careers. In P. H. Gunz & M. A. Peiperl (Eds.), *Handbook of Career Studies* (pp. 350–372). Los Angeles, CA: Sage Publications.

Perlmutter, H. V. (1969). The tortuous evolution of the multinational corporation. *Columbia Journal of World Business*, 4, 9–18.

Recruit Shingaku Soken (2011). Recruit college management 169 (in Japanese). Jul.–Aug., p. 8. Retrieved from souken.shingakunet.com/college_m/2011_RCM169_04.pdf. Accessed February 28, 2012.

Rousseau, D. M. (1995). *Psychological Contracts in Organizations*. Thousand Oaks, CA: Sage Publications.

Schein, E. (1978). *Career Dynamics: Matching Individual and Organizational Needs*. Reading, MA: Addison-Wesley.

Shiraki, M. (1995). *Nihon kigyuo no kokusai jintekishigenkanri* (International human resource management of Japanese companies) (in Japanese) (6th ed.). The Japan Institute for Labour Policy and Training.

Stahl, G. K., Chua, C. H., Caligiuri, P., Cerdin, J., & Taniguchi, M. (2009). Predictors of turnover intentions in learning-driven and demand-driven international assignments: The role of repatriation concerns, satisfaction with company support, and perceived career advancement opportunities. *Human Resource Management*, 48(1), 89–109.

Super, D. E. (1980). A life-span life-space approach to career development. *Journal of Vocational Behavior*, 16: 282–298.

Taggart, J. H. & McDermot, M. C. (1993). *The Essence of International Business*. New York: Prentice Hall.

Taniguchi, M. (2011). Careers in Japan. In J. P. Briscoe, D. T. Hall, & W. Mayrhofer (Eds.), *Careers Around the World* (pp. 266–278). New York and London: Routledge.

Yamagishi, T. & Yamagishi, M. (1994). Trust and commitment in the United States and Japan. *Motivation and Emotion*, 18(2), 129–166.

# 15

# GLOBAL CAREERS

## An Indian Perspective

*Sushanta K. Mishra, Indian Institute of
Management Indore, India, and
Pawan S. Budhwar, Aston University, UK*

## Introduction

In this chapter, we examine the global careers of individual actors in the Indian context. Surprisingly, India is an underresearched context within the literature on careers, despite being an obvious location to study global careers. In this chapter, we focus our attention on global careers in the offshore industry for two reasons.

First, the industry represents a new form of organizational process that embodies a complex interaction of globalization, technology, and transgeographic dynamics. With technological advancements, organizations have the options of moving individuals physically to other locations or delivering their skills through other means. As far as individuals are concerned, there is a shift in the emphasis away from crossing geographical boundaries towards crossing intellectual and cultural ones in their daily interaction with foreign colleagues (Cappellen & Janssens, 2010). As interactions are becoming virtual in nature, people are compelled to think globally and employ cross-cultural skills in their daily interaction with foreign colleagues (Peiperl & Jonsen, 2007). A global career requires that individuals pursue career competencies that are applicable in multiple regions across the world, and develop an orientation that transcends national, regional, and social identities (Cappellen & Janssens, 2010). Hugely important, yet largely neglected, forms of global career are being enacted by individuals operating from one location but catering to the needs of global customers.

Second, the offshore industry is one of the most rapidly growing areas of work globally. It epitomizes some of the key contemporary issues concerning the shifting nature of work, labor relations, economic development, and regulations. These services include call centers, software development, financial services, stock-market research, medical transcriptions, and other such services. According to the

NASSCOM strategic review (2011), the offshore industry, especially IT services exports, excluding exports relating to business process outsourcing (BPO), hardware, engineering design, and product development from India were estimated to grow by 22.7% to record revenues of US$33.5 billion in the fiscal year 2011. Although the offshore industry has received limited attention in the field of careers, they have been explored in other fields, notably work experience, identity, stress outcomes for employees, and labor processes (Das, Dharwadkar, & Brandes, 2008; Noronha & D'Cruz, 2007; Tayler & Bain, 2005).

## The Situation of Global Careers in India

India is a democratic republic, comprising 28 states and seven union territories. It borders Bangladesh, Bhutan, and Burma in the east, China in the north and northeast, Pakistan in the west and northwest, and Sri Lanka in the south. It occupies a strategic location in South Asia for international trade. With a geographic area of 3.3 million km$^2$, India is the second largest country in Asia and the seventh largest in the world. A former British colony, India has emerged as the largest democracy in the world since its independence in 1947.

According to the provisional census report for 2011, the population of India is 1,210 million. India is the birthplace of three of the world's main religions: Hinduism, Buddhism, and Sikhism. Indian society comprises six main religious groups: Hindus, Muslims, Sikhs, Christians, Jains, and Buddhists. There are over 3,000 castes. According to *Ethnologue* (2009 edition: Lewis, 2009), there are a total of 438 living languages present in India. The linguistic diversity index (based on *Ethnologue* 2009 edition data) of India is very high, with a score of 0.93 (0 indicates no diversity, and 1 indicates total diversity). Two languages, namely Hindi and English, are recognized as the official languages. India has one of the largest English-speaking populations in the Asia–Pacific region. The literacy rate for those over 15 years of age is 51%, but literacy is unevenly distributed (Budhwar, 2001). These facts show the diverse nature of the Indian workforce.

In the year 1991, the Indian economy witnessed serious inflation, decelerated industrial production, fiscal indiscipline, very high borrowing (both internal and external), and a low level of foreign-exchange reserves. The World Bank and the IMF agreed to bail out India, on the condition that it changed to a "free-market economy" from a regulated regime. To meet the challenges, a number of reforms were undertaken by the government of India. Subsequent liberalization of the economy changed the thrust of corporate management from "protection" to "competition."

Liberalization of the economy, coupled with technological innovations in the last two decades, has led to the restructuring and reorganization of work. The emergence of information- and technology-driven organizations has expanded the service sector and redefined the notion of time, space, distance, production, consumption, and boundaries across the globe. Services once considered

"non-tradable" across international borders, as they involve person-to-person contact, are now taken for granted. Newer technologies have made the long-distance transfer of information realizable and inexpensive. Rapid change in the global economy, the rise of knowledge work, and rapid technological innovation (Arthur, DeFillippi, & Lindsay, 2008; Pang, Chua, & Chu, 2008) not only changed the way people work, but also altered traditional organizational structures, employer–employee relationships, and the work context, creating changes in how individuals pursue their careers (Pieperl & Jonsen, 2007). These changes have made possible the globalization of services, such that many services previously produced only locally are now being offshored. All these led to the growth of the service sector; for example, the service sector in the Indian GDP accounted for about 55.3% (estimated) in 2010 (Central Intelligence Agency, 2011), compared with 15% in 1950.

As organizations expand beyond geographic boundaries, they seek to blur or minimize the barriers that inhibit communication and productivity across vertical, horizontal, external, and geographical organizational boundaries (Ashkenas, Ulrich, Jick, & Kerr, 1995). When organizations become boundaryless, the careers of the individuals in these organizations gradually shift from the traditional, hierarchical, and linear models to boundaryless careers, which are characterized by fluid arrangements, uncertainty, and flexibility (Arthur & Rousseau, 1996). This chapter discusses the concept of the global career and its relevance in the context of India. There are different approaches to understanding what makes a career global. One way to describe a global career is the centrality of the international element in the career of a person over the long term (Suutari & Taka, 2004). According to this perspective, individuals with global careers have a career track involving multiple international relocations, encompassing various positions and assignments in several countries (Makela & Suutari, 2009). In contrast to the physical movement of people across different geo-locations, Dickmann and Baruch (2011) described how virtual global employees can work from their office (even their home) and be part of a multinational team, engaged in a global project and/or collaborating with a number of contacts in various locations. In this chapter, we hope to broaden the conceptualization of global careers and, in doing so, respond to the call for a wider perspective of global careers, beyond international assignments or inter-organizational moves (Inkson & Thorn, 2010). With the advent of technology, even though organizations become global by crossing multiple geographic boundaries, their employees still continue to work in the global context without crossing the geographic boundaries. Operating across borders, the organizations are required to develop global mindsets and treat the entire world as their home (Adler & Bartholomew, 1992). Briscoe, Hall, and DeMuth (2006: 31) referred to the boundaryless mindset as "the attitude that people hold toward initiating and pursuing work-related relationships across organizational boundaries" and operationalized it as psychological mobility. Thus, global careers do not mean individual careers spanning multiple, physically

**TABLE 15.1** Global IT and IT-enabled-services market

| IT spend by category | Year 2010 | 2011 | 2012 | 2013 | 2014 |
|---|---|---|---|---|---|
| IT services | 574 | 594 | 621 | 652 | 684 |
| BPO | 158 | 167 | 177 | 189 | 201 |
| IT services + BPO | 732 | 761 | 798 | 841 | 885 |
| Software | 282 | 297 | 316 | 337 | 362 |
| Hardware | 599 | 643 | 686 | 727 | 767 |
| Total spend | 1,614 | 1,702 | 1,800 | 1,904 | 2,014 |

*Source*: NASSCOM Strategic Review 2011

separated, geographic boundaries, but, rather, careers crossing multiple psycho-logical boundaries. These changes have raised questions about the practice of global work, and, more specifically, the management and development of global careers (Cappellen & Janssens, 2010). Although researchers have urged for future research to explore the influence of contextual factors on career enactment, there is little career research happening in non-Western countries (Sullivan & Baruch, 2009), such as India. However, India is one of the fastest-growing economies in the world. Globalization, technological advancement, and market pressures have forced organizations in this subcontinent to become global.

According to the NASSCOM strategic review, BPO exports from India were estimated to grow by 14% in the fiscal year 2011 to record revenues of US$14.1 billion. The global IT and IT-enabled servies market is provided in Table 15.1. According to a recent report by NASSCOM, emerging opportunities in both the global and domestic markets can help India reach US$130 billion in IT–BPO revenues and are expected to contribute about 7% to the annual GDP.

The industry is also expected to create about 14.3 million direct and indirect employment opportunities (NASSCOM, 2011).

## The Relevance of Contemporary Career Concepts in India

Liberalization coupled with globalization has changed not only the nature of work but also the concept of the work arena. Scholars have argued for the need to understand the career concepts in this changing work context. Among the numerous new career concepts, the boundaryless career (Arthur & Rousseau, 1996) is by far the most influential. Although research on boundaryless careers has mainly focused on careers that cross organizational boundaries (Sullivan & Baruch, 2009), the original conceptualization of Arthur and Rousseau (1996) was more general, including mobility across different kinds of boundary, such as occupational, cultural, and geographical ones. The literature in the context of

the boundaryless career has highlighted the importance of geographical boundaries (see Sullivan & Arthur, 2006). Makela and Suutari (2009) defined managers with global careers as individuals having three or more international assignments during the course of their careers, in two or more countries. Similarly, Cappellen and Janssens (2005) incorporated multiple international moves in terms of location as one of the key facets of a global career. In fact, it is assumed that crossing geographical boundaries is critical in the development of global careers. The importance of technology is highly underrepresented in this literature. The present chapter argues that crossing the psychological boundary is important, as crossing the geographical boundary can be compensated by technology. Hence, there is a need to understand global careers in the present context. In order to promote understanding of this new career logic, Dickmann and Baruch (2011) introduced the notion of "virtual global employees," meaning that, in today's rapidly changing environment, there is a shift from the traditional, physical movement of individuals across different geo-locations, to working from their office (even their home) and being part of a multinational team, engaged in a global project, and/or collaborating with a number of contacts in various locations. Thus, global careers do not essentially mean individual careers spanning multiple, physically separated, geographic boundaries. Baruch argued that, when organizations cross the geographic boundaries between nation-states, the development of a career system will have to take into account country-specific differences (Baruch, 2004: 216). Baruch further argued that a global mindset—openness and willingness to cross borders, such as geographic and cultural borders—as part of the career make an individual a global manager. Although describing both physical and psychological mobility of individuals in the context of boundaryless careers, Sullivan and Arthur (2006) described the existence of careers having low levels of physical mobility but high levels of psychological mobility. However, they discussed neither the role of technology in work settings nor individuals pursuing their careers in the offshore industry. Throughout this chapter, we have argued that global careers do not mean individual careers spanning multiple, physically separated, geographic boundaries, but rather those crossing multiple psychological boundaries.

## Structural, Cultural and Contextual Difficulties in Pursuing Global Careers in India

There are difficulties that hinder the development of global careers in the Indian context. Based on interviews with seven senior executives (vice presidents and general managers), seven middle-level managers (managers), and six frontline employees (in August 2011), in five different organizations, we discuss below some of the difficulties affecting global careers in the offshore industry. The interviews were conducted by the authors for the purpose of writing this chapter.

## Parental Role

In India, parents play a critical role in the careers of their children. As the offshore industry is relatively new in India, compared with other traditional industries such as automobile, manufacturing, and pharmaceutical, there are limited success stories in this industry. Also, as it is a new industry, parents/guardians have limited understanding about it and, as a result, they do not encourage their children to pursue their careers in this industry. Most employees take it as a stop-gap arrangement, and, hence, the attrition rate is high. However, as this industry matures, more people may start considering it as a career option.

## Age Profile of Employees

As it is a new industry, the average age of its employees is low. Being very young in age, the employees have aspiration levels that are very high, and the maturity level is low. Because of high aspirations, they want to grow fast and, hence, hop from company to company. Also, because of their low maturity level, they are very sensitive to organizational practices. Even a slight sense of discomfort triggers them to quit the job. According to one vice president (HR), the average age of his colleagues in India is about 28–29 years, compared with 45–46 years in Europe. In fact, according to NASSCOM (2006), over 50% of the population in this industry is under 25 years of age. So, there is a huge gap in maturity. Technically, these employees are brilliant, but application of mind (maturity) during customer interactions is low, and that makes a difference when it comes to dealing with uncertainty.

## Women Employees

Traditionally, Indian society is conservative in nature, and, given the odd working hours, it is difficult to attract women members to join this profession. However, as the industry has grown, over the years, there has been an increase in women's participation.

## Language

According to the general manager (HR) of a company, one of the key elements that the organizations focus on is the ease with which the communication between the employee and the client takes place. In this regard, the focus of many organizations is how to reduce the language barrier. So, training on telephone etiquette, drafting of emails, and communication skills is provided. As people from different regions of India have different linguistic backgrounds, they have differences in their accents. Care is taken to normalize the accent and reduce the gap in communication. On the other hand, clients are not uniform in their language skills. For example, accents differ among French, English, or American

clients. Based on the geographic region served by the employees, region-specific training is provided to them. Furthermore, the general manager reported that Indians usually speak faster than their counterparts in other countries. In the initial training programs, they are trained to speak at a slower pace.

## Cultural Awareness

Cultural awareness is essential to understanding why and how other people behave in the way they do, and it will enable effective communication with them. According to one HR manager of an IT offshore organization, as understanding the clients' viewpoint is very important for the success of the business, knowledge about beliefs, norms, and behaviors as practiced in the target country is important. Knowledge of customers' norms and beliefs should reduce or eliminate misunderstanding. For example, while interacting with US clients, the service provider should know about cultural issues such as *Thanksgiving* and so on.

## Religion

The predominant religion of India is Hinduism. Consequently, the majority of people working in offshore industries are from the Hindu religion, and their names are Hindu names. Most of the clients are from other religions, predominantly Christianity and Islam. Generally, the frontline employees use pseudo names, so that it is easier for clients to relate to the service provider. However, some organizations reported that their employees no longer use pseudo names, as clients are becoming familiar with Hindu names. In this industry, every activity, such as taking days off and holidays, revolves around clients. For example, a majority of the respondents reported that it is difficult to get leave during Hindu festivals, compared with getting leave during the festivals at the clients' end, such as *Christmas* or *Eid*.

## Respect for Seniors

India has strong values and cultural norms. Respect for seniors is one of them. To acclimatize the employees to the offshore culture, the organizations' practices are tuned to Western culture, such as calling seniors by their name. Some of the respondents reported that initially they experience dissonance while calling their seniors by name, but over time they get used to this culture.

## Infrastructure

The offshore industry works 24 hours a day, 7 days a week, and, hence, the business requires more IT infrastructure support. Most of the organizations have captive IT units. Being in India, not all the cities have well-developed infrastructures,

and, as a consequence, there are clusters of companies in particular regions. As a result, there is migration of employees from other cities to the developed cities. All these lead to the following issues. First, the cities are becoming overpopulated, leading to related problems with aspects such as accommodation, traffic, etc. For example, in the city of Bengaluru, traffic is a big concern. Second, with companies being in the same city, employees have many options to switch companies, leading to attrition. Among other factors, people prefer organizations where the commuting time is the minimum.

## Safety and Security

As the industry operates around the clock, a safe and secure environment in the work arena, as well as during travel from home to workplace, is equally important. Most of the organizations take special safety measures to ensure that their employees, especially women employees, reach their home safely.

## Time Zones

In an offshore business, the frontline employees need to cater to the needs of their clients. Depending on the geographic region of the client, the frontline employees have to manage their work time. For example, if clients are in Australia, office hours start from early morning every day; in the case of clients in the Middle East, office hours start at about 12:00 noon, and, in the case of US clients, office hours are at night. These timings are not for a short duration. Every day, the frontline employees need to work in that time period. This frequently disturbs individuals' biological cycle. In some cases, different time zones lead to social isolation of the employees. After the night's work, the employees go to their houses, take rest, and get prepared for the next day's work. Thus, communications with parents, relatives, and friends suffer heavily. Whatever interaction they have is with colleagues in the same occupation. Over a time, they get distanced from their social surroundings.

Lohit's story suggests that building a successful global career necessitates understanding nuances of different contexts, knowledge about the business, and the ability to communicate clearly with clients. Experience provides maturity and confidence, which help in dealing with the clients in a better manner. The onus of career growth is on the individuals, as better knowledge and skills will enhance their market value.

Although U.S. companies were quick to use offshore, IT and business-process applications, the offshore phenomenon is not restricted to the US only. One necessity of global business is the need to interact with people who are culturally different (Thomas & Inkson, 2004). Cultural awareness is essential to understand why and how other people behave in the way they do, and it enables effective communication with them. The removal of restrictions on the media industry

## Story of a Virtual Global Career in India

Lohit completed his 4-year engineering degree in computer sciences and decided not to pursue a career in engineering. Instead of joining the software industry, he joined a company in the knowledge-process-outsourcing (KPO) industry as a lead researcher. The company has offices in major cities across six continents, including: Berlin, Dubai, London, New York, Sao Paulo, Singapore, Stockholm, Sydney, and Toronto. The company leverages on the global research base of best practices to produce a portfolio of conferences. Each year, it offers approximately 2,000 worldwide conferences, seminars, and related learning programs. The Indian center caters to the U.S., Dubai, Singapore, Australia, and UK markets. The company has different domains, namely, marketing, sales, and operations. In sales, the job is to carry out research to find out who are the potential clients for a particular concept (product). The conferences, summits, or forums that are organized are business-to-business events, with specific focus on potential clients.

The sales team in which Lohit works focuses on the Middle East. At certain times, such as Ramadan, Eid, etc., the focus shifts to other places, such as South Africa. Although the geographic region is the Middle East, there are subtle differences between the functioning in Dubai and Saudi Arabia. The language of communication is English. Lohit uses a pseudo name (as his name is a Hindu name), as it helps the client relate to the service provider more easily, and that makes the transaction a bit easier. Understanding the way the Middle East market works, its prayer timings, and preferences helps in transactions with clients. According to Lohit, office hours and holidays depend on the particular geographical region that one serves. According to him, at times the service providers have to compromise on festivals, as there are differences in religion, ceremonies, and festivals across nations.

The office duration is 9 hours a day, with a break of about 1 hour 30 minutes. On an average day, he is on a telephone call for about 7 hours. However, according to Lohit, this industry offers growth opportunities. Every day is a learning experience here, because every event has something to offer, at least in terms of exposure. Mistakes do occur, but the company accommodates them. According to Lohit, communication skills are most important. Even though they contact clients in the Middle East, the people with whom they interact are generally managing directors, project directors, or heads of department of some units. Usually, they have a good grasp of the English language. As a lead researcher, most of the communication happens over the telephone, and, thus, understanding the whole concept in this business is important. As long as one communicates the message in a crystal-clear manner, accent does not matter. Knowing the context helps in this business, and it comes through practice. Although Lohit has not visited Dubai, he is familiar with the geography, culture, and working hours in Dubai. According to him, all that comes through experience, which broadens understanding of clients.

Career growth for Lohit is getting the opportunity to learn more about the business, and he aims to be part of the operations unit, where the primary job is to develop concepts for products.

helped people to have access to multiple channels, which helps them to learn the nuances of foreign cultures and speak in a manner that helps in presenting themselves as natives of the same country as that of the client.

Offshore work has also impacted the local context in a significant way. Most importantly, it has generated employment opportunities for local people. Furthermore, the industry has provided the opportunity to interact with people in other locations. These transactions between individuals across different cultural and geographical locations influence, or might influence in the long term, the mindset of people and consequently their tolerance and acceptance of other cultures in their own societies. This adaptation of clients' cultural norms in their daily lives might facilitate the transformation of local societies into multicultural societies. There are visible changes in the dress, drinking, and eating habits in places populated with offshore companies. For an example, one of the respondents reported that the number of McDonalds in the city had gone up to about 27 after its entry in the 1990s. Also, a number of pubs have appeared in the city of Bengaluru. As discussed above, the offshore industry and, specifically, the employees in this industry portray the metamorphosis of their cultural and social lives because of various conditions in which they work, including night shifts, altered social lives, and adaptation to different cultural contexts.

## Critical Remarks

Lohit's story suggests that individuals' focuses are shifting from the organization to the self in terms of gaining skills and knowledge. In a sense, employees take charge of their careers (Hall, 1996) and seek employment that enables them to progress and gives them enough opportunity to acquire knowledge and skills. Thus, success is interpreted as the experience of psychologically meaningful work (Sullivan, 1999), and career growth is derived from self-development rather than from hierarchical advancement within one company (Parker & Inkson, 1999). Thus, research on protean careers and boundaryless careers seems particularly relevant in the context of global careers.

## Conclusions

In this chapter, we have tried to understand the concept of global careers through the experiences of individuals in the Indian offshore industry. We have explored the structural, cultural, and contextual difficulties in pursuing global careers in India. Through the discussions, we have highlighted the fact that a global career can be looked at as a career, not only spanning multiple geographical locations, but also, more importantly, spanning multiple psychological boundaries. The chapter further discussed the complexities involving individuals, organizations, and societies in the context of global careers.

# References

Adler, N. J. & Bartholomew, S. (1992). Managing globally competent people. *Academy of Management Executive, 6,* 52–65.

Arthur, M. B. & Rousseau, D. M. (1996). A career lexicon for the 21st century. *Academy of Management Executive,* 10(4), 28–40.

Arthur, M. B., DeFillippi, R. J., & Lindsay, V. J. (2008). On being a knowledge worker. *Organizational Dynamics,* 37(4), 365–377.

Ashkenas, R., Ulrich, D., Jick, T., & Kerr, S. (1995). *The Boundaryless Organization: Breaking the Chains of Organizational Structure.* San Francisco, CA: Jossey-Bass.

Baruch, Y. (2004). *Managing Careers: Theory and Practice.* New Delhi: Prentice Hall.

Briscoe, J. P., Hall, D. T., & DeMuth, R. L. F. (2006). Protean and boundaryless careers: An empirical exploration. *Journal of Vocational Behavior,* 69, 30–47.

Budhwar, P. S. (2001). Human resource management in India. In P. S. Budhwar & Y. A. Debrah (Eds.), *Human Resource Management in Developing Countries* (pp. 75–90), London: Routledge.

Cappellen, T. & Janssens, M. (2005). Career paths of global managers: Towards future research. *Journal of World Business,* 40(4), 348–360.

Cappellen, T. & Janssens, M. (2010). Enacting global careers: Organizational career scripts and the global economy as co-existing career referents. *Journal of Organizational Behavior,* 31, 687–706.

Central Intelligence Agency (2011). Retrieved from https://www.cia.gov/library/publications/the-world-factbook/geos/in.html#Econ, March 5, 2011.

Das, D., Dharwadkar, R., & Brandes, P. (2008). The importance of being "Indian": Identity centrality and work outcomes in an off-shored call center in India. *Human Relations,* 61(11), 1499–1530.

Dickmann, M. & Baruch, Y. (2011). *Global Careers.* London: Routledge.

Hall, D. T. (1996). Protean careers of the 21st century. *Academy of Management Executive,* 10, 8–18.

Inkson, K. & Thorn, K. (2010). Mobility and careers. In S. C. Carr (Ed.), *The Psychology of Mobility in a Global Era* (pp. 259–278), New York: Springer.

Lewis, M. P. (2009). *Ethnologue: Languages of the World.* Dallas, TX: SIL International.

Makela, K. & Suutari, V. (2009). Global careers: A social capital paradox. *The International Journal of Human Resource Management,* 20(5), 992–1008.

NASSCOM (2006). *Strategic Review 2006: The IT industry in India.* New Delhi: The National Association of Software and Services Companies (NASSCOM).

NASSCOM (2011). *Strategic Review 2011: The IT-BPO sector in India.* New Delhi: The National Association of Software and Services Companies (NASSCOM).

Noronha, E. & D'Cruz, P. (2007). Reconciling dichotomous demands: Telemarketing agents in Bangalore and Mumbai, India. *The Qualitative Report,* 12(2), 255–280.

Pang, M., Chua, B. L. & Chu, C. W. L. (2008). Learning to stay ahead in an uncertain environment. *The International Journal of Human Resource Management,* 19(7), 1383–1394.

Parker, P. & Inkson, K. (1999). New forms of career: The challenge to human resource management. *Asia Pacific Journal of Human Resources,* 37(1), 76–85.

Peiperl, M. & Jonsen, K. (2007). Global careers. In H. Gunz and M. Peiperl (Eds.), *Handbook of Career Studies* (pp. 350–372). Los Angeles, CA: Sage.

Sullivan, S. E. (1999). The changing nature of careers: A review and research agenda. *Journal of Management,* 25, 457–484.

Sullivan, S. E. & Arthur, M. B. (2006). The evolution of the boundaryless career concept: Examining physical and psychological mobility. *Journal of Vocational Behavior*, 69, 19–29.

Sullivan, S. E. & Baruch, Y. (2009). Advances in career theory and research: A critical review and agenda for future exploration. *Journal of Management*, 35(6), 1542–1571.

Suutari, V. & Taka, M. (2004). Career anchors and career commitment of managers with global careers. *Journal of Managerial Psychology*, 22(7), 628–648.

Taylor, P. & Bain, P. (2005). India calling to far away towns: The call centre labour process and globalisation. *Work, Employment and Society*, 19(2), 261–282.

Thomas, D. C. & Inkson, K. (2004). *Cultural Intelligence: People Skills for Global Business*. California: Berrett-Koehler.

# 16

# GLOBAL CAREERS IN THE UNITED STATES

*S. Gayle Baugh, University of West Florida, USA, Sherry E. Sullivan, Bowling Green State University, USA, and Shawn M. Carraher, Indiana Wesleyan University, USA*

## Introduction

In this chapter, we examine some aspects of global careers in the United States. We use contemporary career theory as a lens to examine the situation of immigrants and expatriates, as well as individuals moving outside of the United States. In line with contemporary career theories, we consider how information technology can be leveraged in order to develop a global career without physical migration. In addition, information technology can be coupled with rapid transportation in order to manage a global career without either short-term or long-term relocation. Finally, we turn a critical eye toward what remains problematic in the study of global careers from the US perspective and identify some areas of research that can be explored.

## Contemporary Career Models and Global Careers in the United States

The boundaryless-career concept suggests that the boundaries between industries, occupations, organizations, functions, levels, and even countries have become more permeable (Arthur & Rousseau, 1996; Sullivan & Arthur, 2006). Some, however, have argued that scholars have failed to consider factors that may constrain the degree to which individuals enact or experience boundaryless careers (e.g., Gunz, Peiperl, & Tzabbar, 2007; Sullivan, 1999; Sullivan & Baruch, 2009). Although boundaries in general have become more permeable, the ease of passage between boundaries is not the same for each individual (Sullivan & Arthur, 2006).

The idea that factors may impede the passage across country boundaries is well illustrated by Richardson's (2009) study of how academics' ability to pursue careers

across country borders was influenced by scientific, national, and organizational context. Specifically, those in the scientific disciplines of medicine and engineering were thought to have easier transitions across country borders than those in the arts and humanities. In terms of national context, government actions that restricted the flow of international scholars, such as policies that citizens be given priority for jobs over foreign nationals, were delineated. In terms of organizational context, internationally mobile scholars' ability to obtain secure academic employment has been constrained by a tendency on the part of decision-makers to disregard research productivity, funding, and teaching awards from other countries.

The purpose of this chapter is to examine factors that may enable and impede the global career experiences of the 308.7 million of individuals living in the United States (US Census Bureau, 2010). Dickmann and Baruch (2011, p. 7) broadly define global careers in terms of careers that "progress or evolve outside of a single country."

Individuals with global careers include those who move across physical borders, such as those who immigrate, become expatriates, engage in one or more international assignments, globetrot (i.e., move from project to project throughout the world), and cross country borders on daily, weekly, or monthly commutes. These individuals pursue global careers through physical mobility. However, personnel in the military and diplomatic services who are stationed outside their home country or collaborate across country borders also have global careers. Global careerists can include those workers who may never leave their home country but work as virtual global employees, such as those who are part of multinational teams and work projects (Banai & Harry, 2004; Dickmann & Baruch, 2011).

A number of factors may enable or impede individuals in the US with respect to engaging in different forms of global career (e.g., Al Ariss & Syed, 2011). As depicted in Figure 16.1, there are a variety of factors that can push and pull the immigration of foreign nationals (Al Ariss, 2010; Baruch, 1995). For example, from 1820 to 1850, many Irish immigrated to the US because of push factors, such as the 1845 potato famine, political and religious unrest, and even the lack of potential spouses for women. Many Irish immigrants were attracted to the US because of pull factors, including the increased demand for workers to engage in physical labor, such as digging canals or working on the railroads. The encouragement of family and friends already living in the US and the growth of Irish communities to assist in the transition to a new culture further helped to fuel the increase of immigrants from Ireland. By 1840, the Irish comprised almost 50% of all immigrants and had well-established networks to help others to find lodgings and work. These networks also provided newcomers with a sense of community, based upon shared history, values, and religion (Rosenblum & Brick, 2011).

Likewise, military conflicts (e.g., World War II, Korea, Iraq) and international relations (e.g., diplomats, secret service, CIA) enabled the global careers of many

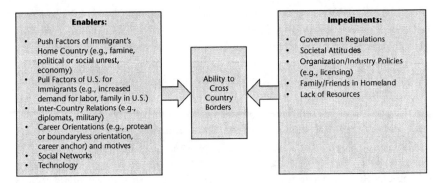

**FIGURE 16.1** Some enablers and impediments to global careers

US citizens. For instance, research has found that the children of military personnel (Cooke, Spears, & Skegg, 1985; Payne, Warner, & Little, 1992), as well as those who moved with internationally mobile parents (Selmer & Lam, 2004), are more likely to have global careers. Politics and societal attitudes can also influence migration (Carr, Inkson, & Thorn, 2005). As a case in point, there was a rise in US citizens moving to Canada during the Vietnam War. More recently, those looking for more liberal attitudes towards same-sex marriages have migrated out of the US.

An enabling factor of increasing importance to today's global careers is the effect of technology. Advances in aviation technology have permitted easier and faster physical passage across country borders. Individuals can more readily visit plant locations in other countries, fly in for meetings, and even commute between countries. Moreover, technological advances have permitted individuals to stay in their own home while working in virtual teams and collaborating with colleagues throughout the world (Carraher, 1998; Dickmann & Baruch, 2011).

In addition to external forces, internal forces influence global careers. Internal factors such as career orientations (Briscoe & Hall, 2006; Suutari & Taka, 2004), career motives (Sullivan & Mainiero, 2008), personality (Boneva & Frieze, 2001), and the desire to engage in self-initiated expatriation (Tharenou, 2009; Tharenou & Caulfield, 2010) or self-directed travel and career-development experiences (Inkson & Myers, 2003) can enable global careers. For example, there are numerous case studies of individuals who were driven by the need for challenging work and chose an employment situation that permitted them to travel throughout the globe or to collaborate with colleagues in other countries (Mainiero & Sullivan, 2006).

Figure 16.1 also depicts forces that may impede the passage between country boundaries. Government regulations and societal attitudes are major obstacles to immigrants and foreign workers. For example, the Chinese Exclusion Act of

1882 began an 80-year restriction on Chinese immigration to the US. Similarly, societal attitudes of the 1880s created barriers for Chinese immigrants, with many employers discriminating against Chinese workers in terms of pay and promotions. Others banned the so-called "rice eaters" from their places of business and excluded them from social activities, blaming the Chinese for rising unemployment rates in the US urban areas.

Organizational (Cappellen & Jansssens, 2010) and professional practices can also discourage the immigration of foreign workers (Al Ariss, 2010; Carr et al., 2005; Zikic, Bonache, & Cerdin, 2010). For example, similar to the situation in a number of other Western countries, many well-educated medical professionals cannot legally practice in the US because of the need for country-specific licenses or accreditations. Other considerations, such as the separation from family and friends (Cappellen & Janssens, 2010) or lack of resources (Al Ariss & Syed, 2011), can also cause potential immigrants to rethink leaving their homelands.

In this chapter, we focus on immigration into the US and the attendant issues of employment and career development. We then examine the phenomenon of migration out of the US. The influence of public policy on physical and psychological mobility will be emphasized.

## Structural, Cultural, and Contextual Opportunities and Difficulties

As an economically developed country, the United States offers many opportunities for global careerists. However, internationally mobile individuals also face obstacles in pursuing career opportunities within the US, and US citizens may encounter impediments in attempting to follow career prospects outside of the boundaries of their own country. We will consider some of these factors next.

### Immigration Policy in the US

As has been noted previously, migration is the result of both *push* and *pull* factors (Al Ariss, 2010; Baruch, 1995; Rumbaut, 1994). "Push" factors involve those reasons in the home country, including poor economic conditions, lack of opportunity, physical deprivation, or objectionable political conditions that cause individuals to look for other opportunities. "Pull" factors may include economic opportunity, potential career mobility, and equal opportunity. The US, as an economically developed country, has a net population increase when both immigration and out-migration are considered. That is, as noted by many researchers, population tends to flow toward those countries that offer greater economic opportunity and away from those that offer less (Rumbaut, 1994).

Many individuals begin their career journey in the US as expatriates, either working for a company based in, or with facilities in, the country or as students seeking advanced education (see the Engineer's Story). After their sojourn in the

US, some individuals choose to extend their stay, whereas others return to their home country or move on to another international assignment (Baruch, Budhwar, & Khatri, 2007; Tharenou & Caulfield, 2010). Among those who choose to stay, some are able to become legal residents, whereas others simply overstay their student or temporary work visa, becoming part of a "shadow" or underground economy. Career experiences differ greatly for these two variations in entry.

The same two entry options exist for individuals who choose to enter the US directly, without first entering as students or expatriates. Although the US benefits from a large number of legal immigrants (about 1 million annually; Monger & Yankay, 2011), desire for entry quickly outstrips the legal options for admission (Donato, Aguilera, & Wakabayashi, 2005). This situation is not surprising, given the focus of US immigration policy on reunification of families (Monger & Yankay, 2011). However, legal and illegal immigrants to the US do not compete for the same jobs. Whereas legal immigrants have options for utilizing their career

---

## The Engineer's Story

As a young child in Bangladesh, Rehan used to watch US television shows, such as *Star Trek* and *Hawaii Five-0*. Like many other children around the globe, US values and culture captured the imagination of this small child and presented a picture of a land of freedom and opportunities. From those early influences, Rehan began to have dreams of coming to the US some day. After completing his bachelor's degree in engineering in Bangladesh, Rehan applied to, and was accepted by, two US universities that offered full graduate assistantships in the Master's program in chemical engineering. He chose the University of Tennessee for his advanced degree and, in about a year, he received several job offers to work for chemical companies. Rehan thought it would be a great idea to start work and then return to the university for a doctoral degree. The employment position would allow him to utilize his engineering skills and to apply for permanent residency status in the US. But, as is so often the case, Rehan loved the challenge of daily troubleshooting and practical chemical engineering problems. He has not yet made the decision to pursue a Ph.D., as he had planned, because he is so engrossed in his work and intrigued by the challenges it offers. Rehan cannot remember any major obstacles to pursuing his engineering career or developing a good life outside of work. However, he does recall that there were some cultural and language barriers. Although good communication skills are important for all upwardly mobile employees, he believes that it is even more so for people from non-English-speaking countries. Rehan now realizes that language and cultural barriers may impede progress to top management roles for talented foreign-born professionals. Rehan still loves his job, but is also facing the hard truth of relatively slow career growth. He still has aspirations to reach the top levels of his company, however. It was always his intent to remain in the US after his education, and so, despite the restricted career progress, a return to Bangladesh is not under consideration.

capital, those who follow the alternative route have a less positive career experience (Bell, Kwesiga, & Berry, 2010).

The US has not always been characterized by controlled borders. Although the Chinese Exclusion Act of 1882 served to bar immigration from that country, there were no limits on immigration from Europe (Benton-Cohen, 2010). In fact, in the early 1900s, the US was experiencing a surge of immigration that has only been equaled in recent times. However, large proportions of these new immigrants were from Southern and Eastern Europe and thus were darker-skinned, less educated, and poorer than previous immigrants. In addition, these individuals were viewed as taking jobs from US-born workers, despite limited evidence that such displacements were actually occurring. Under growing public pressure, Congress passed the Immigration Act of 1907, which limited immigration but did not yet introduce immigration quotas (Benton-Cohen, 2010).

Immigration quotas were instituted in the post-World War I period of greater isolationism. These quotas were based on the ethnic distribution within the US as of the 1890 census, before the large-scale influx of immigrants from Southern and Eastern Europe (Benton-Cohen, 2010). Although legislation set a very small limit on immigration from Europe, it further created an "Asiatic barred zone," which essentially closed the door on immigration from Asia and precluded citizenship for Asians already living in the US. No limits were set on immigration over land, and thus individuals from Canada and Mexico were given free access. The US faces a very different immigration situation today (Hoefer, Rytina, & Baker, 2010), and clearly the seeds of this situation were sown in restrictions on immigration developed in the early part of the last century.

The advent of World War II produced an entirely different immigration situation—that of "war brides" (or, more appropriately, "war spouses," as there were women as well as men who married overseas and wished to bring a spouse home with them). This issue had a dramatic influence on US immigration policy, which was designed to foster family reunification, with less concern directed toward employment opportunities (Wolgin & Bloemraad, 2010). The desire to bring returning soldiers' family together finally overcame the inherent racism in immigration policy in the US. Opportunities were opened for foreign-born spouses and other family members of US citizens, over and above the immigration quotas (still based on the 1890 census figures). From the post-World War II period to the present time, most immigration into the US has been based on family status (Monger & Yankay, 2011).

## Employment and Career Opportunities Among Immigrants

Although little consideration is given to employment opportunities for those entering the US, that omission may not be as serious a concern as it might at first appear. Given that a large portion of new entrants to the US are related to current citizens, they have entered the country with an immediate, although small,

social network with which to launch a job search. In addition, equal-employment-opportunity legislation was designed to ensure that ethnicity would not affect one's ability to obtain employment. Research on how new immigrants utilize their family network will advance our knowledge of careers of immigrants. Examination of the influence of ethnic communities on employment options would also be revealing (Haller, Portes, & Lynch, 2011).

Despite this optimistic assessment, the real state of affairs is not quite so rosy. Whereas immigrants who enter the US with high levels of human capital might find the situation to be reasonably welcoming, those with low levels do not fare so well. Immigrants require access to education and the absence of workplace discrimination in order to experience upward social and economic mobility (Ellis & Almgren, 2009). Without these conditions, the children of immigrants, or the second generation, are in grave danger of assimilating downward mobility—not at all the dream that most new entrants have when they come to the US (Asher, 2011; Haller et al., 2011). Even for individuals with high levels of skills and education, lack of recognition of credentials, lack of knowledge regarding local requirements, and absence of a professional network may hinder career development in a new national setting, as has been the case in other countries (Richardson, 2009; Tharmaseelan, Inkson, & Carr, 2009; Zikic et al., 2010).

Although US immigration policy is directed toward family reunification, there are nonetheless a number of immigrants to the US who come for economic, rather than familial, reasons. Economic immigrants enter the US with H1-B visas, which require employer sponsorship and an employment commitment. This form of visa offers eventual citizenship, after a period of years. However, given that the immigrant enters the US with employer sponsorship, the individual is not completely free to leave his or her current employer. To leave the job, even if career progress is blocked in the current situation, means that the individual will either have to return to the home country and/or begin the process again with a new employer (Somerville & Walsworth, 2009). Further, the terms and conditions of employment are subject to arbitrary change, with little or no recourse on the part of the employee (Avery, Tonidandel, Volpone, & Raghuram, 2010; Somerville & Walsworth, 2009). Thus, although the H1-B visa offers the opportunity for entry and eventual citizenship, with all of its accompanying rights, it may also stymie true career development, through binding the individual to a particular employer, often for periods as long as 10 years. To date, little empirical attention has been directed to this mechanism of potential permanent entry to the US.

In addition to the over 1 million people who enter the US annually with legal immigration status, there are also a large number of individuals who enter without such status (Hoefer et al., 2010). These individuals, who generally enter the US for economic opportunity, have a much more difficult time finding and maintaining employment. The Immigration Reform and Control Act (IRCA) of 1986, which holds employers responsible for ascertaining legal status to work, is aimed at discouraging illegal entry by reducing employment opportunities for

undocumented immigrants. Evidence suggests that such individuals have, instead, been relegated to an informal (or "shadow") economy, where payments are made in cash owing to undocumented status (Donato et al., 2005). The overall result has been lower wages and mistreatment, including uncompensated overtime work, sexual harassment, and unsafe working conditions, rather than the intended failure to hire (Bell et al., 2010; Donato et al., 2005). Indeed, illegal immigration has, over the years, been tacitly approved (although publicly condemned), because it ensures a steady stream of low-wage workers (Rosenblum, 2011).

It is not only undocumented immigrants whose status has become less secure. In the post-9/11 US, immigration policy has been merged with maintaining national security, and both legal and undocumented immigrants have come to be regarded with fear and suspicion (Coleman & Kocher, 2011; Rosenblum, 2011). In recent years, undocumented status has been criminalized to an extent previously unknown (Ismaili, 2010). As a result, fear of detention and deportation has become a part of everyday life for many immigrants, both legal and undocumented (Ismaili, 2010; Mittelstadt, Speaker, Meissner, & Chishti, 2011). Whereas, in the past, immigration enforcement was regarded as a matter of border control, the focus is currently on the management of immigrant populations that have already settled in the US (Coleman & Kocher, 2011).

The insecurity engendered by current immigration policy is exacerbated by the delegation of enforcement authority to state and local officials (Mittelstadt et al., 2011). Given the devolution of authority to local levels, enforcement of immigration policy varies greatly by geography. Some local officials utilize the delegation of powers to escalate routine contact between law enforcement and immigrants to the broader purpose of investigation of immigrant status. Most deportations now begin with routine traffic stops (Coleman & Kocher, 2011). Deportation can occur before criminal adjudication, and detention can continue beyond or in the absence of criminal charges, raising the very real possibility that immigration enforcement may masquerade as public safety (Mittlestadt et al., 2011). Even legal immigrants are subject to detention and have, in some instances, been deported in error, thus raising the level of insecurity for all immigrants in the US (Coleman & Kocher, 2011). The effect of immigration-enforcement policies on employment opportunities and career development for both legal and undocumented immigrants has not yet received much empirical attention.

The pull factors bring some immigrants, both legal and illegal, back to their country of origin. Some immigrants, especially from Mexico and Central America, cycle through periods of expatriation and repatriation, each time making the decision about which location is most desirable (e.g., Tharenou & Caulfield, 2010). Some individuals who expatriate to the US as a result of an employment assignment will return to their country of origin after completion of the assignment. However, a large number of individuals who enter the US enter with the intent to stay and develop their career there (as indicated by Jamil's story). Thus, the focus of the discussion of global careers in the US must include a discussion of immigration into the country.

---

### Persistence Pays Off

Jamil was born in a small village in India and began investing in his future at a very young age. He saved every little reward or gift to put toward his education, rather than spending it on candy or toys. Jamil decided to come to the US at age 19. After extensive research, he decided to enroll at the University in Alabama. Obtaining a student visa was easier in those days (before the events of 9/11), and so, with a scholarship from the university in hand, he embarked upon his career journey. He strengthened his skills in English while pursuing an MBA degree. He also worked as a server at a restaurant chain and focused again on saving for further education. After completing his MBA degree, he worked in the retail industry, but his passion for self-development led him to enroll in a doctoral program in education. Upon receiving his EdD degree, Jamil went to work as a full-time faculty member at a well-known university in Alabama. After 6 years of full-time employment, Jamil feels that his efforts have finally paid off! He views the culture in the US as open and tolerant and feels that he has a wonderful life, with his job, his wife, and his children.

---

In the next section, we will turn our attention to individuals who choose to expatriate out of the US, on either a temporary or a permanent basis. We will explore the migration of US citizens, mobility among members of the military and university students, and the impact of technology on global careers.

## The Migration of US Citizens

Although the US population has frequently been influenced by migration into the country, migration out of the country is also a growing phenomenon. In this section, the movement of US citizens out of the country and into other settings will be examined. Movement outward can be a relatively permanent migration or a more temporary, expatriate assignment. This movement may be facilitated by military service or spending time as an exchange student; further, technology may serve to relieve some of the necessity for migration or expatriation.

## Migration and Expatriation Out of the US

Research has found that there are many factors that enable and impede migration and expatriation, including income differentials between countries, employment levels, immigration laws, relative standards of living (Evans, Goulas, & Levine, 2007), quality of life, family relations (Geist & McManus, 2008), political changes, and societal issues (Carr et al., 2005). Hatton (2010) suggests that the strongest driver for US migration is the pull factor of economic opportunity and increased income potential. In the vignette featuring Fred Michaels, for example,

---

## Migration and Money

In 1985, Dr. Fred Michaels (pseudonym) completed his Ph.D. in business administration with an emphasis on marketing from a prestigious US university. He received multiple offers from universities in the US, Australia, and New Zealand. He accepted a 1-year appointment at a leading university in New Zealand but ended up staying for 12 years. He eventually became an associate professor and department chairperson. He accepted the offer because the salary was well above what he would have been able to earn in the US, and it gave him the opportunity to work at a major research university. Fred and his wife reared four children in New Zealand. Two of the children remained in New Zealand after their parents returned to the US. Fred decided to leave New Zealand when the country's dollar decreased in value to such a level that he was able to earn substantially more in the US.

---

Dr. Michaels migrated to New Zealand for a higher salary and reverse migrated back to the US for economic reasons.

During the 1960s, many US citizens migrated to Mexico City because of the economic opportunities available. Mexico also had the largest concentration of US citizens working abroad at that time, making its expatriate community and social networks highly attractive (Davis, 1980). During the same time period, there was an increase in the number of young men migrating from the US to Canada, owing to the push factor of a draft and the desire to avoid military service in the Vietnam War. Over time, the US has witnessed changes in migration rates in response to other political factors (e.g., the reelection of George W. Bush) and social issues (e.g., same-sex marriages). Interestingly, however, although the attacks of September 11, 2001 have decreased immigration to the US, they did not have much influence on the outward migration of US citizens (Martin & Midgley, 2010).

Today, the top location for both expatriation and migration from the US continues to be Mexico, followed by Canada and countries in the European Union (EU) (Aydemir & Borjas, 2007; Hatton, 2010; Rosenblum & Brick, 2011). Although many believe that lack of foreign-language skills impedes the ability of US citizens to live abroad, this problem may be overstated, in that English is the language of business throughout most of the world (Chiswick & Miller, 2001; Creese, 2010). Instead, it appears that immigration laws are a major factor influencing which countries US citizens choose as targets of migration or expatriation, with Canada having stricter laws than either Mexico or the EU.

Canadian employers are required to provide specific reasons for not hiring each Canadian applicant if the employer desires to consider hiring non-Canadians (Richardson, 2009). Canada's laws are such an obstacle to the immigration of US citizens that it has been called *the 49th parallel effect* (Hunt & Mueller, 2004),

whereby more highly skilled Canadians migrate to the US, but the opposite occurs less frequently (de Hass, 2005). In general, more highly skilled workers in North America tend to move from the North to the South, with many highly skilled Canadians migrating to the US, and many highly skilled US citizens migrating to Mexico. This North–South migration pattern has resulted in a narrowing of wage inequity in Canada, an increase in wage inequity in the US, and a decline in the wages of low-skilled workers in Mexico (Aydemir & Borjas, 2007).

Unfortunately, it is impossible to provide an accurate historical picture of US migration patterns. Although the US government has consistently collected information on immigration patterns since the late 1940s, it has not done a consistent job of collecting similar data on the migration rates of US citizens. Additionally, there have been questions about the accuracy of some of the data (Gibbs, Harper, Rubin, & Shin, 2003). For example, in the 1970s and 1980s, the US Census Bureau estimated annual migration of US born citizens to be at 27,000. During the 1990s, the Census Bureau estimated annual migration of US citizens had jumped to 48,000. However, Gibbs and associates compared the Census Bureau migration data for the 1990s to data from other sources (e.g., immigration data of other countries) and could not reconcile the differences. They suggest that the estimate of 48,000 is too high, and the annual estimate for the 1990s is probably closer to 18,000. Given that US citizens (with passports) are not restricted in their passage across US borders, the government lacks detailed records of how long, and for what purposes, individuals leave the country. Moreover, records from different agencies (e.g., US consulates) are not centralized, and many agencies maintain records for only a certain period of time.

The lack of historical data on migration rates of US citizens suggests that the collection of more accurate information on those who make inter-country moves is needed. In addition to information collected by government agencies, scholars should consider examining migration patterns using theory-driven models. For instance, although money may be an important motivating force for US migration or expatriation (Hatton, 2010), in common with other mobility decisions, migration and expatriation are complex processes, and factors beyond economic gain are usually considered. For future research, scholars could examine how an individual's need for authenticity, balance, and challenge influence his/her decision to expatriate or to migrate (Sullivan, Forret, Carraher, & Mainerio, 2009), or whether those with higher protean or boundaryless orientations are more likely to migrate (Briscoe & Hall, 2006).

Similarly, little is known about reverse migration, i.e., those US citizens who return to the US after a period of living in one or more foreign countries (Chacko, 2007; Shrestha, 2011). Although research has been done on the return of workers to India (Chacko, 2007) and Mexico (Rendall, Brownell, & Kups, 2011; Van Hook & Zhang, 2011), little is known about the reverse migration in other countries, including the US. Studying career motives (e.g., Sullivan et al., 2009)

and orientations (Briscoe & Hall, 2006) may provide important insights about what factors compel individuals to return to their homeland.

### The US Military and Students Abroad

There are two major groups of US citizens who regularly travel outside the US as part of their career progression: members of the US military and university students. Research is just beginning to be completed, however, on how military and study-abroad programs impact global careers.

In 2010, there were approximately 291,651 US military personnel working outside the country. The largest numbers of these individuals were deployed in Afghanistan (36%), Iraq (29%), Germany (19%), Japan (12%), and the Republic of Korea (10%). Prior research has found that military personnel on active duty (Jones, 2010; Oberholster, 2011), as well as those who are retired, are more likely than the general population to move internationally. The vignette about Wesley Learner illustrates how military experience in multiple countries often translates into high-paying, global-career opportunities. Interestingly, Wesley's global career also demonstrates how globetrotting may result in a better work–family balance than a local job.

The spouses and children of military personnel are also more likely to migrate than the general population (Cooke et al., 1985; Payne et al., 1992). Anecdotal evidence suggests that international travel while accompanying a family member in the military may enhance culture awareness, and, thus, these individuals may be more likely to work across country borders. More empirical, theory-driven research on the factors that may foster the global careers of members of military personnel is needed.

A growing number of university students with US citizenship travel outside the country for career purposes. These international-student experiences vary in length from just a few weeks to an entire academic year. Likewise, these student

---

### Global Careers In and Out of the Military

Wesley Learner served in the Military Police for the US Marine Corps for three tours overseas—one in South Korea, one in Japan, and one in Saudi Arabia. Upon retiring from the Marines, he worked 6 months as a sheriff's deputy in his hometown. Wesley's wife worked evenings, while he worked mornings. Wesley usually left for work 3 hours prior to when his children woke for school, and so the family had little time together. He was soon offered four times his deputy's salary to become a full-time security specialist to oil employees working around the world. One week Wesley may be in Saudi Arabia, the next week he may be in Germany, and the next in Malaysia. He enjoys his work and has 1 month off for every month and a half worked, so that he has ample time with his wife and children.

experiences vary in type, including internships as well as combined travel and classroom programs. During the 2009–2010 academic year, approximately 271,000 US students studied abroad, with the top destinations being the UK (12.1%), Italy (10.3%), Spain (9.4%), France (6.3%), and China (5.1%). Although all of the top five destinations saw increases in the number of US students entering for purposes of study, other destinations saw more dramatic changes. Whereas Australia saw a large decrease in the percentage of US students studying there (10.6%), Israel saw the largest percentage increase (60.7%), from 1,958 US students studying there in 2008–2009 to 3,146 in 2009–2010. India also experienced a large percentage increase (44.4%) in students entering from the US (Institute for International Education, 2010).

Between 1995 and 2007, the number of US students studying abroad has more than tripled. In the 2007–2008 academic year, summer tours or programs of 8 weeks or fewer comprised 56% of the programs offered in US universities (Institute for International Education, 2010). Although previous studies have shown that study-abroad programs increase cultural awareness and language skills, few studies have examined the impact of these programs on career outcomes. Likewise, relatively little research has examined how program length affects career outcomes.

In one of the few studies of career outcomes and program length, Norris and Gillespie (2008) reported on a survey of 3,723 alumni of US study-abroad programs from 1950 to 1999. Forty-eight percent of the alumni reported having a global career, defined as working or volunteering in an organization located in a foreign country or in a position in the US that had specific international components. Those pursuing a global career were significantly more likely than those following a domestic career path to agree that the study-abroad program had an impact on their career direction and permitted them to acquire skills that influenced their career path. This effect was stronger for those who studied abroad for a full year, rather than for a shorter time period. Likewise, Carley, Stuart, and Dailey (2011) examined the survey results from 349 alumni of a two-week study-abroad program that took place between 1999 and 2007. This short program had little effect upon students' career choice or probability of working for a multinational company. These findings suggest that longer-duration programs have a stronger effect on the likelihood of students engaging in global careers than short programs. Research that examines specific career paths and outcomes is needed to understand better how study-abroad programs may impact the different types of global career (e.g., expatriate, frequent international business traveler, virtual team member) of university students.

Despite the prevalence of English across a number of countries, many believe that lack of foreign-language training reduces a student's awareness and interest in global-career opportunities. Since 1995, however, both the number of US students studying a foreign language and the diversity of languages studied have increased, with students opting for languages such as Arabic along with the traditional choices of Spanish, French, and German (Furman, Goldberg, & Lusin,

2010). Future research should examine how studying a foreign language impacts the likelihood of US students choosing to study abroad, and how it also impacts global-career outcomes.

## Technology and Global Careers

Has technology changed how US organizations do business? The answer is a resounding "yes," especially the use of communication technologies. Although transatlantic flights have been possible since the 1930s and common since the 1960s, the ease of communication connecting those around the world has had a significant impact on everything from expatriate assignments to virtual global work teams. For example, it is estimated that the cost of a failed expatriate assignment can be between five and ten times the cost of a local hire. The cost of an expatriate who is unable to adjust to the local culture may be up to three times the cost of a premature repatriation, with the highest maladjustment and failure rates being among US expatriates (Carraher, 2005). With modern transnational communication technologies, however, organizations can often identify and solve expatriate adjustment problems earlier than in the past. Additionally, the use of long-distance mentoring via technology may also help smooth the effective transition to an international location, as well as ease the repatriation process (Carraher, Sullivan, & Crocitto, 2008).

Communication technologies have also revolutionized the use of virtual global teams. No longer do international coworkers need to rely on costly communication methods, such as long-distance phone calls, or wait for letters or packages to travel across locations. Instead, centralized Internet systems, meeting platforms, email, Skype, and other technologies (e.g., Second Life) make collaboration across country borders easier and more cost effective, so that individuals around the globe can work together. As illustrated in the next vignette, members of a global work team can be highly effective without the need ever physically to meet face to face, through the use of technologies (Algesheimer, Dholakia, & Gurău, 2011).

### Global Virtual Work Teams

In the late 1990s, two of this chapter's authors were part of an international virtual work team that examined a US-based multinational professional service organization with operations throughout the world. The virtual project team consisted of the chief executive officer for the organization, 59 in-country leaders (from countries including Zambia, Sudan, and China), an internal organizational consultant (working in the US and Sudan), a data-entry specialist (working in the US and Kenya), and ourselves (working in the US). None of the team members was required to travel in order to complete the project.

The number of virtual work teams, such as the one used to complete this volume, is increasing. Nearly 66% of all US Fortune 500 company employees will work within virtual environments at some point in their career. Firms use virtual global work teams so that they can be more flexible (Morris, Marshall, & Rainer, 2002) and cost-effective (Sivunen, 2006; Vroman & Kovacich, 2002). Virtual teams permit organizations to obtain, blend, and apply learning and knowledge quickly within the organization's locations throughout the world (Furst, Reeves, Rosen, & Blackburn, 2004; Lu, Waxon-Manheim, Chudoba, & Wynn, 2006). Many medical teams in the US make use of virtual global work teams and include experts from India and other countries, reducing costs to a fraction of those of a US-based expert. For example, a patient in the US can have an MRI (magnetic resonance imaging) scan performed, with the radiologist in India reporting the results in real time, at a 10% cost saving to the hospital.

Global virtual teams take on the characteristics of general teams; however, the members are geographically dispersed and often use technology-mediated communication mechanisms (Alavi & Tiwana, 2002; Bell & Kozlowski, 2002; McLean, 2007; O'Leary & Cummings, 2007; Piccoli, Powell, & Ives, 2004). Like other types of project teams, virtual global work teams can come together in response to a specific organizational need and, once the goal is reached, the teams can be dismantled (Morris et al., 2002).

Research has found that there are several critical factors that affect the success of virtual work teams, including trust, communication differences, rewards, social skills, and goal clarity (e.g., Bandow, 2001; Goodbody, 2005; Peters & Karren, 2009; Sizoo & Serrie, 2004; Stoner, 1993). Building team collaboration by increasing trust at the formation stage of a global virtual work team helps to maximize the benefits of virtual teamwork (Sarker, Valacich, & Sarker, 2003). Achieving trust requires that the teams have clear goals, expectations, and communication among team members (Bandow, 2001; Stoner, 1993), so that all team members understand the mission of the organization. Lack of trust among teammates can cause individuals to be less willing to contribute to the team, leading to inefficient teamwork, higher costs, longer project cycle, and lower levels of quality (Prati, Douglas, Ferris, Ammeter, & Buckley, 2003).

Virtual global work teams have the additional complications of members being in different time zones and from different cultures, as well as perhaps speaking different languages (Cummings, 2011; Gurung & Prater, 2006; Piccoli et al., 2004), and having different ethical and work standards (Kimble, Li, & Branchflower, 2001). Time-zone differences can have both positive and negative influences on global virtual work team performance. Time differences can introduce flexibility and efficiency. Members of a virtual team can pass work in progress among the members in different time zones, so that the work continues, even when some of the team members are asleep. By contrast, the different time zones can also impose problems when seeking to coordinate meetings or attempting to schedule activities such as teleconferences. Virtual team members should pay special

attention to the day of the week and understand that Friday in their time zone may be the weekend for other team members. For instance, one of this chapter's authors served on a four-person research committee, with three members working in the US and the fourth working in Malaysia. Typically, meetings were scheduled in the early morning for the US members, which made it late evening for the member working in Malaysia. Owing to unusual circumstances, one meeting was scheduled for the afternoon in the US, with the Malay member attending the meeting at 2 a.m. in his time zone. With some care with regard to schedules, most of the issues with time zones can be greatly lessened (Carraher et al., 2008); cross-cultural differences, however, may be more difficult to eliminate.

Cross-cultural differences can make it very difficult for global virtual teams to function effectively (Carraher, 2005; Cummings, 2011; Dickmann & Baruch, 2011; Hobman, Bordia, & Gallois, 2003; Tian & Emery, 2002; Zakaria, Amelinckx, & Wilemon, 2004). Team members may lack the necessary cross-cultural knowledge, awareness, and training to work with others, and these differences can be magnified in the virtual work environment (Davey & Allgood, 2002; Suutari & Burch, 2001; Utley, Kozleski, Smith, & Draper, 2002). Language barriers and communication problems (Domke-Damonte, 2001; Randel, 2003), as well as technological difficulties (Redman & Sankar, 2003), can further complicate the functioning of global virtual work teams. Although cultural diversity can bring a wealth of knowledge, skills, and ways of thinking to a virtual team, it also requires a high level of coordination in order to integrate individuals' differences (Greggas-McQuikin, 2004). If additional coordination is needed, it may be necessary to have some of the team members physically meet face to face.

## Virtual Expatriation

Since the 1990s, US organizations have had an increasingly difficult time recruiting qualified expatriates to move overseas to less desirable locations. Markets in Africa, Eastern Europe, and Asia were opening up, and yet 80% of organizations surveyed reported having employees turn down expatriate assignments owing to dual career issues (Flynn, 2000). A number of organizations turned to virtual expatriates as an alternative to traditional expatriate assignments. For example, from 1997 to 1999, there was a 44% increase in virtual expatriate assignments (Flynn, 1999). Of 270 organizations, employing 65,000 expatriates and operating in 24 European countries, about two thirds of the organizations were using virtual expatriates (Flynn, 1999).

Through the use of Skype, email, online video conferencing, and smart phones, virtual expatriates are using technology to manage in other countries, rather than physically moving to the new location (Huang & Hsu, 2003; Latta, 1999). Virtual expatriates complete their international assignments using electronic media, with some firms using a hybrid approach that includes quarterly, monthly, or biweekly trips to international sites (Solomon, 1998).

Although organizations are increasingly making use of virtual expatriates, the study of these individuals has largely been ignored in the academic literature; hence, we know relatively little about those who take on these roles. In one of the few extant studies, Carraher (1998) examined 172 virtual expatriates who lived in the US but served as managers in Asia and Africa. Nearly 70% of the virtual expatriates were men, and over 80% were married, with most being in dual-career relationships. Like Larry in the vignette, many individuals are becoming virtual expatriates in order to balance work and family.

---

### A New Breed of Global Careerists

Larry Lead lives in Plano, Texas, just outside of Dallas, but he is the manager of marketing for the India operations of a large multinational organization. When first offered the job, he was going to turn it down, because his wife had a great job in Dallas and would have difficulty finding a comparable job in Mumbai, India. However, his supervisor arranged for Larry to become a virtual expatriate. Larry travels to Mumbai for a week every 3 months, but otherwise manages operations from his Plano office using Skype, email, and video conferences.

---

## Commuters, Business Travelers, and Other Global Careerists

Relatively little is known about other types of global career, including those of individuals who commute between country borders and who are frequent business travelers (Dickmann & Baruch, 2011). Much of what we know about these types of global career in the US is from case studies or anecdotal evidence. For example, the Ambassador Bridge between Detroit, Michigan, and Windsor, Canada, is the leading international border crossing in North America. Each day, it is estimated that more than 40,000 commuters, tourists, and truck drivers carrying US$323 million worth of goods cross the bridge. Yet we know little about those workers who use the Ambassador Bridge for their daily commutes.

Similarly, relatively little is known about individuals who traverse the borders of many countries as part of their business travels. For instance, Solomon (1998) completed a case study about the experiences of Stephen Rhinesmith, the president of a Boston-based consulting company. Rhinesmith is a frequent international business traveler, as described by this quote: "Last week I spoke Tuesday in Germany and Friday in Sydney—and I go to Paris tomorrow. Two weeks ago I flew to Vienna on Wednesday, spoke on Thursday morning and came home Thursday afternoon" (Solomon, 1998, p. 14).

We also know little about underground global careerists, who are exploiting technology and the world market for their own gain. Anecdotal evidence suggests there is a great potential for unethical and illegal careers to arise from the global

marketplace. For instance, a top-rated engineer in a US aerospace organization "hired" an engineer in India at about 7% of his own salary to perform his work. At the end of the day, the engineer would email all of his work to his "employee" in India and, when he returned to the office the next morning, the completed work was waiting in his email. Likewise, although there are no published empirical studies of these individuals, from police, government, and media reports, it is well known that many US businesspeople deal in illegal imports and exports, including the trafficking of drugs, people, and weapons.

## Critical Perspectives on Global Careers in the US

This examination of global careers in the US has caused us to reflect critically upon this area. As a result, we offer three major issues that must be confronted before significant progress can be made with respect to the study of global careers. First, it is important to develop a clear differentiation among the different types of global career. Dickmann and Baruch (2011) offer a definition of global careers, but there is little agreement as to how different types of global career should be defined. For example, whereas some studies differentiate between organization-initiated and self-initiated expatriates, other studies do not. Likewise, there is little agreement about what constitutes a long-term assignment versus a short-term assignment, or what is considered occasional versus frequent business travel. Differences in the number of assignments, the length of each assignment, and the various countries in which these assignments take place are often not accounted for in studies of global careers. For instance, should Harry, who travels one week out of every month to one foreign location, and Sally, who travels five consecutive weeks each year among five different foreign locations, both be classified as frequent business travelers, with comparable career experiences? We may be using terms, such as *frequent business traveler*, to describe global careers that are very different in nature.

Scholars should strive to be more precise in defining what type of global career is being examined, so that results across studies can be more readily compared and understood. Additionally, it should be recognized that some individuals might not have "pure forms" of global careers. An individual's career may not be easily or neatly categorized as one specific type of global career. For example, Stan has engaged in long- and short-term expatriate assignments and some business travel to various countries, as well as being a member of a number of cross-national, global, face-to-face and virtual teams. Stan, however, cannot simply be defined as an expatriate manager or a frequent international business traveler or a virtual global team member, but instead has a career that is some hybrid of the three types.

Second, we must begin to examine the psychological aspects of global careers. Much of the literature on global careers seems to focus on the physical crossing of country borders, which can be easily identified, with relatively little attention

being paid to psychological mobility or the interplay between physical and psychological mobility. A theory-driven model that classifies the different types of global careerist by examining psychological as well as physical mobility may be one means further to advance our understanding of global careers.

For example, it may be useful to consider applying Sullivan and Arthur's (2006) reconceptualization of the boundaryless-career concept to global careers. Using this reconceptualization, global careers could be examined in terms of the degree of physical and psychological mobility experienced by the individual, the interaction between these two types of mobility, and how mobility may change over time. Using such a model may also provide a framework better to study factors that impede or enable global careers.

Third, scholarly attention should be directed toward the contextual issues that influence global careers. Each chapter in this volume has examined global careers, considering how the country's geography, history, and other country-specific factors influence the global careers of people living in that country. This has advanced the discussion of how contextual issues impact careers.

Government policies, business needs, and societal attitudes have a strong impact on the careers of those living within the US borders. These within-country policies, business needs, and attitudes also interact with the policies, business context, and attitudes of other countries to create a complex environment in which people work and live. Studying careers within a complex global context is not easy. Career scholars may benefit from partnering with colleagues in many different countries and in other disciplines better to capture global-career experiences.

## Directions for Future Exploration

In this chapter, we have examined the key role of immigration and migration in the global careers of those living in the US. We have also examined the impact of key factors, especially technology, on global careers. We are encouraged by the recent conceptualizations of global careers (e.g., Dickmann & Baruch, 2011) and the increased study of careers that cross country borders. We were quite surprised, however, by the lack of historical data on the migration rates of US citizens. Although the government has already begun to make changes to broaden the scope of its data collection, scholars must also step forward to conduct theory-driven research on why individuals leave the US and why some return after a period of working in other countries.

We are also concerned about the relative lack of empirical research on global careers in the US Most of the research on global careers focuses on organization-initiated expatriate assignments, with scholars more recently studying self-initiated expatriate assignments. We suggest that future research on expatriates concentrate on under-studied areas, such as cross-border mentoring of expatriates, which will contribute to our understanding of expatriates, while also having implications for

other literatures (e.g., mentoring). Research on self-initiated expatriate assignments has already offered some interesting contributions to the literature on global careers and should be continued.

It is clear from our review that scholars also need to devote more attention to less studied types of global career and aspects thereof, such as how being part of an international virtual work team or collaborating with colleagues across national borders affect career outcomes. Although there is a well-established literature on group process and a growing literature on virtual work teams, the influence of different cultures on team process deserves more attention. Cross-border virtual work teams are increasingly being used in organizations and may play an even larger role in the future. More research on how membership in an international virtual work team impacts careers experiences and how outcomes are enacted is needed.

Although there are many benefits to those engaging in boundaryless global careers, such as increased cultural awareness and career competencies, there are also disadvantages to global careers that must be considered. For example, we know relatively little about the experiences of marginalized groups, such as undocumented immigrants, in the global work environment. An undocumented worker in the US is at the mercy of unscrupulous employers. Because of their illegal status, it is difficult to study how the careers of these individuals unfold, or how their career experiences (e.g., fear of deportation, standard of living, working conditions) may impact the career opportunities of their children, i.e., future generations of workers.

Likewise, individuals who frequently travel for business may gain benefits, such as challenging and rewarding assignments, along with some accompanying costs to this type of global career. Those who traverse borders on a regular basis may suffer from unexpected side effects, such as increased stress and health problems, feelings of isolation from family and friends, and lack of deep connections with coworkers. The career of the spouses of frequent business travelers may also be negatively affected, as these spouses may take on a greater share of child-rearing responsibilities, as well as duties related to maintaining the home and finances. Career scholars may benefit from partnering with colleagues in other disciplines, such as sociology and health care, better to understand how marginalized groups, frequent travelers, and others may struggle in the global boundaryless-career environment.

Resolution of the three critical issues identified—the definition of global careers, recognition of the psychological aspects of pursuing a global career, and identification of important contextual factors—will facilitate a more detailed examination of the future research directions discussed. The study of global careers will be of increasing importance, although the nature of global careers may change as they are influenced by advancing technology.

# References

Al Ariss, A. (2010). Modes of engagement: Migration, self-initiated expatriation, and career development. *Career Development International, 15*, 338–358.

Al Ariss, A. & Syed, J. (2011). Capital mobilization of skilled migrants: A relational perspective. *British Journal of Management, 22*, 286–304.

Alavi, M. & Tiwana, A. (2002). Knowledge integration in virtual teams: The potential role of KMS. *Journal of the American Society for Information Science and Technology, 53*, 1029–1045.

Algesheimer, R., Dholakia, U. M., & Gurău, C. (2011). Virtual team performance in a highly competitive environment. *Group & Organization Management, 36*, 161–190.

Arthur, M. B. & Rousseau, D. M. (1996). *The Boundaryless Career: A New Employment Principle for a New Organizational Era.* New York: Oxford University Press.

Asher, C. (2011). The progressive past: How history can help us serve generation 1.5. *Reference & User Services Quarterly, 51*(1), 43–48.

Avery, D. R., Tonidandel, S., Volpone, S. D., & Raghuram, A. (2010). Overworked in America? How work hours, immigrant status, and interpersonal justice affect perceived work overload. *Journal of Managerial Psychology, 28*, 133–147.

Aydemir, A. & Borjas, G. J. (2007). Cross-country variation in the impact of international migration: Canada, Mexico, and the United States. *Journal of the European Economic Association, 5*, 663–708.

Banai, M. & Harry, W. (2004). Boundaryless global careers: The international itinerants. *International Studies of Management and Organization, 34*(3), 96–120.

Bandow, D. (2001). Time to create sound teamwork. *Journal for Quality and Participation, 24*(2), 41–47.

Baruch, Y. (1995). Business globalization—the human resource management aspect. *Human Systems Management, 14*(4), 313–326.

Baruch, Y., Budhwar, P. S., & Khatri, N. (2007). Brain drain: Inclination to stay abroad after studies. *Journal of World Business, 42*(1), 99–112.

Bell, B. S. & Kozlowski, S. W. J. (2002). A typology of virtual teams: Implications for effective leadership. *Group & Organization Management, 27*, 14–33.

Bell, M. P., Kwesiga, E. N., & Berry, D. P. (2010). Immigrants: The new "invisible men and women" in diversity research. *Journal of Managerial Psychology, 25*, 177–188.

Benton-Cohen, K. (2010). The rude birth of immigration reform. *Wilson Quarterly, 34*(3), 16–22.

Boneva, B. S. & Frieze, I. H. (2001). Toward a concept of a migrant personality. *Journal of Social Issues, 57*, 477–491.

Briscoe, J. P. & Hall, D. T. (2006). The interplay of boundaryless and protean careers: Combinations and implications. *Journal of Vocational Behavior, 69*, 4–18.

Cappellen, T. & Janssens, M. (2010). Enacting global careers: Organizational careers scripts and the global economy as co-existing career referents. *Journal of Organizational Behavior, 31*, 687–706.

Carley, S., Stuart, R., & Dailey, M. P. (2011). Short-term study abroad: An exploratory view of business student outcomes. *Journal of Management Policy and Practice, 12*(2), 44–53.

Carr, S. C., Inkson, K., & Thorn, K. (2005). From global careers to talent flow: Reinterpreting "brain drain." *Journal of World Business, 40*, 386–398.

Carraher, S. M. (1998). Manual for the individual-level entrepreneurial orientation scales. Unpublished manuscript, Indiana University.

Carraher, S. M. (2005). An examination of entrepreneurial orientation: A validation study in 68 countries in Africa, Asia, Europe, and North America. *International Journal of Family Business, 2*, 95–100.

Carraher, S. M., Sullivan, S. E., & Crocitto, M. M. (2008). Mentoring across global boundaries: An empirical examination of home- and host-country mentors on expatriate career outcomes. *Journal of International Business Studies, 39*, 1310–1326.

Chacko, E. (2007). From brain drain to brain gain: Reverse migration to Bangalore and Hyderabad, India's globalizing high tech cities. *GeoJournal, 68*, 131–140.

Chiswick, B. R. & Miller, P. W. (2001). A model of destination-language acquisition: Application to male immigrants in Canada. *Demography, 38*, 391–409.

Coleman, M. & Kocher, A. (2011). Detention, deportation, devolution and immigrant incapacitation in the US, post 9/11. *Geographical Journal, 177*(3), 228–237.

Cooke, K. R., Spears, G. F., & Skegg, D. C. (1985). Frequency of moles in a defined population. *Journal of Epidemiological Community Health, 39*, 48–52.

Creese, G. (2010). Erasing English language competency: African migrants in Vancouver, Canada. *Journal of International Migration and Integration, 11*, 295–313.

Cummings, J. N. (2011). Economic and business dimensions: Geography is alive and well in virtual teams. *Communications of the Association for Computing Machinery, 54*(8), 24–26.

Davey, H. & Allgood, B. (2002). Offshore development, building relationships across boundaries: A case study. *Information Strategy, 18*, 13–16.

Davis, J. H. (1980). Americans in Mexico. *Town and Country, 134*, 5007.

de Hass, A. G. (2005). Facilitating parent involvement: Reflecting on effective teacher education. *Teaching and Learning, 19*(2), 57–76.

Dickmann, M. & Baruch, Y. (2011). *Global Careers.* London: Routledge.

Domke-Damonte, D. (2001). Language learning and international business. *S.A.M. Advanced Management Journal, 66*(1), 35–40.

Donato, K. M., Aguilera, M., & Wakabayashi, C. (2005). Immigrant policy and employment conditions of US immigrants from Mexico, Nicaragua, and the Dominican Republic. *International Migration, 43*, 5–29.

Ellis, M. & Almgren, G. (2009). Local contexts of immigrant and second-generation integration in the United States. *Journal of Ethnic & Migration Studies, 35*, 1059–1076.

Evans, J., Goulas, E., & Levine, P. (2007). Military expenditure and migration in Europe. *Defence and Peace Economics, 18*(4), 305. Retrieved December 30, 2011, from ABI/Inform Global. Document ID: 1284671911.

Flynn, J. (1999). E-mail, cell phones, and frequent flyer miles let "virtual" expats work abroad but live at home. *Wall Street Journal*, October 25, 1999, A 26.

Flynn, J. (2000). Multinationals help expatriate couples deal with the strains of living abroad. *Wall Street Journal*, August 8, 2000, A 19.

Furman, N., Goldberg, D., & Lusin, N. (2010). Enrollments in languages other than English in United States institutions of higher education Fall 2009. Modern Language Association of America (MLA). Retrieved from www.mla.org/pdf/06enrollment survey_final.pdf

Furst, S. A., Reeves, M., Rosen, B., & Blackburn, R. S. (2004). Managing the life cycle of virtual teams. *Academy of Management Executive, 18*(2), 6–18.

Geist, C. & McManus, P. A. (2008). Geographical mobility over the life course: Motivations and implications. *Population, Space and Place, 14*, 283–303.

Gibbs, J., Harper, G., Rubin, M., & Shin, H. (2003). Evaluating components of international migration: Native-born emigrants. Washington DC: US Census Bureau, Population Division.

Goodbody, J. (2005). Critical success factors for global virtual teams. *Strategic Communication Management, 9*(2), 18–21.

Greggas-McQuikin, D. (2004). Building unbeatable teams. *Medsurg Nursing, 13*, 5–12.

Gunz, H., Peiperl, M., & Tzabbar, D. (2007). Boundaries in the study of career. In H. Gunz and M. Peiperl (Eds.), *Handbook of Career Studies* (471–494). Thousand Oaks, CA: Sage.

Gurung, A. & Prater, E. (2006). A research framework for the impact of cultural differences on IT outsourcing. *Journal of Global Information Technology Management, 9*, 24–43.

Haller, W., Portes, A., & Lynch, S. M. (2011). Dreams fulfilled, dreams shattered: Determinants of segmented assimilation in the second generation. *Social Forces, 89*, 733–762.

Hatton, T. J. (2010). The cliometrics of international migration: A survey. *Journal of Economic Surveys, 24*, 941–969.

Hobman, E. V., Bordia, P., & Gallois, C. (2003). Consequences of feeling dissimilar from others in a work team. *Journal of Business and Psychology, 17*, 301–325.

Hoefer, M., Rytina, N., & Baker, B. C. (2010). *Estimates of the Unauthorized Immigrant Population Residing in the United States: January 2009.* Office of Immigration Statistics, Policy Directorate, US Department of Homeland Security.

Huang, L. Y. & Hsu, C.-C. (2003). Factors on channel integration decisions of Taiwanese manufacturers in the export market. *Journal of the American Academy of Business, Cambridge, 2*, 312–321.

Hunt, G. L. & Mueller, R. E. (2004). North American migration: Returns to skill, border effects, and mobility costs. *Review of Economics and Statistics, 86*, 988–1007.

Inkson, K. & Myers, B. A. (2003). "The big OE": Self-directed travel and career development. *Career Development International, 8*, 170–181.

Institute for International Education (2010). Open-doors report on US study abroad: Leading destinations. Retrieved from www.iie.org/Research-and-Publications/Open-Doors/Data/US-Study-Abroad/Leading-Destinations/2008-10, February 10, 2012.

Ismaili, K. (2010). Surveying the many fronts of the war on immigrants in post-9/11 US society. *Contemporary Justice Review, 13*(1), 71–93.

Jones, K. (2010). The experiences of World War II US American expatriate veterans of African descent. Unpublished dissertation, Saybrook University.

Kimble, C., Li, F., & Branchflower, A. (2001). Overcoming barriers to virtual team working through communities of practice. Unpublished manuscript.

Latta, G. W. (1999). Expatriate policy and practice: A ten year comparison of trends. *Compensation and Benefits Review, 31*(4), 35–39.

Lu, M., Waxon-Manheim, B., Chudoba, K. M., & Wynn, E. (2006). Virtuality and team performance: Understanding the impact of variety of practice. *Journal of Global Information Technology, 9*, 4–32.

McLean, J. (2007). Prepare for the future. It's happening fast. *British Journal of Administrative Management, 58*, 17–25.

Mainiero, L. A. & Sullivan, S. E. (2006). *The Opt-Out Revolt: Why People Are Leaving Companies to Create Kaleidoscope Careers.* Mountain View, CA: Davies-Black.

Martin, P. & Midgley, E. (2010). Immigration in America 2010. *Population Bulletin Update.* Washington DC: Population Reference Bureau.

McLean, J. (2007). Prepare for the future. It's happening fast. *British Journal of Administrative Management, 58*, 17–25.

Mittelstadt, M., Speaker, B., Meissner, D., & Chishti, M. (2011). *Through the Prism of National Security: Major Immigration Policy and Program Changes in the Decade Since 9/11.* Washington DC: Migration Policy Institute.

Monger, R. & Yankay, J. (2011). *US Legal Permanent Residents: 2010.* Office of Immigration Statistics, Policy Directorate, U. S. Department of Homeland Security.

Morris, S. A., Marshall, T. E., & Rainer, Jr., R. K. (2002). Impact of user satisfaction and trust on virtual team members. *Information Resources Management Journal, 15*(2), 22–31.

Norris, E. & Gillespie, J. (2008). How study abroad shapes global careers: Evidence from the United States. *Journal of Studies in International Education, 13,* 382–397. Retrieved from http://migrationinformation.org/Resources/unitedstates.cfm, February 10, 2012.

O'Leary, M. B. & Cummings, J. N. (2007). The spatial, temporal, and configurational characteristics of geographic dispersion in teams. *MIS Quarterly, 31,* 433–452.

Oberholster, A. J. (2011). The motivation of NPO workers for accepting international assignments. Unpublished dissertation, Nova Southeastern University.

Payne, D. M., Warner, J. T., & Little, R. D. (1992). Tied migration and returns to human capital: The case of military wives. *Social Science Quarterly, 73,* 324–339.

Peters, L. & Karren, R. J. (2009). An examination of the roles of trust and functional diversity on virtual team performance ratings. *Group & Organization Management, 34,* 479–504.

Piccoli, G., Powell, G. N., & Ives, B. (2004). Virtual teams: Team control structure, work processes, and team effectiveness. *Information Technology & People, 17,* 359–375.

Prati, L. M., Douglas, C., Ferris, G. R., Ammeter, A. P., & Buckley, M. R. (2003). Emotional intelligence, leadership effectiveness, and team outcomes. *International Journal of Organizational Analysis, 11,* 21–40.

Randel, A. E. (2003). The salience of culture in multinational teams and its relations to team citizenship behavior. *International Journal of Cross Cultural Management: CCM, 3,* 27–44.

Redman, C. A. & Sankar, C. S. (2003). Results of an experiment comparing the analysis of Chik-fil-A case study by virtual teams versus face-to-face teams. *Journal of SMET Education: Innovations and Research, 55,* 55–62.

Rendall, M. S., Brownell, P., & Kups, S. (2011). Declining return migration from the United States to Mexico in the late-2000s recession: A research note. *Demography, 48,* 1049–1058.

Richardson, J. (2009). Geographic flexibility in academia: A cautionary note. *British Journal of Management, 20*(S1), 160–170.

Rosenblum, M. R. (2011). *US Immigration Policy Since 9/11: Understanding the Stalemate Over Comprehensive Immigration Reform.* Washington DC: Migration Policy Institute.

Rosenblum, M. R. & Brick, M. (2011). *US Immigration Policy and Mexican/Central American Migration Flows: Then and Now.* Washington DC: Migration Policy Institute.

Rumbaut, R. G. (1994). Origins and destinies: Immigration to the United States since World War II. *Sociological Forum, 9,* 583–621.

Sarker, S., Valacich, J. S., & Sarker, S. (2003). Virtual team trust: Instrument development and validation in an IS educational environment. *Information Resources Management Journal, 16*(2), 35–55.

Selmer, J. & Lam, H. (2004). "Third culture kids": Future business expatriates? *Personnel Review, 33,* 430–445.

Shrestha, M. B. (2011). Sibling rivalry in education: Estimation of intra-household trade-offs in human capital investment. Unpublished manuscript.

Sivunen, A. (2006). Strengthening identification with the team in virtual teams: The leaders' perspective. *Group Decision and Negotiation*, *15*, 345–366.

Sizoo, S. & Serrie, H. (2004). Developing cross-cultural skills of international business students: An experiment. *Journal of Instructional Psychology*, *31*, 160.

Solomon, C. M. (1998). Building teams across borders. *Global Workforce*, *3*(4), 14.

Somerville, K. & Walsworth, S. (2009). Vulnerabilities of highly skilled immigrants in Canada and the United States. *American Review of Canadian Studies*, *39*, 147–161.

Stoner, C. R. (1993). Team building: Answering the tough questions. *Business Horizons*, *36*(5), 70–79.

Sullivan, S. E. (1999). The changing nature of careers: A review and research agenda. *Journal of Management*, *25*, 457–484.

Sullivan, S. E. & Arthur, M. (2006). The evolution of the boundaryless career concept: Examining physical and psychological mobility. *Journal of Vocational Behavior*, *69*, 19–29.

Sullivan, S. E. & Baruch, Y. (2009) Advances in career theory and research: A critical review and agenda for future research. *Journal of Management*, *35*, 1542–1571.

Sullivan, S. E. & Mainiero, L. A. (2008). Using the Kaleidoscope Career Model to understand the changing patterns of women's careers: Designing HRD programs that attract and retain women. *Advances in Developing Human Resources*, *10*, 32–49.

Sullivan, S. E., Forret, M. L., Carraher, S. M., & Mainiero, L. A. (2009). Using the Kaleidoscope Career Model to examine generational differences in work attitudes. *Career Development International*, *14*, 284–302.

Suutari, V. & Burch, D. (2001). The role of on-site training and support in expatriation: Existing and necessary host-country practices. *Career Development International*, *6*, 298–311.

Suutari, V. & Taka, M. (2004). Career anchors of managers with global careers. *Journal of Management Development*, *23*, 833–847.

Tharenou, P. (2009). Self-initiated international careers: Gender differences and career outcomes. In S. G. Baugh & S. E. Sullivan (Eds.), *Research in Careers, Vol. 1: Maintaining Focus, Energy, and Options Over the Career*. Charlotte, NC: Information Age.

Tharenou, P. & Caulfield, N. (2010). Will I stay or will I go? Explaining repatriation by self-initiated expatriates. *Academy of Management Journal*, *53*, 1009–1028.

Tharmaseelan, N., Inkson, K., & Carr, S. C. (2009). Migration and career success: Testing a time-sequenced model. *Career Development International*, *15*, 218–238.

Tian, R. J. & Emery, C. (2002). Cross-cultural issues in Internet marketing. *Journal of the American Academy of Business, Cambridge*, *1*, 217–224.

US Census Bureau (2010). Movers by type of move and reason for moving. Current Population Survey, *2010 Annual Social and Economic Supplement: Geographical Mobility: 2009 to 2010*. Retrieved from www.census.gov/population/, February 10, 2012.

Utley, C. A., Kozleski, E., Smith, A., & Draper, I. L. (2002). A proactive strategy for minimizing behavior problems in urban multicultural youth. *Journal of Positive Behavior Interventions*, *4*(4), 196–207.

Van Hook, J. & Zhang, W. (2011). Who goes? Who stays? Selective emigration among the foreign born. *Population Research and Policy Review*, *30*, 1–24.

Vroman, K. & Kovacich, J. (2002). Computer-mediated interdisciplinary teams: Theory and reality. *Journal of Interprofessional Care*, *16*, 159–170.

Wolgin, P. E. & Bloemraad, I. (2010). Our gratitude to our soldiers: Military spouses, family re-unification, and postwar immigration reform. *Journal of Interdisciplinary History*, *41*, 27–60.

Zakaria, N., Amelinckx, A., & Wilemon, D. (2004). Working together apart? Building a knowledge-sharing culture for global virtual teams. *Creativity and Innovation Management, 13*, 15.

Zikic, J., Bonache, J., & Cerdin, J.-L. (2010). Crossing national boundaries: A typology of qualified immigrants' career orientation. *Journal of Organizational Behavior, 31*, 667–686.

# AUTHOR INDEX

Note: page numbers in *italic* type refer to figures; those in **bold** type refer to tables. Spelling and punctuation have been standardized to US usage.

Alexander, C. 122
Arnold, J. 33
Arthur, M. B. 36, 289, 315
Aycan, Z. 230, 241

Barnes, Jeff 249
Bartlett, C. A. 267
Baruch, Yehuda 1–17, 32, **33**, 38, 93, 107, 109, 152, 248, 287, 289, 298, 314
Baugh, S. Gayle 86, 297–322
Benencia, R. 111
Bimrose, J. 33, 43
Black, Conrad 21, 22–23, 26, 27
Black, J. S. 274, 275
Blair, Tony 23
Blenkinsopp, John 31–54
Bloch, A. N. 41, 43
Blustein, D. L. 41
Bodur, M. 239
Bourdieu, P. 9, 48, 59, 63, 73, 81–82, 86, 89
Brewster, C. 168
Briscoe, J. P. 2, 287
Brown, A. 40
Bu, N. 19
Budhwar, Pawan S. 45, 149, 285–296

Cacopardo, M. 111
Callanan, G. A. 282
Cappellen, T. 37, 168, 289
Carley, S. 309
Carr, S. C. 36, 37, 148
Carraher, Shawn M. 297–322
Castles, S. 10, 95, 100
Chretien, Jean 23, 24, 27
Chudzikowski, Katharina 55–77
Conway, N. 36
Costa e Silva, Susana 161–184

Dailey, M. P. 309
David, F. R. 278
de Cieri, H. 154
de Menezes, L. M. 36
DeFillippi, R. J. 36
Demireva, N. 44
DeMuth, R. L. F. 287
Dessler, G. 219
Dickmann, M. 1–2, 32, **33**, 39–40, 107, 109, 152, 168, 248, 287, 289, 298, 314
Doherty, N. 152, 168
Duarte, Paulo 161–184

Erdener Acar, E. 232
Erel, U. 44, 48

# SUBJECT INDEX

Note: page numbers in *italic* type refer to figures; those in **bold** type refer to tables. Spelling and punctuation have been standardized to US usage.

**SERIES ADVISORY EDITOR:
LYMAN L. JOHNSON,
UNIVERSITY OF NORTH CAROLINA AT CHARLOTTE**